W9-BNH-237

AMERICAN VISIONARIES

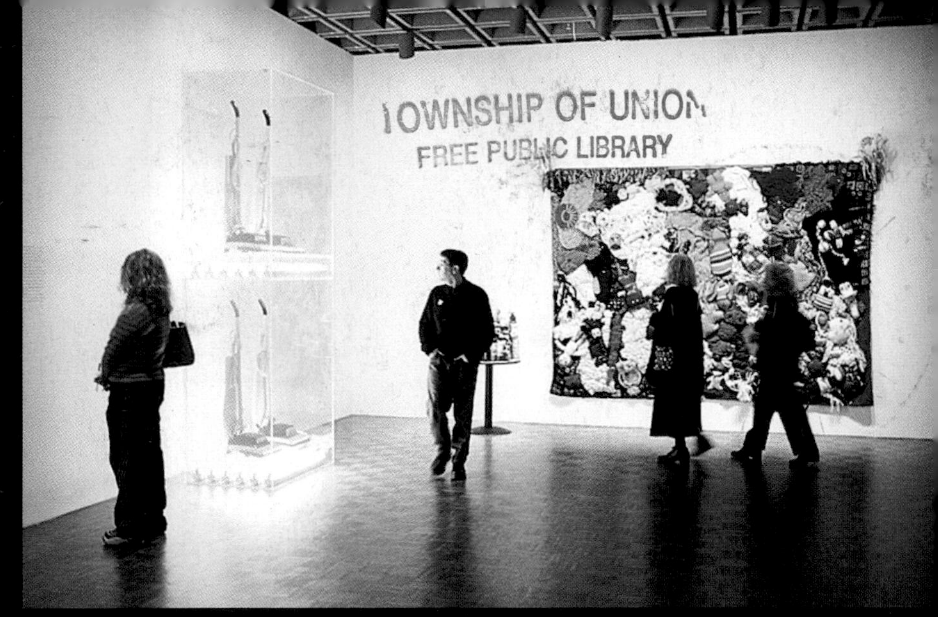

Whitney Museum of American Art, New York
Distributed by Harry N. Abrams, Inc., New York

This book is supported by a grant from Furthermore, a program of the J.M. Kaplan Fund, and by public funds from the New York State Council on the Arts, a State agency.

Research for Whitney Museum publications is supported by an endowment established by The Andrew W. Mellon Foundation and other generous donors.

A portion of the proceeds from the sale of this book benefits the Whitney Museum of American Art and its programs.

Cover: Jenny Okun, *Whitney Window*, 2001
Frontispiece: Photograph by Toshi Kazama ©2000

LIBRARY OF CONGRESS CATALOGING-IN-PUBLICATION DATA
Whitney Museum of American Art
American Visionaries: selections from the Whitney Museum of American Art/ introduction by Maxwell L. Anderson.
p. cm
ISBN 0-8109-6831-2 (cloth : alk. paper)—ISBN 0-87427-127-4 (pbk : alk. paper)
1. Art, American—20th century—Handbooks, manuals, etc. 2. Art—New York (State)—New York—Handbooks, manuals, etc. 3. Whitney Museum of American Art—Handbooks, manuals, etc. I. Anderson, Maxwell Lincoln. II. Title.

N6512.W445 2001
709'.73'0747471—dc21 2001045487

945 Madison Avenue at 75th Street
New York, NY 10021
www.whitney.org

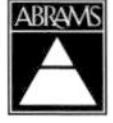

Harry N. Abrams, Inc.
100 Fifth Avenue
New York, NY 10011
www.abramsbooks.com

Abrams is a subsidiary of

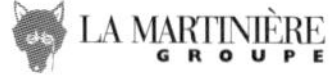

Printed and bound in Germany

12/02

CONTENTS

THE ARTISTS' MUSEUM

Maxwell L. Anderson

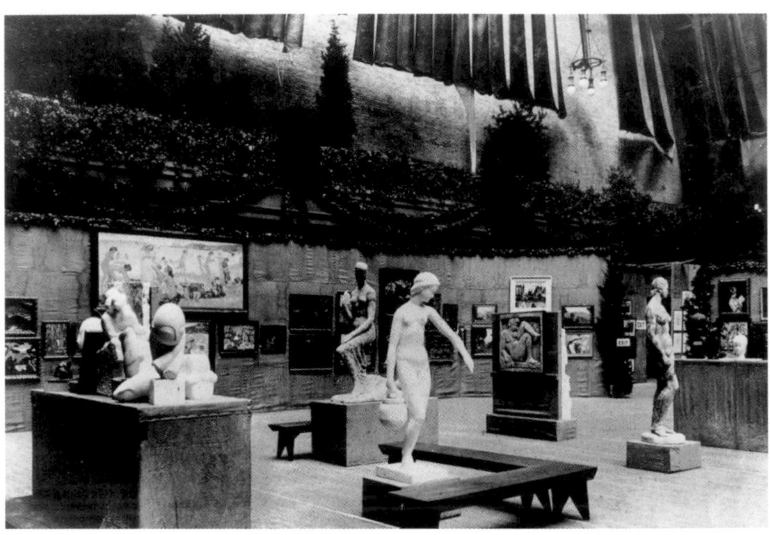

"International Exhibition of Modern Art" (The Armory Show), 69th Regiment Armory, New York, 1913.

From its founding to the fulfillment of its vision today, the Whitney has provided America's artists with a prominent public space for their work to be shown, collected, and studied for the benefit of a broad public. Today this seems like a reasonable mission. At the beginning of the twentieth century, however, support for American art was uncommon and far from mainstream concerns. Although America's political system was its own, its social and cultural scene was still reflexively eyeing the Continent. Museums founded over the course of the previous generation, including The Metropolitan Museum of Art and the Museum of Fine Arts, Boston, were focused exclusively on the art of the Old World. Few art dealers involved themselves with American art and fewer still were prepared to support emerging artists. The only way for an artist's work to be exhibited was through juried shows and art societies, which consistently favored traditionalists. Collectors, too, were primarily interested in Old Masters, save those who were willing to make room for Impressionism, then a thirty-year-old style.

The 1913 Armory Show was a watershed in the history of American art. This huge independent exhibition introduced European modernism to the American public. Never before had international vanguard art been presented in the United States without the comforting passage of time. But the Armory Show was not primarily a European affair. Organized by twenty-five members of the Association of American Painters and Sculptors, fully three-quarters of the works were by Americans. The shockers, however, were such works as Marcel Duchamp's *Nude Descending a Staircase* and Henri Matisse's *Blue Nude*, both of which raised critics' hackles, galvanizing them against contemporary European art. But these same assaults on academic tradition also emboldened a generation of American artists.

Gertrude Vanderbilt Whitney, founder of the Museum, had been an enthusiastic patron of American art since 1907, when she organized an exhibition of the work of younger American artists. The following year she bought four of the seven paintings sold from the controversial exhibition of The Eight, the revolutionary artists who depicted the people and places of ordinary urban life. For the Armory Show, she contributed $1,000 for the decoration of the exhibition.

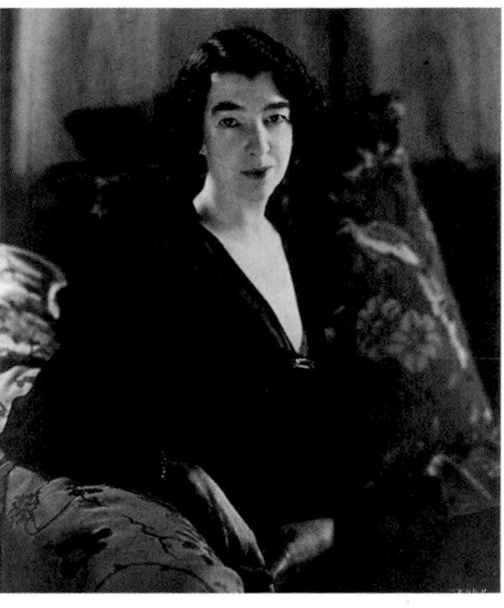

Edward Steichen, *Gertrude Vanderbilt Whitney*, 1937. Gelatin silver print, 16 5/8 x 13 7/16 in. (42.2 x 34.1 cm). Gift of the family of Edith and Lloyd Goodrich 89.7

The year after the Armory Show, Mrs. Whitney's advocacy of American art took its first permanent form. She purchased a brownstone at 8 West 8th Street and opened the Whitney Studio, an exhibition space and social center for young progressive artists. Over the course of the next year, she spearheaded the formation of the Friends of the Young Artists, an organization that assisted needy American artists and held exhibitions in the Whitney Studio. In 1916, John Sloan had his first one-artist exhibition there. The next year, Mrs. Whitney gave $1,500 to defray the expenses of the inaugural exhibition of the Society of Independent Artists, an American group founded in emulation of the French Société des Artistes Indépendants on the principle of "no juries, no prizes."

On May 15, 1918, Mrs. Whitney formally established the Whitney Studio Club and instituted nonjuried annual survey exhibitions of its members'

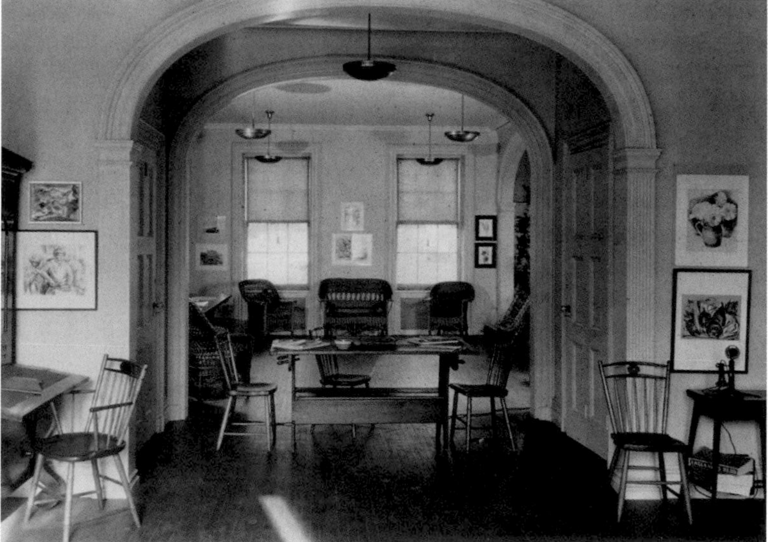

Charles Sheeler, *Office Interior, Whitney Studio Club*, c. 1928. Gelatin silver print, 7 1/2 x 9 3/8 in. (19.1 x 23.8 cm). Gift of Gertrude Vanderbilt Whitney 93.24.1

work. During the next decade, more than eighty-six exhibitions were held at the Studio Club, including twenty-eight one-artist shows. Among these latter were the first solo exhibitions of Edward Hopper (1920) and Reginald Marsh (1924). Membership requirements were simple and democratic: any artist who was introduced by a member could join.

In July 1923, Mrs. Whitney placed an advertisement in *The Arts*, a popular monthly journal. Headed "What Is a Home Without a Modern Picture?" it was part of a crusade to persuade the public to buy works of living American artists. The Whitney Studio Club had by this time become the most active and influential center of liberal art in the country. Ironically, its success led to its demise. By 1928, with membership at four hundred and a waiting list of as many more, it could no longer function as an artists' club. Mrs. Whitney then introduced the Whitney Studio Galleries, whose purpose was to provide a place where artists, particularly younger artists lacking dealers, could show their work without cost or complicated procedures. She herself made regular purchases from among the works exhibited. The Whitney Studio Galleries had a concentration of solo shows of young artists and actively engaged in exhibiting and selling pictures. By 1930, however, the Studio Club and Studio Galleries had fulfilled their original purpose. Interest in American art among dealers, museums, and the public had increased, and the academic hold on the art scene was broken.

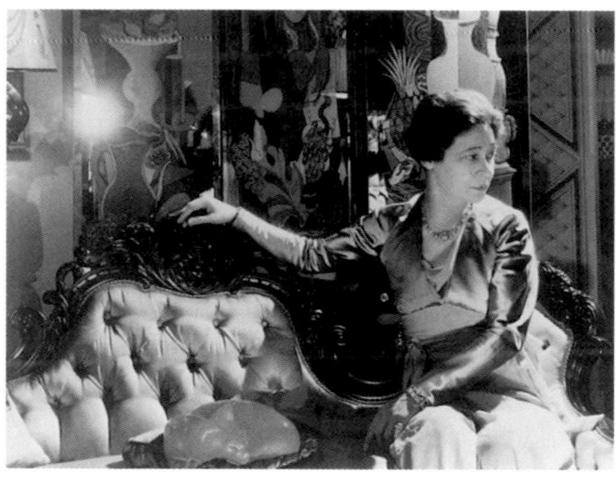

Cecil Beaton, *Juliana Force*, c. 1931. Gelatin silver print, 7 1/4 x 9 1/4 in. (18.4 x 23.5 cm). Gift of Gertrude Vanderbilt Whitney 93.25

Success, meanwhile, had again created a problem: the Whitney collection had grown to some five hundred works by American artists but was in dead storage with no place to show it. In October 1929, Juliana Force, Mrs. Whitney's longtime assistant and the woman who ran the Studio Club and Studio Galleries, made her way uptown to The Metropolitan Museum of Art, at Mrs. Whitney's behest. She sat down with its director, Dr. Edward Robinson, and formally offered the Whitney collection to the Metropolitan. Dr. Robinson flatly rejected the offer.

In mid-November, two weeks after the stock market crash that would usher in the Depression, The Museum of Modern Art was founded as an advocate of European modernism. In the meantime, Mrs. Whitney's stalwart commitment to contemporary American artists still lacked a dedicated institutional advocate. Juliana Force, however, had long harbored a desire to start a museum rather than see the collection incorporated into the Metropolitan. The founding of the Modern only added fuel to the fire lit by Robinson's rebuff, pushing Mrs. Whitney to the realization that her patronage of American art could only continue effectively under the formal aegis of a separate, independent institution. Weeks of feverish and secretive planning culminated in a press conference on January 3, 1930, at which Force announced that Mrs. Whitney had decided to endow the first museum devoted to American art. Mrs. Whitney was at the time on a trip to France, but her spirit was everywhere apparent. In her public statement, Force proclaimed that the Whitney would be an institution for the nation's artists:

> *Ever since museums were invented, contemporary liberal artists have had difficulties in "crashing the gate." Museums have had the habit of waiting until a painter or sculptor had acquired a certain official recognition before they would accept his work within their sacred portals. Exactly the contrary practice will be carried on in the Whitney Museum of American Art.*

A press conference two months later, however, presented a more pragmatic and museological mandate:

> *While this museum will emphatically not be a repository for relics, no museum can be a place for experiment. It is no longer necessary for this organization to help young artists to gain a hearing. What is now needed is a depot where the public may see fine examples of America's artistic production, and it is this need which we hope to fill...our objective will be the formation of a collection of pictures and other works of art whose merit alone make them worthy of being preserved in a public collection.*

The seeming contradiction between these two statements anticipated what would become the Whitney's dual purpose: to be both the incubator of new work and a museum committed to engaging a broad public with the best art made in the United States.

November 16, 1931, marked the opening of the Whitney Museum of American Art in adjoining brownstones on West 8th Street, remodeled by Noel & Miller, Architects. Juliana Force was appointed first director of the Museum, which at this point contained more than six hundred works of art, acquired over a period of twenty-five years. Although now operating as a chartered institution, the

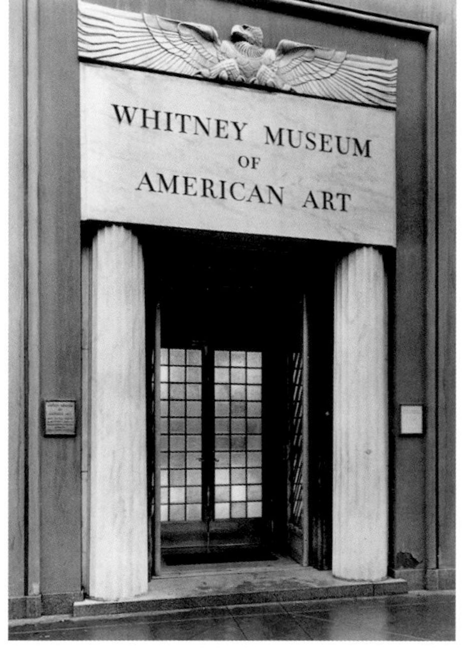

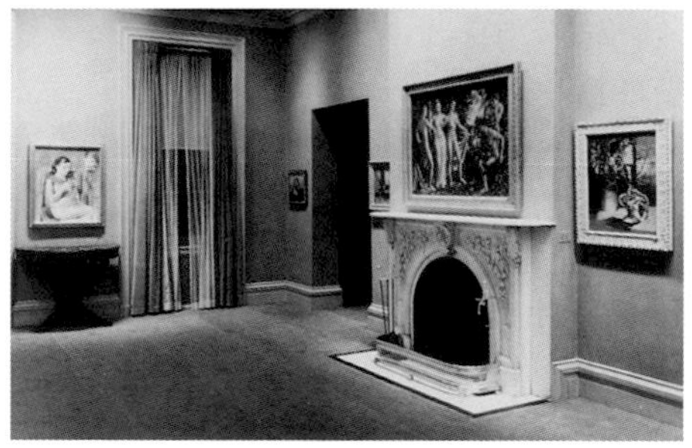

TOP: Whitney Museum of American Art at 10 West 8th Street, c. 1931.

BOTTOM: "First Biennial Exhibition of Contemporary American Painting," 1932.

Museum maintained policies originally formulated for the Whitney Studio Club. It continued, for example, the tradition of nonjuried exhibitions surveying new American art in the form of Biennials, the first of which took place in 1932. For the "First Biennial Exhibition of Contemporary American Painting," artists—among them Grant Wood, Arshile Gorky, and Georgia O'Keeffe—were invited to submit works of their own choosing. The critical reception was cool. Malcolm Vaughan was among the many who found the survey lacking, opining that "an artist never knows his best works."

Such reactions initiated what became a venerable tradition of critical disparagement of Whitney Biennials. But the arrows lose their sting with hindsight, which reveals that many of America's greatest artists have received their debut in these Whitney exhibitions.

A $20,000 acquisition fund was also created in 1932, the money to be spent on purchases from each Biennial. The emphasis was on buying works by artists not already in the collection. Moreover, as part of its policy of support for living artists, the Whitney extended the privilege of purchasing Biennial works to the public. At the 1932 Biennial, twenty-eight works were bought by the Museum and seven by private collectors as well as museums such as the Metropolitan. The Whitney also found other ways to declare its commitment to living artists: the first three curators of the Whitney—Edmund Archer, Lloyd Goodrich, and Hermon More—were themselves artists; More and Goodrich would later direct the institution.

In 1934, only two years after its founding as the first museum of national art, works from the Whitney's Permanent Collection were chosen to represent America in the 19th Venice Biennale. A year later, the Museum mounted "Abstract Painting in America," the first exhibition of its kind, which anticipated the founding of the American Abstract Artists group in 1936. The Museum failed to take advantage of its own exhibition, however, purchasing no works from it for the collection.

A formal Board of Trustees was also created in 1935, and it included Flora Whitney Miller, the daughter of Gertrude Vanderbilt Whitney. The Board continued to reinforce the Museum's mission. By 1936, for example, Biennial artists were being paid a rental fee for each work submitted to the exhibition. This was the first recognition by an American museum of any form of artists' rights, which are enshrined in European law but were then new to this nation.

Among other landmarks in the Whitney's practice of supporting living artists was the 1941 Annual entitled "Artists Under Forty," which highlighted the talents of a younger generation, including the first display of the work of David Smith. The Museum's role in promoting American art also went beyond the organization of exhibitions. In 1942, in cooperation with thirty other museums and college art departments, the Whitney helped establish the American Art Research Council to advance research and record the work of leading artists, past and present.

Gertrude Vanderbilt Whitney died that same year, having seen her original dream realized more fully than anyone could possibly have anticipated. Her legacy thrives to this day. But initially her death left the Museum in an uncertain state. The 1943 "Gertrude Vanderbilt Whitney Memorial Exhibition" led to a period of renewed discussion of a merger with The Metropolitan Museum of Art. A Whitney Wing was proposed for the Metropolitan, to be built with the $2.5 million Mrs. Whitney bequeathed to the Whitney Museum. After the "Memorial Exhibition," the Whitney reopened solely for the 1943–44 Annual while the leadership considered the merger with the Metropolitan.

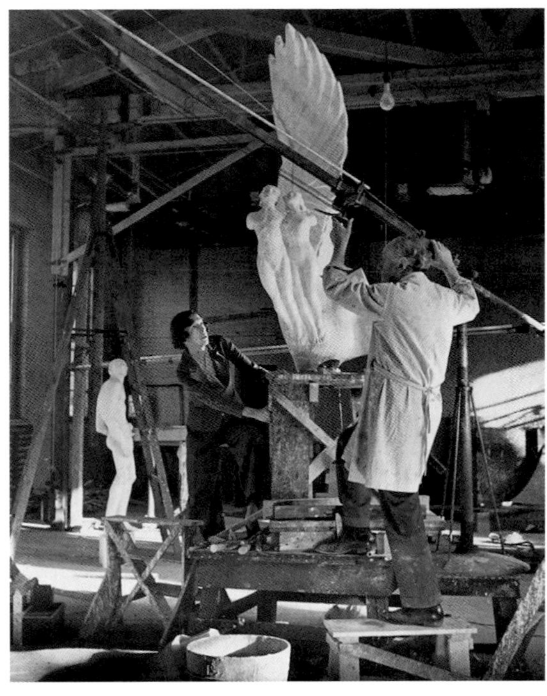

Gertrude Vanderbilt Whitney with her assistant, Salvatore F. Bilotti, in her sculpture studio on MacDougal Alley, c. 1939. At center is the maquette for her sculpture *Spirit of Flight*, exhibited at the 1939 World's Fair in New York.

In 1945, exhibitions at the Whitney recommenced, making an immediate mark on the art world. The Annual of that year heralded the emergence of the New York School, with first-time presentations of the work of William Baziotes, Hans Hofmann, Mark Rothko, and Mark Tobey. Of the 165 artists in the exhibition, fifty-four were having an inaugural showing at the Whitney. As already evidenced by the 1935 "Abstract Painting in America" show, the Museum's record of exhibiting abstract art was often daring and advanced. The following year "Pioneers of Modern Art in America" was mounted, and the work of Jackson Pollock was shown, while Willem de Kooning appeared in a Whitney exhibition in 1948. The Whitney's acquisitions record for advanced art, however, continued to be less adventurous than its exhibitions, especially during the period of Abstract Expressionism.

Another major exhibition of 1945 was "European Artists in America," featuring thirty-seven European painters and sculptors then working in this country. The exhibition highlighted the important contributions of international artists to American art. Thereafter, exhibitions routinely included European immigrant artists, recognizing the influence of European modernism in America.

During all these exhibitions, merger discussions with the Metropolitan had continued. Finally, on November 11, 1945, three years after the initial proposal, the Metropolitan announced that it would build a new wing to house the Whitney Museum of American Art. The Museum of

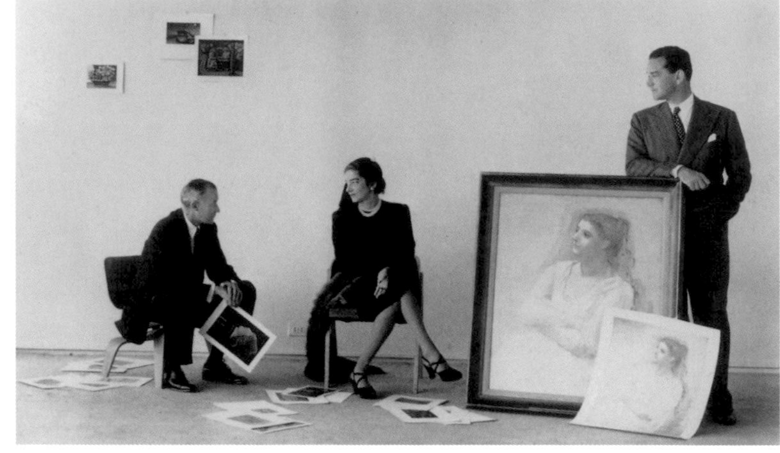

TOP: Museum presidents discuss the Three Museum Agreement. Left to right: Roland L. Redmond, The Metropolitan Museum of Art; Flora Whitney Miller, Whitney Museum; John Hay Whitney, The Museum of Modern Art. Photograph by Arnold Newman, 1947.

OPPOSITE PAGE TOP: Hermon More, director of the Whitney Museum, with architect Auguste L. Noel, reviewing the architectural plans for the Museum's new building on West 54th Street, 1953.

MIDDLE: Flora Whitney Miller with the first group of non-family Trustees elected to the Board, 1961. Left to right: David M. Solinger, B.H. Friedman, John I.H. Baur, Roy R. Neuberger, Lloyd Goodrich, Arthur G. Altschul, Michael H. Irving.

BOTTOM: Facade of the Whitney Museum of American Art at 22 West 54th Street, c. 1954. Noel & Miller, Architects; Philip Johnson, exterior design consultant.

Modern Art, however, was loath to see its two sister institutions go forward alone with a merger that would reshape the New York museum scene. The Modern's intervention led, in September 1947, to the "Three Museum Agreement." The core concept behind this agreement was that MoMA would turn over all work more than a century old, on a rolling basis, to the Metropolitan, and would cease collecting American art in deference to the Metropolitan's Whitney Wing, whose collection would be expanded.

The agreement fell apart a year later. On September 30, 1948, the Whitney formally withdrew from the Three Museum Agreement. A terse press release read: "The aims of the two institutions [the Whitney and the Metropolitan] in relation to contemporary art have proved to be so divergent that the Trustees of the Whitney Museum have decided to abandon the plans for coalition."

The collapse of the merger plan emboldened the almost twenty-year-old Whitney to take independent strides, as did a new administration. The Museum began a fresh commitment to the work of living artists. In November 1948, following the death of Juliana Force, Hermon More became the Museum's second director, a position he would hold for a decade, and he appointed Lloyd Goodrich associate director. One of their initial decisions was to deaccession the pre-twentieth-century art that the Museum had been collecting along with the art of the present. In December 1949, M. Knoedler & Company handled the sale of most of the Whitney's eighteenth- and nineteenth-century works. In a press release describing the sale, the Museum stated that it "has...decided, in order to use its resources and facilities most effectively for the benefit of American art, to concentrate on contemporary art." Although the Whitney continued to hold historical exhibitions and publish books on American art history, the sale focused its institutional mandate on contemporary art and artists.

The failure of the Three Museum Agreement had not put an end to the Whitney's collaborative ventures. In May 1949, The Museum of Modern

Art had offered the Whitney a plot of land it owned on 54th Street for a much needed building expansion. Once the Whitney agreed to relocate, in December 1949, the two museums announced plans that, from the Whitney's vantage, would further the cause of contemporary American art. These plans included joint touring exhibitions, lending art to each other, coordinating exhibition programs, and collaborating on research problems.

On October 26, 1954, the Whitney moved from its original 8th Street location to 22 West 54th Street. There were by then 1,300 works in the Permanent Collection. From 1958 to 1968, Lloyd Goodrich served as the Whitney's third director, with John I.H. Baur as associate director. (Baur had been curator of painting and sculpture since 1951.)

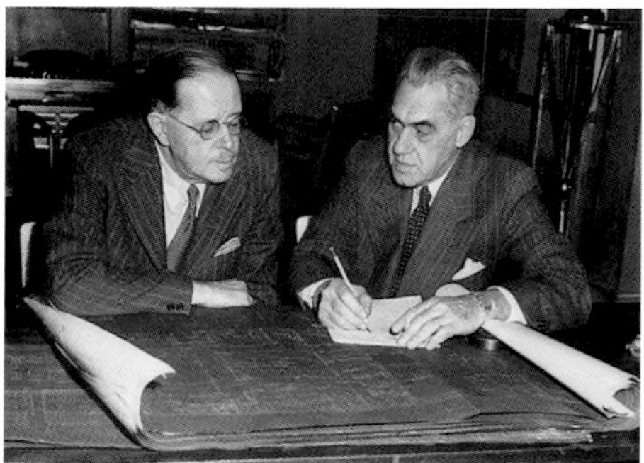

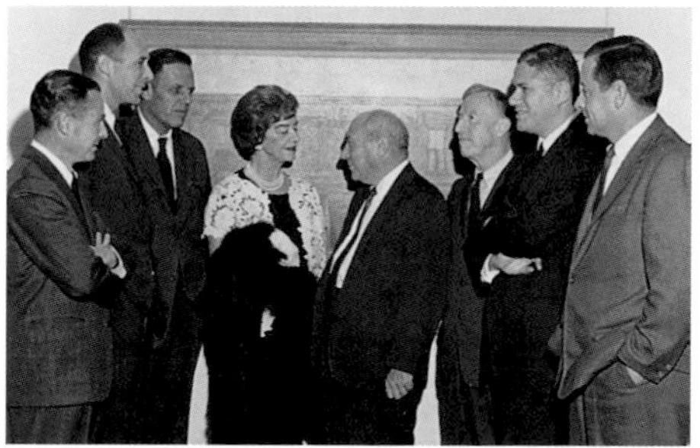

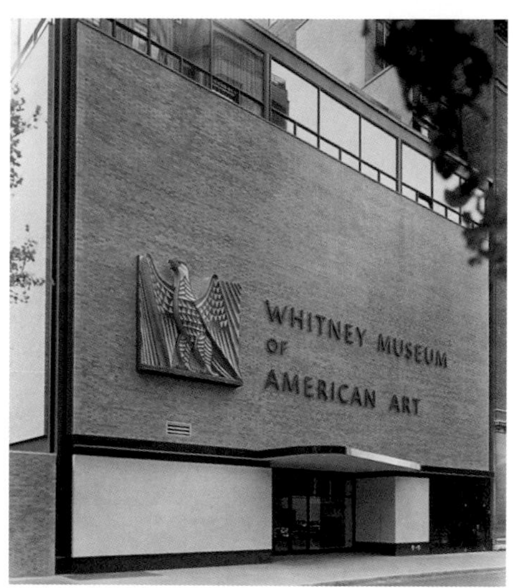

One of the most publicized Whitney exhibitions of the 1950s was the contemporary American art section of the "American National Exhibition in Moscow," which opened in 1959 at the Moscow Fair in Sokolniki Park. This ambitious exhibition, organized to implement an East-West cultural exchange agreement signed by the United States and the Soviet Union in 1958, included three decades of American art, beginning in 1928. It swiftly became a political football. Representative Francis E. Walter, chairman of the infamous House Un-American Activities Committee, charged that artists in the exhibition were largely Communists and demanded that the exhibition be censored. President Eisenhower, however, refused to order the withdrawal of any works from the exhibition.

In 1961, the Board of Trustees was expanded to include nonfamily members—an important step designed to broaden and professionalize the ambitions of the institution. In 1963–64, with the midtown building becoming increasingly cramped, a campaign to build new headquarters at 945 Madison Avenue was initiated. More gifts to the collection followed; beginning in 1966 and continuing for many years to come, Howard and Jean Lipman donated an extraordinary group of more than one

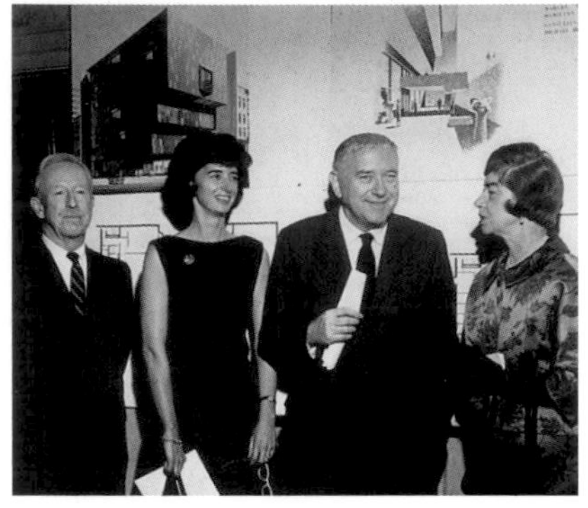

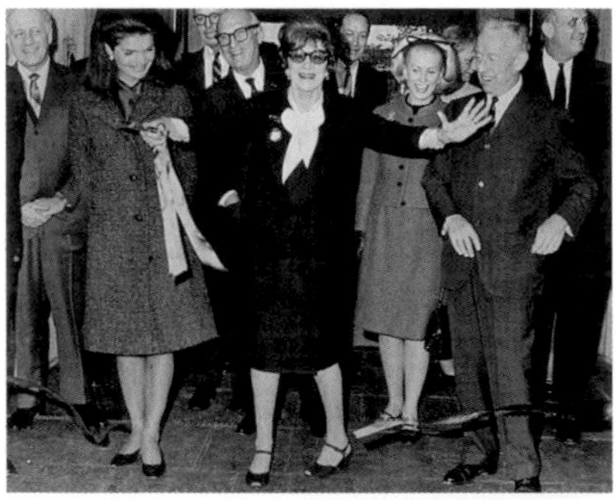

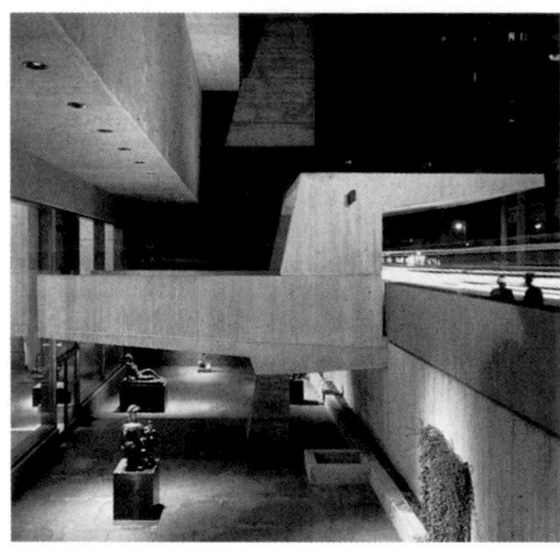

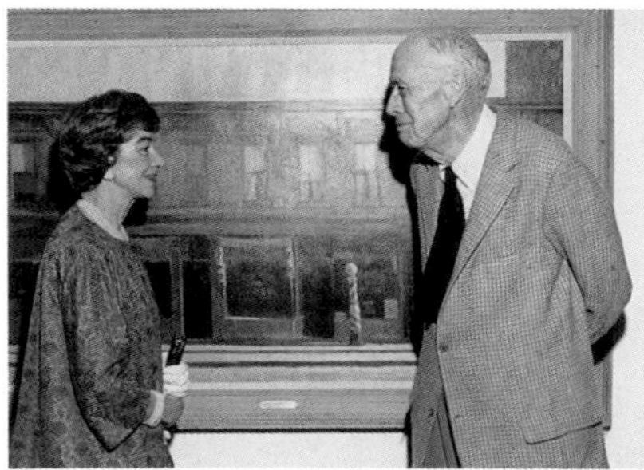

hundred sculptures, creating one of the strongest museum collections of post-World War II American sculpture. A commitment to serving a wider public in the new building led to the establishment of an Education Department in the summer of 1966.

On September 27, 1966, Jacqueline Kennedy helped inaugurate the Whitney's new building at 945 Madison Avenue and 75th Street, designed by Marcel Breuer, with his partner, Hamilton Smith, and Michael Irving, consulting architect. By then, the Permanent Collection had grown to 2,000 works. That same year, David M. Solinger was appointed president of the Museum, a position he held until 1974. Solinger was the first Museum president outside the Whitney family and was instrumental in retooling the Museum's finances to put the institution on a more stable footing.

The 1960s witnessed a significant expansion of the Museum's scope, collections, and outreach. The Independent Study Program was formed in 1967 to give advanced students the opportunity to study in New York with artists, critics, dealers, and the Museum staff. Various features of the program enabled students to organize exhibitions, pursue art practice, curatorial work, art historical scholarship, and critical writing. The appointment of John I.H. Baur as director in 1968 brought a leading art historian to the helm of the Museum. Baur, who served until 1974, accepted the Josephine N. Hopper Bequest—the entire artistic estate of Edward Hopper, more than 2,500 objects, the largest gift of a single artist's work ever made to an American museum. Under Baur's directorship, the Museum focused its attention on the diversity of contemporary art, and the collection and exhibitions programs soon grew more expansive, not only in number but in media. He established the Painting and Sculpture Acquisition Committee, and photography began to be collected in 1970. That same year, the Whitney presented its first exhibition devoted to architecture, on Paolo Soleri, and formed an

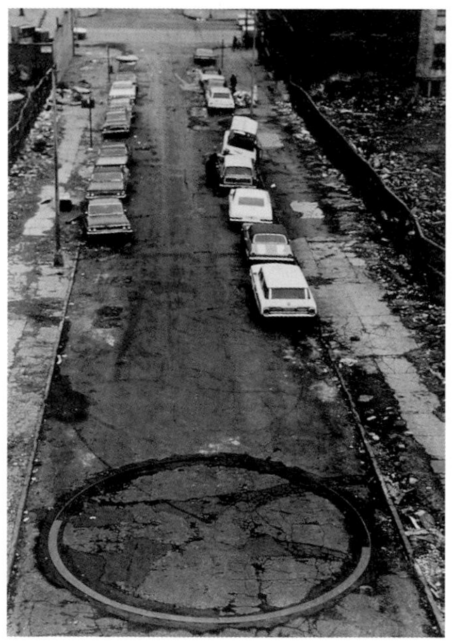

Richard Serra's off-site sculpture *To Encircle Base Plate Hexagram Right Angles Inverted,* from the 1970 Annual. Photograph by Peter Moore © Estate of Peter Moore/VAGA, N.Y.

OPPOSITE PAGE TOP: Left to right: Museum director Lloyd Goodrich with Flora Miller Irving, architect Marcel Breuer, and Flora Whitney Miller at the announcement of the plans for the new building, December 11, 1963.

SECOND FROM TOP: Flora Whitney Miller (center) at the dedication ceremony for the new Whitney Museum at 945 Madison Avenue, September 27, 1966. Left to right: Jacqueline Kennedy, president of the National Committee, with National Committee members William A. Marsteller and Nathan Cummings, Robert W. Sarnoff, Trustee, Marylou Whitney, and Lloyd Goodrich, Museum director.

SECOND FROM BOTTOM: Entrance ramp and sculpture court of the Whitney Museum, looking south from 75th Street, 1966.

BOTTOM: Flora Whitney Miller with Edward Hopper in front of his 1930 painting *Early Sunday Morning,* 1961.

Architecture Committee to plan future shows in the field. The Film Department was created in 1970 as well. Site-specific sculptures, such as Dennis Oppenheim's *Decomposition—Whitney Museum* and Michael Heizer's *City Depression*, had been featured in the 1968 Sculpture Annual, while the 1970 Annual included off-site installations by Richard Serra, Robert Smithson, and Keith Sonnier.

At year's end in 1970, the Whitney staged New York's first major exhibition of the new art form of video, and a New American Filmmakers Series (later renamed New American Film and Video Series) was launched to support the work of independent, noncommercial American filmmakers. Within the next two years, the Whitney mounted the multimedia survey "Contemporary Black Artists in America" and, in the maelstrom of the Vietnam War, the Whitney was the East Coast venue for "Executive Order 9066: The Internment of 110,000 Japanese Americans." Organized by the California Historical Society, it was the Museum's first exhibition dedicated to photography.

In 1973, the Whitney launched a concept that would later revolutionize the museum world with the opening of its first branch museum, at 55 Water Street. The only cultural facility of its kind at the time to serve the Lower Manhattan community, the site also functioned as a curatorial laboratory for the Independent Study Program.

Since the 1930s, the original Whitney Biennials had been turned into Annuals, with each year's exhibition focusing on different media. In 1973, the program changed back to a biennial schedule, and the exhibition that year combined all media. The shift was made in acknowledgment of new art practices that crossed boundaries, rejecting traditional categories of art making in favor of hybrid processes.

The directorship of Thomas N. Armstrong III (1974–90) brought a new emphasis on acquiring works of individual artists in depth. Armstrong also wanted to build the collection so as to represent every phase of American art at its best. To this end, he retooled the Biennial to feature younger artists who had not been shown in New York and, in the Permanent Collection, sought to balance art from the first half of the twentieth century with contemporary art.

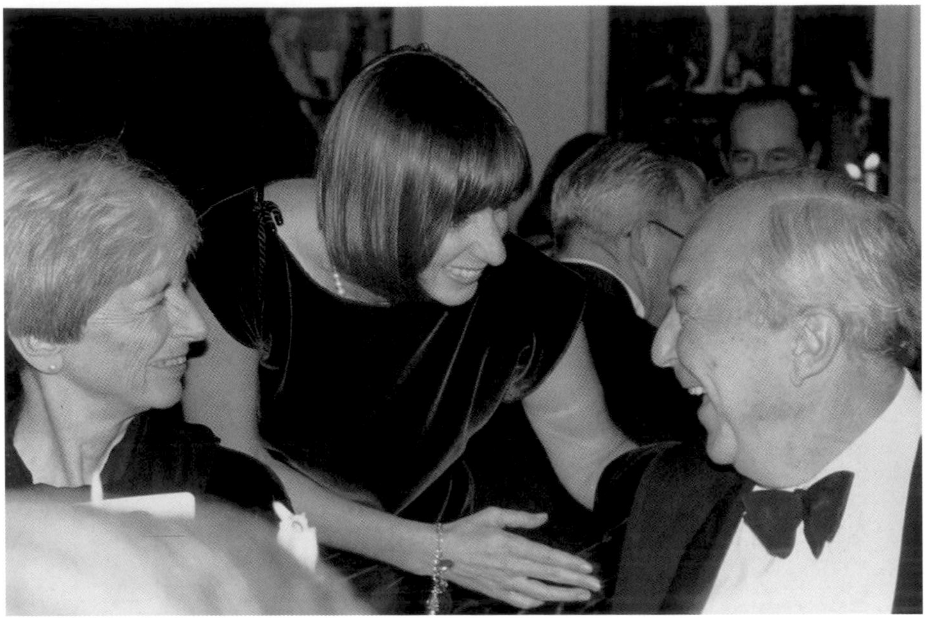

Flora Miller (Irving) Biddle (left) and her daughter Fiona Donovan, with Jasper Johns at lenders' dinner for "The Drawings of Jasper Johns," 1991.

Throughout Armstrong's tenure, the Board of Trustees played a vital role in the institution, led first by Howard Lipman as president (1974–77; he continued to serve as Trustee until 1992). The Board began to take on a more important role in safeguarding the Museum's solvency while honoring its historic mission. Lipman was succeeded by Flora Miller (Irving) Biddle, who served until 1985 and remained an active Board member until 1999, when she was elected Honorary Trustee. Gertrude Vanderbilt Whitney's granddaughter was and continues to be a steadfast champion of contemporary art. Fiona Irving Donovan, Gertrude's great-granddaughter, became a Trustee in 1977 and still serves on the Board. Leonard A. Lauder began serving as a Trustee in 1977 (he became president in 1990 and chairman in 1994). Through his continuing generosity, he has had a more significant impact on the Whitney than any other nonfamily Trustee—Lauder has been responsible for more major acquisitions than any individual in the Museum's history. He was preceded as president by William S. Woodside (1985–90), who stayed on as a Trustee until 1995.

To celebrate the Museum's fiftieth anniversary, the National Committee was reestablished by Armstrong in 1980. The committee members, outstanding patrons of art from across the nation, enlarged the scope of the Museum's collecting and exhibition activities by funding purchases and supporting traveling exhibitions of Whitney works.

Armstrong's tenure was highlighted by significant additions to the Permanent Collection as well as an exhibition program that encompassed both the past and present. The 1968 Hopper Bequest became the nucleus of two large and extraordinarily popular exhibitions between 1979 and 1981

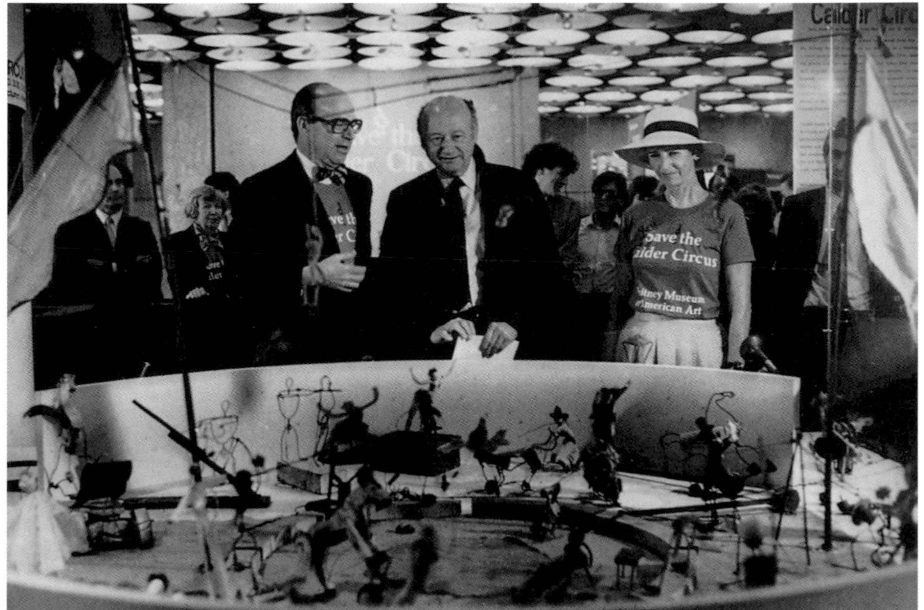

May 5, 1982, press conference announcing the Museum's successful fund-raising campaign to purchase *Calder's Circus*. Left to right: Museum director Tom Armstrong, Mayor Edward I. Koch, and Flora Miller (Irving) Biddle.

that presented landmark surveys of Hopper's paintings, prints, and illustrations. In 1978, the Museum received the Felicia Meyer Marsh Bequest—more than 850 paintings, oil studies, drawings, and sketches by her husband, Reginald Marsh, which formed the basis of a major exhibition in 1979. The 1977 Lawrence H. Bloedel Bequest enlarged the collection yet further.

Armstrong's mandate to collect and exhibit the works of individual artists in depth was fulfilled in a series of nine exhibitions called "Concentrations," which, over a period of two years, showed the Whitney's holdings of American masters Maurice Prendergast, Charles Sheeler, John Sloan, Charles Burchfield, Gaston Lachaise, Stuart Davis, Georgia O'Keeffe, and Alexander Calder. In 1981, the Permanent Collection went on continuous view for the first time, when the third floor was dedicated to an installation of masterworks that remained in place until 1989. A unique addition to the collection was *Calder's Circus*, which had been on loan since 1970. Installed in the Lobby, it had long delighted visitors, from children to art critics. In 1982, the Calder family decided to sell the ensemble, and within a few hectic months of strenuous campaigning, the Whitney raised $1.25 million to purchase the work; half the amount was donated by the Robert Wood Johnson Jr. Charitable Trust.

The idea of major museums opening branches seems commonplace today, but it was still a novel conception in the 1980s, when the Whitney opened three branches in five years. The Downtown Branch had been in operation since 1973. In 1981, the Museum extended its reach from Lower Manhattan to suburban Connecticut with the inauguration of a branch in the headquarters of Champion International Corporation in Stamford, which remained open until 2000. Midtown Manhattan was the locus for the next branch, at the headquarters of Philip Morris Incorporated on Park Avenue and 42nd Street. Opened in 1983, it is still in operation, providing the bustle of commuters, businesses, and tourists with an opportunity to break up the day with a museum visit. The Whitney's fourth branch (1986–92) was established at the headquarters of the Equitable Life Assurance Society on Seventh Avenue between 51st and 52nd Streets. The Downtown Branch, in the meantime, was searching for a new home, which it found in 1988. The Whitney Museum of American Art, Downtown at Federal Reserve Plaza, which remained in operation until 1992, was funded by a partnership of Park Tower Realty and IBM.

Exhibitions at the branch museums reached into the Permanent Collection for works not normally on view and, at the same time, mounted shows of young and lesser-known artists, whose innovative work had often never been seen in a solo museum exhibition. The operation of the branch museums signaled a remarkable and productive collaboration between corporate America and a nonprofit art institution, a collaboration that brought American art, new and old, into local communities.

TOP: Bill Viola (foreground) working with Museum director David A. Ross on the catalogue for the 1998 "Bill Viola" exhibition.

BOTTOM: "Black Male: Representations of Masculinity in Contemporary American Art," 1994.

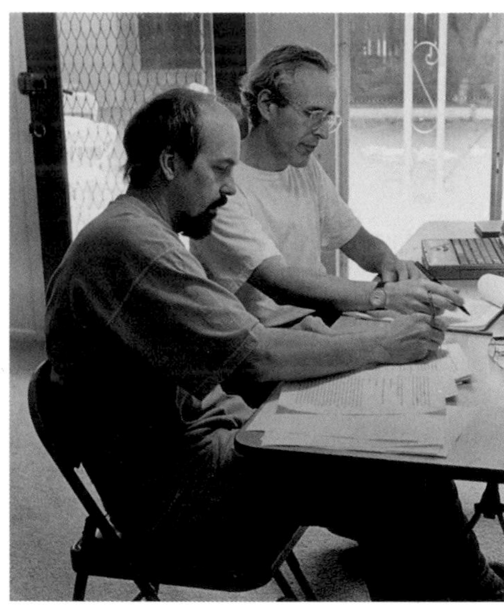

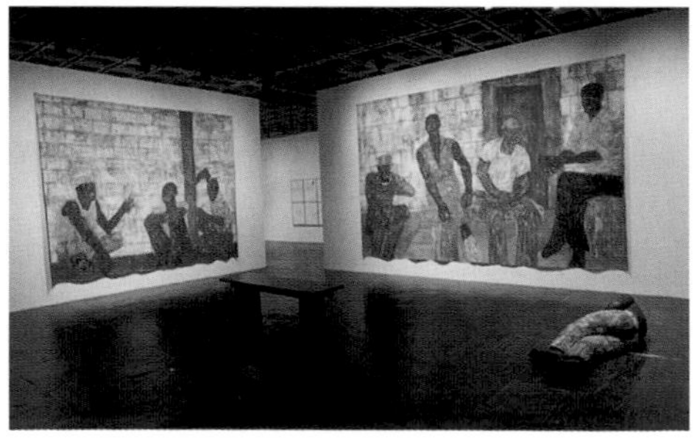

A short listing of some of the major exhibitions of the later 1970s and 1980s reveals the Museum's ongoing commitment to the past, present, and future. In addition to the Hopper and Marsh shows, the Whitney mounted "Jasper Johns," the largest international traveling exhibition of the work of an American artist (1977), and the first museum retrospectives of Cy Twombly (1979), Nam June Paik (1982, the most comprehensive exhibition ever devoted to a single video artist), Cindy Sherman (1987), Frank Gehry (1988), and Robert Mapplethorpe (1988). "New Image Painting" (1978), including works by Jennifer Bartlett, Neil Jenney, Susan Rothenberg, and Joe Zucker, gave a name to a vanguard reconsideration of recognizable imagery in the art of the 1970s; "Disney Animation and Animators" (1982) presented the first thoroughgoing examination of animation as an art form; and "New American Art Museums" (1982), a traveling exhibition, assessed contemporary architectural solutions to the needs of art museums.

Armstrong's departure in 1990 was involuntary and led to some disaffection with the Museum in parts of the art world. The Board ultimately appointed David A. Ross as the Whitney's sixth director in 1991. During Ross' tenure, Gilbert C. Maurer, a Trustee since 1983, served as president; he was succeeded in 1998 by Joel S. Ehrenkranz, who has materially strengthened the commitment of Board members to the Whitney's mission. Ross presided over an extraordinarily energetic period in the Whitney's history, in which major additions to the Permanent Collection were paralleled by imaginative exhibitions that embraced new art and new media as well as new ideologies.

Under Ross' aegis, a Photography Acquisition Committee and Film & Video Committee were established to develop these areas and increase acquisitions. In 1994, the Charles Simon Bequest, gift of a longtime Trustee, provided the Museum with eighty major works, including seventeen John Marin paintings and watercolors; the Permanent Collection now holds works that represent the full range of Marin's art. Four years later, the Whitney acquired fifteen oils and gouaches by Ad Reinhardt, making the collection the largest single holding of Reinhardt's work in the United States.

Among one-artist shows of the 1990s were those devoted to Agnes Martin (1992), Jean-Michel Basquiat (1992, his first retrospective), Richard Avedon (1994), Nan Goldin (1996), and Bill Viola (1998), the latter curated by Ross himself. Thematic exhibitions ranged from "Making Mischief: Dada Invades New York" (1996) to "Black Male: Representations of Masculinity in Contemporary American Art" (1994), which explored stereotypical representations of race and gender from a variety of opposing stances. A novel series of three shows entitled "Views from Abroad: European Perspectives on American Art Drawn from the Whitney Collection" invited curators from Amsterdam, Frankfurt, and London to offer their personal takes on American art in exhibitions shown at the Whitney and at their own institutions.

By the 1980s, it had become clear that the Whitney's burgeoning collection and exhibition programs had outgrown the capacity of the Breuer building. In 1985, plans for an expansion, designed by Michael Graves, failed to muster unanimous support among the Whitney's key stakeholders and had to be abandoned. It was then decided to expand within the Breuer building itself by transforming the fifth floor offices into exhibition galleries. The administrative arm of the Museum (also in need of more space) would move around the corner into renovated brownstones on 74th Street. In 1996, after the purchase of an

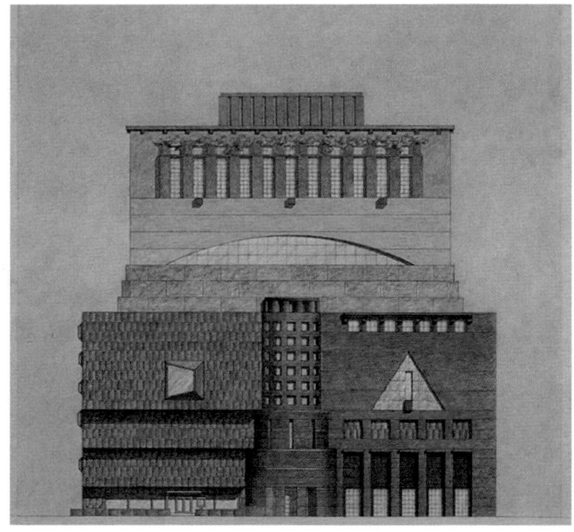

Michael Graves, *Madison Avenue Elevation—Scheme 1, for Proposed Whitney Museum Extension*, 1985. Michael Graves Architect, Princeton.

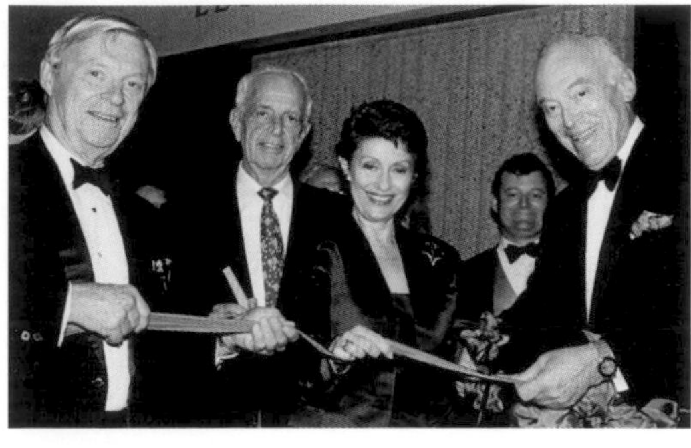

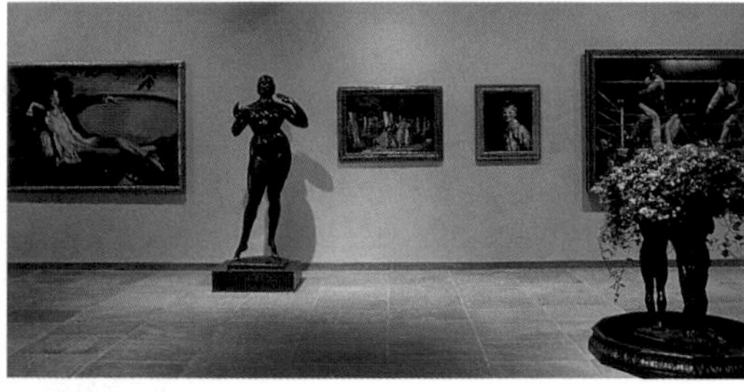

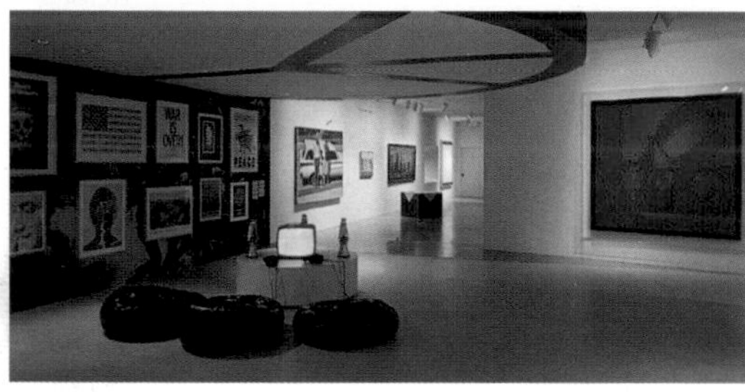

additional brownstone, construction began on the administrative wing, designed by Richard Gluckman and David Mayner Architects. The following year, with the offices vacated, the Gluckman-Mayner renovation of the Breuer building got underway. In the spring of 1998, the Whitney's first custom-designed Permanent Collection exhibition space, the Leonard & Evelyn Lauder Galleries, opened on the fifth floor.

The Lauder Galleries are dedicated to art from 1900 to 1950. Plans for a Permanent Collection exhibition of works from the latter half of the century on the second floor were postponed to accommodate "The American Century: Art & Culture 1900–2000." Conceived by David Ross, the two-part exhibition, which ran from April 1999 to February 2000, was the most ambitious in the Museum's history, twice filling 30,000 square feet of exhibition space with a comprehensive, authoritative survey of twentieth-century art in its social and cultural context.

Following Ross' departure for the San Francisco Museum of Modern Art, the undersigned became the Whitney's seventh director in the fall of 1998. I had the pleasure of overseeing the final preparations for "The American Century" and organizing the museum-wide 2000 Biennial. After the Biennial closed, the Mildred and Herbert Lee Galleries on the second floor were reinstalled with a permanent exhibition of works dating from c. 1950 to the present.

TOP: Left to right: Gilbert C. Maurer, Louis Gartner, Evelyn Lauder, William Lauder, and Leonard A. Lauder at the ribboncutting ceremony opening the Leonard & Evelyn Lauder Galleries, March 31, 1998.

MIDDLE: Leonard & Evelyn Lauder Galleries, installation view, 1998.

BOTTOM: Part II, 1950–2000, of "The American Century: Art & Culture 1900–2000."

Over the past three years, the Whitney has built on the strong legacy of previous directors, adding to the collection, staging exhibitions that draw from the work of emerging artists and from renowned as well as underappreciated twentieth-century masters, and forcefully making a case for the art of our new century through acquisitions, exhibitions, and public programs. A $5 million gift from Trustee Robert Wilson has launched the Museum's first program in conservation. In 2000, two adjunct curators were hired to oversee the Museum's efforts in architecture and new media arts, respectively. A commitment to providing broad public access to our collections led to the development of a dynamic website, including webcast interviews with artists, a random-access audio tour in the Museum using state-of-the-art players, and an expansion of our public hours, with a near doubling of membership and attendance since 1998.

In 2001, during Leonard Lauder's chairmanship and Joel Ehrenkranz's presidency, the Museum engaged visionary architect Rem Koolhaas to help us write our next chapter, which will entail the first substantial growth in more than forty years. Although our plans are at an early stage as of this writing, we are for the first time envisioning adequate space both for the Permanent Collection and for educational programs.

An invigorated commitment to supporting living artists led to Chuck Close's appointment to the Whitney's Board of Trustees in 2000, the first artist in this capacity. Thanks to Trustee Melva Bucksbaum, the Whitney now has an extraordinary vehicle for the recognition of an individual artist's achievement. In March 2000, she created a $2 million endowment to "honor a living American artist whose work demonstrates a singular combination of talent and imagination." The award of $100,000 is given every two years to an artist exhibiting in the Biennial. One of the largest prizes offered in the visual arts, the Bucksbaum Award heralds a renewal of the Museum's long-standing mission: to be the artists' museum.

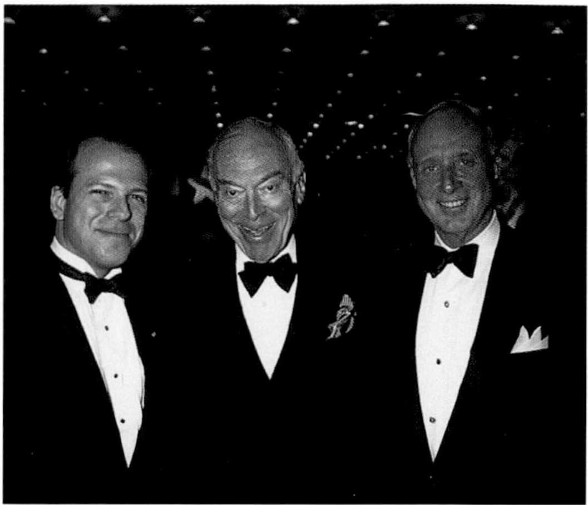

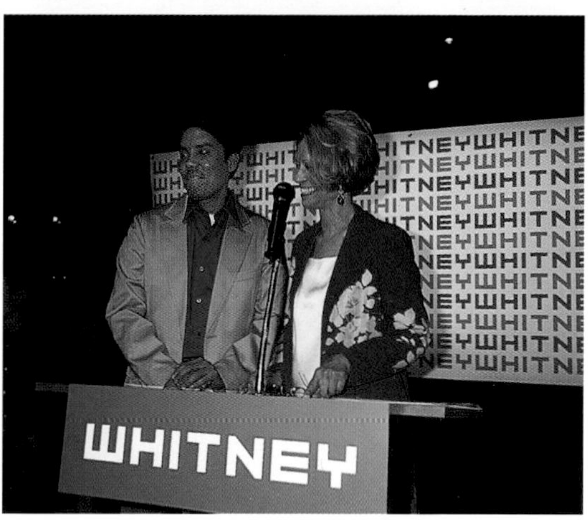

TOP: Left to right: Maxwell L. Anderson, Leonard A. Lauder, and Joel S. Ehrenkranz at the Whitney's American Art Award dinner, June 12, 2000.

BOTTOM: Paul Pfeiffer receiving the first Bucksbaum Award from Melva Bucksbaum, May 1, 2000.

Curators, other professional staff, volunteers, trustees, and patrons have shaped the Whitney in the course of its first seventy years. A brief essay cannot do justice to the hundreds whose generosity of spirit, intelligence, and professionalism have kept the Whitney's abiding commitment to American artists alive and flourishing. This handbook is accordingly dedicated to the artists who are the Whitney's reason for being and to the patrons, collectors, critics, and scholars who have long considered the support of artists a fundamental necessity.

This brief recap of the Museum's history makes it evident that, like other major art institutions, historical circumstances have given the Whitney numerous natural strengths and presented a number of challenges. The process of building a collection is one of developing these assets and overcoming inherited weaknesses. For seventy years, an enlightened succession

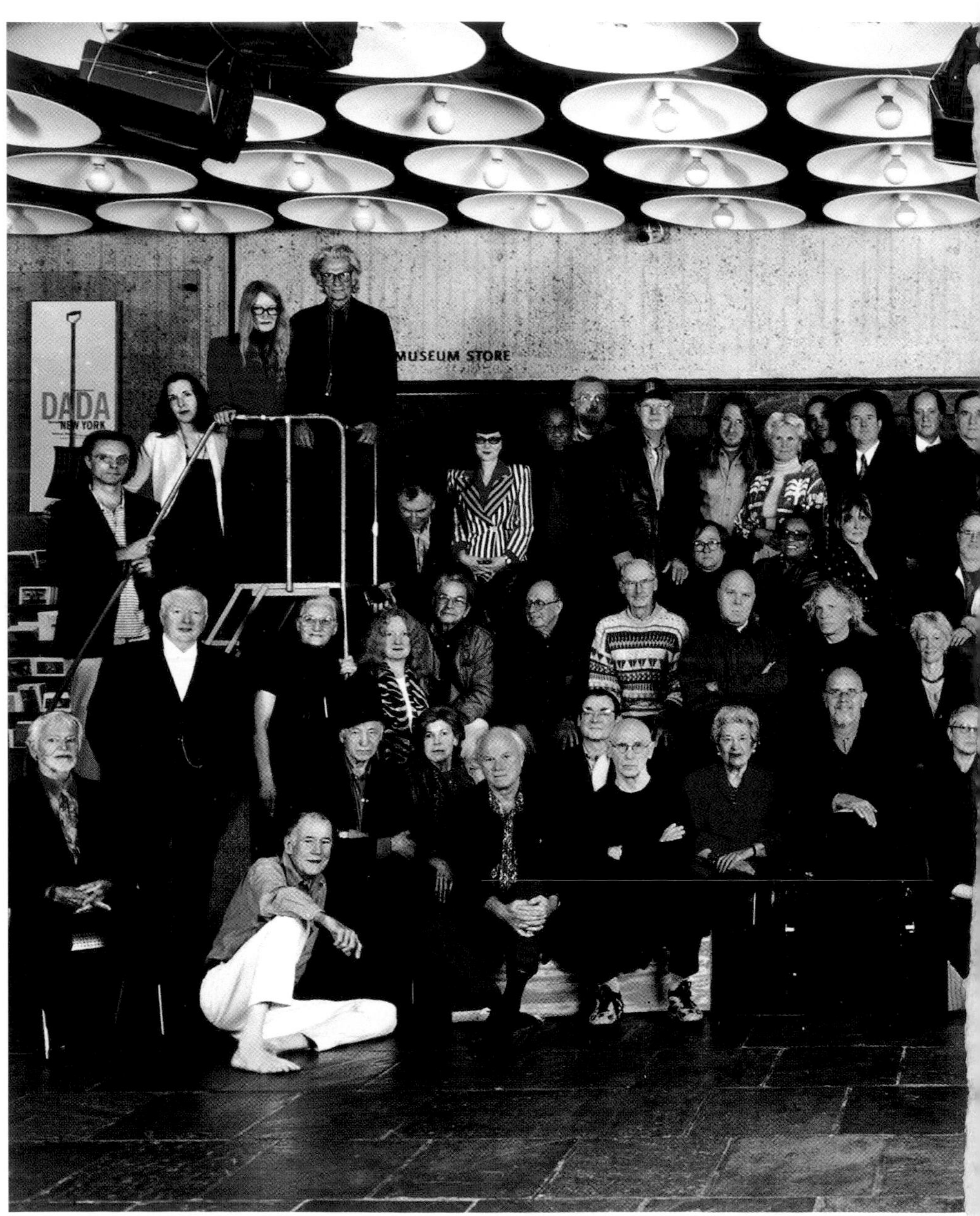

Group portrait of eighty-two artists whose work was exhibited in Part II, 1950–2000, of "The American Century: Art & Culture 1900–2000."

of directors, curators, and patrons has been doing just that. As the 377 works in this handbook attest, today the Whitney takes pride in a Permanent Collection—now comprising nearly 13,000 objects created by 2,450 artists—through which one can recount the entire history of American art in the twentieth century—and the history being made in the twenty-first.

Photographed by Timothy Greenfield-Sanders on September 24, 1999, in the Lobby of the Museum. ©Timothy Greenfield-Sanders, 1999.

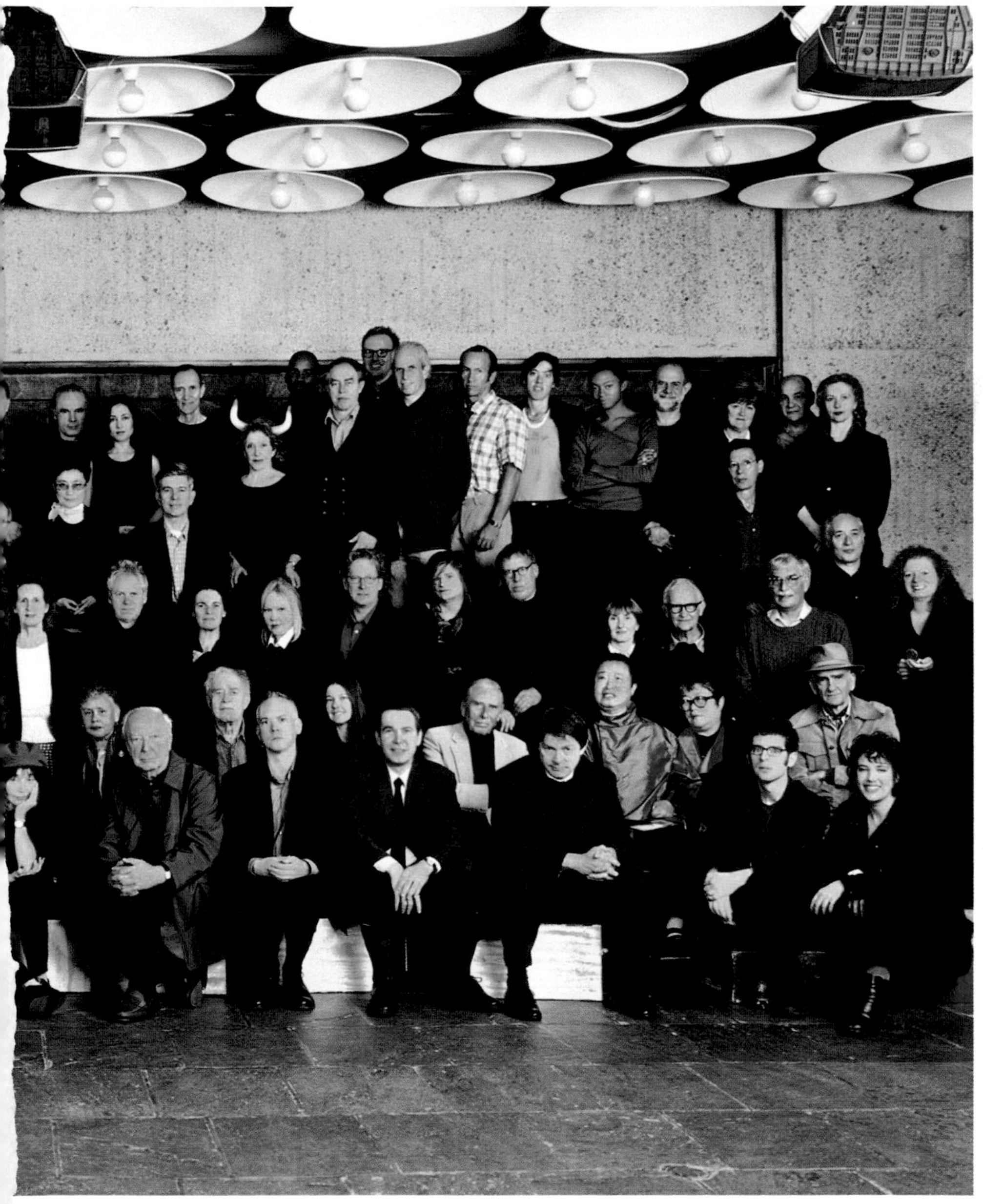

ARTISTS

Vito Acconci
Robert Adams
Doug Aitken
Josef Albers
Carl Andre
Janine Antoni
Polly Apfelbaum
Ida Applebroog
Diane Arbus
Richard Artschwager
Richard Avedon
Milton Avery
Alice Aycock
Peggy Bacon
John Baldessari
Lewis Baltz
Matthew Barney
Jean-Michel Basquiat
William Baziotes
Romare Bearden
Robert Bechtle
George Bellows
Lynda Benglis
Thomas Hart Benton
Dawoud Bey
Isabel Bishop
Ross Bleckner
Oscar Bluemner
Peter Blume
Lee Bontecou
Jonathan Borofsky
Louise Bourgeois
Patrick Henry Bruce
Charles Burchfield
Scott Burton
Paul Cadmus
Ingrid Calame
Alexander Calder
Peter Campus
Federico Castellon
Vija Celmins
John Chamberlain
Christo and Jeanne-Claude
Larry Clark
Chuck Close
Sue Coe
Willie Cole
Bruce Conner
John Coplans
Joseph Cornell
Petah Coyne
Ralston Crawford
John Currin
John Steuart Curry
Douglas Davis
Stuart Davis
Jay DeFeo
Beauford Delaney
Charles Demuth
Richard Diebenkorn
Burgoyne Diller
Jim Dine
Mark di Suvero
Arthur G. Dove
Elsie Driggs
Guy Pène du Bois
Carroll Dunham
Jimmie Durham
William Eggleston
Nicole Eisenman
Sally Elesby
Richard Estes
Philip Evergood
Tony Feher
Lyonel Feininger
John Ferren
Dan Flavin
Robert Frank
Helen Frankenthaler
Jared French
Lee Friedlander
Adam Fuss
Ellen Gallagher
William J. Glackens
Fritz Glarner
Robert Gober
Nan Goldin
Leon Golub
Félix González-Torres
Arshile Gorky
Adolph Gottlieb
Dan Graham
Philip Guston
Peter Halley
Jane Hammond
David Hammons
Duane Hanson
Keith Haring
Marsden Hartley
Tim Hawkinson
Mary Heilmann
Michael Heizer
Robert Henri
Eva Hesse
Gary Hill
Lewis Hine
Jenny Holzer
Edward Hopper
Roni Horn
Peter Hujar
Robert Indiana
David Ireland
Robert Irwin
Neil Jenney
Alfred Jensen
Jess
Jasper Johns
Joan Jonas
Joe Jones
Kenneth Josephson
Donald Judd
Alex Katz
Mike Kelley
Ellsworth Kelly
Edward Kienholz
Franz Kline
Willem de Kooning
Jeff Koons
Joseph Kosuth
Lee Krasner
Barbara Kruger
Walt Kuhn
Gaston Lachaise
Liz Larner
Louise Lawler
Jacob Lawrence
Blanche Lazzell
Rico Lebrun
Charles LeDray
Lee Mingwei
Alfred Leslie
Sherrie Levine
Helen Levitt
Sol LeWitt
Roy Lichtenstein
Glenn Ligon
Mark Lombardi
Morris Louis
Louis Lozowick
George Luks
Vera Lutter
Stanton Macdonald-Wright
Robert Mangold
Robert Mapplethorpe
Brice Marden
John Marin
Reginald Marsh
Kerry James Marshall
Agnes Martin
Gordon Matta-Clark
Jan Matulka
Anthony McCall
Allan McCollum
Susan Meiselas
Ray Metzker

Richard Misrach
Joan Mitchell
Lisette Model
Abelardo Morell
Robert Morris
Robert Motherwell
Vik Muniz
Gerald Murphy
Elizabeth Murray
Elie Nadelman
Peter Nagy
Bruce Nauman
Alice Neel
Shirin Neshat
Louise Nevelson
Barnett Newman
Isamu Noguchi
Kenneth Noland
Georgia O'Keeffe
Claes Oldenburg
Catherine Opie
Tom Otterness
Tony Oursler
Nam June Paik
David Park
Philip Pearlstein
Raymond Pettibon
Paul Pfeiffer
Jack Pierson
Adrian Piper
Lari Pittman
Jackson Pollock
Fairfield Porter
Richard Pousette-Dart
Maurice Prendergast
Stephen Prina
Martin Puryear
Robert Rauschenberg
Charles Ray
Man Ray
Ad Reinhardt
Matthew Ritchie
Larry Rivers
Liisa Roberts
Tim Rollins + K.O.S
James Rosenquist
Martha Rosler
Theodore Roszak
Susan Rothenberg
Mark Rothko
Michal Rovner
Edward Ruscha
Robert Ryman
Alison Saar
Betye Saar
David Salle
Lucas Samaras
Glen Seator
George Segal
Richard Serra
Ben Shahn
Joel Shapiro
Charles Sheeler
Cindy Sherman
Everett Shinn
Shahzia Sikander
Gary Simmons
Laurie Simmons
John F. Simon, Jr.
Charles Simonds
Lorna Simpson
Aaron Siskind
John Sloan
David Smith
Kiki Smith
Tony Smith
Robert Smithson
Raphael Soyer
Edward Steichen
Pat Steir
Frank Stella
Joseph Stella
Louis Stettner
Clyfford Still
Jessica Stockholder
John Storrs
Sarah Sze
Yves Tanguy
Diana Thater
Paul Thek
Wayne Thiebaud
Bob Thompson
Mark Tobey
Fred Tomaselli
George Tooker
James Turrell
Richard Tuttle
Cy Twombly
Bill Viola
Andy Warhol
Max Weber
Weegee (Arthur Fellig)
Carrie Mae Weems
Lawrence Weiner
H.C. Westermann
Fred Wilson
Robert Wilson
Garry Winogrand
Jackie Winsor
Terry Winters
David Wojnarowicz
Steve Wolfe
Martin Wong
Grant Wood
Christopher Wool
Andrew Wyeth
Marguerite Zorach

Notes to the Artists' Pages

An asterisk (*) indicates that a work was exhibited in a Whitney Annual or Biennial.

Dimensions are in inches followed by centimeters; height precedes width precedes depth. Dimensions followed by the word "sight" have been measured within the frame or mat opening.

In the accession number of a work, the first set of digits refers to the year of acquisition—two digits for the twentieth century, four for the twenty-first. The number after a decimal point indicates the sequence of the work's addition to the Permanent Collection that year. For example, 90.3 is the third work acquired in 1990; 2001.23 is the twenty-third work acquired in 2001. Promised gifts are preceded by the letter P. For works accessioned in a group, the year is followed by the group accession number and the individual item number within the group. For example, 89.15.5 and 89.15.6 refer to the fifth and sixth works in a group.

As indicated by a comparison of the date of accession with the date of the work, a significant number of works were acquired within two years of their completion.

VITO ACCONCI

b. 1940

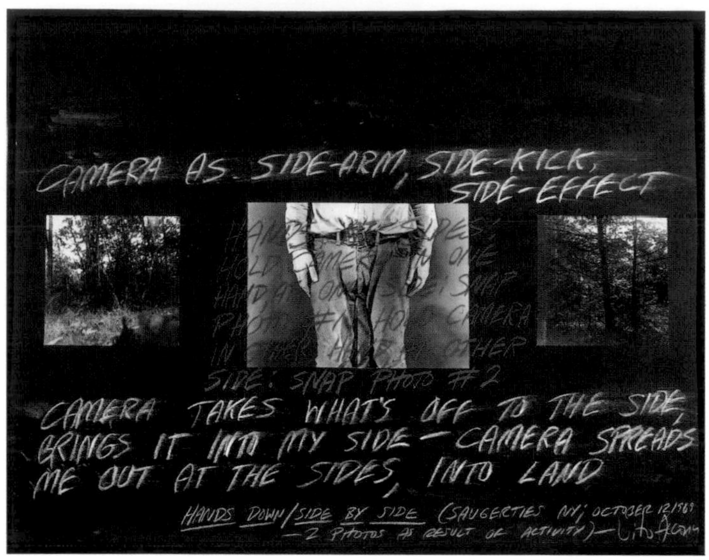

In his highly charged performances and single-channel videos made in the 1970s, Vito Acconci challenged the aesthetic notions of mainstream society with vulgar and sometimes shocking explorations of human psychology and the body. Yet these works dealt with a serious issue: how difficult it is to know and fully accept oneself, and how frustrating are our efforts to know and understand others.

Hands Down/Side by Side, one of Acconci's earliest works, records a simple performance, or "action": standing and staring straight ahead at a landscape setting, Acconci held a camera in his right hand, at hip level, the lens pointed to the right, his left hand at his side; he then repeated the process with his left hand, pointing the camera to the left. The landscape photographs that resulted appear at the edges of *Hands Down/Side by Side*. The central image of Acconci's midsection is a means of preserving and explaining the action. It announces that the photographs were not taken from the vantage of a standing figure holding a camera at eye level, but from the level of the artist's lowered hands. The red-lettered text written over this photograph describes the process in words, while the white-lettered text above and below plays on the concept of hands at sides to personalize the camera as Acconci's "side-arm," "side-kick," and "side-effect"; it is what "spreads me out at the sides, into land."

Acconci uses photography to locate his body in a particular place, while also "extending" his vision to the parts of his body that lack eyes. In doing so, he exposes the limitations of human perception. With only two eyes, set at the same height and oriented in the same direction, our experience and memory of our body in space can only be partial, and we must rely on language, other people, and recording technology to understand and remember ourselves in the world.

Hands Down/Side by Side, 1969
Gelatin silver prints and chalk on paperboard, 29 7/8 x 39 15/16 in. (75.9 x 101.4 cm)
Purchase, with funds from the Photography Committee 92.12

ROBERT ADAMS

b. 1937

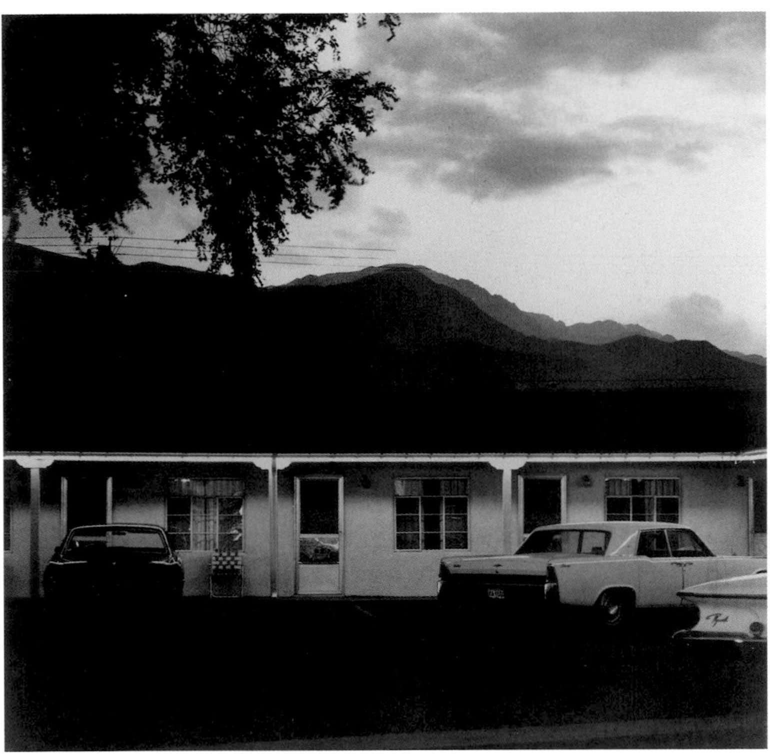

Robert Adams' 1970 photograph of a motel in Colorado Springs captures a moment that seems at once uncannily familiar and lost forever. The motel's silvery gray tones create a precisely linear horizontal bar across the picture; as the tails of unmistakably American-make automobiles edge into the foreground, a distant mountain range fades, like a fairy tale, into the mist. Adams' work is often placed under the rubric of New Topographics, which describes a group of photographers who used large-format cameras that rendered their subjects in exacting, often hyper-real detail. Their photographs explore the complicated, compromised beauty of natural landscapes eroded by the effects of industrialization.

Adams shares the New Topographics sense of social commitment: he is a longtime resident of the Colorado Front Range and a participant in activist efforts to restore and maintain local natural resources and lands. His photographs, however, lack moralistic overtones. In *Motel*, the contrast between the grandeur of the mountain range and the banality of the motel and automobiles is presented in neutral, as it were. Both nature and technology are just there. Deeply influenced by Edward Hopper's surreal light (p. 143), which imbues *Motel* with an almost forlorn sense of quiet, Adams' photograph sets up a subtle interplay between the motel—familiar icon of American suburbia—and the mountain range that lends this particular scene its lonely majesty.

Motel, 1970
Gelatin silver print mounted on paperboard, 5 7/8 x 5 15/16 in. (14.9 x 15.1 cm)
Purchase, with funds from the Photography Committee 96.12

DOUG AITKEN

b. 1968

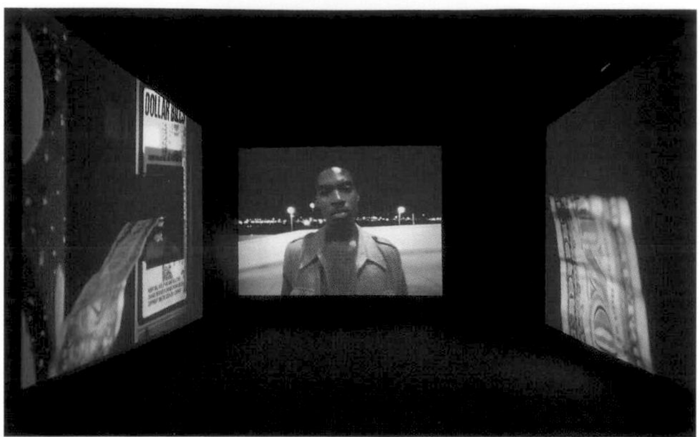

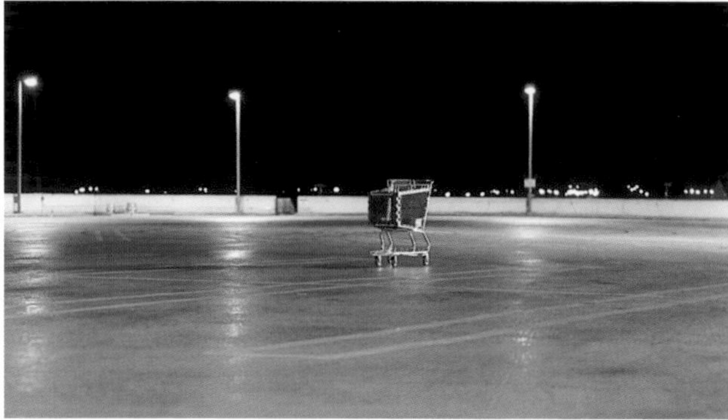

Doug Aitken is a multidisciplinary artist whose works include video, photography, and installations. His art is notable for its extremely high production values: high resolution images and tight editing call to mind the look of Hollywood cinema more than the experimental film and video familiar to the art world. Nevertheless, Aitken's art is extremely poetic: using the tools of the commercial film and video industry, he creates haunting works that explore various aspects of life in our increasingly alienating, globalized society.

Electric Earth, Aitken's most ambitious video installation to date, is a multiroom, multiscreen piece that surrounds the viewer with a loosely structured narrative about a young man in a big city. Walking along the deserted outskirts of Los Angeles at night, the youth seems to be overwhelmed, emotionally and physically, by everyday sights—a blinking streetlight, a wheel spinning on a shopping cart, the motions of a bill stuck in the slot of a soda machine, a car window, flickering fluorescent lights, and airplanes flying overhead. Each of these events creates rhythms and motions that are mimicked in his own body. The feeling of being literally absorbed into this "electric earth" is echoed in the enveloping nature of the installation itself, which surrounds the viewer with synchronized, large-scale video images.

* ***Electric Earth***, 1999
8-laserdisc installation and architectural environment, dimensions variable
Purchase, with funds from the Painting and Sculpture Committee and the Film and Video Committee 2000.145

JOSEF ALBERS

1888–1976

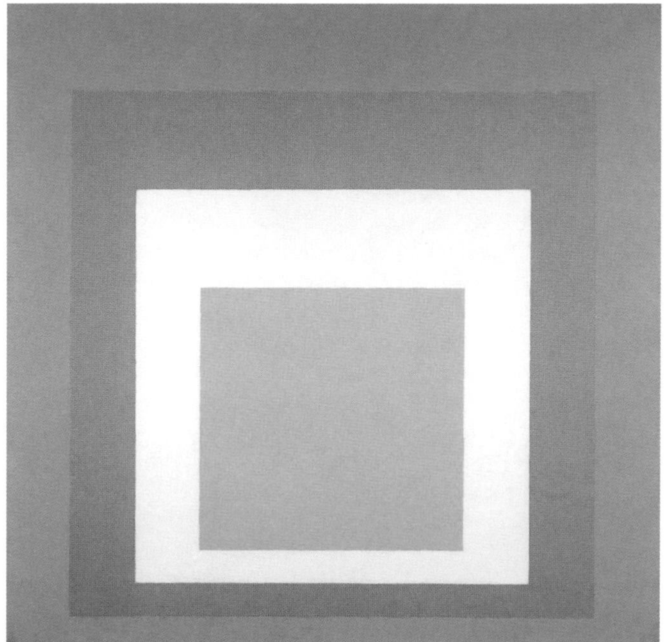

Josef Albers devoted his professional life to a systematic examination of the optical effects of color. The *Homage to the Square* series, begun in the summer of 1949, occupied him for twenty-five years. Each one of the thousand works in different media presents four superimposed squares of different colors—and each one reveals how our perception of a single color and whether it appears to project or recede depend on that color's interaction with adjacent colors. "*Ascending*" is typical of the paintings in the series. Albers squeezed the paint directly from the tube and then, using a palette knife, spread it evenly on masonite panels, which he preferred to more conventional canvas. Within the restrictive format of four squares, Albers, like a composer writing imaginative variations on a single melodic theme, created countless color combinations in which the value and effect of individual colors change markedly from work to work.

Josef Albers' teaching career and published writings were as influential as his art. At the Bauhaus in Germany, Black Mountain College in North Carolina and, beginning in 1950, the Yale University School of Art, he devised practical exercises that enabled his students to learn theories of color through direct experience. His now classic book, *Interaction of Color*, was published in 1963. Albers also drew analogies between color and human behavior: "Color," he wrote, "behaves like man...first in self-realization and then in the realization of relationships with others." In other words, just as red may appear more intense next to yellow than next to blue, individuals act differently in different company. Life, in Albers' vision, like color, is dynamic and unpredictable.

Homage to the Square: "Ascending", 1953
Oil on composition board, 43 1/2 x 43 1/2 in. (110.5 x 110.5 cm)
Purchase 54.34

CARL ANDRE

b. 1935

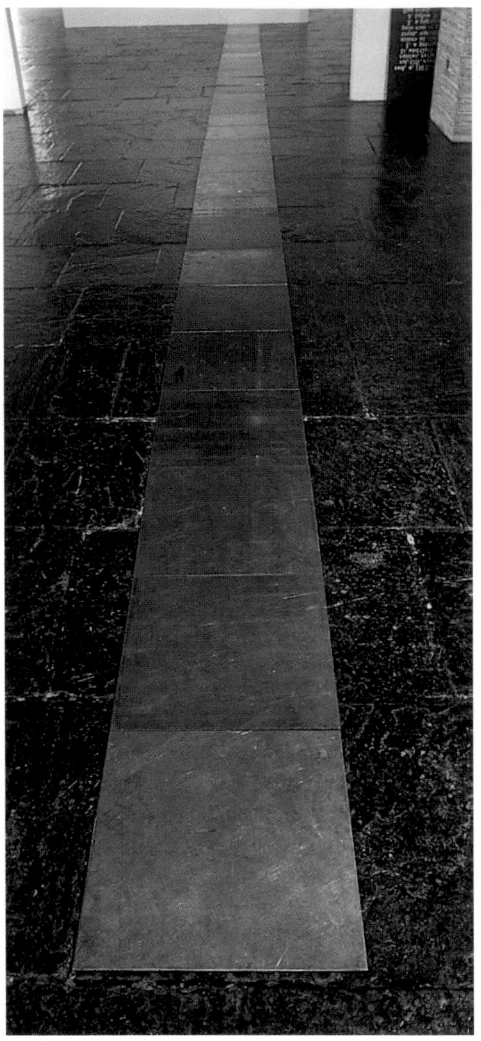

Both a poet and an artist, Carl Andre became one of the leading figures of Minimalism in the 1960s. Like other artists associated with the movement, such as Donald Judd (p. 160) and Tony Smith (p. 292), Andre focused his energies primarily on sculpture. His works from the mid-1960s and after challenged the basic premises of traditional sculpture, particularly its verticality and its finite quality—the way "the top of the head and the bottom of the feet were the limits of sculpture." Andre's sculptures, by contrast, were emphatically horizontal, "running along the ground," as he put it, like roads rather than buildings.

Twenty-Ninth Copper Cardinal is composed of twenty-nine identical and interchangeable square copper plates set on the floor. Extending single file from the base of a wall, the plates are laid down, one against the next, without being attached. The work belongs to the series *Copper Cardinals*, which Andre began in 1973. All are composed of square plates—in linear format if the number of units constitutes a prime number (for example, twenty-nine), or in rectangular format if it does not. Andre, who wanted the viewer to walk on his floor plate pieces, referred to the long format of *Twenty-Ninth Copper Cardinal* as a "causeway": "They cause you to make your way along them or around them or to move the spectator over them." As one stands on the work (especially toward the middle) there is a sense that it extends beyond the twenty-nine squares—that it continues beyond sight—an effect that again defies the conventional limits of sculpture.

Twenty-Ninth Copper Cardinal, 1975
Copper, 29 units, 3/16 x 20 x 20 in. (.5 x 50.8 x 50.8 cm) each, 3/16 x 20 x 580 in. (.5 x 50.8 x 1,473.2 cm) overall
Purchase, with funds from the Gilman Foundation, Inc. and the National Endowment for the Arts 75.55

JANINE ANTONI

b. 1964

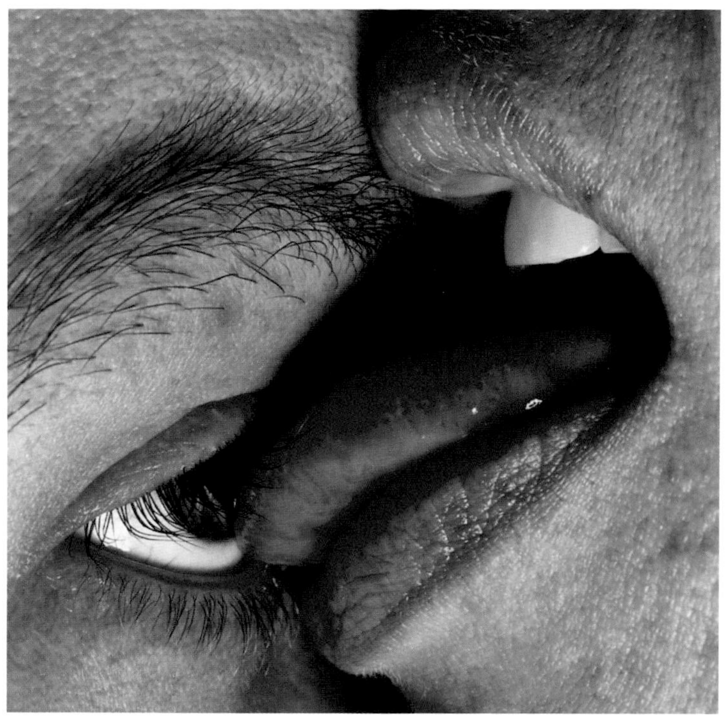

Janine Antoni often employs her own body as an instrument to make art. In her well-known work *Gnaw*, for example, shown in the Whitney's "1993 Biennial Exhibition," she nibbled at a 600-pound cube of chocolate and a 600-pound cube of lard with her teeth, then recycled the gnawed pieces into replicas of candy boxes and lipstick tubes. The 1999 photograph *Mortar and Pestle* is a much more confrontational work, in which Antoni wanted to capture the sense of something "a little closer than intimate." It is difficult to look casually at *Mortar and Pestle*, a close-up view of the artist's tongue (the pestle) being thrust into her husband's open eye (the mortar). The image is startling and impossible to ignore.

Antoni harnesses the natural ability of photography to come up closer on something than is possible or likely in human experience. She then enlarges the image beyond life size—a mouth and a browed eye fill a square photograph that measures 4 feet by 4 feet. Moreover, the precision of photographic detail enables us to feel the moment of contact. To what end? *Mortar and Pestle* probes the nature of relationships through an unflinching vision of trust and intimacy. Normally, the human eye instinctively blinks shut to ward off foreign objects, to protect sensitive tissue from harm. The open eye, then, marks a repudiation of such defense mechanisms. In this sense, it serves a larger metaphorical function, signaling a willingness to surrender one's vulnerability to another. Though *Mortar and Pestle* may initially provoke an uneasy response, it is ultimately a celebration of trust.

Mortar and Pestle, 1999
Chromogenic color print mounted on aluminum, 47 15/16 x 47 15/16 in. (121.8 x 121.8 cm)
Purchase, with funds from Joanne Leonhardt Cassullo and the Dorothea L. Leonhardt Fund at the Communities Foundation of Texas 99.53

POLLY APFELBAUM

b. 1955

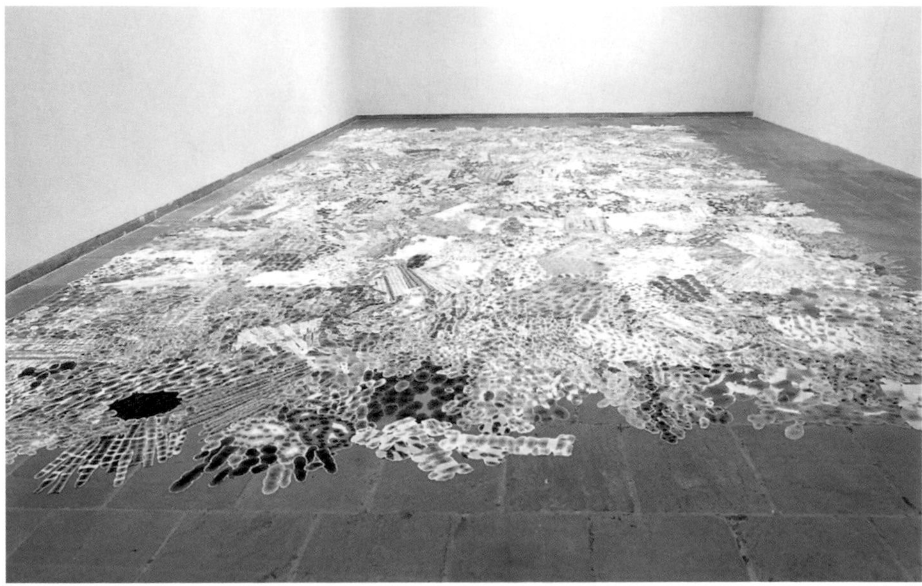

As part of a widespread cultural interest in gender and its social construction, many artists in the 1980s and 1990s alluded to femininity by incorporating women's clothing and domestic handicraft in their art works. The installations Polly Apfelbaum began making in the early 1990s with cut and dyed fabric are clearly connected to this practice. In formal terms, however, the staining of the fabric and its helter-skelter arrangement on the floor establish a retrospective link to 1950s abstract traditions—the Abstract Expressionist works of Jackson Pollock, who dripped paint onto canvases spread on the floor (p. 242); Color Field paintings such as those by Helen Frankenthaler, Morris Louis, and Kenneth Noland (pp. 110, 189, 225), in which paint was poured onto unprimed canvas; and the "scatter art" of the Postminimalists, in which various materials were allowed to occupy the space of a room in almost haphazard fashion.

For *Ice*, Apfelbaum cut hundreds of small pieces of synthetic crushed velvet and stained them with the 104 available colors of commercial fabric dye. She refers to the stain by which she achieves each color as "a calligraphic mark, a signature, a fingerprint, but then it also becomes just a blot of color." To produce *Ice*, Apfelbaum arranged the dyed pieces in increasingly elaborate patterns of color, with each tiny bit of velvet overlapping the others. The allusion to ice is twofold: it is a substance often found underfoot, slippery and unstable; but, most pertinent for Apfelbaum's installation, ice can also refract light with prismatic splendor, an effect recreated by the sheen of the velvet.

Ice, 1998
Synthetic velvet and dye, dimensions variable
Purchase, with funds from the Painting and Sculpture Committee 98.74

IDA APPLEBROOG

b. 1929

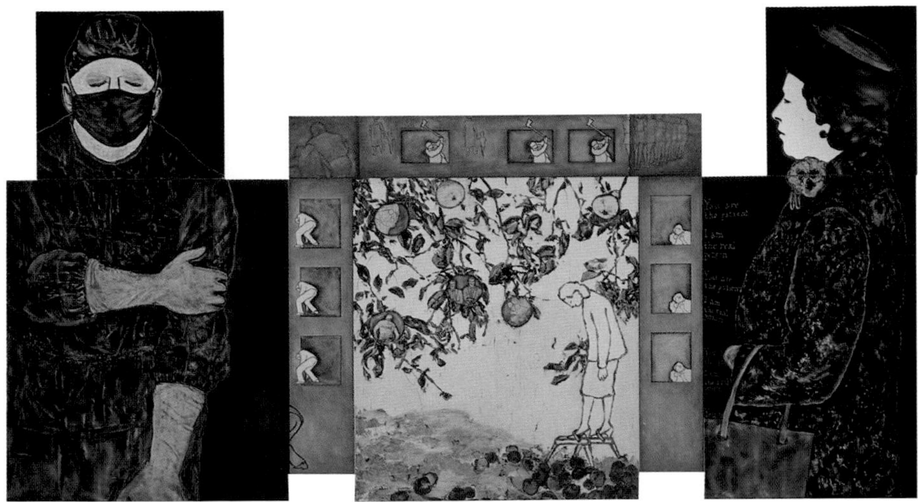

Ida Applebroog combines images culled from newspapers, magazines, and television with her own invented characters to create absurd yet poignant paintings that explore the misuse of power. Made up of eight panels of varying size, *Emetic Fields* is part of a series that uses imagery and terminology from the medical profession as a metaphor for societal dysfunction—"emetics" are drugs used to induce vomiting.

Applebroog's unconventional palette emphasizes "body" colors—bile greens, blood reds, and piss yellows. The central canvas shows a woman in a surreal orchard of oversize fruit, like a latter-day Eve about to be expelled from Eden. Contained within some of the fruit are images of intimidating-looking men that mark this field as a domain of patriarchy. Each of the woman's feet is bound to a strange, stiltlike contraption that is either confining her to this menacing environment or helping her negotiate its terrain.

On three sides of the central canvas are narrow bands of simple repeating images that resemble film frames or comic strip sequences and have been a signature convention of Applebroog's since she began her career in the 1970s. Evoking unrelated streams of partial memories, these framed images depict mundane yet cryptic scenes—a man bending down to pick up a stone, another wielding an ax, still another embraced in a kiss.

Adding to the elusive narrative are two larger-than-life figures on either end: at left, a surgeon and, at right, Queen Elizabeth II. Their colossal size, pressing in from the flanks, insinuates other dynamics of control—of doctors over patients and governments over their citizens. But Queen Elizabeth appears like an ordinary housewife, self-assured but staid, while the closed-eyed surgeon, clutching his arm, seems vulnerable. The repeating texts on the queen's canvas read: "You are the patient" and "I am the real person," leaving open to question who is sick and who is well, who has power, who does not.

Emetic Fields, 1989
Oil on canvas, 110 7/16 x 204 5/8 in. (280.5 x 519.8 cm) overall
Gift of Jean Lignel 99.100a–h

DIANE ARBUS
1923–1971

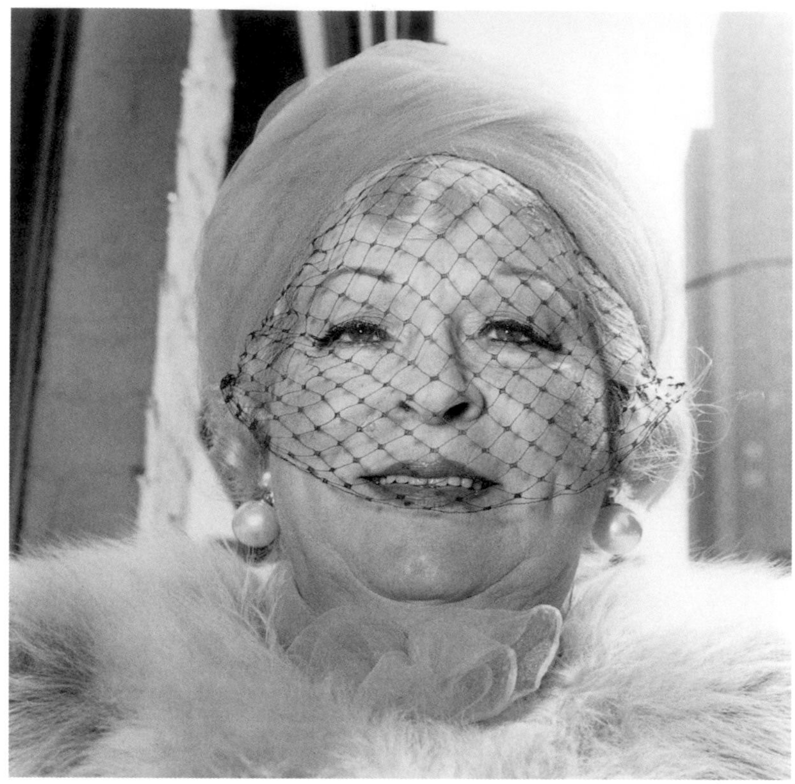

A snapshot is by definition an amateur, unstylized photograph that betrays the haphazard spontaneity of a moment—or so it was understood before Diane Arbus redefined it. Around 1962, Arbus took the 2 1/4 x 2 1/4-inch camera, which had always been considered a formal portrait camera, and began using it on city streets and in private homes, with minimal preparatory staging. Arbus captured American society as its social fabric was unraveling during the tumultuous 1960s.

Woman with a Veil on Fifth Avenue, N.Y.C. occupies an important position within Arbus' oeuvre: its image of a bourgeois woman represents a counterpart to the midgets, giants, hermaphrodites, transsexuals, and circus performers who were often the subjects of her unflinching photographs. But neither in these photographs nor in *Woman with a Veil* is there any hint of moralistic judgment or sociopolitical grandstanding. Instead, Arbus gives full flight to her subject's wonderful euphoria as it appears to spread to Manhattan's misted skyscrapers. From the lush softness of fur to the perfect luster of oversize pearl earrings, Arbus recorded a moment of splendor, as if she shared in her subject's delight with the world. Her photographic eye focused on what makes people unique and, in the process, respected each of her subjects for their individuality.

Woman with a Veil on Fifth Avenue, N.Y.C., 1968
Gelatin silver print, 10 1/2 x 10 1/4 in. (26.7 x 26 cm)
Purchase, with funds from Ann G. Tenenbaum, Thomas H. Lee, and the Photography Committee 97.15

RICHARD ARTSCHWAGER

b. 1923

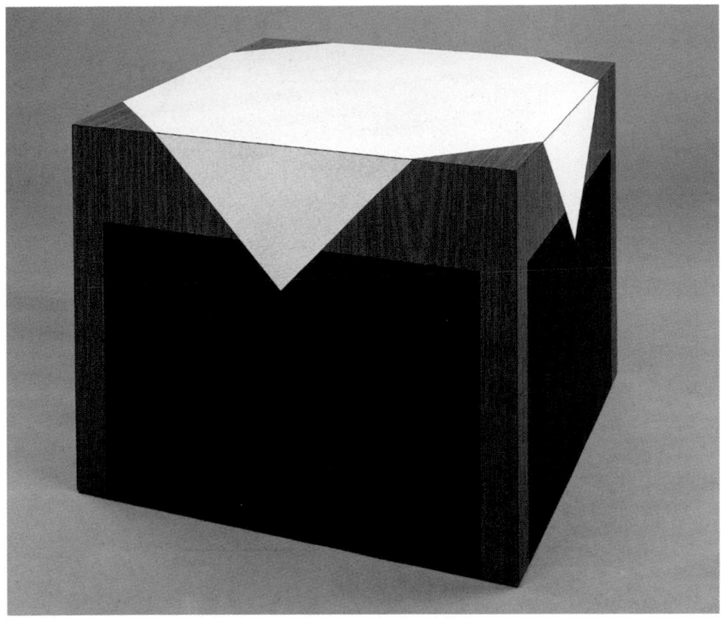

Richard Artschwager worked as a cabinet- and furnituremaker in New York until a 1958 fire in his studio led him to reconsider his profession. When, in his mid-thirties, he decided to become an artist, he also decided that sculpture could be made out of virtually anything. Before long, he hit upon the idea of relating the materials and form of his art to the grammar of domestic furniture, including chairs, tables, mirrors, windows, and doors.

But Artschwager's work distinguishes itself from the conventions of handcrafted furniture in many respects. *Description of Table*, for example, consists of a simple plywood cube inlaid with pieces of black, white, and faux wood-grain Formica. Cold in appearance and industrially produced, Formica is a material disdained by craftsmen for its tacky cheapness—"the great horror of the Age," Artschwager called it. Yet Artschwager used it precisely because it was *of* the age and because it could achieve certain illusionistic effects. Like the Cubists' use of mass-produced faux wood-grain papers to represent tabletops in their still-life collages, Artschwager's use of Formica functions simultaneously as image and object, as a representation and as the thing itself. *Description of Table* also recalls the reductive geometries of Minimalist sculptures such as Tony Smith's *Die* (p. 292). Uncharacteristic of Minimalism, however, is the suggestion of something beyond geometry—a cloth-draped table, with the black rectangles below evoking the table's empty, negative space. But *Description of Table* is not in fact a table: it is art—"mental furniture," in the words of one critic—witty, wry, and full of contradiction. "I use visual perception," Artschwager explained, "as a way of bringing people into my space." *Description of Table* both draws us in and frustrates our expectations of the table's particular, mundane usefulness.

Description of Table, 1964
Melamine laminate on plywood, 26 1/8 x 31 7/8 x 31 7/8 in. (66.4 x 81 x 81 cm)
Gift of the Howard and Jean Lipman Foundation, Inc. 66.48

RICHARD AVEDON

b. 1923

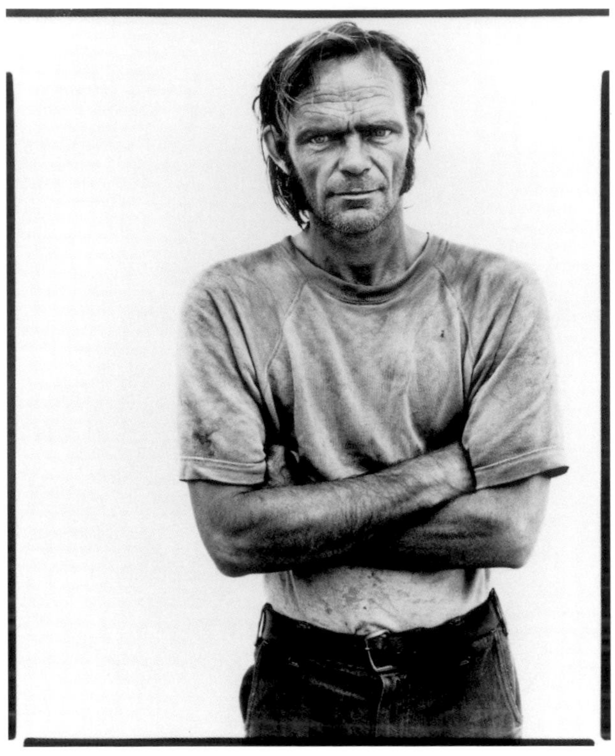

For the past forty years, Richard Avedon, as renowned for his fashion photography as for his stark portraits, has been reinventing the photographing of human subjects. Avedon freed fashion models from their stiff poses and erased the personal accoutrements and backgrounds that had tied photographic portraiture to its painterly precedents. Some of his most powerful portrait work appears in his book *In the American West*, a series of portraits he took between 1979 and 1984 and published in 1985. *Bill Curry, drifter, Interstate 40, Yukon, Oklahoma, 6/16/80* is one of the photographs in the book. Here, as in all the portraits, Avedon focused not on the rugged cowboys or heroic adventurers of the American myth of the West, but on society's neglected casualties—the poor and the misfit, among them impoverished farmers, slaughterhouse workers, and waitresses as well as drifters, degenerates, and snake charmers.

Blown up to the impressive scale shared by all the subjects in the book, Avedon's portrait of Bill Curry is a study in factual detail. Avedon began his career in the Merchant Marine during World War II, photographing autopsies and making identification photos. This training in the minute dissection and documentation of the human body developed in Avedon's mature photography into a preference for stark, detailed images, whether the subject is an elegant fashion model or a forgotten man in a forgotten place. The portrait of Bill Curry, an otherwise anonymous man crossing his arms against his chest, is filled with what Avedon refers to as his photographs' "confrontational erotic quality." Whether pride, self-confidence, trust, or scorn lie behind Curry's piercing eyes, the rich grays and seamless white background that characterize Avedon's prints spark a visceral immediacy, a disorienting sense of intimacy with a subject we cannot know.

Bill Curry, drifter, Interstate 40, Yukon, Oklahoma, 6/16/80, 1980
Gelatin silver print mounted on aluminum, 47 x 37 9/16 in. (119.4 x 95.4 cm)
Gift of Norma and Martin Stevens 98.24

MILTON AVERY
1885–1965

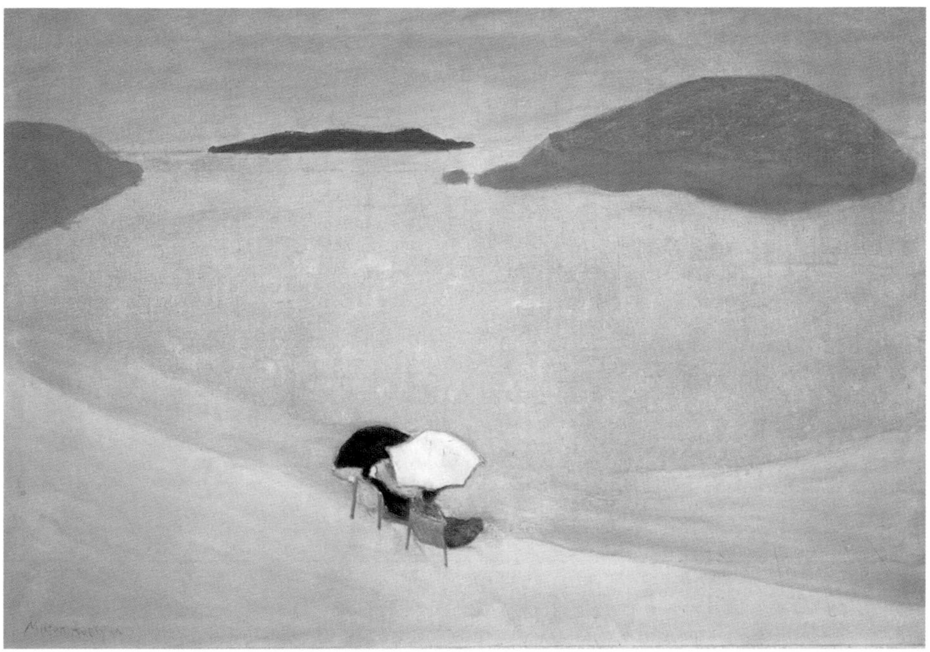

In *Sea Gazers*, Milton Avery distills an expansive landscape vista into a few interlocking flat bands of color. The serenity of this seascape, inspired by summers on the New England coast, owes much to the economy of compositional form, with the two figures beneath umbrellas reduced to a few spare shapes. "I always take something out of my pictures," the artist said. "I strip the design to essentials." Avery applied the oil paint with watercolor technique, using multiple layers of thin, diluted washes. This fluid handling of pigment reveals his remarkable gifts as a colorist: whether land- and seascapes, domestic interiors, or portraits, all his works are marked by luminous palettes, richly saturated hues, and subtle modulation of tones. Color for Avery represented not only form—an expanse of light blue in the *Sea Gazers* delimits the sea, a triangle of beige the beach—but also emotion. His juxtaposition of harmonious gradations of blue, green, and brown in *Sea Gazers* contributes to the work's tranquil mood, a mood that marked many of his paintings.

Born and trained in Connecticut, Avery moved to New York in 1925. Although he worked productively until his death forty years later, by mid-century his representational painting was often overlooked, as abstract and gestural painters came to dominate the art world. Nonetheless, Avery proved an important influence on a younger generation of American artists. Early abstract paintings by Adolph Gottlieb and Mark Rothko (pp. 124, 263), for example, are indebted to Avery in their thinly applied pigments and limited color palettes.

Sea Gazers, 1956
Oil on canvas, 30 x 44 in. (76.2 x 111.8 cm)
Lawrence H. Bloedel Bequest 77.1.3

ALICE AYCOCK

b. 1946

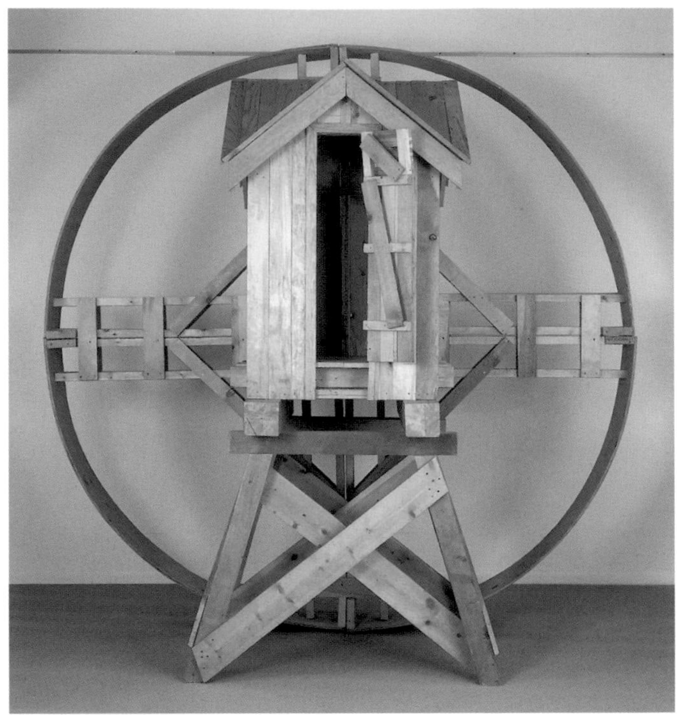

Using forms borrowed from vernacular architecture and the basic methods and ordinary materials of carpentry, Alice Aycock has assembled sculptures that express remarkably diverse narratives. Aycock's father was a builder who had studied architecture and engineering; her art school teachers were Minimalist sculptors. Accepting the influence of both, she pursued eclectic interests, from ancient mythology to modern chemistry, medieval painting to the design of nuclear reactors.

In *Untitled (Shanty)*, Aycock uses her idiosyncratic touch to transform a common building type into an object of mystery that transcends the original function of its architecture. She elevates the structure (quite literally) on splayed stilts and frames it within a wooden ring, toward which it reaches with ladderlike wooden arms. The materials and construction methods suggest practical use, but the building has no function; the open door invites entry, but the shanty is too small for human scale. The configuration, moreover, evokes a number of different images: a five-pointed star, a Tantric circle, and Leonardo da Vinci's Vitruvian man—an ideally proportioned man with outstretched limbs touching the contour of a perfect circle. Although one foot of the sculpture seems planted in Renaissance humanism and the other in Eastern mysticism, the plainspoken materials are rooted in the Pennsylvania farm country where Aycock grew up.

Untitled (Shanty), 1978
Wood, 54 x 30 x 30 in. (137.2 x 76.2 x 76.2 cm)
Base, 45 x 36 x 42 in. (114.3 x 91.4 x 106.7 cm)
Diameter of wheel, 107 1/2 in. (273.1 cm)
Gift of Raymond J. Learsy 84.71.1

PEGGY BACON
1895–1987

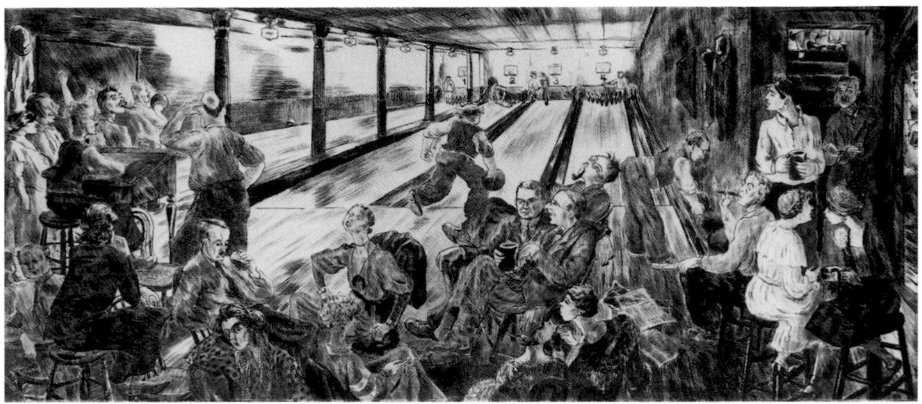

In the 1920s and 1930s, Peggy Bacon earned a reputation as a clever caricaturist and perceptive chronicler of the flourishing New York artistic community that she knew well. Her drypoint print *The Ardent Bowlers* is both a group portrait and a caricature, an eyewitness account and a satire. The print depicts a weekly gathering at a bowling alley on Third Avenue. Each figure is a portrait of someone Bacon knew, based on numerous sketches. In fact, the artist claimed that she "never faked a figure to fill a composition." Most of the participants have been identified and include the artists Yasuo Kuniyoshi, Reginald Marsh (p. 198), Bacon, and her husband, Alexander Brook.

The Ardent Bowlers, however, does not document a particular evening, but rather records the artist's general impression of her friends. Though not precisely a caricature, it recalls Bacon's well-known satiric portraits of the previous decade, in which, as she put it, she wanted to convey "a spicy and clairvoyant comment upon the subject's peculiarities." In *The Ardent Bowlers*, physical features are exaggerated for comic effect, and the title itself is subtly humorous. Few of the "ardent" bowlers are actually paying attention to the game. Instead, they chat among themselves, suggesting that their passion is conversation, not bowling. Bacon's satiric portraits were never mean-spirited, but she eventually became uncomfortable with caricature and abandoned it by the mid-1930s.

The Ardent Bowlers, 1932
Drypoint: sheet, 11 3/8 x 18 5/8 in. (28.9 x 47.3 cm); plate, 6 x 13 15/16 in. (15.2 x 35.4 cm)
Purchase 32.85

JOHN BALDESSARI

b. 1931

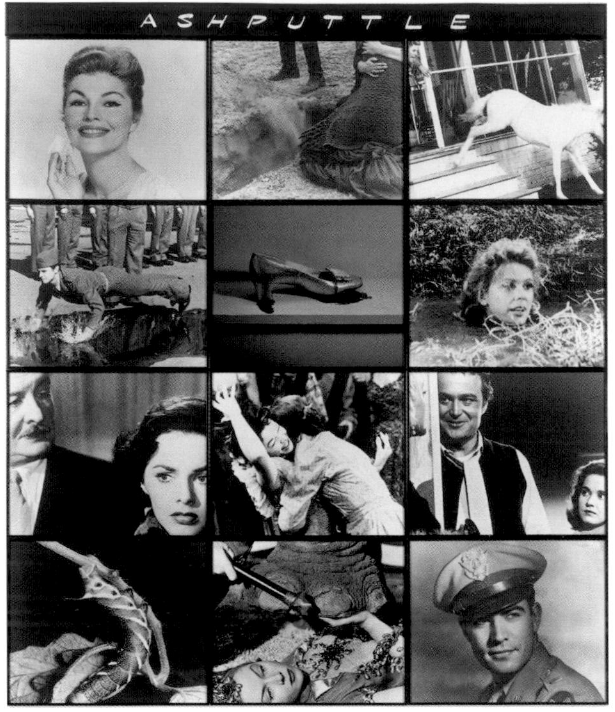

Since the mid-1960s, John Baldessari has subverted conventions about how a work of art is made, what is represented in it, and how we understand it. Early on in his career, Baldessari, a major figure of West Coast Conceptual art, abandoned easel painting in favor of film stills, photographs, and other ready-made media imagery, which he uses to explore our visual culture and how it determines ideas about artistic originality and narrative expectations.

Ashputtle exemplifies the way Baldessari uses appropriated imagery to question traditional narrative structure. It is one of six works based on the fairy tales compiled in the nineteenth century by the Brothers Grimm, born in Kassel, Germany. (Baldessari conceived the series for an exhibition in Kassel.) The title is a clever variant of Aschenputtel—the fairy-tale character known in English as Cinderella. In the piece, the artist placed eleven black-and-white film stills in a grid arrangement. One of the images in the center section is a color snapshot of the familiar and emblematic slipper; the other stills come from a variety of old films, none of them having anything to do with Cinderella. The images encourage us to seek narrative connections: how, for example, do the male authority figures—the military officers and the father—fit into the Cinderella story? But the cropped nature of the film stills and their seemingly arbitrary juxtapositions leave the answers to all such questions open-ended. This unfixed narrative, however, is precisely what Baldessari intends. As critic Coosje van Bruggen noted, Baldessari's series of fairy tales reveals the collective authorship of narratives: we constantly reinvent stories, he reminds us, out of the tissue of earlier stories.

***Ashputtle**, 1982
11 gelatin silver prints, 1 silver dye bleach print (Cibachrome), and text panel, 84 x 72 in. (213.4 x 182.9 cm) overall
Purchase, with funds from the Painting and Sculpture Committee 83.8a–m

LEWIS BALTZ

b. 1945

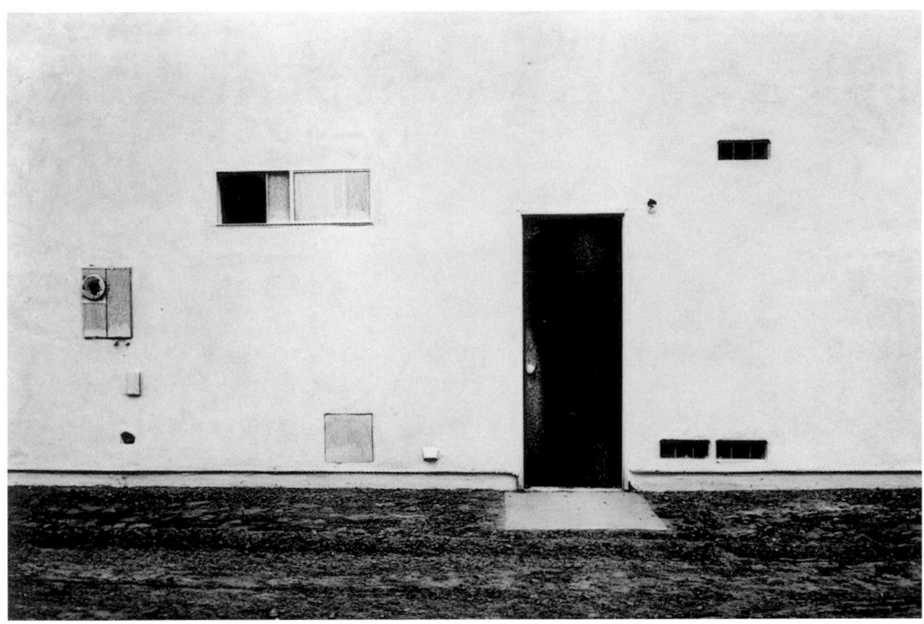

Lewis Baltz began photographing the West Coast's new subdivisions and industrial parks in the late 1960s, at the height of postwar America's rapid flight from city to suburb. In 1975, he was included in the George Eastman House exhibition "New Topographics"—a small group of influential photographers (including Robert Adams, p. 27) who used large-format cameras to capture the exquisite detail of mundane elements of landscape and architecture. Their dispassionate observations of the decay and artifice of the modern American West challenged the romanticized visions of earlier landscape photographers. Within New Topographics work, Baltz's photographs typically struck an aesthetic balance between bland, man-made structures and the despoiled landscapes within which they resided.

The Tract Houses, a series made between 1969 and 1971, comprises twenty-five black-and-white photographs of the exteriors of new, vacant suburban homes on the outskirts of Los Angeles. Like *Tract House #17*, most of the photographs, taken dead-on and close up, are architectural details that suppress three-dimensionality and emphasize the vernacular minimalism of these austere, mass-produced buildings: chimneys, windows, doors, and air vents are reduced to simple geometric shapes. *Tract House #17* shows the broad side of a house, on which squares, rectangles, and small circles serendipitously create an asymmetrical grid. The image, at once formally harmonious and socially oppressive, has a deadpan quality that makes it difficult to determine Baltz's agenda. One thing is clear: the photographer's profound interest in these unremarkable places compels viewers to take them seriously and to consider other seemingly banal sites as worthy subjects for art.

Tract House #17, 1971
Gelatin silver print mounted on paperboard, 5 11/16 x 8 1/2 in. (14.4 x 21.6 cm)
Purchase, with funds from the Wilfred P. and Rose J. Cohen Purchase Fund, the John I.H. Baur Purchase Fund, the Grace Belt Endowed Purchase Fund, and the Photography Committee 93.70q

MATTHEW BARNEY

b. 1967

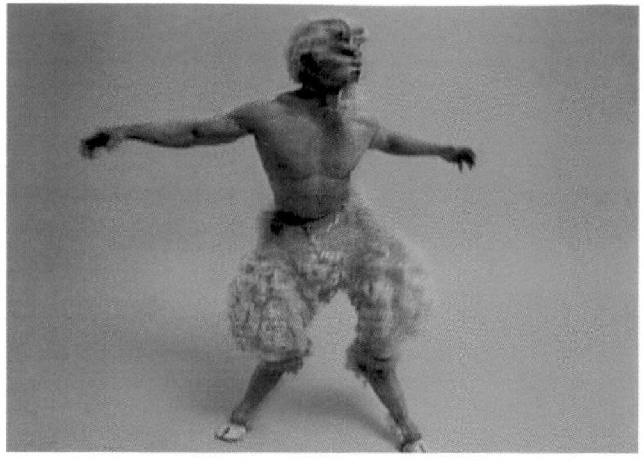

Throughout the 1990s, Matthew Barney developed a personal, highly idiosyncratic body of art: constellations of videos, performances, sculptures, installations, and photographs involving complex artificial symbolic systems drawn from biology, myth, history, and fiction. The early *Drawing Restraint* series is based on the process of muscular growth—the fact that muscles must encounter resistance in order to become stronger. To make the drawings, Barney donned restraints that kept him from reaching the paper without difficult contortions. In the video installation *Drawing Restraint 7*, he transferred this notion of struggle into a world of satyrs competing to be the most virile. Wearing prostheses that hinder movement, including stiltlike cloven hooves, Barney's satyrs wrestle, chase each other's tails, and battle to remove their opponents' horns.

The extraordinarily complex *CREMASTER* series of films and related art works contains a more expansive notion of biological potential born of resistance. In imagery that ranges from the sexual differentiation of the fetus to more individually determined physical and mental acts, Barney sees a vital, struggling force at work, both in acts of will and in biological or instinctual processes. In *CREMASTER 2: Drone Ensemble*, a set of photographs featuring "characters" from the *CREMASTER 2* film, Barney presents this struggle through animals who are both individualized and communal: the bull, a symbol of strength yet also a member of a herd; the bee who labors in a collective community for a single queen; and the dog who, as a pet, signals our tendency to project human characteristics and individuality onto animals. Harking back to Barney's earlier pieces involving prostheses, the works are framed in a self-lubricating plastic normally used for internal prostheses, such as artificial knees.

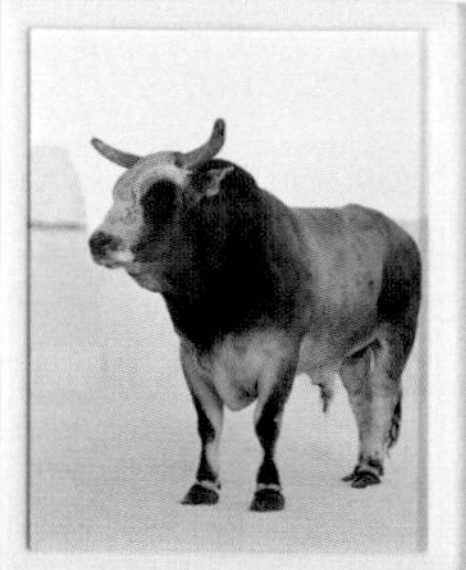

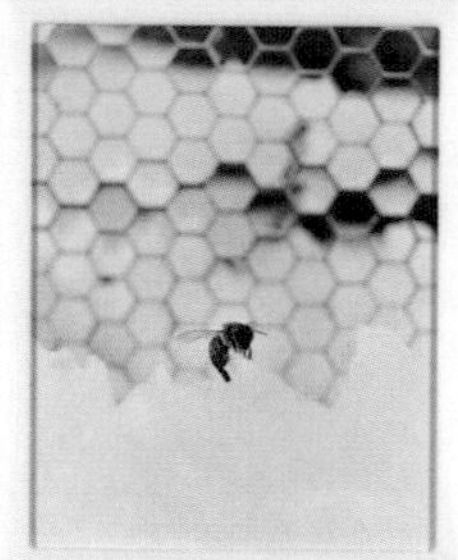

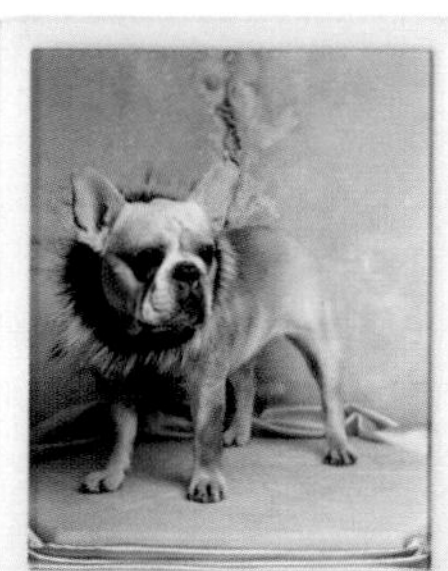

Drawing Restraint 7, 1993
Video monitors, laserdisc players, silent color laserdiscs, steel, plastic, and fluorescent lighting fixture, dimensions variable
Purchase, with funds from the Painting and Sculpture Committee 93.33

CREMASTER 2: Drone Ensemble, 1998
3 chromogenic color prints in acrylic frames, 41 1/2 x 33 7/8 in. (105.4 x 86 cm) each
Purchase, with funds from the Photography Committee, Steven Ames, Anne and Joel Ehrenkranz, Arthur Fleischer, Kathryn Fleck, and Elizabeth Kabler in honor of Sondra Gilman Gonzalez-Falla 99.161a–c

JEAN-MICHEL BASQUIAT

1960–1988

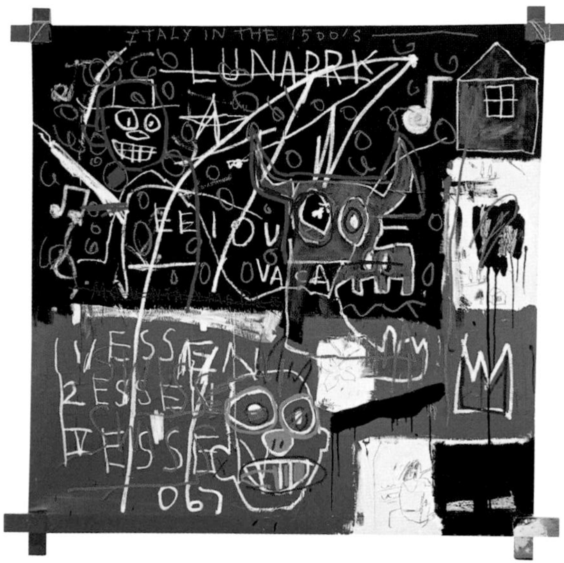

Born in Brooklyn, Jean-Michel Basquiat was among a group of young, New York-based artists (including his friend Keith Haring, p. 131) who emerged in the early 1980s as the art and music worlds welcomed a new style, infused with urban hip-hop. Basquiat, born to a Haitian father and Puerto Rican mother, first gained public notoriety with the cryptic graffiti messages he placed in the SoHo neighborhood of Manhattan. Around 1980, he began painting on canvas, consciously evoking the clandestine, unpolished look of graffiti or "primitive" art, an effect compounded by materials that appear to have been scavenged from the street—such as the exposed crossbars latched with twine at the corners of *"LNAPRK"*. Yet the content of Basquiat's work combines references to art history, in which he was well versed, with notations on colonialism, racism, and African-American jazz or sports legends. He integrated these various subjects by fluidly shifting between writing and drawing—deploying words, as he said, "like brushstrokes."

The references in *"LNAPRK"* are less politically motivated than in other Basquiat works of the period. Painted after a visit to Italy, the work is named for an amusement park outside Milan (Luna Park is also the name of one of the first amusement parks of the early twentieth century in New York's Coney Island). In the upper section, a simplified bull stands just above "Vaca," the Spanish word for cow. The words "Mountain Maple" appear crossed-out in red, just above the lower half; in a white patch beneath the bull is a leaf from a mountain maple tree. At top, "Italy in the 1500's" refers to the flowering of the Renaissance and may have been taken from the contents page of a history or art history book, which Basquiat frequently raided for his paintings. The crown near the bottom right is Basquiat's "tag," or signature, from his days as a graffiti artist and appears often in his art. When asked what the subject matter of his work was, he summed it up as "royalty, heroism, and the streets."

"LNAPRK", 1982
Synthetic polymer and oil stick on canvas, 73 1/2 x 72 1/4 in. (186.7 x 183.5 cm)
Gift of June and Paul Schorr in honor of the 60th Anniversary of the Whitney Museum of American Art 91.83

WILLIAM BAZIOTES

1912–1963

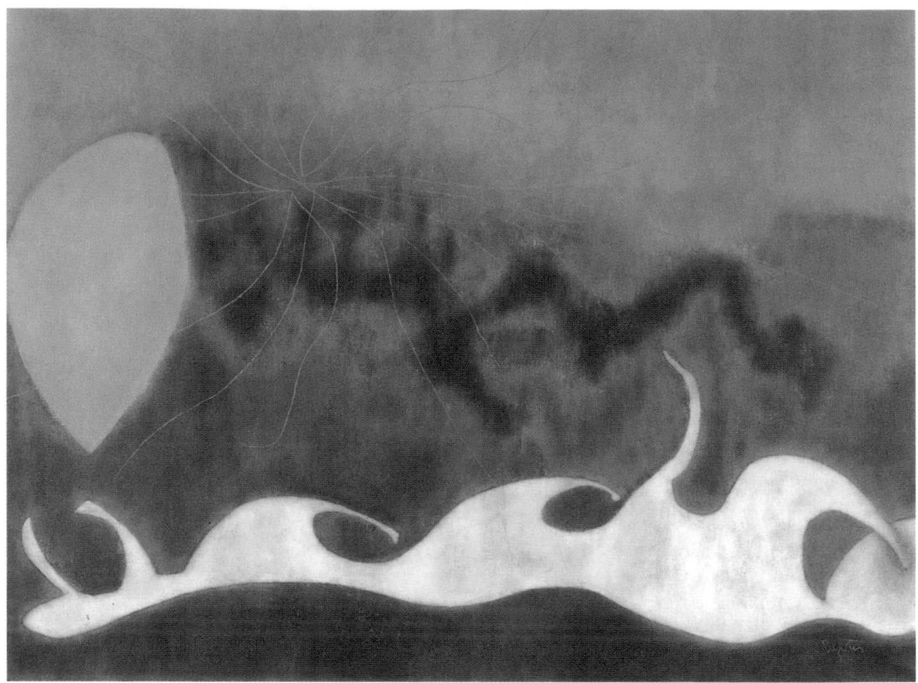

William Baziotes was a key figure in American art's shift toward abstraction in the 1940s and 1950s. Friendly with the French Surrealists living in New York during World War II, he was one of the first American artists to incorporate their ideas about automatism, a form of unstructured expression that draws on the unconscious. Thanks to his discussions with contemporaries such as Robert Motherwell (p. 213) and Jackson Pollock (p. 242), the concept became a pivotal part of the burgeoning movement of Abstract Expressionism. Yet rather than respond to automatism by emphasizing speed and spontaneity, as other Abstract Expressionists did, Baziotes worked slowly and meditatively. Applying many layers of paint, which he thinned with turpentine and linseed oil, he created the subtle washes of undulating color that became his trademark.

Baziotes, moreover, never abandoned figuration for abstraction. The curvilinear shapes in his paintings evoke natural forms—fossils, bones, or cellular organisms. Fascinated by paleontology and botany, he was a frequent visitor to the fossil and dinosaur displays at the American Museum of Natural History in New York. *The Beach* was inspired by the memory of a trip to New Smyrna, Florida, in 1944. "The dryness, the heat, and the fossils on the beach depressed me considerably," he recollected many years later. In 1955, this barren landscape and its primordial creatures found their way into the bottom and left portion of *The Beach*. The more comforting imagery of the Pennsylvania mountains, viewed from Baziotes' porch, seems to emerge from the center of the canvas.

The Beach, 1955
Oil on canvas, 36 x 48 in. (91.4 x 121.9 cm)
Purchase 56.12

ROMARE BEARDEN
1912–1988

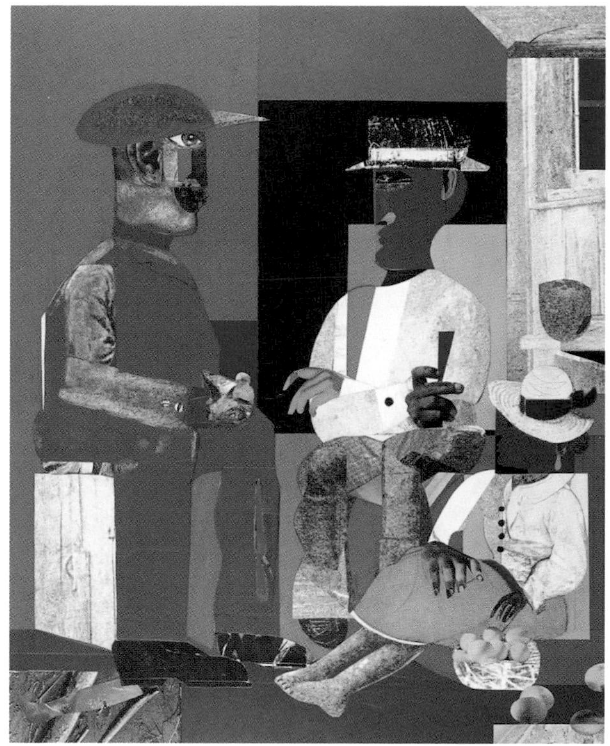

Romare Bearden's formal training began at New York's Art Students League in the late 1930s. In 1950–51, while studying philosophy in Paris, he became further engaged with the work of Pablo Picasso, particularly with the collage technique he had invented in the early years of the century. Collage—the unexpected juxtaposition of disparate materials, especially cut paper—became Bearden's principal method in the mid-1960s.

The decade of the 1960s in America was fraught with sociopolitical strife. As an African-American, Bearden was particularly concerned with the struggle for civil rights. He believed in a connection between art and social reality, stating that "whatever increases the self-awareness of black people will therefore enlarge the opinion they have of themselves—as well as the opinion other people have of them." *Eastern Barn*, composed of photograph and magazine cutouts and various pieces of painted and mottled paper, shows three seated figures engaged in conversation. The collage medium calls attention to the intentionally disjunctive structure of the picture: three-dimensional figures are rendered resolutely flat; there are shifts in scale—heads, feet, and hands are disproportionate to bodies; and the bodies in turn outsize the interior barn space in which they are located. The interlocking fragments of Bearden's collages conjure images of his childhood in the rural South and later in industrial Pittsburgh, and evoke as well syncopated jazz rhythms, Harlem street culture, and the restless vitality of city life.

Eastern Barn, 1968
Collage of paper on board, 55 1/2 x 44 in. (141 x 111.8 cm)
Purchase 69.14

ROBERT BECHTLE

b. 1932

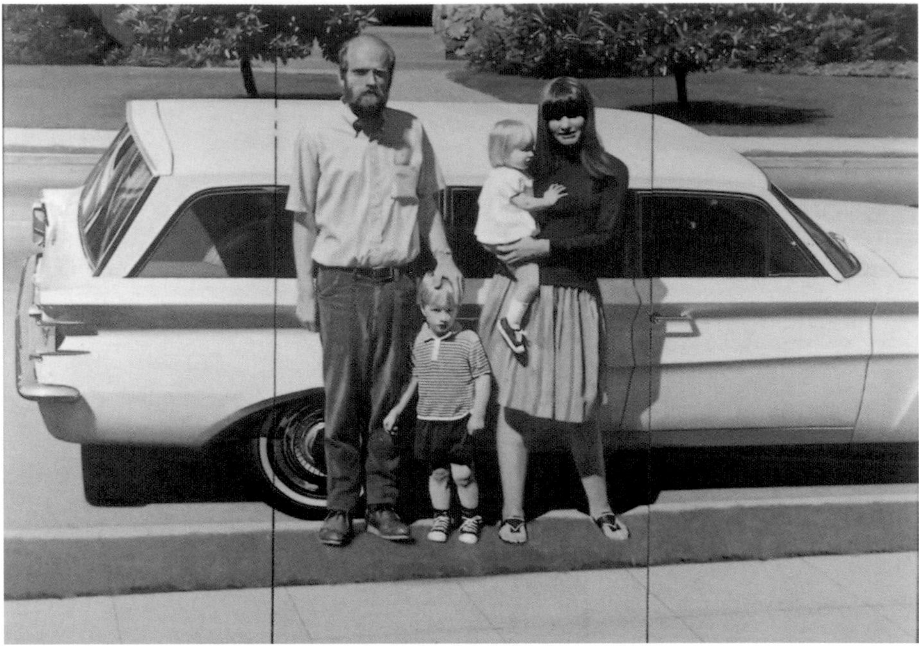

California artist Robert Bechtle has been called "the poet of the parked car." The inclusion of people in *'61 Pontiac* is unusual, as most of the artist's paintings depict empty cars, streets, houses, and yards in Oakland or San Francisco. Bechtle, often linked to other Photo-Realist artists, including Chuck Close and Richard Estes (pp. 74, 103), derives the images in his polished paintings from snapshots. He says that he prefers the camera's impartiality, its facility for depicting quotidian subject matter in a straightforward way. Indeed, this work shows Bechtle with his wife and children, but they might be any 1960s family. From a distance, the painting is indistinguishable from a photo; only when approached close up can the viewer discern its three separate panels and minute brushstrokes. The work is suffused with the harsh glare of the California sun, which makes it difficult to determine the time of day and flattens its subjects into muted washes of color. Bechtle's unique talent resides in his ability to present images from familiar, middle-class life in a neutral fashion and, at the same time, to render them curiously fascinating. One quality that runs through his work is a persistent stillness: his subjects seem incapable of motion, frozen in time—as if in a photograph.

'61 Pontiac, 1968–69
Oil on canvas, 59 3/4 x 84 1/4 in. (151.8 x 214 cm)
Purchase, with funds from the Richard and Dorothy Rodgers Fund 70.16

GEORGE BELLOWS

1882–1925

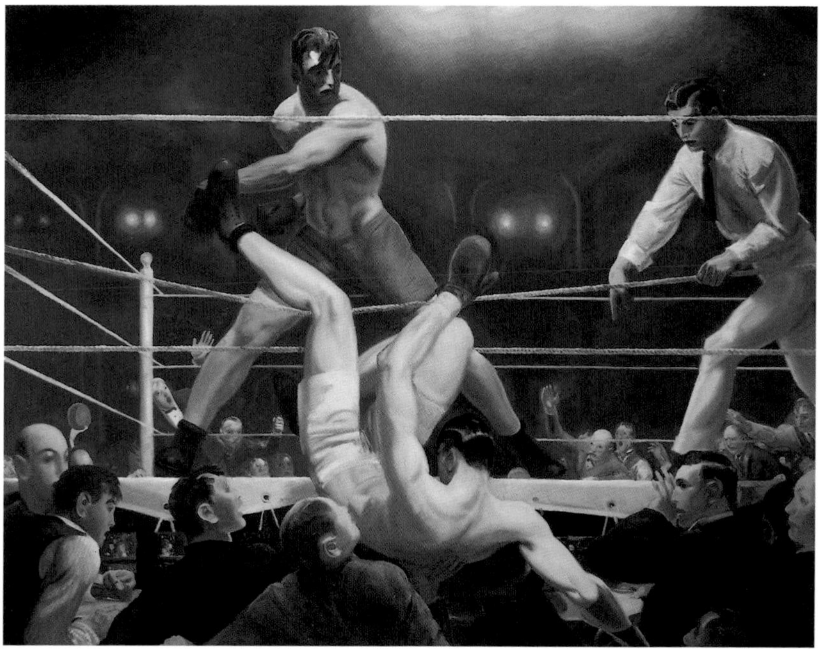

One of the foremost urban realists in early twentieth-century New York, George Bellows remained committed to representational art throughout his career. To supplement his income as a painter, he also worked as a sports illustrator for daily newspapers. He was an avid sports fan, and the events he covered often found their way into his art. Between 1907 and 1924, he used the prizefight as the subject of six major oil paintings and numerous drawings and prints. On September 14, 1923, the *New York Evening Journal* assigned Bellows to cover Jack Dempsey defending his heavyweight title against the Argentinean boxer Luis Firpo. A crowd of 90,000 attended the fight at New York's Polo Grounds. Short and dramatic, it became one of the most famous bouts of the century. In the first round, Dempsey sent Firpo to the floor seven times before the Argentinean knocked the champion out of the ring with a blow to the jaw. Dempsey went on to win the fight by a knockout in the second round, but in this painting, produced the following summer, Bellows chose to represent the drama of Dempsey falling out of the ring, feet in the air and arms flailing.

Ironically, the dramatic stop-action effect of Dempsey and Firpo, seen from the vantage of a ringside viewer, is created by the geometry Bellows imposed on the composition. An activating diagonal begins at the falling fighter's lowered right arm and extends upward through his left leg. A second diagonal begins with the referee's pointing right arm and continues through Dempsey's right thigh and the left arm of the man he's falling on. These two diagonals form an energetic cross-axis that stabilizes the composition, as does the triangle formed by Firpo's straight, steady legs.

Dempsey and Firpo, 1924
Oil on canvas, 51 x 63 1/4 in. (129.5 x 160.7 cm)
Purchase, with funds from Gertrude Vanderbilt Whitney 31.95

LYNDA BENGLIS

b. 1941

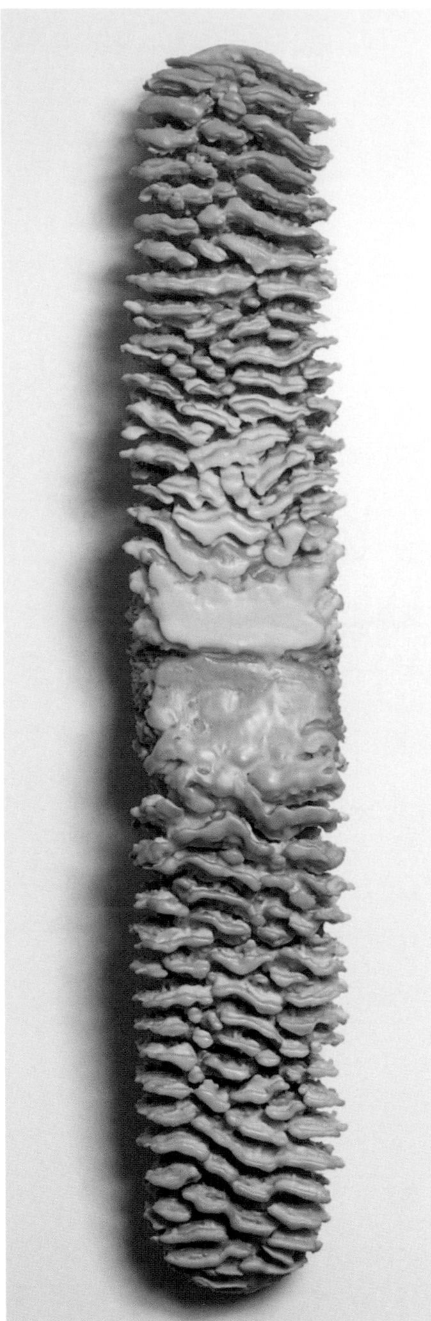

Lynda Benglis recalled that when she moved to New York at the height of the Minimalist movement in 1964, she felt compelled "to make something that related to the body, that was humanistic, and not machine-like." Benglis used organic materials to fashion objects that suggest the human body through corporeal motifs and malleable forms. Her works of the mid-1960s, like those of Eva Hesse (p. 138), are a rebuttal to the precise geometry and rigid materials of Minimalist sculpture.

In *Travel Agent*, Benglis' labor-intensive process becomes an integral part of the structure. Working outward in both directions from the center of a masonite panel, she painstakingly layered pigmented wax in pinks, greens, yellows, and blues. The resulting accumulation records her repetitive motions of applying the wax. Toward the center, Benglis lightly torched and/or ironed the wax, creating a smooth surface. *Travel Agent* elicits a visceral response, both because the narrow stalagmite fingers of wax evoke the linings of internal organs and because the sensuous but fragile surfaces entice us to touch. "Although the forms are not specifically recognizable," Benglis explained, "the feelings are."

Travel Agent remained in Benglis' possession for more than decade. She began to rework it in 1977, and considered it finished the following year. Few other wax-based works from this early stage in her career still exist because she burned many of them to warm her unheated studio.

Travel Agent, 1966 and 1977–78
Pigmented beeswax and gesso on masonite, 36 1/4 x 6 3/4 x 5 1/2 in. (92.1 x 17.2 x 14 cm)
Gift of Dr. Lawrence Werther 91.88.1

THOMAS HART BENTON

1889–1975

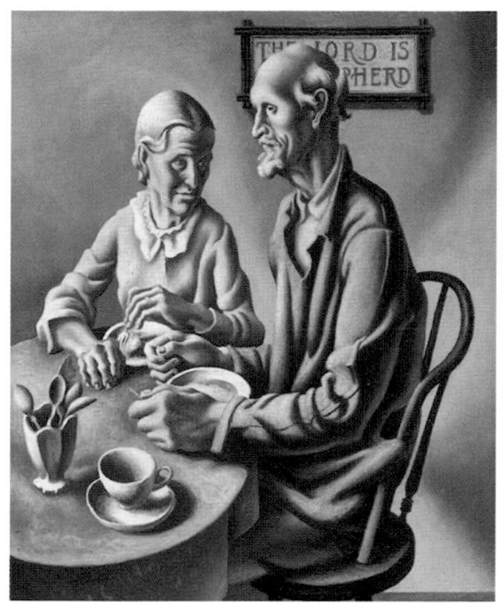

Thomas Hart Benton's *The Lord Is My Shepherd* is one of the early landmarks of American Regionalist art. Along with John Steuart Curry, Joe Jones, and Grant Wood (pp. 83, 158, 330), among others, Benton developed a nationalistic narrative art that sought to preserve the values of rural or small-town America. *The Lord Is My Shepherd* was painted on Martha's Vineyard, off the Massachusetts coast. It portrays George and Sabrina West, who lived down the hill from the barn where Benton worked every summer from 1920 until his death. The Wests, a hard-working couple with three children, were deaf-mutes. This may explain the prominence of their hands, but these hands are also roughened from manual labor, while their somber gazes reflect weariness after a strenuous day. The title of the painting, drawn from the sampler on the wall, speaks of the Wests' piety and humility.

More than two decades later, Benton's figurative style remained relatively unchanged, but *Poker Night (from "A Streetcar Named Desire")* presents an altogether different world. Benton had been commissioned by producer David O. Selznick to create a painting based on Tennessee Williams' play *A Streetcar Named Desire*. The painting was intended as a surprise gift for Selznick's wife, Irene, herself a producer, who brought the play to Broadway in 1947. Benton's work captures the sexual tension and undertone of violence in the story of Blanche DuBois (holding up a mirror), her sister Stella (leaning over the armchair), and Stella's husband, the hot-tempered Stanley Kowalski (standing at the table in a white undershirt). The scene Benton depicted is one of the play's most dramatic and memorable moments, when Blanche taunts a drunk and angry Stanley with her refined airs.

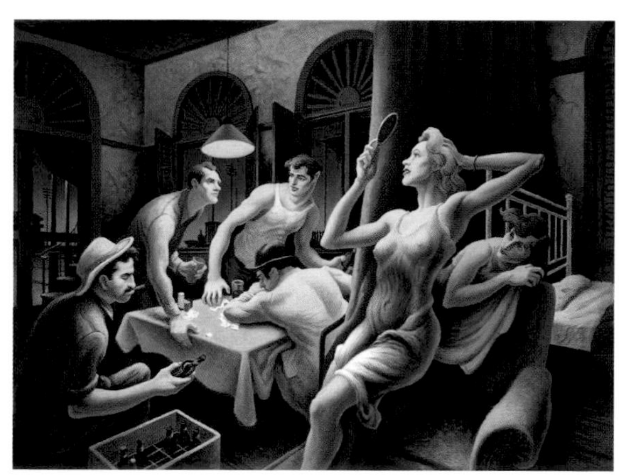

The Lord Is My Shepherd, 1926
Tempera on canvas, 33 1/4 x 27 3/8 in. (84.5 x 69.5 cm)
Purchase 31.100

Poker Night (from "A Streetcar Named Desire"), 1948
Tempera and oil on panel, 36 x 48 in. (91.4 x 121.9 cm)
Mrs. Percy Uris Bequest 85.49.2

DAWOUD BEY
b. 1953

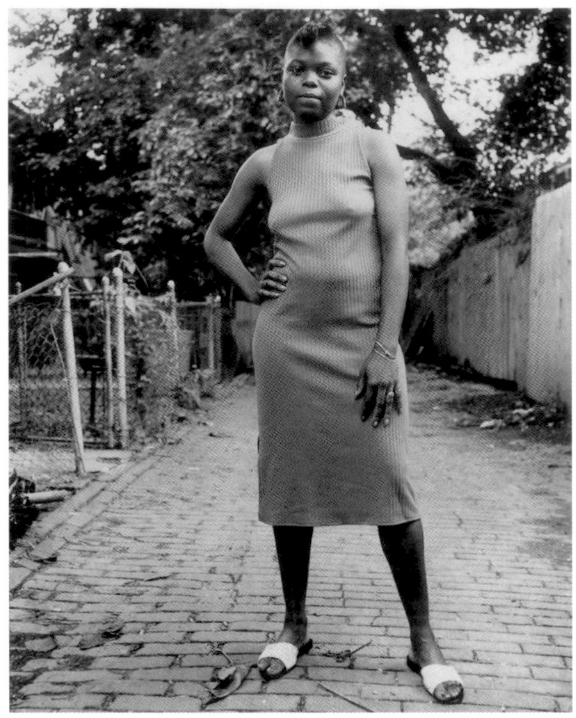

In 1969, Queens-born Dawoud Bey visited The Metropolitan Museum of Art for the first time to see "Harlem on My Mind," a seminal exhibition that documented the cultural capital of black America with more than seven hundred photographs. Galvanized by the realization that photography could be a powerful means of forging a positive memory for the African-American community, Bey began creating *Harlem USA* (1975–79), a collective portrait of the neighborhood. He roamed the streets of Harlem, photographing residents with a 35mm camera his godmother had given him.

Bey practiced traditional street photography in Harlem and in other American black communities until the late 1980s, when he became concerned about the "implicit power relationships acted out in the process of photographing people, particularly those on the margins of society." He dispensed with the unobtrusive 35mm snapshot camera and began working with the Polaroid camera, as in *A Young Woman Between Carrolburg Place and Half Street, Washington, DC.* The Polaroid camera was larger, had to be mounted on a tripod, and required a slow set-up process that enabled Bey to establish and sustain contact with his subject. The camera instantly produced a sheet of film that peeled apart into a 4 x 5-inch negative and a black-and-white positive, which Bey gave to the subject. He later used the negative to make enlarged prints.

The young woman, gazing calmly into Bey's camera, is thus complicit in the making of the image. The directness of her pose and glance brings to mind Walker Evans' photographs of Depression-era sharecroppers and James Van Der Zee's portraits of Jazz Age Harlemites. Like his predecessors, Bey conveys the dignity and spirit of his individual subjects, producing a collective image that enriches the community they come from.

A Young Woman Between Carrolburg Place and Half Street, Washington, DC, 1989
Gelatin silver print, 22 x 17 in. (55.9 x 43.2 cm)
Purchase, with funds from the Photography Committee 99.156

ISABEL BISHOP

1902–1988

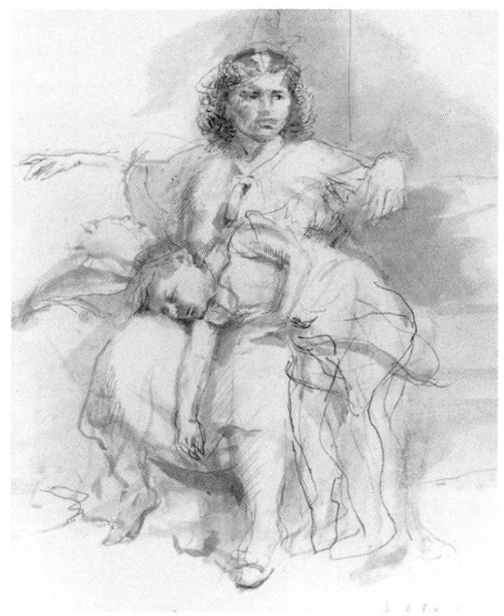

Isabel Bishop's drawings, etchings, and paintings depict familiar urban types isolated from the robust hubbub of the city. For six decades, she found her subjects primarily on New York City's Union Square, which she could view from a window in her studio. Bishop was the only female member of the 14th Street School (14th Street borders Union Square on the south), a group of painters, including Reginald Marsh and the Soyer brothers (pp. 198, 294), who were captivated by the energy of city life. Her interest, however, lay not in New York's monumental crowds and rapid pace, but in the solitary reverie and intimate conversations of the career girls, young mothers, and unemployed men she observed from her window.

Bishop's drawings were the heart and soul of her meticulous working process, in which she teased out the natural momentum of a gesture, the vitality in casual actions such as yawning, chatting, or drinking. The fluid lines and atmospheric ink wash of *Waiting* suggest restless folds of clothing, shifting limbs, and the watchful serenity of a private moment between a mother and child.

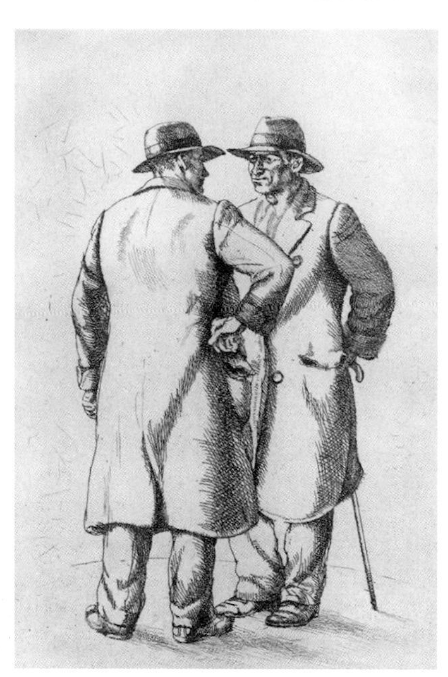

Bishop often turned to the more laborious medium of etching to verify whether, as she put it, there was "any idea in the drawing." When an idea engaged her, she drew and etched it over and over before finally turning it into a painting. Her process was so rigorous that she seldom completed more than four paintings in a year. Some images, especially those depicting men, never reached the canvas stage. For the exchange between out-of-work men in *Conversation*, the incisive, monochromatic quality of the etching medium seemed a more suitable conveyor of somber mood than a painted palette.

Waiting, 1935
Ink on paper, 7 1/8 x 6 in. (18.1 x 15.2 cm) sight
Purchase 36.31

Conversation, 1931
Etching: sheet, 11 1/4 x 9 1/2 in. (28.6 x 24.1 cm); plate, 5 15/16 x 4 in. (15.1 x 10.2 cm)
Felicia Meyer Marsh Bequest 80.31.142

ROSS BLECKNER

b. 1949

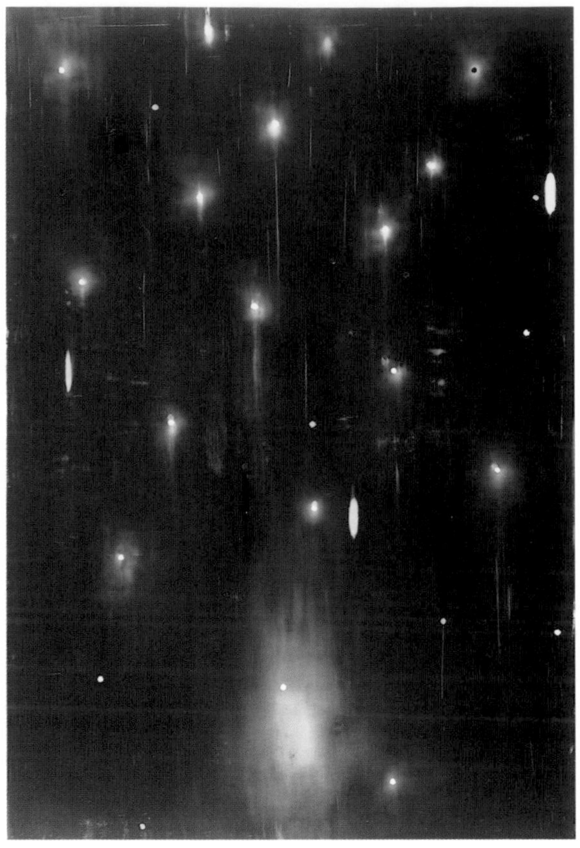

Ross Bleckner's *Count No Count* suggests the expanse of the nighttime sky filled with a constellation of softly glowing stars. At the same time, the painting hints at a more abstract, even spiritual, sense of illumination. Bleckner blends wax into oil paint to make the surface more luminous, conveying what he describes as "this almost continual light that comes from inside." Indeed, all of Bleckner's works, from his 1970s geometric paintings of all-over circles and pulsating stripes to more recent paintings with funereal imagery such as candelabras, flowers, and urns, engage the formal and symbolic qualities of light.

In *Count No Count*, various kinds of illumination are shown across a broad dark expanse: starlike bright white circles, oval yellow-tinted forms, thin white streaks, and a hazy, indistinct glow in the lower center. Together, these marks defy simple explanation, seeming to allude simultaneously to everything from the cosmos, to wood grain, to a supernatural apparition. Combining a sense of vast space with suggestions of strong emotions and natural forces, *Count No Count* evokes the "sublime" landscapes of eighteenth- and nineteenth-century Romanticism—landscapes designed to produce a sense of awe before the divinity manifest in natural phenomena. Ultimately, however, Bleckner's work, as it subtly shifts between abstraction and representation, illumination and darkness, inspires not awe but quiet reverie.

Count No Count, 1989
Oil and wax on canvas, 108 x 72 1/8 in. (274.3 x 183.2 cm)
Purchase, with funds from the Painting and Sculpture Committee 89.28

OSCAR BLUEMNER

1867–1938

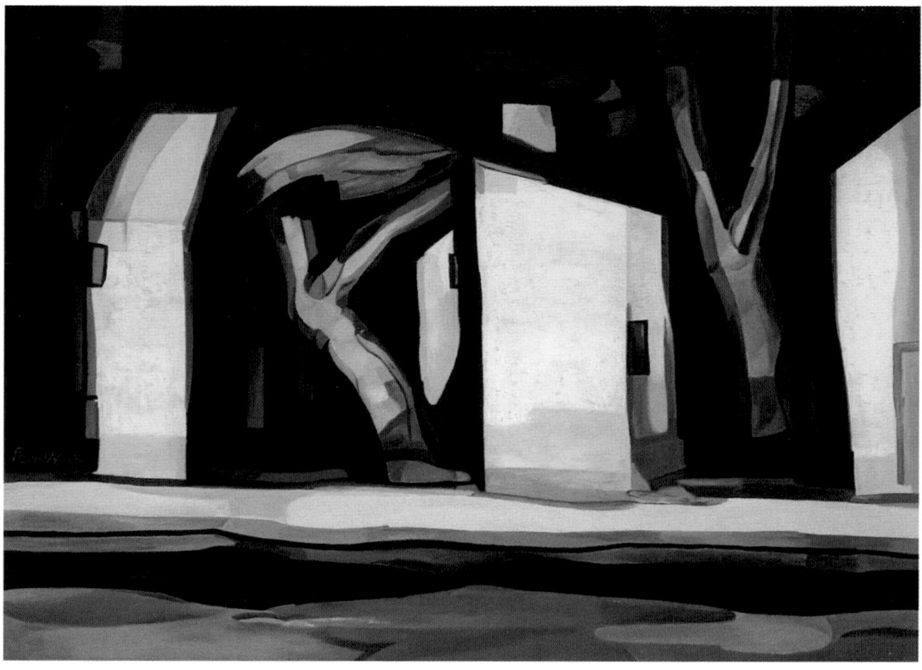

Oscar Bluemner, German émigré architect turned painter, had his first one-artist exhibition in New York in 1915. His prismatic, boldly geometric canvases—bursting with factories, barns, and winding country roads—were in step with the non-naturalistic approach to color and form practiced by American modernists. But Bluemner soon rejected his early canvases, noting that "there is too much in the pictures...too much idea."

What engaged Bluemner were the mystical and emotive properties of color and shape. The idea that colors represented primary emotions, first proposed in the early nineteenth century by Johann Wolfgang von Goethe, became the guiding principle of his art. "When you FEEL colors," Bluemner said, "you will understand the WHY of their forms." In his system, red, for example, the most vital color, was a warning; it was also the symbol of power, energy, and life. Yellow was light and warmth, and black was sorrow and society; the two colors together, as seen in *A Situation in Yellow*, stirred up "an exquisite sensation."

The painting, completed in the last decade of Bluemner's life, offers dark trees and yellow buildings rendered luminescent by overlapping glazes of pure pigment; Bluemner called this process "tone building." He likened the composition of a painting to musical structure and orchestration: pigment was a key on the piano; the shifts in tones were octaves and harmonies. With its chromatic vibrancy and unified rhythm, *A Situation in Yellow* strikes a dark, shimmering chord.

A Situation in Yellow, 1933
Oil on canvas, 36 x 50 1/2 in. (91.4 x 128.3 cm)
Gift of Nancy and Harry L. Koenigsberg 67.66

PETER BLUME

1906–1992

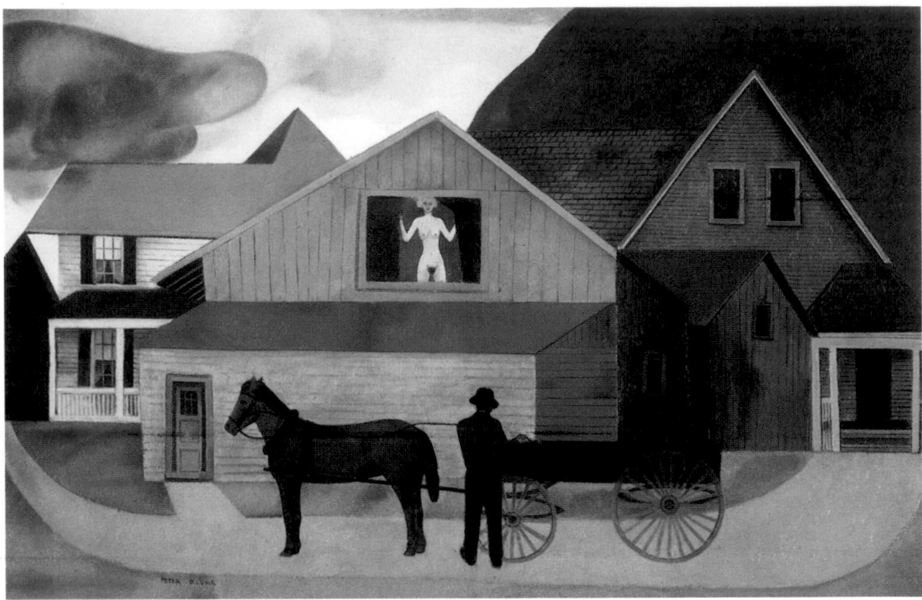

Peter Blume completed *New England Barn* the year he turned twenty. The painting reveals a precocious self-assurance and foreshadows the meticulous but dreamlike compositions he produced later in his career. Borrowing European Surrealist strategies, Blume brought together images that seem unrelated and, sometimes, incompatible, as in the nude woman who stands rather matter-of-factly in the open door of an otherwise ordinary hayloft. Yet even at this youthful stage, Blume was beginning to develop a distinctly American strain of Surrealism. *New England Barn*, with its geometric architecture and earthy palette, resembles contemporaneous Precisionist paintings, which frequently depicted factories, farms, and other utilitarian buildings (pp. 81, 96, 277).

As a fifteen-year-old student at the Educational Alliance, a settlement house project on New York's Lower East Side, Blume had learned to draw the human figure, first from casts of antique sculpture and then from a live model. He later boasted, "I began working away with great facility....and I moved to the head of my class in no time at all." *New England Barn* conveys the artist's youthful self-confidence in rendering the human figure as well as his desire to forge a style independent of the art he saw around him.

New England Barn, 1926
Oil on canvas, 24 x 36 in. (61 x 91.4 cm)
Gift of Leonard Spigelgass 61.14

LEE BONTECOU

b. 1931

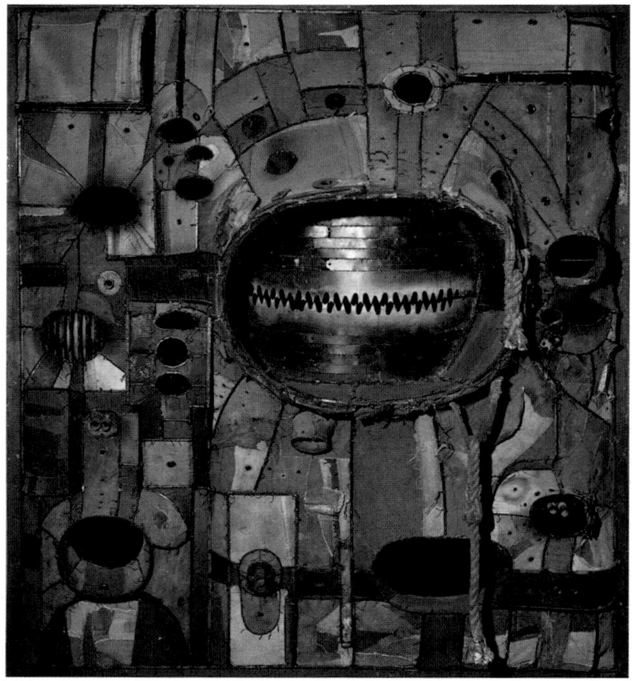

Lee Bontecou's *Untitled, 1961* is a hybrid of painting and sculpture. An assemblage of canvas and objects such as grommets, saw blades, and rope, it hangs on the wall like a painting but projects more than 2 feet into the room. Bontecou combined disparate processes to create this work, welding the metal armature and then suturing fragments of canvas to it with copper wire. (She scavenged most of her canvas from bags and conveyor belts discarded by the laundry beneath her New York studio.) Working with stitched canvas fragments enabled her to produce three-dimensional forms, such as the elliptical cavities backed with black velvet, that would have been impossible with a single length of fabric.

The visual allusions generated by Bontecou's configuration range wide, from destructive man-made devices to organic and geological structures—riveted airplane engines, celestial black holes, gun barrels, volcanoes, human orifices, and the segmented shells of insects. Bontecou courted this ambiguity, and her work is a conflation of the anatomical and the mechanical, the biological and the geological. Artist and critic Donald Judd (p. 160) noted this constant shift of meanings. Bontecou's imagery, he wrote in 1963, "extends from something as social as war to something as private as sex, making one an aspect of the other." Yet for Bontecou, her work was also a response to the historical moment in which it was created. "I wish my work to represent or to be a part of my time... I want them to be things and facts inside us—from war to the wonders of the space age."

Bontecou was one of the most prominent young American artists in the 1960s, and the only woman in gallerist Leo Castelli's stable of artists, a group that included such luminaries as Jasper Johns, Robert Rauschenberg, and Frank Stella (pp. 154, 248, 297). In the early 1970s, however, Bontecou withdrew from the art world, leaving New York and rarely exhibiting her later work.

Untitled, 1961, 1961
Welded metal, canvas, wire, and rope, 72 5/8 x 66 x 25 7/16 in. (184.5 x 167.6 x 64.6 cm)
Purchase 61.41

JONATHAN BOROFSKY

b. 1942

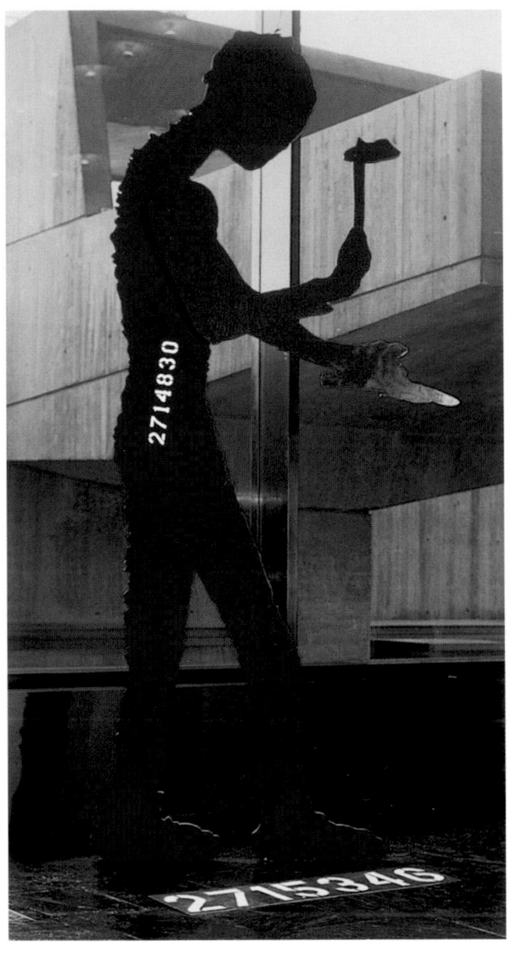

The hammering man is one of several recurring figures who populate Jonathan Borofsky's work. Other members of the family include men with briefcases, runners, chattering men, and sad-eyed clowns. The Whitney's *Hammering Man at 2715346* is 13 feet high, with a motorized arm that activates a constant motion of hammering. The figure first appeared in a 1976 wall drawing Borofsky made of a man hammering a shoe, itself drawn from a *Book of Knowledge* illustration of a Tunisian shoemaker; four years later, Borofsky introduced the motif as a sculpture.

Although the hammering man was based on a book illustration, much of Borofsky's imagery comes from dreams, which he explores in his waking moments with a creative discipline derived from his study of Zen Buddhism. In 1968, he decided to confine his art activity to the recording of his thoughts. A year later, he started to count continuously from one, toward infinity, in an effort to regulate what he called "mind chatter." He then assigned numbers to each subsequent art work to represent the moment in the counting process when the work was created (at 2,715,346 for *Hammering Man*); these numbers also serve as a kind of signature. In this sense, the works are an extension of the artist's ongoing accounting and indicate the importance to Borofsky of subordinating individual works to an expansive—indeed, theoretically endless—family of related sculptures, drawings, ideas, and dreams.

Not all of Borofsky's conceptions, however, remain confined to his inner world. He has applied them to a variety of topical issues, from domestic defense spending to workers' strikes in Poland. The latter, in fact, was invoked, as a written slogan ("Strike") in one *Hammering Man* installation, in which hammering as a generic form of labor was equated with striking as a politically motivated refusal to work.

Hammering Man at 2715346, 1981
Painted wood and masonite with metal stripping and motor, 156 x 66 x 13 1/2 in.
(396.2 x 167.6 x 34.3 cm) variable
Gift of Robert and Jane Meyerhoff 90.30a–b

LOUISE BOURGEOIS

b. 1911

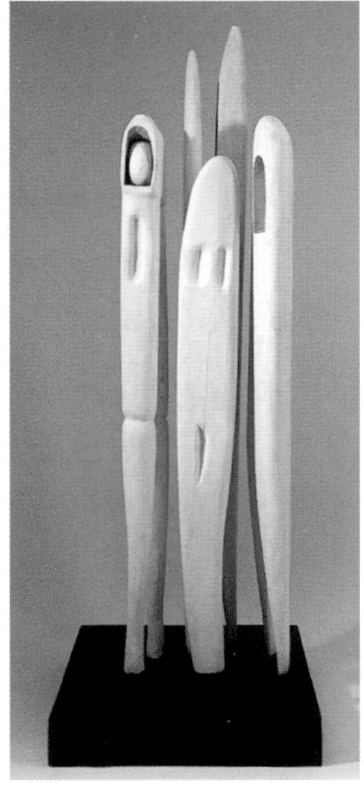

Louise Bourgeois' work, executed in a variety of media, has a thematic consistency. In one way or another, it explores the relationship of the individual to the group and, specifically, of the child to the family. Bourgeois was born in France to a family of artisans and as a child helped her parents restore antique tapestries. Deeply troubled, however, by her father's open infidelity, she found family life unbearable.

Bourgeois emigrated to New York in 1938 and soon embarked on a series of carved and painted wood sculptures, which she called "Personages," that evoked the upright human form. *Quarantania*, an early example from this series, consists of five elongated forms huddled on a pedestal, in a "duel," as she put it, "between the isolated individual and the shared awareness of the group." When Bourgeois described such works as "the drama of one among many," she alluded to her own childhood. The group in *Quarantania* not only resembles human figures, but also sewing needles or weaving shuttles, the tools of her family's trade.

In early sculptures like *Quarantania*, references to Bourgeois' childhood are veiled in abstraction; in recent years, she has confronted her memories more directly. *Pink Days and Blue Days* incorporates clothing from the artist's life, including a silk coat embroidered with the doting nicknames she was given as a child: "Louise, Lise, Lison, Lisette, Louison, Louisette." Yet there is something sinister in this sweetness, for the lace baby gowns hang from bones. This eerie juxtaposition and its dark autobiographical implications echo the Surrealist emphasis on the unconscious, which had engaged Bourgeois while she was living in Paris and remains a subtle current in much of her work.

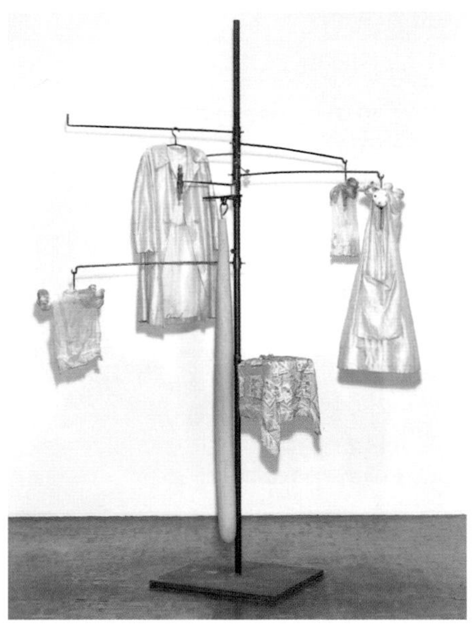

Quarantania, 1941
7 wooden pine elements on a wooden base, 84 3/4 x 31 1/4 x 29 1/4 in. (215.3 x 79.4 x 74.3 cm)
Gift of an anonymous donor 77.80

Pink Days and Blue Days, 1997
Steel, fabric, bone, wood, glass, rubber, and mixed media, 117 x 87 x 87 in. (297.2 x 221 x 221 cm) overall
Purchase, with funds from The Lauder Foundation, Evelyn and Leonard Lauder Fund, the Painting and Sculpture Committee, the Tom Armstrong Purchase Fund, Danielle Lemmon, and the Jack E. Chachkes Endowed Purchase Fund 97.101a–s

PATRICK HENRY BRUCE

1881–1936

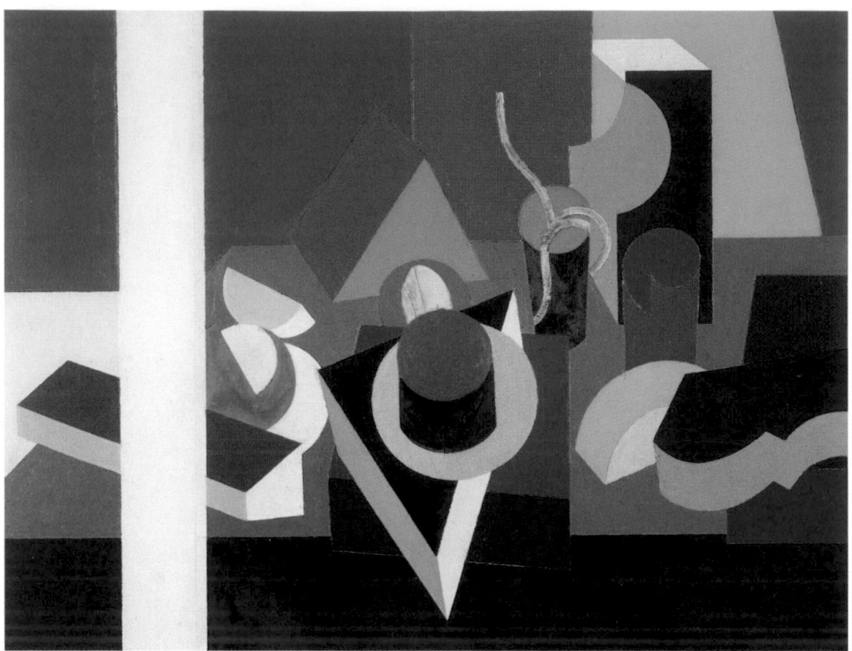

Although Patrick Henry Bruce was the great-great-grandson of the Revolutionary War orator Patrick Henry, he spent most of his adult life in Europe. In the years preceding World War I, he was one of the few American artists accepted by the Parisian avant-garde. After the war, however, Bruce felt increasingly isolated and became convinced that his art would never be understood. He destroyed much of his work and eventually committed suicide, shortly after returning to New York in 1936.

Only about one hundred of Bruce's paintings survive, about half of them still lifes, a genre that appealed to the aloof, analytical artist. In the late 1910s, he began a series of abstracted still lifes to which he gave generic French titles such as *peinture* ("painting") or *nature morte* ("still life"). One of these works is *Painting*, as it is now known. It depicts an arrangement of objects Bruce found around his studio: oranges, drinking glasses, architectural moldings. Yet these specific objects have little personal or sentimental value; they are merely vehicles in the artist's obsessive search for "absolutes," in which an orange, for example, becomes a sphere, its surface uniform and undimpled. Bruce rendered his geometric forms from different vantage points, so that the varying perspectives simultaneously create and destroy the illusion of depth. The vertical white bar cutting the canvas at left marks the forward edge of the space, but its pure abstraction serves to underscore the two-dimensionality of the concept. In *Painting*, Bruce walks a tightrope between the specific and the absolute, between depth and flatness. Keeping these competing forces in balance was a feat he struggled with to the end.

Painting, c. 1921–22
Oil on canvas, 35 x 45 3/4 in. (88.9 x 116.2 cm)
Gift of an anonymous donor 54.20

CHARLES BURCHFIELD

1893–1967

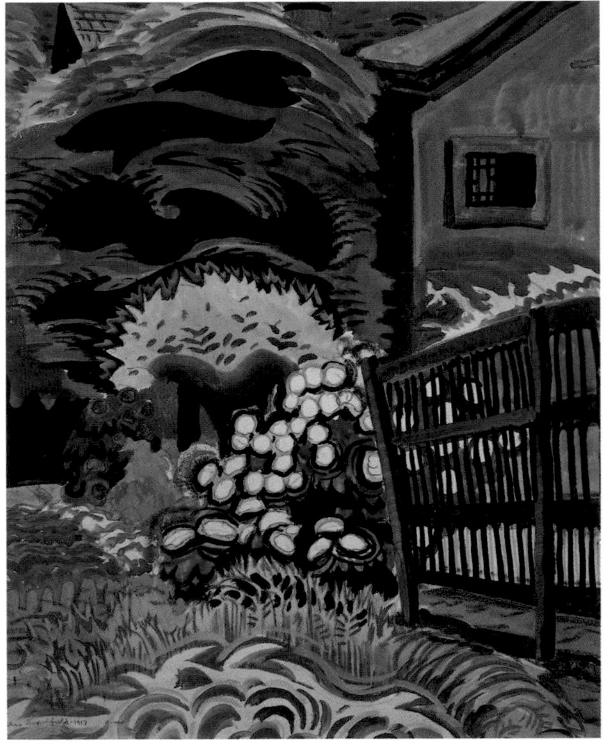

Charles Burchfield spent most of his life as an "inlander," living in Salem, Ohio, and Buffalo, New York—far from the East Coast art world. His visionary watercolor landscapes are intensely individualistic, and yet he was never far from the mainstream of American modernist art. Like many of his contemporaries, Burchfield viewed nature as a source of revelation. Each season, every time of day, called forth a distinct mood that he wanted to capture.

Burchfield painted *Noontide in Late May* soon after returning to Ohio from a brief and unhappy sojourn in New York City. This vivid, exuberant watercolor reflects the artist's enchantment with his own hometown. His neighbor's backyard becomes a fantastic landscape of spring blooms so full of life they seem to pulsate on the page. *Noontide in Late May* was created during Burchfield's "golden year"—a vernal season of intense creativity and abundant artistic growth.

An April Mood, begun nearly thirty years later when the artist was in his fifties, is also set in the springtime—though earlier in the season, when the trees are still bare. Burchfield, who kept detailed weather records in his diaries, was acutely aware of the changing seasons as well as their emotional import. He remarked that he intended *An April Mood* to represent "the anger of God, frowning on delinquent mankind." It is a forsaken landscape that has not yet seen the redemption of spring. The dark clouds of *An April Mood* cast doubt that spring will ever come.

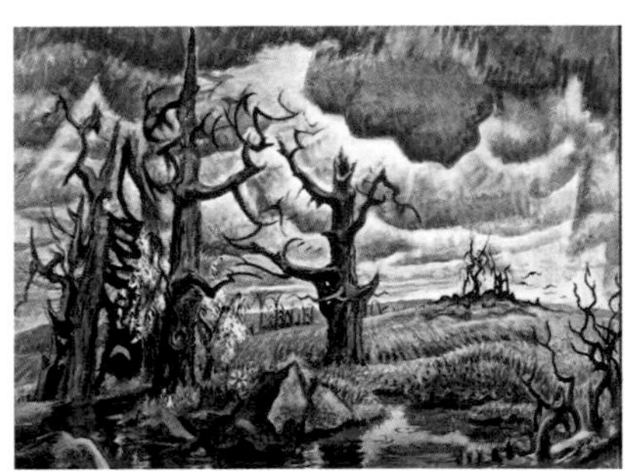

Noontide in Late May, 1917
Watercolor and gouache on paper, 22 x 17 15/16 in. (55.9 x 45.6 cm)
Purchase 31.408

An April Mood, 1946–55
Watercolor and charcoal on paper, 40 x 54 in. (101.6 x 137.2 cm)
Purchase, with partial funds from Mr. and Mrs. Lawrence A. Fleischman 55.39

SCOTT BURTON

1939–1989

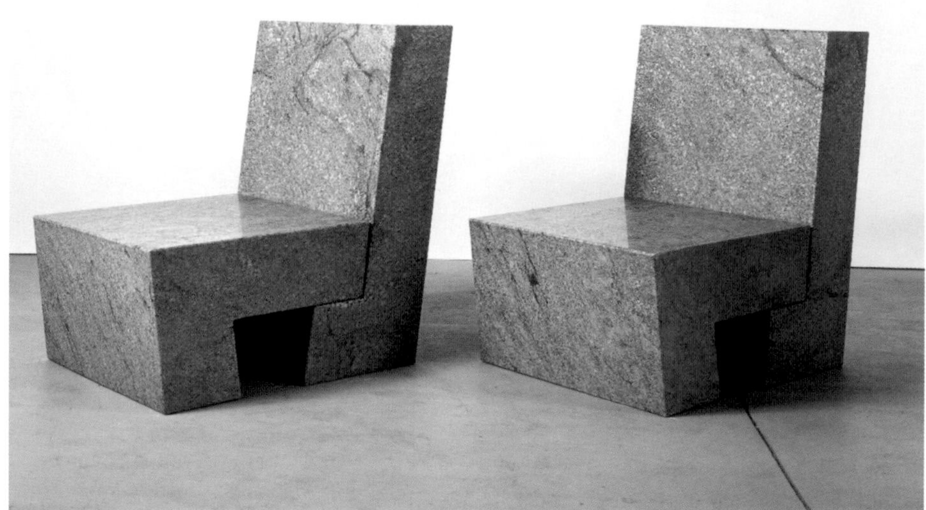

The work for which Scott Burton is best known, the furniture-sculpture hybrids of the 1980s, are constructed of solid stone, rolled steel, brushed aluminum, or laminated wood—and every one of them is designed to be used as furniture as well as looked at as an art work. Burton held that art should serve the public, and his chairs, many of them intended for public places, are functional sculptures. In their spare, almost impersonal elegance, they also express Burton's belief that a work of art should transcend any single artist's emotional or intellectual concerns. These principles led Burton, in the late 1980s, to devote his time to projects for public spaces, including the plaza in front of the World Financial Center in Manhattan (created in collaboration with Siah Armajani).

Burton began his career as a performance artist, creating highly formalized vignettes that examined, in slow motion, the behaviors of real bodies in space and time. The furniture work is also concerned with the disposition of bodies in space, since all furniture is both accommodating and reflective of the form of the human body—especially chairs, with their arms, legs, backs, and bottoms. *Pair of Two-Part Chairs, Obtuse Angle* is made of heavily veined polished granite. The ample laps, broad, straight backs, and solid seats exemplify this latent anthropomorphism. The title refers to the construction of the piece, each chair being made of two parts, with the supporting part set at an obtuse angle.

Pair of Two-Part Chairs, Obtuse Angle, 1984
Polished granite, 33 x 24 x 33 in. (83.8 x 61 x 83.8 cm) each
Purchase, with funds from the Lemberg Foundation, Inc. 84.32a–d

PAUL CADMUS

1904–1999

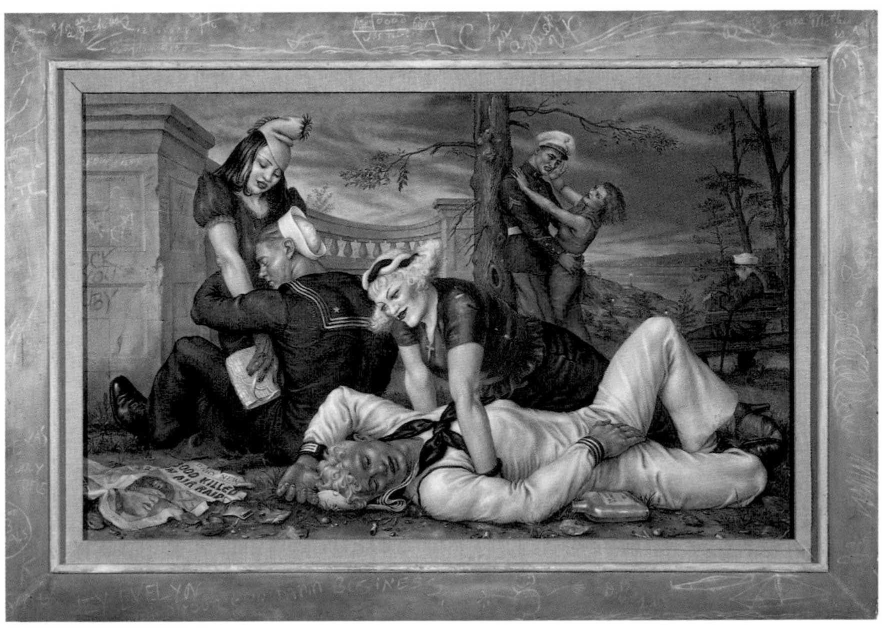

In the art of Paul Cadmus, a classical style of painting often merges with biting social satire. His interest in the musculature and anatomy of the human form took him back to the Italian Renaissance, particularly the work of the fifteenth-century masters Andrea Mantegna and Luca Signorelli. Cadmus' subject matter, however, was truly contemporary, sometimes risqué, and it frequently mocked various aspects of modern American life.

Cadmus' proclivity to satirize, as well as his technical concerns with rendering the body, can be seen in *Sailors and Floosies*, the third painting in a trilogy of works on the theme of sailors that he completed between 1933 and 1938. The sailors' muscular physiques, hardly contained in their tight uniforms, testify to Cadmus' knowledge of the figure. Even the bare arms of the women show an almost exaggerated musculature. Meanwhile, the sleeping sailor in the foreground, with one arm raised over his head, assumes the well-known Renaissance posture of the sleeping Venus. The Venus in this picture, however, is not the reclining figure but, in Cadmus' acerbic transformation, one of the floosies who frequent sailors' on-shore haunts.

Cadmus' trilogy generated intense controversy in its time. Pro-Navy critics thought that depicting the bawdy antics of sailors on leave cast the Navy in a bad light, while others felt that the theme represented a realistic portrayal of what sailors actually did. Heightening the debate were the subtle homoerotic allusions in the other two paintings of the trilogy. Together, the three works epitomize the visual dialogue Cadmus strove to create between a satirical take on modern life and the human figure in an idealized, classical mode.

Sailors and Floosies, 1938
Oil and tempera on panel, 33 1/2 x 48 3/8 in. (85.1 x 122.9 cm) with frame
Gift of Malcolm S. Forbes 64.42a–b

INGRID CALAME

b. 1965

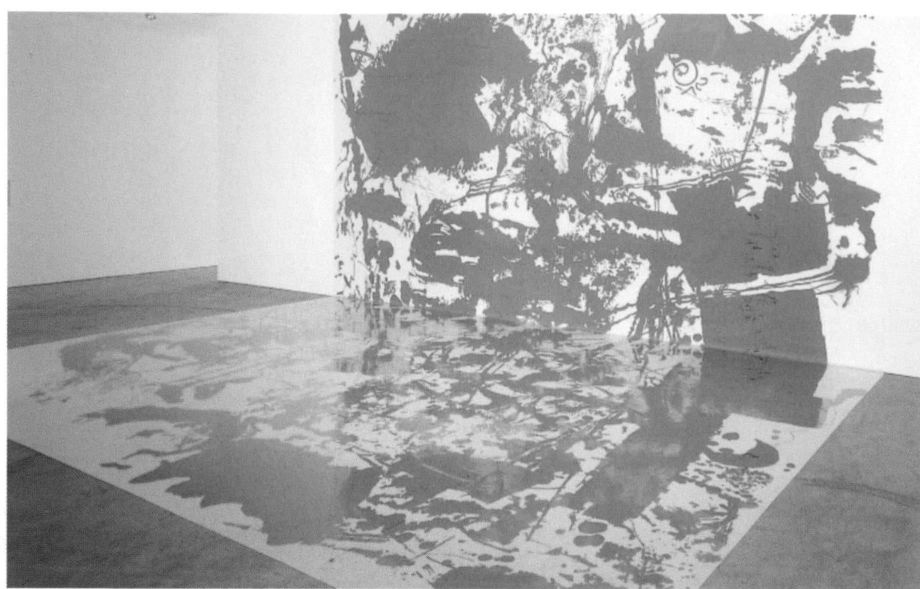

At first glance, Ingrid Calame's monumental *b-b-b, rr-gR-UF!, b-b-b* seems to be a gleeful assortment of Pollock-like spills and splatters of paint (p. 242). On closer inspection, however, it becomes apparent that each abstract mark is applied in a smooth layer of dense enamel paint, its edges delineated with a razor-sharp precision that contrasts with the characteristically gestural and spontaneous techniques of the Abstract Expressionists. Rather than plumb the recesses of her unconscious, Calame finds her marks through an infinitely more extroverted, painstaking process: she roams the streets of Los Angeles, tracing the "lacy stains left by the evaporation of nameless fluids," which she categorizes and archives.

b-b-b, rr-gR-UF!, b-b-b is an arrangement of these stains, grouped in "constellations" that are classified according to the sources of the stains (where they come from or what they were found on) and then retraced onto a mylar surface. In contrast to her deliberate working method, Calame whimsically names her works for the uncontrollable exclamations—sighs of pleasure, groans of pain, paroxysms of fear—that accompany physical experiences. This painting, which appears to dribble down the wall and onto the gallery floor, bears an onomatopoeic title that sounds like what paint—if it could talk—might utter when flung at a wall at high speed. Calame's fascination with the remnants of fluids and urban waste is transformed into self-conscious abstractions whose synthetic, saturated palette strips these remnants of their messy origins. It is as if the monochromatic stains—two generations removed from the dirty California tarmac—have been gathered and sanitized for our protection.

b-b-b, rr-gR-UF!, b-b-b, 1999
Enamel on mylar, 348 x 300 in. (883.9 x 762 cm) overall
Purchase, with funds from the Painting and Sculpture Committee 2000.146a–e

ALEXANDER CALDER

1898–1976

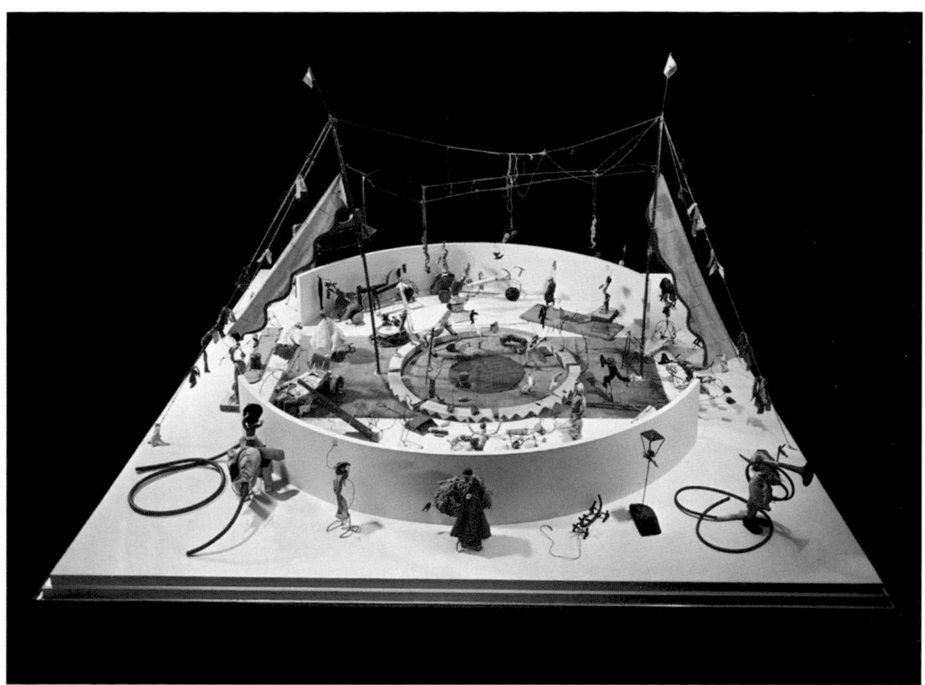

The Whitney Museum has long been engaged with the work of Alexander Calder, one of the twentieth century's most innovative sculptors. With seventy works in a broad range of media, the Museum's Calder holdings rank among the most extensive in the world.

Though he began his professional career with a degree in mechanical engineering, by age twenty-five Calder decided to become an artist, following in the footsteps of his father and grandfather, both well-known sculptors. Having moved to Paris in 1926, he soon began to fabricate dozens of tiny figures and props for what would become his most renowned work, *Calder's Circus*. Making use of simple, available materials such as wire, cork, fabric, and string, he constructed ingeniously articulated animals, clowns, and acrobats, which he manipulated while narrating their actions in English or French and providing sound effects with whistles and bells. A phonograph often provided musical accompaniment. Calder transported his miniature circus between New York and Paris in several suitcases and gave performances on both sides of the Atlantic in his studios and in the

Calder's Circus, 1926–31
Wire, wood, metal, cloth, yarn, paper, cardboard, leather, string, rubber tubing, corks, buttons, rhinestones, pipe cleaners, and bottle caps, dimensions variable, 54 x 94 1/4 x 94 1/4 in. (137.2 x 239.4 x 239.4 cm) overall
Purchase, with funds from a public fundraising campaign in May 1982. One half the funds were contributed by the Robert Wood Johnson Jr. Charitable Trust. Additional major donations were given by The Lauder Foundation, the Robert Lehman Foundation, Inc., the Howard and Jean Lipman Foundation, Inc., an anonymous donor, The T.M. Evans Foundation, Inc., MacAndrews & Forbes Group, Incorporated, the DeWitt Wallace Fund, Inc., Martin and Agneta Gruss, Anne Phillips, Mr. and Mrs. Laurance S. Rockefeller, the Simon Foundation, Inc., Marylou Whitney, Bankers Trust Company, Mr. and Mrs. Kenneth N. Dayton, Joel and Anne Ehrenkranz, Irvin and Kenneth Feld, Flora Whitney Miller. More than 500 individuals from 26 states and abroad also contributed to the campaign 83.36.1–56

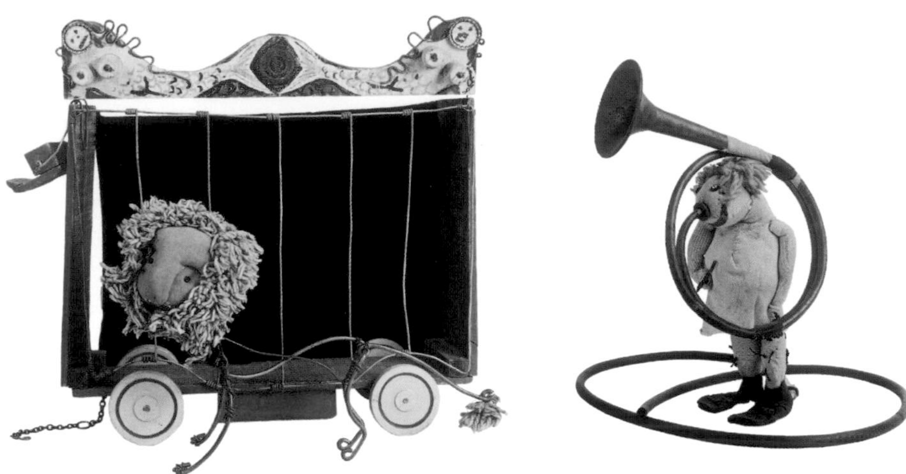

apartments of friends or art patrons. On at least one occasion the sculptor Isamu Noguchi (p. 224) operated the phonograph, a task later taken up by Calder's wife, Louisa. These performances introduced the kineticism that would become the defining characteristic of Calder's art, leading first to the wire sculptures of the late 1920s and eventually to the invention of his abstract mobiles in the early 1930s. The *Circus* performances attracted the attention of several important European modernists and helped foster Calder's reputation within the European avant-garde.

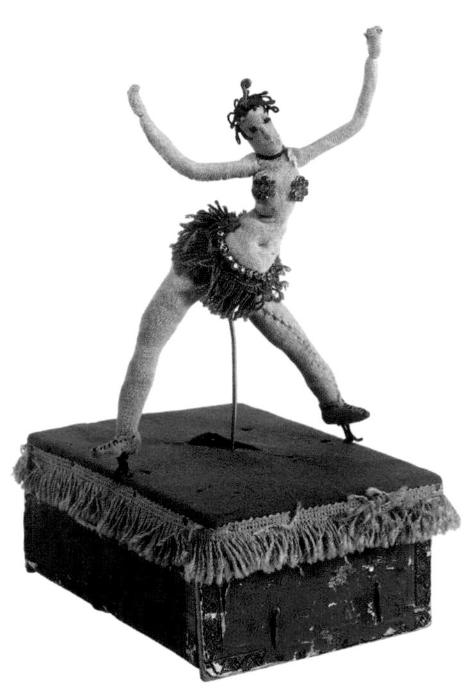

While at work on the *Circus*, Calder began composing sculpture solely from wire, a medium with which he had worked since childhood. With remarkable dexterity, he transformed wire into compositions representing narrative subjects, his favorite circus themes, or uncanny likenesses of his friends, family, or current celebrities. Essentially continuous line drawings in space, the wire sculptures could be suspended so that they moved, or mounted on a base, where they remained virtually static.

Details of ***Calder's Circus***

ALEXANDER CALDER

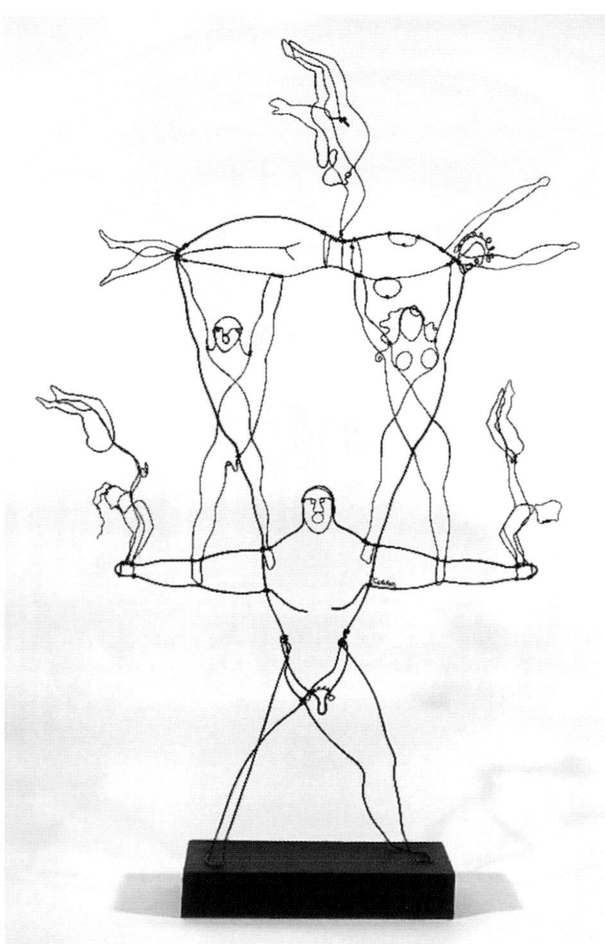

At more than 5 1/2 feet in height, *The Brass Family* is one of the artist's largest, most ambitious works in wire, realized with astonishing economy of means and fluidity of form. In 1930, due in part to an epiphanic visit to the Paris studio of Piet Mondrian, founder of the abstract style known as Neo-Plasticism (p. 91), Calder himself turned to abstraction. The following year, he made his first "mobiles," a term coined by his friend Marcel Duchamp. At first set in motion by motors or manual cranks, the mobiles eventually moved only by a touch of the hand or currents of air. A large standing mobile from 1931, *Object with Red Discs*, embodies the simple geometry and precise balance of forms that characterized Calder's early abstract work. A black wooden ball at the end of a long steel rod provides ballast for a structure of wire, small spheres, and red metal disks held in a delicately cantilevered poise.

The Brass Family, 1927
Brass wire and painted wood, 66 3/8 x 40 x 8 in. (168.6 x 101.6 x 20.3 cm)
Gift of the artist 69.255

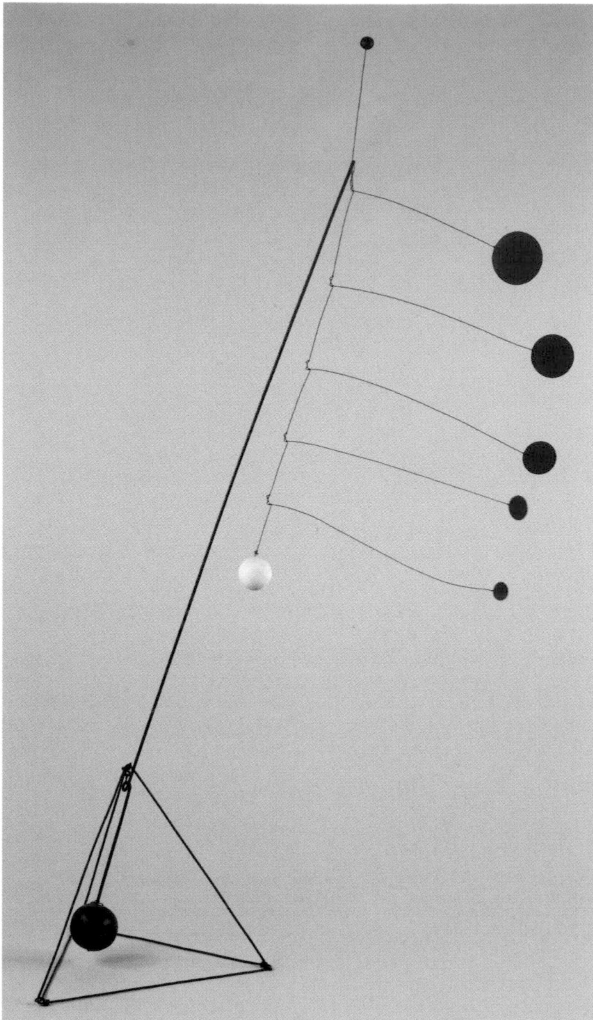

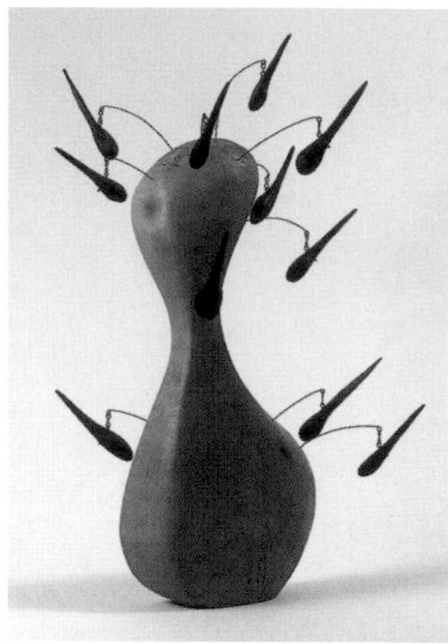

During World War II, Calder relied increasingly on wood for his sculpture, due to domestic shortages of metal. A skilled wood carver since the late 1920s, he embarked on a new group of constructions in 1942 called *Constellations*, an imaginative response to the biomorphic Surrealism of his friends Joan Miró and Jean Arp. For *Wooden Bottle with Hairs*, Calder carved a curving, bottle-shaped form to which he attached small, pointed objects that dangle from wires and chains and jiggle threateningly when disturbed.

As materials became plentiful again, Calder returned to his favorite medium, sheet metal. For the next thirty years, until his death in 1976, he was periodically occupied with large-scale outdoor works and frequent public commissions. In 1932, Arp had invented the term "stabile" for Calder's immobile objects. *Seven-Legged Beast*, made at Segre's Iron Works

Object with Red Discs, 1931
Painted steel rod, wire, wood, and sheet aluminum, 88 1/2 x 33 x 47 1/2 in. (224.8 x 83.8 x 120.7 cm) with base
Purchase, with funds from the Mrs. Percy Uris Purchase Fund 86.49a–b

Wooden Bottle with Hairs, 1943
Wood and wire, 22 3/8 x 13 x 12 in. (56.8 x 33 x 30.5 cm) overall
50th Anniversary Gift of the Howard and Jean Lipman Foundation, Inc. 80.28.2a–l

ALEXANDER CALDER

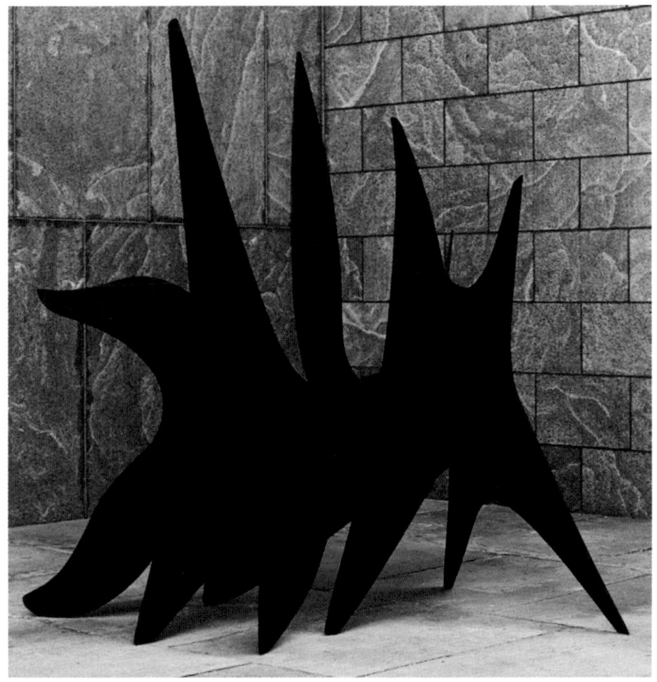

in Waterbury, Connecticut, typifies the artist's mid-size stabiles of the 1950s: interlocking, organic forms in black painted steel (Calder's preferred color for stabiles), and a vague resemblance, despite its abstract nature, to a strange, prehistoric creature. Though substantial in scale and weight, the stabile sits gracefully aloft, its seven "feet" seeming hardly to touch the ground. Like his stabiles, Calder's mobiles occupy space not through volumetric form but through multiple planar shapes that branch into space. For his mature, wind-driven mobiles, Calder sought the random movement induced by air currents, but controlled it through carefully calibrated systems of weights and balances. In large cut-metal mobiles such as *Big Red*, with its 9 1/2-foot span, the full composition spins slowly through 360 degrees, while subsidiary systems within form their own independent kinetic compositions.

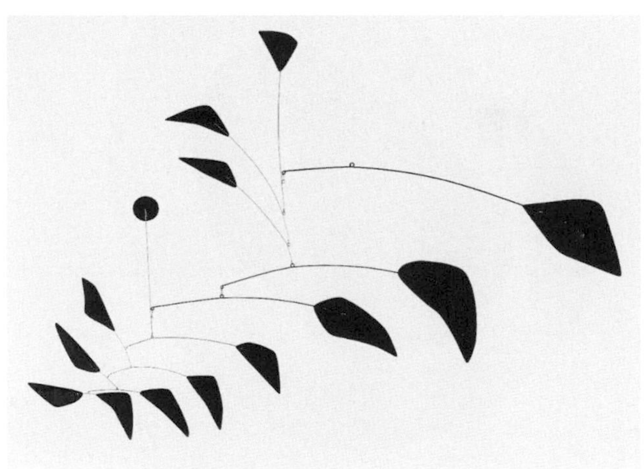

Seven-Legged Beast, 1957
Painted steel, 84 x 84 x 48 in. (213.4 x 213.4 x 121.9 cm)
Gift of Louisa Calder 83.45

Big Red, 1959
Sheet metal and steel wire, 74 x 114 in. (188 x 289.6 cm)
Purchase, with funds from the Friends of the Whitney Museum of American Art, and exchange 61.46

PETER CAMPUS

b. 1937

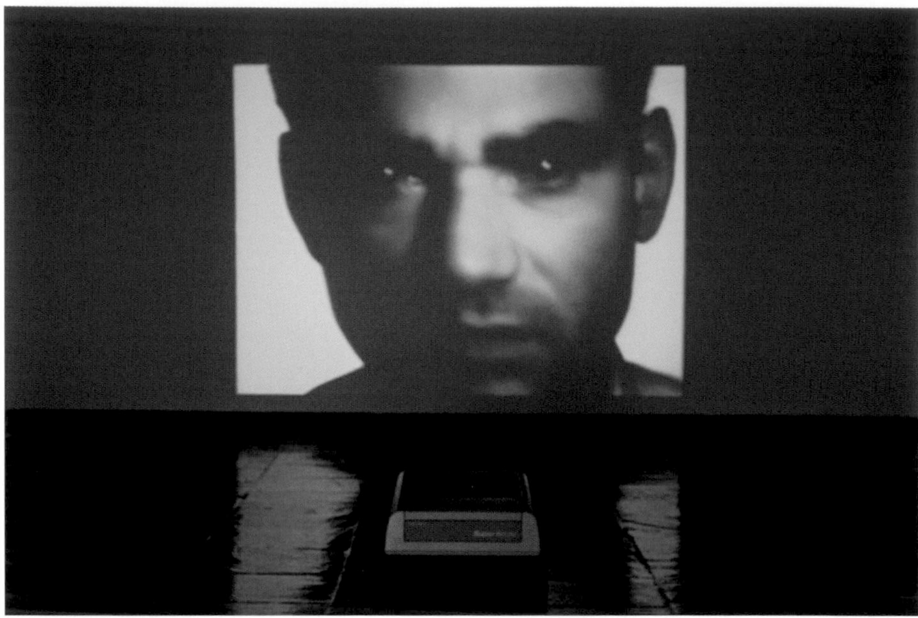

Peter Campus is one of the most influential pioneers of video art. In the 1970s, he created a series of seminal video installations that engaged viewers in an existential confrontation with images of themselves, using a closed-circuit camera to produce large, mirrorlike projections in a darkened gallery space. *Head of a Man with Death on His Mind* marks Campus' transition into new territory: instead of live projections of the viewer seen within the gallery, he introduced prerecorded images. It was no longer the viewer's self, but a projected other who was subject to internal scrutiny.

In *Head of a Man with Death on His Mind*, an 8-foot-high projection of a man's face stares at us from the end wall of the darkened gallery. One side of the face is in heavy shadow; on the other, the nose and forehead are sharply highlighted. The eyes glint ominously, the pupils like pinholes, as if the light were emanating from inside the eyes rather than reflecting external illumination. The stillness of the image, along with the stark contrasts of light and shadow and the work's monumental scale, give this two-dimensional projection a sculptural character. In the brooding, intensely morbid countenance, there is a tension between the motionless surface and the mental activity behind the features, symbolized by the open pupils. Light, in Campus' work, becomes a powerful means of externalizing the workings of the inner self.

Head of a Man with Death on His Mind, 1978
Video projection, dimensions variable
Promised gift of The Bohen Foundation P.91.4

FEDERICO CASTELLON

1914–1971

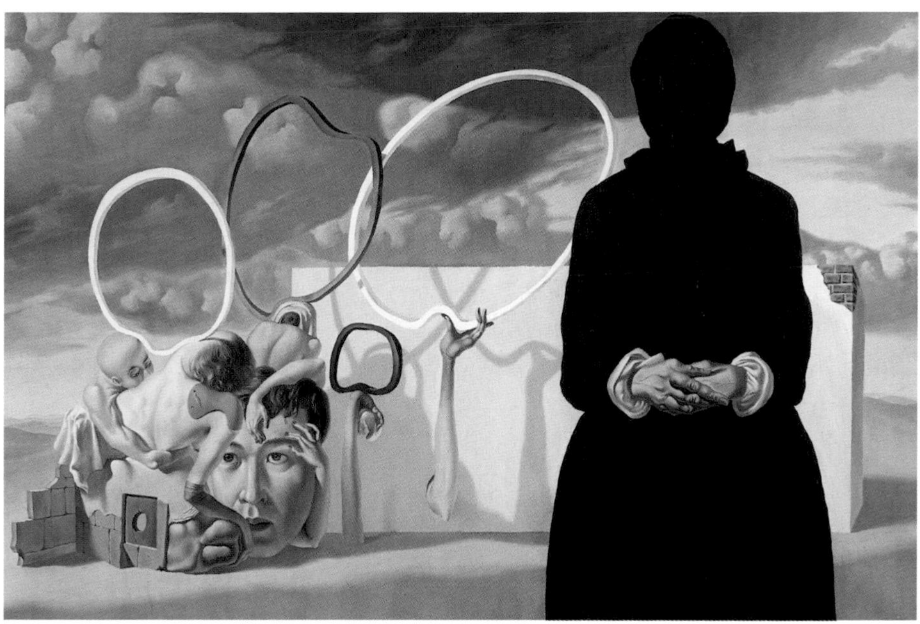

Federico Castellon's dreamlike painting *The Dark Figure* employs the visual vocabulary of Surrealism: dismembered and deformed bodies, crumbling architecture, wilted forms. Castellon, however, unlike the Surrealists, was not concerned with the workings of his unconscious but with more universal symbols. Although he resisted discussing the specific allusions in his work, it is difficult to separate *The Dark Figure* from the historical context in which it was painted. Born in Spain and raised in Brooklyn, Castellon returned to his homeland in 1934 on a fellowship from the Spanish Republic. There he came into contact with several leading Surrealists, including Salvador Dalí. Castellon's fellowship was cut short, however, when he was drafted into the Spanish Army. He returned to America, narrowly escaping involvement in the Spanish Civil War.

Castellon painted *The Dark Figure* in 1938, as Francisco Franco's right-wing troops threatened to dissolve the Spanish Republic, and as the rise of fascism endangered all of Europe. *The Dark Figure* depicts a landscape of despair—buildings lie in ruin, storm clouds lurk overhead. The face of the robed figure in the foreground is obscured, like an executioner's. Only the hands, painted in meticulous detail, are clearly visible. The figures at left cower, as if expecting these hands to commit some unspeakable crime. The colossal head in their midst bears the artist's features. Castellon looks on, unblinking, a silent seer.

The Dark Figure, 1938
Oil on canvas, 17 x 26 1/8 in. (43.2 x 66.4 cm)
Purchase 42.3

VIJA CELMINS

b. 1939

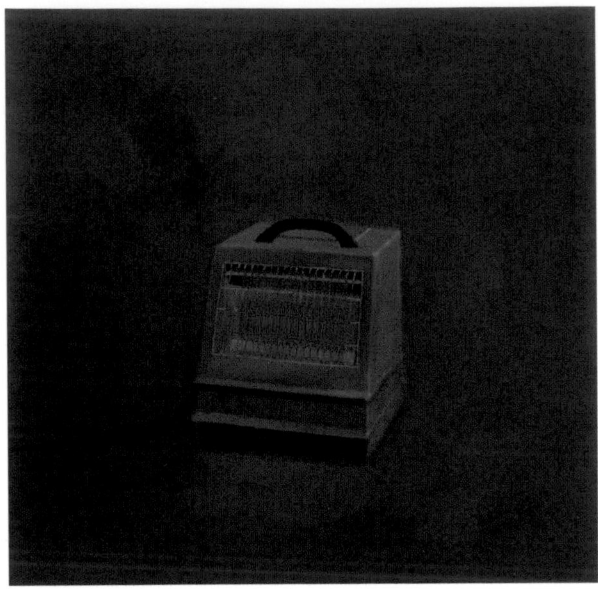

A meticulous realist, Vija Celmins is often associated with the Minimalist painters of the 1960s, because her dispassionate, precise approach reflects their aversion to emotional engagement. The early painting *Heater*, for example, was made when Celmins was a graduate student at UCLA and engaged in a methodical depiction of the contents of her studio. The painting is composed entirely of tonal gradations of gray, except for the glowing coils of the heater, which seem to radiate warmth from the picture surface. But the heater stands alone on the canvas, and only slender cast shadows anchor it to the ground. What, we can well ask, is it heating?

A similar separation of a subject from its normal narrative associations characterizes the later *Ocean Surface Woodcut*. The surface of the ocean here is neutral—neither stormy nor serene—no boats serve to indicate the extent of the area depicted, and no horizon line fixes the water in a physical place. Since the late 1960s, the ocean has been one of Celmins' favorite subjects, one she has returned to time and again. Yet all her subjects, whether man-made or natural, grow progressively elusive with extended viewing. What is gained through such viewing, however, is an appreciation of Celmins' commitment to factuality, to precise calibrations of weight, shape, and texture. Like a reliable reporter, she objectively records the physical condition of objects and the spaces around them.

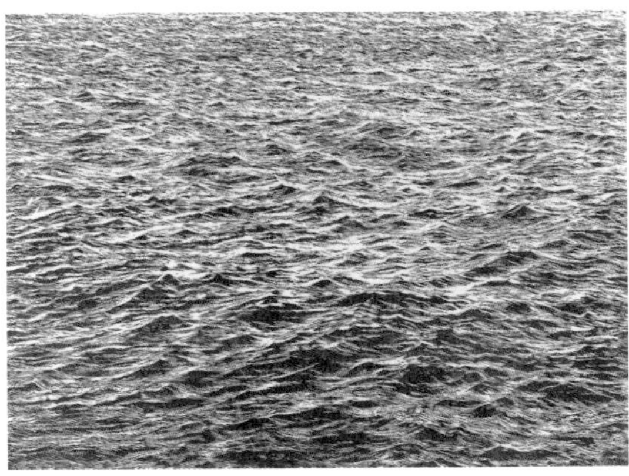

Heater, 1964
Oil on canvas, 47 7/16 x 48 in. (120.5 x 121.9 cm)
Purchase, with funds from the Contemporary Painting and Sculpture Committee 95.19

Ocean Surface Woodcut, 1992
Woodcut: sheet, 19 3/8 x 15 1/2 in. (49.2 x 39.4 cm); image, 8 13/16 x 11 15/16 in. (22.4 x 30.3 cm)
Purchase, with funds from the Print Committee 92.34

JOHN CHAMBERLAIN

b. 1927

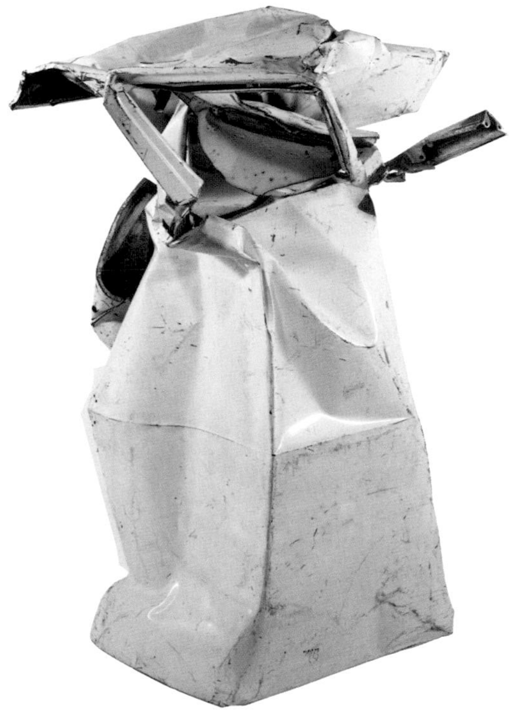

John Chamberlain is best known for the sculptures he began to make in the late 1950s from crushed automobile metal, an unconventional medium for fine art. Finding sources of inspiration in his everyday environment, he created works of surprising beauty from materials others discarded. He once remarked: "Everybody makes sculpture every day, whether in the way they wad up a newspaper or the way they throw the towel over the rack."

Despite the violence suggested by wrecked automobiles, in *Velvet White* Chamberlain manipulates the material as one might crumple or crush a bolt of the softest fabric, fitting two already-compressed pieces of metal together, one on top of the other, to assemble the work. As a symbol of the automotive industry, a leader in America's post-World War II economic boom, the salvaged metal also alludes to the cycle of production and disposal that helped fuel the newly developed consumer culture in the 1950s and 1960s.

Beyond its allusions to American life, *Velvet White* encompasses the drama and gestural physicality of 1950s Abstract Expressionism (Chamberlain was particularly influenced by the work of Franz Kline, p. 165), as well as Pop art's appropriation of America's commodity culture. Chamberlain also explores the nature of the sculptural object, particularly its three-dimensional presence and potential for varying profiles. By maintaining the irregularity of the crushed metal he found, he forces the viewer to walk around the jagged, voluminous form of *Velvet White* to experience it in full.

Velvet White, 1962
Painted and chromium-plated steel in two parts, 80 3/4 x 53 x 49 3/16 in. (205.1 x 134.6 x 124.9 cm) overall
Gift of the Albert A. List Family 70.1579a–b

CHRISTO AND JEANNE-CLAUDE

b. 1935 b. 1935

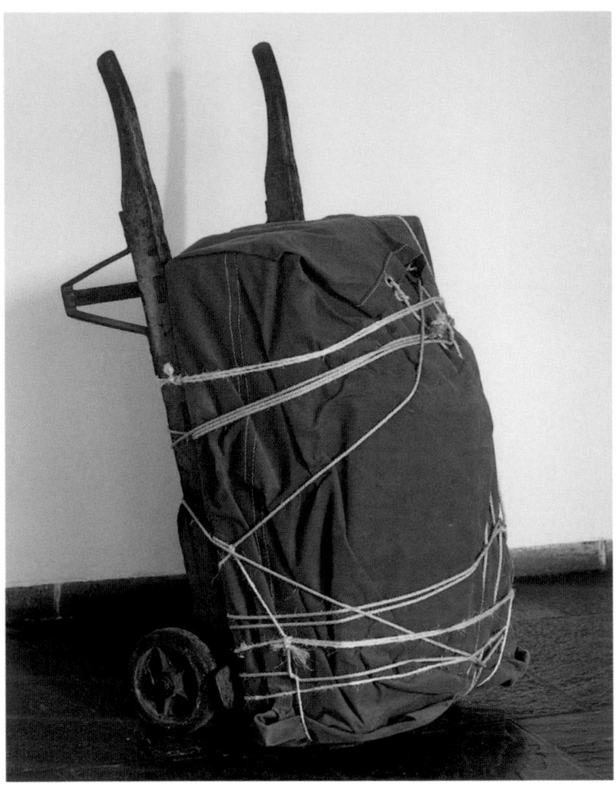

Christo and Jeanne-Claude are renowned for their wrapped buildings, bridges, and land surfaces—such as the wrapping of Berlin's Reichstag in a million square feet of aluminum-colored fabric (1995). These projects have provoked an intense, forty-year dialogue on the relationship between public art and institutional politics, urban and rural life, and what is visible and what is concealed.

Beginning in 1958, this wrapping technique was also applied to smaller objects. Unlike the public projects, whose interiors are often known, even if not visible, the nips and folds of the workmanlike brown canvas tied with ordinary household rope in *Package on Hand Truck* are carefully designed to suggest—but never specify—the contents within. What is emphasized here is the work's poverty of means, signified by the tarpaulin and common rope as well as by the hand truck, which replaces the noble pedestal of traditional sculpture. The same hand truck also insists on the mobility of the work. *Package on Hand Truck*, therefore, is everything the wrapped structures are not: it is movable and inelegant, and its interior remains mysterious. Our response to it strikes no political chord, but rather a personal note. Each viewer must decide whether the hidden contents are puzzling, playful, or threatening.

Package on Hand Truck, 1973
Metal, tarpaulin, wood, and rope, 51 15/16 x 24 1/4 x 29 in. (131.9 x 61.6 x 73.7 cm)
Gift of Mr. and Mrs. Albrecht Saalfield 74.74

LARRY CLARK
b. 1943

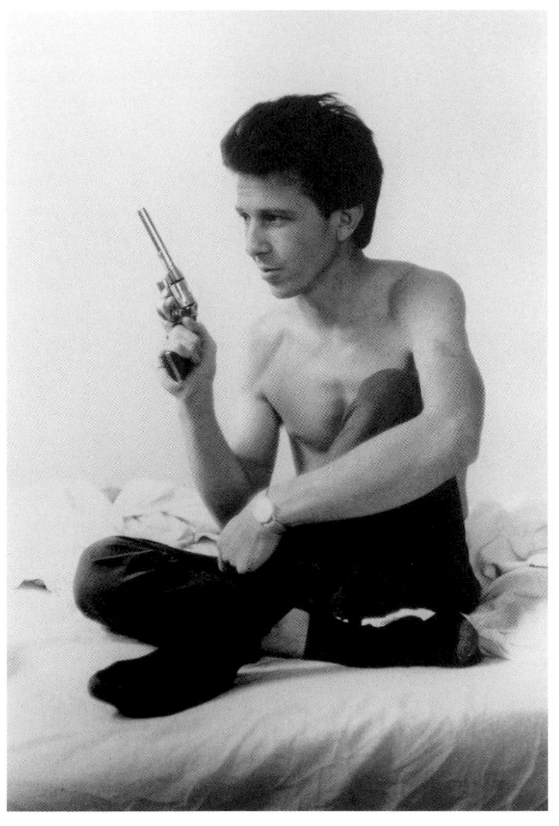

Throughout his career, filmmaker and photographer Larry Clark has repeatedly returned to the themes of youth, drugs, sex, and violence, which he explored in his earliest work, *Tulsa*, a book of photographs published in 1971. *Tulsa* comprises three sections of striking black-and-white images of Clark's own subculture, taken in 1963, 1968, and 1971 on trips back to his Oklahoma hometown. Unlike most photojournalistic representations of life on the margins, the photographer here is as much participant as he is observer (Clark himself appears in one of the late photographs in the book). Seen together, the images offer a kind of cinematic narrative that traces the lives and deaths of Clark's amphetamine-addicted friends. Early photographs capture young men and women in states of reverie, staring into mirrors or looking out of car windows, injecting speed. The later images increasingly reveal the intrusion of violence and the casual presence of handguns.

This untitled photograph shows Clark's friend Billy Mann, one of two sitters identified by name in the book. Mann, who died of an overdose in 1970, is bare-chested, sitting cross-legged on a bed in front of a plain white wall and holding a poised gun in his right hand; his pensive expression is directed at something outside the frame. The opposite page contains one of the book's sparse captions: "death is more perfect than life."

Clark's dry, epigrammatic remark is characteristic of the matter-of-fact sentiments expressed in *Tulsa*. The intimate photographs are unsparing yet free of moral judgment. Although the subject matter is squalid, the Tulsa photographs are carefully framed and dramatically lit. With its white backdrop, pale light, and affected pose, the portrait of Mann in fact resembles a studio picture. Here, as in many of the photographs, Clark's aesthetic concerns cloak his desolate subjects in an armor of toughness and grace.

Untitled, 1972
Gelatin silver print, 8 7/16 x 5 3/4 in. (21.4 x 14.6 cm)
Purchase, with funds from the Photography Committee 92.111.2

CHUCK CLOSE

b. 1940

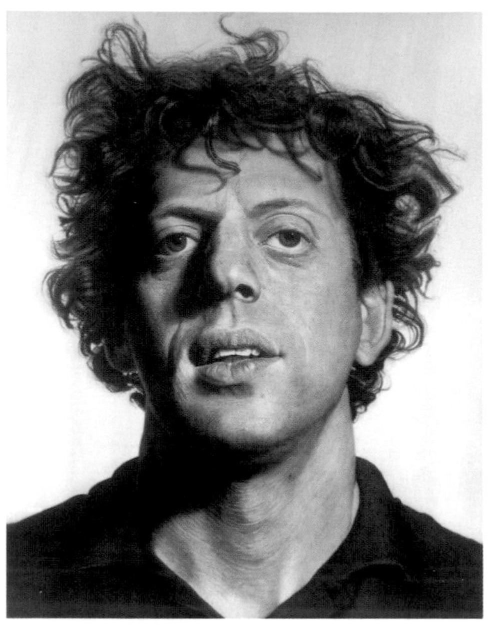

Many critics labeled Chuck Close a Photo-Realist when he introduced his first major works—eight large-scale paintings of faces, made between 1968 and 1970. Although these canvases do contain remarkably accurate detail, such as that found in the paintings of Robert Bechtle and Richard Estes (pp. 46, 103), Close's work has more in common with the conceptually based, systematic art of Sol LeWitt (p. 184).

Phil is a portrait of Close's longtime friend, innovative composer Philip Glass. In this and other early "heads" (as Close dubs them), each face is strictly frontal and set against a neutral ground. The artist limited his palette to diluted black acrylic paint, applied with an airbrush, which adds to the photographic quality of the image. For each head, he took an 8 x 10-inch photograph of the sitter, overlaid the snapshot with a penciled grid, and then painted a vastly enlarged blowup of each square onto the canvas. Despite this drastic change of scale from snapshot to canvas, the face nonetheless retains the candid, slightly awkward character of the original image.

A decade later, in 1979, Close produced a series of huge, high-resolution Polaroids, such as *Self-Portrait/Composite/Nine Parts*. As he explained, "It was the first time I considered myself a photographer." Whereas the grid hidden beneath the painted surface of *Phil* is drawn in pencil, here it asserts itself emphatically as a design element. The nine clearly demarcated and misaligned modules highlight the tension between the part and the whole and reveal how discrete bits of information coalesce in the creation of an image.

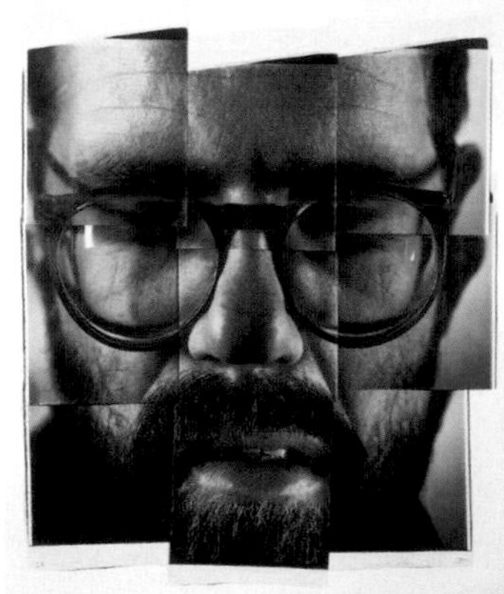

Phil, 1969
Synthetic polymer on canvas, 108 x 84 in. (274.3 x 213.4 cm)
Purchase, with funds from Mrs. Robert M. Benjamin 69.102

Self-Portrait/Composite/Nine Parts, 1979
9 internal dye diffusion transfer prints (Polaroids) mounted on canvas, 76 1/2 x 61 1/2 in. (194.3 x 156.2 cm) overall
Gift of Barbara and Eugene Schwartz 91.30

SUE COE

b. 1951

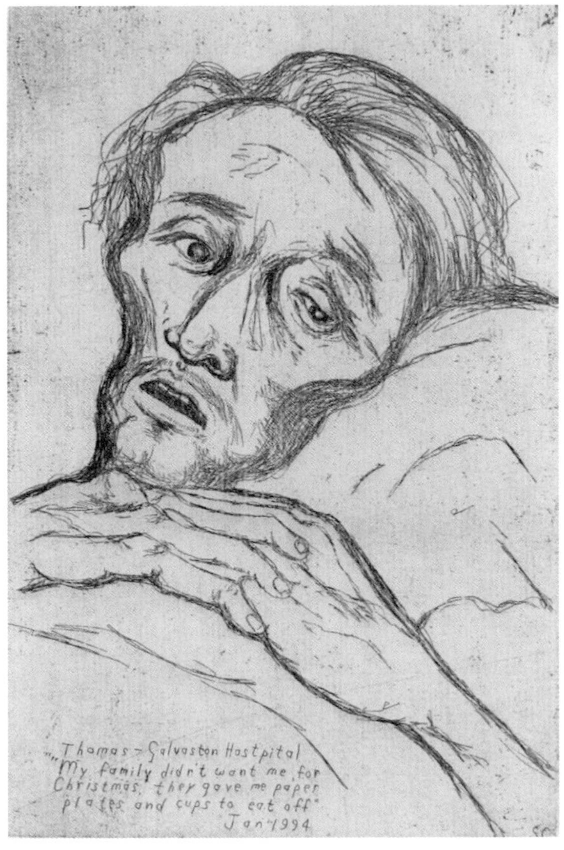

In early 1994, Sue Coe was invited to visit the infectious disease ward of a Galveston, Texas, hospital by her close friend and fellow artist Dr. Eric Avery. Her *AIDS Suite*, a portfolio of ten prints, etchings, and photoetchings, records the frustrated isolation and dejection, the overwhelming sense of abandonment, imprinted on the faces of the people suffering from AIDS.

Thomas—Galvaston Hostpital (the last two words are misspelled in the etched legend below the image) depicts the emaciated face and hands of an AIDS patient, propped up on a pillow. The text of the legend, presumably the man's own words, reads: "My family didn't want me for Christmas, they gave me paper plates and cups to eat off." Against an ignorant public's fear of contamination, Coe shows the magnitude of individual pain and suffering brought on by the AIDS epidemic. In the tradition of 1920s and 1930s Social Realist art (p. 275), she believes that exposing injustice and inequality will move people to take action.

The British-born Coe has been firmly committed to political art throughout her career. Her drawings, prints, and paintings have tackled such charged issues as South African apartheid, rape, homelessness, prisoners' rights, and vivisection. She publishes her work in the popular press and chooses to sell prints in large editions at a low price. Bridging the gap between illustration and fine art, Coe challenges the established categories of the art market. In America, she remarks, "the great art is in magazines and newspapers. It's called commercial art but in fact it's less commercial than gallery art."

Thomas—Galvaston Hostpital, 1994
Drypoint: sheet, 13 x 9 3/4 in. (33 x 24.8 cm); plate, 8 13/16 x 5 3/4 in. (22.4 x 14.6 cm)
Purchase, with funds from the Print Committee 94.74.9

WILLIE COLE

b. 1955

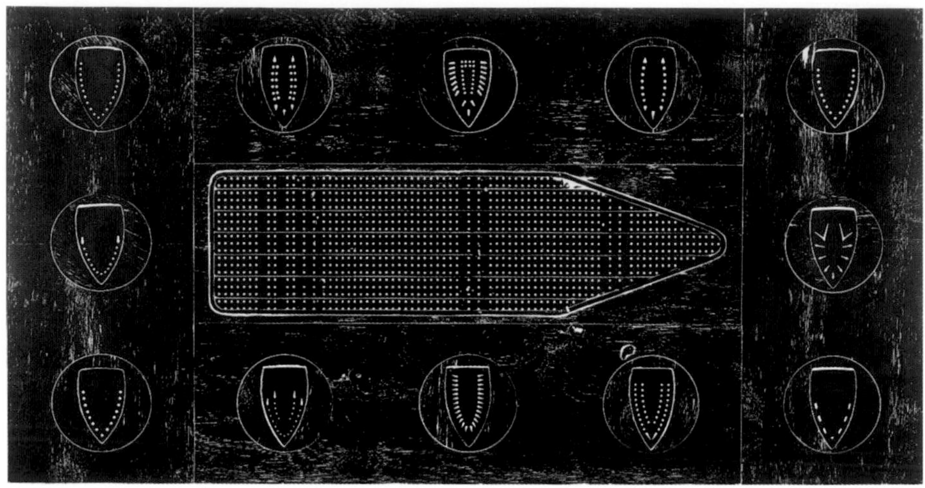

Willie Cole takes familiar household objects apart and imagines what else they could become, what else they could mean. Discarded ironing boards he finds near his studio in Newark, New Jersey, become shields; irons become idols. Cole is drawn to materials that recall the domestic labor of his African-American ancestors, even as they reflect the heritage of African art.

Stowage is an unusual variant on the woodblock print, which Cole created by embedding an ironing board and the soleplates of twelve irons into wood, forcing the objects down until they were flush with the surface and then applying ink to the whole. To the artist, the images formed by the base of the irons suggest the distinctive markings associated with different African tribes, for each brand of iron leaves its own recognizable pattern. The perforated metal ironing board reminds Cole of illustrations from nineteenth-century books on slave trading that showed Africans stowed on slave ships like so much cargo. *Stowage* thus represents the physical voyage from Africa to America and the conditions slaves endured as they made the ocean passage. Yet the print also alludes to a cultural voyage. Cole believes that "when one culture is dominated by another culture, the energy, or powers, or gods of the previous culture hide in vehicles in the new culture." In *Stowage*, Cole suggests that African spirituality still inhabits the domestic tools used by slaves and their descendants in America—that the brutal crossing did not sever an essential kinship to the ancestral homeland.

Stowage, 1996
Woodcut with metal relief printing: sheet, 55 1/2 x 104 5/8 in. (141 x 265.7 cm);
image, 49 1/2 x 94 7/8 in. (125.7 x 241 cm)
Purchase, with funds from the Print Committee 98.8.2

BRUCE CONNER
b. 1933

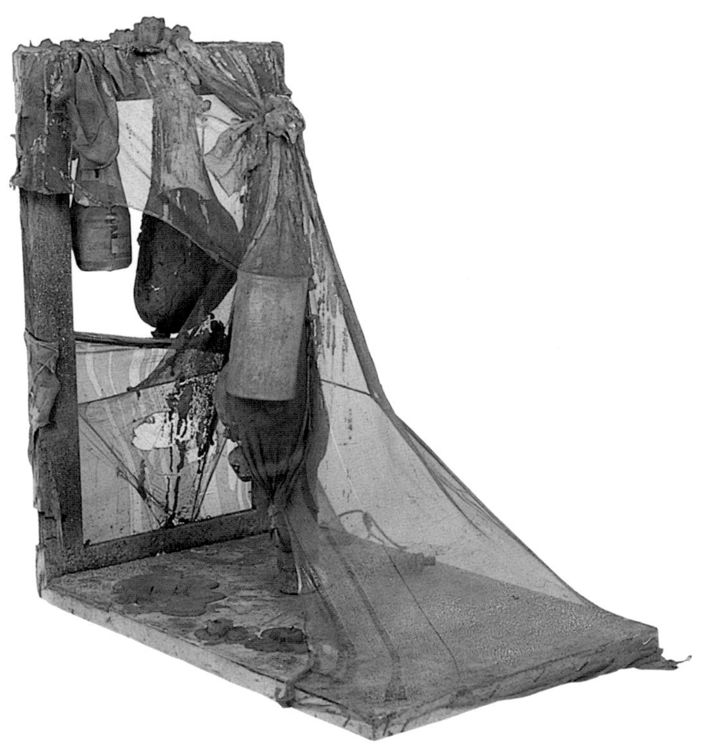

Bruce Conner, a defiant Bay Area individualist, has had one of the most complex careers in twentieth-century American art: experimental filmmaker, photographer, painter, draftsman, sculptor of junk assemblages, experimental lighting technician, occultist, visionary, peyote proselytizer—a fugitive spirit whose life and work cannot be held down to a few conventional categories.

Not surprisingly, Conner spurned bourgeois ideals of art as an expression of privileged creativity that produces a beautiful and eternal object. As a West Coast member of the Beat Generation in the 1950s, he challenged artists to deliver new forms appropriate for the age, forms based on new values—spontaneity, impurity, the degraded, and the marginal. In his portrait of the Beat poet Allen Ginsberg, he thumbed his nose at the conventions of portraiture, which for centuries had demanded high standards of likeness. Conner's portrait of his friend is evocative rather than representational. Through junk materials—including a tin can, a nylon stocking, candles, wax, and spray paint—casually joined together in the discontinuous, abstract language of assemblage, Conner portrays the spirit of the dark, unorthodox poet whose famous book-length poem *Howl* (1956) begins: "I have seen the best minds of my generation destroyed by madness."

Portrait of Allen Ginsberg, 1960
Wood, fabric, wax, tin can, glass, feathers, metal, string, and spray paint, 20 x 11 1/4 x 21 3/8 in.
(50.8 x 28.6 x 54.3 cm)
Purchase, with funds from the Contemporary Painting and Sculpture Committee 96.48

JOHN COPLANS

b. 1920

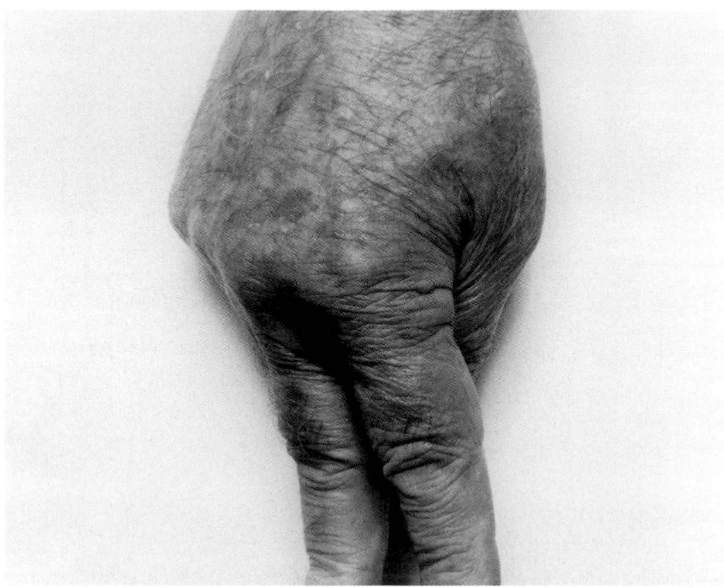

John Coplans began his career as an abstract painter, participating in the first survey of British postwar abstract art at London's Redfern Gallery in 1957. But he quit painting in 1962 to explore other careers: first as founding editor of the vanguard journal *Artforum*, later as a museum curator and author. In 1980, at the age of sixty, Coplans took up photography and has since become known for his unusual self-portraits, which take the form of details of his manifestly aging body. His photographs—all of which he refers to as self-portraits—never reveal his face, however, an absence that lends his images both an abstract and an unindividualized character.

Coplans considers his work to be "an investigation into myself and the universal," but his subject is also the non-idealized, and—for some—abject terrain of the elderly male body that American youth-and-beauty-oriented culture excludes from its popular representations and its psychic field of vision. In *Self-Portrait, Fingers Standing, No. 2*, the seventy-nine-year-old Coplans presses the viewer into looking very closely at his aging hands. The sheer scale of the work—24 x 31 inches—magnifies the abstraction: we are confronted with a prosaic wrinkle in time, but also with an index of—and a glimpse into—a mortality that our antiseptic contemporary culture prefers to repress.

On another level, this *Self-Portrait*, like many of Coplans' later photographs, is about transformation. Beyond the transformations of old age, Coplans investigates the transformations that art can render. So enlarged and isolated from the body are his fingers and the back of his hand that the image also reads as the bent back of a figure, with the two fingers serving as legs. Ultimately, Coplans' entwined digits affirm that art and life are flourishing in the still-capable hands of the octogenarian artist.

Self-Portrait, Fingers Standing, No. 2, 1999
Gelatin silver print, 24 x 31 in. (61 x 78.7 cm)
Gift of an anonymous donor 2000.307

JOSEPH CORNELL

1903–1972

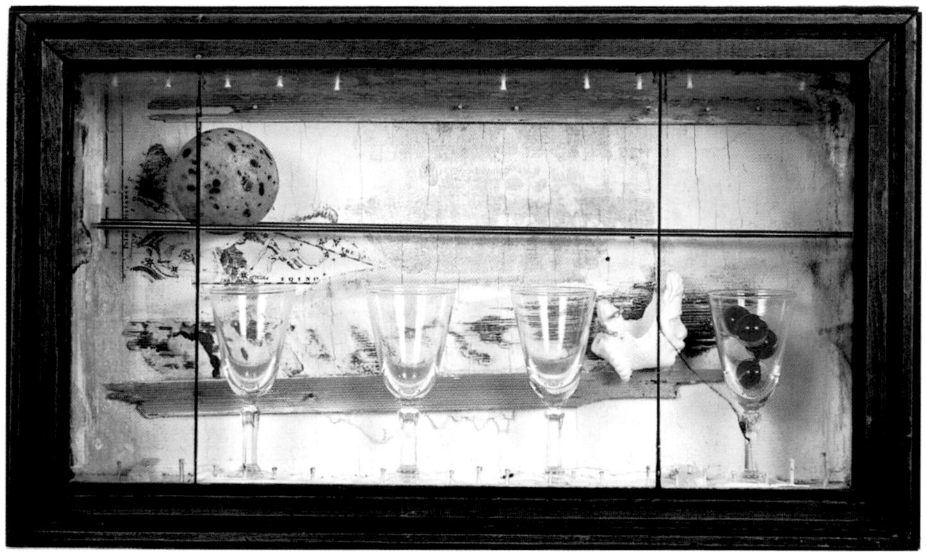

Often described as a Surrealist, Joseph Cornell shared neither the Surrealists' faith in chance occurrences nor their fascination with the subconscious, the irrational, the unpredictable. Instead, he methodically collected newspaper clippings, photographs, seashells, and Dutch clay pipes and filed them carefully away in the basement of his home in Flushing, New York. His art works consist of selections of these objects, placed in glass-covered, framed boxes. The things Cornell collected were related, even if tenuously, to his favorite subjects: nineteenth-century sopranos, the ballet, European literature, and astronomy. In fact, he was a lifelong student of astronomy, poring over articles and books on the subject and regularly observing the constellations from his backyard.

Although his reading kept him informed about the latest scientific discoveries and theories, Cornell preferred a simpler, more mechanical image of the universe. *Celestial Navigation* recalls the clockwork universe of an orrery—an eighteenth-century apparatus that explained the solar system with miniature revolving planets. Like an orrery, the box contains moving parts: the larger blue ball rolls along metal tracks, while the marbles can be switched from one cordial glass to another. Cornell placed these movable orbs against a backdrop of the "fixed" stars by pasting fragments of constellation maps to the walls of the box. In *Celestial Navigation*, Cornell invokes the myths, images, and theories once used to explain the predictable yet baffling patterns of the night sky. The box is his model of an ordered, though perhaps not entirely knowable, universe.

Celestial Navigation, n.d.
Box construction with wood, glasses, marbles, plaster head, painted cork ball, metal rods, nails, paper collage, tempera, and painted glass, 9 5/8 x 16 1/4 x 4 in. (24.5 x 41.3 x 10.2 cm)
60th Anniversary Gift of Estée Lauder, Inc. 92.24

PETAH COYNE

b. 1953

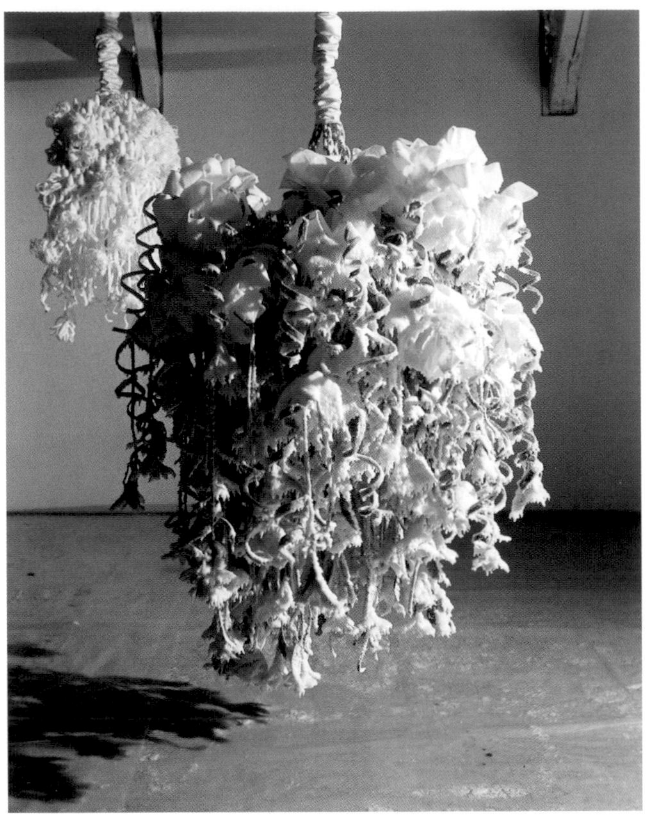

Petah Coyne's early work included fearsome sacks of dirt, sticks, wire, and tar that were also suspended from the ceiling, though they often seemed torn from the earth or from inside some primal body. Her more recent pieces have grown increasingly explicit in their references to femininity and religion. Coyne calls the group of sculptures to which this untitled work belongs her "girls." And, she says, they're "tough at the core." This buoyant, lacy, fragile-seeming white wax confection is built around wire armatures suspended from the ceiling by heavy gauge chains—a resilience at the core that is as important symbolically to Coyne's feminist and spiritual concerns as it is to the structure of the piece. Yet this work and others in the group cannot be reduced to a simple opposition of strength and fragility. In their resemblance to great Rococo chandeliers, they are also images of self-immolation, since the blazing light they evoke would also spell their molten ruin.

Coyne's indirect references to the body and organic matter connect her work to that of the Postminimalists, a generation of artists, including Lynda Benglis and Eva Hesse (pp. 48, 138), who turned away from the stark geometry of Minimalism to explore the more visceral, thematically rich aspects of material, process, and form.

Untitled, #824, 1996
Wax and mixed media, dimensions variable, approximately 96 x 46 x 53 in. (243.8 x 116.8 x 134.6 cm)
Gift of an anonymous donor in honor of Ronald and Linda Daitz 99.98

RALSTON CRAWFORD

1906–1978

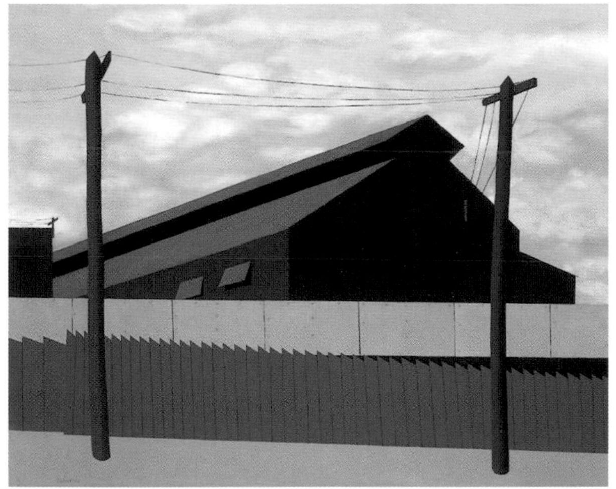

During the Depression, Ralston Crawford's Precisionist paintings of highways, grain elevators, and steel foundries captured America's enduring optimism about technology and progress. After World War II, however, his work became increasingly abstract, and his cool, analytical approach was sidelighted in an art world dominated by the spontaneity of Abstract Expressionism.

Steel Foundry, Coatesville, Pa. exemplifies Crawford's Precisionist phase. Like Elsie Driggs and Charles Sheeler (pp. 96, 277), he focused on an icon of industrial might, but in a modernist key: the foundry's architecture is reduced to an arrangement of flat, monochromatic planes, while the dark silhouette is made more imposing by the background of white wispy clouds. The saw-toothed fence and telephone poles cast an almost homey note, further setting off the starkness of the foundry.

In the postwar years, the Precisionist faith in technology was sorely tested. In 1946, on assignment for *Fortune* magazine, Crawford witnessed the Navy's atomic bomb tests at Bikini Atoll in the Marshall Islands. Then, during a 1951 trip to Cologne, Germany, he saw firsthand the destruction even conventional weapons can cause. Crawford photographed Cologne's ruins and returned to Paris to produce a series of lithographs inspired by his observations. He based *Cologne Landscape #6* on a photograph he had taken of a bombed-out building, whose ruins he translated into splintered, jagged forms. Yet Crawford had not lost his optimism entirely. Describing his Cologne lithographs, he wrote of "the cracked-up, rotten, manure-heap facets of this society," but also of "the good and noble aspects of human existence now and in all societies."

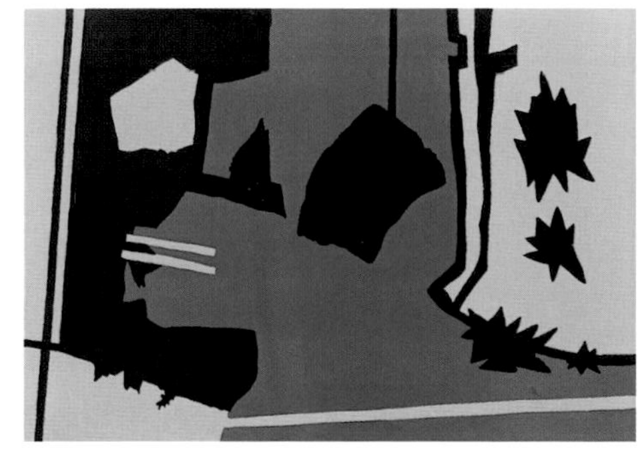

Steel Foundry, Coatesville, Pa., 1936–37
Oil on canvas, 32 x 40 in. (81.3 x 101.6 cm)
Purchase 37.10

Cologne Landscape #6, 1951
Lithograph: sheet, 19 3/4 x 25 3/4 in. (50.2 x 65.4 cm); image, 14 7/8 x 21 1/8 in. (37.8 x 53.7 cm)
Gift of Charles Simon 71.77

JOHN CURRIN

b. 1962

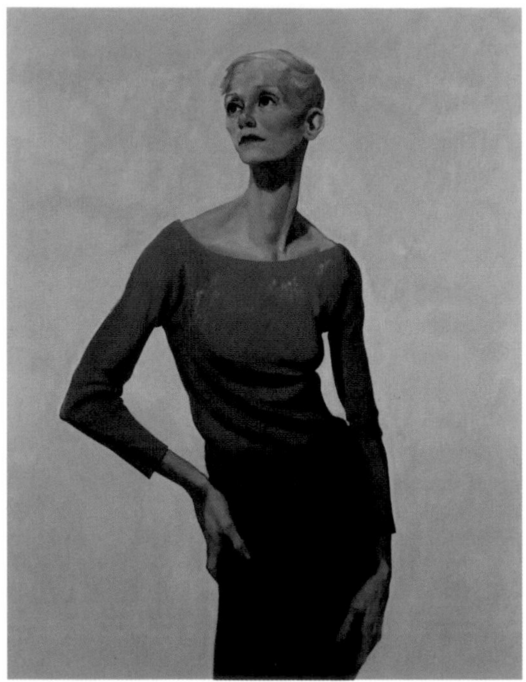

In the mid-twentieth century, during the heyday of Abstract Expressionism, it seemed inconceivable that vanguard art would ever again involve the figure. Yet even critic Clement Greenberg, the most ardent champion of abstraction, had to admit, "connoisseurs of the future may prefer the more literal kind of pictorial space. There have been reversals of taste before." Indeed, by the 1980s, the figure had reemerged as a strong presence in contemporary art, often in the guise of styles that hark back to past traditions.

John Currin's work draws on a variety of influences—from the painterly realism of Old Master art to fashion magazines to kitschy pinup posters—to create deceptively naturalistic portraits. The thinness, delicate features, elegantly indifferent pose, and stylish clothing of the subject in *Skinny Woman* give her the look of a contemporary fashion model. Yet Currin's treatment of the figure radically accentuates the elongation of her limbs, recalling the distortions of El Greco and other sixteenth-century Mannerist artists. Her *contrapposto* pose, with its sinuous S-curve and hand resting on one hip, pays homage to Classical Greek and Roman statuary and its echoes in the Renaissance. Undercutting the "high art" seriousness of these references, Currin gives the woman's face an almost overly sentimental appearance reminiscent of the plaintive, wide-eyed look of thrift-store portraits of children and animals. By combining elements from various periods and sources, Currin creates an uneasy composite image that, despite its apparent simplicity, provides fertile ground for the imagination.

Skinny Woman, 1992
Oil on canvas, 50 1/8 x 38 1/16 in. (127.3 x 96.7 cm)
Purchase, with funds from The List Purchase Fund and the Painting and Sculpture Committee 92.30

JOHN STEUART CURRY

1897–1946

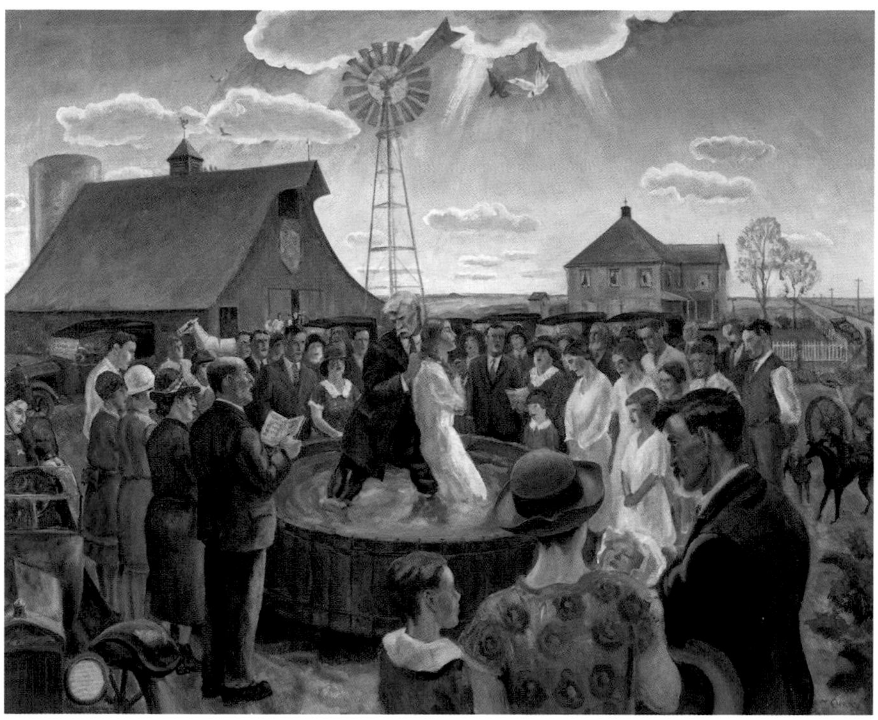

John Steuart Curry's *Baptism in Kansas*, spun from childhood memories, marked the beginning of a career inextricably linked to the Kansas town he had left a decade before. The painting, first exhibited in 1928 at The Corcoran Gallery of Art in Washington, D.C., was immediately welcomed by both critics and the public for its vigorous portrayal of rural religious fervor. This novel departure from the urban imagery and abstracted landscapes of American modernism forecast the emergence of Regionalism, the movement that glorified grassroots, rural values during the poverty-stricken years of the Great Depression.

Curry's fellow Midwesterners Thomas Hart Benton and Grant Wood (pp. 49, 330) joined him at the helm of Regionalism. *Baptism in Kansas*, however, typifies Curry's unique vision of an idealized American heartland. In his vision, the natural disasters that plagued the Midwest—tornadoes, floods, droughts, and blizzards—are matched only by the fundamentalist zeal of its inhabitants. This dramatic baptismal scene recalls one that Curry saw in 1915, when the local creeks were parched and the only suitable site for the ceremony was a water tank. The dynamic stance of the ashen-faced preacher predicts the baptismal submersion about to occur; the circle of pious hymn singers, the row of Model T's, and the receding countryside provide a tranquil counterpoint. Above, the birds and aureole of sunlight speak of a harmony—if only temporary—between the gathered worshipers and their harsh, unpredictable homeland.

Baptism in Kansas, 1928
Oil on canvas, 40 x 50 in. (101.6 x 127 cm)
Gift of Gertrude Vanderbilt Whitney 31.159

DOUGLAS DAVIS

b. 1933

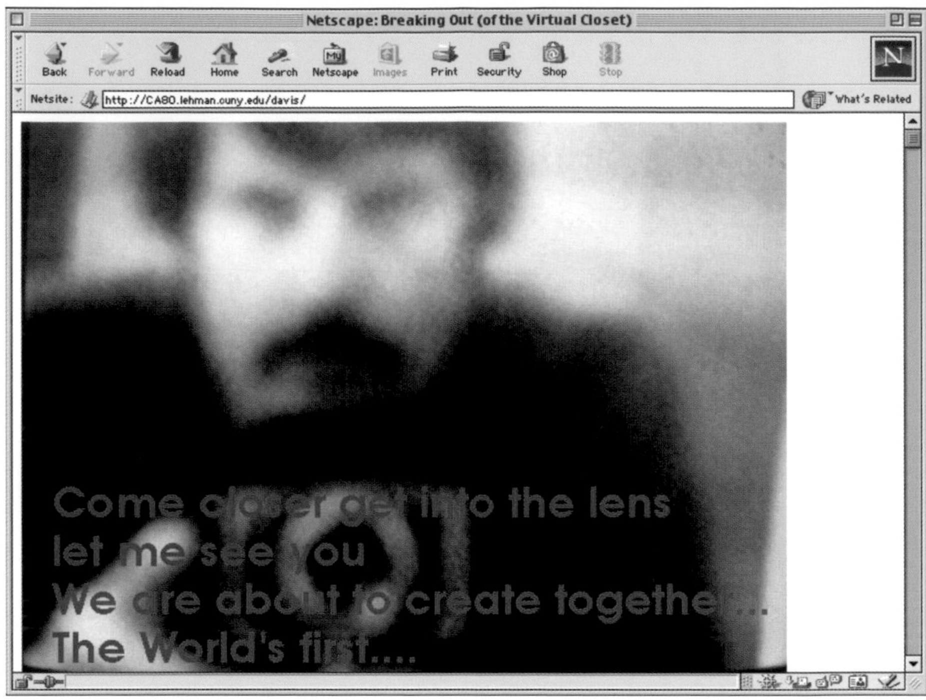

In 1995, the Whitney Museum acquired its first work of Internet art, Douglas Davis' *The World's First Collaborative Sentence*. Commissioned by the Lehman College Art Gallery, Bronx, New York, in conjunction with "Interactions," its 1994 survey exhibition of the artist's work, *Sentence* is an ongoing textual and graphic performance on the World Wide Web that is maintained on the Lehman website but owned by the Whitney Museum. Visitors to the site may add their own contributions to the *Sentence*—there are more than 250,000 to date, separated into twenty-one "chapters," in dozens of languages and with a remarkable range of images and graphics. Any subject may be addressed, but no contribution can end with a period, as the *Sentence* is infinitely expanding.

Douglas Davis, well known for his video work, had been experimenting with "long-distance art" in the form of live satellite video and intercontinental performances for quite some time. It seemed natural that he would further explore these concepts in the new medium of the Internet. *The World's First Collaborative Sentence* is a classic work of net art, documenting the earliest stages of a new art form. With its collaborative, polyvocal, multilingual, and boundless nature, the sentence has become a microcosm of the Internet itself. As a decidedly low-tech "multi-user environment" that allows for combinations of textual, visual, and aural components, it is a collective space which, in its broad array of voices and topics, achieves fluent transitions between the prosaic and the sublime.

The World's First Collaborative Sentence, 1994
Diskette, 3 3/4 x 3 1/2 in. (9.5 x 8.9 cm)
Gift of Barbara Schwartz in honor of Eugene M. Schwartz 95.253

STUART DAVIS

1892–1964

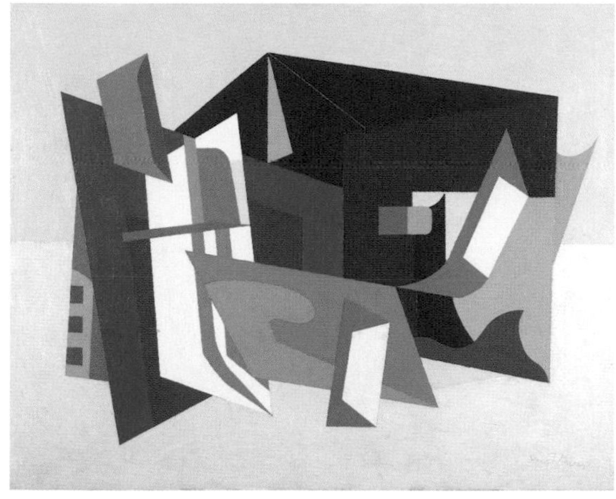

In 1907, at the age of fifteen, Stuart Davis quit high school and moved to New York. Eventually, the city's billboards, street signs, newspapers, and ragtime rhythms found their way into his urbane semi-abstractions. "All of my pictures," he said, "have their originating impulse in the impact of the contemporary American environment." But Davis was also among the first Americans to translate developments in modern European art into an American vernacular. Works such as *Egg Beater No. 1*, based on an actual eggbeater he nailed to a table in his studio, incorporate the generalized forms, flattened interlocking planes, and non-imitative color of Picasso's Synthetic Cubism.

The high degree of abstraction in *Egg Beater No. 1* was a departure for Davis, who

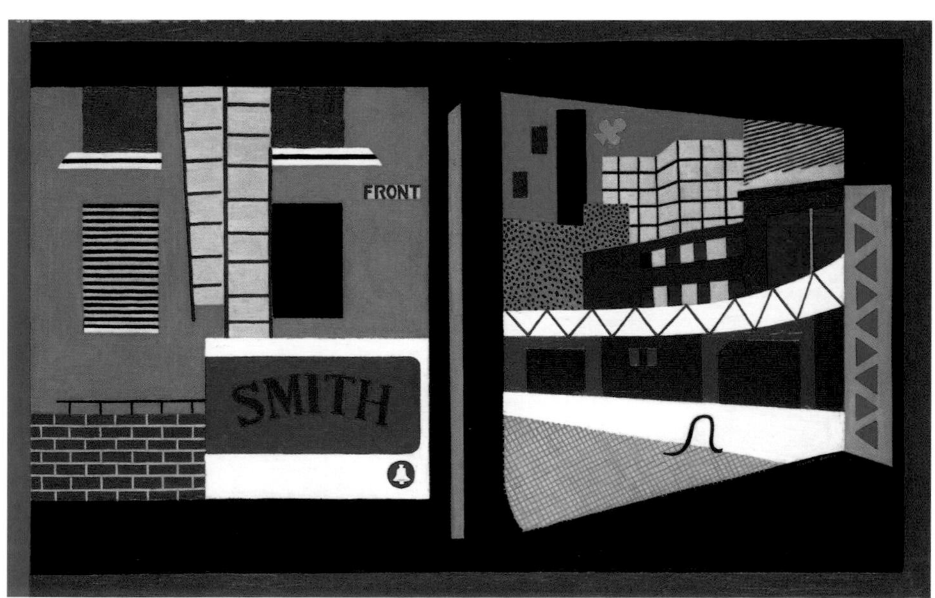

Egg Beater No. 1, 1927
Oil on canvas, 29 1/8 x 36 in. (74 x 91.4 cm)
Gift of Gertrude Vanderbilt Whitney 31.169

House and Street, 1931
Oil on canvas, 26 x 42 1/4 in. (66 x 107.3 cm)
Purchase 41.3

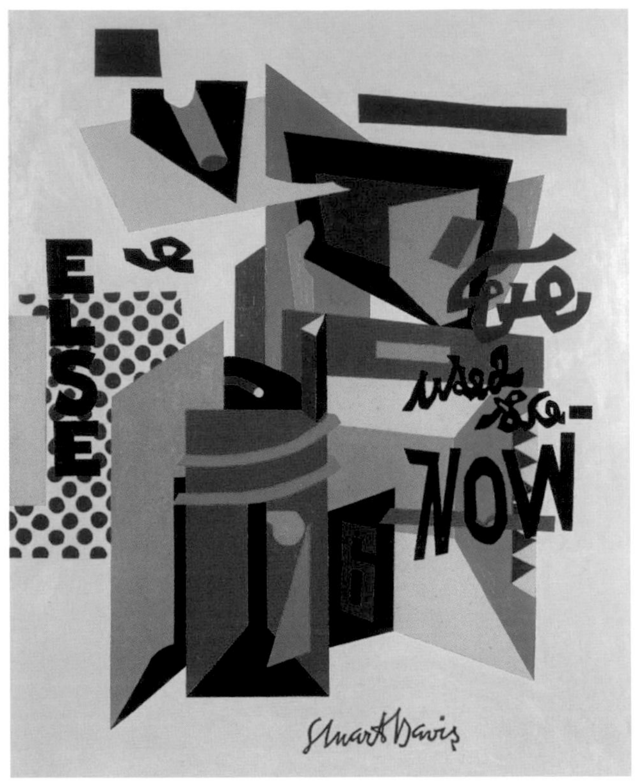

never considered himself an abstractionist. More typical, and more recognizable, is *House and Street*, the artist's interpretation of the tenements and commercial skyscrapers on Front Street in Lower Manhattan. Using the graphic language of signs, words, and advertisements, Davis rendered the scene in a bold modern palette. In addition to the sign designating the street, Davis included the name Smith at left, which probably derives from a campaign poster for Alfred E. Smith, then governor of New York, who was seeking his party's nomination in the 1932 presidential race. The composition, moreover, is divided into two simultaneous, yet distinct street views, what Davis referred to as a "mental collage."

The jazzy mix of everyday objects, words, and chromatic energy is also characteristic of *Owh! in San Paõ*, made twenty years later but based on an earlier painting that likewise presented a geometric reduction of a coffeepot. In the later variation, Davis copied the coffeepot but added the words "else," "used to be," and "now," referring perhaps to the temporal gap between the two pictures. Davis' introduction of a commercial vocabulary and everyday objects helped make *Owh! in San Paõ* one of his most influential paintings, anticipating the pictorial concerns of the later Pop artists who appropriated the imagery of consumer culture, as in Andy Warhol's *Green Coca-Cola Bottles* (p. 316).

Owh! in San Paõ, 1951
Oil on canvas, 52 1/4 x 41 3/4 in. (132.7 x 106 cm)
Purchase 52.2

JAY DEFEO
1929–1989

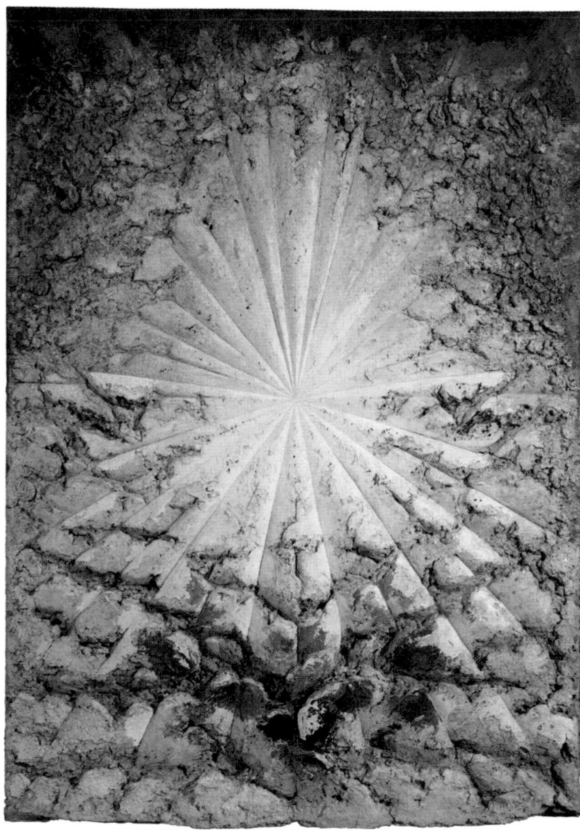

During the 1950s, in what became known as the Bay Area art scene, a tightly knit group of bohemian artists, among them Jay DeFeo, experimented with new ways of making and defining art. "Perhaps more than anyone else, Jay DeFeo has epitomized a historic era in Bay Area art, when art was something one lived twenty-four hours a day, and involved not just the making of paintings or sculptures but the salvage of meanings and purpose itself," wrote critic Thomas Albright.

The Rose, DeFeo's chief work, testifies to the artist's sense of purpose. Nearly 11 feet tall and weighing more than a ton, it is a monumental painting-assemblage. DeFeo began *The Rose* in 1958 with a single idea—that the work "would have a center." Two years later, it was illustrated in an exhibition catalogue under the title *Deathrose*, although DeFeo refused to lend the actual work to the exhibition because it was still unfinished. For the next six years, she kept applying thick paint, then chiseling away at it, and applying more paint; eventually, she attached the original canvas of *Deathrose* to a larger canvas that serves as the support for the work she later titled *The Rose*. DeFeo also incorporated fragments of objects from her daily life into *The Rose*, including, according to eyewitnesses, pearls, beads, and barrettes. The result is a monument to the process of painting as the defining act of an artist's existence. And, indeed, *The Rose* reflects not only a work carved out of life, but a life shaped by work. The clarity and concision of its starlike center fades at the gouged-out edges, where the painstaking sculptural work of adding and subtracting paint evokes the drama of the artist's struggle.

The Rose, 1958–66
Oil with wood and mica on canvas, 128 7/8 x 92 1/4 x 11 in. (327.3 x 234.3 x 27.9 cm)
Gift of the Estate of Jay DeFeo and purchase, with funds from the Contemporary Painting and Sculpture Committee and the Judith Rothschild Foundation 95.170

BEAUFORD DELANEY

1901–1979

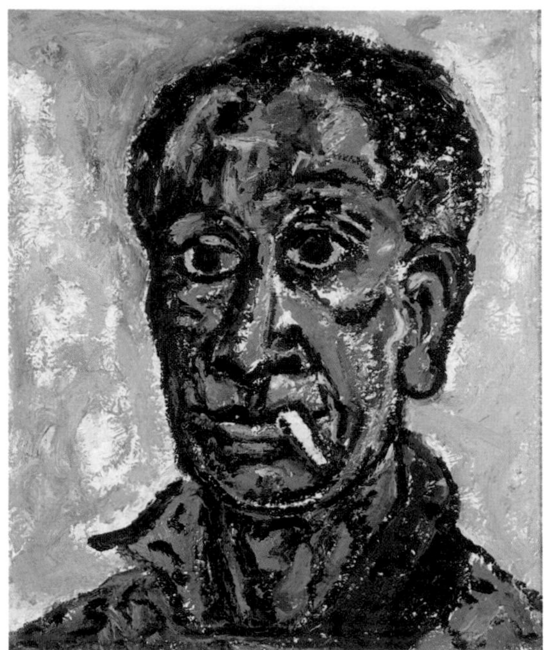

Although Beauford Delaney's evocative portraits and abstracted cityscapes were admired by such writers and poets as James Baldwin, Countee Cullen, and Henry Miller, wider acclaim eluded the African-American artist. The son of a minister, he left his Knoxville, Tennessee, home at twenty-four to study art in Boston. From then on, he struggled to earn a living as an artist and inhabited a succession of cheap, cramped studios in New York's Harlem and Greenwich Village, and, finally, in Paris.

Delaney painted *Auto-Portrait* in his mid-sixties, while living in a studio his friends helped him acquire in Paris. It was one of the most fertile phases of his career, even though he was recovering from a nervous breakdown he had suffered in 1961. In his self-portrait, Delaney seems uncertain, anxious, troubled. A cigarette hangs from the corner of his mouth, as if forgotten. The hardships of his life can be traced in the craggy, heavy lines of his face. His eyes, bordered in thick, black paint, are just slightly out of alignment, giving him an unsettled, searching look.

Delaney's portrait of himself reveals the more troubling, more nuanced, perspective of a man constrained, not only by persistent racial stereotypes, but by the romanticized myth of the struggling artist. In a glowing essay published in 1945, Henry Miller portrayed Delaney as an almost saintly ascetic, devoted to his art. Miller wrote that "logic, our crazy logic, dictates that the environment of the creative individual must be composed of all the ugly, painful, discordant and diseased elements of life."

Auto-Portrait, 1965
Oil on canvas, 24 x 20 in. (61 x 50.8 cm)
Purchase, with funds from the Wilfred P. and Rose J. Cohen Purchase Fund, the Richard and Dorothy Rodgers Fund, the Katherine Schmidt Shubert Purchase Fund, and the Mrs. Percy Uris Purchase Fund 95.2

CHARLES DEMUTH

1883–1935

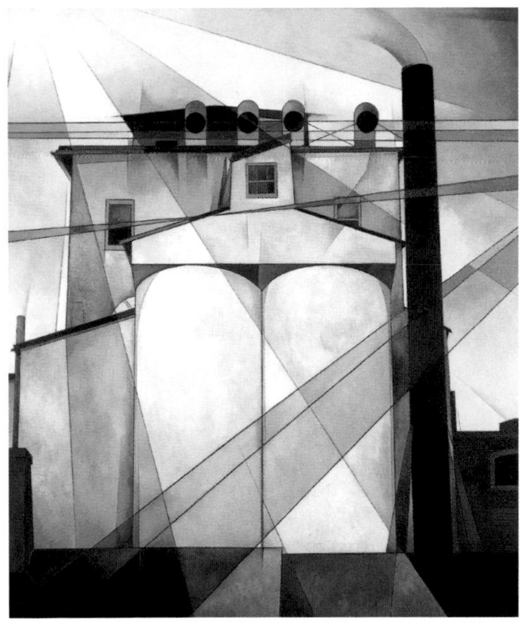

My Egypt, depicting a grain elevator owned by John W. Eshelman and Sons in Demuth's hometown of Lancaster, Pennsylvania, is a tour de force of Precisionist painting, which used modernist aesthetic principles to represent the architectural landscape of twentieth-century America. Demuth's grain elevator rises up, along with Elsie Driggs' steel mill and Charles Sheeler's automobile plant (pp. 96, 277), as a testament to the place of industry at the pinnacle of American achievement.

In *My Egypt*, a series of diagonal planes creates force lines that visually convey the dynamism of an industrial nation. The two white beams descending from the upper left also suggest rays emanating from a latter-day heaven. Indeed, in these years, belief in the power of American industry to lead the nation to a glorious future had taken on the intensity of a religion. The title reinforces this meaning by implicitly comparing American industry to the great pyramids of Egypt, one of the legendary Seven Wonders of the World. Demuth also intended the title to allude to the slave labor that built the pyramids, thus intimating the dehumanizing effect of industry on the nation's workers. *My Egypt* nevertheless remains a brilliant fusion of representation and abstraction that transforms a functional structure into a national icon.

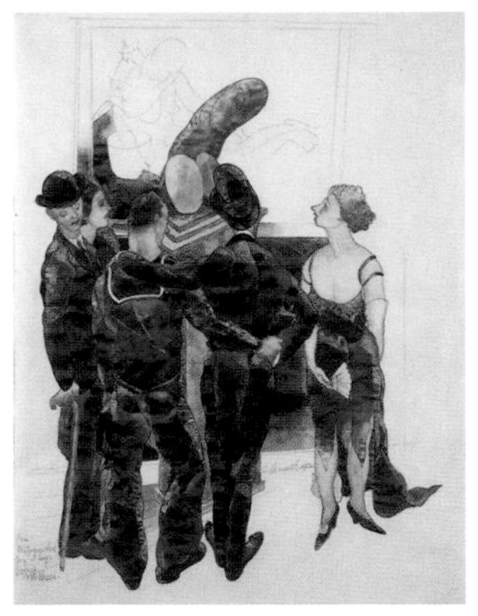

Demuth's watercolors of the same period explored an entirely different subject matter: sex and amorality. *Distinguished Air*, based on a short story by Robert McAlmon, portrays a provocative woman in evening dress, a male homosexual couple, and a heterosexual couple. All are at an art exhibition, viewing Constantin Brancusi's famous sculpture *Princess X*, whose overtly phallic form belies its innocuous title.

My Egypt, 1927
Oil on composition board, 35 3/4 x 30 in. (90.8 x 76.2 cm)
Purchase, with funds from Gertrude Vanderbilt Whitney 31.172

Distinguished Air, 1930
Watercolor on paper, 16 3/16 x 12 1/8 in. (41.1 x 30.8 cm) irregular
Purchase, with funds from the Friends of the Whitney Museum of American Art and Charles Simon 68.16

RICHARD DIEBENKORN

1922–1993

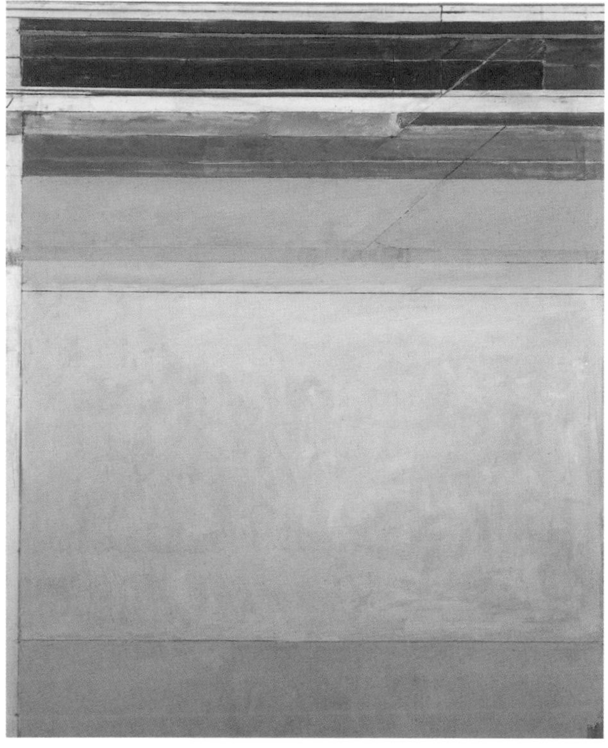

Richard Diebenkorn is best known for the *Ocean Park* series of landscape abstractions he began in 1967 after moving to Santa Monica. For the next twenty-five years, inspired by his Ocean Park neighborhood, he made landscape his primary subject matter. These abstract paintings marked a shift for Diebenkorn, who during the 1950s was associated with a style known as Bay Area Figurative art, practiced by artists around San Francisco, including David Park (p. 235).

Conceived as a series and numbered sequentially, the *Ocean Park* paintings are all tall, rectangular canvases, most of them divided by horizontal and vertical lines. Some seem to depict physical elements of landscape—the conjunction of ocean and sky or bands of colored clouds at sunset—while others imply more intangible elements such as space, atmosphere, or light. Diebenkorn's primary expressive tool is always color, which he uses to convey both structure and atmosphere. One of the later works in the series, *Ocean Park #125*, delicately balances compressed bands of color in the upper portion, an open expanse of gray-blue at center, and a lone yellow vertical running along the left edge. The work's monumental scale and large central field envelop the viewer, much like the paintings of two of Diebenkorn's early teachers, Mark Rothko and Clyfford Still (pp. 263, 300). As in many *Ocean Park* paintings, vestiges of earlier compositional decisions and marks, what Diebenkorn called "crudities," can still be seen beneath washes of color. Two barely visible diagonals in the black band at top right signal the original, more leftward placement of the two parallel diagonals that run through the black and blue bands. For Diebenkorn, revealing the process that yielded the finished painting—"the stumbling," as his friend Wayne Thiebaud (p. 307) described it—was crucial to the character of the work.

Ocean Park #125, 1980
Oil on canvas, 100 x 81 in. (254 x 205.7 cm)
Purchase, with funds from the Charles Simon Purchase Fund, the Painting and Sculpture Committee, and anonymous donors, by exchange 80.36

BURGOYNE DILLER

1906–1965

In the mid-1930s, Burgoyne Diller was one of the first American artists to adopt the strict grammar and limited vocabulary of Neo-Plasticism, also known as De Stijl. This systematic approach to painting, advocated by the Dutch artist Piet Mondrian, replaced the curves of nature with a man-made geometric order. The rules were simple: only right angles and straight lines were permitted; the palette was restricted to primary colors, plus black and white; and any illusion of depth was to be avoided. These rules, though straightforward, made the task of painting both ascetic and more exacting. In Diller's *First Theme*, the large white rectangle on the left precisely balances the two smaller forms to the right. The narrow, yellow rectangle overlaps the imaginary vertical axis ever so slightly. The three elements are thus subtly arranged so that the perfectly square canvas never quite divides into two halves but remains one impeccable, integrated whole.

Diller embraced Neo-Plasticism as a universal language that transcended boundaries of class, race, and nationality. To him it was an inherently egalitarian style. Yet many viewers found such abstraction too dry, elitist, and foreign. For Diller, however, the geometric calculations of De Stijl yielded paintings well suited to an industrialized nation. Like the modern architecture of factories, Neo-Plasticism offered a pure experience, free of unnecessary and antiquated embellishments.

First Theme, 1938
Oil on canvas, 30 1/16 x 30 1/16 in. (76.4 x 76.4 cm)
Purchase, with funds from Emily Fisher Landau 85.44

JIM DINE

b. 1935

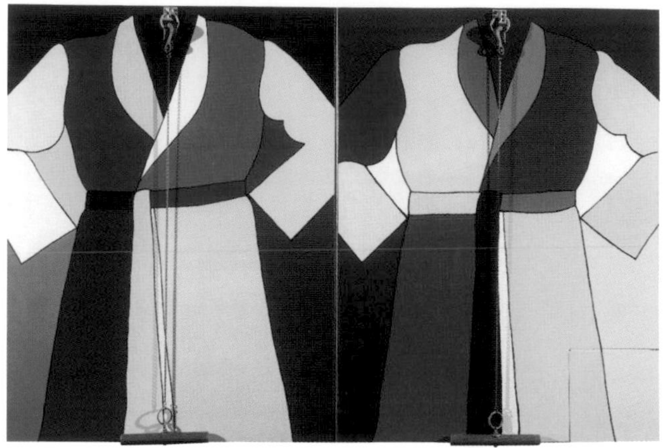

Bathrobes are a signature motif among the brushes, neckties, hearts, and palettes that make up Jim Dine's autobiographical iconography. They also provide one of the most enigmatic keys to his work. "I don't have a bathrobe to paint from," he explained. "What I use is what I've used from the very beginning—a newspaper ad which I clipped out of *The New York Times* back in 1963. The ad shows a robe with the man airbrushed out of it. Well, it somehow looked like me, and I thought I'd make that a symbol for me." In *Double Isometric Self-Portrait (Serape)*, solid, arbitrarily colored blocks are painted in a flat, nongestural manner. The "portrait" is emptied of the person within, void of any individualizing trace of the brush, and doubled by the diptych form. At what would be the back of each robe's neck—had it not been painted the same color as the background—Dine affixed a ring, from which hangs a hook attached to an inoperable pulley system. Dine leaves it to us to decide what doesn't work: the culture of advertising, with its impersonal stereotypes, or the conventions of portraiture, with its idealized claim to represent the individual.

By the time he began the bathrobe series in the early 1960s, Dine had achieved renown in the new world of Pop art. Like other Pop artists, he appropriated media imagery and made the material of everyday life a legitimate subject for representation. Life and art had already come together for Dine in the late 1950s, when he participated in the events known as Happenings. Happenings merged performance art with the messy spontaneity of real life. In his *Car Crash #2* print, Dine documents one such performance, which reenacted an actual car crash he survived. His stage set, costume, and performance then became the material for pseudo-documentary photographs. As he did later in the bathrobe portraits, Dine challenged the traditional visual means by which we record our autobiographies.

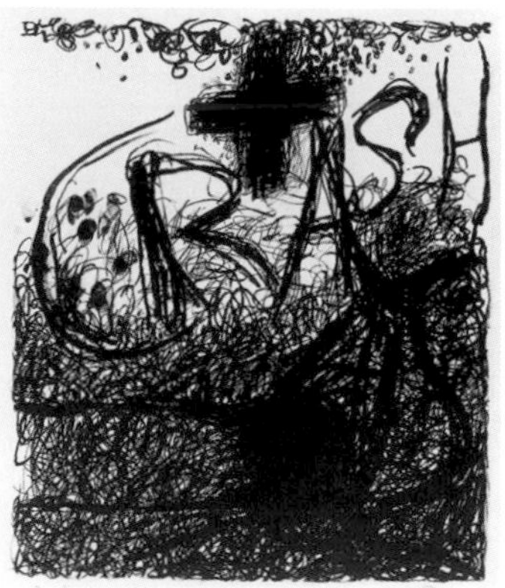

Double Isometric Self-Portrait (Serape), 1964
Oil with metal rings and hanging chains on canvas, 56 7/8 x 84 1/2 in. (144.5 x 214.6 cm)
Gift of Helen W. Benjamin in memory of her husband, Robert M. Benjamin 76.35

Car Crash #2, 1960
Lithograph: sheet, 29 7/8 x 22 3/16 in. (75.9 x 56.4 cm); image, 21 x 18 in. (53.3 x 45.7 cm)
Purchase, with funds from the Print Committee 2000.248.2

MARK DI SUVERO

b. 1933

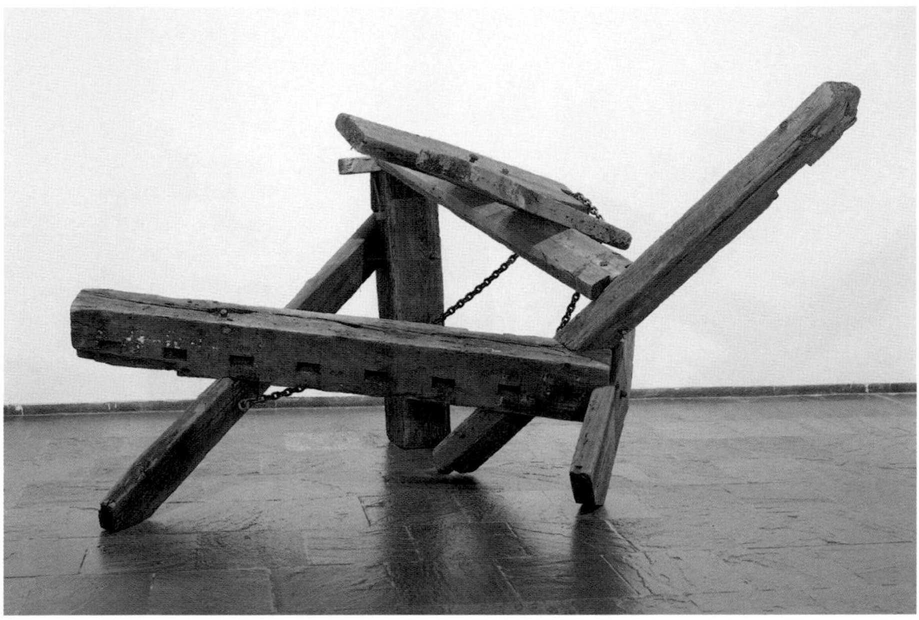

Viewing the first major exhibition of Mark di Suvero's sculptures at a New York gallery in 1960, critic Sidney Geist had a "sense of participating in a historical moment....From now on, *nothing will be the same*." The centerpiece of the show was *Hankchampion*, named in honor of the artist's younger brother, Hank, an attorney who championed civil rights. The work reflects the young sculptor's successful attempt to "give an emotional charge to space." Di Suvero arranged eight massive, weathered wooden beams and a long metal chain in a bold, asymmetric configuration that echoes the wide, gestural brushstrokes of such Abstract Expressionists as Franz Kline (p. 165), whom di Suvero particularly admired. Moreover, like other sculptors of the 1950s and 1960s, among them John Chamberlain and Louise Nevelson (pp. 71, 222), di Suvero worked with found materials—*Hankchampion*'s beams were reclaimed from junkyards in downtown Manhattan.

The composition also represents a youthful artist's response to the expected stability of traditional sculpture as well as of post-and-lintel construction. Di Suvero torqued static horizontals and verticals into dramatic, surging diagonals that convey a world of precarious dislocation rather than equilibrium. One senses that, despite the weighty mass of the beams, touching a single element would cause the entire structure to collapse.

Hankchampion, 1960
Wood and chains, 80 x 151 x 112 in. (203.2 x 383.5 x 284.5 cm) overall
Gift of Mr. and Mrs. Robert C. Scull 73.85

ARTHUR G. DOVE

1880–1946

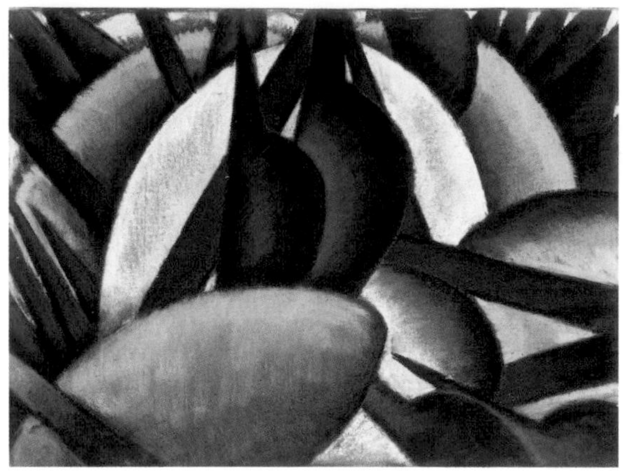

One of the first American artists to pursue abstraction, Arthur G. Dove was committed to translating nature into an abstract vocabulary of color and shape, to recording the sensations experienced in nature rather than its precise forms. Although part of the New York art world, he always lived and worked outside the city—on farms in Westport, Connecticut, and upstate New York, at a yacht club, and, between 1929 and 1933, on a 42-foot yawl on Long Island Sound. Throughout his career, whatever aesthetic turn his work took, nature remained at the heart of his creative process.

In the sensuous *Plant Forms*, Dove fixed the animating life force of nature into an abstract pattern of curvilinear and straight lines, with subtle tonal gradations giving volume to each shape. *Plant Forms* is executed in pastel, a medium Dove turned to in 1911. But rather than apply it to paper, he used it on canvas and wood supports, which made the

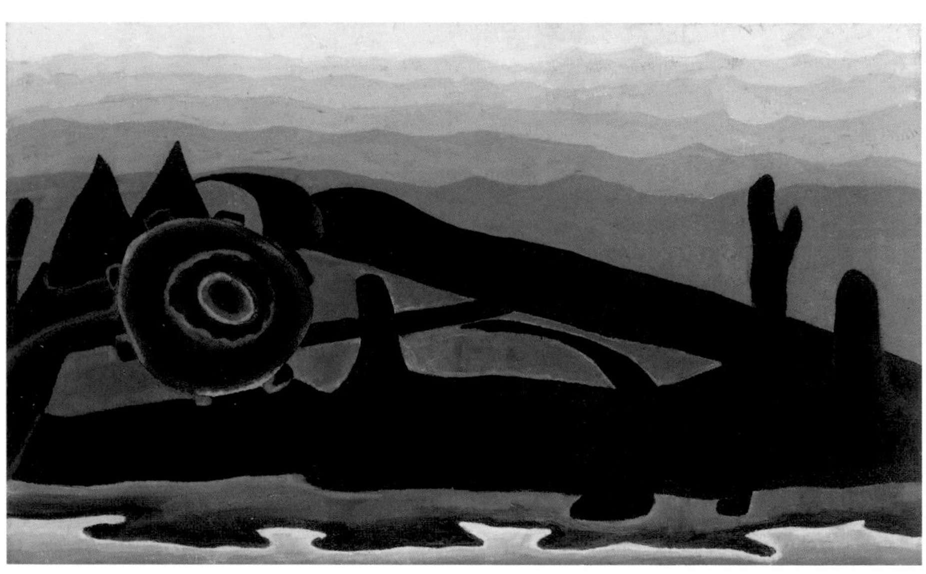

Plant Forms, c. 1912
Pastel on canvas, 17 1/4 x 23 7/8 in. (43.8 x 60.6 cm) sight
Purchase, with funds from Mr. and Mrs. Roy R. Neuberger 51.20

Ferry Boat Wreck, 1931
Oil on canvas, 18 x 30 in. (45.7 x 76.2 cm)
Purchase, with funds from Mr. and Mrs. Roy R. Neuberger 56.21

pastel more visibly substantial. In addition, since pastel is a luminous medium, we seem to be looking through seven or eight successive layers of enlarged, swelling vegetation.

Ferry Boat Wreck is also steeped in nature, but it was prompted by a specific event. During the thirties, Dove was a resident caretaker for a yacht club in Oyster Bay, Long Island. *Ferry Boat Wreck* is an abstracted interpretation of a wreck he witnessed not far from his home. The dark forms of the sinking boat are outlined against a jagged strip of sand in the foreground and successive bands of waves that merge into gray-blue-green clouds. The disk of concentric orange stripes—the sun or the moon—sounds a hopeful note that pierces the ocean's gloom.

An entirely different tone, witty and intellectual, pervades the collages and assemblages that Dove produced from 1924 to 1930, which transform quirky and found images into imaginative landscapes and portraits. In *The Critic*, Dove used newspaper clippings and advertising scraps to depict an art critic on roller skates vacuuming up the experience of art. The critic, in Dove's sardonic view, is literally empty-headed, his monocle unused. It is an unseeing, unthinking person who will render judgment on works of art.

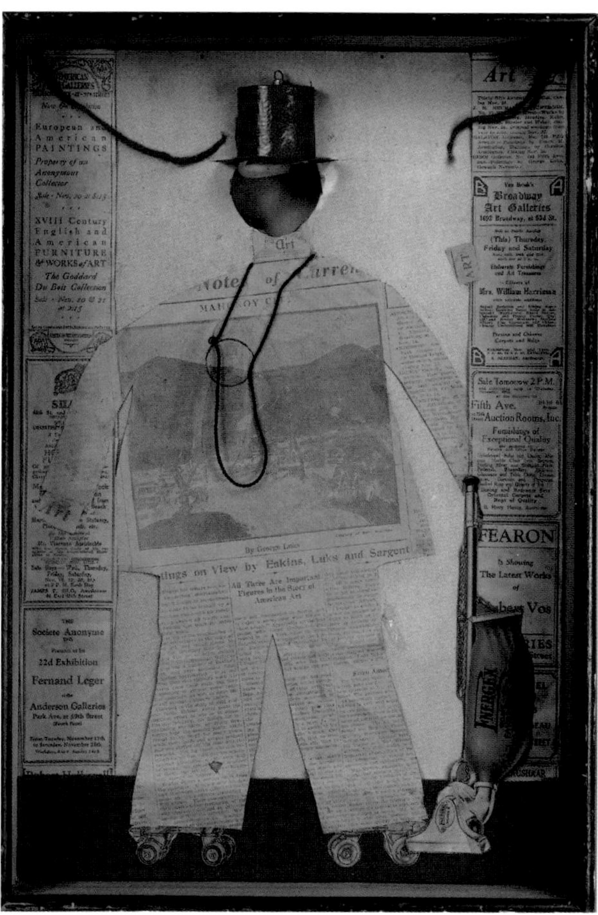

The Critic, 1925
Collage of paper, newspaper, fabric, cord, and broken glass, 19 3/4 x 13 1/4 x 4 3/4 in. (50.2 x 33.7 x 12.1 cm)
Purchase, with funds from the Historic Art Association of the Whitney Museum of American Art, Mr. and Mrs. Morton L. Janklow, the Howard and Jean Lipman Foundation, Inc., and Hannelore Schulhof 76.9

ELSIE DRIGGS

1898–1992

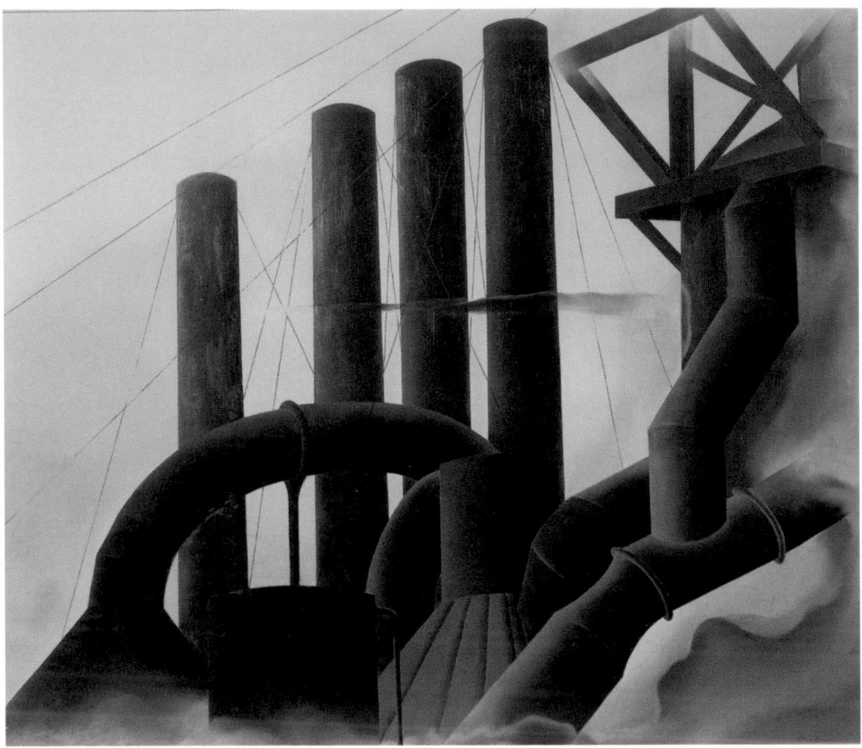

In the 1920s and 1930s, a group of artists known as Precisionists produced austere, sharply delineated portraits of factories and modern machinery that, like *Pittsburgh*, not only depict America's emergent industrial landscape, but express society's faith in technology and progress (pp. 89, 277). *Pittsburgh* recalls a train ride that Elsie Driggs took as a child past the city's steel mills at night. Years later, remembering the sulfurous hues tinting the nocturnal sky from the spewing smokestacks, she returned to Pittsburgh to make studies for a painting. She discovered, however, that the mill was using a new process and the smoky discharge no longer colored the sky. She sketched the buildings anyway and returned to her studio to paint *Pittsburgh* with a palette of grays.

Driggs exhibited the painting in New York, where her gallery declared it an exemplar of a "new classicism." The artist, in response, called *Pittsburgh* her "Piero della Francesca," referring to the fifteenth-century Italian painter in whose frescoes she saw monumental religious themes rendered in a hushed, reverential mood. In *Pittsburgh*, Driggs created a devotional image for a twentieth-century faith. Yet the monolithic gray smokestacks rising above the haze seem inescapably dark and menacing. Was Driggs questioning America's newfound faith in technology? Or is it only we, with our anxieties about global pollution, who perceive the environmental threat in those mighty shafts?

Pittsburgh, 1927
Oil on canvas, 34 1/4 x 40 in. (87 x 101.6 cm)
Gift of Gertrude Vanderbilt Whitney 31.177

GUY PÈNE DU BOIS

1884–1958

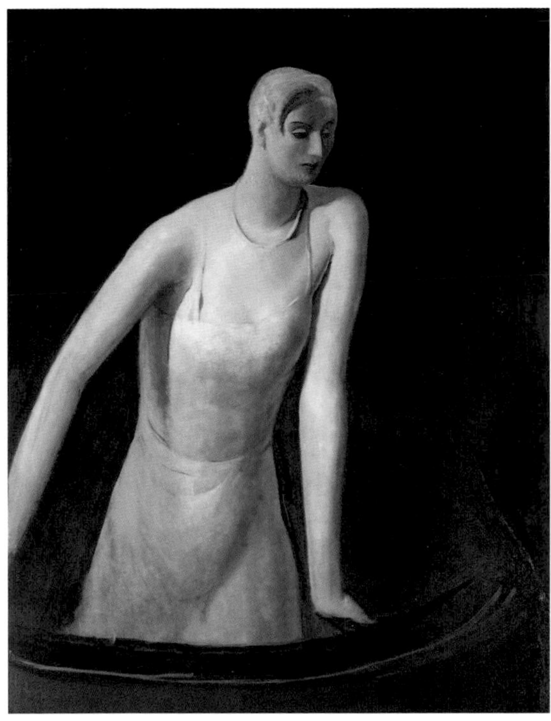

With his elegant portraits of bland, plump businessmen and chic but vacuous flappers, Guy Pène du Bois satirized New York and Paris society of the 1920s. One of his favorite settings was the opera, which he attended as a music critic for the *New York American* and as the guest of Gertrude Vanderbilt Whitney. From his seat at the opera, du Bois studied the rich and the powerful; he then returned to his studio to paint what he had observed. *Opera Box* portrays a refined, statuesque woman looking down from an upper tier of the house; her expression is distant, self-absorbed, impenetrable.

Du Bois' engagement with everyday life—or the everyday life of the very wealthy—has been credited to his teacher, the pioneering realist Robert Henri (p. 137). Du Bois shared the urban realists' interest in contemporary subject matter. However, he also belonged to a tradition of social satire that included the French nineteenth-century cartoonist and painter Honoré Daumier.

Opera Box is a subtle satire—a trenchant commentary on the drama that enfolds offstage, in the theater's audience. The sole occupant of an opera box is lit as if on stage, her luminescent, marmoreal skin set against a dark, velvety backdrop. Although her regal demeanor masks any individual personality, it suggests the woman knows—or hopes—that she is being watched. Like a sculpture set in the niche of the opera box, she poses for all to admire.

Opera Box, 1926
Oil on canvas, 57 1/2 x 45 1/4 in. (146.1 x 114.9 cm)
Purchase 31.184

CARROLL DUNHAM
b. 1949

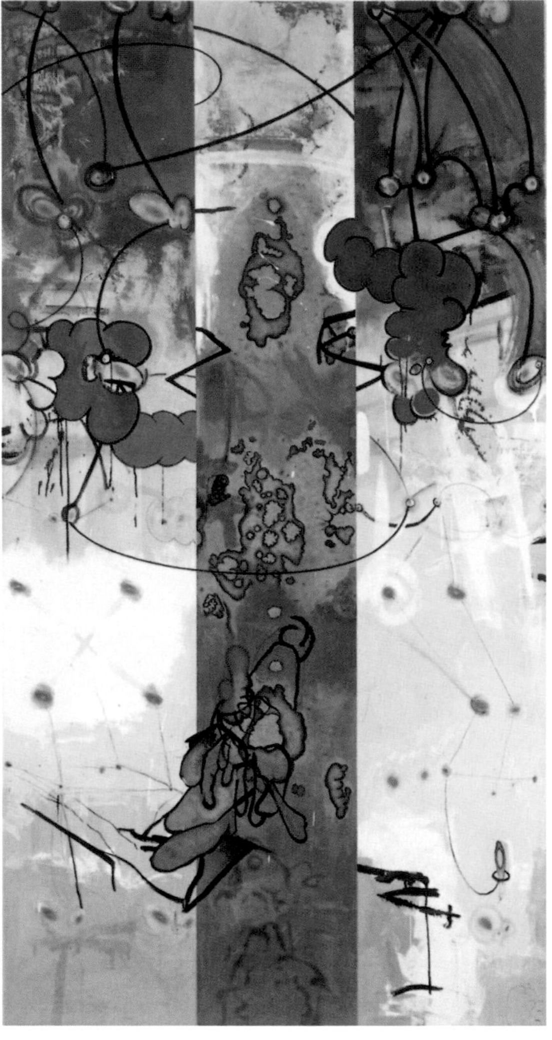

In the 1980s, Carroll Dunham, drawing on the legacy of both Pop imagery and Postminimalist abstraction, developed a graphic language that absorbs the street-level vitality of graffiti but is as fast and loopy as cartoons, and often as lighthearted. At the same time, there is an explosive energy in Dunham's work that is often close to violent and never far from sexual.

Between 1982 and 1987, Dunham generally used wood veneer as a painting surface, exploiting the pattern of the grain in composing each image. In *Pine Gap* (so called because two vertical panels of pine veneer are separated by a central one of elm), the wood's knots are turned into visual highlights, while other linear incidents on the veneer become the basis of rough-edged forms whose color-saturated edges resemble the contours in solarized photographs. These forms come well within the orbit of figuration yet stop short of narrative representations. The outlines of intestinal shapes and of male genitalia, readily discernible, float freely in a high-colored field also punctuated with sweeping black lines that suggest trajectories of objects in motion. Critic Klaus Kertess has praised the "exquisite derangement" of Dunham's work, a description that perfectly captures its distinctive balance of mayhem and precision.

Pine Gap, 1985–86
Mixed media on wood veneers, 77 x 41 in. (195.6 x 104.1 cm)
Purchase, with funds from The Mnuchin Foundation 86.36

JIMMIE DURHAM

b. 1940

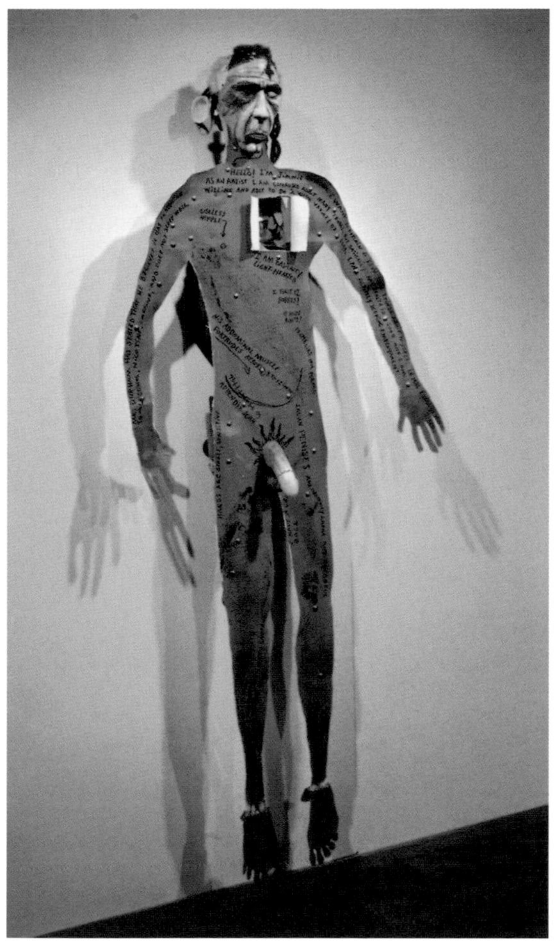

Artists have been creating images of themselves for centuries, but few have approached the project of self-representation with the irony and skepticism of Jimmie Durham. A Wolf Clan Cherokee, born in Washington, Arkansas, and trained at the École des Beaux-Arts in Geneva, Durham brings a complex personal identity to his self-portrayals in performances, poetic texts, and sculptures. His 1986 *Self-Portrait*, a life-size canvas cutout, is painted reddish brown in allusion to the derogatory epithet "redskin" and adorned with a brightly colored wooden face and penis. The body is inscribed with a series of texts that probe the artist's precarious sense of self. One, for example, reads: "My skin is not that dark, but I am sure that many Indians have coppery skin." Rather than attempt to mirror Western preconceptions or resurrect a lost "authentic" Indian self, Durham mines the gap between stereotype and self-perception to reveal an irretrievable absence at the heart of his own Native American identity. Other phrases on the body, such as "I have twelve hobbies and 11 house plants," point more generally to the difficult and, at times, seemingly absurd task of explaining oneself to another. At once the record of a particular individual and an invitation to broad philosophical reflection, Durham's work encourages viewers to consider where the truth of identity lies: in the ground of our physical bodies, in our response to the expectations of others, or in those aspects of ourselves that forever elude representation.

Self-Portrait, 1986
Canvas, wood, paint, metal, synthetic hair, fur, feathers, shell, and thread, 78 x 30 x 9 in. (198.1 x 76.2 x 22.9 cm)
Purchase, with funds from the Contemporary Painting and Sculpture Committee 95.118

WILLIAM EGGLESTON

b. 1937

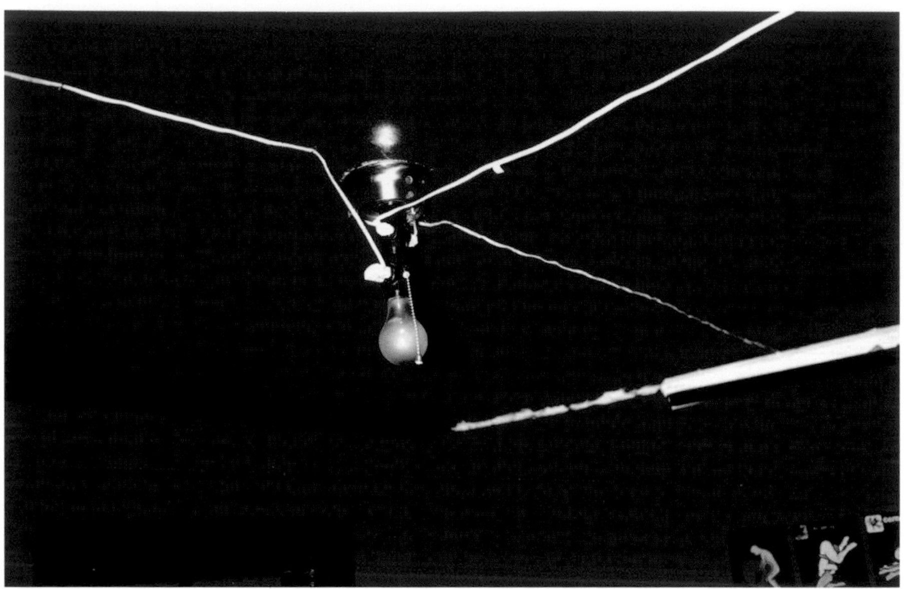

The photographer William Eggleston describes his selection of subjects as "democratic." He trains his lens on banal things, such as the red ceiling in the guest room of a friend's house. The thousands of photographs Eggleston has shot over the years form an eccentric, aggregate portrait of Memphis, Tennessee, and the Mississippi Delta. Working primarily with dye transfer prints, a technique of printing color photographs that yields pure and intense color, Eggleston records this world, not in muted shades of black and white, but in raw, sometimes garish hues.

Describing *Greenwood, Mississippi*, he explained, "When you look at the dye [the red dye that is part of the process of a dye transfer print] it is like red blood that's wet on the wall. The photograph was like a Bach exercise for me because I knew that red was the most difficult color to work with." *Greenwood, Mississippi* is shot from what might be called a moth's-eye view. The photograph isolates a section of ceiling and upper wall, a "subject" that would not normally be considered appropriate for high art. The lightbulb is dimmed, and we don't see enough of the lurid red room to determine the character of the space or its occupants. The room could be anyone's, in any place; and in this inclusiveness lies the inherently democratic nature of Eggleston's work.

In 1976, Eggleston was the subject of the first exhibition of color photography at The Museum of Modern Art, New York. Though widely panned by the critics, the exhibition gave a new artistic legitimacy to color photography, which until then had been deemed suitable only for advertising and commercial work.

Greenwood, Mississippi, 1973
Dye transfer print, 11 5/8 x 17 7/8 in. (29.5 x 45.4 cm)
Gift of Anne and Joel Ehrenkranz 94.111

NICOLE EISENMAN

b. 1963

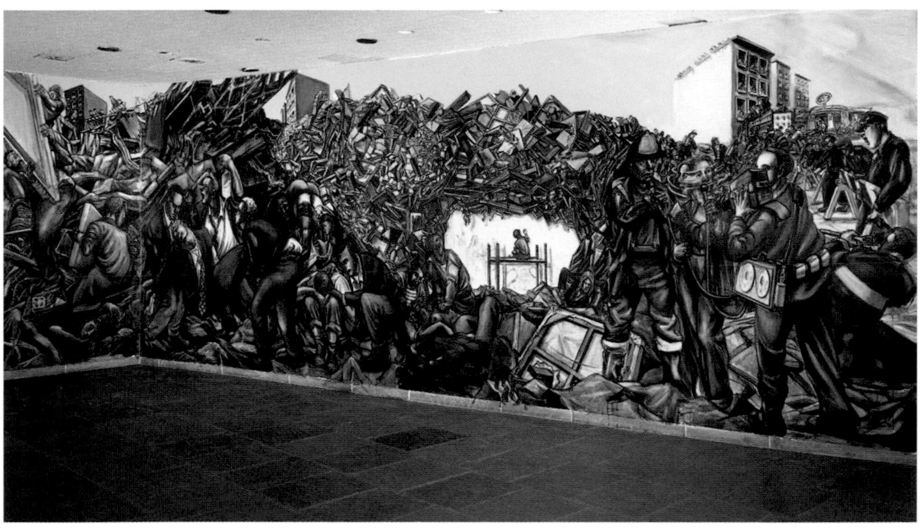

Created for the Whitney's "1995 Biennial Exhibition," *Exploding Whitney Mural* is a candid, sardonic fantasy: at the center of this epic composition, an artist sits on a scaffold, calmly painting a mural, while the Whitney collapses around her. The painter is Nicole Eisenman herself, and she goes about her work blithely ignoring the cataclysm. The mural surface teems with toppled architecture, injured men and women, rescue workers, newscasters, and a crushing mountain of ruined paintings. When the dust settles, her painting alone will remain. The idea for the composition arose when Eisenman, who specializes in mural painting, was invited to participate in the Biennial but was assigned a wall in the Lower Gallery, rather than one in the more prestigious galleries upstairs. "I felt really annexed," she said. "One way to be more central would be to blow up the whole museum so that my wall would be the only one left."

Eisenman, thirty-two years old when this mural was executed, is known for her brash, iconoclastic work. Her muscular figurative style has roots in the art of earlier eras: she points to Michelangelo and Picasso, for example, as important influences. She is also often linked to a more local tradition of epic mural painting, as represented by (among others) Thomas Hart Benton and Reginald Marsh (pp. 49, 198), who both produced public murals in New York in the 1930s. Although her other murals often depict the war between the sexes, sometimes from a frankly lesbian perspective, Eisenman resists being identified as an activist artist. More central to her work is a disarming use of humor. "Humor is an inlet," she explains. "You can seduce people with it and make them happy, and then you can sort of slap them across the face and say, 'Look again.'"

* ***Exploding Whitney Mural***, 1995
Latex paint and ink, approximately 166 x 360 in. (421.6 x 914.4 cm)
Purchase, with funds from an anonymous donor 96.113

SALLY ELESBY

b. 1942

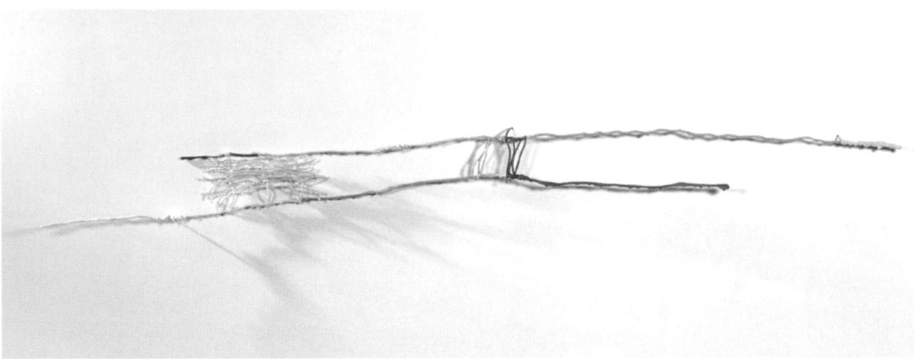

Los Angeles-based Sally Elesby's *Horizontality with Green and Brown* is a whimsical work designed to confound conventional distinctions between sculpture and painting or drawing. The work consists of three-dimensional "lines"—in reality, painted wires on a metal framework—that hang on a wall. The sculpture, therefore, can be read as a painting, with the lines forming a composition that is seen against the "background" of the wall. The shadows that the piece casts on the wall then form another network of lines, though these have no material substance, which completes the work. The indefinite character of *Horizontality* is intensified by Elesby's use of paint. The thin wires were coated with adhesive and then dipped repeatedly in paint, giving the liquid a physicality that transforms it into sculptural material.

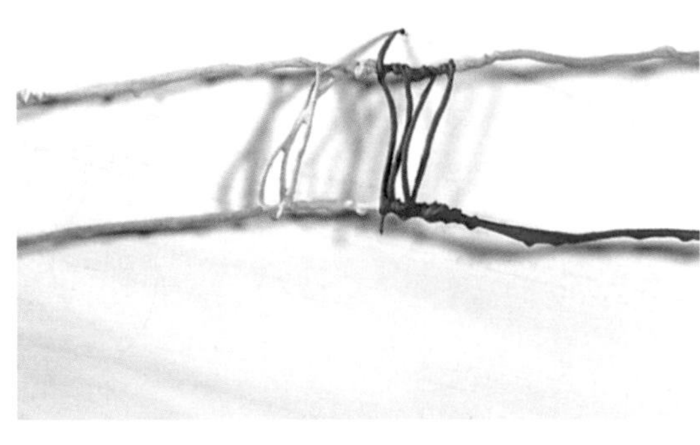

Horizontality with Green and Brown is also a study in the principles of color and balance—a study more commonly associated with painting than with sculpture. As the work of Josef Albers (p. 29) demonstrates, the effect of any one color depends on its relationship to other colors in a painting. Highly saturated colors look "heavier" than less intense hues. The consequent weight of the deep blue line at lower right, however, is countered by the longer stretch of pink and tightly coiled yellow above. At left, the mass of pale green "scrawls" is equivalent in force to the short, bright red line segment above, while the green tendrils also seem to support (with some difficulty) the pale yellow line trailing off below. Through these and other plays of color, Elesby has wittily reinterpreted the classical concept of a balanced composition.

Horizontality with Green and Brown, 2000
Oils on wire and colored glue, 6 x 74 x 5 1/2 in. (15.2 x 188 x 14 cm)
Purchase, with funds from the Contemporary Committee 2000.368

RICHARD ESTES

b. 1932

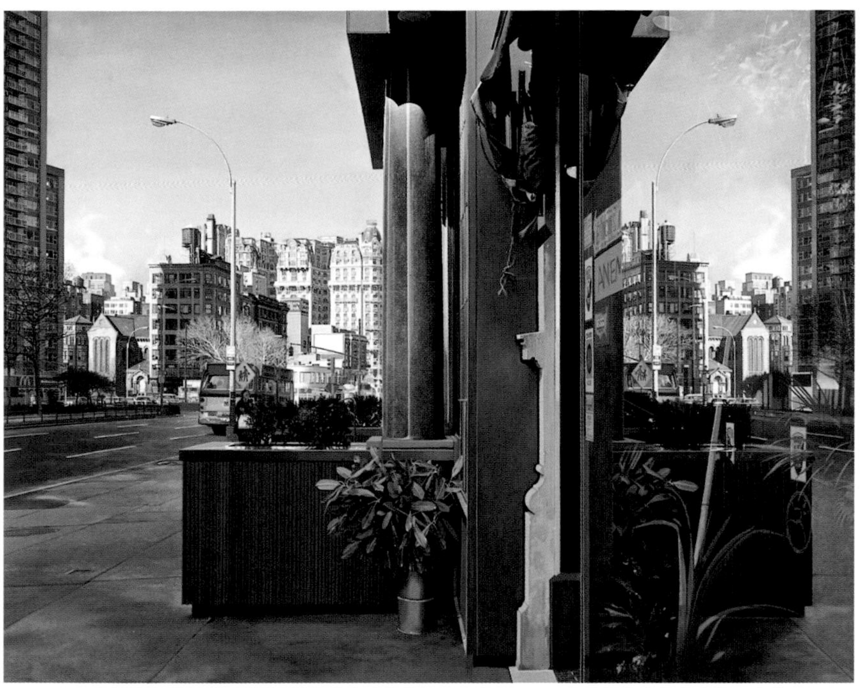

In the late 1960s, a group of artists began to use photographic aids as a basis for painting. Richard Estes is among the leading Photo-Realists, along with Robert Bechtle and Chuck Close (pp. 46, 74), and his canvases, with their luminous precision and finely rendered detail, can be mistaken for photographs. Estes often shoots five or six rolls of film in preparation for a single painting, blowing up details and combining elements from several photographs as source material. He paints deserted, litter-free streets in late afternoon light, usually including large expanses of glass store windows that both reflect the scene depicted and transparently reveal what lies behind them. Estes takes small liberties in his otherwise lifelike paintings—streets and buildings intersect in perspectivally inaccurate ways, and people, storefronts, and signs are added or subtracted.

This painting features one of the artist's favorite landmarks, the Ansonia Hotel near his apartment on Manhattan's Upper West Side. The large scale of the work—it is 4 feet high and 5 feet wide—makes Estes' gleaming verisimilitude all the more remarkable. In one sense, however, the high degree of realism in *Ansonia* is deceptive, for the painting features a uniform sharp focus that would be impossible with natural vision or with a camera. "When I look at things," Estes explained, "some things are out of focus. But I don't like to have some things out of focus and others in focus because it makes very specific what you are supposed to look at, and I try to avoid saying that. I want you to look at it all. Everything is in focus."

Ansonia, 1977
Oil on canvas, 48 x 60 in. (121.9 x 152.4 cm)
Purchase, with funds from Frances and Sydney Lewis 77.33

PHILIP EVERGOOD

1901–1973

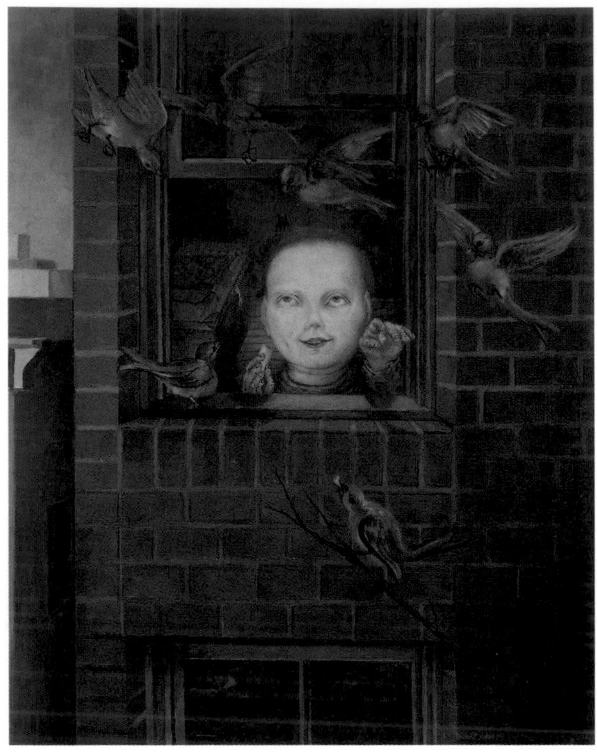

Philip Evergood's art defies easy classification. With his strong political conscience and sensitive eye for everyday experience, Evergood could be called a Social Realist. Yet his paintings also possess an odd, disjointed quality reminiscent of Surrealism. *Lily and the Sparrows*, like much of Evergood's work, refers to a particular incident. "I happened to stop at the curb, just dreaming," the artist recalled, "and looked up, and here was an amazing sight. A little, bald-headed, white beautiful face was in a window with little bits of crumbs—alone."

Evergood named the child Lily and painted her pale face from memory. He rendered the hands in exquisite detail, articulating each fingernail and joint. Yet he also relied on imagination. The inside of Lily's home would not have been visible to a pedestrian on the street. Evergood skewed the perspective to reveal a fictitious interior with sparse furnishings. All the colors seem unnatural, restricted to drab browns, except for the lurid red brick and Lily's luminous face and hands.

In *Lily and the Sparrows*, Evergood recorded not just the physical facts he had seen, but the metaphysical reverie it inspired. For him, the face of an ordinary child in a window assumed an otherworldly aura. His painting of that child recalls a medieval scene from the life of a saint, for the ethereal but impoverished Lily is sharing her bread with the sparrows.

Lily and the Sparrows, 1939
Oil on composition board, 30 x 24 in. (76.2 x 61 cm)
Purchase 41.42

TONY FEHER

b. 1956

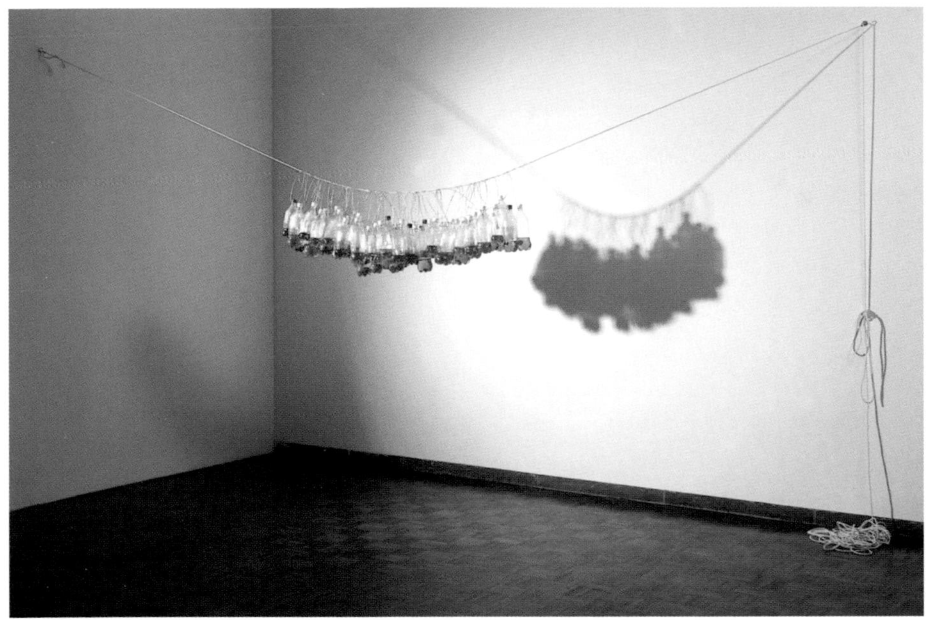

Tony Feher's work is often composed of random detritus; he assembles found and discarded materials such as marbles, bottles, Styrofoam, loose change, and scraps of carpet and wood into striking arrangements which highlight the fragility as well as the durability of the cast-off materials. Transforming the mundane into the ethereal and the rough into the delicate, Feher's art serves as a reminder that beauty can be found in the everyday. In their incorporation of commonplace objects as primary materials, these sculptures relate to the work of many other American artists of the 1980s and 1990s, among them Félix González-Torres, David Hammons, Mike Kelley, and Alison Saar (pp. 121, 129, 162, 267).

In *Suture*, fifty-seven Coca-Cola liter bottles hang from steel wire hooks on an arc of clothesline. Stripped of their labels, the bottles are partially filled with red-tinted water that echoes the occasional red plastic bottle cap punctuating the cluster. The work reminded Feher of a surgery scar on his belly, and the title *Suture* alludes to the design of his stitches. *Suture* calls attention to its own physical presence in real space and time: condensation clouds the plastic bottles and refracts light from inside the gallery, and the work is hung across the span of a corner rather than on a single wall. Feher would like the viewer to be encompassed by the sculpture, "with the rope disappearing out of your peripheral vision."

Suture, 1997
57 plastic bottles, water, food coloring, wire, and rope, dimensions variable
Purchase, with funds from Andrew Ong and the Painting and Sculpture Committee 97.110

LYONEL FEININGER

1871–1956

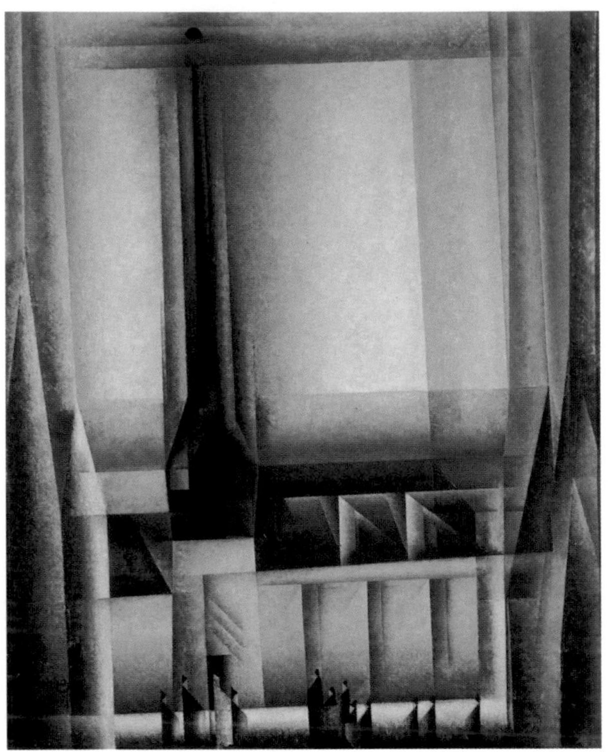

The Gelmeroda church in the German city of Weimar was one of Lyonel Feininger's most beloved subjects; it was not far from the Bauhaus school where he taught in the years following World War I. Although born in New York, Feininger spent more than half his life in Europe and was closely allied with the avant-garde in both France and Germany. Yet he also looked to the past for inspiration: *Gelmeroda, VIII* is a modernist painting of a traditional church.

Feininger once remarked that he was interested in painting the space around objects, not objects themselves, and his Gelmeroda is set into the sky like a faceted jewel. Church and sky, constructed from diaphanous veils of paint, are equally immaterial. The spire appears to quiver, as if only momentarily crystallized from the gray ether. The solemn churchgoers at the lower edge seem similarly incorporeal, reduced to a group of translucent triangles. Yet the figures establish the scale of the architecture and provide a human presence. As Feininger explained, "I shall probably never in my pictures represent humans in the usual way—all the same whatever urges me is human." Gelmeroda's spire pierces the sky, connecting these earthbound creatures to the heavens. The effect, however, is not one of traditional hierarchy, but of unity: in Feininger's painting, heaven and earth are merely facets of a single, ethereal reality.

Gelmeroda, VIII, 1921
Oil on canvas, 39 1/4 x 31 1/4 in. (99.7 x 79.4 cm)
Purchase 53.38

JOHN FERREN

1905–1970

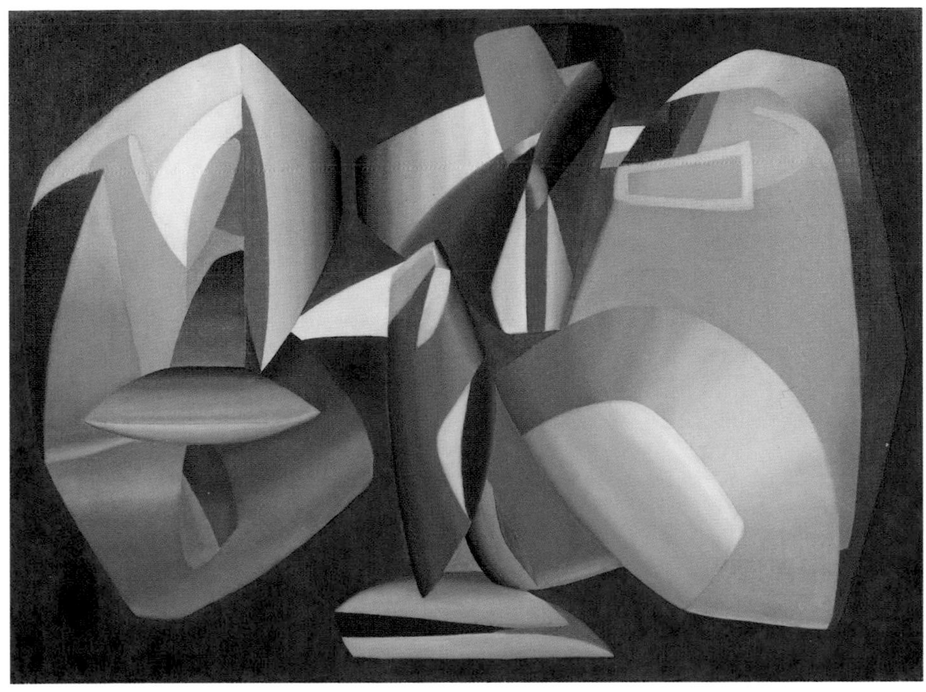

John Ferren's rich and varied career reads like an encyclopedia of twentieth-century abstraction. In the years preceding World War II, he befriended leaders of the European avant-garde and briefly joined the Abstract American Artists group; after the war, he worked, along with other artists of the New York School, as an Abstract Expressionist. Yet despite the impressive range of Ferren's achievements as an abstract painter, he actually began his career as a sculptor. Although *Composition on Green* is informed by Ferren's contact with other modernist painters, it also suggests the lasting impact of his early training in sculpture.

Composition on Green consists of a single, contiguous mass of abstract forms set against a dark green backdrop. At first glance, the forms appear to float, untethered to the edges of the canvas. Yet they are grounded by a pedestal-like appendage that runs parallel to the lower edge, as if the entire mass were precariously balanced on an invisible table. The painting is like an image of a sculpture, with curved and twisted forms modeled from subtle gradations of color. On the right, however, an expansive patch of cerulean blue undermines this resemblance. Like an open window, it pierces the green backdrop and suggests an infinite space beyond. Although Ferren demonstrates a sculptor's concern for weight and volume, as a painter he is not limited by the laws of physics. The blue opening announces that this mass of interlocking forms, despite its apparent bulk, is but an illusion.

Composition on Green, 1936
Oil on canvas, 29 x 39 1/2 in. (73.7 x 100.3 cm)
Purchase, with funds from the Friends of the Whitney Museum of American Art 78.54

DAN FLAVIN

1933–1996

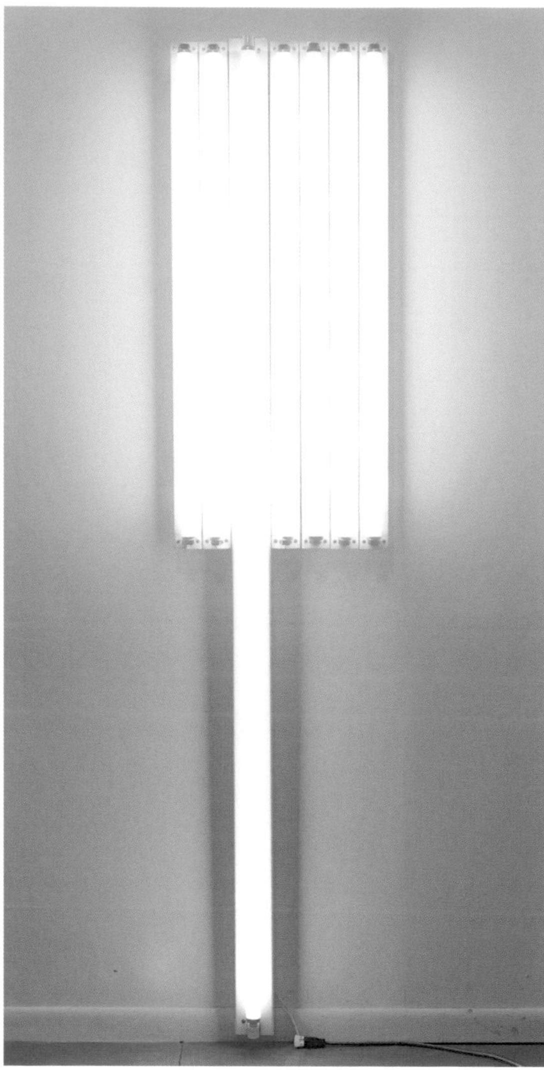

One of the most significant developments in twentieth-century art was the introduction of non-art materials as legitimate vehicles of expression. Dan Flavin's forty-year exploitation of fluorescent light tubing is one of the most remarkable achievements in this long tradition. Using a minimum of means, he realizes a maximum of effect, as the incandescence of light is not merely depicted, but made into the physical subject of the work. In *Untitled*, six identical white fluorescent tubes are balanced against a seventh, double their length. The abstract, architectural tension of the arrangement produces an almost religious, elegiac rhythm.

Flavin's use of prefabricated industrial materials had an important precedent in the art of Marcel Duchamp, the early twentieth-century exponent of Dada, who conceived of "ready-mades"—found objects re-presented as works of art. The common materials Flavin uses depend on electricity, which operates, in turn, only in conjunction with the surrounding elements—the tubes, the wiring, the wall, the room. Yet all these elements are forgotten when we look at the work. The effect is nearly magical: as the light dilates before us, the tubes themselves all but disappear, and we find ourselves in a real world of light. Flavin's fluorescent sculptures, by holding abstraction and reality in a visibly ethereal balance, offer a concise, sophisticated paradigm of twentieth-century art.

Untitled, 1966
Fluorescent lights, 96 x 21 x 3 1/2 in. (243.8 x 53.3 x 8.9 cm)
Gift of Howard and Jean Lipman 71.214

ROBERT FRANK

b. 1924

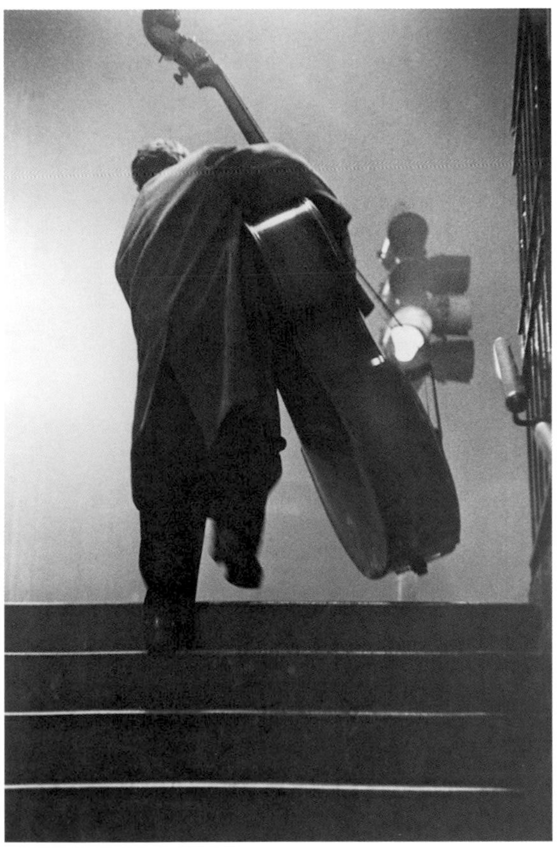

"Black and white is the vision of hope and despair," Robert Frank said of his work. Son of a Jewish-German father, Frank was born and raised in Switzerland and emigrated to America in 1947. The photographs he made in the late 1940s and 1950s provide an alternative view of a world in the process of change. At a time when images were filled with optimism, the unheroic quality of Frank's street photographs offered an implicitly critical perspective of the postwar scene.

Between 1949 and 1953, Frank traveled back and forth between Europe and the United States. This photograph of a man, presumably a musician, exiting an underground station while carrying an upright bass was made in London. (The work was previously titled *New York Subway*; however, Frank recently discovered by looking at his contact sheets that it was taken in London.) Characteristic is the sense of malaise that permeates the scene, a foggy image of an ambiguous figure, perhaps on his way home. Here, as in all his pictures, Frank eschews conventional and idealizing approaches to photographic narratives such as one might then have found in the pages of *Life* and *Vogue* (for which Frank also worked) in favor of personal reportage. He captures a spontaneous and uncertain scene using a low, tilted angle to introduce the street's bleak, gray atmosphere.

Like the work of the American Beat poets he later befriended, Frank's photography breaks through the glossy and optimistic facade of 1950s culture to plumb its darker, melancholy side. In 1958, after traveling across the country on a Guggenheim Fellowship, Frank published *The Americans*, a series of portraits of everyday people taken with such blunt candor that critics at first derided it as "un-American." Such candor, however, is the foundation of Frank's photography. "I'm always looking outside," he explained, "trying to look inside. Trying to say something that's true."

London, 1952–53
Gelatin silver print mounted on paperboard, 13 1/2 x 8 11/16 in. (34.3 x 22.1 cm)
Purchase, with funds from the Photography Committee in memory of Eugene M. Schwartz 95.169

HELEN FRANKENTHALER

b. 1928

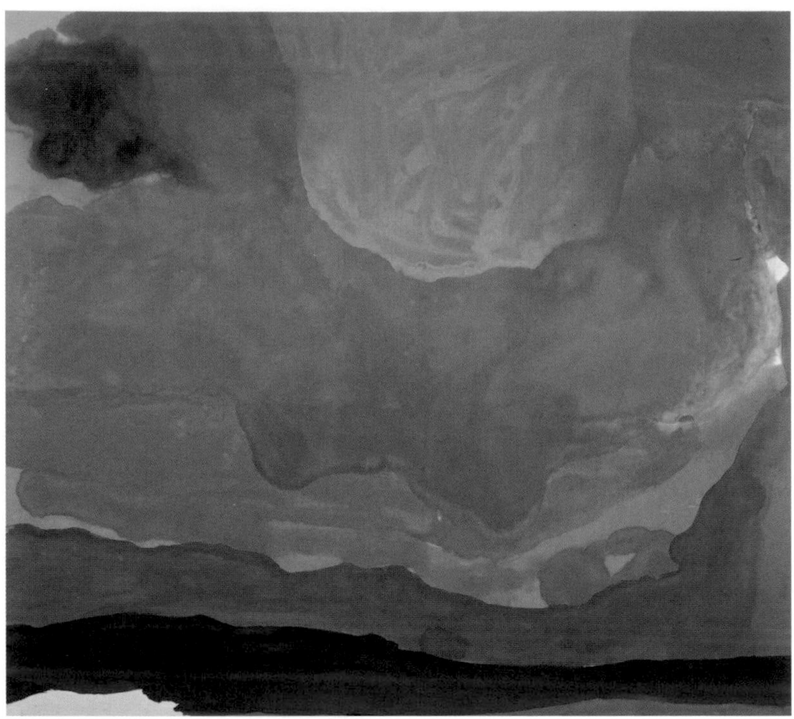

In 1952, Helen Frankenthaler developed an innovative method for applying paint directly onto unprimed canvas. This procedure, which came to be known as "stain painting," helped make Frankenthaler one of most important artists of the male-dominated group of Abstract Expressionists. Building on Abstract Expressionism's concern with the physical properties of paint and the gestures and actions of the painting process, Frankenthaler extended Jackson Pollock's famous "drip" technique (p. 242) in a new, more lyrical direction. Like Pollock, she placed her canvas directly on the floor and poured paint from above, largely without the aid of a brush. But her paint was thinned to a watery liquid, and rather than Pollock's curvilinear, loopy forms, Frankenthaler's paintings display broad expanses of color that often come close in appearance to the vaporous fields of Mark Rothko (p. 263).

Unlike Pollock and Rothko, however, Frankenthaler never entirely abandoned a commitment to representation. Although the reference is often subtle, her paintings consistently evoke natural scenes. The undulating forms in *Flood*, for example, relate to a simplified landscape, with layers of sky, cloud, mountain, forest, and water. The zones of oranges, pinks, green, and purple, moreover, evoke different emotional states, billowing surges of feeling. Hue and shape become conveyors of place and emotion. In a statement she provided for the Whitney's records on *Flood*, Frankenthaler wrote: "I think of my pictures as explosive landscapes, worlds and distances, held on a flat surface."

* ***Flood***, 1967
Synthetic polymer on canvas, 124 x 140 in. (315 x 355.6 cm)
Purchase, with funds from the Friends of the Whitney Museum of American Art 68.12

JARED FRENCH

1905–1988

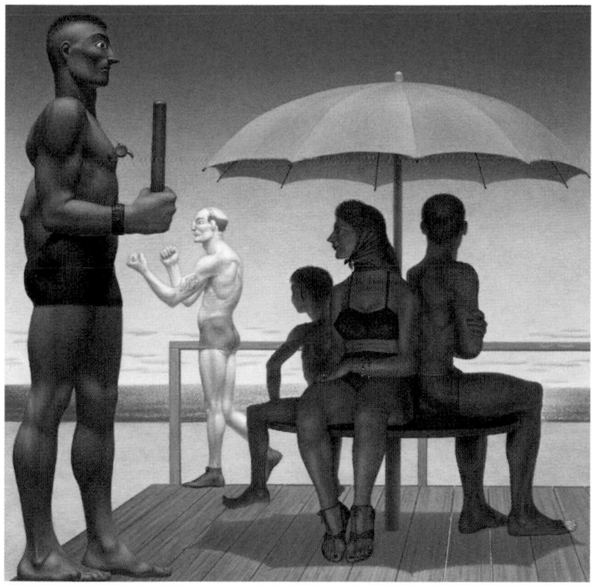

Although Jared French began *State Park* during a summer on Fire Island, a beach community off Long Island's south shore, he did not consider it a painting of a particular beach. Instead, his entranced figures inhabit a barren, dreamlike landscape. French's fascination with the unconscious suggests Surrealist influences, but he in fact drew on many sources, both contemporary and historical.

In the early 1930s, French traveled through Europe with Paul Cadmus (p. 61), the beginning of a lifelong relationship that was both professional and romantic. When they returned to the United States, French married the artist Margaret Hoening, who joined Cadmus and French during their summers on Fire Island. There the three artists formed a collaborative photographic project they dubbed PAJAMA, combining the first two letters of each of their names. They photographed one another on the beach, and the rigid, classical poses they assume in these images convey the same sort of mythic drama enacted in *State Park.*

The tanned lifeguard in the foreground has the fixed, lidless eyes and stiff stance of a kouros, an Archaic Greek statue of a nude youth. At the rear of the deck is a slightly paunchy, balding man in a boxer's stance, while a family of three gathers beneath the shade of a large pink umbrella. Who is the lifeguard protecting, and from what? No threats are visible: the sky is clear, the ocean calm, the beach unpopulated. The disposition of the figures suggests that the guard may be shielding the nuclear family from an imagined threat—the threat of homosexuality posed by the lone man at back. Ironically, the members of the family sit with their backs to each other, implying that their tenuous bond survives only by constantly patrolling the borders of "normalcy."

State Park, 1946
Egg tempera on composition board, 23 1/2 x 23 1/2 in. (59.7 x 59.7 cm)
Gift of Mr. and Mrs. R.H. Donnelley Erdman 65.78

LEE FRIEDLANDER

b. 1934

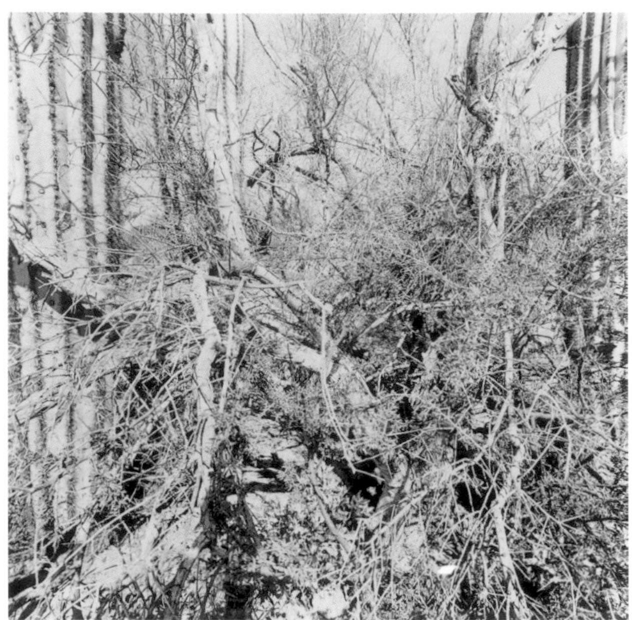

Lee Friedlander is frequently regarded as a photographer of the American "social landscape," a term he himself coined in 1963 to describe his densely layered photographs of populated sidewalks, reflective shop windows, and roadside motel rooms illuminated by flickering television screens. His concern, however, was never with a straightforward documentary, for he habitually allowed telephone poles, chain-link fences, and other elements to bisect or even obscure his subjects. He spent, in his own words, "about twenty-five years wondering what would be around the next corner and testing what it would look like with my camera." This restless curiosity about the formal composition of the physical world has led him to photograph a wide variety of subject matter, including natural landscapes, which he began to consider a "real subject" in the late 1980s.

Friedlander first visited the Sonora Desert around that time and continued to make pictures there for twelve years. He was transfixed by the Southwest's dry, alien terrain, just as earlier twentieth-century American photographers had been. But whereas his predecessors had isolated the archetypal saguaro cactus and vast sandy expanses, Friedlander was drawn to the impenetrable thicket of the desert forest. In *Sonora*, the sun-bleached brush, trees, and cactus are transformed into a complicated abstraction that fills the frame and obscures pictorial depth. In fact, the compressed composition and dense details create an image where the conventional hierarchy of space—foreground, middleground, and background—breaks down. "I discovered a long time ago," Friedlander said, "that my photographs contain a foreground that is not passive." The *Sonora* series is also unusual for its high-key printing, which accentuates the blinding brightness of the natural sunlight.

Sonora, 1995
Gelatin silver print, 14 3/4 x 14 13/16 in. (37.4 x 37.6 cm)
Purchase, with funds from the Photography Committee 96.165

ADAM FUSS

b. 1961

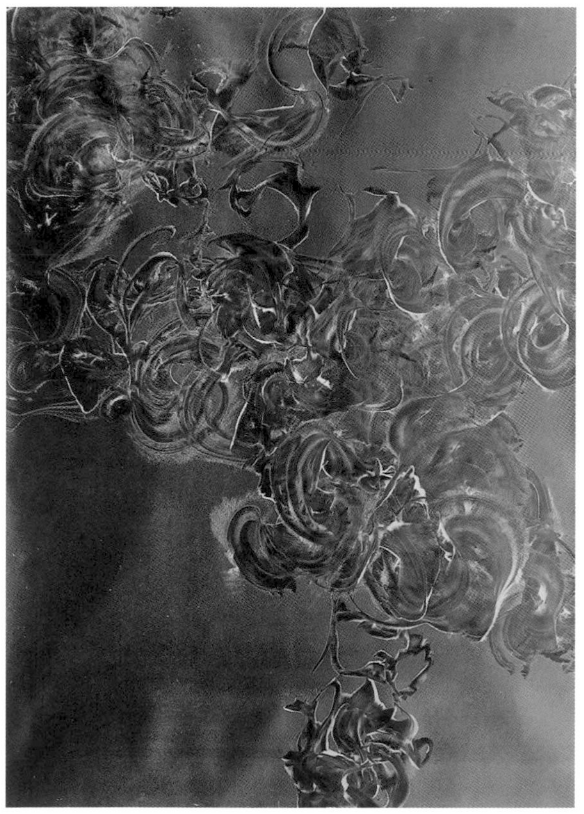

Adam Fuss works with two of the elements essential to photography: light and light-sensitive paper. Since moving from London to New York in the early 1980s, he has experimented widely with photograms. A photogram is produced without a camera by arranging objects on photographic paper and then exposing the arrangement to light. The objects block the light from the paper, so that the areas they cover come up white when the paper is developed. If the objects are transparent, they filter light, resulting in a toned area. A photogram is therefore a unique negative print comprising light forms intermixed with dark areas of exposed paper, somewhat like an X-ray. The history of the photogram extends as far back as photography, beginning with the 1833 "leaf drawings" of pioneer photographer William Henry Fox Talbot and continuing into the twentieth century with Man Ray's "rayographs" (p. 251).

The ghostly ripples of *Untitled* trace the sleek movements of snakes that Fuss allowed to slither freely over a large sheet sprinkled with talcum powder. The ethereal character of the light-marked surface betrays neither the animals' physical weight nor the mass of the channeled paths they left. Although the swirling patterns can be read as an allusion to Abstract Expressionist painting (p. 242), Fuss himself speaks of the way the image's seductive immateriality and suggestive spirituality transcend both the mundane source and the direct physicality and literalness implicit in the photogram process.

Untitled, 1988
Gelatin silver photogram, 61 11/16 x 43 1/2 in. (156.7 x 110.5 cm)
Purchase, with funds from Kathryn Fleck and Michèle Gerber Klein 2000.220

ELLEN GALLAGHER

b. 1965

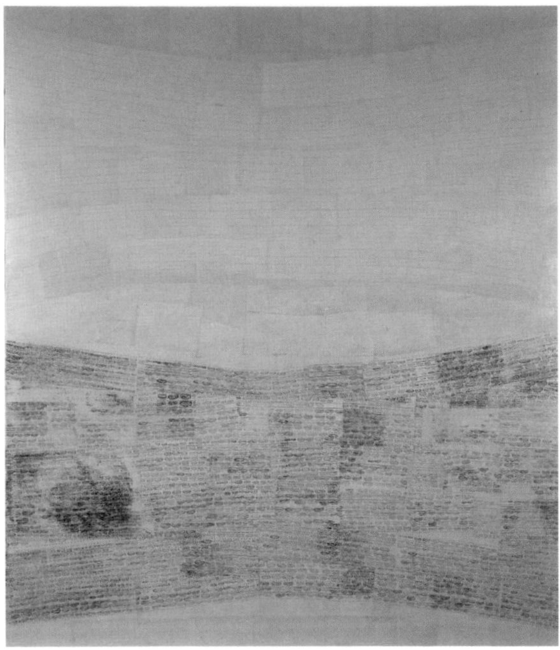

Using ink and paper on canvas, and employing painstaking detail, Ellen Gallagher brings a graphic, even writerly sensibility to painting. From a viewing distance adequate to take in a work of this size (*Afro Mountain* is nearly 7 feet high and 6 feet wide), it seems a serenely poised example of late Minimalist abstraction; the delicate lines and subtle tones suggest the work of Agnes Martin (p. 201), whom Gallagher admires. But when the painting is inspected closely, at a more intimate range, its gentility and reticence fall away. Crammed between the bowed horizontal lines are hundreds of drawings of wide-lipped mouths. Borrowed from the stock imagery of minstrel shows, this derogatory stereotype of a black physiognomic feature, drawn on sheets of paper affixed to the canvas, resist its formal constraints with all the force of long-suppressed anger. Once noted, the lips warp the painting's smooth surface in uncontrollable ways.

Gallagher, who first gained widespread attention when she was included in the Whitney Museum's "1995 Biennial Exhibition," is a New Englander; her father is African-American and her mother is Irish. Both insider and outsider with respect to this country's main racial communities, she has developed a remarkably subtle language for expressing the uneasy sense of affiliation—and the hidden uncertainties—that are characteristic of contemporary culture. As we look first from a distance and then more closely at *Afro Mountain*, we engage in a sharply divided, two-step process of assimilation that tests our assumptions about both art and race with exceptional, even uncomfortable, clarity.

* ***Afro Mountain***, 1994
Ink and paper on canvas, 83 7/8 x 72 1/4 in. (213 x 183.5 cm)
Gift of an anonymous donor 95.71

WILLIAM J. GLACKENS

1870–1938

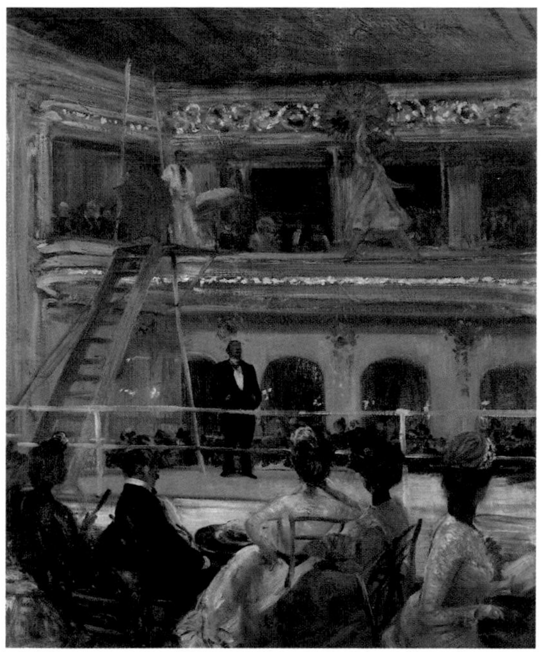

William Glackens was one of several successful Philadelphia newspaper illustrators who, under the tutelage of Robert Henri (p. 137), abandoned the murder-and-mayhem scenes of journalism. Along with George Luks, Everett Shinn, and John Sloan (pp. 191, 279, 287), he instead used his draftsman's skills to capture the everyday spontaneity of American urban life. He began painting just before he moved to New York in 1896 and always favored refined middle-class subjects. Using impetuous brushstrokes to apply layers of thick pigment, Glackens caught the swift pace of fashionable New Yorkers as they shopped, promenaded, dined and, as in *Hammerstein's Roof Garden*, watched the spectacular cabaret-style entertainment that was a novelty in turn-of-the-last-century America.

Roof gardens were a summertime innovation, providing open-air entertainment to urban audiences when stifling heat forced the indoor theaters below to close. Opera impresario Oscar Hammerstein owned several such sites throughout the city, and this one, the Palace Roof Garden, sat atop his adjoining Victoria and Republic Theatres. In *Hammerstein's Roof Garden*, Glackens casually framed the changing mores of post-Victorian society and the sweeping impact of new technologies. He depicted a well-lit public arena in which men and women sit side by side watching exotic vaudevillian performers; daubs of creamy white and yellow pigment register the filigreed tangle of electric lights that made nighttime theater possible. In his generally muted palette, vivid colors are limited to the tightrope walker's cerulean blue dress and the red umbrella—bright splashes of bohemia balanced high above the genteel audience.

Hammerstein's Roof Garden, c. 1901
Oil on canvas, 30 x 25 in. (76.2 x 63.5 cm)
Purchase 53.46

FRITZ GLARNER

1899–1972

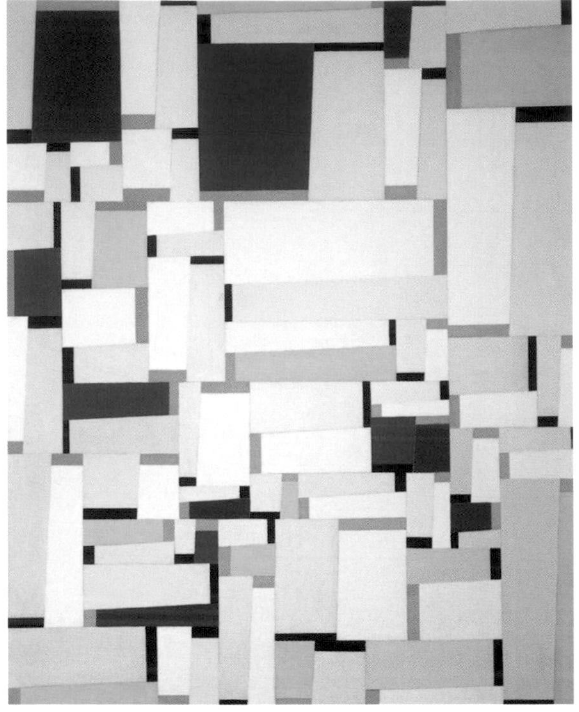

In 1936, the Swiss-born painter Fritz Glarner emigrated to the United States, where he was joined four years later by the Dutch artist Piet Mondrian, the leading proponent of Neo-Plasticism (p. 91). The two men had known each other in Europe, but their relationship flourished on foreign soil. Until Mondrian's death in 1944, they met regularly at the Dutch artist's New York home, discussing their systematic approach to painting.

During this period, Glarner began to produce what he called *Relational Paintings*, a series that occupied him until his death. His work, like Mondrian's, was governed by a strict set of rules. Unlike Mondrian, he permitted diagonal lines, but only to emphasize horizontal and vertical elements. Glarner also expanded on Neo-Plasticism's limited palette, using shades of gray in addition to black, white, and primary colors. He felt that this broader palette allowed him to achieve a balanced relationship between competing colors and shapes.

In this *Relational Painting*, the shades of gray cause the brilliant white forms to advance, while the black bars seem to recede. Angles just slightly off ninety degrees lend the composition a jumbled energy. Yet closer analysis reveals that the entire painting is built on a scaffolding of interlocking rectangles. A diagonal line divides each rectangle into two differently colored trapezoids. Black and gray bars, placed at opposite ends of these two trapezoids, obscure the painting's underlying geometry. Thus, while adhering to the elementary rules he established for his *Relational Paintings*, Glarner created works of striking dynamism and complexity.

****Relational Painting***, 1949–51
Oil on canvas, 65 x 52 in. (165.1 x 132.1 cm)
Purchase 52.3

ROBERT GOBER

b. 1954

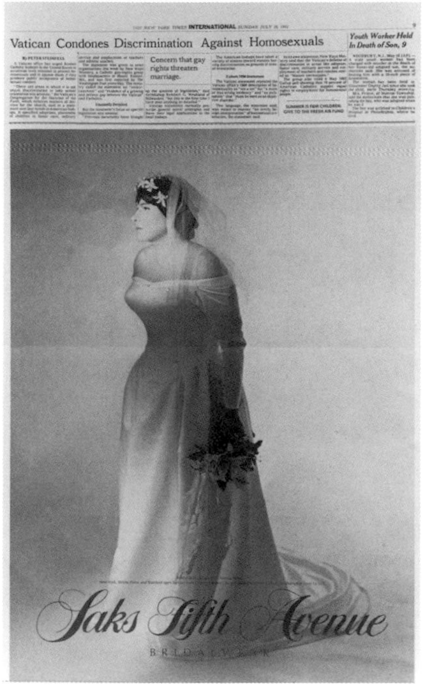

At a time when artists are turning more frequently to industrial fabrication and the incorporation of readymade, off-the-shelf objects in the creation of sculpture, Robert Gober painstakingly handcrafts works that are highly realistic, yet often disturbingly altered. Among his signature pieces are empty, strangely proportioned sinks and drains, whose evocative forms are at first barely distinguishable from industrially fabricated objects.

Gober has also produced work of a more political nature. The untitled photolithograph of 1992–96 resembles a page from *The New York Times*, but it was Gober who selected and montaged the news stories and advertisement and inserted himself into the bridal gown. The transvestite bride underscores the message of the news reports, which present an unsettling portrait of American values. One story about the Vatican condoning discrimination against homosexuals in cases of adoption and foster care is juxtaposed with another about a New Jersey youth worker who murdered her adopted son. The implication is that no one group of people can be declared "safe" for children.

Less obviously political, although still engaged with the inequities of contemporary society, is the lifeless, paraffin male leg protruding from the wall in the 1991 untitled sculpture. The leg is meticulously fitted with individual and highly realistic hairs, which give it a profound sense of intimacy. The overall effect of the severed leg is not only shocking but melancholy and, for the artist, deeply rooted in the mortality of AIDS. While the phallic associations of the protruding candle are undeniable, the candle also suggests a vigil, a sense of time passing, running out, and of bodies melting away.

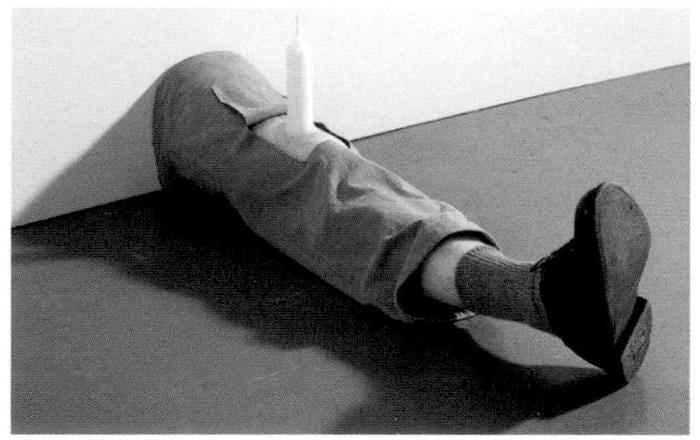

Untitled, 1992–96
Photolithograph: sheet and image, 22 7/16 x 13 9/16 in. (57 x 34.5 cm)
Purchase, with funds from the Print Committee 97.5

Untitled, 1991
Wax, cloth, wood, leather, and human hair, 13 1/2 x 7 x 37 1/2 in. (34.3 x 17.8 x 95.3 cm)
Purchase, with funds from Robert W. Wilson 92.6

NAN GOLDIN
b. 1953

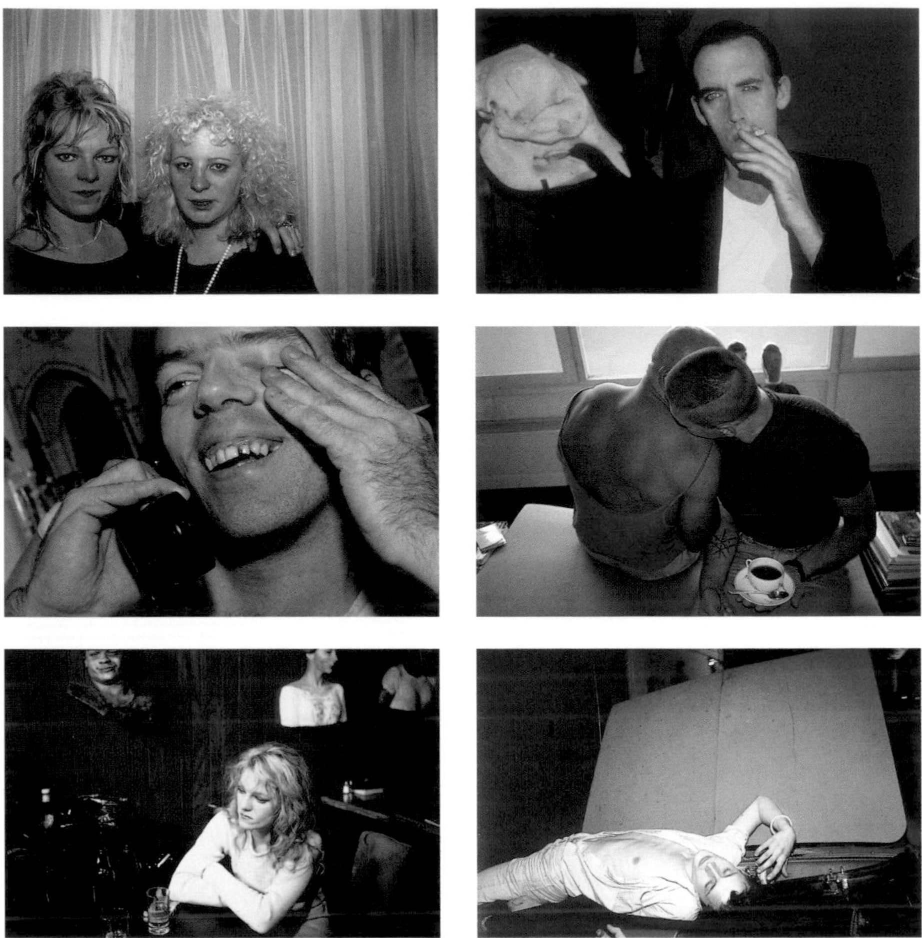

"My work comes from the snapshot," Nan Goldin says. "It's the form of photography that is most defined by love. People take them out of love, and they take them to remember—people, places, and times. They're about creating a history by recording a history. And that's exactly what my work is about." Drawing on the candid photographs of marginal Americans taken by Robert Frank (p. 109) and others, Goldin shoots diaristic photographs of her friends that explore the visual vocabulary of their poses as well as the squalid glamour of bohemian addiction. She tenderly records women looking into mirrors, girls in bathrooms and barrooms, sleeping women, battered women, empty beds, drag queens lying in bed, along with various forms of sex and sexuality.

The Ballad of Sexual Dependency is Goldin's most influential work to date—"the diary I let people read," she says. Using the amateur format of the slide show on a monumental

* ***The Ballad of Sexual Dependency***, 1976–92 (detail)
690 slides with audiotape, computer disk, and titles, dimensions variable
Purchase, with funds from The Charles Engelhard Foundation, the Mrs. Percy Uris Bequest, the Painting and Sculpture Committee, and the Photography Committee 92.127a–b

scale, Goldin created a chronicle of East Village punk bohemia through an always changing compilation of nearly seven hundred slides, accompanied by such songs as The Velvet Underground's "All Tomorrow's Parties" and, from Kurt Weill and Bertolt Brecht's *Threepenny Opera*, "The Ballad of Sexual Dependency," from which the work draws its title. Goldin began showing *The Ballad* as early as 1978 in downtown New York clubs and bars, and she continued to add to and adjust the selection of images and music until 1992.

Goldin turns her attention away from figures in interior settings to figureless landscape views in *Trees by the River, Munich*. But the absence of human presence in this color photograph speaks not so much of the untrammeled beauties of nature as it does of loss. Like the deeply emotive colors in *The Ballad*, the subtle, blurry tones of *Trees by the River* convey a sense of sad beauty. Ultimately, Goldin's photograph is not a landscape of trees and a river, but a landscape of the mind, a metaphor for memory and the passage of time.

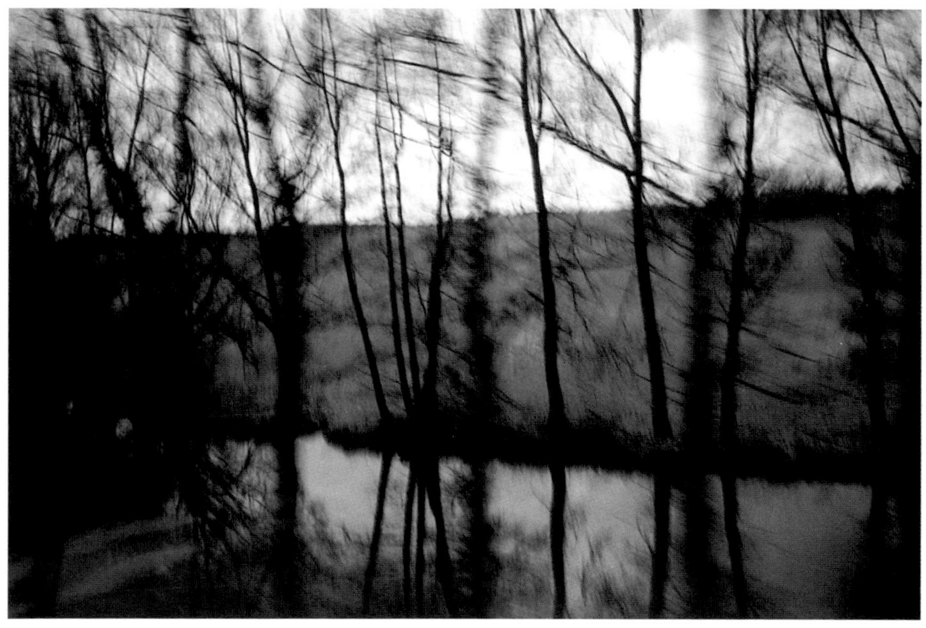

Trees by the River, Munich, 1994
Silver dye bleach print (Ilfochrome), 27 7/16 x 40 in. (69.7 x 101.6 cm)
Gift of the artist and Matthew Marks Gallery 2001.239

LEON GOLUB

b. 1922

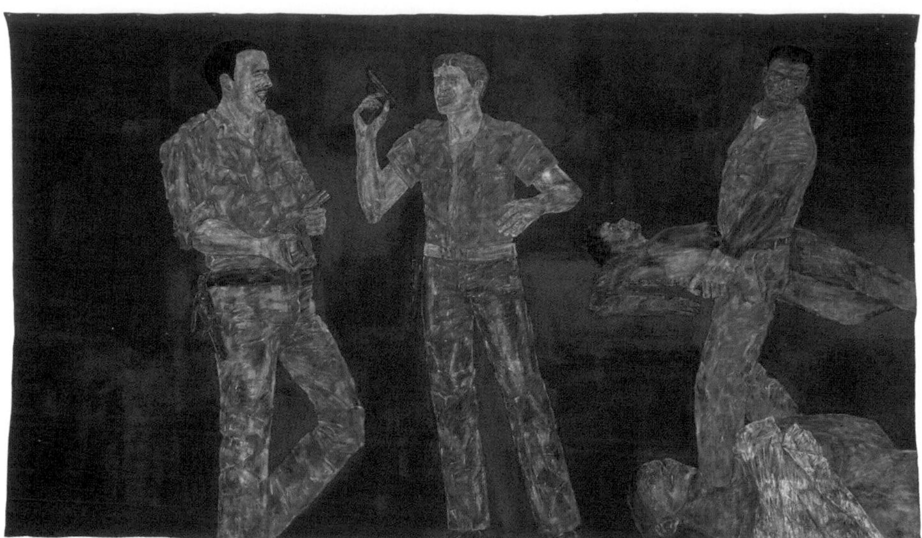

A depiction of five male figures in the aftermath of an execution, 10 feet high and more than 15 feet wide, Leon Golub's *White Squad I* is both instantly legible and physically overwhelming. For forty years, Golub's painting has been vehemently political. The poses, actions, and faces of his painted figures are based on photographs of "political criminals," all housed in an enormous archive he has compiled from newspaper and magazine photographs of scenes of terror in Latin America, China, and elsewhere.

Golub's unique working process mimics the physical violence of what he depicts: with the canvas laid on the ground, he builds up the figures in acrylic, then pours solvent on them and scrapes away until only a delicate skin of paint remains. "What you see finally," Golub explained, "is a paint film which has been in a sense 'smashed back' into the tooth of the canvas." In *White Squad I*, two men lie dead, a standing man with gloved hand straddling the body of the foreground victim. The other two men brandish the guns apparently used for the executions. The figures are flattened like cutouts against a background of unscraped mottled red, so that they evoke their sources in two-dimensional photographs. Their gestures and deeply etched grimaces—again as in photojournalism—are at once realistic and awkward. This caught-in-the-act character evokes not only the institutionalized violence captured in the original photographs, but the ease with which the camera translates reality into newsworthy images.

White Squad I, 1982
Synthetic polymer on canvas, 120 x 184 in. (304.8 x 467.4 cm)
Gift of the Eli Broad Family Foundation and purchase, with funds from the Painting and Sculpture Committee
94.67

FÉLIX GONZÁLEZ-TORRES

1957–1996

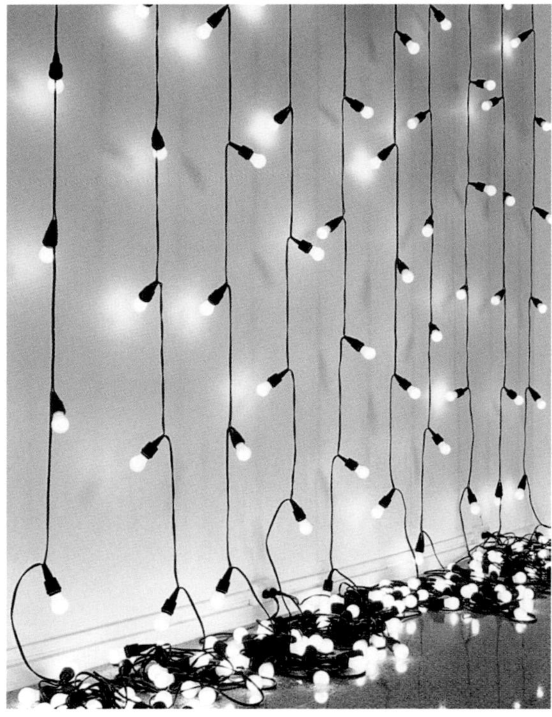

The work of Félix González-Torres, one of the most provocative and prolific artists of the early 1990s, radically questions our ideas about what it means to make a work of art, to own one, and to interpret one. *Untitled (America)* consists of twelve strings of lightbulbs, containing a total of 504 bulbs. It is typical of the artist's conception of the art work as a collaboration between the artist and the owner. *Untitled (America)* can be shown in any way the owner desires: indoors or outdoors; hanging from the ceiling, across the wall, or on the floor; as one long line, several smaller ones, or even as a big tangle of bulbs and wires in a corner. González-Torres' notion of collaboration often extended to the viewing public as well. Among other signature works, for example, were piles of candy for viewers to take and for the owner to replace at will, and stacks of paper printed with images that passersby could appropriate and use as posters.

González-Torres' open-ended works nevertheless tend to steer the viewer into thoughts of a personal or political nature. In this piece, such thought is provoked by the title. A Cuban immigrant to the United States, González-Torres subtitled many of his works "America," a sort of blank symbol that left viewers free to impose their own interpretations. Does "America" refer to the United States, or to North and South America, or just to Latin America? Does the word—and thus the art work—mean something different to someone for whom America is a destination or an ideal, rather than a point of origin? Despite the work's extreme simplicity, *Untitled (America)* allows for a complicated range of individual interpretations, and this openness to multiple meanings is crucial to an understanding of González-Torres' art.

Untitled (America), 1994–95 (detail)
12 light strings, each with 42 15-watt lightbulbs and rubber sockets, dimensions variable
Purchase, with funds from the Contemporary Painting and Sculpture Committee 96.74a–l

ARSHILE GORKY

1904–1948

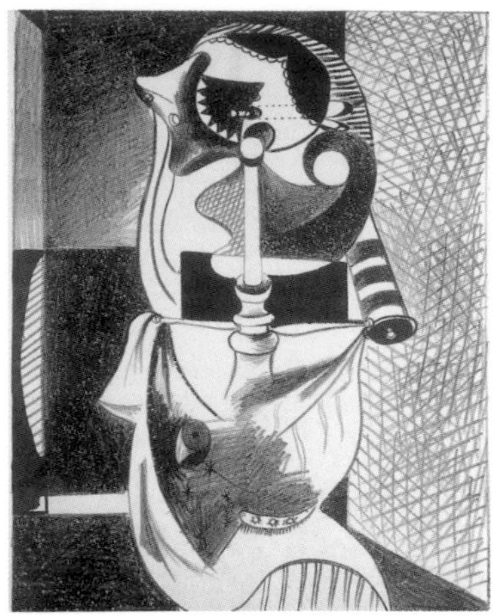

Arshile Gorky is often considered a transitional figure in the history of modernism—a bridge between Surrealism and Abstract Expressionism. In fact, he fits neatly into neither camp. He was too fond of tradition to endorse Surrealism's focus on the unconscious, too deliberate in his working methods to embrace the spontaneity of Abstract Expressionism. Yet, in a broader sense, the term transitional is apt. Gorky's art, like his persona, always seemed to be in the midst of becoming something else.

In 1920, Vosdanik Adoian left his native Armenia for America, where he changed his name. He adopted the surname of Maxim Gorky, claiming to be the Russian writer's nephew. Determined to become a great artist, he diligently mimicked the work of Cézanne and Picasso. *Mannikin* reveals Gorky's mastery of Synthetic Cubism, but with its misplaced eye and monstrous, malformed head, the lithograph also signals the growing impact of biomorphic Surrealism on Gorky's work.

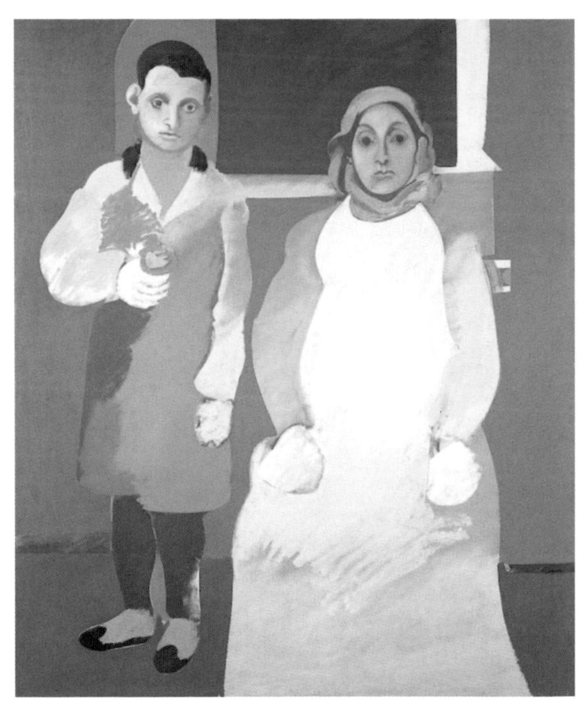

While advancing his career as an artist in America, Gorky never forgot his homeland and the trauma of the Ottoman Turks' campaign of genocide against the Armenians. In 1915, Gorky, his mother, and sister were sent by the Turks on a death march. All three survived, but Gorky's mother died four years later, never having recovered her health. He was haunted by her loss. A photograph of him at age eight, standing beside his mother,

Mannikin, 1931
Lithograph: sheet, 15 x 11 1/2 in. (38.1 x 29.2 cm);
image, 14 1/2 x 11 1/4 in. (36.8 x 28.6 cm)
Purchase 74.36

The Artist and His Mother, c. 1926–36
Oil on canvas, 60 x 50 in. (152.4 x 127 cm)
Gift of Julien Levy for Maro and Natasha Gorky in memory of their father 50.17

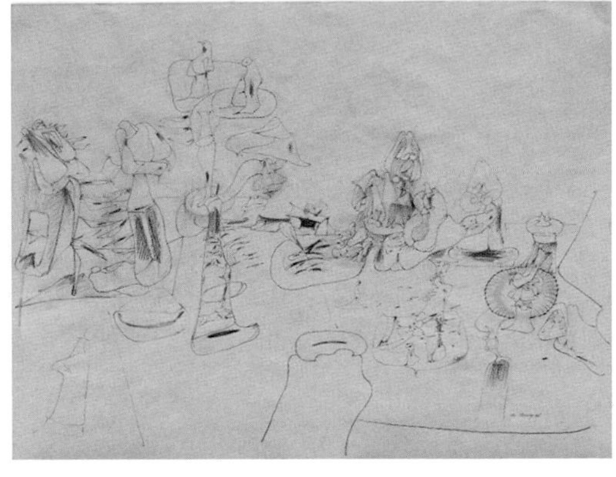

became a crucial link to his past, and Gorky made two paintings of the subject. *The Artist and His Mother*, however, is not simply a copy of a photograph, but a meditation on memory. His mother's expressive face, as well as his own, are precisely delineated, while other areas of the painting seem, like memory itself, fuzzy, unfinished, mutable.

By the early 1940s, Gorky had transformed the dry, brushy paint handling of *The Artist and His Mother* into loosely applied veils of thin paint. The sensuous, flowing biomorphism of the 1946 *Drawing* and the works in the *Betrothal* series seem to anticipate the spontaneity of Abstract Expressionism. *The Betrothal, II*, however, only appears spontaneous—Gorky actually made numerous studies for the painting, exploring the same fluid, biomorphic forms over and again. These forms, along with the title, suggest themes of sexuality and procreation. Attenuated shapes emerge from the yellowish background, as if on the verge of metamorphosis.

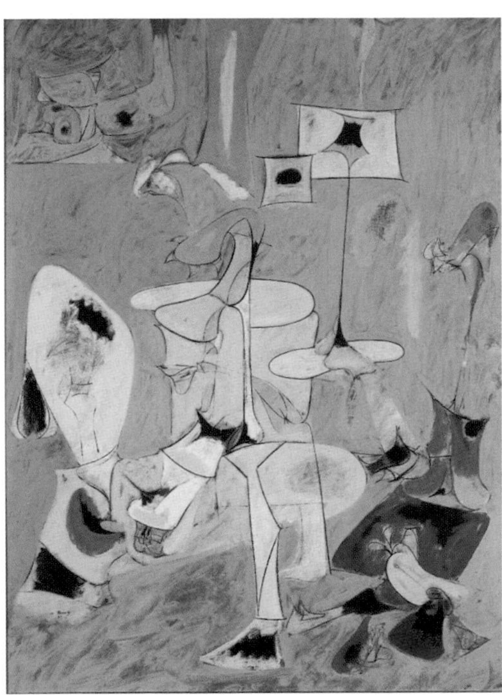

The same year he completed *The Betrothal, II* a series of tragedies began to strike Gorky, including a studio fire, a crippling car accident, and cancer. In 1948, nearing the age of forty-four, he committed suicide. His art would forever remain in a state of transition.

Drawing, 1946
Graphite and colored crayon on paper, 19 1/16 x 25 1/16 in. (48.4 x 63.7 cm)
50th Anniversary Gift of Edith and Lloyd Goodrich in honor of Juliana Force 82.48

The Betrothal, II, 1947
Oil on canvas, 50 3/4 x 38 in. (128.9 x 96.5 cm)
Purchase 50.3

ADOLPH GOTTLIEB

1903–1974

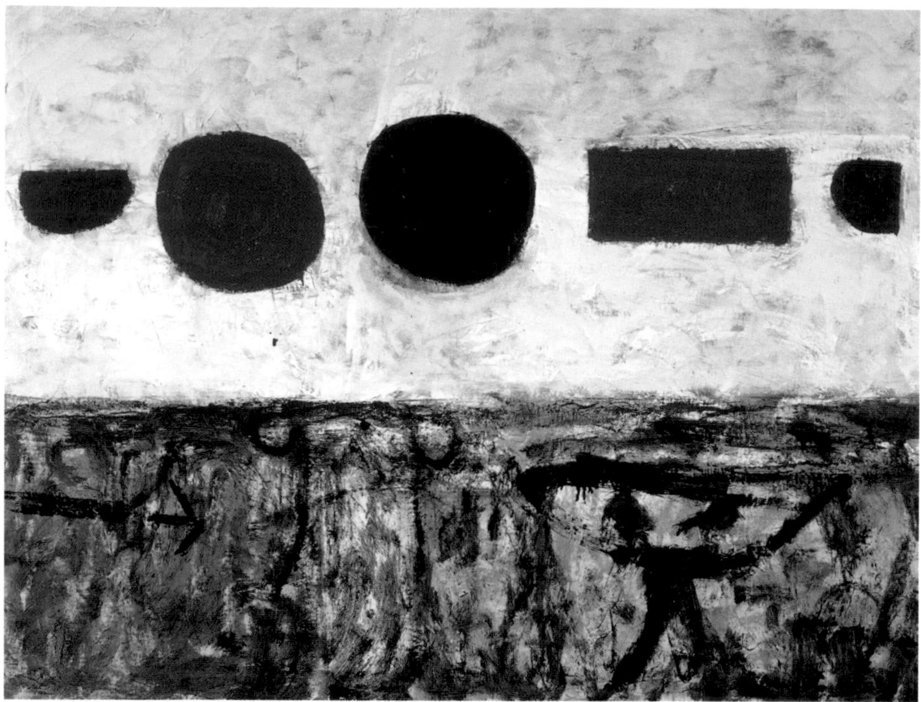

The Frozen Sounds, Number 1 is the first in a series of paintings entitled *Imaginary Landscapes*, produced by Abstract Expressionist Adolph Gottlieb between 1951 and 1957. Each painting is divided into two parts, separated by a horizontal line midway across the canvas. The densely filled bottom half is rendered in heavy, visible brushwork, while an opaque white upper half contains several geometric forms. In the lower part of this painting, a few recognizable images—an arrow and what appear to be parts of stick figures—are painted in black amid thick abstract strokes of ocher, gray, and white. In the upper part, five simple black and red shapes seem to be suspended in an expanse of white.

Some critics have interpreted Gottlieb's middle line as a horizon that divides a sky filled with suns, stars, and crescent moons from a turbulent earthly world—a world, in 1951, still reeling from the horrors and destruction of World War II and living under the cold war threat of atomic devastation. Gottlieb, however, left interpretation to the critics and put the matter more simply: "it interests me to juxtapose things that are so...unrelated and I have to find some way of establishing a relationship and of bringing them together." Indeed, much of Gottlieb's work takes as its subject the conflict and unification of opposites. In *The Frozen Sounds* we see coexisting dualities—figuration and abstraction, light and dark, earth and sky, sun and moon, and, in a more interpretative coupling, calm and chaos.

The Frozen Sounds, Number 1, 1951
Oil on canvas, 36 x 48 in. (91.4 x 121.9 cm)
Gift of Mr. and Mrs. Samuel M. Kootz 57.3

DAN GRAHAM

b. 1942

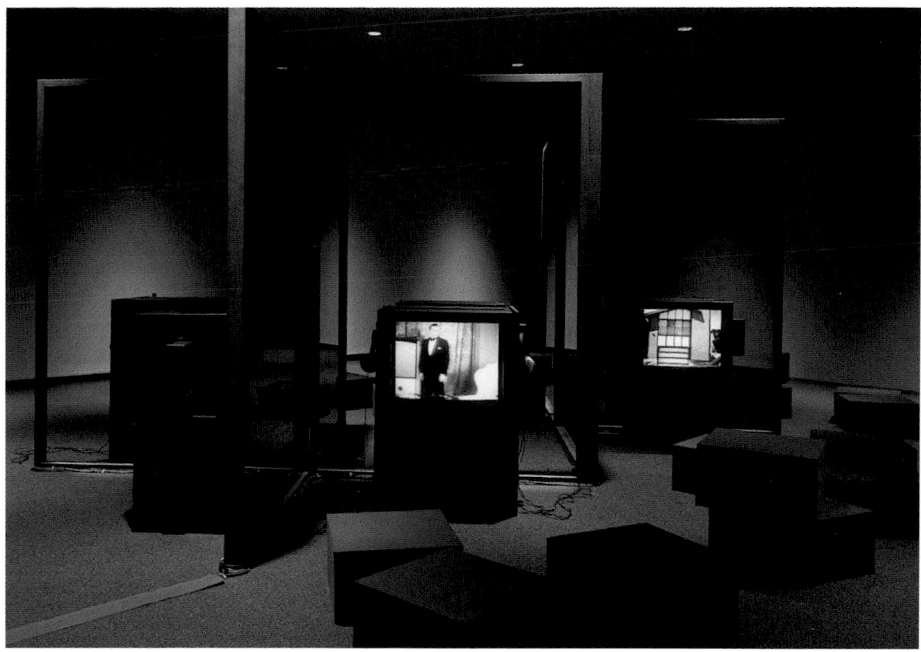

Since the 1960s, Dan Graham has used performance, video, and reflective architectural structures to explore the social nature of perception. By blurring the boundaries between public and private space, he reveals how environment affects the way we see. Video has played an important role in this enterprise since the early 1970s. In *Three Linked Cubes/Interior Design for Space Showing Videos*, Graham creates an architectural structure that is both a sculptural installation and a functional viewing space. Video monitors and seating are placed within three areas defined by five intersecting, rectilinear panels made of two-way mirrors or glass. The reflective panels allow varying degrees of visibility and reflection between one area and another. Viewers are invited to watch three programs of single-channel videotapes, some showing works by the artist, others showing popular films and cartoons, selected by the artist or curator. While watching the videotapes, each viewer can also see the other viewers and catch a glimpse of his or her own reflection. The private, often domestic experience of viewing television or video is thus transformed into a self-conscious public event.

Three Linked Cubes, like other Graham works, creates a viewing environment that replaces the familiar domestic space with a reflective architectural form. Through this process, Graham fuses the intimate experience of television viewing with the social observations taking place across the reflective planes of the architectural space.

Three Linked Cubes/Interior Design for Space Showing Videos, 1986
Wood-framed clear and two-way mirrored glass panels, approximately 96 x 280 x 80 in.
(243.8 x 711.2 x 203.2 cm), panels approximately 90 x 60 in. (228.6 x 152.4 cm) each
Gift of The Bohen Foundation and purchase, with funds from the Painting and Sculpture Committee 94.34a–r

PHILIP GUSTON

1913–1980

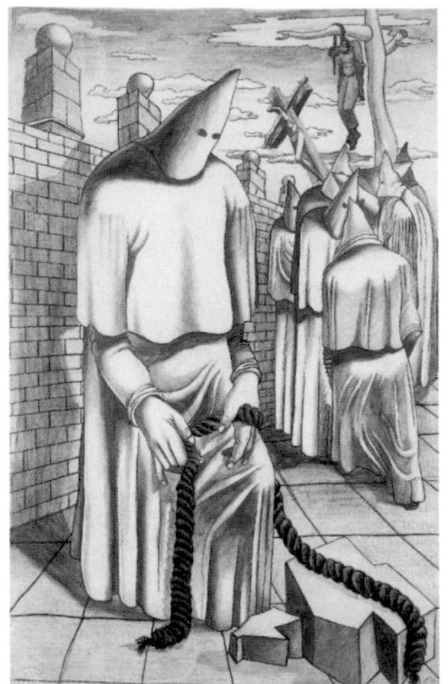

In the mid-1950s, Philip Guston earned critical acclaim for scintillating abstract paintings that crossed lyrical colors with bold, gestural brushwork. He had first received notice, however, more than twenty years earlier for figurative studies such as the small *Drawing for Conspirators*, an accomplished political allegory based on social unrest in Los Angeles. This haunting lynching scene reveals Guston's youthful integration of both historical and contemporary painting, from the monumentality of Renaissance figures to the disquieting fantasies of the Surrealists and the sociopolitical stance of the Mexican muralists.

The later *Dial*, by contrast, exemplifies the shimmering networks of luminous color that were the hallmark of Guston's groundbreaking abstractions. The work's richly textured surfaces offer a nuanced record of Guston's creative process—a mélange of assured gestures and tentative touches, spontaneous choices, and carefully reworked passages. The subtly modulated pastel hues on the edges of the canvas deepen toward the center into more resolute juxtapositions; similarly, the translucent layers of sensuous brushwork congeal at center into a dense, quivering accumulation of painted matter. At once torrid and serene, *Dial* is one of Guston's most accomplished abstractions and marks his affinity with Abstract Expressionist painters seeking to express emotional states without reference to recognizable subjects. Yet *Dial* also reveals the difficulty of creating pure abstractions, for it bears vague suggestions of organic forms and sublime sensations—an impenetrable wood, a fog heavy with vapor, or the flickering glints of sunlight on water.

Drawing for Conspirators, 1930
Graphite, ink, colored pencil, and crayon on paper, 22 1/2 x 14 1/2 in. (57.2 x 36.8 cm) irregular
Purchase, with funds from The Hearst Corporation and The Norman and Rosita Winston Foundation, Inc. 82.20

Dial, 1956
Oil on canvas, 72 x 76 in. (182.9 x 193 cm)
Purchase 56.44

PETER HALLEY

b. 1953

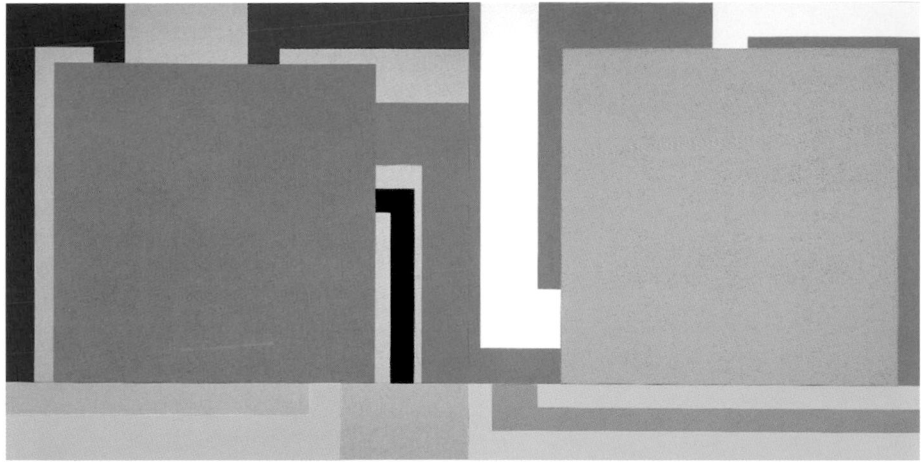

Peter Halley seems, at first glance, to have inherited the legacy of geometric abstractionists such as Burgoyne Diller and Fritz Glarner (pp. 91, 116), who advanced modernist ideas in America in the 1930s and 1940s. Halley's concerns, however, lie elsewhere. He prefers to think of his paintings not as abstractions, strictly speaking, but as representations of the connective arrangements of urban society. Having spent much of his life in New York City, he was impressed by "the functional role that geometry served in a giant city of that sort, the role that geometry had in housing and in moving people, in commerce, in the control of everyday life. I began to see the city as something of a geometric machine in which geometry was the most efficient means of moving people and things."

Halley calls the main panels in his large paintings "cells." In *The Acid Test*, two cells with stuccolike surfaces of orange and blue are superimposed on a network of smoother conduit forms. Painted in bright, often Day-Glo colors in startling, quivering juxtapositions, Halley's compositions are also reminiscent of the iconography of the information age—electronic systems, flowcharts, and computer software diagrams. The overlaps and interruptions of his circuit-grids evoke the systems and infrastructures that arrange and connect—but also isolate—people in contemporary society.

The Acid Test, 1991–92
Synthetic polymer, polymer emulsion, and fluorescent paint on canvas, 4 parts,
90 1/8 x 182 5/16 in. (228.9 x 463.1 cm) overall
Purchase, with funds from the Louis and Bessie Adler Foundation, Inc. and the Painting and Sculpture Committee
92.28a–d

JANE HAMMOND

b. 1950

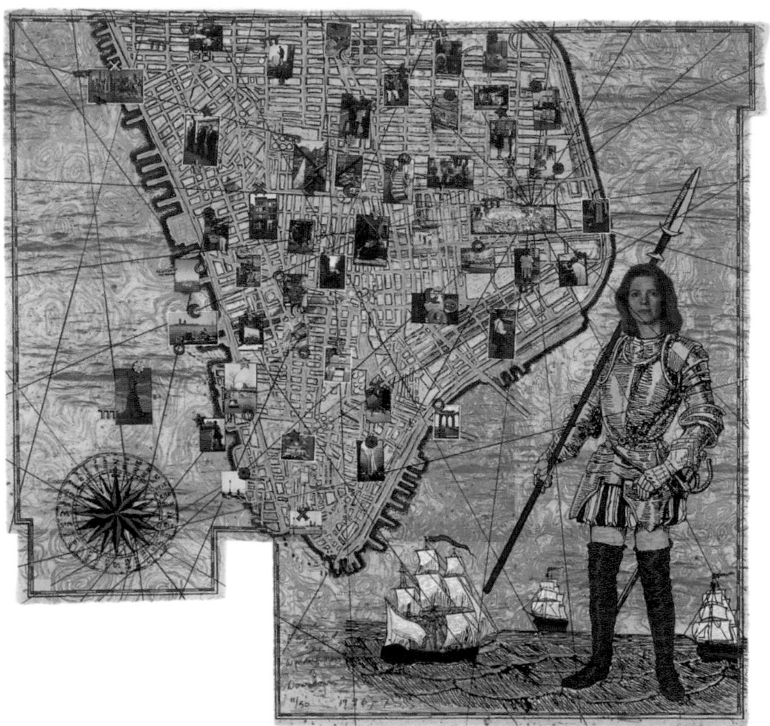

In 1993, Jane Hammond asked the poet John Ashbery to provide a list of titles that would serve as catalysts for future works of art. He complied with forty-four potential titles, including "The Wonderfulness of Downtown." To Hammond, the phrase suggested a self-portrait in the guise of a triumphant conquistador posing before a map of Lower Manhattan.

"The Wonderfulness of Downtown" recalls European maps of the New World and its treasures: tall ships sail in the harbor; at lower left, an old-fashioned compass with radiating lines serves as a navigational aid. But the print also presents a contemporary world. Snapshots of the artist's neighborhood—her home, grocery store, dry cleaners—are displayed like points of interest in a tourist's guide, though their placements do not necessarily correspond to their actual locations.

Hammond's fascination with mapmaking dates back to her childhood, when she marked off 50 square feet of land and methodically attempted to identify and classify everything she found there. The exercise may have been futile, but it taught Hammond that no one systematic analysis can describe every feature of a landscape. In her map of downtown Manhattan, she provides detailed images of certain selected places, but cannot hope to capture a teeming city, always in flux. The wonderfulness of New York is not only a physical experience, but also an emotional one, beyond the reaches of mapmaking.

"The Wonderfulness of Downtown", 1996–97
Color lithograph, screenprint, and collage: sheet and image, 59 x 62 1/2 in. (149.9 x 158.8 cm) irregular
Purchase, with funds from the Print Committee 97.109.5

DAVID HAMMONS

b. 1943

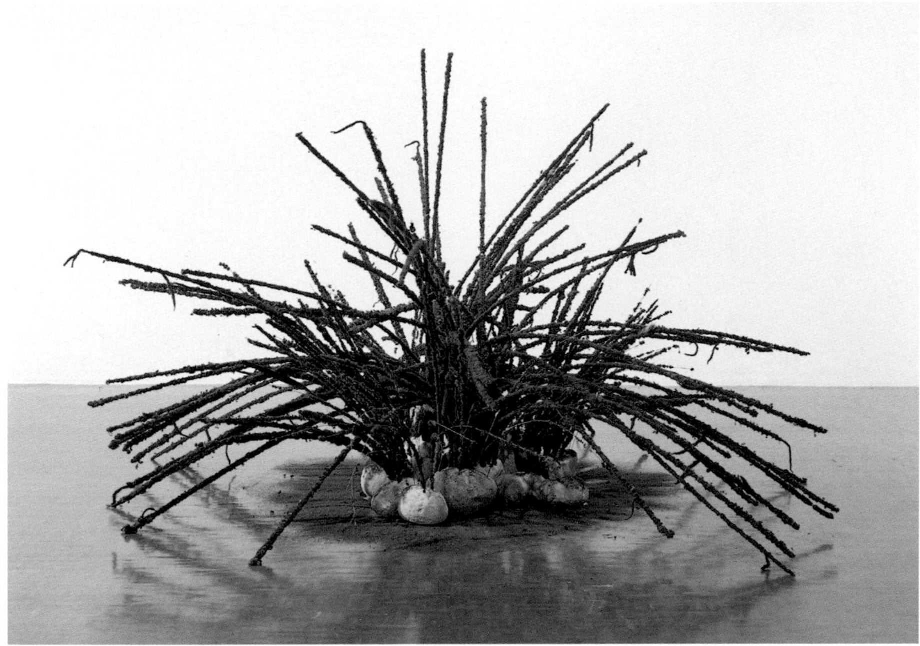

David Hammons finds inspiration in the streets and everyday life of his Harlem community, where he gathers ordinary, discarded, or even ephemeral materials and uses them in performance works or transforms them into sculptures. Hair trimmings, empty liquor bottles, fried chicken wings, barbecued ribs, grease, dirt, snow, paper bags, inner tubes, record fragments, bottle caps, coal, fan blades, shovels, and chains have all at one time or another found a place in his art. Hammons' evocative use of everyday materials echoes the work of artists such as Picasso and Joseph Cornell (p. 79) and alludes as well to vernacular African-American traditions of making art out of whatever is at hand.

Strange things happen when ordinary materials not usually found together are combined. In Hammons' untitled work, we are confronted with an array of spiky tendrils erupting out of a base of smooth stones. This plantlike apparition is composed of bits of kinky black hair attached to long metal wires. Pieces of hair inevitably fall beneath and around the work, echoing natural processes of change and decay. Hardly a comforting bouquet, this work combines the organic and inorganic, plant and animal, to evoke a surreal, otherworldly life-form. Like much of Hammons' art, the piece creates an uncanny sensation of the strangeness that lies just below the surface of the familiar.

Untitled, 1992
Copper, wire, hair, stone, fabric, and thread, 60 in. (152.4 cm) height
Purchase, with funds from the Mrs. Percy Uris Bequest and the Painting and Sculpture Committee 92.128a–u

DUANE HANSON
1925–1996

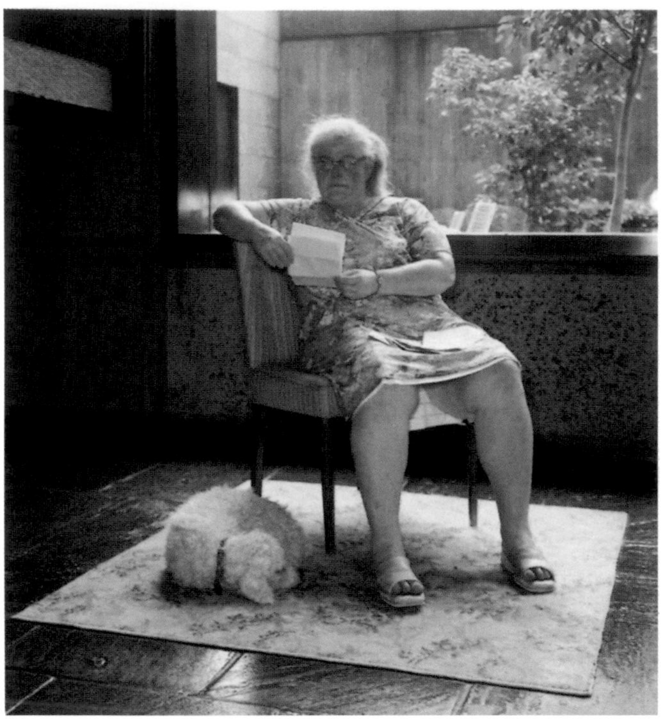

From tourists to construction workers to museum security guards, Duane Hanson's lifelike sculptures present a cross-section of American society. Hanson often spent as long as a year on a single figure—locating models, making polyvinyl casts directly from their bodies (a method he developed in 1967), assembling and painting the casts, and finally outfitting the sculptures with the appropriate attire and accessories. Despite the extreme realism of the figures, they are not necessarily likenesses of specific people. Hanson often took body parts from one model's cast and incorporated them into another, or gave the same figure different hair, skin, and clothing to create another character. The pile of letters in *Woman with Dog*, for example, is addressed to a Minnie Johnson in Florida, though the model for the work was someone else who lived near Hanson's Florida studio.

Hanson's works are therefore not portraits of actual people in their environments, but realistic fictions that illuminate the "everyday types of things that people do," which for Hanson constituted "the common denominator" that runs through all levels of American society. When seen in a museum context, these works effect a kind of superrealism that forcibly focuses our attention on the psychological temperaments and emotions of otherwise "invisible" Americans. As Hanson wrote about *Woman with Dog*, "I wanted a credible, unpretentious working class type of woman at mail time enjoying the fellowship of a friendly letter and her pet dog."

Woman with Dog, 1977
Cast polyvinyl, polychromed in acrylic, with cloth and hair, 46 x 48 x 51 1/2 in.
(116.8 x 121.9 x 130.8 cm) overall
Purchase, with funds from Frances and Sydney Lewis 78.6

KEITH HARING
1958–1990

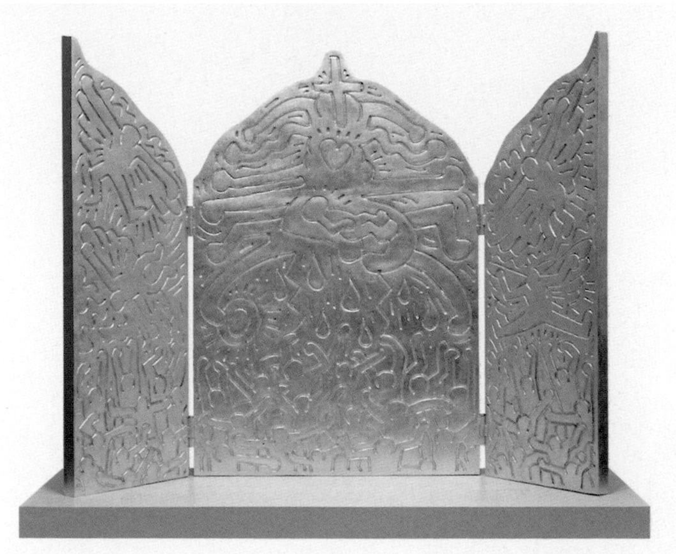

Keith Haring's art began on the streets of New York, where he used subway billboards and sidewalks as surfaces for brightly colored, cartoonlike drawings. Haring saw an affinity between the fluidity of the line in subway graffiti and his own drawing style: "It seemed like it was coming from the same generation and place I was coming from." His first works were drawn with chalk on empty black advertisement panels in the subway, usually before a watchful public, who always wanted to know what the drawings meant. Because the process did not allow for mistakes, Haring evolved a quick, free-flowing, and spontaneous style that was to become his signature.

The same style and the same integration of art and street life characterizes Haring's found-object sculptures, where he used detritus—refrigerator doors, discarded cribs, stuffed animals—as surfaces to paint and draw on. Haring also made fully independent sculptures such as *Altar Piece*, and they too bear the marks of his style. This cast bronze work, issued in an edition of nine, consists of a center panel flanked by two wings, the whole covered in gold leaf. It was Haring's friend Sam Havadtoy, an interior designer, who suggested the altarpiece format when Haring asked for advice about covering up a fireplace in his new apartment. Instead of a brush, Haring used a loop knife to carve free lines into clay, and the images that emerged were religious, in keeping with the tripartite form of a medieval altarpiece: angels with wings, an all-encompassing massive Christ figure at the top of the central panel with a cross and heart, arms embracing a baby, tears falling from Christ onto a crowd of figures raising their arms up toward heaven. One side panel represents a fallen angel, while the other depicts the resurrection of Christ. *Altar Piece* is Haring's final work; it was cast in bronze after his death.

Altar Piece, 1990
Bronze with gold leaf, 59 1/2 x 70 7/8 x 16 3/4 in.
(151.1 x 180 x 42.6 cm) overall
Gift of Yoko Ono and Sam Havadtoy 96.186a–g

MARSDEN HARTLEY

1877–1943

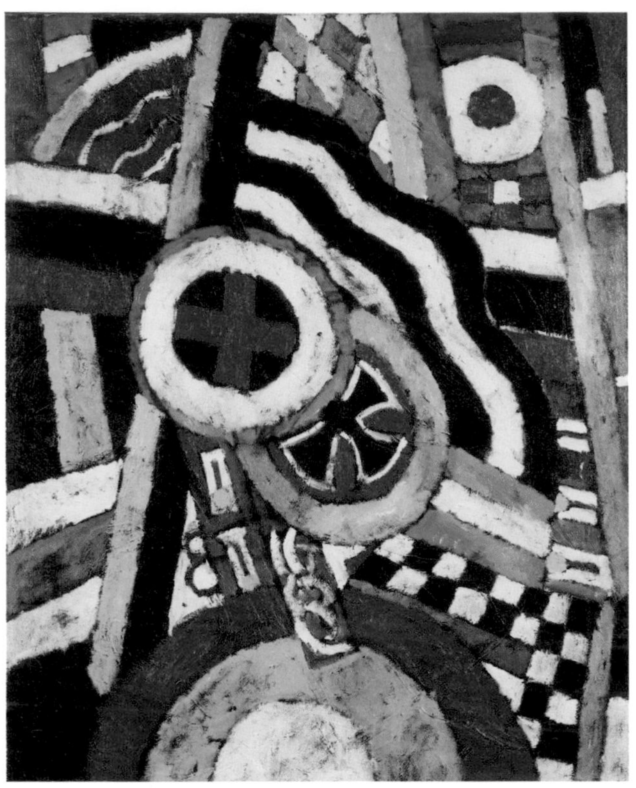

In his life and his art, Maine native Marsden Hartley was a perpetual wanderer: he never remained in one place for long, never settled on a particular style. In Europe, just before World War I, he became a pioneering American modernist, creating highly personal, Cubist-influenced paintings. Although he later rejected the abstraction of these early works, his art remained essentially subjective—even more so late in life, when he returned to Maine. Equally consistent was his use of rough-textured brushwork as an expressive tool.

In 1912, Hartley sailed for Europe, settling first in Paris and, later, in Berlin. Life in the imperial German capital—the intensity of the crowds, the constant spectacle of military pageantry—thrilled him, and he began to incorporate military imagery into his paintings. The outbreak of World War I deeply troubled him, and he was devastated by the death of Karl von Freyburg, a young officer who for Hartley embodied the classical ideal of masculine beauty and youth. A month later, in tribute to von Freyburg and his world, Hartley began a series of abstract paintings on German military themes—*War Motifs*, as he called them—which reflected his simultaneous repulsion and fascination with the war. Such works as *Painting, Number 5* integrate flags, the Iron Cross, and epaulettes through a pictorial vocabulary of coarse brushwork, dramatic colors, and tightly knit patterns.

Painting, Number 5, 1914–15
Oil on canvas, 39 1/2 x 31 3/4 in. (100.3 x 80.6 cm)
Gift of an anonymous donor 58.65

MARSDEN HARTLEY

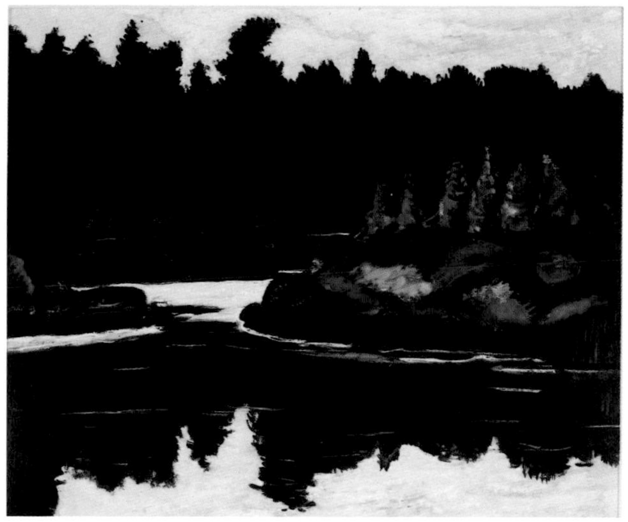

Hartley exhibited his *War Motif* paintings shortly after he returned to New York in December 1915, but they received a lukewarm reception, in part due to their military imagery. He spent the next decade and a half on the move—between New York, New Mexico, Massachusetts, Bermuda, New Hampshire, Mexico, France, and Germany. During these peripatetic years, his work, almost exclusively landscapes and still lifes, grew increasingly dramatic and emotionally expressive. In 1937, he resettled in Maine, determined to become the state's "first painter."

Works such as *Robin Hood Cove, Georgetown, Maine* describe the rugged natural simplicity Hartley associated with Maine. The palette is softer than in earlier works, and the mood more tranquil, perhaps reflecting his belief that his birthplace was the source of his "private strength, both spiritually and aesthetically." In *Robin Hood Cove*, as well as in the charcoal drawing *The Lighthouse, #1*, Hartley sacrificed elegance and the sophisticated modernism he once practiced for the expressiveness of mood and emotion. His reduction of forms into massive, almost carved shapes projects a sense of solemn grandeur. In capturing what he perceived as the archaic severity and elemental strength of Maine, Hartley's late landscapes convey the sense of spiritual renewal he found when, after decades of traveling, he returned to his roots.

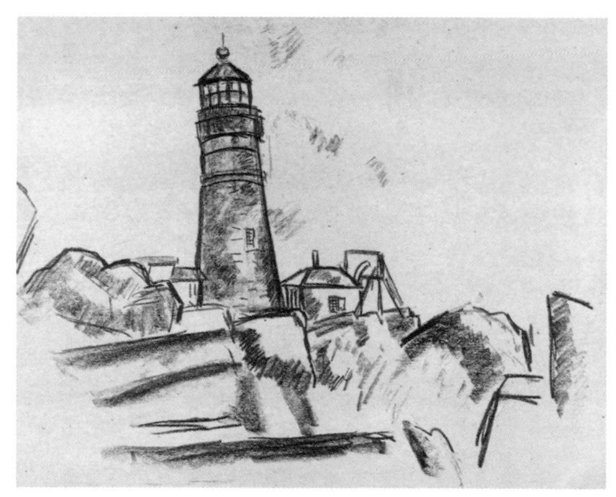

Robin Hood Cove, Georgetown, Maine, 1938
Oil on board, 21 3/4 x 25 7/8 in. (55.3 x 65.7 cm)
50th Anniversary Gift of Ione Walker in memory of her husband, Hudson D. Walker 87.63

The Lighthouse, #1, 1941
Charcoal on cardboard, 21 15/16 x 27 13/16 in. (55.7 x 70.6 cm)
Charles Simon Bequest 96.60.29

TIM HAWKINSON

b. 1960

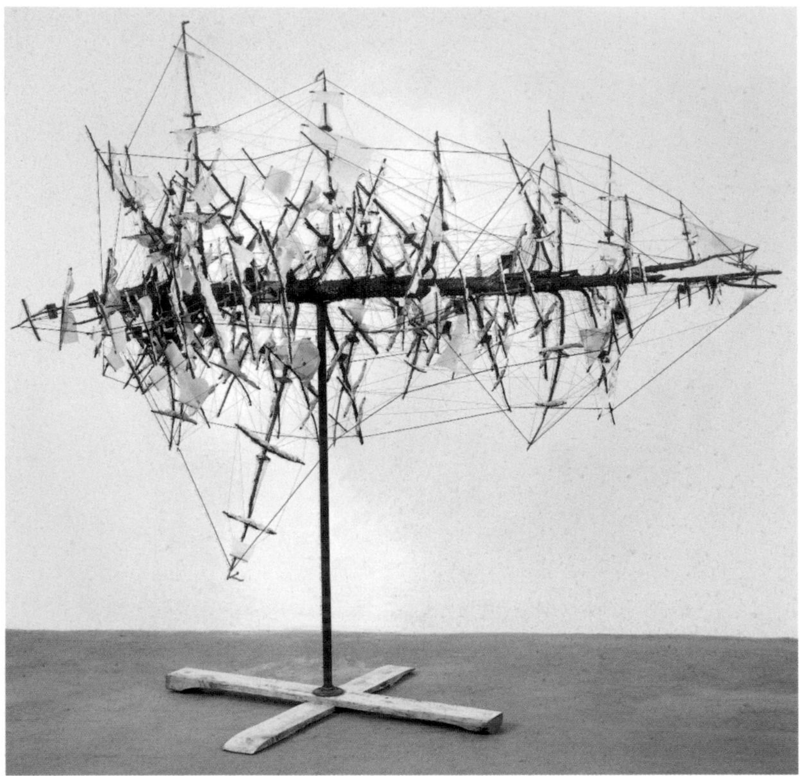

Tim Hawkinson's *Das Tannenboot* is a visual pun derived by combining the German word for Christmas tree (*Tannenbaum*) with that for boat (*Boot*). *Das Tannenboot* is a Christmas tree, stripped of its needles, turned on its side, and then outfitted with little sails and rigging. The resulting work defies easy description. It is delicate, strangely beautiful, and yet—with its mass of barren branches and sails like dead leaves—somewhat melancholy. Laid out horizontally, the conical symmetry of the fir tree creates a mirror effect above and below the stem that suggests a fantastically inefficient flotilla sailing across a reflective body of water; or else just a useless structure that is nearly all sail and no boat. Yet despite these illusionistic or metaphorical possibilities, the work is absolutely literal: in the end, *Das Tannenboot* is exactly what it says it is—a tree-boat.

Hawkinson's creative twisting of language suggests affinities with such Conceptual artists as Joseph Kosuth, Edward Ruscha, and Lawrence Weiner (pp. 169, 265, 320). Hawkinson's art, however, also has a strong and sometimes extravagant visual presence, as is apparent in *Das Tannenboot*. This combination of Conceptual linguistic ploys and high-powered aesthetic effects is typical of much West Coast art of the past two decades, including the work of Sally Elesby and Mike Kelley (pp. 102, 162).

Das Tannenboot, 1994
Christmas tree, fabric, elastic, string, and metal, 66 x 70 x 43 in. (167.6 x 177.8 x 109.2 cm)
Gift of Eileen and Peter Norton 96.49

MARY HEILMANN

b. 1940

Mary Heilmann came to New York in 1974, "the year," she says, that "painting died." Her own work responded to the prevailing influences of Minimalism and Conceptualism. "My early paintings made use of very pure, non-inflected color and placed no emphasis on emotional content," she explained. They were "made with one move, one idea." She also drew freely on such modernist masters as Josef Albers (p. 29), Piet Mondrian, and Kasimir Malevich, all abstractionists who explored the expressive possibilities inherent in color and composition.

Big Bill, created with an unusual combination of tempera and synthetic polymer, reveals Heilmann's engagement with the way paint lies on the surface, with the speed and fluency possible with varying brushwork, and with the emotional resonance of color. Above all, *Big Bill* explores the psychological effects of slightly skewing geometric forms, of keeping them just fractionally off-balance. Heilmann, who originally studied pottery, continues to think like an object-maker: "When I make a painting, I'm like a kid stacking blocks; I push the shapes around in my mind....I was a potter first, and that's an activity that also depends upon geometry." Heilmann's paintings, however, for all these self-described constraints, convey a very painterly sense of freedom.

Big Bill, 1987
Tempera and synthetic polymer on canvas, 43 3/16 x 40 3/16 in. (109.7 x 102.1 cm)
Gift of Evelyn Meyers 92.26

MICHAEL HEIZER

b. 1944

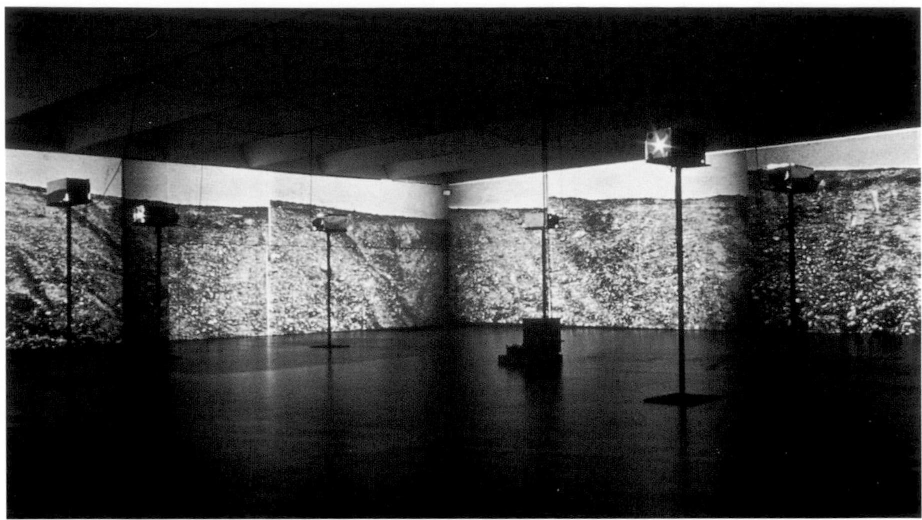

In 1970, in a Munich suburb, Michael Heizer created *Munich Depression*, a 16-foot-deep void with gently sloping sides that reached 100 feet in diameter. It was part of a group of early outdoor sculptures dealing with negative space. Viewers experienced the work in two ways: from a distance, where it appeared to interrupt the flat surface of the ground; and from within, where, having walked down its sides, they saw not only the gravel and earth interior but a distinct horizon line and the open sky above. After completing *Munich Depression*, Heizer made the photographic projection installation *Actual Size: Munich Rotary*, a 360-degree view of *Munich Depression* projected from large photographic glass plates made from Heizer's own negatives and screened through six custom-made projectors.

Like *Munich Depression*, Heizer's granular, black-and-white, actual-size projections of the gravel and earth sides, horizon, and ribbon of sky explore how optical perception is determined by location. The gallery, which normally allows us an exterior view of sculptures, here defines a negative space that encloses us in an interior. During the 1960s and 1970s, many Land artists used photography to document their outdoor work. By contrast, *Actual Size: Munich Rotary* both documents *Munich Depression* three-dimensionally, as a projective space, and creates a parallel, independent work. Yet there is an inherent distortion in the photographic recording process, which renders precise re-presentation impossible. In the tension between the real space of *Munich Depression* and the photographic space of *Actual Size: Munich Rotary*, Heizer makes visible the fact that reality lies somewhere between what we observe and what we know.

Actual Size: Munich Rotary, 1970
6 steel projectors designed by Marit Ambats, 6 black-and-white glass photographic slides, and 6 steel pipes with wood platforms, and steel bases, dimensions variable
Gift of Virginia Dwan 96.137a–jj

ROBERT HENRI

1865–1929

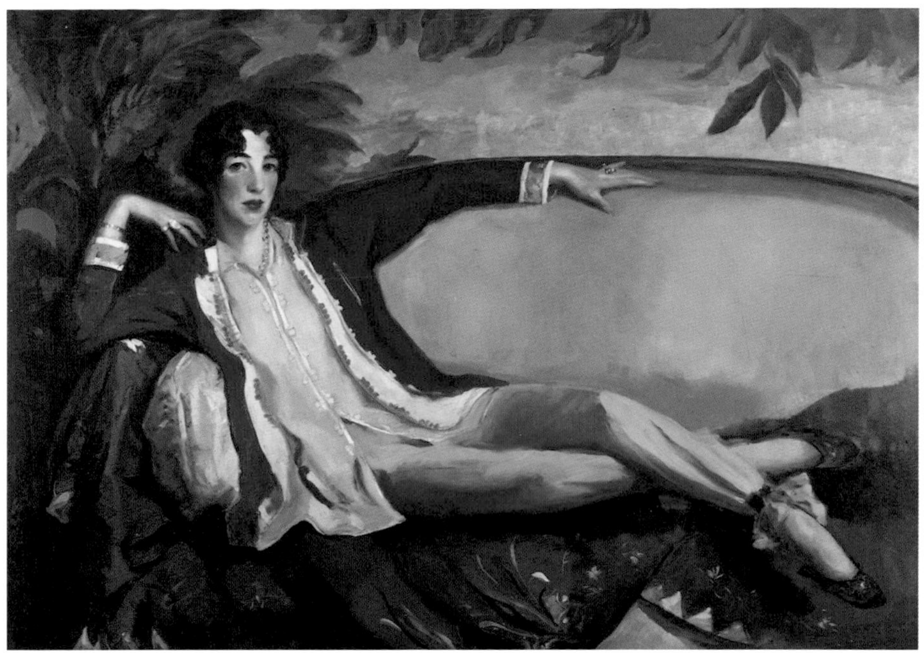

Gertrude Vanderbilt Whitney, founder of the Whitney Museum, commissioned this portrait in 1916 from Robert Henri, leader of the urban realists who had shocked the New York art world barely a decade earlier with their images of unremarkable people and commonplace city life (p. 287). By 1916, Mrs. Whitney, a professional sculptor, was an active patron of American artists, and the Whitney Studio Club in Greenwich Village, precursor of the Museum, was a lively center for the support and exhibition of new American art.

When Henri's portrait was finished, Mrs. Whitney's husband, Harry Payne Whitney, refused to allow her to hang it in their Fifth Avenue home. He didn't want his friends to see a picture of his wife, as he put it, "in pants." Mrs. Whitney's attire and self-possessed demeanor were highly unusual for a well-bred woman of her day. In this painting, Henri transformed the traditional genre of a recumbent female—usually a nude courtesan or the goddess Venus—into a portrait of the quintessential "modern" woman, dressed in elegant silk lounging pajamas, her hair bobbed, and her arms and legs casually arranged in an open, free-spirited pose. Fittingly, the portrait was never displayed in the Whitneys' opulent town house; Mrs. Whitney had it hung in her Greenwich Village studio, which in 1931 became the first home of the Whitney Museum.

Gertrude Vanderbilt Whitney, 1916
Oil on canvas, 50 x 72 in. (127 x 182.9 cm)
Gift of Flora Whitney Miller 86.70.3

EVA HESSE

1936–1970

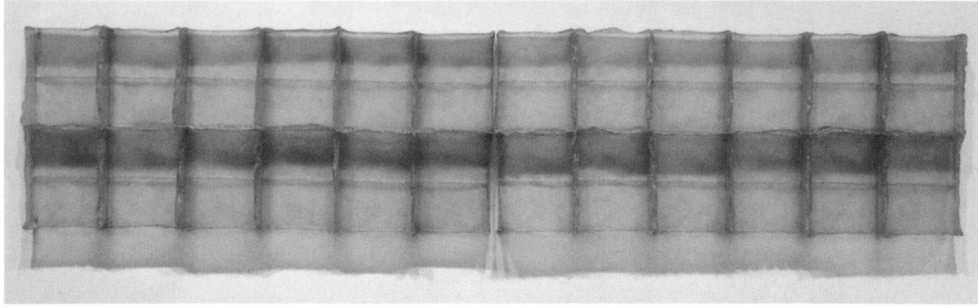

Although Eva Hesse employed the seriality of Minimalism in her sculptures of the 1960s, her works, unlike the reductive abstractions of Minimalism (p. 30), take the human body as a point of departure. Hesse used nontraditional art materials—pliable and unstable substances such as latex, cheesecloth, rope, and resin—to create sculptures that resemble living organisms with translucent, skinlike surfaces. The unstructured nature and subtle tactility of her work is in part a reaction against the industrial look and rigorous modularity of Minimalism, which she said reminded her of the concentration camps of World War II. Born in Germany to Jewish parents, Hesse had fled from the Nazis with her family when she was three years old.

Sans II was originally a five-part sculpture that stretched 35 feet across when it was first exhibited in 1968. Each of the five traylike segments was then sold separately, though the Whitney Museum now has two of them in the Permanent Collection. Hesse applied no decorative color to *Sans II*—the beige and yellow tones are natural to the fiberglass and resin. As she explained, "Color is whatever comes out of a material and keeps it what it is."

Untitled (Rope Piece), a slightly later work, at first seems relatively chaotic. But the configuration was made to hang from precisely thirteen points on the wall and ceiling, and is fixed where the ropes are glued together with latex. While the work was in progress, Hesse described it as "very ordered," and she was uncertain whether to "make it more structured...or leave it changeable." The resulting configuration of dangling and looping ropes manages to combine structure with chaos. "Chaos," Hesse said, "can be structured as non-chaos. That we know from Jackson Pollock" (p. 242).

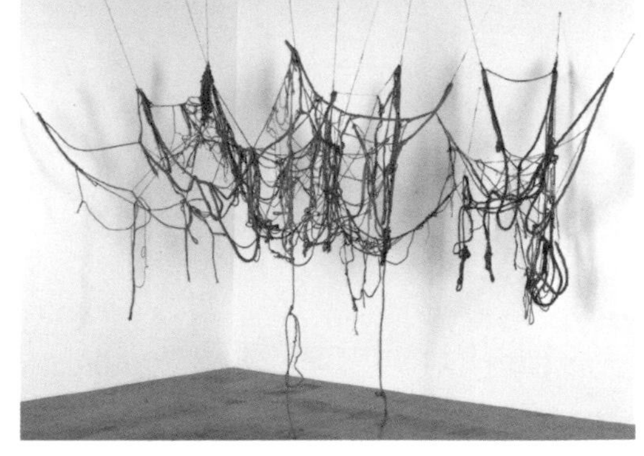

Sans II, 1968
Polyester resin and fiberglass, 38 x 170 3/4 x 6 1/8 in. (96.5 x 433.7 x 15.6 cm)
Purchase, with funds from Ethelyn and Lester J. Honig and the Albert A. List Family 69.105

Untitled (Rope Piece), 1969–70
Latex over rope, string, and wire, dimensions variable
Purchase, with funds from Eli and Edythe L. Broad, the Mrs. Percy Uris Purchase Fund, and the Painting and Sculpture Committee 88.17a–b

GARY HILL

b. 1951

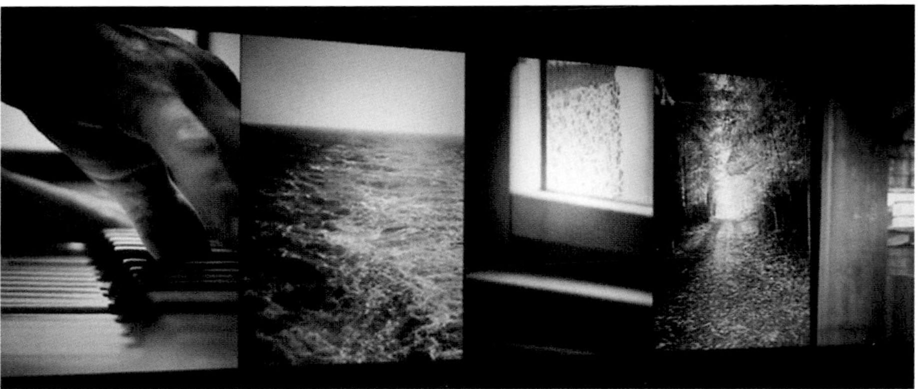

Since his first experiments with video in the mid-1970s, Gary Hill has used the time-based, feedback properties of the medium to explore the nature of perception. In *Circular Breathing*, a series of large black-and-white images appears sequentially, from left to right, across a wall of the gallery, in five sections. The continually changing sequences—for example, hands playing the piano, a close-up of a young girl reading, the wake of a boat in the sea, the edge of a window—all suggest fragments of narrative. As each successive image appears, its speed, and the speed of its accompanying sound—such as the turning of a page, a phrase of Erik Satie's piano music, the chopping of wood—are "shared" with the previous ones in a gradual process of slowed-down action and sound. Eventually, all five images reach an almost photographic stillness and the sound nearly grinds to a halt. As soon as the five images are on the screens, the one on the right slides off, and the others follow suit until we are confronted with five blank screens. The first image and its sound then reemerge from the left at original speed, and the process resumes, creating a continuous loop in space and time.

The reading of the images from left to right follows the structure of Western reading and writing. In each of the sequences, a swift action in the first image—the turning of a page or the emphatic inscription of a period at the end of a sentence—triggers the appearance of the rest of the sequence. The images, even as they slow down, begin to flicker rapidly in a strobe effect, accompanied by a loud, agitated sound. An obscure narrative appears to build, but the sequences yield no logic, and the images slide across our vision like half-remembered fragments of a dream. The viewer's focus is shifted from the habitual linearity that compels a literal meaning to the deep perceptual questioning that lies at the heart of all Gary Hill's work.

Circular Breathing, 1994
Single-channel video and sound installation: 5 color video projectors, laserdisc player, computer-controlled video switcher, dimensions variable
Promised gift of Pamela and Richard Kramlich P.95.3a–q

LEWIS HINE

1874–1940

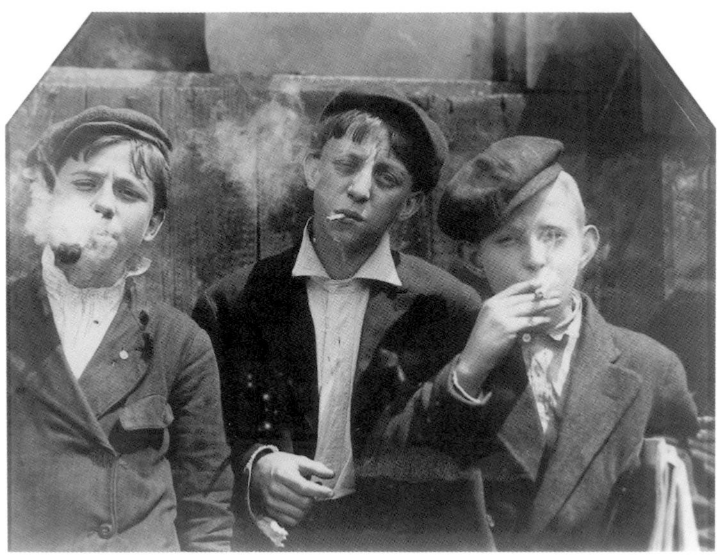

Lewis Hine championed humanist ideals in his chronicles of ordinary life. A schoolteacher with a background in sociology, around 1904 he began to photograph immigrants recently arrived on Ellis Island in New York Harbor. Hine was a pioneer in employing photography in the interest of social reform, and his images provide a compassionate look at the often maligned and unwelcome newcomers. These photographs, along with Hine's portrayals of the impoverished American working class or Europeans made destitute by World War I, are landmarks in the history of documentary photography.

Newsies at Skeeter Branch, St. Louis, Missouri is part of Hine's most influential series of photographs, made while on staff at the National Child Labor Committee from 1908 to 1918. Hine took more than five thousand photographs of children on the street or at work in factories, mills, mines, and canneries. The images were published in newspapers and pamphlets, alongside articles advocating labor reform or with detailed captions recording names, locations, and dates. With their wrenching visions of exploited children and lost innocence, these photographs served as powerful weapons in the battle for stricter child labor laws.

In *Newsies at Skeeter Branch*, three precocious newspaper boys pose before the camera, in a frontal composition characteristic of Hine's work. Cockily gazing into the lens with cigarettes in their mouths, the boys show a street savvy unsuited to their young years. As a group in the Child Labor series, the newspaper boy pictures draw attention to the hazards of the work—the children move in city traffic, work late hours, or sell newspapers in pubs and brothels. Yet, as in this photograph, there is also a celebratory tone, as Hine captures the boys' dignity and vitality of spirit. "I wanted to show the things that had to be corrected," he noted, and "I wanted to show the things that had to be appreciated."

Newsies at Skeeter Branch, St. Louis, Missouri, c. 1910
Gelatin silver print, 3 5/16 x 4 5/16 in. (8.4 x 11 cm)
Gift of Barbara Schwartz in memory of Eugene Schwartz 98.77.1

JENNY HOLZER

b. 1950

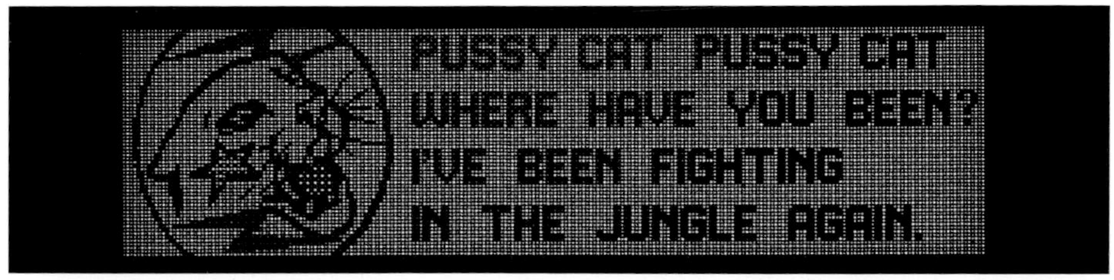

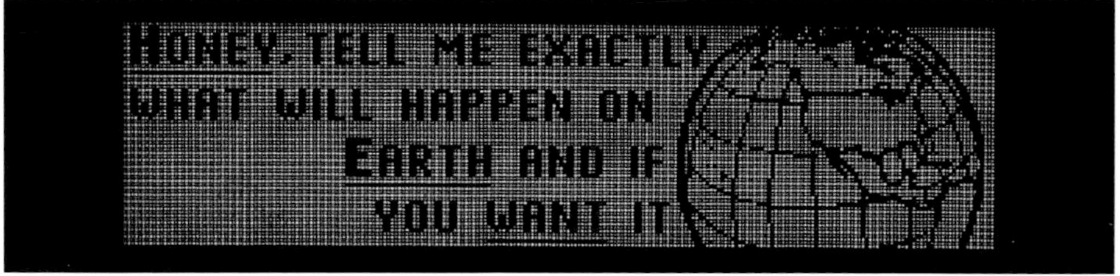

Like a number of artists who emerged during the 1980s, including Barbara Kruger, Louise Lawler, Martha Rosler, and Cindy Sherman (pp. 171, 175, 260, 278), Jenny Holzer deploys the codes of mass media to challenge the politics of representation—the verbal and pictorial signs that define gender, sexuality, and class. For Holzer, "art is an instrument of social transformation." Her strident yet poetic messages often exploit modern technology, such as LED signs—the electronic signs that blink throughout Times Square and along the Las Vegas Strip. Holzer's often publicly sited works confront passersby with rapidly changing phrases—for example, PROTECT ME FROM WHAT I WANT or MONEY CREATES TASTE.

Holzer employs a similar technology in *Unex Sign #1*, from *The Survival Series*. In this series, she broadcasts what she describes as "alternative public service messages" that explore urban conditions of "fear, panic, and withdrawal." Like other works in the series, this one combines images with open-ended questions and often unexpected responses—PUSSY CAT PUSSY CAT WHERE HAVE YOU BEEN? I'VE BEEN FIGHTING IN THE JUNGLE AGAIN. The nursery-rhyme innocence of the question is undermined by the stark answer and, in the drawing, by the transformation of a gentle pet into a feline beast. Though their precise meaning remains elusive, such messages speak with disarming simplicity of the modern conditions of desperation and alienation.

Unex Sign #1 (Selections from The Survival Series), 1983
Spectrocolor machine with moving graphics, 30 1/2 x 116 1/2 x 11 5/8 in. (77.5 x 295.9 x 29.5 cm)
Purchase, with funds from the Louis and Bessie Adler Foundation, Inc., Seymour M. Klein, President 84.8a–c

EDWARD HOPPER

1882–1967

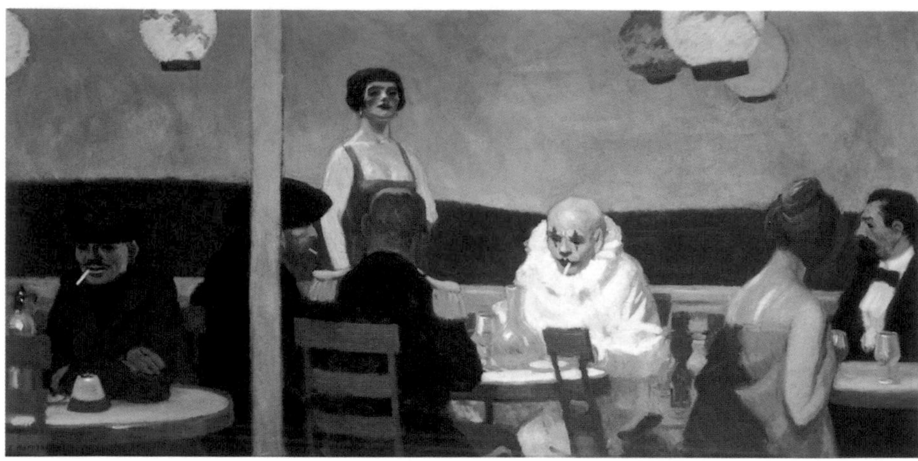

Generations of Americans have responded deeply to Edward Hopper's art, to the spartan canvases that reflect the emptiness, and sometimes the almost heroic plainness, of modern American life. As a young artist, Hopper studied with Robert Henri (p. 137) and other realists who advocated a commonplace subject matter, keyed to everyday American experience. Some of Hopper's early paintings, however, show the effects of the three trips to Paris he made between 1906 and 1910, when he became enamored of French culture. *Soir Bleu* is an imagined re-creation of a French café, with a cast of characters ranging from the well-dressed couple at right, to the decadent clown and rouged woman at center, to a rough-looking man seated alone at left, whom Hopper, in a study for the painting, identified as a pimp. When *Soir Bleu* was first exhibited in 1915, the critics dismissed it as an "ambitious fantasy" and rejected its exotic, foreign subject.

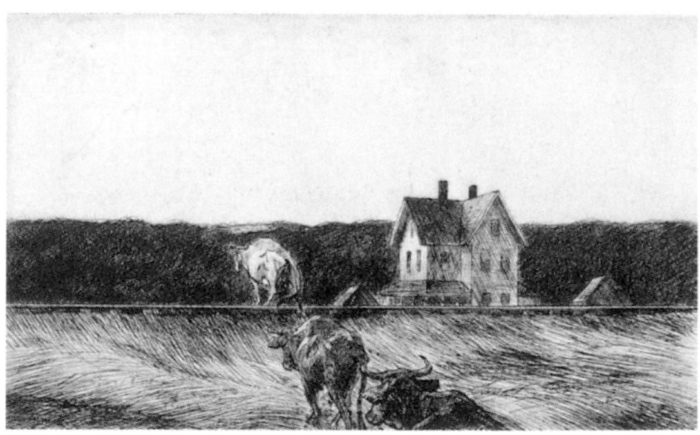

Hopper first won critical acclaim with the etchings of American life that he began to produce in 1915 and that launched his mature style. The richly etched tonalities and spare components of *American Landscape* encapsulate the Americanness of the simple gabled farmhouse behind the railroad tracks. In the painting *Railroad Sunset*, a signal tower stands starkly

Soir Bleu, 1914
Oil on canvas, 36 x 72 in. (91.4 x 182.9 cm)
Josephine N. Hopper Bequest 70.1208

American Landscape, 1920
Etching: sheet, 13 3/8 x 18 1/4 in. (34 x 46.4 cm); plate, 7 5/16 x 12 5/16 in. (18.6 x 31.3 cm)
Purchase 31.690

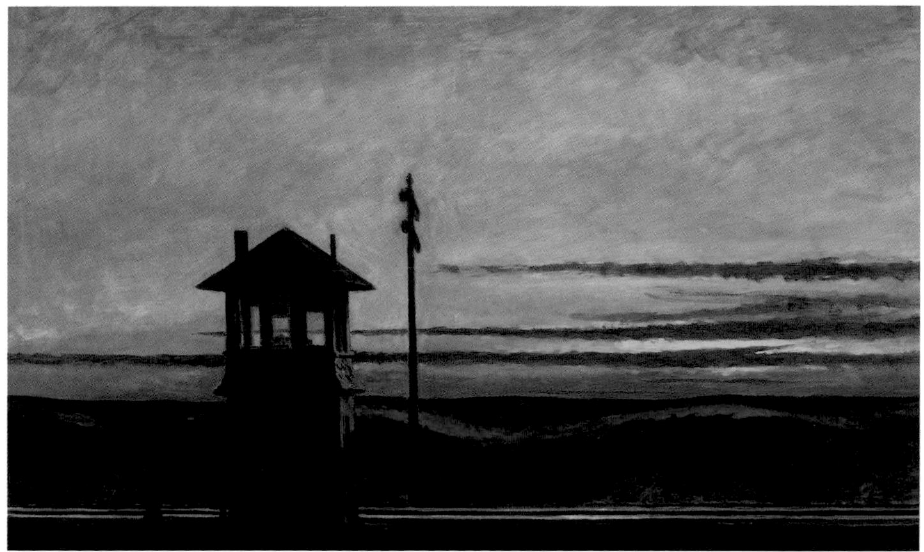

against undulating green hills and the spectacular colors of sunset. In both works, railroad tracks slice through the pastoral countryside, as if Hopper had glimpsed America from the window of a passing train.

For all their apparent realism, Hopper's mature oil paintings rarely record actual sites with precision. He sketched assiduously, but then fabricated most of his compositions in the studio. Among his preparatory works were watercolors, typically executed at the site. Watercolors such *Light at Two Lights* therefore tend to be more descriptive, filled with the details and textures Hopper often eliminated in the final painting—but radiant with the subtle nuances of the Cape Cod light reflecting off the lighthouse and plain New England dwellings.

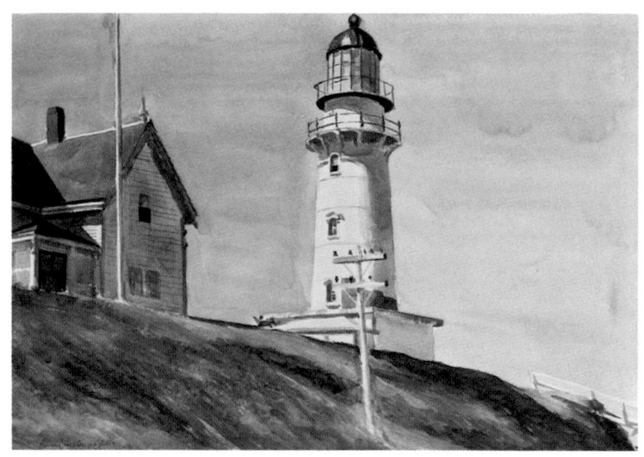

Although Hopper described *Early Sunday Morning* as "almost a literal translation of Seventh Avenue," he has in fact reduced the New York City street to bare essentials: the window

Railroad Sunset, 1929
Oil on canvas, 29 1/4 x 48 in. (74.3 x 121.9 cm)
Josephine N. Hopper Bequest 70.1170

Light at Two Lights, 1927
Watercolor on paper, 13 7/8 x 20 in. (35.2 x 50.8 cm)
Josephine N. Hopper Bequest 70.1094

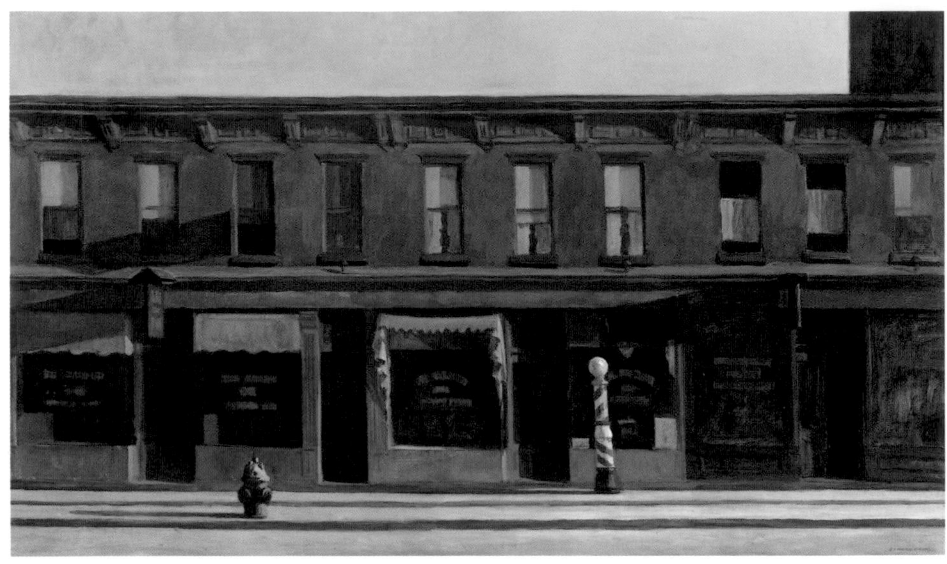

signs are illegible and architectural ornament is merely suggested. The long, early morning shadows in the painting, moreover, would never appear on a north-south street like Seventh Avenue, but they create the apprehensive atmosphere of empty buildings on an unpeopled street at the start of day.

Hopper found drama in the most mundane moments. In a drawing for the etching *Evening Wind*, a woman crouches expectantly before curtains that billow as if from a sudden gust of wind. Forty years later, he painted *A Woman in the Sun*, whose nude subject stands in a shaft of light from a nearby window. In both works, the outside world enters private, interior spaces through an open window. In *Second Story Sunlight*, the drama between an older woman reading and a young woman preening in a bathing suit occurs on the porch. Hopper would not explain their relationship, describing *Second Story Sunlight* simply as "an attempt to paint sunlight as white with almost no yellow pigment in the white. Any psychological idea will have to be supplied by the viewer."

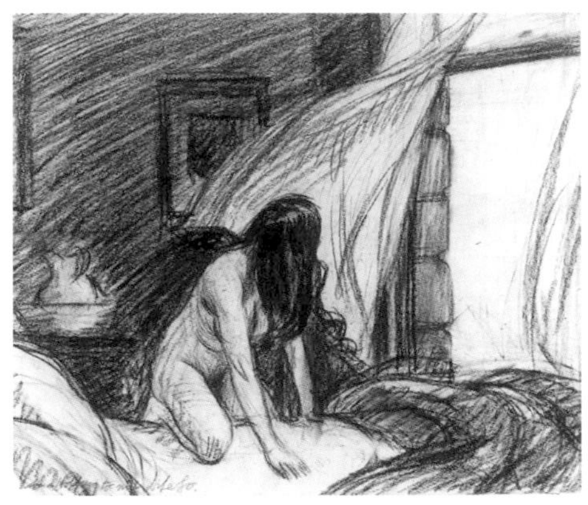

Early Sunday Morning, 1930
Oil on canvas, 35 3/16 x 60 1/4 in. (89.4 x 153 cm)
Purchase, with funds from Gertrude Vanderbilt Whitney 31.426

Study for Evening Wind, 1921
Conté and charcoal on paper, 10 x 13 15/16 in. (25.4 x 35.4 cm)
Josephine N. Hopper Bequest 70.343

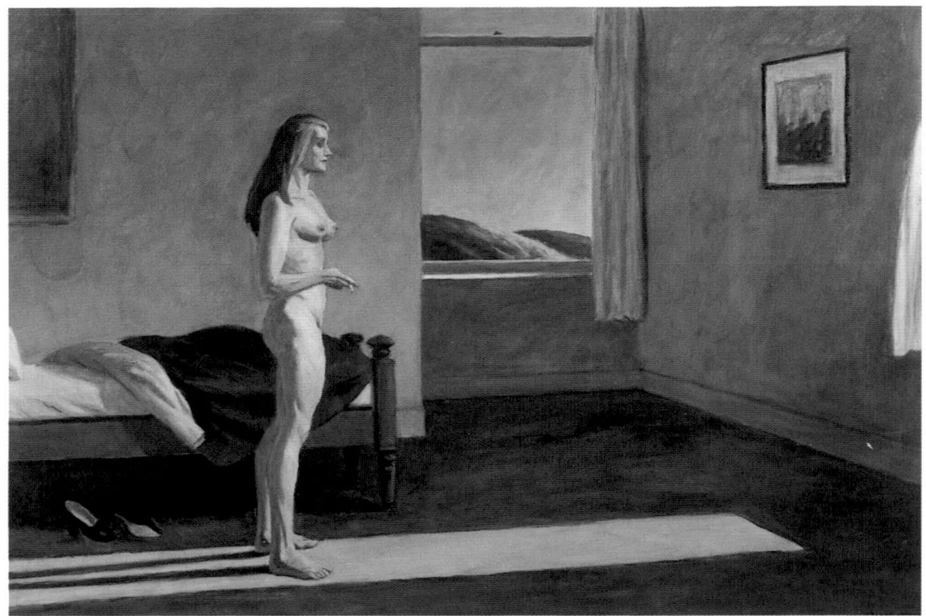

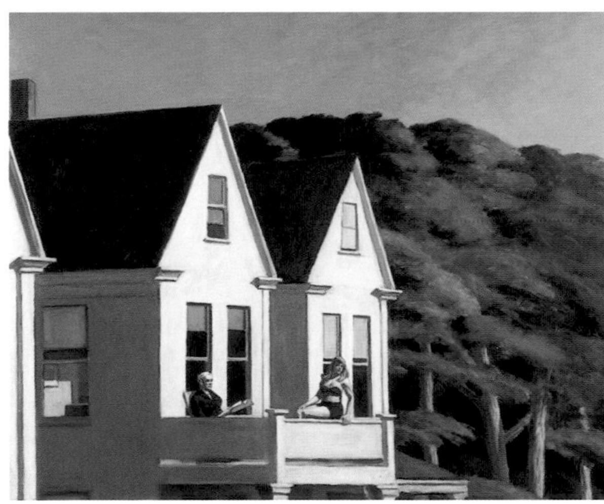

Inevitably, viewers do interpret Hopper's art psychologically. With a judicious and sober brushstroke and a minimum of detail, he could evoke scenes of great drama and longing. In his images of the lighthouses and rocky coasts of New England, of railroads crossing the countryside, or of the streets and interiors of the city, America continues to find in Hopper's art a compelling reflection of itself.

A Woman in the Sun, 1961
Oil on canvas, 40 1/8 x 61 1/4 in. (101.9 x 155.6 cm)
50th Anniversary Gift of Mr. and Mrs. Albert Hackett in honor of Edith and Lloyd Goodrich 84.31

Second Story Sunlight, 1960
Oil on canvas, 40 1/8 x 50 3/16 in. (101.9 x 127.5 cm)
Purchase, with funds from the Friends of the Whitney Museum of American Art 60.54

RONI HORN

b. 1955

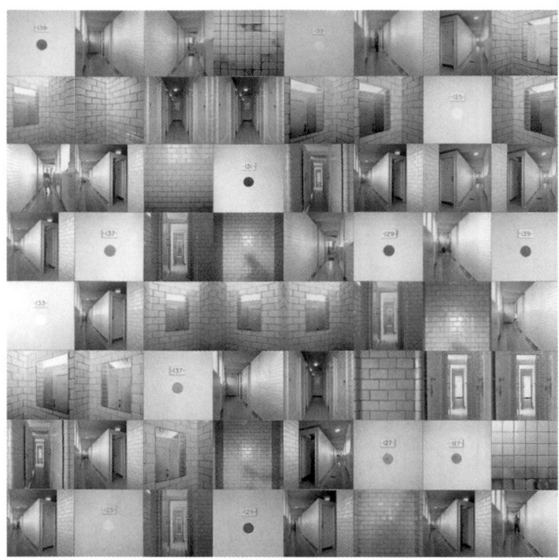

Since the mid-1970s, New York-born artist Roni Horn has produced sculptures, drawings, photographic installations, and books that defy art historical classification. Some of her sculptures, for example, in their geometric forms and industrial materials, seem to reflect the language of 1960s Minimalism, but they reject the Minimalist idea of the sculpture as a self-contained object, unresponsive to its environment. In fact, it is the very relationship between the work, its site, and the viewer that is the subject of Horn's art. "A work always comes together twice," she explains, "first, for the artist, and, second for the viewer. For me that second coming together is really an essential part of the experience."

This "second coming together"—the viewer's visceral response—even defines Horn's two-dimensional work. In *Ellipsis (II)*, she photographed the changing rooms of a public swimming pool in Reykjavík, Iceland, a country to which she has traveled regularly since 1975. A labyrinth of rooms, hallways, and doors with peepholes, the area is covered with white tiles that curve around corners to form a single continuous surface. The doors are specially designed to close off one room while opening another. As a result, the architecture obscures boundaries between inside and outside, here and there. Horn mirrors this spatial effect in *Ellipsis (II)* through a dynamic arrangement of sixty-four tile-shaped images of doors, hallways, and walls. Through repetition, inversion, and scale—the work measures 8 x 8 feet—she invites the viewer to look across and through the expansive surface, initiating an unending voyeuristic journey encouraged by the mazelike architecture itself. As Horn commented on the viewing experience: "In *Ellipsis* you don't really see what you're looking at until you've seen it all, until you've looked at all of the sixty-four photographs. In the cumulative differences and similarities of the images and in the search it poses—the experience of the original space unfolds."

Ellipsis (II), 1998
64 gelatin silver prints mounted on Sintra, 96 x 96 in. (243.8 x 243.8 cm) overall
Purchase, with funds from Anne and Joel Ehrenkranz, the Photography Committee, and the Contemporary Committee 2001.13

PETER HUJAR

1934–1987

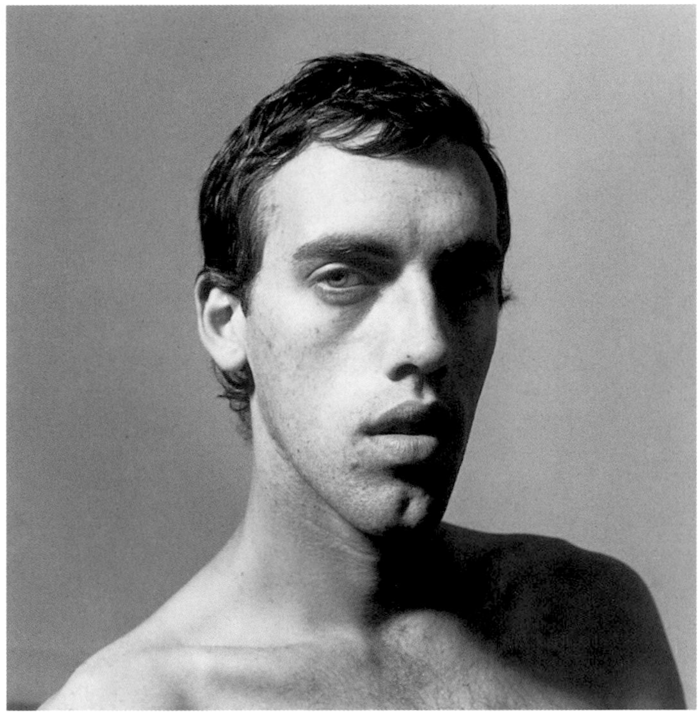

Peter Hujar began his photographic chronicle of New York's downtown subculture in the early 1970s, after abandoning the commercial and fashion work that had occupied him for two decades. Close friends, casual acquaintances, and famous strangers visited Hujar's East Village loft, where he photographed them sitting on a wooden chair or reclining on his bed. In this intimate environment, artifice fell away. By respecting the sense of vulnerability a portrait subject feels in front of the camera, Hujar was able to draw out the person behind the public facade. In his studio, even movie stars and transvestite divas shed their public plumage.

In 1981, Hujar met the artist David Wojnarowicz, twenty years younger and at the beginning of his own career. Their intense, enduring relationship was an affinity of opposites: Wojnarowicz's fiery, politically charged art (p. 327) belonged to a world far different from Hujar's seductive, slyly classical photographs. But portraiture is a collaborative venture, and this image fuses their disparate sensibilities. In Hujar's lens, Wojnarowicz's steady gaze—augmented by the dramatic shadows on his face and shoulder—is reminiscent of the homoerotic youths who appear, lips parted and hair tousled, in Caravaggio's late sixteenth-century paintings. Wojnarowicz's expression, at once willful and submissive, marks the complexity of a friendship that lasted until Hujar died of an AIDS-related illness in 1987. Wojnarowicz, who tested HIV-positive soon after, died in 1992.

David Wojnarowicz, 1981
Gelatin silver print, 14 3/4 x 14 13/16 in. (37.5 x 37.6 cm)
Purchase, with funds from the Photography Committee 93.76

ROBERT INDIANA

b. 1928

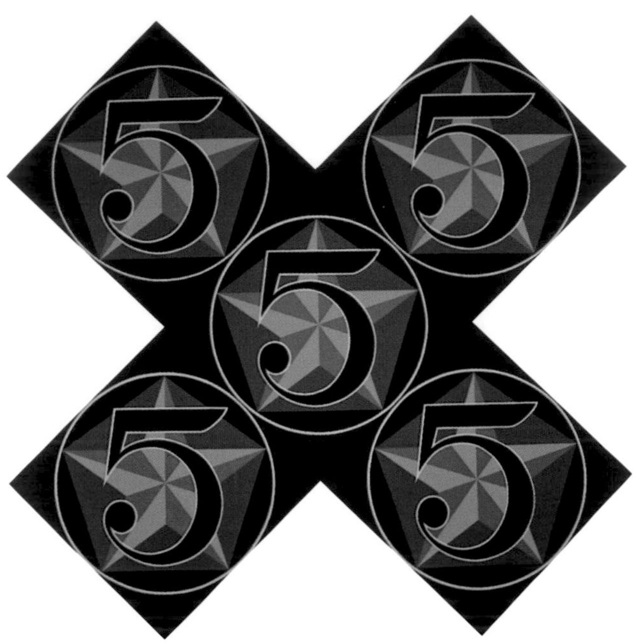

Shortly after moving to New York City in 1954, Robert Clark changed his name to Robert Indiana, intending the switch to commemorate his Midwestern roots. Much of the imagery in Indiana's signlike paintings alludes to small-town America's billboards, highway signs, roadside motels, and restaurants. Like many Pop artists of the 1960s, Indiana transforms familiar words, letters, and numbers into large, vibrantly colored icons derived from the emblems of advertising and consumer culture. His paintings, he said, are about "that happy transmutation of the Lost into the Found, the Neglected into the Wanted, the Unloved into the Loved."

The X-5 is one of a series of five works that Indiana made in homage to Charles Demuth's *The Figure 5 in Gold* (1928), one of his favorite paintings. Demuth's painting, in turn, was inspired by the vision in William Carlos Williams' poem "The Great Figure": "...I saw the figure 5 in gold on a red fire truck moving...through the dark city." Indiana reworked the hard-edged, stencil-style figures and bold colors of Demuth's image into an unusually structured work of layered geometries—the numeral superimposed on a star and a pentagon set within a circle, each of these configurations repeated on five separate canvas squares arranged into an X-shape.

The X-5 was Indiana's first black, white, and gray painting, though he had used the X-shaped canvas in previous works. The form was inspired by the danger crossing signs at railroad tracks. Not only did Indiana have a penchant for vernacular signs, but his grandfather had been an engineer on the Pennsylvania Railroad.

The X-5, 1963
Oil on canvas, 108 x 108 in. (274.3 x 274.3 cm)
Purchase 64.9a–e

DAVID IRELAND

b. 1930

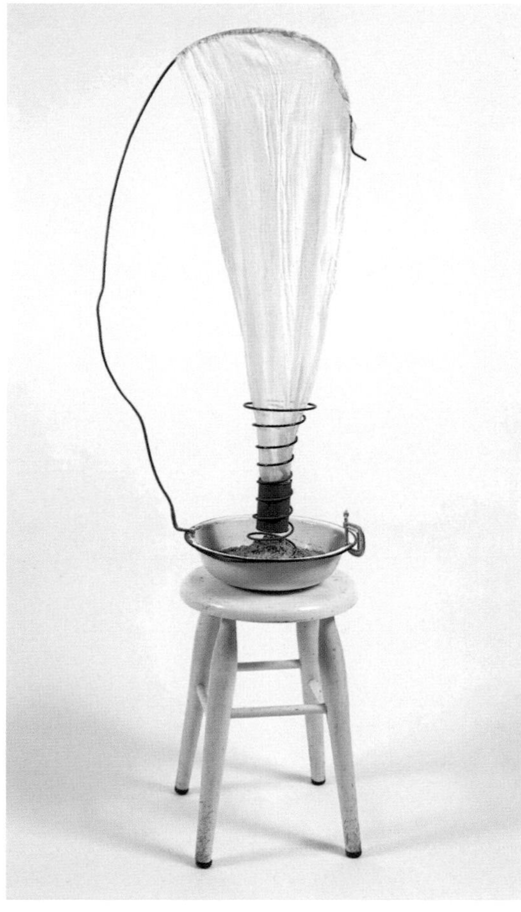

In David Ireland's *Northwest Version #2*, white fabric and a metal clamp are attached to an assembly of concrete, copper wire, a metal pan, and an oil can, all resting on a painted stool. The San Francisco-based artist makes his sculptures with uneventful, mundane materials—cement and dirt, paper and tar, sawdust and sheetrock—and often includes household materials such as rubber bands, brooms, and used furniture. Ireland's sculptures stand on the border between art and non-art, forcing us to reconsider traditional definitions of what art is or can be, what materials are legitimate, and where art can be located. "I like the piece not to have a flag on it that says it's a work of art." In this respect, Ireland is an heir to Marcel Duchamp, who in the early twentieth century placed ready-made objects such as a urinal, a bicycle wheel, and a shovel in art institutions as a means of expanding the definition of art.

Beyond these commonplace materials, the composition of Ireland's sculpture is suggestive of some kind of crude experiment or energy circulation system. From a bed of concrete, the thin wire coils up around the oil can and veil-like cloth, which evokes steam, smoke, or heat. The outer wire simultaneously suspends the cloth and maintains its vertical orientation while returning the flow of energy back to the basin where it began. The simple wooden stool on which the sculpture sits, however, makes the work look as if it would be more at home in a kitchen or a barn than in a scientific laboratory. This use of raw, everyday materials to symbolize energy flows recalls the work of the German artist Joseph Beuys, who in the 1960s and 1970s used materials such as felt and fat to create metaphoric transformers of social and spiritual energy.

Northwest Version #2, 1987
Metal pan, cedar oil, painted oil can, concrete, copper wire, metal clamp, and fabric on painted wood stool, 53 1/8 x 17 3/4 x 12 in. (134.9 x 45.1 x 30.5 cm) overall
Gift of Kelli and Allen Questrom 95.12a–b

ROBERT IRWIN

b. 1928

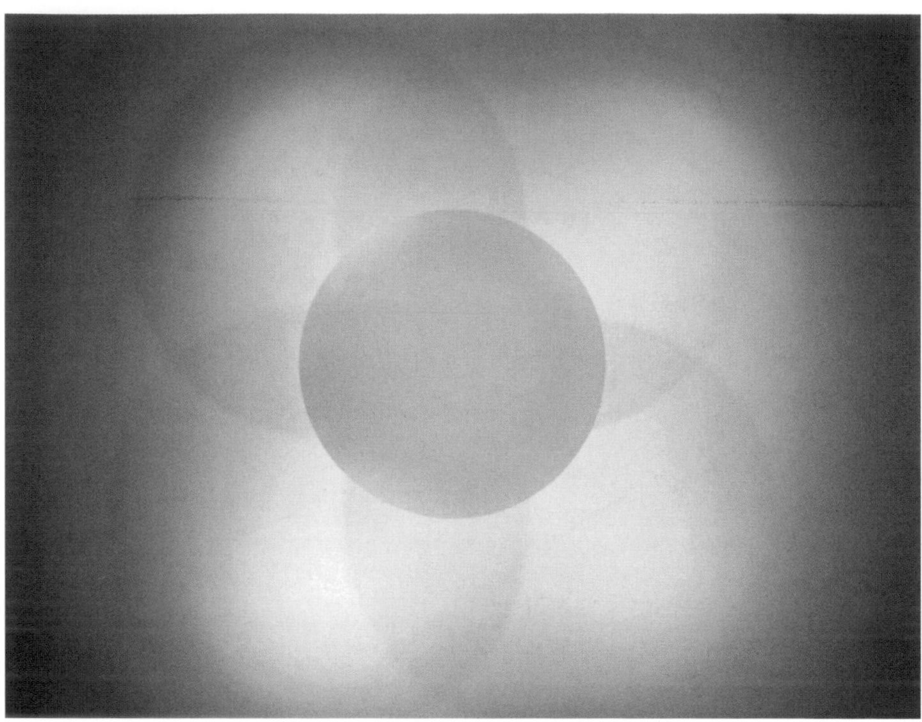

In the 1960s, Robert Irwin was among a group of artists, including Dan Flavin and James Turrell (pp. 108, 312), who turned light into a medium for artmaking. Unlike art made with physically tangible materials, such works change appearance not only in different settings, but often in the course of a single extended viewing as well. The result—and the artists' intention—is to make the viewer's perception of the environment and the viewing experience itself essential parts of the art work. In Irwin's work, which hovers on the borders between painting, sculpture, and installation art, light and space are the primary materials, while the physical components used to create the visual effects are secondary.

No Title is composed of a gently convex, curved aluminum disc that slightly projects from the wall on which it is mounted. Spray-painted in subtle modulations of pale, opaque acrylic, the disc is surrounded by four symmetrically placed incandescent floodlights of equal intensity. These lamps, combined with the lights in the gallery, cast ethereal geometric shadows on the wall behind and allow the viewer to perceive fine gradations of color and light. Nearly imperceptible tints of pink and green, for example, appear around the edges of work, and shadows overlap in petal-like forms. *No Title* is one of a series of disc paintings that began with a question Irwin posed: "How do I paint a painting that does not begin and end at an edge but rather starts to take in and become involved with the space or environment behind it?"

No Title, 1966–67
Synthetic polymer on aluminum with 4 floodlights, diameter, 48 in. (121.9 cm); depth, 13 in. (33 cm)
Purchase, with funds from the Howard and Jean Lipman Foundation, Inc. 68.42a–e

NEIL JENNEY

b. 1945

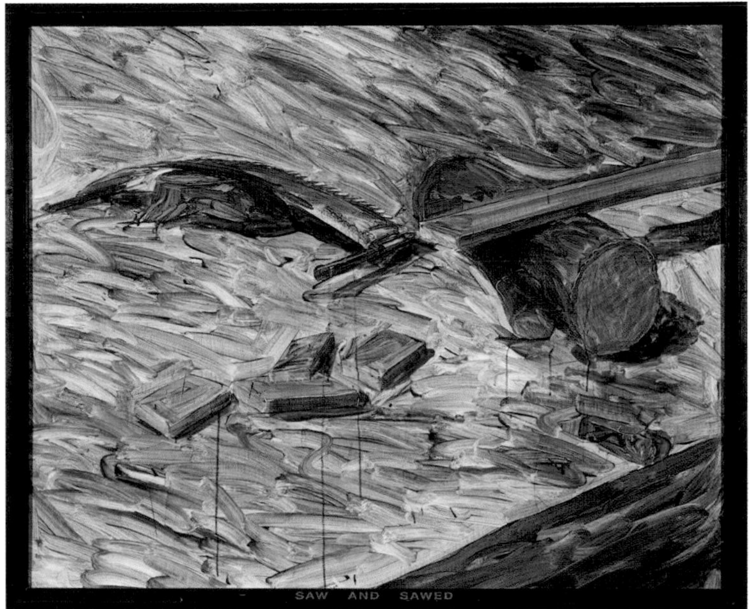

In the late 1960s, reacting against the dominance of abstraction, Neil Jenney began a series of paintings that were unabashedly realist, depicting simple, recognizable objects. Affectionately dubbed "bad paintings" by the artist, they were early examples of a trend later called New Image.

Jenney's bad paintings typically featured pairs of related images: a crying girl and a broken doll, a fish and a pole, a saw and lumber. The artist explained: "I'm interested in showing objects existing with and relating to other objects because I think that is what realism deals with." In *Saw and Sawed*, a crosscut saw rests on the stump of a tree; a sawed-off section of a trunk is at right, another crosses the corner below. The saw represents an action, the stump and trunk segments describe the aftermath. In this group of related objects, however, there are in fact two "aftermaths," for the pieces of planed wood at center and right record the milling of the tree into usable lumber.

All the objects are rendered in wide smears of paint that mimic the gestural brushwork of Abstract Expressionism (pp. 165, 166). But Jenney uses paint to represent objects, not to express subjective experience. His palette is also direct and uncomplicated, as if pulled from a small box of crayons: the grass is Kelly green, the wood a simple brown.

Jenney reinforces his straightforward realism with a black wooden frame that creates the illusion of a window; the title of the work is painted at the bottom. Yet beneath the artist's seemingly prosaic imagery lies a more somber message. The action depicted is irreversible: once sawed, a tree cannot be rendered whole again. In the past three decades, the ecological concerns implicit in this early painting have become central to Jenney's work.

Saw and Sawed, 1969
Oil on canvas, 58 1/2 x 70 3/8 in. (148.6 x 178.8 cm) with frame
Gift of Philip Johnson 77.65

ALFRED JENSEN

1903–1981

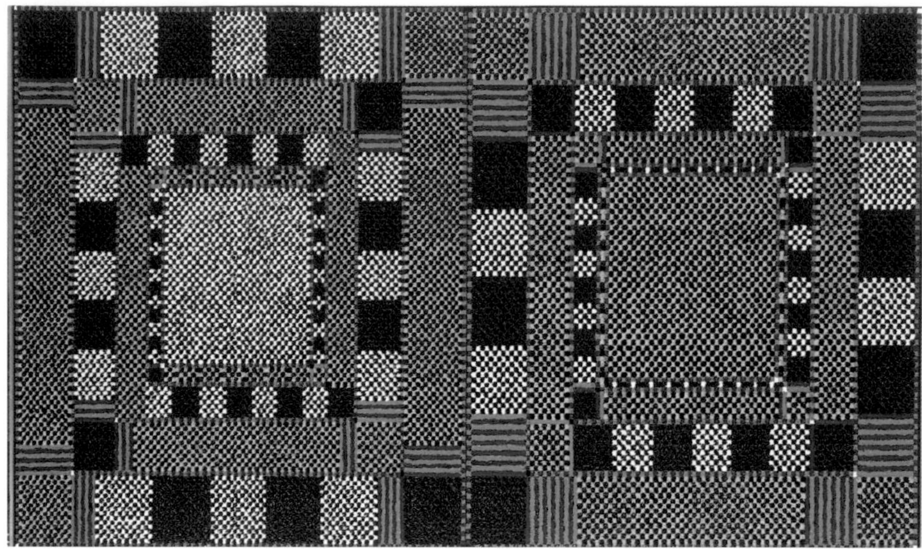

Alfred Jensen did not begin to produce his thickly painted, intricately patterned canvases until he was in his fifties. Born in Guatemala, he spent the first half century of his life traveling and studying art but never settled on a particular style. He also read widely and was fascinated by a variety of subjects, including Goethe's color theories, the Mayan calendar, and the *I Ching*. For years he made detailed diagrams based on his readings until finally, in 1957, he realized that these drawings could provide subjects for his paintings.

Timaeus III and IV is Jensen's diagram of the perfect year, as described in Plato's *Timaeus*. In a perfect year, the spheres of the heavens align: the sun, the moon, and the planets reach their hypothetical starting points simultaneously. In response to Plato's account of the proportions that supposedly govern the spacing and movements of the spheres, Jensen said that the left-hand panel of his *Timaeus* expresses "the proportions three, seven, eleven, and fifteen." Although the width of each square does increase by increments of four, outward from the center, Jensen's logic is difficult to follow, and the mathematical relationship between his painting and Plato's text remains tenuous at best. Jensen's abstruse paintings may fail to elucidate complex systems, but they demonstrate his compulsion to make sense of the world and to find truth—in a diagram.

Timaeus III and IV, 1966
Oil on canvas, 60 x 100 in. (152.4 x 254 cm) overall
Purchase, with funds from the Friends of the Whitney Museum of American Art 67.29

JESS

b. 1923

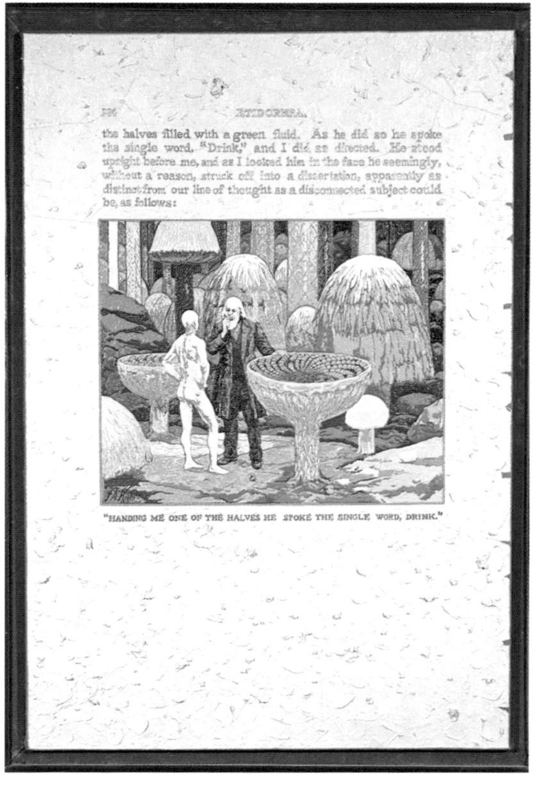

In 1949, Burgess Collins, an amateur painter, abandoned his day job as a chemist on an atomic defense project after having a dream that the world would end in twenty-six years. Deciding that "art was far more meaningful than making plutonium," he moved to San Francisco, changed his name to Jess, and pursued a career as a painter.

Jess described his working method as one of "rescuing and resurrecting images": his paintings are derived from reproductions in his large archive of pictures—a disparate collection of black-and-white book and magazine illustrations, postcards, and old photographs. A close friend of many writers and poets in San Francisco, he also integrated texts or literary references into most of his paintings. Often these texts were taken from the original source of the illustration, particularly in the case of children's books.

Between 1959 and 1976, Jess produced a series of thirty-two works entitled *Translations*. These works, he explained, "translated nineteenth-century images through time to the present." The *Translation* paintings are interpretations of black-and-white reproductions of color images, which Jess knew only in their black-and-white state. Each one is accompanied by a text, inscribed on the back or within the painting, that Jess pulled from diverse sources. *"Handing Me One of the Halves He Spoke the Single Word, Drink": Translation #23* is based on an illustration by J. Augustus Knapp found in John Uri Lloyd's 1894 book *Etidorpha, or the End of the Earth.* Jess copied the image onto canvas with a pencil and then painted it in a heavily impastoed, paint-by-numbers style. The palette of green tones belies the black-and-white source he worked from. The text on the back of the painting is also from Lloyd's book and discusses time, eternity, and the human soul.

"Handing Me One of the Halves He Spoke the Single Word, Drink": Translation #23, 1969
Oil on canvas mounted on wood, 30 x 20 in. (76.2 x 50.8 cm)
Purchase, with funds from the Mrs. Percy Uris Purchase Fund, Mrs. Laila Twigg-Smith, Dr. Jack Chachkes, the John I.H. Baur Purchase Fund, the Wilfred P. and Rose J. Cohen Purchase Fund, the Julia B. Engel Purchase Fund, and gift of Odyssia Skouras 93.20

JASPER JOHNS

b. 1930

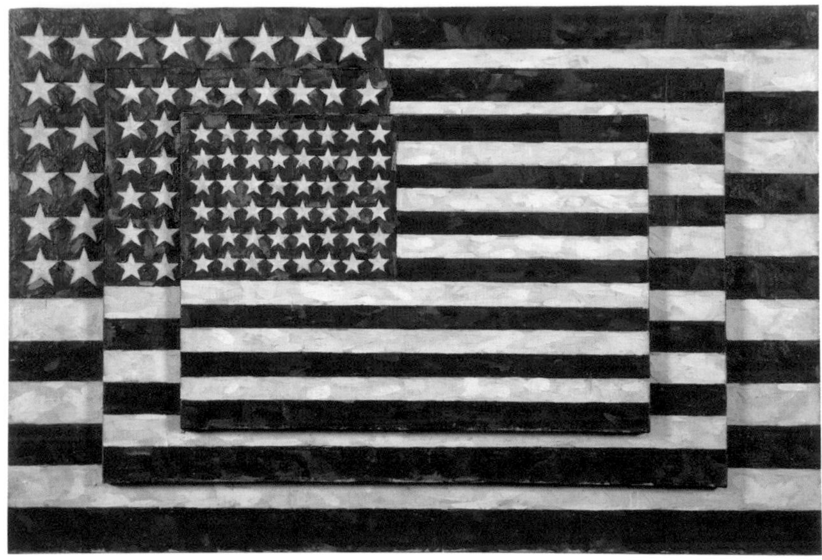

Beginning in the mid-1950s, Jasper Johns explored the boundary between abstraction and representation through the use of familiar icons such as the target, the alphabet, numbers, and the American flag. As Johns described them, these signs are "things the mind already knows," things that are "seen and not looked at, not examined." By altering their context, color, or pattern, he drew attention to the relationship between sight and thought, perception and conception. In *Three Flags*, America's national banner appears superimposed on itself in three different scales. Similarly in *White Target*, Johns removed all color from the bull's-eye motif and made each concentric circle of equal value, thereby confounding our expectations of what a target looks like and what it is used for. The visual emphasis in both these works shifts from their emblematic significance to the geometric patterns and the variegated texture of the picture surface. Johns painted with encaustic, a mixture of pigment suspended in warm

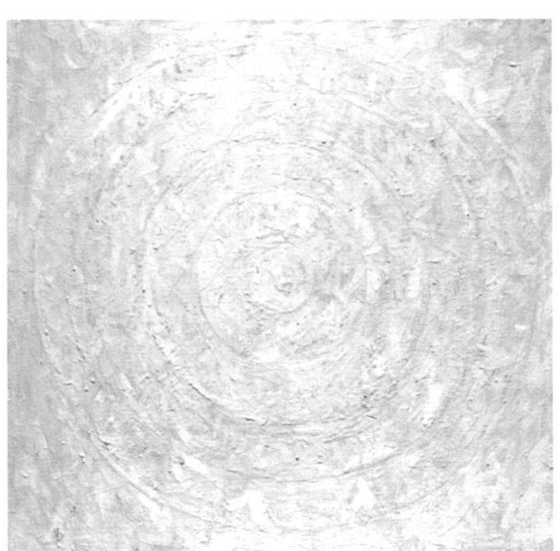

Three Flags, 1958
Encaustic on canvas, 30 7/8 x 45 1/2 x 5 in. (78.4 x 115.6 x 12.7 cm)
50th Anniversary Gift of the Gilman Foundation, Inc., The Lauder Foundation, A. Alfred Taubman, an anonymous donor, and purchase 80.32

White Target, 1957
Encaustic on canvas, 30 x 30 in. (76.2 x 76.2 cm)
Purchase 71.211

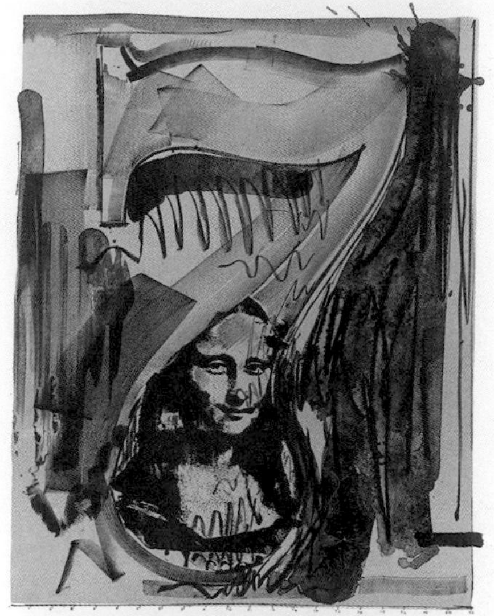

wax, which congeals as each stroke is applied. The resulting accumulation of discrete marks creates a sensuous and almost sculptural surface.

Johns continued to explore similar iconography in the 1960s and 1970s, expanding his repertoire to include printmaking. In lithographs such as the 1968 *Black Numeral* series, to which *Figure 7* belongs, he returned to the numbers that had been the subjects of some of his earlier paintings. *Figure 7* therefore becomes part of Johns' increasingly self-referential examination of commonplace images. He also included a familiar face from art history, that of the *Mona Lisa*. She sits in the curve of the 7 not only in reference to Leonardo

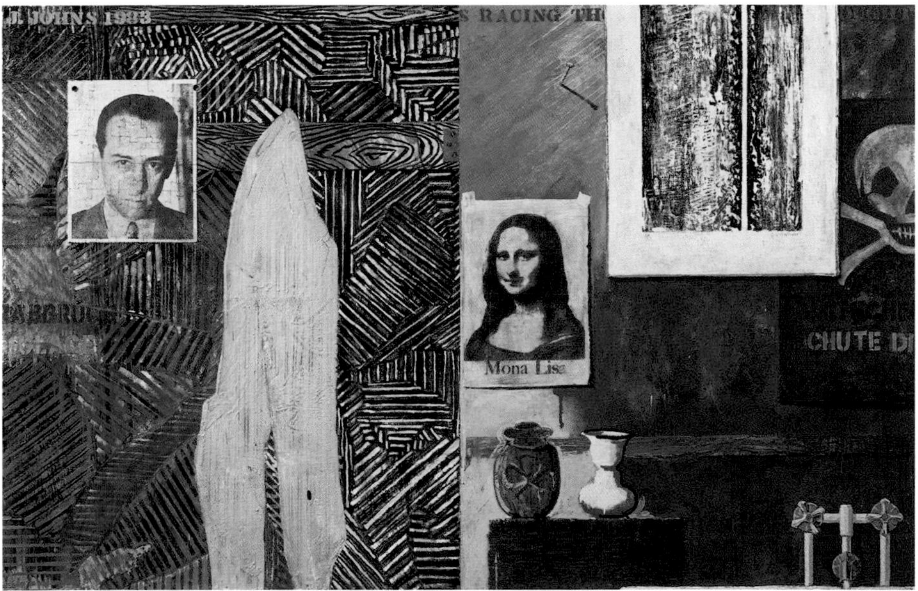

Figure 7, 1968
Lithograph: sheet, 37 x 30 in. (94 x 76.2 cm); image, 27 3/4 x 21 7/16 in. (70.5 x 54.5 cm)
Gift of Robert Simons 85.46.8

****Racing Thoughts***, 1983
Encaustic and collage on canvas, 48 x 75 1/8 in. (121.9 x 190.8 cm)
Purchase, with funds from the Burroughs Wellcome Purchase Fund, Leo Castelli, the Wilfred P. and Rose J. Cohen Purchase Fund, the Julia B. Engel Purchase Fund, the Equitable Life Assurance Society of the United States Purchase Fund, The Sondra and Charles Gilman, Jr. Foundation, Inc., S. Sidney Kahn, The Lauder Foundation, Leonard and Evelyn Lauder Fund, the Sara Roby Foundation, and the Painting and Sculpture Committee 84.6

JASPER JOHNS

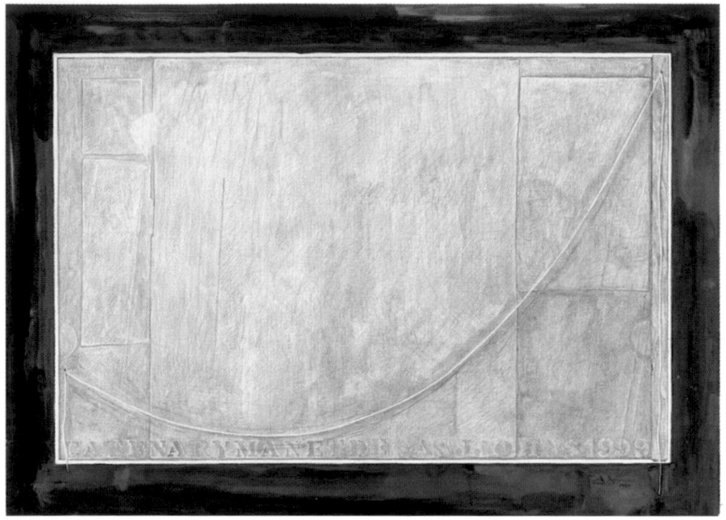

da Vinci, but as well to Marcel Duchamp—an artist much admired by Johns—who in 1919 defaced a reproduction of the *Mona Lisa* with a mustache and exhibited it as his own work.

In the 1980s, in paintings such as *Racing Thoughts*, Johns drew on both autobiographical and art historical sources to create works with complex layers of associations. *Racing Thoughts* depicts the bathroom of his former country house (note the wicker hamper and running faucet at bottom in the right half). Attached to the center of the canvas is a handkerchief bearing an image of the *Mona Lisa*, by now a well-known player on Johns' stage. The words "Racing Thoughts" are inscribed in stencil-like letters across the top of the right half, separated by an image of a lithograph Johns owns by Barnett Newman (p. 223). A sign in German and French at the right edge warns of falling ice; the message continues at the left edge. All of this suggests a kind of coded picture of art history and the artist's world, a reading reinforced in the left half by the jigsaw puzzle portrait of Johns' dealer, Leo Castelli.

In the drawing *Catenary (Manet-Degas)*, from the *Bridge* series, Johns personalizes the peculiar fate of Édouard Manet's painting *The Execution of Maximilian* (1867–68), which had been cut into sections that were sold off separately. Edgar Degas later managed to recover four of the fragments and partially reconstructed the work by gluing the pieces to a larger canvas in positions corresponding to their original placement. The faint rectangular outlines in the main gray section of Johns' drawing represent the contours of the four sections in Degas' reconstruction. The curved line running from the bottom left to the top right depicts a string making a catenary curve—a curve formed by dropping a string from two fixed points (and used frequently in the design of suspension bridges). The catenary unites the fragments of the composition and metaphorically links Manet and Degas to Johns in a larger art historical context. This chain is reinforced by the stenciled letters at the bottom that read "CATENARYMANETDEGASJ.JOHNS1999."

Catenary (Manet-Degas), 1999
Graphite, watercolor, and ink on paper, 24 3/8 x 33 5/8 in. (61.9 x 85.4 cm)
Promised gift of The American Contemporary Art Foundation, Inc., Leonard A. Lauder, President P.2001.48

JOAN JONAS
b. 1936

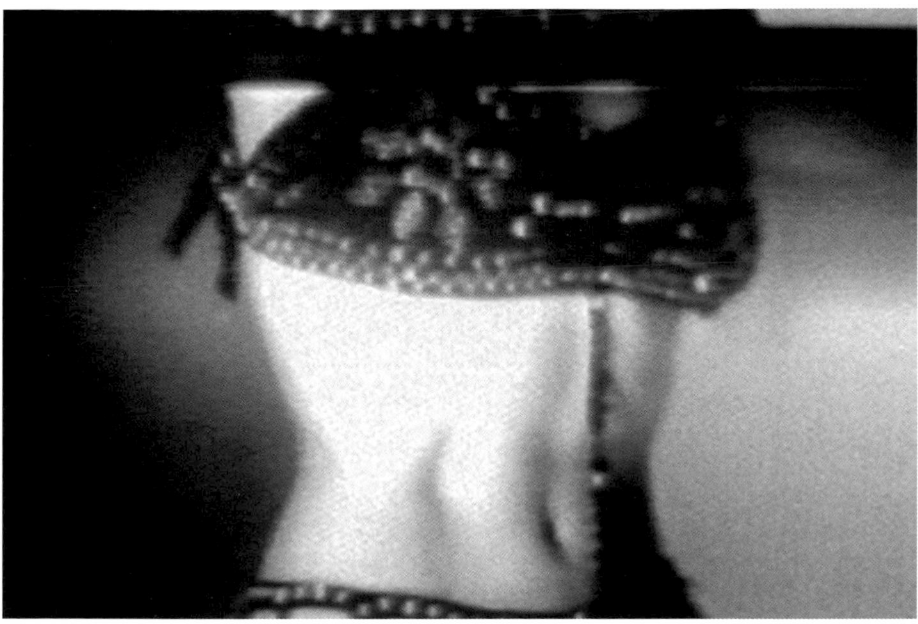

In the experimental climate of the late 1960s and early 1970s, artists used the moving image to extend their sculptural practice into a time-based form, using film, video, and performance. Joan Jonas produced some of the most important works of the period in these media, among them *Vertical Roll*, widely considered a seminal work in single-channel video.

In *Vertical Roll*, the video monitor's vertical hold is used as a formal device to rupture the perceived wholeness of the image on the screen. Interrupting the electronic signal, a rolling black bar scrolls relentlessly downward, revealing a segment of the image for a fraction of a second, in a staccato rhythm that echoes the process of blinking. Each "blink" offers a fleeting glimpse of a section of Jonas' body as she performs in front of the camera—either garbed in a feather headdress, wearing a mask, in a belly dancer's costume, or nude. Legs, fabric, mask, face, and arms appear in a series of tantalizing flashes, constructing a body that slides elusively away from clear definition.

The rhythm of the images is punctuated by the sound of Jonas relentlessly banging a silver spoon on a surface, which introduces an assertive tone. In her refusal to sustain her image within a fixed pictorial space, Jonas uses the mirrorlike qualities of the video camera to present herself as a sequence of fragments, suggesting the impossibility of reading identity as something singular and unified.

Vertical Roll, 1972
Video, black-and-white, sound; 19:38 minutes
Purchase, with funds from the Film and Video Committee 2000.189

JOE JONES
1909–1963

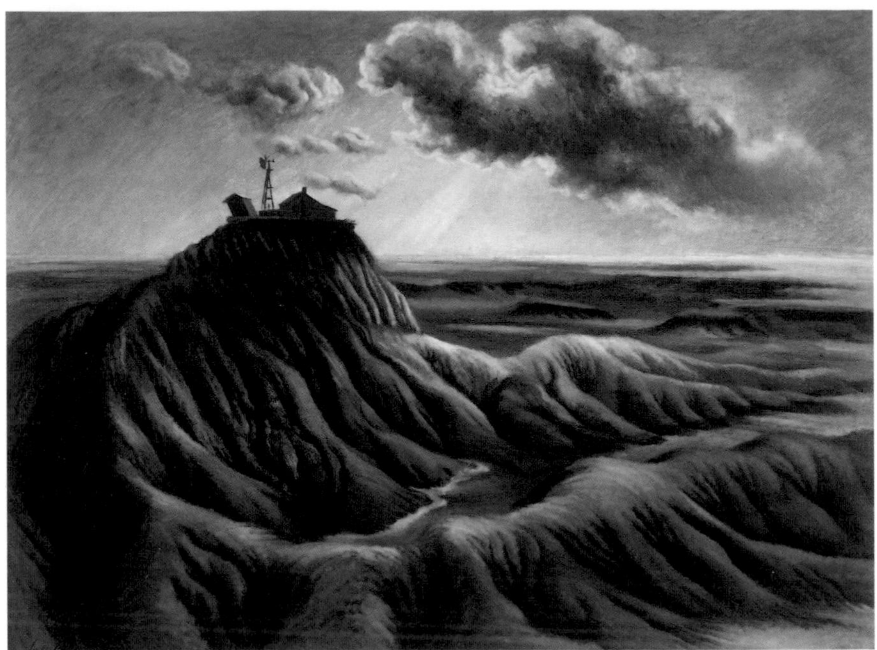

Although Joe Jones' paintings of wheat fields and farms resemble Regionalist works of the 1930s, the St. Louis native's leftist politics distinguish him from more conservative contemporaries such as Thomas Hart Benton and Grant Wood (pp. 49, 330). Jones' father was a house painter, and the young man at first adopted his father's vocation. Even after he turned his brush to canvas, he continued to wear coveralls, identifying himself proudly with the working class. He had little formal art education and rejected modernism and the East Coast establishment as too elitist. He also embraced Communism, which put him at odds with residents of his hometown.

Despite his political leanings, Jones was, like the Regionalists, sympathetic to the traditional values of the nation's heartland. His *American Farm* dramatizes the disastrous effects of the Great Depression while championing the resiliency of Midwestern farmers. The painting is one of a group produced under the auspices of the Works Progress Administration, which employed artists on government projects during the Depression. Jones was commissioned to record drought conditions on American farms. Although the landscape of *American Farm* is gouged by soil erosion, he clearly did not intend this painting to be an accurate historical record. Instead, he cast the Midwestern farmer in the role of Noah, with the farm perched like the ark atop Mount Ararat after the Flood. The barn and windmill, overlooking a ravaged landscape, have survived the disaster, while the sun, barely peeking through dark clouds, hints at Jones' undampened faith in the endurance of American farm life.

American Farm, 1936
Oil and tempera on canvas, 30 x 40 in. (76.2 x 101.6 cm)
Purchase 36.144

KENNETH JOSEPHSON

b. 1932

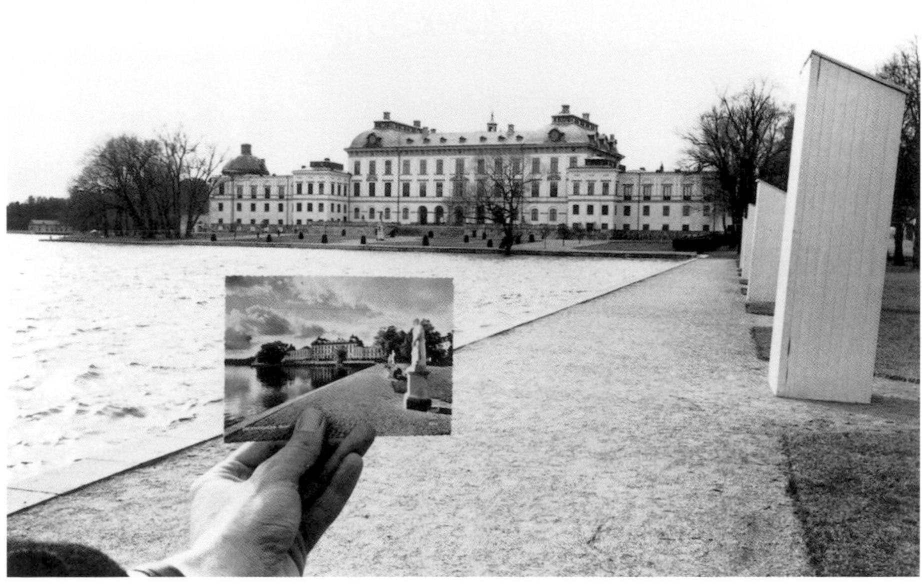

Kenneth Josephson was one of the first postwar American artists to practice a self-referential mode of photography. While his images vary in subject matter—street photography, light studies, family photographs, nudes, and landscapes, to name a few—they all reveal his fascination with photography as a medium. During the 1950s, Josephson studied with key figures in the history of American photography and emerged from his training with a reverence for photography's unique image-making capabilities.

Drottningholm, Sweden is part of Josephson's well-known *Images within Images* series and reflects one of the most prominent motifs in his work, the image placed within another image. "It was always magical, how you could put this realistic image in any setting of your choosing and the way that would affect and change that setting." By juxtaposing the idealized postcard image with what he himself encounters on a gray winter day, Josephson encourages the viewer to find both similarities and differences between the two images, thereby raising questions about photographic truth versus illusion. Further, by photographing the postcard being held in his own hand, he makes the viewer keenly aware of the photograph as a discrete object—one that you can hold, examine, and manipulate. "I like the idea of including a piece of me in the photograph...because it refers back to the act of me taking the picture and involves the viewer in understanding how the picture is being made."

Drottningholm, Sweden, 1967
Gelatin silver print, 10 15/16 x 13 7/8 in. (27.8 x 35.2 cm)
Purchase, with funds from the Photography Committee 2000.237

DONALD JUDD
1928–1994

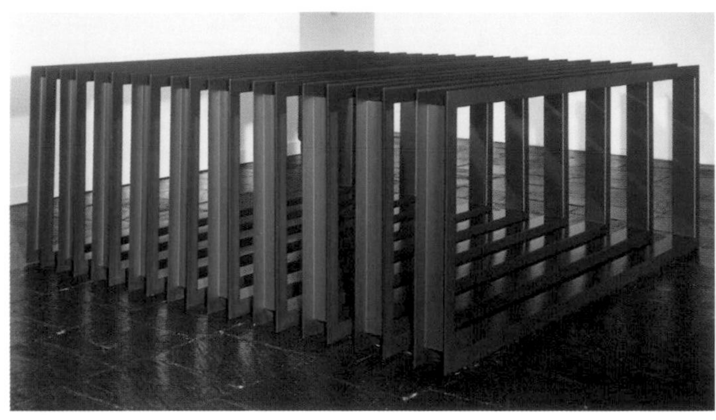

Although he disliked the categorization, Donald Judd is considered one of the leading proponents of Minimalism (pp. 30, 292) and is best known for the cubic and rectilinear sculptures he had fabricated from industrial materials beginning in the early 1960s. Abstract sculpture became Judd's primary form of art because its three-dimensional nature mitigated the potential for illusionism. A well-respected and articulate art critic, he explained in 1965 that "actual space is intrinsically more powerful and specific than paint on a flat surface."

Judd often composed his sculptures of multiple identical units set at regular intervals. The works were placed on the floor without a pedestal or directly on the wall in vertical, cantilevered "stacks." These arrangements created an interplay of solid forms and the voids in between. The 1966 untitled sculpture demonstrates this rhythmic organization of space as well as Judd's willingness to use decorative color. For this work, he employed automotive paint, specifically, the color known as 1958 Chevy Corvette Regal turquoise metallic.

Judd also experimented widely with the sculptural format of a floorbox, as in the 1968 untitled work. Fabricated from steel and a vibrant amber plexiglass, it displays a complex relationship not of solid and void, as in the earlier work, but of open and enclosed volumes. The enclosed volumes are rendered visible by the transparent plexiglass, whose amber tint also colors the space. Whereas in traditional hollow sculpture, we must imagine what fills an interior, in Judd's work we see what he called "actual space" with a directness that encompasses the inside as well as the exterior.

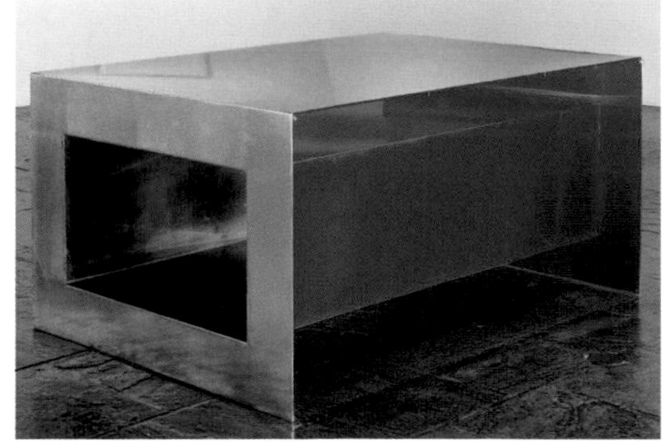

Untitled, 1966
Painted steel, 48 x 120 x 120 in. (121.9 x 304.8 x 304.8 cm)
Gift of Howard and Jean Lipman 72.7a–j

Untitled, 1968
Stainless steel and plexiglass, 33 x 68 x 48 in. (83.8 x 172.7 x 121.9 cm)
Purchase, with funds from the Howard and Jean Lipman Foundation, Inc. 68.36

ALEX KATZ

b. 1927

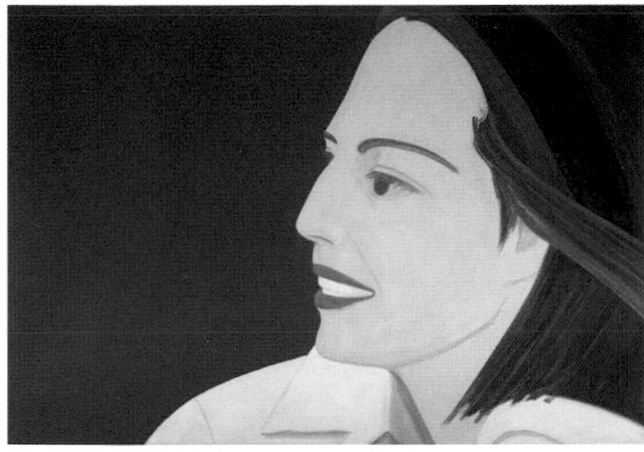

As a young artist in the 1950s, Alex Katz, seeking a way out of the gestural Abstract Expressionist painting then dominating the New York art world, began to make collages of figures out of cut paper. In his later paintings, he retained the flat, unmodeled look of these cut-paper works. In 1958, he met his future wife, Ada, who became his most prominent model. In *The Red Smile*, he painted a profile of his wife's face set against a smooth red background. Although the portrait bears Ada's features, its simplified, almost billboard-style rendering seems generic rather than specific—an effect reinforced by the large scale, nearly 7 x 10 feet. Katz's broad, unmodulated expanses of color resist a three-dimensional reading, which allies his work with the large geometric sculptures of Minimalist art that reduced form to bare essentials (pp. 30, 160, 292). The contemporaneous interest of Pop artists in billboard advertisements also influenced Katz to produce bigger and more aggressive images.

Apple Blossoms, painted more than thirty years later, parallels *The Red Smile* in its monumentality—it is 8 feet tall and 10 feet wide—and insistent two-dimensionality. The trees with green foliage and white blossoms do not literally represent a landscape; rather, the daubs of paint and lyrical strokes activate the entire surface of the canvas, so that the elements of pictorial landscape are abstracted into a flat pattern.

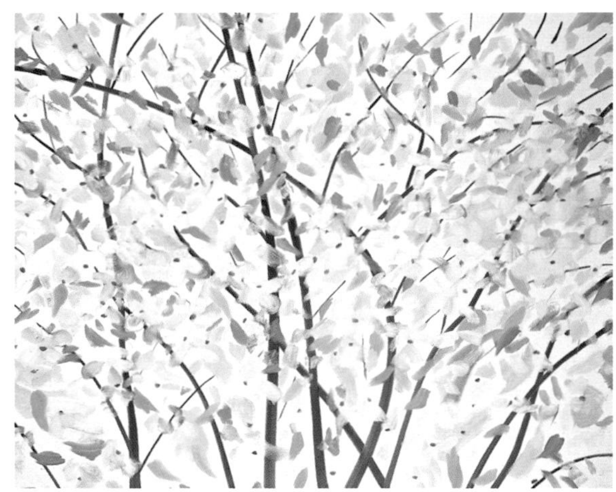

Katz's work finds a balance between abstraction and realism. The intimate portrait and landscape become occasions for the exploration of distilled form and color, while at the same time poetically evoking the character of their subjects.

The Red Smile, 1963
Oil on canvas, 78 3/4 x 114 3/4 in. (200 x 291.5 cm)
Purchase, with funds from the Painting and Sculpture Committee 83.3

Apple Blossoms, 1994
Oil on canvas, 96 x 120 3/16 in. (243.8 x 305.3 cm)
Purchase, with funds from the Contemporary Painting and Sculpture Committee, the Wilfred P. and Rose J. Cohen Purchase Fund, the Katherine Schmidt Shubert Purchase Fund, the David M. Solinger Purchase Fund, the Grace Belt Endowed Purchase Fund, and the Louise and Bessie Adler Foundation, Inc. 97.46

MIKE KELLEY

b. 1954

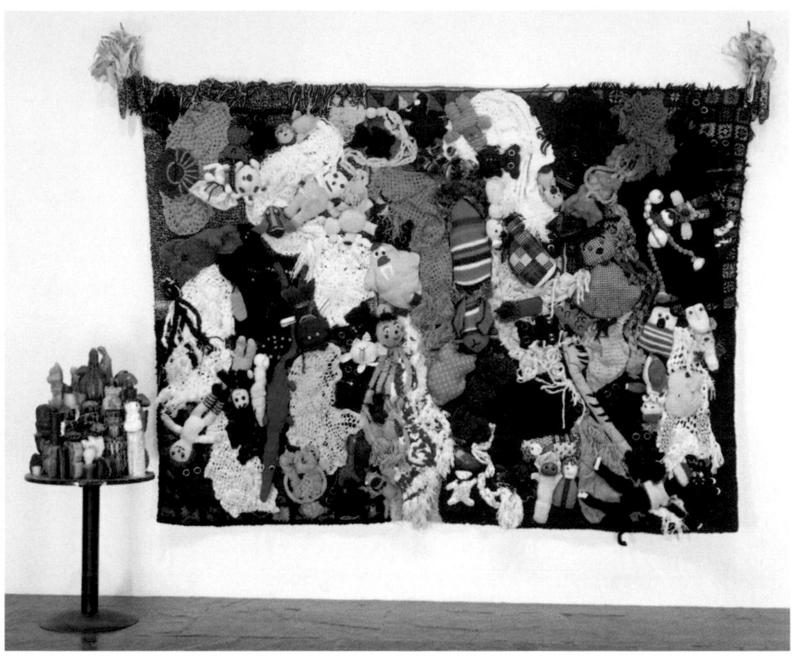

Within his diverse body of work, which includes sculpture, drawing, video, performance, and painting, Los Angeles-based Mike Kelley makes art that questions what it means to grow up in America. His works are often based on his own experience as the child of a blue-collar Catholic family in the Midwest in the 1950s and 1960s. *More Love Hours Than Can Ever Be Repaid* is a chaotic assemblage of used, handmade dolls and blankets that the artist found in thrift stores. The title does not designate to whom more love hours are owed, but simply suggests the condition of loving something too much, or of receiving too little in return—like the cast-off items that make up the sculpture. The title also carries associations of guilt: do we expect children to repay the time and love lavished on them? When parents and relatives create these toys and blankets, are the countless hours of stitching, knitting, or crocheting a kind of penance?

In the related work *The Wages of Sin*, a collection of melted candles becomes an altar to the power of teen angst and the imminent approach of adulthood. When Kelley was a teenager in the 1960s, such colorful, mass-produced candles were part of the psychedelic trappings of youth culture, a declaration of independence from the parental world. Yet this independence, when confronted by the dolls and blankets in *More Love Hours*, comes with a newfound sense of guilt—for the abandonment of parents, comforting stuffed toys, and safety blankets, as well as for experimentation with forbidden things. But what does sin earn, and how are its wages spent? Collectively, Kelley's works evoke a child's rite of passage to the adult world of labor, guilt, and atonement.

***More Love Hours Than Can Ever Be Repaid* and *The Wages of Sin*, 1987**
Stuffed fabric toys and afghans on canvas with dried corn; wax candles on wood and metal base, 90 x 119 1/4 x 5 in. (228.6 x 302.9 x 12.7 cm) plus candles and base
Purchase, with funds from the Painting and Sculpture Committee 89.13a–e

ELLSWORTH KELLY

b. 1923

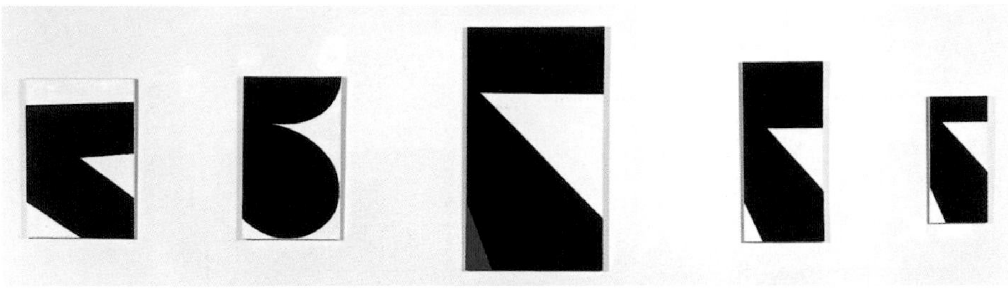

Ellsworth Kelly's complex, often massively scaled geometric abstractions are frequently grounded in something actually seen. *Painting in Five Panels* is one in a series of Kelly's "figure-ground" paintings, which explore the relationship between background and foreground elements, between positive and negative spaces. Like other figure-ground abstractions, *Painting in Five Panels* began with a visual observation—in this case, a visit to the Philadelphia Museum of Art in 1954, where Kelly was intrigued by the way five small, differently sized paintings by the Spanish Cubist Juan Gris were hung on the wall. He liked "the way the five Gris pictures worked together, reinforcing each other." Kelly proceeded to make five smaller paintings in varying scales designed to be hung together as one work. Each panel features a black shape set against a white ground, though in the largest, central panel, Kelly added a slice of green at the lower left. His investigation of figure-ground relationships, however, extended beyond the visual effects of the individual canvases to encompass the wall spaces between and around each work. For *Painting in Five Panels*, he specified the order of the panels and exactly how many inches each panel should be hung from the floor and from the adjacent panels.

Atlantic, which Kelly painted the following year, was the first work in which he reversed the black-white scheme, here placing a white area on top of a black ground. *Atlantic* derives its abstracted curves from a shadow, cast by telephone poles, that Kelly observed on a book he was reading on a bus. The facing pages of the book and its central fold are mirrored in the painting's diptych structure. Kelly first translated the shadow, curved by the bowing of the book, into a group of drawings in 1955, then into a smaller painting, and finally into the grand scale of *Atlantic*—more than 9 feet wide.

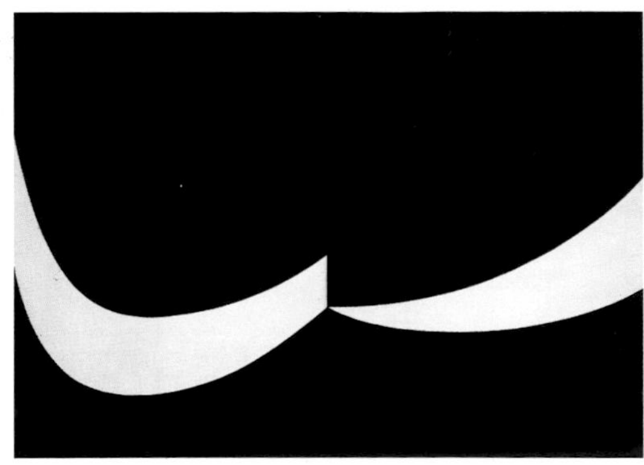

Painting in Five Panels, 1955
Oil on canvas, 36 x 140 5/16 in. (91.4 x 356.5 cm) overall
Promised gift of Charles H. Carpenter, Jr. P.94.9

Atlantic, 1956
Oil on canvas, 2 panels, 80 x 114 in. (203.2 x 289.6 cm) overall
Purchase 57.9a–b

EDWARD KIENHOLZ

1927–1994

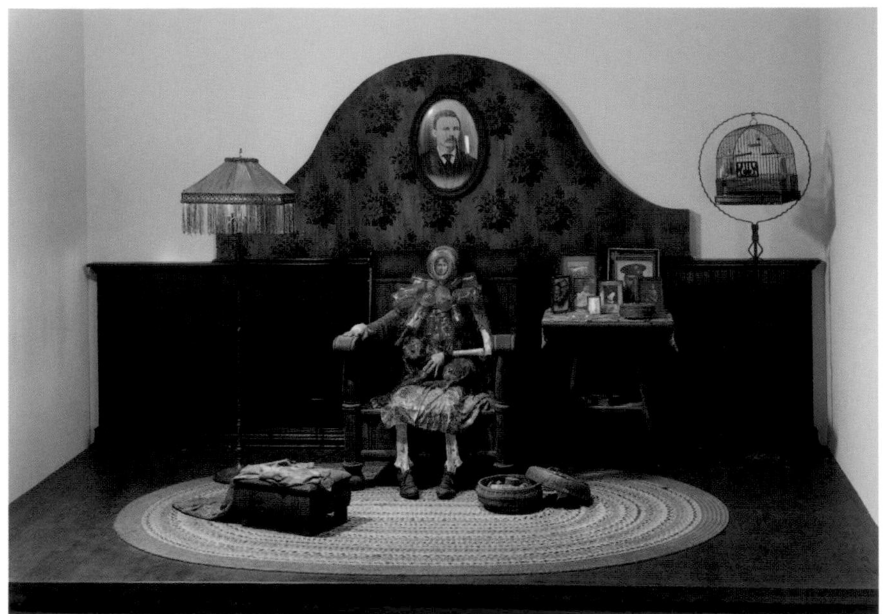

Edward Kienholz believed that the human condition and its cultural setting could be comprehended only through the commonplace, the discordant, and the discarded. In the late 1950s, his art took the form of repulsively attractive, found-object assemblages; in 1961, he made the first of many life-size tableaux such as *The Wait*—environmental installations that expose social and political inequities.

The Wait, one of Kienholz's best-known—and most morbid—works, investigates the plight of the aged. An old woman, embalmed in plastic coating and constructed of cow bones (with a deer skull for the back of her head), sits at the center of a maudlin interior. A matriarch of obsolescence, she lives in a cell of memory. Her attendants are a broken lamp beneath a tattered shade and the feeble chirps and fettered flight of a live, caged parakeet. Her youth is recalled in the bottled photograph of an innocent, late adolescent face that serves as her own face. She is adorned with a grim and heavy necklace of sixteen glass jars containing crosses and gold figurines that stand for events of her past—in the artist's words, "her childhood on a farm and move on to girlhood, waiting for her man, marriage, bearing children, being loved, wars, family, death and then senility, where everything becomes a hodgepodge."

In this vision of imminent death, even the most common domestic activities, symbolized by the crocheting and sewing equipment, must be set aside. Kienholz's work, unlike any other sculpture of the era, injected emotional and moral indignation into postwar American art.

The Wait, 1964–65
Tableau: wood, fabric, polyester resin, flock, metal, bones, glass, paper, leather, varnish, black-and-white photographs, taxidermed cat, live parakeet, wicker, and plastic, 13 units, 80 x 160 x 84 in. (203.2 x 406.4 x 213.4 cm) overall
Gift of the Howard and Jean Lipman Foundation, Inc. 66.49a–m

FRANZ KLINE

1910–1962

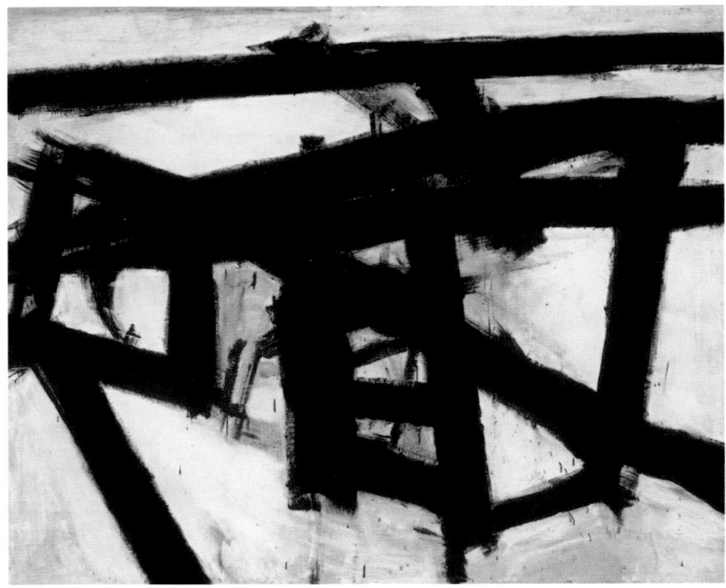

Although an important figure of Abstract Expressionism, Franz Kline never intended his paintings to be records of spontaneous expression, as they were assumed to be for Willem de Kooning and Jackson Pollock (pp. 166, 242). Rather, his paintings are often carefully composed of elements taken from earlier sketches and studies. Kline's signature black and white canvases, which he produced from around 1949 to 1961, were inspired in part by the experience of seeing his small-scale drawings projected onto a wall. He was fascinated by the way something as simple as an intersection of lines became forceful and dramatic when enlarged and isolated: "There's an excitement about the larger areas, and I think you confront yourself much more with a big canvas." By magnifying details in his paintings, Kline was perhaps also influenced by the work of his photographer friends, among them Aaron Siskind (p. 286).

Mahoning, nearly 7 feet high and more than 8 feet long, was painted with quick, broad motions in fast-drying enamel paint. It is based on a sketch (also owned by the Whitney Museum) that Kline made on the page of a telephone book. Atypically, Kline incorporated collage elements into *Mahoning*—sheets of paper are affixed to the canvas under layers of paint. Critics have sometimes cited Japanese calligraphy as a source for works such as *Mahoning*, but Kline pointed out that he was not painting black symbols on a white field. "Calligraphy is writing, and I'm not writing....I paint the white as well as the black, and the white is just as important." Kline titled many of his paintings after locations near Wilkes-Barre, Pennsylvania, where he grew up, though they are not meant to represent landscapes in any way. Mahoning is the name of two separate towns in Pennsylvania as well as a county in western Ohio.

Mahoning, 1956
Oil and paper collage on canvas, 80 x 100 in. (203.2 x 254 cm)
Purchase, with funds from the Friends of the Whitney Museum of American Art 57.10

WILLEM DE KOONING

1904–1997

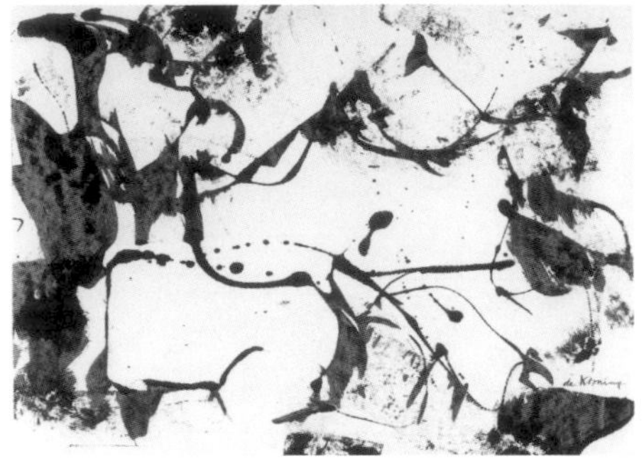

A leading artist among the Abstract Expressionists, Willem de Kooning never believed that abstraction and representation were mutually exclusive: "I'm not interested in 'abstracting' or taking things out or reducing painting to design, form, line, and color. I paint this way because I can keep putting more things in it—drama, anger, pain, love, a figure, a horse, my ideas about space. Through your eyes it again becomes an emotion or an idea." This slippage between representation and abstraction can be seen throughout de Kooning's work. In drawings such as *Landscape, Abstract,* the artist allowed loose, gestural marks to suggest landscape and body forms even though the work remains resolutely abstract.

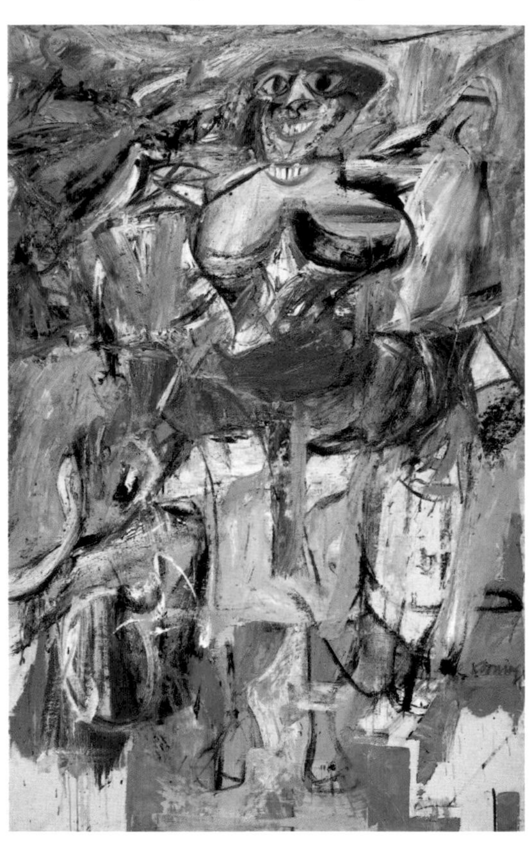

A standing woman is clearly visible in *Woman and Bicycle*, despite the painterly integration of the body into its surroundings. The female figure is one of the most traditional subjects in the history of art, but the woman in de Kooning's painting is distinctly of the 1950s. Her bright yellow dress, high heels, and garish smile reflect the specifically American gender stereotypes of the time, to which de Kooning, an immigrant from the Netherlands, was repeatedly drawn for the famous series of woman paintings he made between 1950 and 1953. In *Woman and Bicycle*, a second toothy grin hangs like a necklace and indicates an earlier placement of the mouth.

In the late 1950s, de Kooning began dividing his time between

Landscape, Abstract, c. 1949
Oil on paper mounted on board, 19 x 25 1/2 in. (48.3 x 64.8 cm)
Gift of Mr. and Mrs. Alan H. Temple 68.96

Woman and Bicycle, 1952–53
Oil on canvas, 76 1/2 x 49 in. (194.3 x 124.5 cm)
Purchase 55.35

WILLEM DE KOONING

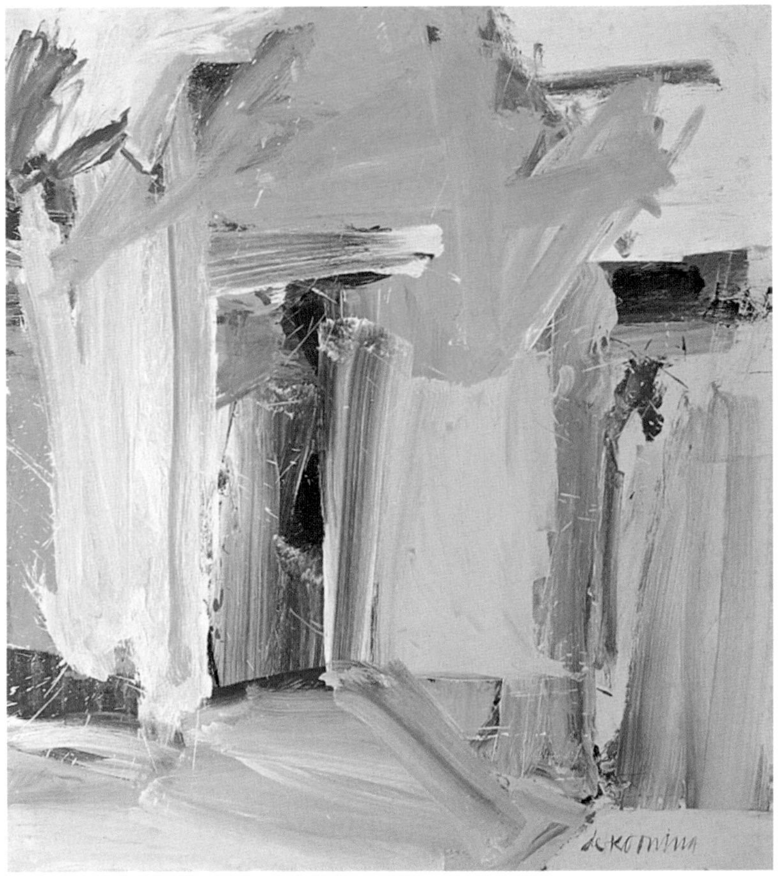

New York and eastern Long Island, then a rural area. His paintings of this period, as he described them in 1960, reflect the change in his surroundings: "They're emotions, most of them. Most of them are landscapes and highways and sensations of that, outside the city—with the feeling of going to the city or coming from it." That same year he painted *Door to the River*, with brushstrokes (made with housepainter's brushes) that Frank Stella (p. 297) described as "wide, wet, and wristy." The broad strokes of pink, yellow, brown, and white form a doorlike rectangle in the center of the canvas, beneath which lies a passage of blue, perhaps evoking the river in the title.

Door to the River, 1960
Oil on canvas, 80 x 70 in. (203.2 x 177.8 cm)
Purchase, with funds from the Friends of the Whitney Museum of American Art 60.63

JEFF KOONS

b. 1955

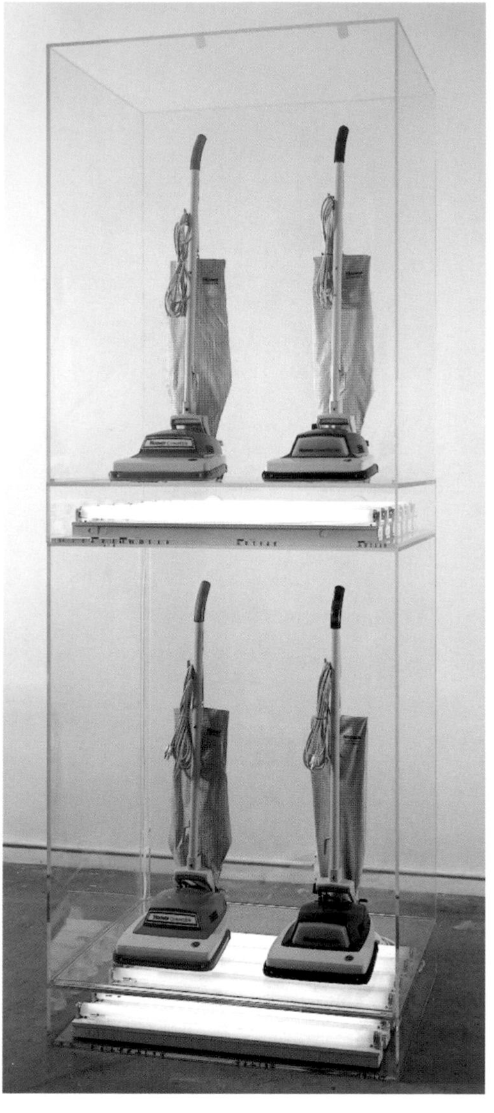

One of the most scandalous and successful artists of the 1980s, Jeff Koons adapted the Pop sensibility of Claes Oldenburg and Andy Warhol (pp. 229, 316) to make wry comments on the materialism and consumer obsessions spreading throughout society during the economic boom of the 1980s. Much of his subject matter was drawn not from the high-end products coveted by the well-to-do, but from kitsch—stuffed toys and cheap ceramic figurines. Koons copied these objects, sometimes on a monumental scale, in the finest porcelain, crystal, and stainless steel. He also proved himself to be a master manipulator of the media, running flashy ads in art magazines that featured pictures of himself rather than of his work. He succeeded in promoting an image of the artist as star, as tastemaker, and as bestower of cultural integrity.

New Hoover Convertibles is from one of Koons' earliest series of works, called *The New*. With an irony worthy of Marcel Duchamp, who in 1917 exhibited a urinal as a work of art, Koons placed brand-new, store-bought vacuum cleaners in an immaculate, minimal display case that protects them from the dust and surface grime they are designed to remove. Rather than scooting through dirt, the machines hover over bright, sterile fluorescent lights. By thoroughly transforming the expected context and use of the vacuum cleaners, and by raising domestic appliances to the immortal realm of fine art, Koons makes us question not only the art collector's impulse, but society's obsessions with cleanliness, efficiency, and newness.

New Hoover Convertibles, Green, Blue; New Hoover Convertibles, Green, Blue; Double-Decker, 1981–87
Vacuum cleaners, plexiglass, and fluorescent lights, 22 units, 116 x 41 x 28 in.
(294.6 x 104.1 x 71.1 cm) overall
Purchase, with funds from The Sondra and Charles Gilman, Jr. Foundation, Inc., and the Painting and Sculpture Committee 89.30a–v

JOSEPH KOSUTH

b. 1945

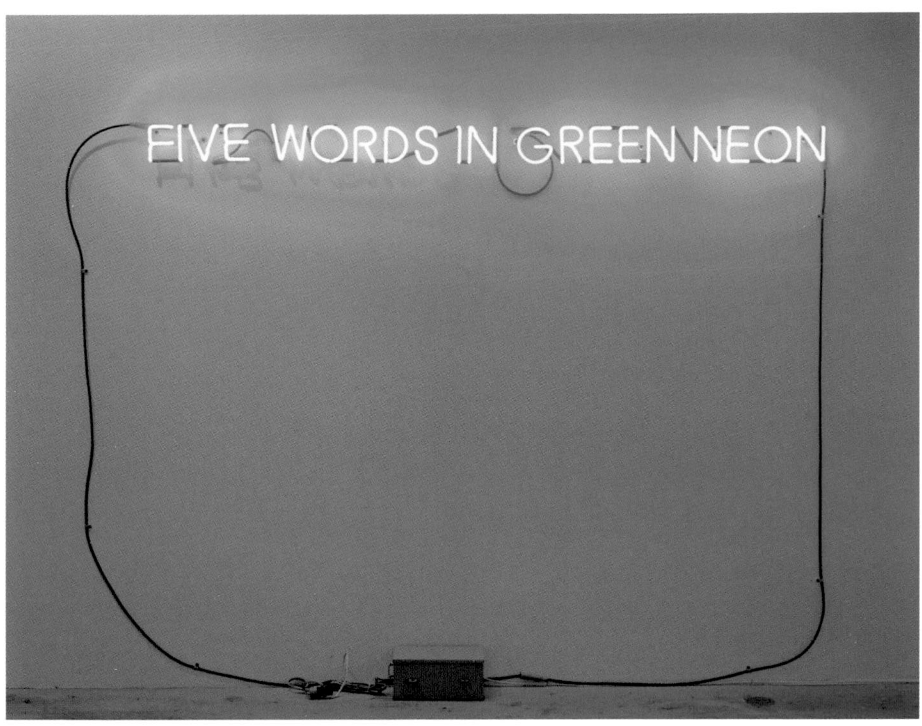

In 1969, Joseph Kosuth published the first part of his three-part manifesto "Art After Philosophy" in a London journal and instantly became a leading theorist and practitioner of Conceptual art. "Being an artist now," he wrote, "means to question the nature of art." Traditional art forms such as painting could only summon antiquated considerations of aesthetic value or taste. Art needed to define itself anew by abandoning conventional means of expression.

Five Words in Green Neon anticipates Kosuth's written manifesto by a few years but clearly reflects its assertion that Conceptual art is based "on the understanding of the linguistic nature of all art propositions." The work, comprising only the words of the title constructed in green neon tubing, makes language its content by collapsing description and image into each other. *Five Words in Green Neon* is not only the title of the work but all that we see. Art, Kosuth reveals, does not reside in the object itself, but in our ideas about the object. This object is meant to be displayed within a museum or gallery context, amid works whose meanings are far less self-evident. The contrast between Kosuth's object and traditional art challenges our instinctive assumptions about the nature of art and draws attention to the way perception is determined by language.

Five Words in Green Neon, 1965
Neon tubing, 62 1/8 x 80 5/8 x 6 in. (157.8 x 204.8 x 15.2 cm) overall
Purchase, with funds from Leonard A. Lauder 93.42a–c

LEE KRASNER

1908–1984

In the mid-1940s, Lee Krasner was one of the first to adopt the artistic innovations that would soon become known as Abstract Expressionism. She had already committed herself to abstraction before World War II, when she joined the American Abstract Artists, a group dedicated to furthering the cause of abstract art at a time when most American artists were painting in a realist style.

From 1946 to 1949, Krasner, who was married to Jackson Pollock (p. 242), made a series of small-scale works she called the *Little Image* paintings, in which she sought "a merging of the organic with the abstract." These canvases, with thick paint surfaces and all-over compositions, can be separated into three groups. In the first, Krasner fractured the surface into a mosaic of color, while in the second she covered the surface with weblike traceries.

She referred to works of the third type, including *White Squares*, as "hieroglyphic." Krasner was fascinated by ancient languages. Raised as an Orthodox Jew, she learned to copy (though not to read) Hebrew letters, which fostered a lifelong interest in the abstract character of writing dissociated from meaning and ultimately led to the marks of her "hieroglyphic" works.

White Squares is covered in a dense, white lattice of open squares, with an evenness that recalls a page of text. Yet the traces of yellow, blue, and green visible beneath the black ground give the painting a sense of depth. The concentric rectilinear forms may evoke another of Krasner's fascinations, foraminifera—spirally arranged marine organisms. Indeed, Krasner had a collection of crystals, shells, and foraminifera, which perhaps explains why the painting was originally titled by a friend (and inscribed on the stretcher) "Passion for Collecting."

White Squares, c. 1948
Oil on canvas, 24 x 30 in. (61 x 76.2 cm)
Gift of Mr. and Mrs. B.H. Friedman 75.1

BARBARA KRUGER

b. 1945

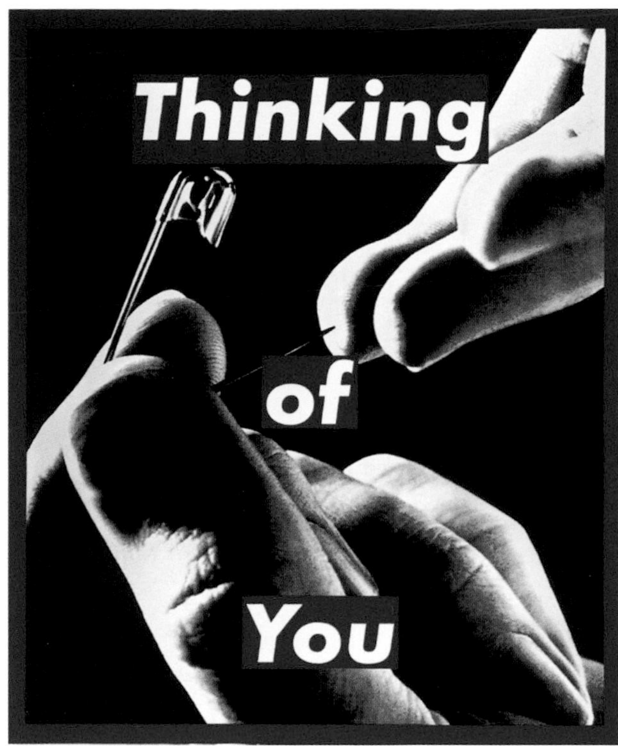

Barbara Kruger began her career as a graphic designer of book jackets and magazines, including an eleven-year stint as art director for *Mademoiselle*. When she left the commercial world and took up artmaking in 1979, it was to expose the very institutions she had once served. She is now an image scavenger, culling vintage images from the mass media, which she juxtaposes with slogans and phrases such as "Thinking of You," "I Shop Therefore I Am," and "Your Body Is a Battleground." Displayed not only in galleries and museums, but also in traditionally non-art contexts such as billboards, newspapers, magazines, bus stops, and train stations, Kruger's "picture practice," as she calls it, addresses the impact of the media on the formation of identity, gender, sexuality, race, class and, above all, power relations.

Thinking of You incorporates an enlarged close-up of a found photograph of a safety pin pricking someone's index finger and interrupted by the phrase "Thinking of You," written in Kruger's signature font—Futura Bold Italic—and contained in her signature lacquered red frame. Typical here is Kruger's use of a shifting pronoun—in this case "You"—to replicate the mass media's implication of the viewer into its web of insinuating messages. Like the safety pin, Kruger's tactic pricks at our sense of self-awareness as objects of media attention. Who is being addressed? How does the media create desire for the commodity being sold? How do we critically read media imagery? Kruger's work lifts the veil that conceals the sublimated messages directed to our unconscious needs and desires.

Untitled (Thinking of You), 2000
Photographic screenprint on vinyl, 123 x 101 in. (312.4 x 256.5 cm)
Purchase, with funds from the Katherine Schmidt Shubert Fund 2000.217

WALT KUHN

1877–1949

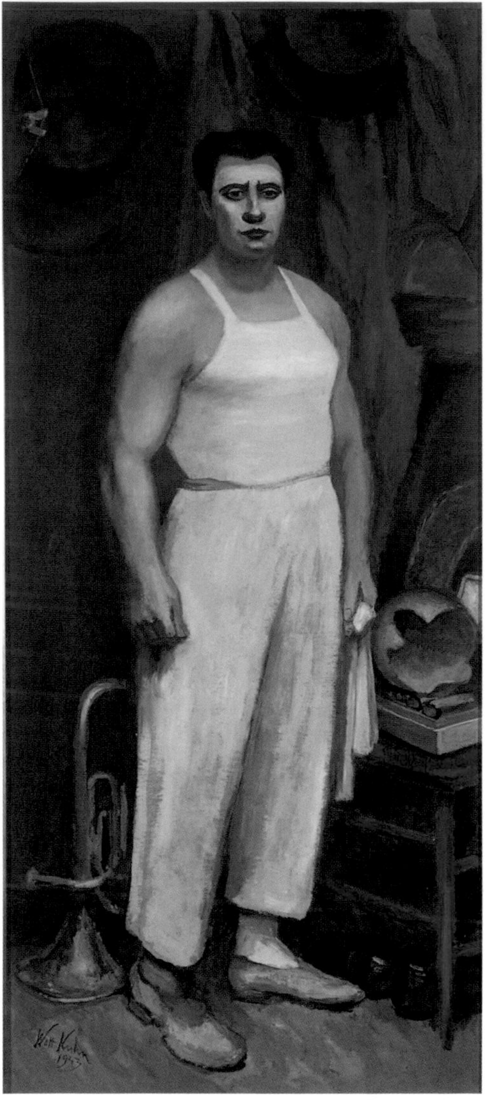

Although *Clown in His Dressing Room* represents one of Walt Kuhn's most familiar subjects, the artist did not begin to paint his somber, reflective portraits of circus performers until the 1920s, when he was in his fifties. By then he had already established himself as an artist—and had worked as a cartoonist, set decorator, and traveling bicycle racer. Kuhn was one of the organizers of the 1913 Armory Show, which introduced America to European vanguard art, and he himself experimented with modernist ideas. Yet he was never entirely satisfied with his work. A health crisis, at age forty-eight, led him to rediscover the theatrical subjects that had always fascinated him: clowns, acrobats, and other characters of the stage and circus.

For the next twenty years, Kuhn produced memorable portraits such as *Clown in His Dressing Room*. His models were often professional performers—but not celebrities—whom he auditioned for their roles in his paintings. He designed the theatrical costumes but allowed his models to select from these costumes and pose themselves. Each portrait was thus a collaborative production, with Kuhn serving as ringmaster to a melancholy parade of performers. Like many of Kuhn's portraits, *Clown in His Dressing Room* is set backstage. The performer is not yet in costume; his colorless attire and white makeup contrast with the vivid red and green clothing behind him. He stands with a casual resignation, as if posing for an official portrait. Kuhn presents the clown not as an individual, but as a type—as the humble but ennobled figure behind the painted mask.

Clown in His Dressing Room, 1943
Oil on canvas, 72 x 32 in. (182.9 x 81.3 cm)
Gift of an anonymous donor 50.1

GASTON LACHAISE

1882–1935

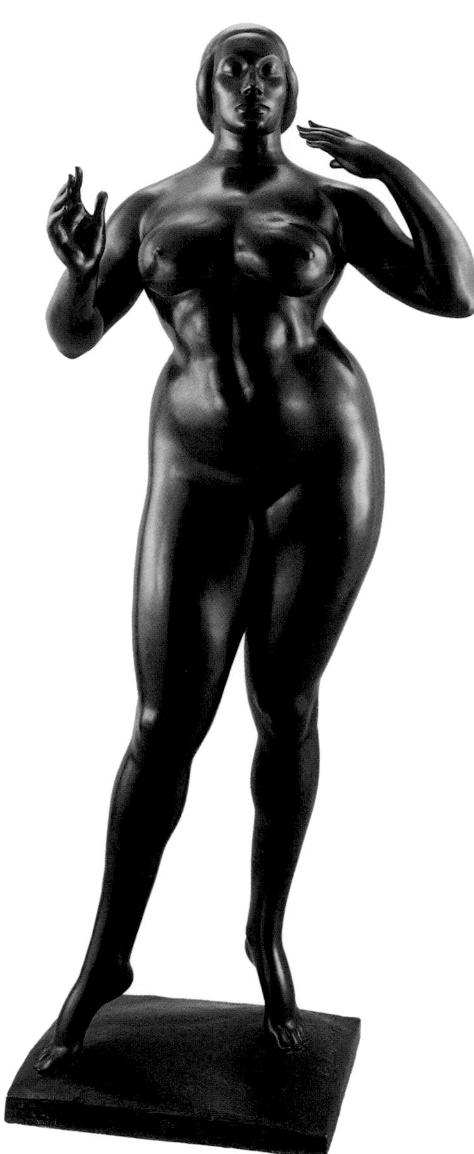

The French-born sculptor Gaston Lachaise produced a remarkably diverse and inventive body of work on a single subject: the shapely form of the American woman who was first his mistress and later his wife. When Lachaise chanced upon Isabel Dutaud Nagle at the Luxembourg Gardens in Paris, he was a promising young sculptor, trained in the academic tradition. Though Isabel was married and ten years his senior, he followed her back to America, where he would remain for the rest of his life.

In 1912, Lachaise created a plaster portrait of his beloved Isabel; known as *Standing Woman*, it was later cast in bronze. The sculpture, with swelling breasts and hips and a narrow, high waist, is taller than the actual Isabel. Lachaise was always fascinated by mass, whether it was made of flesh or metal. Yet his *Standing Woman* is perched on improbably tiny feet, making her bulk seem somehow airy. She appears both massive and weightless, earthy and ethereal.

Lachaise called Isabel "the Goddess I am searching to express in all things." She was not just a model, but an enduring muse, an archetype of womanhood. It is not surprising that critics have often compared his portraits of Isabel to such prehistoric fertility figures as the Venus of Willendorf. Yet the ancient sculpture looks squat and earthbound beside Lachaise's buoyant *Standing Woman*. Isabel rises as if toward eternity, her arms tentatively seeking a gesture.

Standing Woman, 1912–27
Bronze, 69 1/2 x 26 15/16 x 17 in. (176.5 x 68.4 x 43.2 cm)
Purchase 36.91

LIZ LARNER

b. 1960

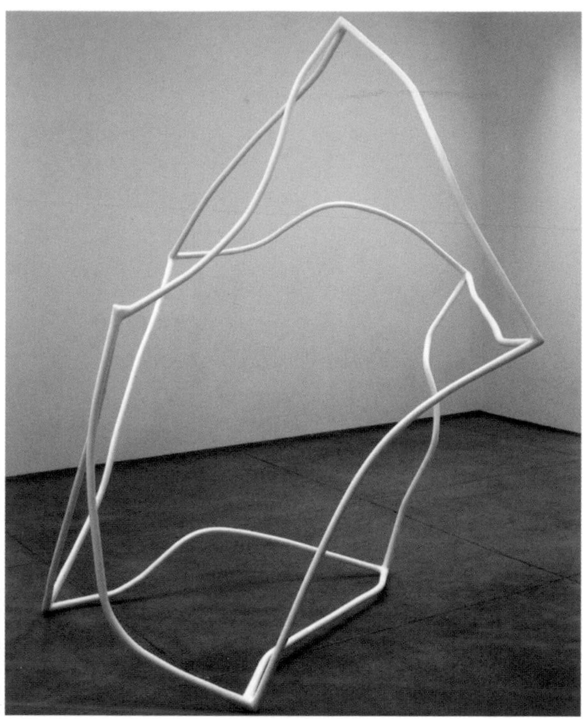

Although California artist Liz Larner revisits aesthetic territory first charted by Minimalist sculptors of the 1960s, her work ventures onto new ground. Like the Minimalists, she often explores perceptions of geometric form. But whereas the shapes of Minimalist sculpture seem as straightforward as a simple cube (p. 292), Larner's configurations resist easy identification.

Two or Three or Something recalls a Minimalist cube that has been reduced to a skeleton, then bent and contorted. The edges and corners seem to have a will of their own, swooping up off the floor or torquing, as if trying to walk themselves right out of the gallery. Larner constructed this complex armature from steel wrapped in paper and then tinted with watercolor paints. *Two or Three or Something* is therefore both painterly and sculptural; or, as the title suggests, it vacillates between two and three dimensions and an undefinable middle ground.

Larner explains that she employs "line to make forms that could not be perceived at all if I were to use solid volume." Conversely, she uses sculpture to investigate shapes that cannot be appreciated in a line drawing: her work demands viewing from all angles. A former student of photography, she believes that the best sculpture defies photographic reproduction. Larner's work hinges on the physical experience of objects. *Two or Three or Something* cannot be comprehended by stationary looking; to understand the work fully, you must walk around it.

Two or Three or Something, 1998–99
Steel, paper, and watercolor, 101 x 84 x 64 1/2 in. (256.5 x 213.4 x 163.2 cm)
Purchase, with funds from the Contemporary Committee 2001.31

LOUISE LAWLER

b. 1947

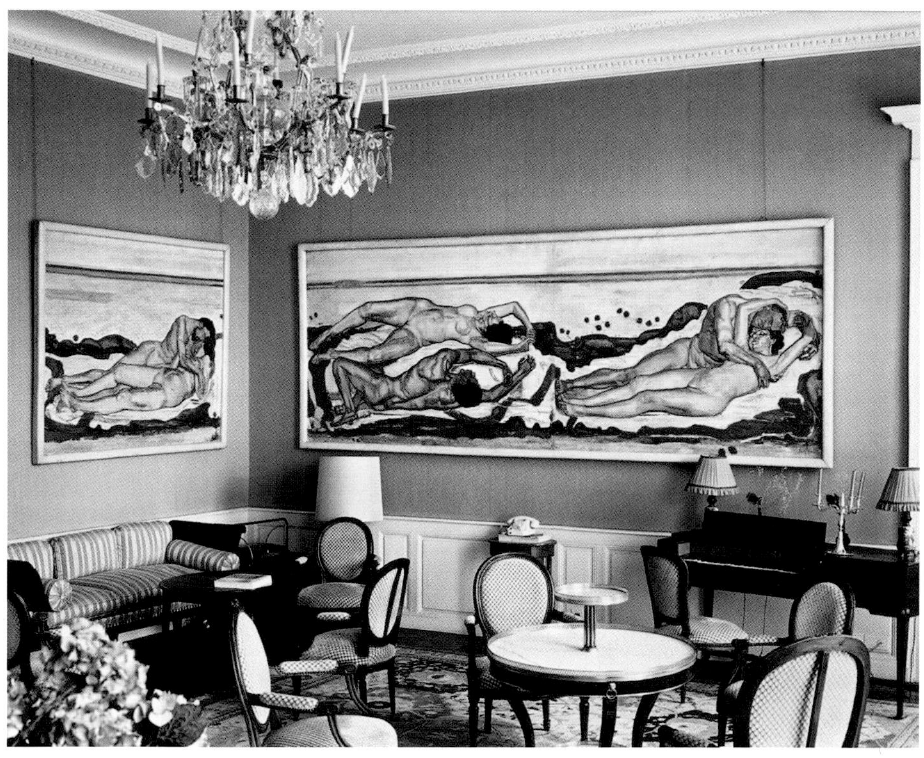

Louise Lawler's photographs examine the institutional contexts, commodity structures, and social sites where art gets seen, sold, and displayed—galleries, museums, private collections, auction houses, and art storage facilities. Lawler's work enables us to reflect on the often unseen impact that context exerts on the functions of art and the ways we understand it.

Salon Hodler documents the salon of a Swiss collector that is filled with rare antiques and dominated by two turn-of-the-last-century Symbolist paintings by the Swiss artist Ferdinand Hodler. But whereas the painted scenes are warm with lovers' embraces, in Lawler's photograph the salon itself, as critic Rosalind Krauss observed, takes on the cold, clinical, generalized air of an upscale hotel lobby. By presenting Hodler's paintings in this kind of setting, Lawler reveals them as dispassionate signs of wealth, class, and rarefied taste.

Implicit in Lawler's work, however, is the realization that different environments would bring to light other aspects of Hodler's canvases—their painterly eroticism on a museum wall, their commodity value on an auction house podium. Her photographs make the case that art is not a static language with fixed meanings; it is, on the contrary, fluid and mutable, always subject to shifting contexts, changing times, and altering collaborations.

Salon Hodler, 1992–93
Silver dye bleach print (Ilfochrome) mounted on paperboard, 48 x 57 7/16 in. (121.9 x 145.9 cm)
Purchase, with funds from the Photography Committee 94.23

JACOB LAWRENCE

1917–2000

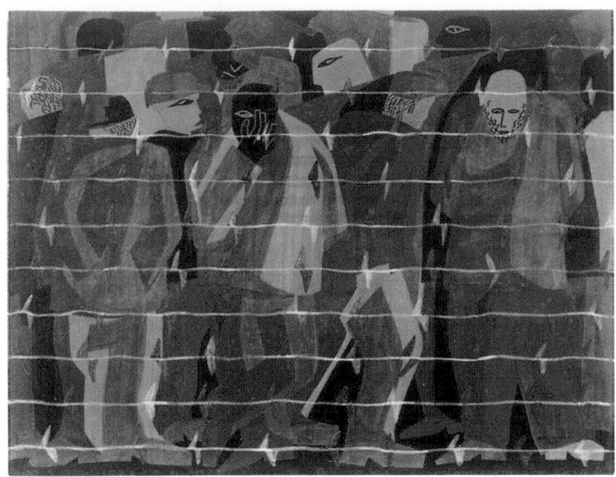

In 1941, twenty-four-year-old Jacob Lawrence had an exhibition at New York's Downtown Gallery—and quietly made history. Lawrence was the first African-American artist to be shown by a major commercial New York gallery. The work on view, *The Migration of the Negro* (1940–41), was a sixty-panel series that treated the African-American struggle for freedom with the grandeur of an epic. Early in his career, Lawrence had discovered that painting a series of works on one central theme was the most effective way to convey a story. The five series that preceded the *War Series* of 1946–47 were all narrative cycles based on history, whereas the *War Series* derived from personal experience. Produced almost a year after Lawrence's discharge from the Coast Guard, the fourteen panels present a sequence of self-contained reflections on the sense of displacement, regimentation, and community that Lawrence felt during his wartime service. *Reported Missing* shows both white and black American soldiers as prisoners of war, huddled together behind barbed wire. In their shared anxiety and misery, the question of race has become irrelevant.

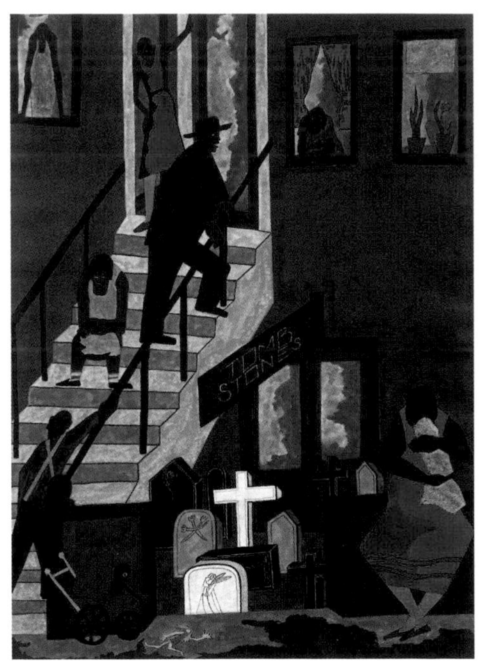

Also characteristic of Lawrence's work in the 1940s are subjects drawn from the streets and interiors of Harlem. Although he believed that you cannot "tell a story in a single painting," he occasionally worked outside the series structure. In bright, bold colors, *Tombstones* encapsulates the full sweep of life within the African-American community, from the cradle—the baby in a carriage at left, the mother and child at right—to the grave, marked at center by the tombstone seller's wares.

War Series: Reported Missing, 1947
Egg tempera on composition board, 16 x 20 in. (40.6 x 50.8 cm)
Gift of Mr. and Mrs. Roy R. Neuberger 51.18

****Tombstones***, 1942
Gouache on paper, 28 3/4 x 20 1/2 in. (73 x 52.1 cm) sight
Purchase 43.14

BLANCHE LAZZELL

1878–1956

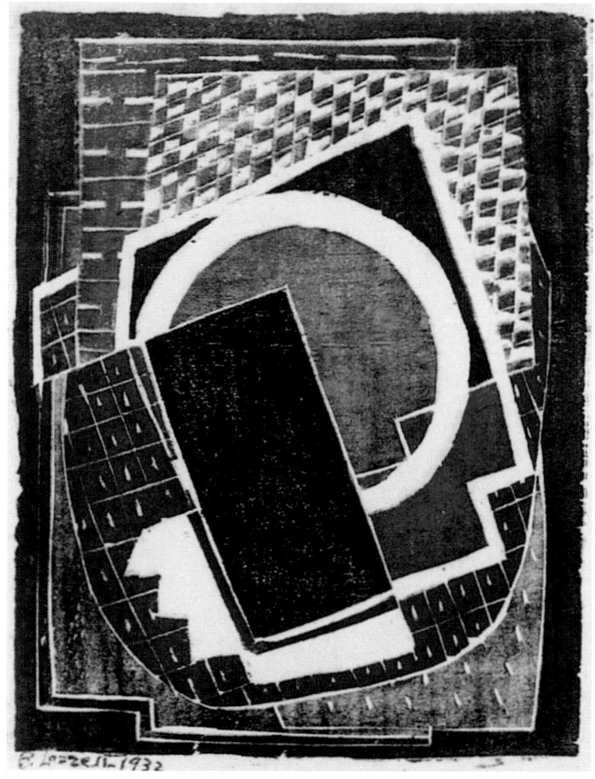

In the summer of 1949, the artistic community of Provincetown, Massachusetts, celebrated the careers of four artists in the region recognized as early proponents of abstract art. The celebration took the form of a series of exhibitions, lectures, performances, and discussions. One exhibition was devoted to the career of Blanche Lazzell, the only woman in the group, with a survey of her color blockprints, drawings, and paintings. Lazzell, a native of Morgantown, West Virginia, had studied in Paris in the years prior to World War I. In 1923, she returned to Paris to study with Fernand Léger, Albert Gleizes, and André Lhote. With Léger and Gleizes in particular, Lazzell mastered the lessons of planar abstraction—simplifying her forms by deleting details to reduce a composition to its most essential parts. Her works are enlivened by an almost Fauvist palette that can give her more identifiable images a lively, decorative appeal.

Abstract principles sustain much of Lazzell's work but are most visible in the series of non-representational blockprints and paintings she created after 1923. Her 1932 color block print *Untitled (Abstraction)* closely adheres to the compositional formulas espoused by Gleizes—interlocking, superimposed forms that create a lively two-dimensional surface. Although small in physical size, the image has the monumentality and scale of a painting or sculptural relief.

Untitled (Abstraction), 1932
Woodcut: sheet, 9 1/8 x 5 3/8 in. (23.2 x 13.7 cm) irregular; image, 5 9/16 x 4 1/4 in. (14.1 x 10.8 cm)
Purchase, with funds from the Print Committee 2000.41

RICO LEBRUN

1900–1964

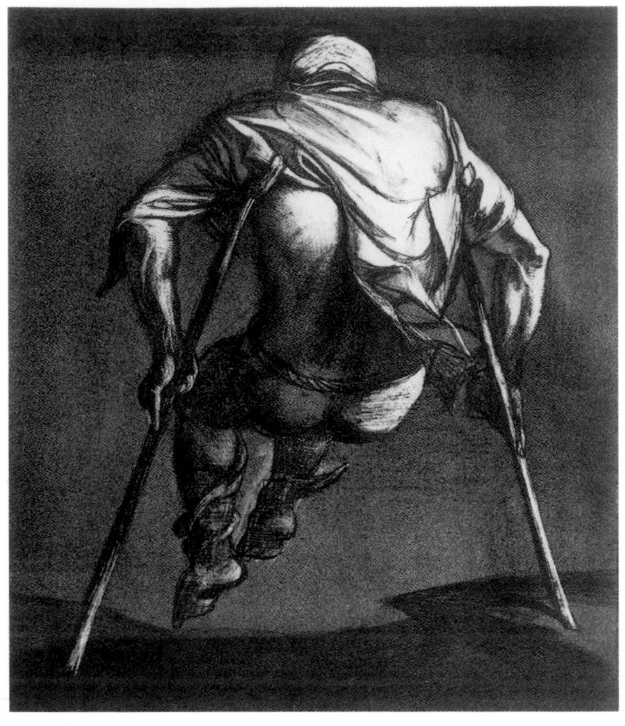

Little American art at mid-century could equal the psychological intensity of Rico Lebrun's figurative paintings, drawings, and prints. For Lebrun, the human being was an inexhaustible subject, a crucible that illuminated the ongoing crises of his time and their profound repercussions. His paintings and extensive corpus of drawings are marked by an intensity of focus on emotionally charged gesture and body movement.

Born and trained in Italy, Lebrun was profoundly influenced by the Italian and Spanish artists of the Mannerist and Baroque periods. After emigrating to New York in the 1920s, he spent long hours in the print rooms at The Metropolitan Museum of Art and the New York Public Library, studying the prints and drawings of the master draftsmen of the past: the beggars and lonely people who populate Rembrandt's etchings and Francisco Goya's *Disasters of War*, a series of horrific etchings prompted by the atrocities of Napoleon's war in Spain. The full impact of these studies can be seen in Lebrun's first lithographs of beggars and cripples, produced at the Colorado Springs Fine Arts Center in 1945. *Rabbit*, the most enigmatic of these prints in both imagery and title, has long been ranked among the important American prints of the period. In this strange image of a cripple hovering over a barren landscape, Lebrun captured the anxiety and uncertainty that pervaded civilization after the devastation of World War II. *Rabbit* does not present a victorious figure, but a survivor about to enter unknown terrain. In his willingness to go on despite fear and physical debility, he represents the enduring heroism of humankind.

Rabbit, 1945
Lithograph: sheet, 19 15/16 x 14 7/8 in. (50.6 x 37.8 cm); image, 17 1/8 x 12 3/4 in. (43.5 x 32.4 cm)
Purchase, with funds from the Print Committee 98.41.4

CHARLES LeDRAY
b. 1960

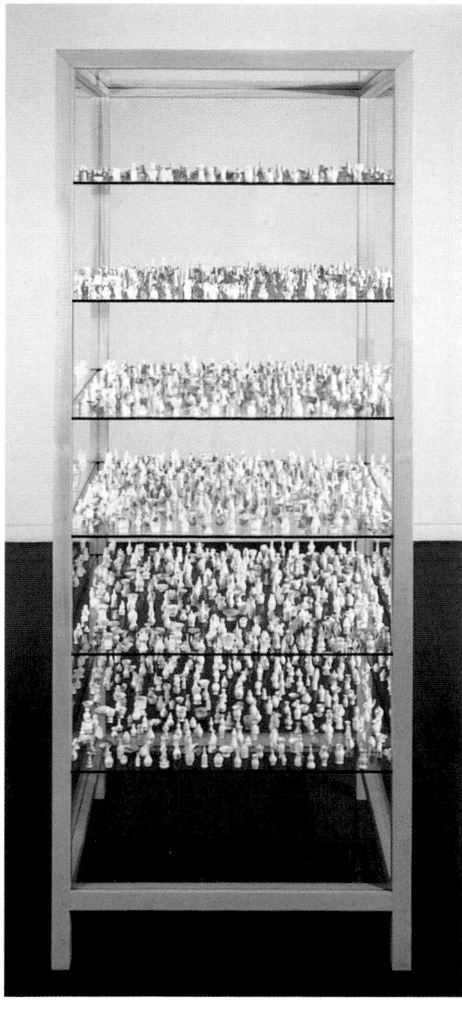

Charles LeDray's mode is the miniature. At the beginning of his career, he created tiny but highly detailed hand-sewn garments. Such painstaking craftsmanship and minute scale are equally evident in *Milk and Honey*. Two years in the making, it comprises a wood-framed glass cabinet with six glass shelves holding two thousand miniature, hand-thrown porcelain vessels—and no two are alike. These small pitchers, pots, bowls, and beakers, some characterized by simple symmetry, others by ornate detail, represent a veritable encyclopedia of ceramic styles, from Sung pottery to freehand twentieth-century vessels. All are glazed in varying shades of white, forming a ghostly, subtly differentiated array.

LeDray's work is open to a variety of interpretations. The miniature scale suggests that we are looking into a private world, perhaps the world of childhood or of childhood memories, while the sealed glass vitrine that contains the vessels speaks of obsessive collecting and proud display. The title refers to the biblical description of "a land of milk and honey"—the Promised Land vouchsafed to the Israelites enslaved in Egypt. LeDray's land of milk and honey seems to be a kind of multicultural utopia in which historical, stylistic, and cultural distinctions remain, even as they are subsumed into a common unity. Throughout history, vessels such as these have symbolized fecundity and plenty. Reduced to miniature scale, their symbolism is undiminished; indeed, the very abundance of the vessels implies a world of unending regeneration.

The labor-intensive creation of the garments and vessels in LeDray's work can be associated with the introduction of craft techniques to high art by feminist artists in the 1970s. The use of such techniques by a man indicates a broadening of the categories of artmaking in the 1990s and of the artist's options for self-definition.

Milk and Honey, 1994–96
2,000 porcelain objects, glass, and wood, 77 x 30 x 30 in. (195.6 x 76.2 x 76.2 cm) overall
Purchase, with funds from the Contemporary Painting and Sculpture Committee 96.75a–b

LEE MINGWEI

b. 1964

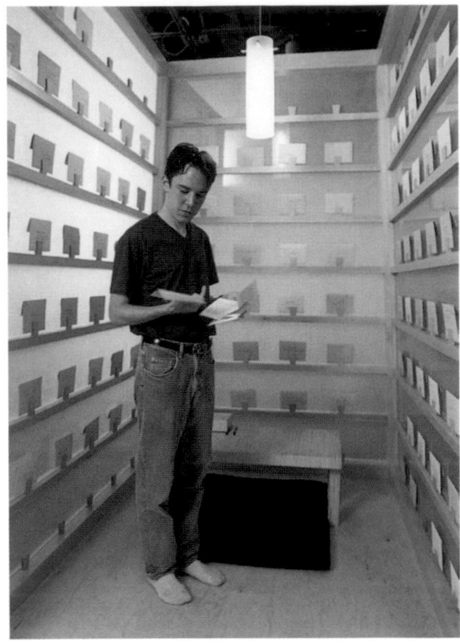

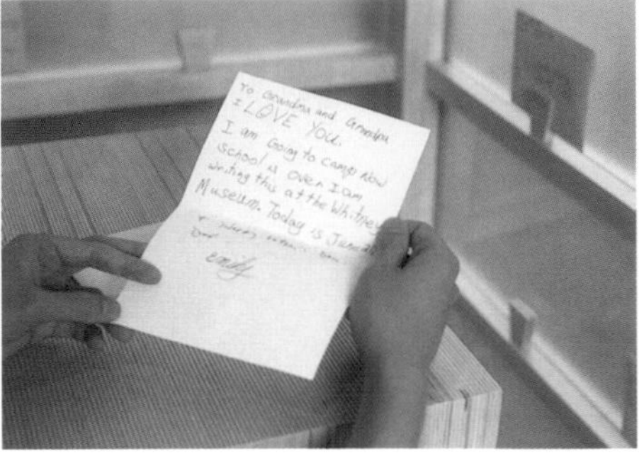

Inspired by the long letters the artist wrote to his grandmother shortly after her death, Lee Mingwei's *Booth from "The Letter-Writing Project"* encourages viewers to compose, in the artist's words, "the letters we have always intended to write but have put off with excuses." The work consists of three freestanding booths, each offering stationery, envelopes, and a quiet space in which to write. Lee asks that we reflect on three things: gratitude, insight, and forgiveness, which correspond respectively to the three positions of meditation in Ch'an Buddhism: standing, sitting, and kneeling. Lee, born in Taiwan, has been immersed in Buddhism since childhood, when he spent summers as an apprentice at a Ch'an monastery.

Each of the booths in *Booth from "The Letter-Writing Project"* provides one of the three meditative positions for writing. Letters and addressed envelopes can be clipped inside the booth for others to read, or they can be inserted in envelopes and sealed. The blurred form of the writer surrounded by letters is visible through the translucent glass panels of the booths. Addressed letters are collected and mailed weekly, while those to the deceased are burned by the artist. By aestheticizing a familiar ritual, *Booth from "The Letter-Writing Project"* heightens our awareness of the potential for change—of "becoming," in the Buddhist conception. Lee's installation also engages in a dialogue with the museum setting itself. Museums have long been regarded as places where the contemplation of beautiful things can lead to a transcendent experience. In *Booth from "The Letter-Writing Project"*, the path to transcendence comes not from the contemplation of objects, but from the consideration of everyday activities.

Booth from "The Letter-Writing Project", 1998
Wood and glass, dimensions variable
Gift of the artist in honor of Flora Miller Biddle and purchase, with funds from Joanne Leonhardt Cassullo and the Dorothea L. Leonhardt Fund at the Communities Foundation of Texas 99.54

ALFRED LESLIE

b. 1927

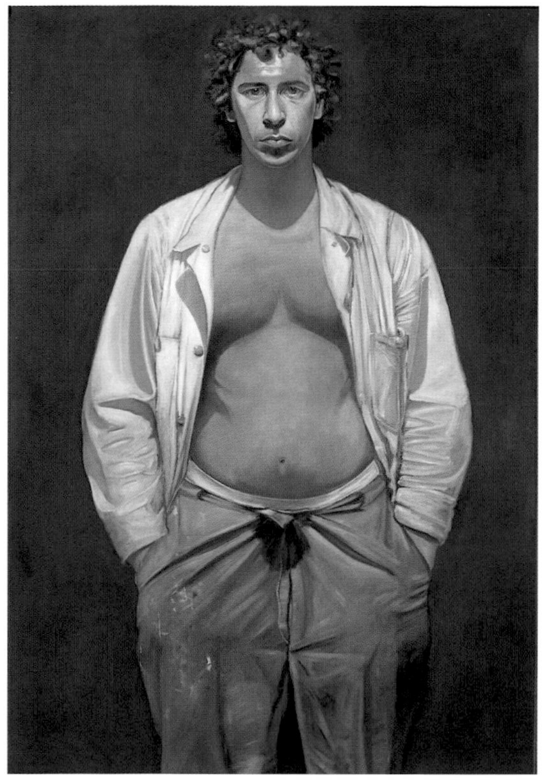

In the late 1940s, Alfred Leslie was among the youngest of the pioneers of Abstract Expressionism. By 1961, however, he was producing groundbreaking films (*Pull My Daisy*) and a form of realism he dubbed "confrontational": portraits of family and friends made from four separate, head-on views of the subject's head, chest, stomach, and hands, each seen from a different eye level, but all seamlessly fused to look like a single perspective view.

These concept-driven figures are isolated against a flat, dark ground, a seemingly endless non-space, and rise beyond life size to monumental scale, so that, as Leslie explained, "there could be no question but that they were meant for public viewing and an institutional life and service." The subjects look directly at the viewer, but their faces are devoid of perceptible emotions; they convey no information about themselves, nor do we know what they are thinking.

In this arresting and influential 9-foot-high self-portrait, Leslie paints himself in a three-quarter-length, frontal pose. Dressed in conventional artist's garb, he confronts the viewer head-on, his gaze somber, his stomach bulging above an unzipped fly and paint-splattered trousers. Leslie's intention has never been to duplicate a photographic effect, but rather to "readmit without excuses the human figure" and by doing so extend the narrow boundaries defined by abstract painting of the late 1950s.

In October 1966, a fire in Leslie's New York City studio destroyed twenty years of work. The Whitney self-portrait, painted shortly after the fire, is one of the few remaining works that exemplify Leslie's concerns in the early and mid-1960s.

Alfred Leslie, 1966–67, 1966–67
Oil on canvas, 108 x 72 in. (274.3 x 182.9 cm)
Purchase, with funds from the Friends of the Whitney Museum of American Art 67.30

SHERRIE LEVINE
b. 1947

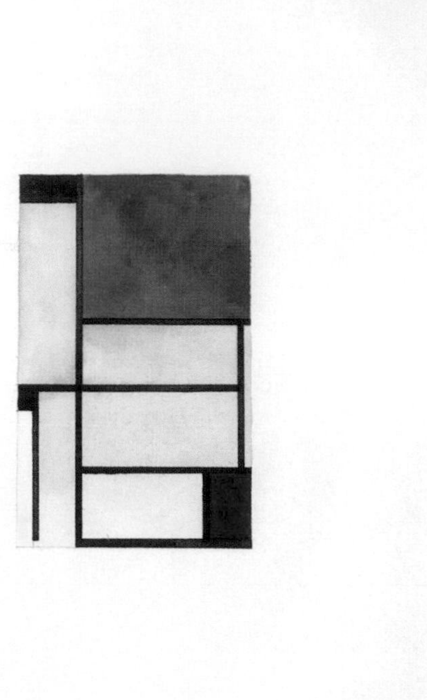

Sherrie Levine says that her work explores "ideas about representation, Modernism, memory, desire, influence, that Oedipal relationship artists have with the past." Along with other image-scavengers, such as Jeff Koons and Barbara Kruger (pp. 168, 171), who also emerged during the early 1980s, Levine has been at the center of discussions about "appropriation," the term used to describe the practice of borrowing imagery from other artists in the service of one's own artmaking. Levine's work, labeled postmodernist by critics, takes aim at the rhetoric of modernism—its demand that art be authentic and original—through a self-conscious use of copying.

Levine begins with the recognition that our sense of art history is determined less by originals than by the reproductions we see in books and magazines and on postcards. Her first appropriations in the late 1970s took the form of collages, pictures cut out of books and magazines and glued onto boards. *After Piet Mondrian* belongs to a later series of watercolors in which Levine copied reproductions of paintings by modern masters such as Vincent van Gogh, Joan Miró, and Piet Mondrian (p. 91). She traced the images from illustrated plates in books onto uniform, 11 x 14-inch pieces of paper—regardless of the format of the original. All the images are watercolors of approximately the same size, which creates a new commonality among originally disparate works. In this way, Levine subtly, almost transparently, asserts her own identity against the mythically august role played by these modern male masters. She herself has suggested that her appropriations address what literary critic Harold Bloom described as "the anxiety of influence," the age-old struggle of artists with their predecessors.

After Piet Mondrian, 1983
Watercolor on paper, 13 15/16 x 11 in. (35.4 x 27.9 cm)
Purchase, with funds from The Norman and Rosita Winston Foundation, Inc. and the Drawing Committee 91.6

HELEN LEVITT

b. 1913

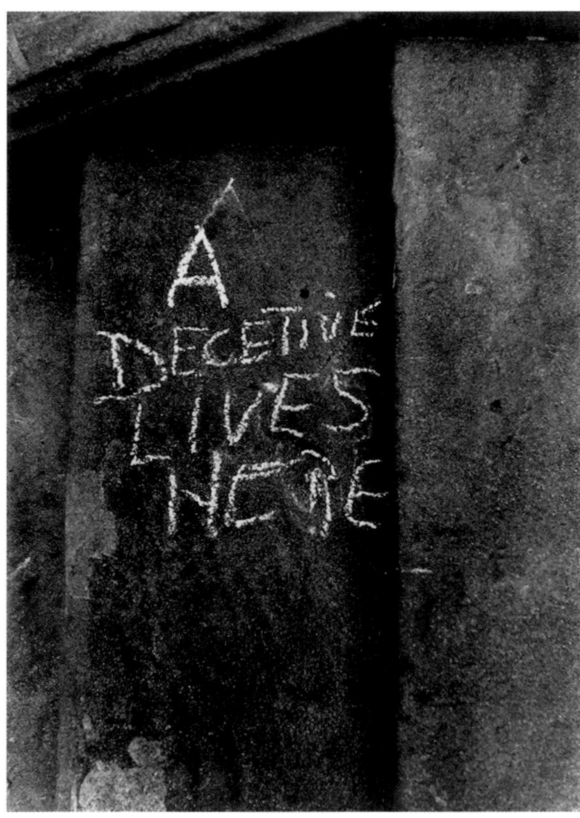

In the 1930s, the images of most professional photographers dealt with poverty and social injustice from a general, humanitarian perspective. The street photography of Brooklyn-born Helen Levitt, however, combines a profound realism with lyrical beauty. Levitt's photographs capture the often gritty stage of New York street life; her interest in vernacular urban subjects is particularly evident in her numerous images of the uninhibited play of children. At the same time, each photograph is remarkable for its subtle beauty; each is a poem about mysterious truths and personal tenderness.

On her way to a school in East Harlem, where she briefly taught in 1937, Levitt began photographing the children's chalk drawings she chanced upon in the streets and on sidewalks. Between 1937 and 1945, she made scores of close-up photographs of such transitory graffiti, which would otherwise have disappeared in the next rainstorm. *New York City* documents a child's scrawl on the stairs of a neighborhood stoop: "A DECETIVE LIVES HERE"—presumably intended to mean "a detective lives here." The endearing innocence of the child's spelling error counters the implication of adult deception, personified by a detective's characteristic stealth. By bearing witness to this anonymous youngster's ephemeral markings, Levitt's photograph gives voice to a child's uncanny ability to see and speak the truth.

To critics of the 1930s and 1940s, Levitt's work resonated with the kind of magical relationships promoted by Surrealism, which similarly celebrated the discovery of the strange and the fantastic in ordinary objects, anonymous things, and chance encounters.

New York City, 1940
Gelatin silver print, 8 x 5 3/4 in. (20.3 x 14.6 cm)
Purchase, with funds from the Photography Committee 97.98.9

SOL LEWITT

b. 1928

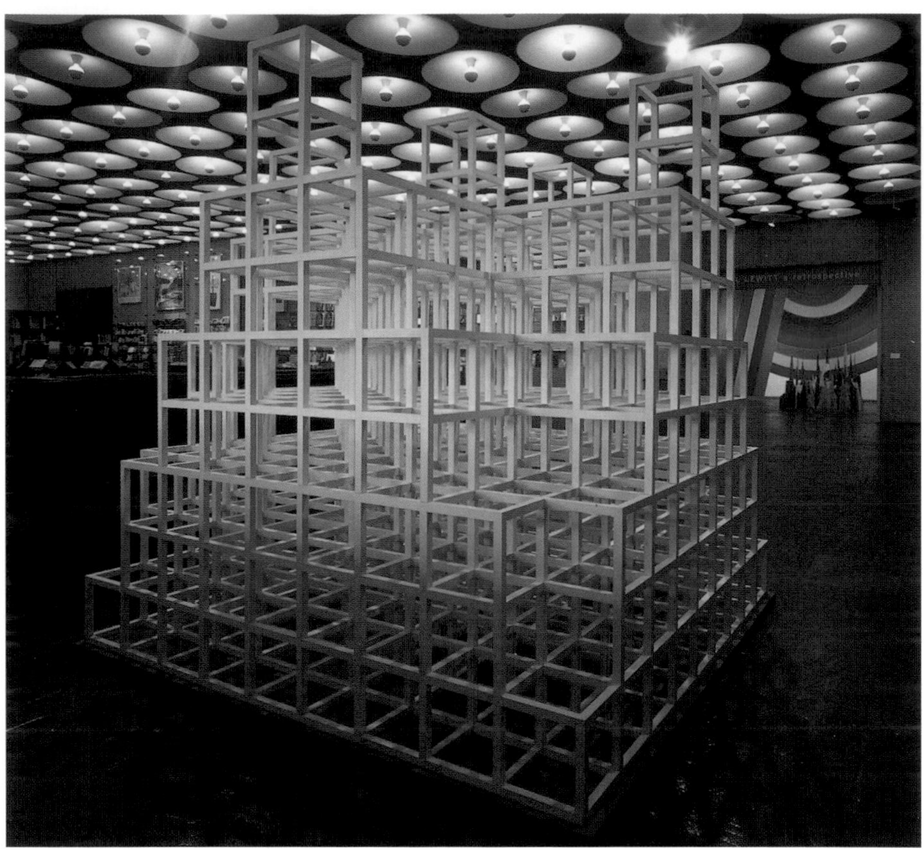

One of the pioneers of Conceptual art, Sol LeWitt gives primacy to the originating idea of a work of art rather than to its execution. Seeking a way to escape the dominance of Abstract Expressionism—with its large-scale paintings and emotionally loaded brushwork—he began in the early 1960s to explore a new method of making art, and in 1967 explained it in an essay entitled "Paragraphs on Conceptual Art." This influential text coined the term for a burgeoning movement which, LeWitt declared, "is made to engage the mind of the viewer rather than his eye or emotions."

LeWitt had already been developing these ideas in three-dimensional objects he called "structures." Based on the unit of an open rather than solid cube, the works peel away what he perceived as the decorative skin on traditional sculpture, revealing their underlying skeleton, or structure. Though he has created structures in a range of scales and shapes—the permutations growing more intricate over the last four decades—LeWitt has

Five Towers, 1986
Painted wood, 8 units, 86 9/16 x 86 9/16 x 86 9/16 in. (219.9 x 219.9 x 219.9 cm) overall
Purchase, with funds from the Louis and Bessie Adler Foundation, Inc., Seymour M. Klein, President, the John I.H. Baur Purchase Fund, the Grace Belt Endowed Purchase Fund, The Sondra and Charles Gilman, Jr. Foundation, Inc., The List Purchase Fund and the Painting and Sculpture Committee 88.7a–h

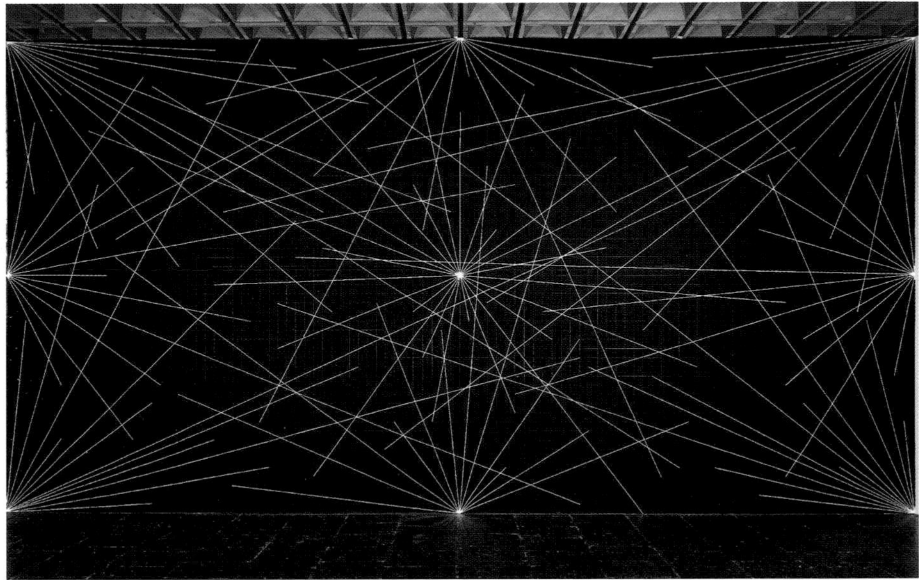

maintained the use of white cubes with a ratio of 1:8.5, that is, the open space between the edges of a cube is 8.5 times the width of each edge. *Five Towers*, a later, more complex structure, rises more than 7 feet high, culminating in four towers on each corner of a square, with a fifth tower in the center.

LeWitt has also sought to realize his ideas in other media, perhaps most famously in his wall drawings. In 1968, he drew directly on a gallery wall, a process that eliminated the intermediary surfaces of paper and frame, thereby taking the flatness of drawing literally. Since then, he has made almost a thousand wall drawings, nearly all accompanied by a set of instructions that enables others to execute them. This approach separates the conception of the work from the craft of fabricating it. LeWitt's written instructions, like the blueprints of an architect or the note-filled staves of a composer, often mark the end of his involvement in the realization of a work. *Wall Drawing #289*, when executed according to the instructions given in the title, covers four walls (one wall is shown here). The exact angle and length of the lines are determined by those who draw them, and the work's precise configuration and scale may be adapted to fit a variety of architectural contexts. Consequently, the wall drawing can differ significantly with each realization. Its only permanent, concrete form is a certificate of authenticity and a set of instructions.

Wall Drawing #289: A six-inch (15cm) grid covering each of the four black walls. White lines to points on the grids. 1st wall: 24 lines from the center; 2nd wall: 12 lines from the midpoint of each of the sides; 3rd wall: 12 lines from each corner; 4th wall: 24 lines from the center, 12 lines from the midpoint of each of the sides, 12 lines from each corner, 1976
White crayon lines and black graphite grid on black walls, dimensions variable
Purchase, with funds from the Gilman Foundation, Inc. 78.1.1–4

ROY LICHTENSTEIN
1923–1997

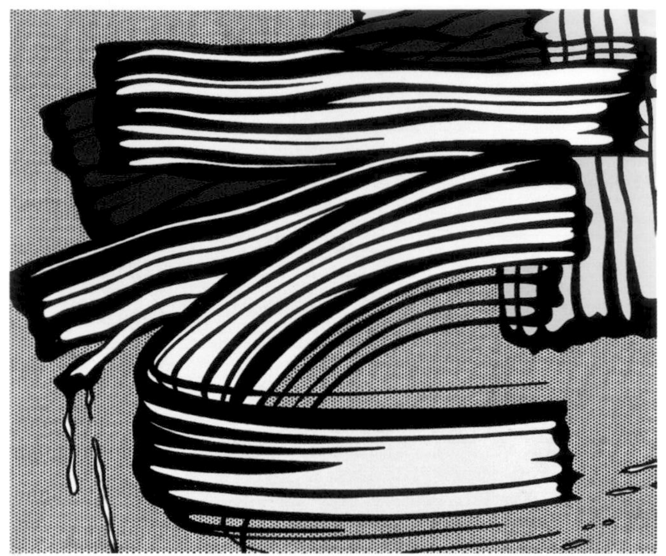

Little Big Painting is one of a number of works Roy Lichtenstein made in 1965 and 1966 in which he chose painting itself, specifically brushstrokes of paint, as his subject matter. These works were in part a wry commentary on the previous generation's most hallowed gestural painters, such as Franz Kline and Willem de Kooning (pp. 165, 166). Although Lichtenstein had immense respect for some of the Abstract Expressionists, he caricatured those painters' signature brushstrokes in a flattened, stylized depiction, even mimicking the drips of paint that would have originally indicated the speed of the artist's hand movements.

Lichtenstein's process, by contrast, was far from speedy, and his labor-intensive work itself constitutes an ironic comment on Abstract Expressionism's gestural method. He began by painting brushstrokes onto clear acetate sheets, and then overlapping the sheets to create a composite arrangement that he projected onto a canvas. He drew the outlines of the projected image onto the canvas, making any adjustments he deemed necessary, and painted the strokes with flat colors. Lastly, he painted the background, a field of blue Ben-Day dots—the regular, mechanically made dots often used to create shades of color in commercial printing and especially in comic books.

Lichtenstein's careful, premeditated rendering of Abstract Expressionism's spontaneous brushstrokes and his explicit reference to comic books parodies the elevated, almost mythical standing of his predecessors. The appropriation of comic book illustration style and the elimination of all surface texture typifies Pop art's preference for the "cool" modes of mechanical reproduction rather than the "hot" emotionalism and tactility of Abstract Expressionism. "One of the things a cartoon does," Lichtenstein noted, "is to express violent emotion and passion in a completely mechanical and removed style."

Little Big Painting, 1965
Oil and synthetic polymer on canvas, 68 x 80 in. (172.7 x 203.2 cm)
Purchase, with funds from the Friends of the Whitney Museum of American Art 66.2

GLENN LIGON

b. 1960

Glenn Ligon borrowed the words repeated across *Untitled (I Do Not Always Feel Colored)* from a 1928 essay by Zora Neale Hurston, "How It Feels to Be Colored Me," in which Hurston says she did not perceive herself as black until she lived outside the tight-knit African-American community she grew up in. As Ligon explains it, Hurston understood that if "one can become colored, then color is a social construction." *Untitled (I Do Not Always Feel Colored)* is one of five works Ligon based on Hurston's writings. The passages he selected all contain the word "I," a pronoun he says "functions simultaneously as Hurston's voice, my voice, and the voice of the painting, positioned in between us."

Ligon transferred the words by rubbing oilstick through a plastic stencil onto the gessoed surface of a door, a support he likes because its proportions suggest the human body. As he worked his way down the door, the text became progressively smudged and illegible because the greasy oilstick left a residue that adhered to the stencil. The smearing created a series of meaningful effects for Ligon: "It makes the words cast shadows, bleed into one another, [so that] their meanings seem less fixed....The smearing also creates a visual interaction with the gesso ground, a metaphor for the interaction between blacks and whites in the construction of racial identity." Moreover, the repetition evokes a common form of punishment for children: the task of writing an apologetic sentence again and again until the point sinks in, while fatigue makes the child's handwriting increasingly sloppy. From block-letter clarity at top to near abstraction at bottom, Ligon's work moves from simple declarative statements through incantation to marks of pure guttural emotion.

Untitled (I Do Not Always Feel Colored), 1990
Oil stick and gesso on panel, 80 x 30 1/16 x 1 1/2 in. (203.2 x 76.4 x 3.8 cm)
Promised gift of The Bohen Foundation in honor of Tom Armstrong P.91.2

MARK LOMBARDI
b. 1900

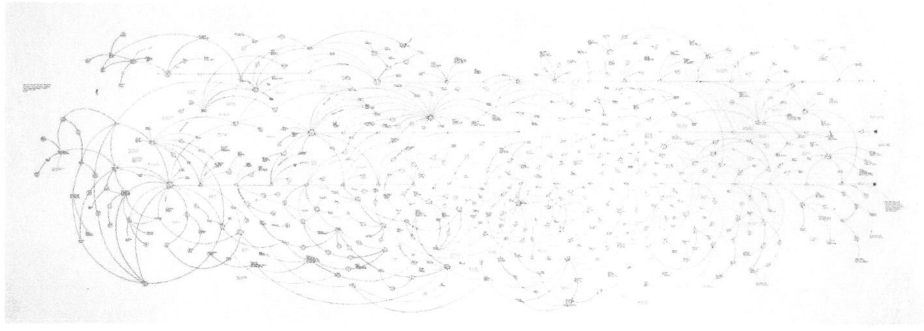

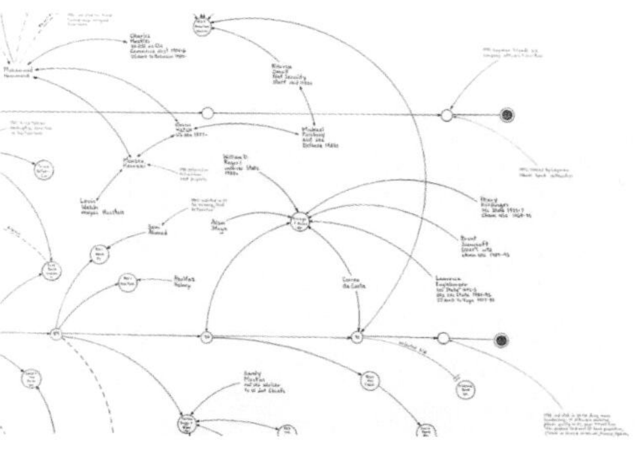

An art historian, librarian, gallery owner, and museum curator, Mark Lombardi was also, throughout his various careers, a practicing artist. But it was not until 1994, when he was in his mid-forties, that a doodle he made while talking to a friend on the telephone led him to begin the remarkable body of drawings that was to bring him critical acclaim and recognition. As in this spectacular, mural-size example, Lombardi uses delicate, skeinlike diagrams to chart the patterns of collusion between corporate and governmental bodies—between power and money—that often span continents and decades.

A prodigious researcher who relied entirely on the public record, Lombardi maintained files with more than 12,000 entries. Having identified a particular nexus of scandalous affiliation, he made small rough pencil drawings before proceeding to larger, more precise ones. But because his investigations were ongoing, even the large-scale drawings were never conclusively finalized. *BCCI, ICIC & FAB* concerns, in part, a money-laundering scandal of the 1980s, which revolved around an Arab bank headquartered in London. As described by Lombardi himself, BCCI "was used not only by drug dealers and con men but also by the governments of the U.S., U.K., Saudi Arabia and the Gulf Arab states to funnel support to Afghan guerrillas fighting Soviet occupation, to pay off friends and adversaries alike and conduct secret arms sales to Iran."

The circles on the drawing identify main participants, the solid lines show "some type of influence or control," a double arrow "mutual relationship or association," a dotted line "flow of money, loans or credits," a squiggle "sale or transfer of an asset," and a double hyphen a "blocked or incomplete transaction." *BCCI, ICIC & FAB* has the text-based character of Conceptual art, specifically recalling the investigative reporting style of the seminal Conceptual artist Hans Haacke.

BCCI, ICIC & FAB, 1996–2000
Graphite on paper, 52 5/16 x 139 in. (132.9 x 353.1 cm)
Purchase, with funds from the Drawing Committee and the Contemporary Committee 2000.250.1

MORRIS LOUIS

1912–1962

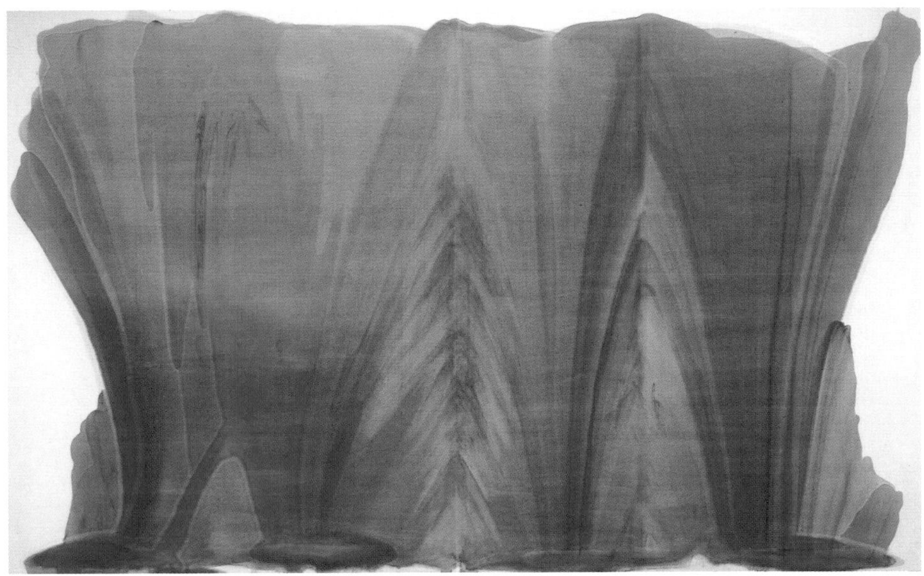

In the mid-1950s, young American artists such as Morris Louis inevitably looked to the example of Jackson Pollock (p. 242), whose Abstract Expressionist style had revolutionized contemporary painting. Louis, along with Helen Frankenthaler and Kenneth Noland (pp. 110, 225), sought to extend Abstract Expressionism, retaining its monumental scale and improvisational technique but discarding its emphasis on expressionistic gesture.

Louis' first mature works were the series of *Veil* paintings he began in 1954 and took up again in 1957–59; *Tet* is one of the works in this later group. The series was initially inspired by Louis' 1953 encounter with the "stain" technique of Frankenthaler. Indeed, Louis considered Frankenthaler's art "a bridge between Pollock and what was possible." Following her lead, he began pouring highly diluted paint onto unprimed canvas, without the aid of a brush. But whereas Frankenthaler placed her canvas directly on the floor, Louis leaned his at an angle against a wall so that the paint flowed down its expanse, following the law of gravity. The results, however—luminous, diaphanous veils of color—appear entirely weightless, as pools of commingled color flow freely down and into the raw canvas. This tension between the physicality of the paint and its visual transformation into pure, disembodied color lies at the heart of Louis' endeavor.

Tet refers to the ninth letter of the Hebrew alphabet; it was among the titles assigned to Louis' work after his death by Clement Greenberg, the noted critic and the artist's close friend.

Tet, 1958
Synthetic polymer on canvas, 95 x 153 in. (241.3 x 388.6 cm)
Purchase, with funds from the Friends of the Whitney Museum of American Art 65.9

LOUIS LOZOWICK

1892–1973

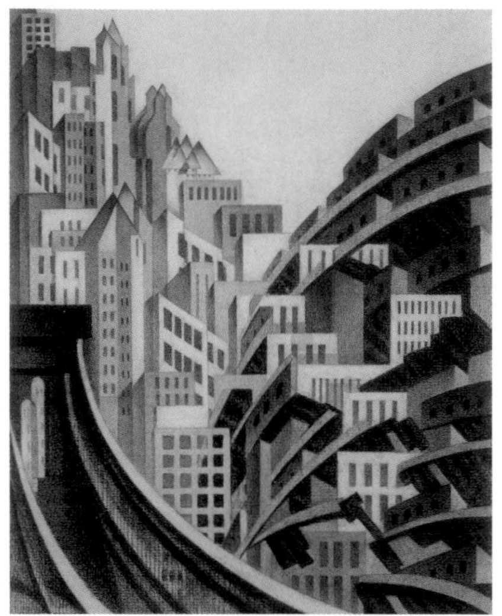

Louis Lozowick left New York in 1919 for a five-year sojourn in Europe. Unlike most of his contemporaries, he did not linger in the ateliers of Paris. Instead, he gravitated to Berlin, where he came into contact with the art and theories of the Russian Constructivists and other avant-garde movements of Central and Eastern Europe, many of them concerned with expressing the energy of modern technology and city life. Lozowick returned to New York in 1924, convinced that industrial complexes and the urban environment were the quintessential subjects for contemporary American art.

This vision was first manifest in a group of distinctive drawings, lithographs, and paintings, including *New York*, that exploit a range of surface textures and tonal blacks to encapsulate the geometry of utilitarian factory buildings, tank structures, and curving el tracks that weave their way through the gridded mass of soaring skyscrapers and apartment buildings. To Lozowick there was beauty in a steel plant—in the cylinder of a tank set above a corner of the rectilinear grid of the factory, the whole unified by a counterpoint of tubular pipes and duct work. The lithograph *Corner of Steel Plant* well illustrates Lozowick's essay "The Americanization of Art," written for the "Machine Age Exhibition" at New York's Steinway Hall in 1927: "The dominant trend in America today, beneath all the apparent chaos and confusion, is towards order and organization which find their outward sign and symbol in the rigid geometry of the American city: the verticals of its smoke stacks, in the parallels of its car tracks, the squares of its streets, the cubes of its factories, the arc of its bridges, the cylinders of its gas tanks...."

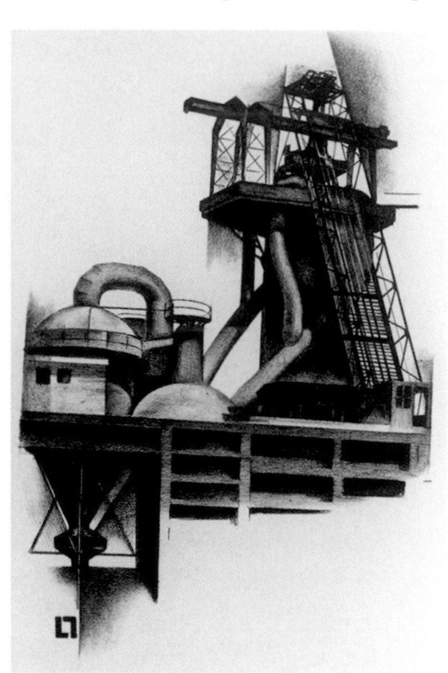

New York, c. 1925
Carbon pencil on paper, 12 13/16 x 10 in. (32.5 x 25.4 cm)
Purchase, with funds from the Richard and Dorothy Rodgers Fund 77.15

Corner of Steel Plant, 1929
Lithograph: sheet, 13 1/4 x 9 7/16 in. (33.7 x 24 cm); image, 11 7/16 x 7 13/16 in. (29.1 x 19.8 cm)
Purchase, with funds from The Lauder Foundation, Leonard and Evelyn Lauder Fund 96.68.202

GEORGE LUKS
1867–1933

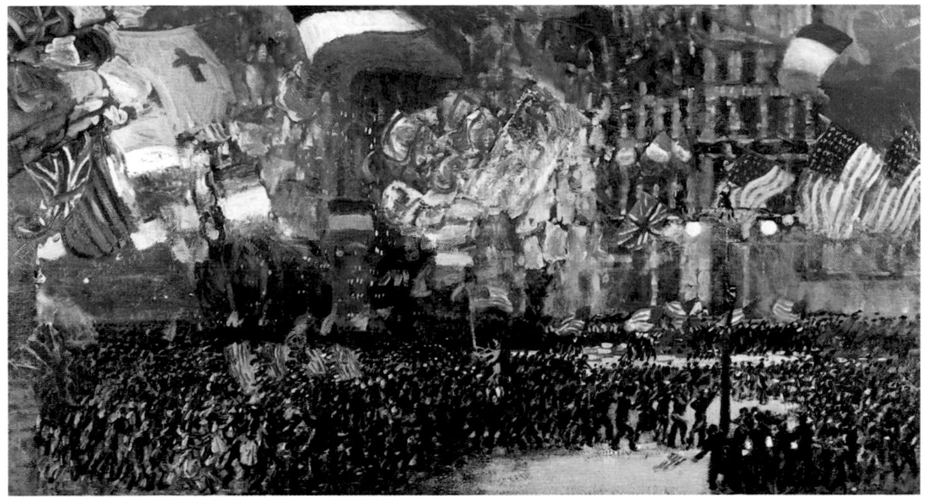

George Luks' *Armistice Night* records the frenzied, flag-waving celebrations that marked the end of World War I. Luks' skill at capturing the essence of an event in a few swift strokes was acquired during his years as a newspaper illustrator in Philadelphia at the turn of the last century. Before the advent of photojournalism, newspapers dispatched illustrators to cover breaking news. Although they often took notes and made quick sketches on-site, they usually completed their work back in the newsroom, relying on memory and, sometimes, inventing details. The influential artist and teacher Robert Henri (p. 137) encouraged Luks and other Philadelphia newspaper illustrators, among them William Glackens, Everett Shinn, and John Sloan (pp. 115, 279, 287), to become painters and move to New York. Eventually, they pioneered a new brand of realism, centered on the kind of contemporary, urban subjects they had covered as newspapermen.

In the newsmaking event depicted in *Armistice Night*, as in his earlier illustrations, Luks does not deliberate over details; the painting is a blur of flags, faces, and fireworks. Blue smoke obscures the buildings in the background, and few individuals stand out in the quickly rendered crowd. The details of *Armistice Night* may be blurry, but the exuberant mood is clear. As always, Luks was more committed to capturing the spirit of the moment—the action, the human drama—than to rendering visual facts.

Armistice Night, 1918
Oil on canvas, 37 x 68 3/4 in. (94 x 174.6 cm)
Gift of an anonymous donor 54.58

VERA LUTTER
b. 1960

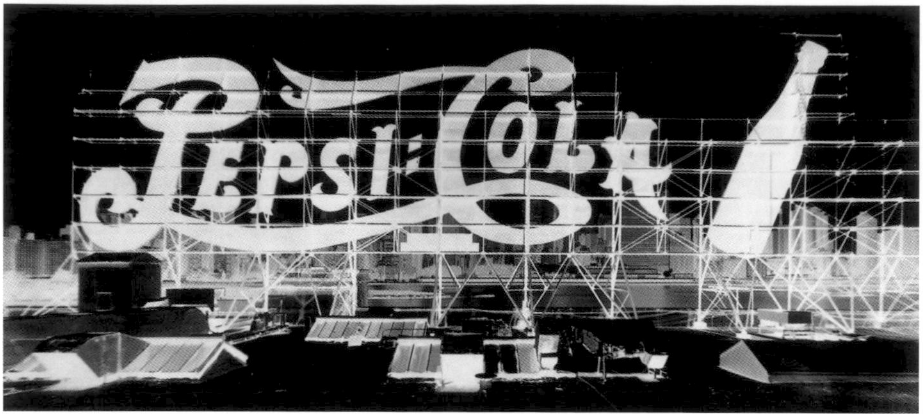

Vera Lutter creates large-scale images of modern industrial and urban settings using the earliest and most rudimentary photographic device, the camera obscura. The camera obscura ("dark room"), which dates back to the Renaissance, operates on the basic principle of photography: when light from a room passes through a small hole into a darkened chamber, an inverted image of the illuminated area is projected onto the opposite wall of the darkened chamber. Lutter, like Abelardo Morell (p. 211), produces her images by transforming entire rooms into camera obscuras—either existing rooms or enclosed spaces she constructs, as in this photograph of a Pepsi-Cola sign atop a building in an industrial area of the borough of Queens in New York City.

Pepsi-Cola, Long Island City, IV: May 19, 1998 was made by placing a large sheet of photosensitive paper on the interior wall facing the aperture of the darkened, room-sized camera obscura, set up behind the Pepsi sign on the roof of the building. The inverted image was exposed onto the paper for several hours. The result is a unique photographic negative print (Lutter has turned it right side up for presentation). The lengthy exposure required by the camera obscura challenges modern photography's reputation as a medium that instantaneously captures a single fleeting moment.

In anticipation of the reversal of the image in the negative print, Lutter built the camera obscura *behind* the sign so that it would read correctly in the exposed image. As a result, the sign normally viewed from Manhattan, across the river, shows Manhattan in the background rather than Queens. Through such visual disparities, a familiar urban icon looks strange, while the long exposure time, which records only stable objects, makes a city known for its constant change and movement seem eerily serene.

Pepsi-Cola, Long Island City, IV: May 19, 1998, 1998
Gelatin silver print on canvas, 55 1/4 x 123 in. (140.3 x 312.4 cm)
Purchase, with funds from the Photography Committee 2000.219

STANTON MACDONALD-WRIGHT

1890–1973

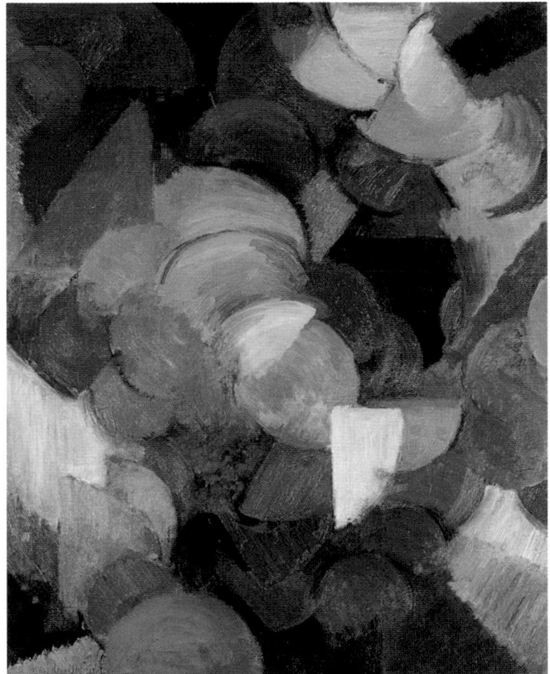

Shortly before World War I, Stanton Macdonald-Wright and fellow artist Morgan Russell coined the term Synchromy to distinguish their kaleidoscopic canvases from other early manifestations of modernism. Meaning "with color," the word also evokes "symphony" and thus suggests a relationship between Synchromy and music. In a catalogue essay for the first exhibition of Synchromist painting, mounted in Munich in 1913, the artists declared: "Whenever man had a desire for heavenly intoxication, he turned to music. Yet color is just as capable as music of providing us with the highest ecstasies and delights."

Both Russell and Macdonald-Wright had studied in Paris with the Canadian painter and color theorist Percyval Tudor-Hart, and both were immersed in the science of perception. In a later treatise on the subject, Macdonald-Wright compared the color spectrum to a musical scale; by combining certain colors, an artist could achieve a kind of visual harmony.

In *"Conception" Synchromy*, Macdonald-Wright limited his palette to few harmonious hues. As in music, it was the interval between the colors that mattered: a certain shade of yellow, for example, demanded a certain shade of bluish green. To establish this system of relationships, he built the painting outward from a wedge of deep yellow at the center. "The first line, color, or tone placed on a canvas," he explained, "dictates every line, color, and tone that follows it." As one of Macdonald-Wright's first truly non-objective compositions, *"Conception" Synchromy* does not mirror an external reality, but explores the melodic nature of color itself.

"Conception" Synchromy, 1915
Oil on canvas, 30 x 24 in. (76.2 x 61 cm)
Gift of George F. Of 52.40

ROBERT MANGOLD
b. 1937

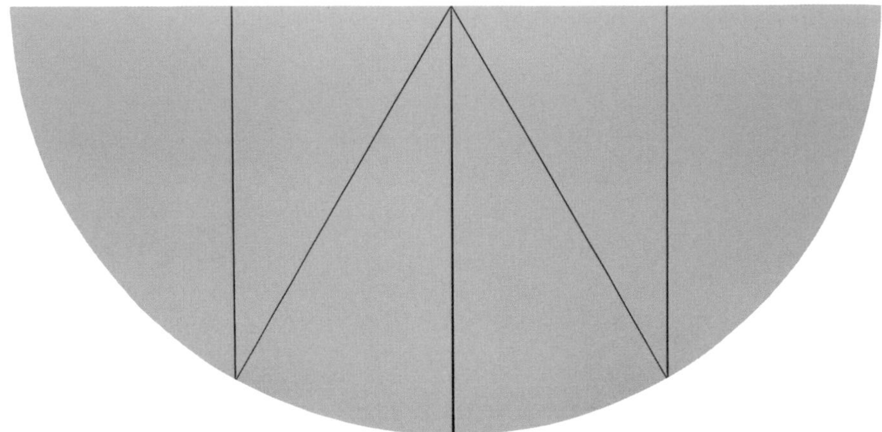

In 1967, the year this painting was executed, Robert Mangold wrote a kind of manifesto called "Flat Art." It began with the bold, uppercase declaration, "ART SHOULD BE TAKEN AT FACE VALUE," and went on to observe, "One thing that is true of flat, two-dimensional art is that flat art can be seen instantly, totally." Made of oil-based commercial paint sprayed onto board, *1/2 Manila Curved Area* is indeed available all at once. The title describes exactly what we see, and the painting's overall form and regular internal divisions are instantly accessible to the eye and mind. Digressive compositional devices, such as shifts in scale or gestural brushwork, are avoided in favor of workmanlike technique and simple declarative geometry. *1/2 Manila Curved Area* is one of a series of Mangold's *Area* paintings, all based on negative shapes; here, the curved form, or half-circle, is loosely deduced from the shape of a segment of sky as it would be seen in a valley between two rolling hills. In Mangold's term, these paintings represent "an architectural kind of air."

Mangold arrived in New York in 1962 and soon associated himself with such leading artists as Sol LeWitt and Robert Ryman (pp. 184, 266). Like them, he articulated a commitment to rigorous formal simplicity and non-art materials and techniques, but he resisted Minimalism's reductiveness of design. As in *1/2 Manila Curved Area*, his works offer subtle permutations of geometric form and nuanced rhythms of line, shape, and color.

***1/2 Manila Curved Area**, 1967
Oil on composition board, 4 panels, 77 1/4 x 144 1/2 in. (196.2 x 367 cm)
Purchase, with funds from the Friends of the Whitney Museum of American Art 68.14a–d

ROBERT MAPPLETHORPE

1946–1989

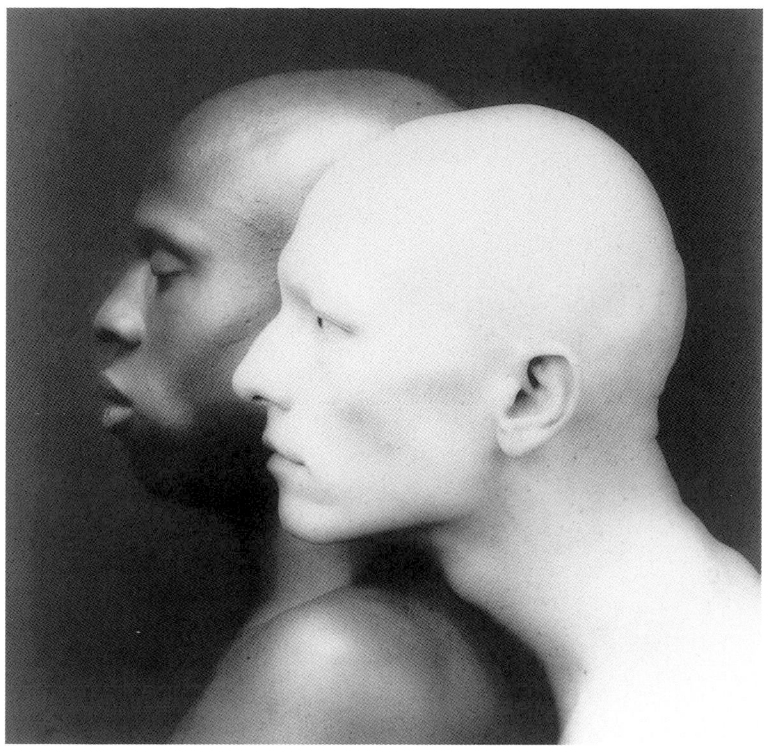

In this luminescent black-and-white photograph, Robert Mapplethorpe portrays two of his friends—a black man, Ken Moody, and a white man, Robert Sherman. The subjects are rendered in profile and appear unusually still, a quality that would later mark Mapplethorpe's still-life photographs of flowers. Set against a uniform dark background, the work highlights its own contrasts: closed eyes and open eyes, black and white, texture and smoothness, tension and harmony. In this study of quiet, classical beauty, even the men's physical imperfections—a wrinkle here, a scar there—appear smooth and polished. These extraordinary effects result from Mapplethorpe's punctilious engagement with the details of the photographic process, from the selection of film and paper to nuances of staging and lighting. He often shot five or six rolls of film to produce a single photograph. "I don't want anything to be questionable," he said. "If I'm doing a head, it has to be in the right position, where the nose hits the cheek."

Mapplethorpe began working in New York in the late 1960s, and from then until his death in 1989 developed an impressive body of photographic work comprising portraits—friends, celebrities, and fashion models—nudes, and still lifes. His photographs grew out of his fascination with physical beauty, though their frequent engagement with homoerotic and sadomasochistic themes made them controversial.

Ken Moody and Robert Sherman, 1984
Gelatin silver print, 15 1/8 x 15 3/16 in. (38.4 x 38.6 cm)
Gift of The Robert Mapplethorpe Foundation 97.103.3

BRICE MARDEN

b. 1938

Brice Marden's *Summer Table* may at first seem to be a Minimalist work in the style of Frank Stella's spare, geometric *Gran Cairo* (p. 297). *Summer Table* is divided into three equally sized but differently colored panels, all free of obvious representational reference as well as any sign of brushstrokes; indeed, Marden used a spatula to smooth out the paint, creating a matte but luminous surface. However, he also left a strip of canvas at the bottom with drips and splashes of paint, thus displaying the process that is camouflaged in the rest of the work. This evidence of process relates Marden's work to the gesture-filled Abstract Expressionist canvases of the 1950s. *Summer Table*, moreover, is not a "pure" abstraction. Like the work of Ellsworth Kelly (p. 163), it is based on an observation—in this case, Marden's recollection of a table he saw on the Greek island of Hydra, set out with glasses of lemonade and Coca-Cola, as well as the colors of the surrounding garden and sea. As the work progressed, the formal aspects of the panels took over, creating stronger colors with a visually tense interplay between the bright central panel and its flanks.

Nature has continued to be an important foundation for Marden's work. In the drawing *Bridge Study*, a study for a painting of the same name, he transformed the palm trees in the balmy Caribbean island of St. Barthélemy (known to Americans as St. Bart's) into gestural calligraphy. Marden took his title from the Ming Dynasty poet Han Shan, whose poems describe a bridge that one crosses to meet the immortals. Writhing black and white organic lines spill across the surface and beyond the edges of the drawing. With swirling energy, the lines form interlocked organic shapes that give an almost figural character to the whole.

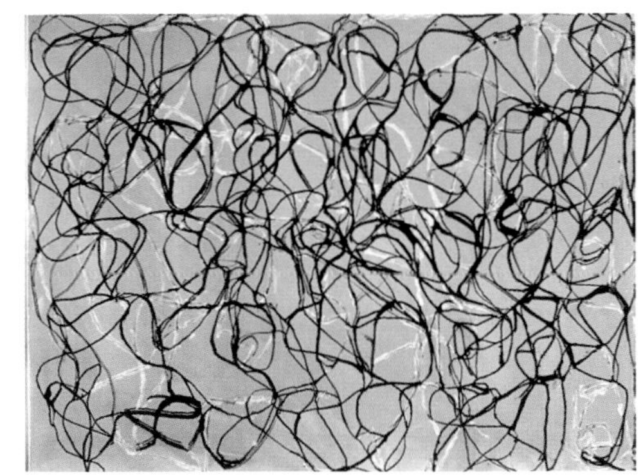

Summer Table, 1972
Oil and wax on canvas, 3 panels, 60 x 105 5/16 in. (152.4 x 267.5 cm) overall
Purchase, with funds from the National Endowment for the Arts 73.30

Bridge Study, 1991
Ink and gouache on paper, 26 15/16 x 34 7/16 in. (68.4 x 87.5 cm)
Purchase, with funds from the Drawing Committee and The Norman and Rosita Winston Foundation, Inc. 92.27

JOHN MARIN

1870–1953

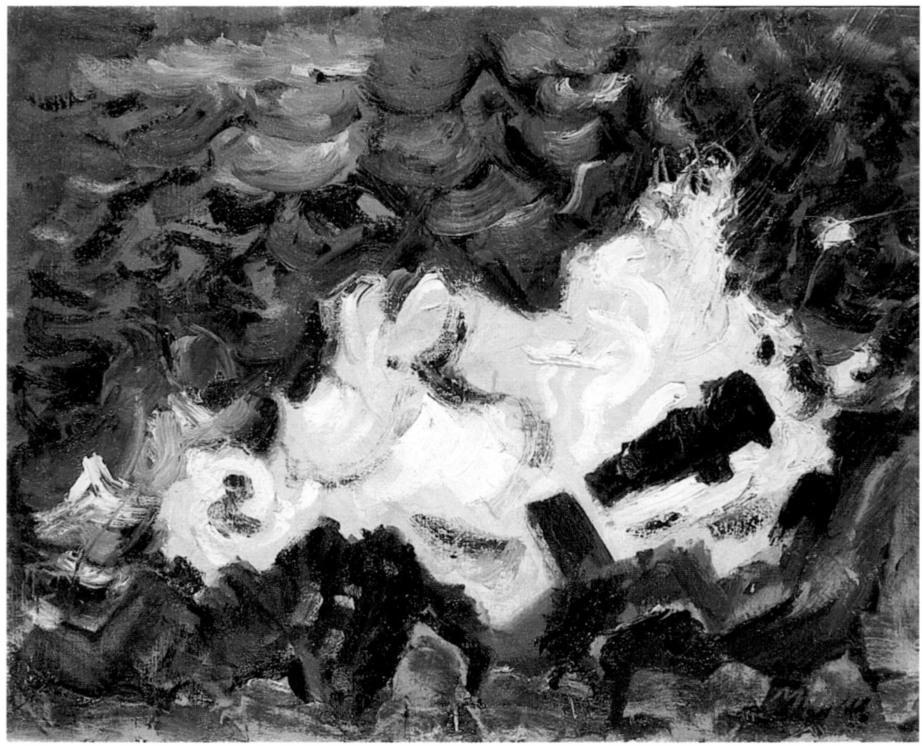

During the 1930s, John Marin, one of the most renowned watercolorists in the history of American art, was primarily committed to painting in oil. His application of paint to canvas, however, is not unrelated to watercolor, for his brushstrokes are remarkably rapid, fluid, and even impetuous, anticipating Abstract Expressionist gestures of the 1950s (pp. 165, 166, 242). Whether using watercolor or oil, Marin was a master at exploiting a medium, and he delighted in accentuating each material's unique characteristics.

Wave on Rock exemplifies not only Marin's painterly technique, but his devotion to nature as subject matter. He spent his childhood in small-town New Jersey and on a peach farm in Delaware, making sketches of the natural world around him. In 1914, he began summering in Maine, where he became entranced with the state's pastoral and marine grandeur. These settings inspired his later land- and seascapes, including *Wave on Rock*. The improvisational character of the brushstrokes suggests the quick recording of a moment, while the thick viscosity of the paint conveys the hard sharpness of the rocks and the impenetrable blueness of the sea. At the same time, the layered, frantic strokes convincingly emulate the choppy sea and the crashing of foaming waves on jagged terrain. In Marin's work, it is the medium itself that produces a sensation of immense energy, force, and movement.

Wave on Rock, 1937
Oil on canvas, 22 3/4 x 30 in. (57.8 x 76.2 cm)
Purchase, with funds from Charles Simon and the Painting and Sculpture Committee 81.18

REGINALD MARSH
1898–1954

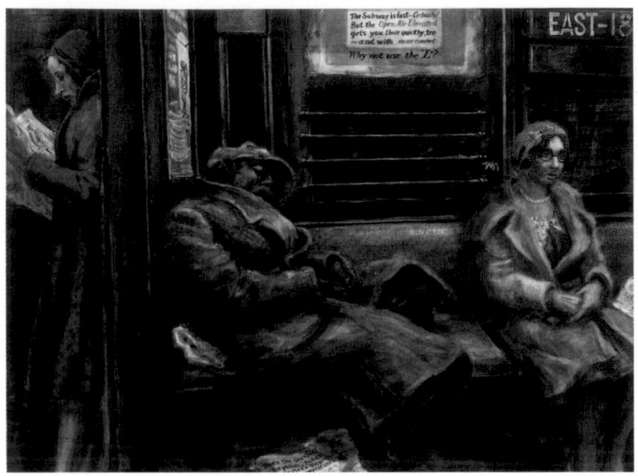

Although born into a wealthy family, Reginald Marsh preferred the crowded public beaches of New York's Coney Island to exclusive summer resorts, the burlesque to the opera. With a homemade sketchbook in his pocket, he frequented the places where ordinary folk gathered. These sketchbooks provided the raw material for an art that captured the character types and the pace of urban America in the 1930s. In *Why Not Use the "L"?*, the individual expressions of the three passengers range from distraction and exhaustion to apprehension—familiar guises to anyone who has used urban transport. (The "L," or "el," was the nickname for the elevated trains that once rose above many New York streets.) The walls of the car are papered with actual advertisements—including the one used to title this painting—which Marsh had carefully copied into his notes.

Marsh sometimes used the city's ubiquitous posters, billboards, and movie marquees to make insightful connections with the depicted figures. In *Twenty Cent Movie*, the advertising copy for the coming attractions—"Human Emotions Stripped Bare," "Joys of the Flesh," "Who Is Without Sin"—provides a social as well as a visual background to the "real" men and women, spread across the foreground as if on a stage set. In an era when the Hollywood movie star was the nation's dominant icon, Marsh's characters reflect the longings and romantic aspirations projected from the cinematic screen. The women's clothing and makeup are cheap imitations of the latest Hollywood styles, while the

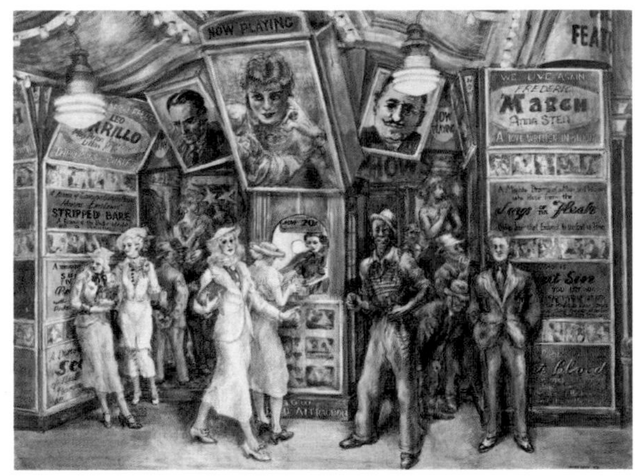

Why Not Use the "L"?, 1930
Egg tempera on canvas, 36 x 48 in. (91.4 x 121.9 cm)
Purchase 31.293

Twenty Cent Movie, 1936
Egg tempera on composition board, 30 x 40 in. (76.2 x 101.6 cm)
Purchase 37.43

REGINALD MARSH

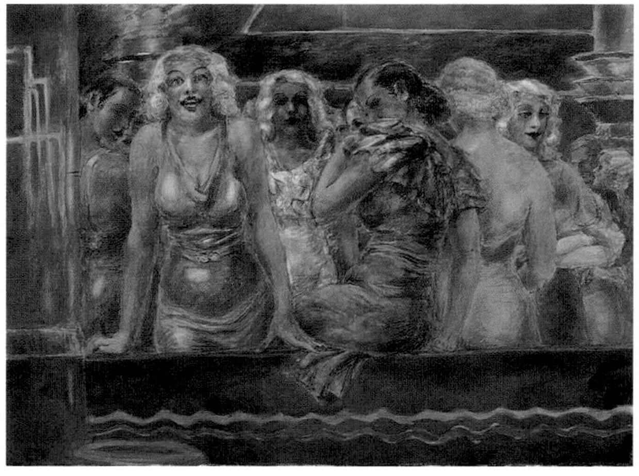

men pose like their filmic counterparts or scrutinize the placards, peering into a fantasy world.

In *Ten Cents a Dance*, the hostesses also emulate the Hollywood ideal of femininity—part siren, part baby doll, part bombshell. The setting is a dancehall, another phenomenon of urban life in the 1930s. Marsh's calendar entries for 1933 record several visits to a particular dancehall, where he deftly sketched the women lounging about, seductively waiting for an invitation to dance. Such halls were open only to men, who purchased rolls of tickets that allowed them, for the price of ten cents, to dance with any available hostess.

Although Marsh's art mirrors modern life, it does not send social or political messages. At the height of the Depression, Marsh produced works such as *Bread Line—No One Has Starved*. The print depicts a pathetic procession of destitute men as they wait in resignation for public assistance. Crammed into a narrow pictorial space, with little distinction among them, the men represent poverty rather than the effects of poverty on individuals. Although Marsh no doubt had compassion for the poor, this collective typecasting turns the bread line into yet another element in the metropolitan landscape, different only in mood from the movie theaters, beaches, railcars, burlesque shows, and dancehalls that pervade Marsh's art.

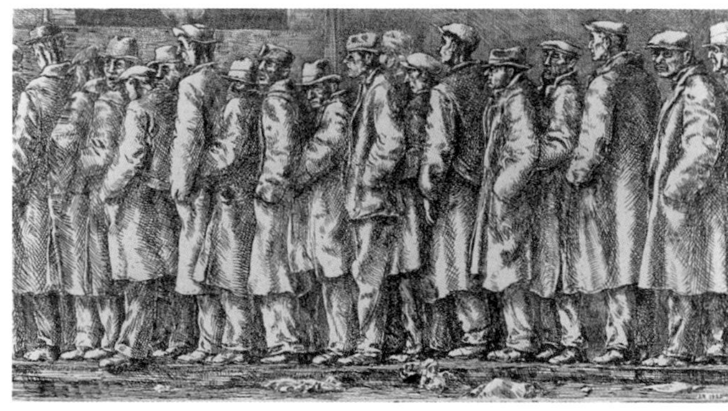

Ten Cents a Dance, 1933
Egg tempera on panel, 36 x 48 in. (91.4 x 121.9 cm)
Felicia Meyer Marsh Bequest 80.31.10

Bread Line—No One Has Starved, 1932
Etching and engraving: sheet, 9 7/8 x 14 1/8 in. (25.1 x 35.9 cm) irregular; plate, 6 3/8 x 11 7/8 in. (16.2 x 30.2 cm)
Katherine Schmidt Shubert Bequest 82.43.1

KERRY JAMES MARSHALL

b. 1955

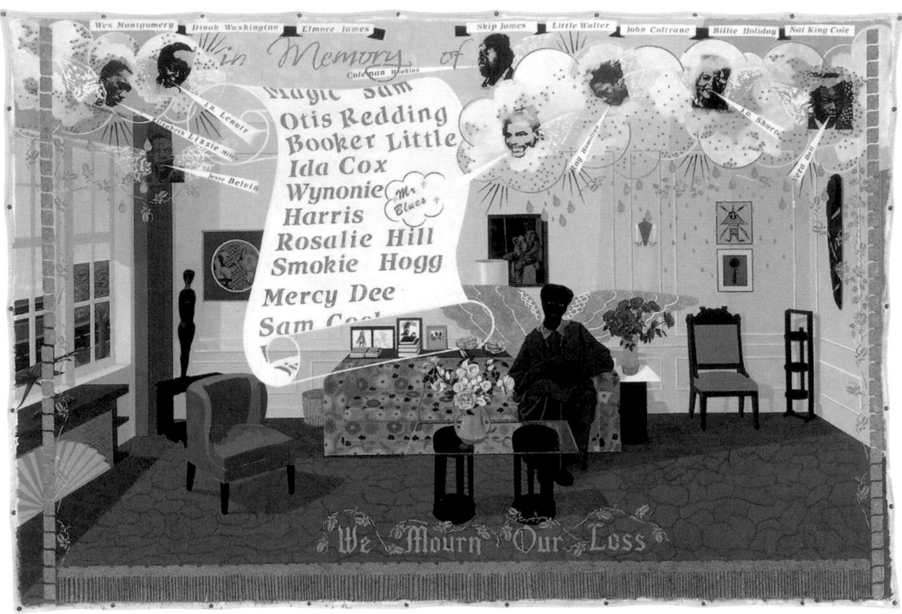

At the center of the 13-foot-wide *Souvenir IV*, painted on unstretched canvas and pinned to the wall like a ceremonial banner, is a scroll honoring major African-American musicians. Above, cloud-haloed heads float like angels, trumpeting the names of other artists; still more are named in the banderoles at the upper margin. “We Mourn Our Loss” is written at bottom in the style of a nineteenth-century needlepoint sampler. The same lament appears in the other paintings in the *Souvenir* series, which are dedicated to artistic and political leaders, most but not all of them African-American. *Souvenir IV*’s setting, also repeated in the series, is a tidy, well-appointed living room, with a sofa at center occupied by a very properly dressed and posed older black woman. Her bearing has such dignity and calm that it is easy to overlook the massive pair of wings at her shoulders. If the words in *Souvenir IV* speak of an elegy, this image adds a note of poignant celebration.

By his own account, Marshall’s upbringing was crucial to his work: “You can’t be born in Birmingham, Alabama in 1955...move to Watts in ’63, and grow up in South Central near the Black Panthers headquarters and see the kinds of things that I saw in my developmental years, and not speak about it.” But throughout his career—which began with collages reminiscent of Romare Bearden (p. 45) and has been linked with the politically oriented paintings on unstretched canvas of Leon Golub (p. 120)—Marshall has avoided conventional summaries of African-American experience. Instead, he explores the rarely acknowledged optimism that flourishes amid difficult circumstances, and the pride that outlives mourning for fallen heroes.

Souvenir IV, 1998
Synthetic polymer and glitter on paper on canvas with grommets, 107 1/2 x 157 1/2 in. (273.1 x 400.1 cm)
Purchase, with funds from the Painting and Sculpture Committee 98.56

AGNES MARTIN

b. 1912

In 1957, after more than a decade of painting abstractly, Agnes Martin arrived at what came to be her signature compositional style, stressing symmetrical and repetitive elements "with neither space nor forms nor symbols," as she put it.

The 6-foot-square format of *Milk River* remained standard for all of Martin's paintings until 1993. Two borders frame the central square. The outermost is plain canvas, while the wider border just inside, made up of mottled paint, acts as a transition to the large white inner square. This center square is patterned horizontally with hand-drawn, highly controlled, red pencil lines, which are incised into the thin layer of paint. The repetitive nature of the lines creates a strong sense of systematic and geometric order. Yet because they are hand-drawn, the lines are slightly imperfect, as are the contours of the rectangles. Such irregularities, along with the subdued color, soften the effect of Minimalist rigidity.

In the 1970s, Martin shifted from the grid format to compositions with horizontal bands of color defined by thin graphite lines. In the 1990 *Untitled #5*, she explores the horizontal juxtaposition of closely valued hues: a pale blue and yellow are diluted to a highly transparent, almost watercolor consistency. As in the earlier *Milk River*, the seeming regularity of the composition is foiled by imperfections in the rendering of the bands and lines that represent what Martin calls the "memory of perfection"—the means by which she seeks to express a sense of serenity, truth, and innocence.

Milk River, 1963
Oil on canvas, 72 x 72 in. (182.9 x 182.9 cm)
Purchase, with funds from the Larry Aldrich Foundation Fund 64.10

Untitled #5, 1990
Synthetic polymer on canvas, 72 x 72 in. (182.9 x 182.9 cm)
Gift of Leonard A. Lauder 97.93

GORDON MATTA-CLARK

1945–1978

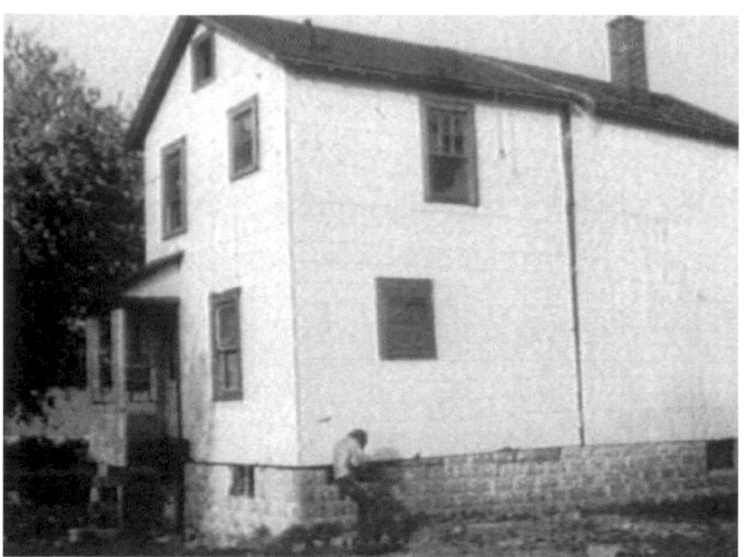

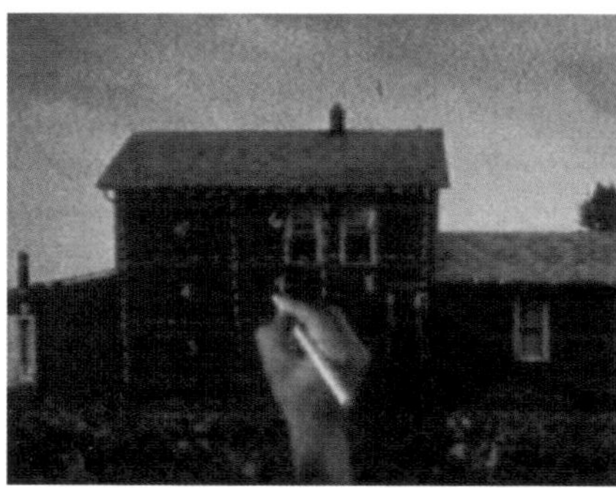

Gordon Matta-Clark was a key figure in the experimental New York art scene of the early 1970s. The son of the Surrealist painter Matta, he trained as an architect, and his work represents a radical fusion of architecture, sculpture, photography, film, and performance. In 1971, he began a series of what he called "cuttings," in which he opened up buildings by cutting shapes into their walls and floors, creating new vistas and passages and revealing hidden spaces. These cuttings merged the formal language of sculpture (line, volume, light, surface) with issues popular in the 1970s (the rupturing of established social and architectural structures) and a utopian concern with urban decay.

Splitting is a film made in 1974 that documents an architectural-sculptural performance. Over a period of months, Matta-Clark sliced a New Jersey house scheduled for demolition in half, chiseling away at its foundations and transforming it into a temporary sculptural environment. The rear section of the house was set on a lowered foundation, creating a wedge of space between the two halves that exposed a series of sliced rooms and introduced light and air into cramped spaces. This splitting implied both a rupturing of the fabric of domestic space and a liberation of the individual from the isolation of middle American suburbia. Like the accompanying series of photographs, sketches, and an artist's book, Matta-Clark's film *Splitting* operates as both a document of the performative event and a parallel work.

Splitting, 1974
Super-8mm film transferred to videotape, black-and-white and color, silent; 11 minutes
Purchase, with funds from the Film and Video Committee 2000.161

JAN MATULKA

1890–1972

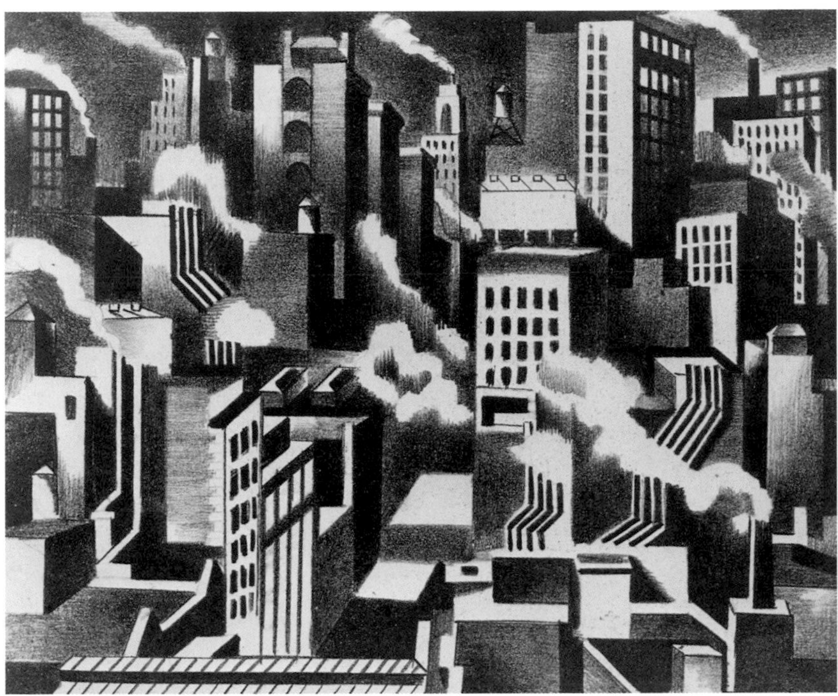

In the mid-1920s, Jan Matulka returned to America after a succession of extended visits to Paris and his native Czechoslovakia. Settling more or less permanently in New York, he enrolled in classes at the Art Students League, where he studied painting and printmaking and produced a series of lithographs that depict the urban landscape.

In *New York—Evening*, Matulka portrays the city as an endless jumble of windows, walls, and smokestacks, with neither stars nor streets to serve as guideposts. A billboard, illuminated by four overhead spotlights near the upper center, is strangely blank. Matulka's attitudes toward his adopted hometown are almost as impossible to read: the print seems neither to celebrate nor to condemn the modern city. Instead, Matulka reduces New York to an abstract pattern of black and white.

In fact, *New York—Evening* reveals more about the artist's experiences in Europe than it does about the American metropolis. In Paris as well as in Prague, Matulka encountered Cubism and its offshoots. The multiple perspectives of his lithograph, which fragment the view, owe much to the Cubist townscapes of Pablo Picasso and Georges Braque as well as to the cityscapes of Fernand Léger.

From 1929 to 1931, Matulka taught a class at the Art Students League that became renowned as a training ground for progressive artists. Although his career faltered in the late 1930s, his knowledge of the European avant-garde and his considerable skills as an artist and teacher formed an enduring legacy to the city he inhabited for the rest of his life.

New York—Evening, 1925
Lithograph: sheet, 14 7/16 x 19 1/2 in. (36.7 x 49.5 cm);
image, 13 1/4 x 16 in. (33.7 x 40.6 cm)
Purchase 77.9

ANTHONY McCALL

b. 1946

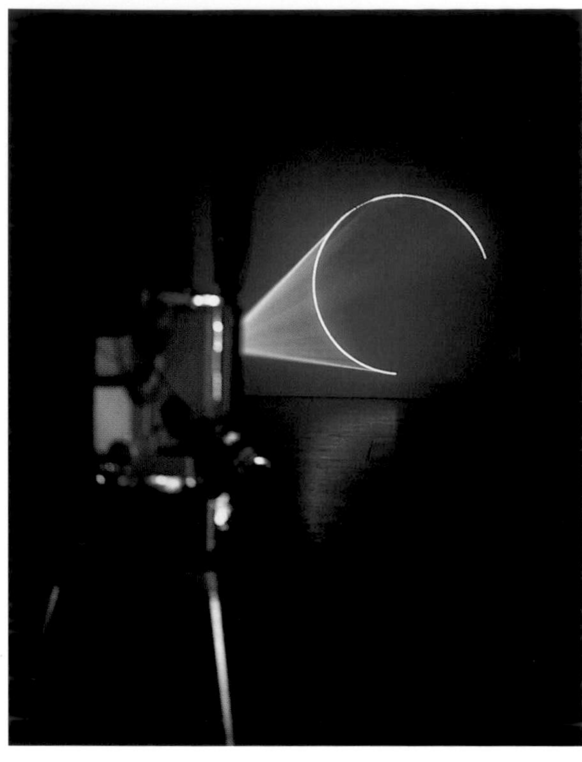

During the 1970s, artists and filmmakers created a new kind of film. Rejecting the narrative demands of Hollywood cinema as well as the more abstract content of independent films, they addressed the specific properties of the film medium—surface, light, projection, frames, time—often in the context of the gallery rather than the cinema auditorium. In 1973, Anthony McCall made *Line Describing a Cone*, the first film to occupy a three-dimensional presence in space. In a complete reversal of conventional cinematic viewing, the audience stands in a darkened gallery, watching the film by looking directly at the light beam as it emanates from the projector. Over a period of thirty-one minutes, a slim pencil of light slowly evolves, first into a curved plane of light and then into a large hollow cone. The forward plane of the cone takes the form of a circle in the process of being drawn and projected onto the wall.

As McCall observed, the process of the film's realization becomes its content. The structure of *Line Describing a Cone* was born out of his desire to create a complete art work from this single idea. We are invited to look into the hollow cone, to lie under it, stand inside it, or walk through it, disappearing into its volume like mist, only to reappear on the other side, like Alice in *Through the Looking-Glass*. Freed from the frontality of the film screen, we can experience an infinitude of multiple viewpoints and planes by physically moving around the film beam. The ephemeral three-dimensional form does not traverse two opposite points in space, but describes the area between them through the tangible presence of light. In dismantling the space of conventional cinema, the fleeting yet tangible solidity of *Line Describing a Cone* fuses the properties of film, sculpture, performance, and Conceptual art.

Line Describing a Cone, 1973
16mm film, black-and-white, silent; 31 minutes
Purchase, with funds from the Film and Video Committee 2001.248

ALLAN McCOLLUM

b. 1944

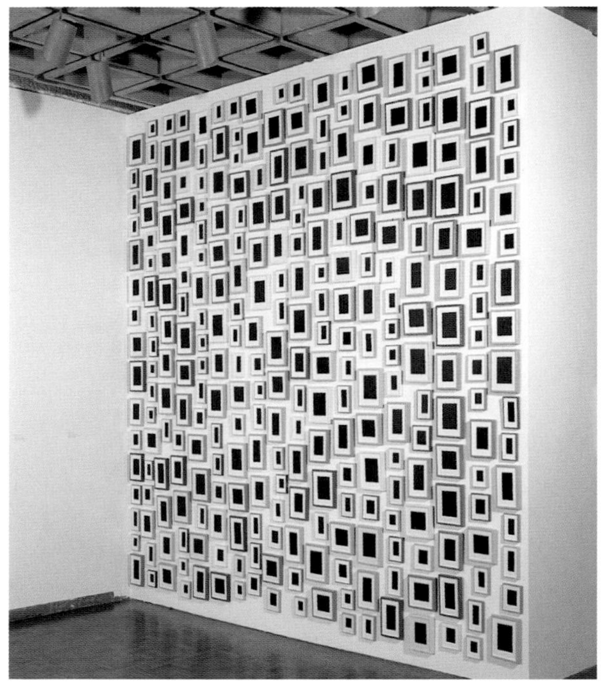

Constructed over a seven-year period, Allan McCollum's *288 Plaster Surrogates* is an installation of 288 cast plaster objects that resemble framed art works in varying shapes, sizes, and colors, each enclosing a black center where one would expect to find an image. By using the classical sculpture process of casting, and by emptying his "surrogates" of any overt content, McCollum inverts the traditional conception of form as a carrier of content. "What is it we want from art that our belief in 'content' works to hide from us?" McCollum has asked. To help answer the question, he gives us art without that troublesome content. All the variations in size and arrangement—the seemingly random placement in vertically aligned rows of differently sized framelike forms in a muted rainbow running from rose to butter-yellow—do little to compromise the invariability of the solid, glossy black centers. What we see when we try to read into each form is simply our own reflection.

Like other contemporary artists, such as Louise Lawler and Fred Wilson (pp. 175, 322), McCollum also uses his work to confront larger issues of the ideological relations between art and institutions, including the museum. In *288 Plaster Surrogates*, he isolates and emphasizes two recognized conventions of art display, framing and the arrangement of works on the wall, in order to indicate that these seemingly tangential elements of art may actually be crucial to our understanding of form and perception of meaning. McCollum proposes that the systems of display perpetuated by art institutions do not necessarily preserve the purity of the work of art, but rather establish a set of viewing conditions that play an important role in determining our responses.

288 Plaster Surrogates, 1982–89
Enamel on solid-cast hydrocal, dimensions variable
Gift of Joan and Jerome Serchuck 2000.190a-bbbbbbbbbbbb

SUSAN MEISELAS

b. 1948

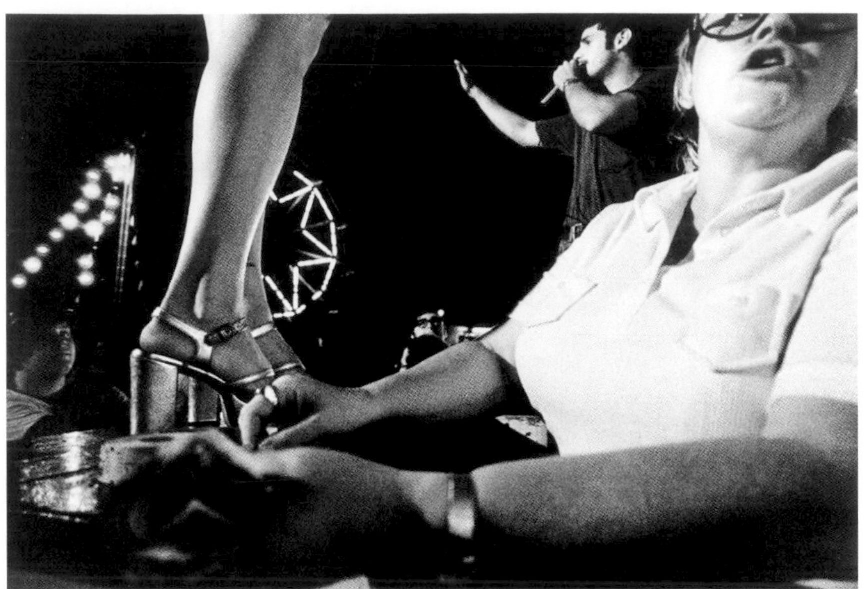

"Watch it! Watch it right now! Stop the music! You're gonna see burlesque, striptease, hootchie-kootchie, and daddy-o it's all the way. The show starts right now—now's the time to go." So begins the "girl show" bally call that introduces Susan Meiselas' 1976 book *Carnival Strippers*, a compilation of more than seventy photographs and texts excerpted from taped interviews and overheard conversations. The work evolved between 1972 and 1975, when Meiselas spent summers traveling with women who performed striptease for small-town carnivals in New England, Pennsylvania, and South Carolina. She views *Carnival Strippers*, her first work, as a depiction of "people struggling to define themselves on their own terms," a description that also applies to her later photographs of war zones in Central and South America.

The book *Carnival Strippers* combines text and image and juxtaposes the various, and often conflicting, perspectives of the strippers, talkers (the men stationed outside the tents to lure customers), show managers, and audience who make up this world. In one of the photographs, *Patty's Show, Tunbridge, Vermont*, Meiselas frames the participants of the show in a single photograph. Patty, a show manager and former stripper, dominates the foreground in uncomfortable proximity to the viewer. In the background, the talker beckons customers, who listen and watch intently. At left, as if perched on an auction block, are the cropped legs of a stripper. Dramatically positioning her camera below the stage, Meiselas propels the viewer into the space of the photograph. Yet her subjects remain psychologically inaccessible because each one is a partial form, visually isolated from the others. While the hazy lights of the Ferris wheel signal the carefree joy of the carnival-goers, the disorienting composition reflects a less sanguine view of the subject.

Patty's Show, Tunbridge, Vermont, 1974
Gelatin silver print, 7 5/8 x 11 1/2 in. (19.4 x 29.2 cm)
Purchase, with funds from the Photography Committee 2000.32

RAY METZKER

b. 1931

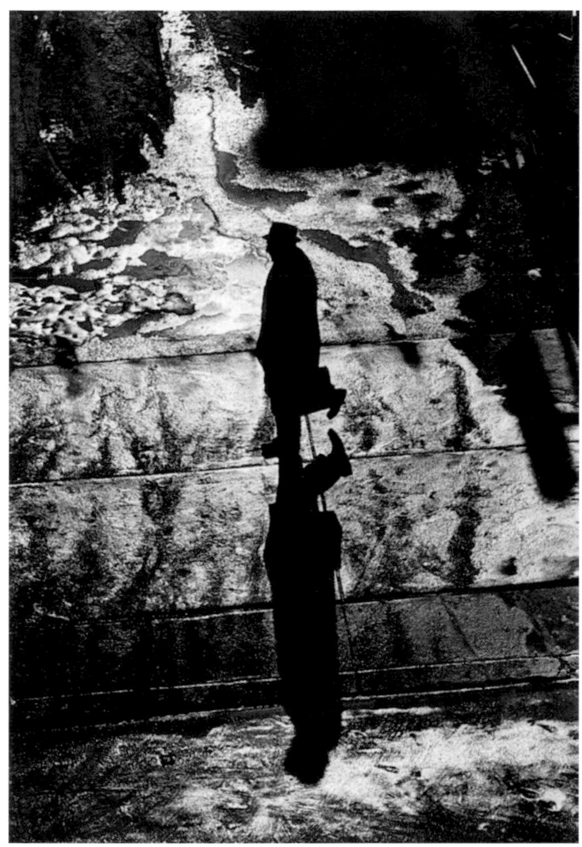

As a student at Chicago's Institute of Design in the 1950s, Ray Metzker developed a strong aesthetic sensibility that led to a body of photographic work rich in formal experimentation. From his teachers Harry Callahan and Aaron Siskind (p. 286), Metzker learned to see the abstract qualities in the world around him, responding particularly to the patterned effects of light and accentuating the tonal variation and graphic contrasts that are unique to black-and-white photography.

Philadelphia, made soon after Metzker graduated from the institute and returned from a trip to Europe, shows a lone man on a rainy, nocturnal street. This is not, however, an image of solitude or alienation, of the kind familiar in the work of Edward Hopper (p. 142). Here, the eye immediately goes beyond psychological effects to study the extraordinary spread of textures, light, and shadow. Metzker uses the slick, oily surfaces of the urban street to accentuate the brilliant, irregular illumination from an unseen streetlamp. The man, with hat, overcoat, and cane, steps through silvery black puddles like a silhouette, his shadow doubling beneath him. In the real world, shadows are ephemeral, but in a photograph they are solid shapes. Metzker uses the man's shadow to create a long central axis that begins in the foreground and moves up the picture plane to the tapering path in the background at top. He also frames the scene to exclude a horizon line. With no break between ground and sky, the vertical sweep of street and shadow locks the viewer's focus on a complex pattern of textures and light.

Philadelphia, 1964
Gelatin silver print, 8 3/4 x 5 7/8 in. (22.2 x 14.9 cm)
Purchase, with funds from Henry M. Buhl in honor of Sondra Gilman Gonzalez-Falla 2000.94

RICHARD MISRACH

b. 1949

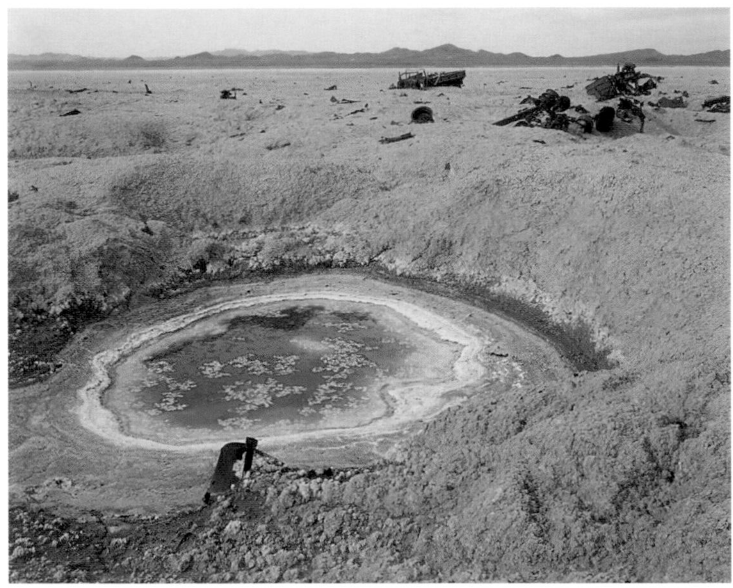

Richard Misrach has been photographing deserts of the American West since the mid-1970s, focusing on landscapes visibly altered by human activity. Most of his work, including the series *Bravo 20: The Bombing of the American West*, falls under the broad theme of what he calls *Desert Cantos*, which are subdivided into *The Terrain*, *The Flood*, *The Event I*, and *The Fires*. For the *Bravo 20* series, Misrach spent nearly two years in an isolated northwest corner of Nevada's Great Basin desert, prompted by a recent discovery that the United States Navy had been illegally treating these public lands as a bombing range since 1952. Using his van as a makeshift darkroom, Misrach documented this besieged area, which the military euphemistically calls "Bravo 20."

In *Bomb Crater and Destroyed Convoy, Bravo 20 Bombing Range, Nevada*, the Humboldt Mountains rise up behind an apocalyptic landscape. A giant crater dominates the picture, surrounded by the scattered, rusted remains of a blown-up military vehicle. Filled with blood-colored water, the crater suggests an open wound. Here, water, the essential life-sustaining source, has been literally and symbolically contaminated. The image, however, is aesthetically engaging, because Misrach intentionally injects formal elegance into his troubling compositions: "I believe that beauty is a very powerful conveyor of difficult ideas. It engages people when they might otherwise look away." By heralding the natural beauty of the American desert, he can more effectively show it as the victim of human abuse.

Misrach also collaborated with his wife, Myriam, to produce a book dedicated to Bravo 20, in which he argues that the area should be turned into a national park—"America's first environmental memorial," a permanent reminder of "our failing stewardship of this Earth."

Bomb Crater and Destroyed Convoy, Bravo 20 Bombing Range, Nevada, 1986
Chromogenic color print mounted on paperboard, 38 7/8 x 49 1/8 in. (98.7 x 124.8 cm)
Purchase, with funds from The Sondra and Charles Gilman Jr. Foundation, Inc. 93.72

JOAN MITCHELL

1926–1992

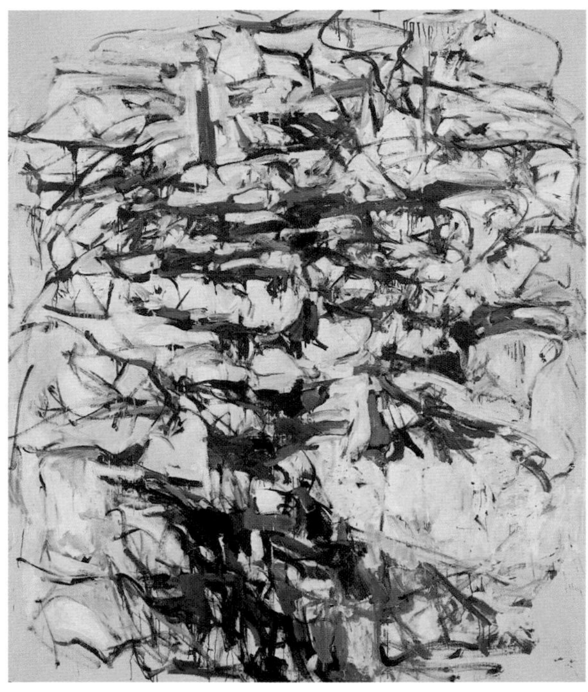

Joan Mitchell was one of the few women who rose to prominence in New York's male-dominated art world of the 1950s. Although she painted in an Abstract Expressionist style, she differed from contemporaries such as Jackson Pollock (p. 242) by placing a greater emphasis on her surroundings. Mitchell referenced landscape in many of her paintings, usually by evoking the physical sensations of her environment, such as light, sound, and movement. Although the horizontal green slashes in *Hemlock* may bring to mind a hemlock tree, Mitchell titled the work after it was completed. The title derives from a passage in a 1916 poem by Wallace Stevens, "Domination of Black," which contains several references to hemlock, including: "Out of the window,/I saw how the planets gathered/Like the leaves themselves/Turning in the wind./I saw how the night came,/Came striding like the color of the/heavy hemlocks...."

Mitchell likened her painting to poetry. It was not, she said, "an allegory or a story. It is more like a poem." In *Hemlock*, the variations of short and long brushstrokes as well as the alternation between flashes of blue or green and larger areas of milky white create a sense of rhythm and movement. The white paint appears both behind and on top of the other colors, which blurs the definition of foreground and background, as in the works of Mitchell's contemporary Franz Kline (p. 165). This ambiguity became one of Mitchell's stylistic hallmarks, and is present in the landscape-inspired works in an Abstract Expressionist style that she continued to paint until her death in 1992.

Hemlock, 1956
Oil on canvas, 91 x 80 in. (231.1 x 203.2 cm)
Purchase, with funds from the Friends of the Whitney Museum of American Art 58.20

LISETTE MODEL

1901–1983

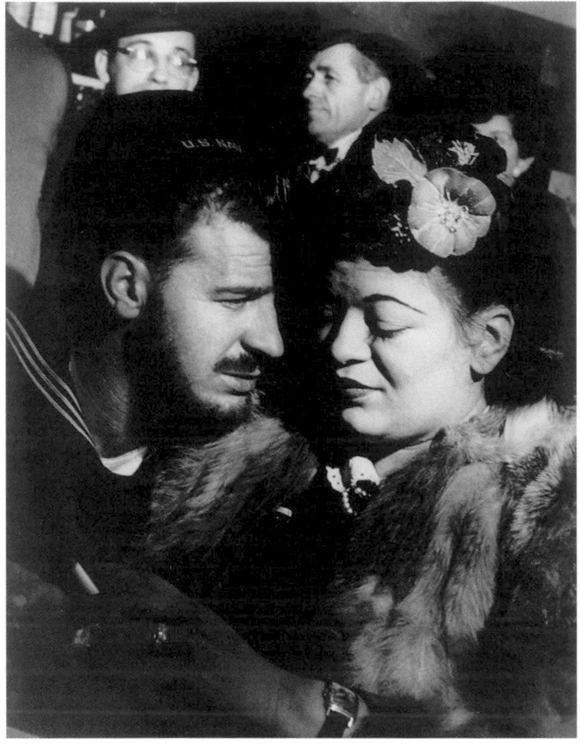

Vienna-born Lisette Model moved with her family to France in the 1920s. Her clear-eyed facility for capturing human eccentricities and excesses was apparent in her first series of photographs, taken while visiting her French mother in Nice in 1937. Using a borrowed Rolleiflex camera, Model strolled down the Promenade des Anglais, making uncompromising photographs of idle gamblers and aging upper-middle-class matrons at their leisure. She moved to New York the following year, and the city became, for her, a grand stage filled with extreme, sometimes grotesque subjects. Unlike the social documentary photographers who had roamed Depression-era New York, Model portrayed her slice of America up close and lurid—and often blurred or sunk in a murky darkness that hinted at the nation's uneasy wartime psyche.

Model gravitated naturally to Sammy's, the only Bowery saloon with a cabaret license in the early 1940s. Its bawdy floor show attracted both the uptown elite and the downtown have-nots. Nicknamed "the poor man's Stork Club," Sammy's provided Model—and fellow photographer Weegee (p. 318)—with a crowded gallery of misfit entertainers and colorful audience members. The sailor and the woman in *Sammy's, New York*, whom Model isolates from the rest of the bar, are absorbed in an intimate exchange. The theatrical light on their faces, the camera's low vantage point, and the extremely close framing—all characteristic of Model's work—escalate moody intensity. A passing moment, caught and registered, is transformed into a persistent, ambiguous image. "We photograph not only what we know but also what we don't know," Model once said. "What counts is sincerity, realism and truth. The art of the split second is my means of exploring."

Sammy's, New York, 1940–44
Gelatin silver print, 13 3/4 x 10 13/16 in. (34.9 x 27.5 cm)
Purchase, with funds from the Photography Committee 97.98.12

ABELARDO MORELL

b. 1948

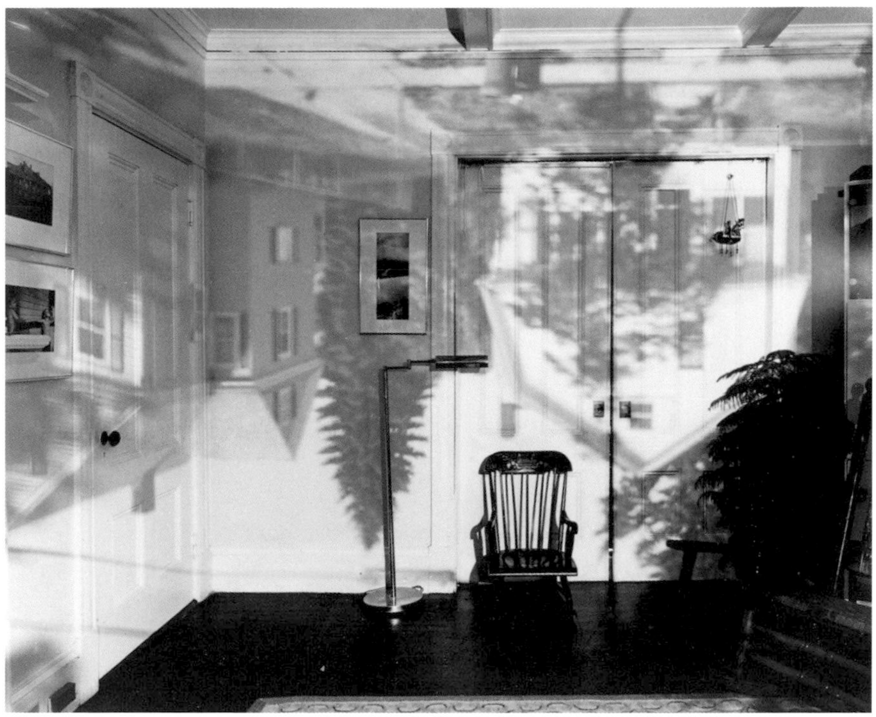

Cuban-born Abelardo Morell began his career as a street photographer, but in 1986 his focus shifted to everyday objects and interiors. Among these images are experiments with the camera obscura. The camera obscura ("dark room") is based on the long-known principle that light entering a darkened space through a small hole will project an inverted image of the illuminated area onto the opposite wall of the darkened space. Like his contemporary Vera Lutter (p. 192), Morell turns entire rooms into camera obscuras. To create *Camera Obscura Image of Houses Across the Street in Our Living Room*, he covered all the windows in his living room with black plastic and made a 3/8-inch hole in the material, thus transforming his living room into a photographic device. He then placed a large-format camera within the room to photograph the projected image of his neighbors' houses.

The resulting work merges both the public and the private realms, a connection underscored by the juxtaposition of the projected image of trees across the street with the leafy plant inside the room. This inside-outside world is an imaginary place, but one that exists for the viewer as well as for the artist. "What made me fall in love with photography," Morell explains, "was that I could make things in life all mine in a picture. While that feeling is still in me, I hope that my images are open enough to invite the imagination of others too." Indeed, the empty chair and reading lamp beckon the viewer to enter both the dreamlike world of fiction and the space of the photograph.

Camera Obscura Image of Houses Across the Street in Our Living Room, 1991
Gelatin silver print, 18 x 22 7/16 in. (45.2 x 57 cm)
Purchase, with funds from Anne and Joel S. Ehrenkranz 2000.19

ROBERT MORRIS

b. 1931

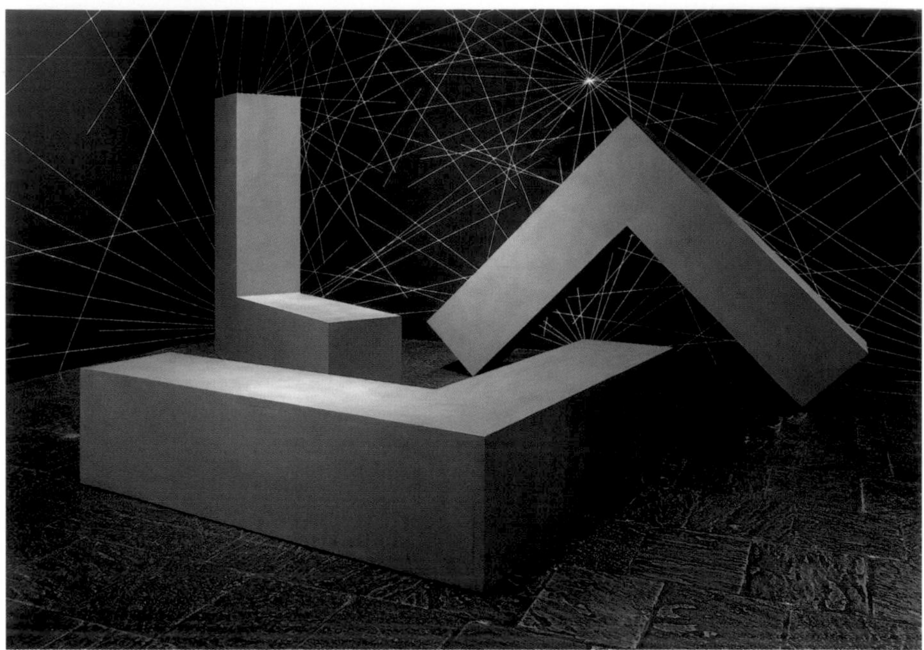

Untitled (L-beams) is one of the canonical works of Minimalism. Beginning in the 1960s, Morris and other Minimalists, including Carl Andre and Donald Judd (pp. 30, 160), used reductive geometry to stress the art work's presence in the viewer's physical space rather than the illusionistic pictorial spaces set off by a picture frame or sculpture pedestal. By eliminating narrative and anecdote in favor of geometry, Minimalist sculpture forces the viewer to acknowledge that perception has a physiological basis: what we see and how we react to it depends on the position of our bodies in relation to the work.

Morris' huge L-beams, for instance, powerfully demonstrate a simple perceptual principle: even though the three beams are exactly the same shape and size (each is composed of two 8-foot-long pieces), their variant placements—an upright L, flat on the ground, and turned on end to form a triangular shape—make them read as different forms. This principle becomes more complicated when, in the physical presence of the sculpture, we realize that the three configurations also create different psychological responses. An object low to the ground elicits a sense of superiority, while those that rival or exceed us in height reduce our sense of self.

Like Morris' work, much Minimalist art, such as that of Tony Smith (p. 292), references human scale in order to produce an empathetic response to masses and forms, even when they are pure geometry. Thus, the seemingly hard-edged, emotionless look of Minimalist sculptures such as *Untitled (L-beams)* in fact produces a visceral response that calls attention to the physical and psychological processes at work in the act of looking.

Untitled (L-beams), 1965
Stainless steel in 3 parts, dimensions variable
Gift of Howard and Jean Lipman 76.29a–c

ROBERT MOTHERWELL

1915–1991

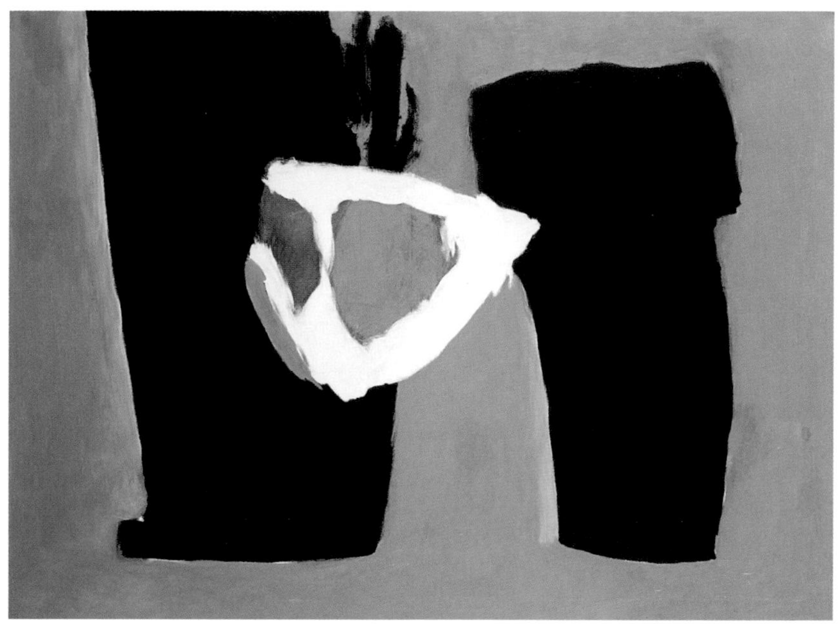

Afternoon in Barcelona is a work from Robert Motherwell's *Iberia* series, inspired by his travels to Spain in the late 1950s. Set within an expansive field of ocher, a triangular gray and white shape connects two large black forms. These groupings of rectangles were a constant of Motherwell's painting vocabulary; he called the configuration a "dolmen," after the prehistoric megaliths composed of upright stones supporting a horizontal slab. The artist may also have meant to evoke his impressions of the Barcelona bullring here: the forms that structure the painting, like the black bulls and yellow sand of the ring, are at once interactive and independent.

The diverse techniques in *Afternoon in Barcelona*—gestural brushstrokes and linear rhythms, rounded biomorphisms and angular geometries, abstraction and representation—speak to Motherwell's unique status as an Abstract Expressionist who had fully absorbed the lessons of the European avant-garde. In fact, his grandly scaled abstractions are often infused with the organic spontaneity of Surrealism. He was inspired by the Surrealists' automatism—drawing or painting without intellectual mediation, in an attempt to delve below conscious intentions. He called automatism a "plastic weapon with which to invent new forms," and indeed the rough-hewn, brushy shapes of *Afternoon in Barcelona* appear to have been executed without deliberation. Motherwell's passion for Spain is also famously recorded in his *Elegies to the Spanish Republic* series, a group of more than 150 paintings, made between 1948 and his death in 1991, that lament the destruction of the Spanish Republic by fascist forces in the civil war of 1936.

Afternoon in Barcelona, 1958
Oil on canvas, 54 x 72 in. (137.2 x 182.9 cm)
Gift of Robert and Jane Meyerhoff 79.35

VIK MUNIZ

b. 1961

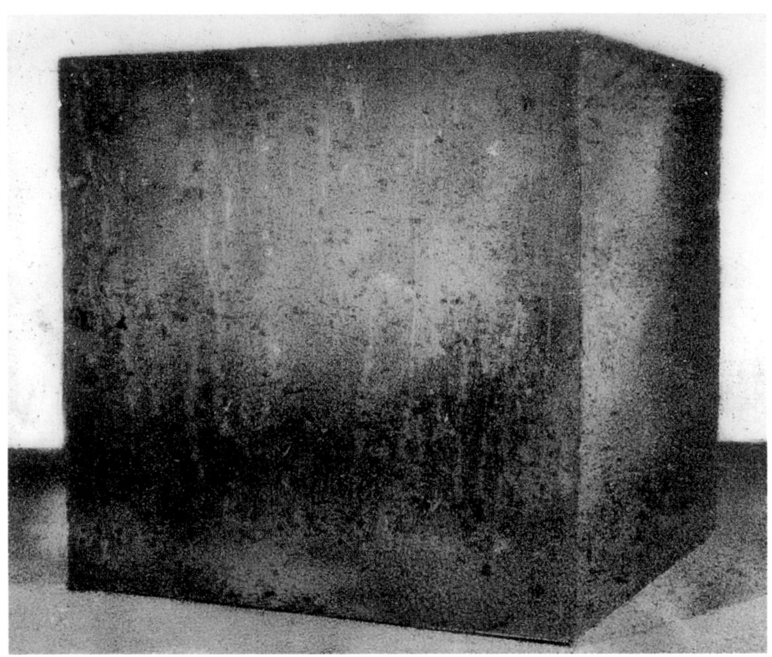

Brazilian-born Vik Muniz is constantly engaged in the process of translating recognizable images created by other artists or photographers (sometimes both) into new languages and new materials. "I prefer representations of representations," the artist says, "to the things themselves."

In *The Things Themselves: Pictures of Dust* series—created expressly for an exhibition at the Whitney Museum in 2001—Muniz worked with installation photographs of Minimalist and Postminimalist art exhibited at the Whitney over the last four decades. Using dust gathered from the Museum's galleries and offices, he made drawings based on these photographs; he then photographed and enlarged them with color film. *Picture of Dust*, nearly 6 feet high, is a photograph of the artist's dust drawing of a photograph of Tony Smith's 1962 sculpture *Die* (p. 292), as it was installed in a Whitney Museum exhibition in 1994. "I became interested in Minimalist art," Muniz explains, "because it attempts to avoid interpretation and historical contextualization. Minimalist art refers to nothing but itself."

Muniz draws on the irreverent Dada legacy of Marcel Duchamp, whose own collection of studio dust was photographed by Man Ray (p. 251) in 1920. But Muniz's primary concern is the fidelity of images—the assumed truth-value of photographs—which he subverts over and over. By bringing dust into the translation, he plays with various levels of illusion, leading us to ask whether we can really believe what we see. To what extent does a photograph ever truly capture—in the words of Edward Weston, one of twentieth-century America's most renowned photographers—"the thing itself"?

Picture of Dust (Tony Smith, Die, 1962, installed at the Whitney Museum in "From the Collection: Photography, Sculpture, and Painting," July 14, 1994–February 26, 1995), 2000
Chromogenic color print, 71 1/2 x 89 in. (181.6 x 226.1 cm)
Gift of Brent Sikkema, New York, and the artist 2001.56

GERALD MURPHY

1888–1964

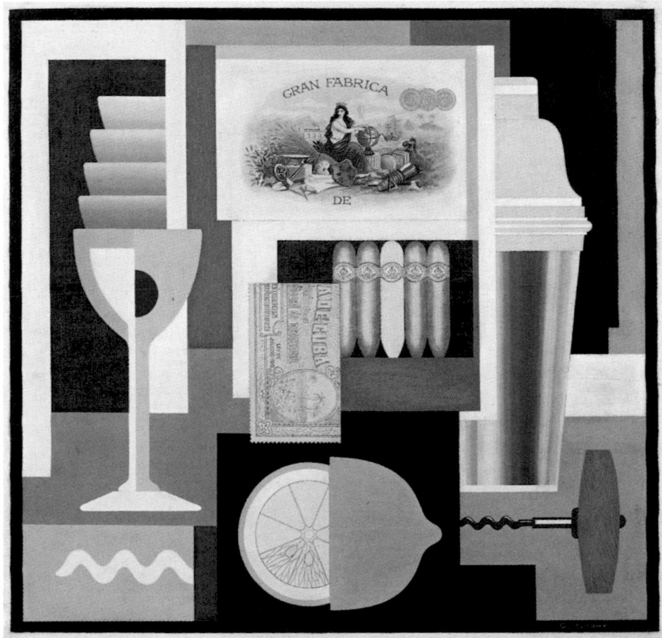

Gerald Murphy was one of the foremost members of the so-called Lost Generation, the artists and writers who flocked to Paris after World War I to work in the city's vanguard artistic environment. His friendships with the international cast of creative spirits who flourished in Paris during the 1920s—including Pablo Picasso, Fernand Léger, and Igor Stravinsky—committed him to the idea of artistic experimentation.

During his short, seven-year career as an artist, Murphy produced only about fourteen paintings. Key among them is *Cocktail*, a bold, stylized depiction of what he called utilitarian "objects in a world of abstraction"—a world of flattened, sometimes fragmented geometric shapes and spatially illogical sizes and juxtapositions. *Cocktail* is in fact a radical still-life painting, reminiscent of French Cubism and of the industrial aesthetic of the American Precisionists (pp. 81, 277). Yet it is also unique in its autobiographical approach. The depicted accoutrements of a typical 1920s bar tray were based on Murphy's memory of his father's bar accessories. It has been suggested that the centrally placed cigar box is especially significant. The five cigars represent Murphy, his wife, and their three children. The illusionistic depiction of the box cover, which alone took Murphy four months to complete, shows a robed woman surrounded by items that allude to Murphy himself: an artist's palette, a boat (he was an avid sailor), and a machine wheel, much like the one pictured in another Murphy painting, *Watch*. Ultimately, *Cocktail* celebrates a ritual that was forbidden during Prohibition in America but became a distinctive feature of life for expatriates living in Europe during the Roaring Twenties.

Cocktail, 1927
Oil on canvas, 29 1/16 x 29 7/8 in. (73.8 x 75.9 cm)
Purchase, with funds from Evelyn and Leonard A. Lauder, Thomas H. Lee, and the Modern Painting and Sculpture Committee 95.188

ELIZABETH MURRAY
b. 1940

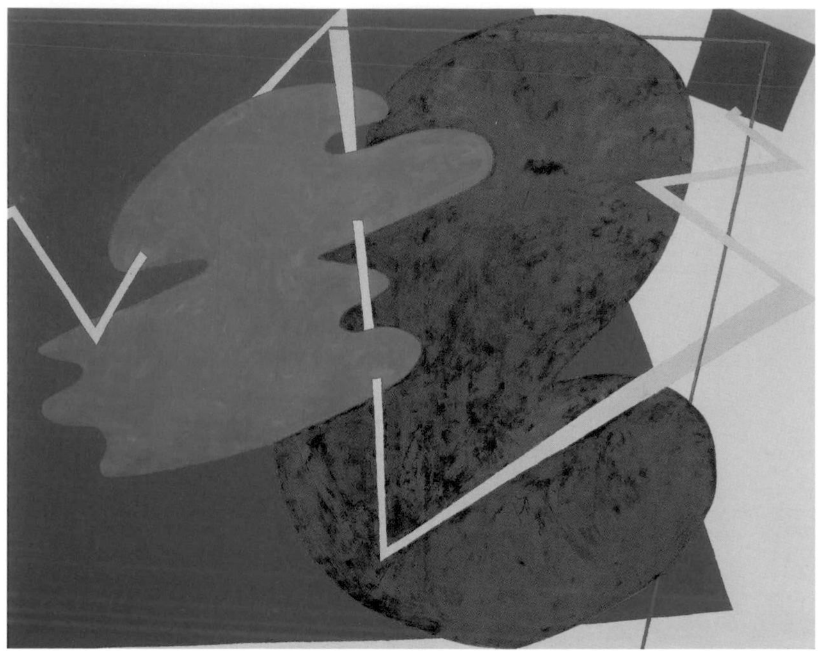

Using lines, shapes, and colors that have the clarity and bounce associated with comic strips as well as a simplicity of form derived from reductive abstraction, Elizabeth Murray has forged a distinctively exuberant vocabulary. *Children Meeting* was made at a time when that vocabulary was just being consolidated. The painting, Murray recalls, "grew out of a confidence about being able to lay down the colors and put in the goofy shapes that were beginning to emerge....I'd never allowed myself to use that zany purple; it's a very hard color because it doesn't have a clear emotion for me." Her comment implies the importance of psychological associations in her work; equally important is the implicit presence of figuration, even in painting that seems resolutely abstract. Small children engaged in joyous, boisterous play can be discerned in the jostling green and pink forms of the 1978 *Children Meeting*, and it is not coincidental that Murray was then a young mother who witnessed such play every day.

Born in Chicago, Murray studied there and in California before moving to New York in 1967, where she encountered the rigorous abstraction of the Minimalists. After early experimentation with Pop-related work in several media, she produced a series of small, Minimalist-influenced abstract paintings. But from the late 1970s on, her pictorial language, though it remained abstract, took on a rollicking and cartoonlike tone. Describing the balance between the representational and the abstract in a work such as *Children Meeting*, Murray remarked, "Abstraction is about intuiting other realities; sometimes there is a remarkable conjunction between the realities intuited and the realities of the world."

Children Meeting, 1978
Oil on canvas, 101 3/16 x 127 in. (257 x 322.6 cm)
Purchase, with funds from the Louis and Bessie Adler Foundation, Inc., Seymour M. Klein, President 78.34

ELIE NADELMAN

1882–1946

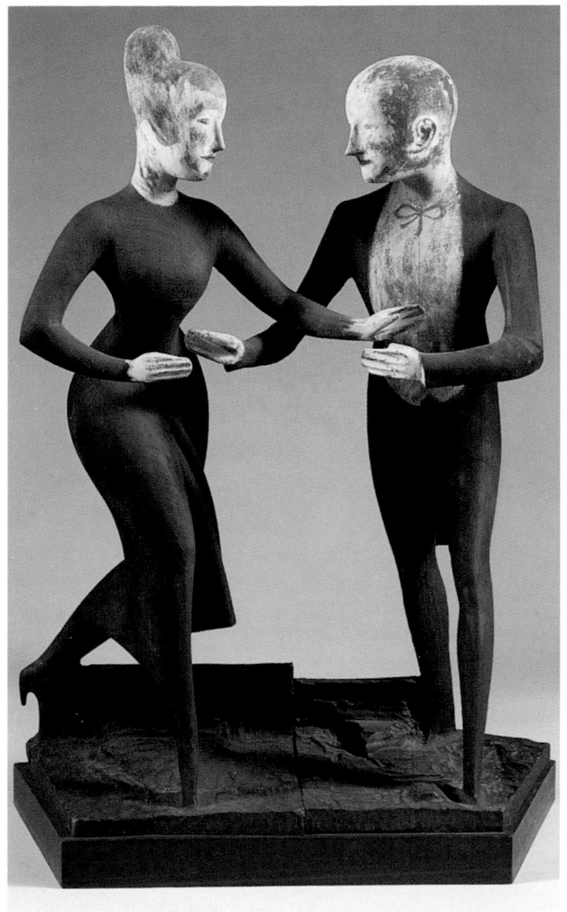

Scenes of entertainment and high society inspired the Polish immigrant artist Elie Nadelman. After his arrival in the United States in 1914, Nadelman, a self-taught sculptor, became a key figure in the movement to synthesize classicism and abstraction in American sculpture. He also began to represent genre subjects—dancers, hostesses, pianists, conductors, and circus performers—all rendered with the sleek simplicity of style for which he is best known.

The exploration of these genre subjects paralleled Nadelman's burgeoning passion for American folk art, as did his use of painted wood rather than more traditional bronze or marble. *Tango* is a primary example of Nadelman's marriage of classical sculpture and popular American subject matter. The natural cherry wood is used to indicate the bodies and outer garments, while hands, faces, and the man's shirt are painted in white gesso or other colors. The slim, elongated woman and man are caught up in the tango, a new Argentine dance that swept across America just before World War I. The tango is a dance of passion, and although Nadelman's couple has succumbed to its rhythm, they appear impervious to its sensuality. Nadelman captures the dance's stylized elegance rather than its sweat, energy, and sexuality. Moreover, he avoided the most recognizable tango step, where the dancers stride forward with hands joined and arms clasped tightly about each other's back, and selected instead a moment in the choreography when the dancers separate. The blocks of wood from which the man and woman were carved are also separate, as are the bases on which they rest.

Tango, c. 1919
Painted cherry wood and gesso, 3 units, 35 7/8 x 26 x 13 7/8 in. (91.1 x 66 x 35.2 cm) overall
Purchase, with funds from the Mr. and Mrs. Arthur G. Altschul Purchase Fund, the Joan and Lester Avnet Purchase Fund, the Edgar William and Bernice Chrysler Garbisch Purchase Fund, the Mrs. Robert C. Graham Purchase Fund in honor of John I.H. Baur, the Mrs. Percy Uris Purchase Fund, and the Henry Schnakenberg Purchase Fund in honor of Juliana Force 88.1a–c

PETER NAGY

b. 1959

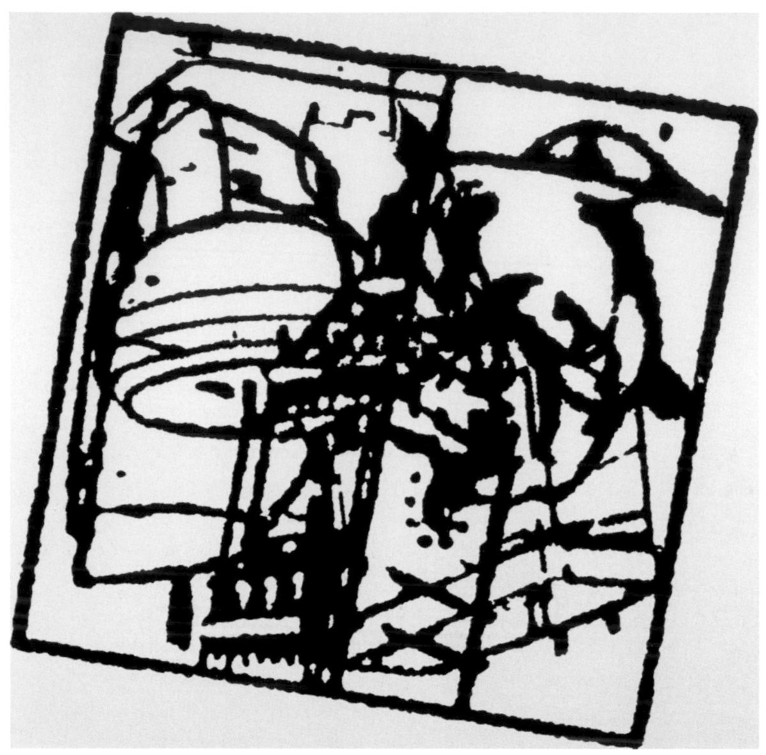

Peter Nagy's paintings of the late 1980s and early 1990s were based on accumulations of illustrations, diagrams, and logos that he duplicated over and over, often with a photocopier. He then enlarged and painted these repeatedly copied images on canvas, a process that transformed the originals into Rorschach-like abstractions whose prior character or function is no longer discernible. *State of Degeneracy*, from the so-called *Cancer Series*, shows a lopsided field of forms, few of which resolve into recognizable imagery. One that does, the upside-down toilet at upper left, is no doubt a reference to Marcel Duchamp's infamous urinal, turned ninety degrees and submitted as a "ready-made" to a New York art exhibition in 1917.

As the titles of both the work and the series suggest, Nagy's painting is intended to evoke the malevolent and incomprehensible processes of cancerous disease. However, Nagy's own duplicating technique is not an allusion to the uncontrollable reproduction of destructive cells or an attempt to represent cancer in a biological or medical sense. Rather, *State of Degeneracy* uses this ravenous affliction as a metaphor for the confusing and all-consuming power of the mass media. As information and imagery become evermore ubiquitous, insistent, and reiterative, we seem to be in danger, Nagy's painting warns, of losing our sense of direction, place, and perhaps even identity.

State of Degeneracy, 1988
Synthetic polymer on canvas, 48 x 48 3/16 in. (121.9 x 122.4 cm)
Gift of Steve Shane 98.39

BRUCE NAUMAN

b. 1941

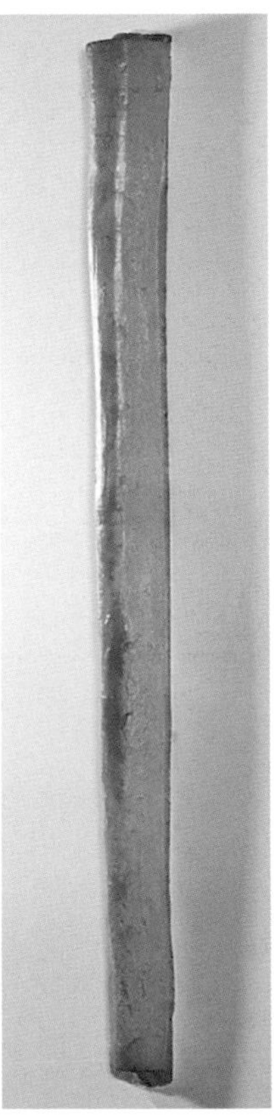

For more than forty years, Bruce Nauman has been experimenting with an extraordinary range of materials, from sculpture to video to holograms. His career began in the 1960s, concurrent with the emergence of Conceptual art, a movement in which artists employed language and documentation to express their ideas. Although Nauman defies categorization as a Conceptualist, he regularly incorporated text in his work, often exploring the relationship between language and the human body. In *Six inches of my knee extended to six feet*, he apparently used his own body as subject, connecting casts of a 6-inch section of his knee until they measured nearly 6 feet. Each 6-inch section of fiberglass might be a recognizable representation of a knee, but as a whole the work is abstracted and ambiguous. Without the descriptive title, it is unlikely that we could identify the anatomical source. In addition to being explanatory, the title cleverly manages to convert not only inches but knees into feet.

In *Self-Portrait as a Fountain*, one of eleven photographs in a portfolio, Nauman questions the traditional role of the artist in society. He depicts himself shirtless, with raised arms and open palms, spewing out an arc of water, in imitation of the nude statues customarily found in decorative fountains. Thus he offers himself as both a fountain and a work of art. During these years, Nauman had used the statement "The true artist is an amazing luminous fountain" in a number of text-based works. This playfully literal illustration of the statement pokes fun at the myth of the serious artist as a prolific genius who spews forth a steady stream of masterpieces.

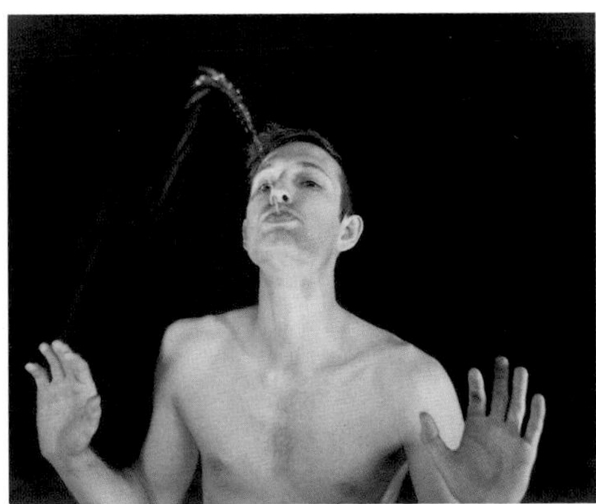

Six inches of my knee extended to six feet, 1967
Fiberglass, 68 1/2 x 5 3/4 x 3 7/8 in. (174 x 14.6 x 9.8 cm)
Partial and promised gift of Robert A.M. Stern 91.115

Self-Portrait as a Fountain, 1966–67 and 1970
Chromogenic color print, 20 1/16 x 23 15/16 in. (51 x 60.8 cm)
Purchase 70.50.9

ALICE NEEL
1900–1984

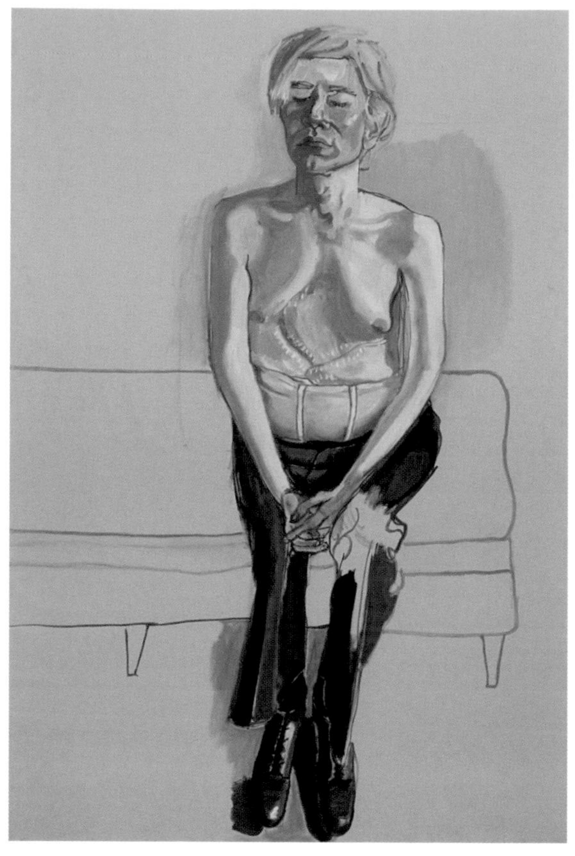

Dubbed by an art critic a "collector of souls," Alice Neel painted an extraordinary variety of people during her prolific, sixty-year career. Her sitters ranged from the notable to the unknown and included family members, neighbors in Spanish Harlem (where she lived for more than twenty years), nude pregnant women, fellow artists, curators, gallerists, a taxi driver, a museum guard, a New York City mayor, and an archbishop.

Neel's 1970 painting of Andy Warhol (p. 316) captures the vulnerability of an artist whose work and public persona were famous for their cool detachment. As in all her portraits, Neel painted Warhol in her own home, which doubled as her studio. His slender, androgynous body is outlined in Neel's trademark ultramarine blue. She shows Warhol with his eyes closed and shirt removed, exposing his pale, scarred torso and the supportive corset he was forced to wear after he had been shot in 1968 by Valerie Solanis—a woman who frequented The Factory, Warhol's studio, and who founded S.C.U.M. (Society for Cutting Up Men), of which she was the sole member. Though reflecting the brightened palette of Neel's work in the 1960s, this canvas is limited to notably cool hues, such as the lonely swatch of pale, icy blue surrounding Warhol's upper body and head. In Neel's spare composition, the only item in the background is the outline of her couch. Depicting him as isolated, wounded, and withdrawn, the "collector of souls" shows us an unexpected, and perhaps more profound, side of Warhol.

Andy Warhol, 1970
Oil on canvas, 60 x 40 in. (152.4 x 101.6 cm)
Gift of Timothy Collins 80.52

SHIRIN NESHAT

b. 1957

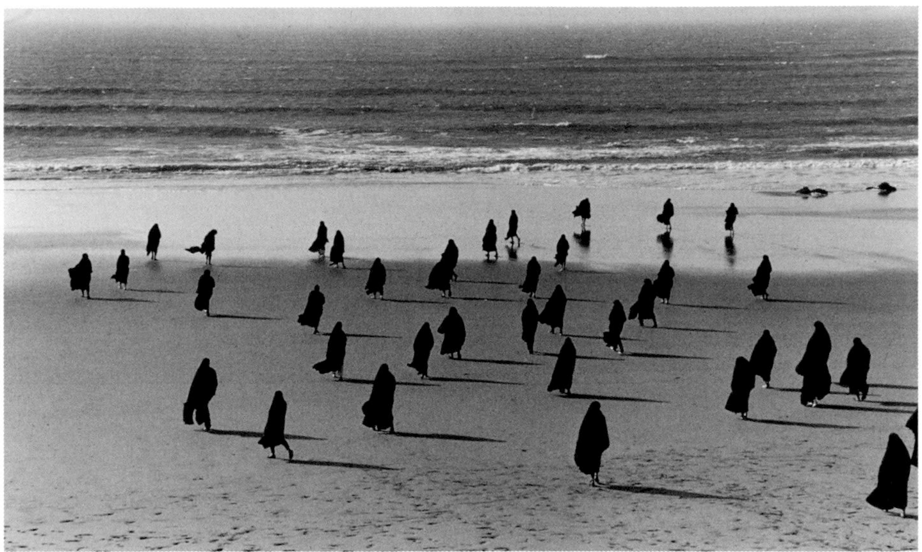

Shirin Neshat, born in Iran, has lived in the United States since 1974. Her work over the last decade, from photographic self-portraits to more recent video installations, has concentrated on the social and cultural definition of women in the contemporary Islamic world. *Rapture* is a two-screen, black-and-white video projection in which an allegorical narrative unfolds on facing walls of the gallery. This division of the film space facilitates the central theme of the narrative, the differences between Muslim men and women. The work opens with facing shots of a fortress and an expanse of desert. The fortress is soon occupied by dozens of men, uniformly clad in black trousers and white shirts, while the desert is gradually crossed by rows of women wrapped in black chadors, the head veil and shawl traditionally worn as a sign of modesty. Neshat's now gendered spaces suggest ready associations (woman=nature, man=culture) as well as contrasts—the men are symbolically entrenched in the tradition and authority of Islam, while the women are both protected and imprisoned by their veils.

Against an evocative soundtrack sung by Iranian composer Sussan Deyhim, a rhythmic dynamic ensues between action and gaze. As the women watch silently, the men across the floor act out a series of mundane activities: carrying ladders and leaning them against the wall; engaging in shoving matches; playing card games. The women then start to ululate in a shrill, taunting burst, following which they fall into silent prayer. In the denouement, the men watch from a parapet as the women approach the seashore and set six of their own to sea in an oarless boat. Caught in the space that divides these two perspectives, party to neither, the viewer is merely witness to the emblematic displays that comprise this choreographed and charged interchange.

****Rapture***, 1999
Video installation, black-and-white, sound; 13 minutes, dimensions variable
Purchase, with funds from the Painting and Sculpture Committee and the Film and Video Committee 99.86

LOUISE NEVELSON
1899–1988

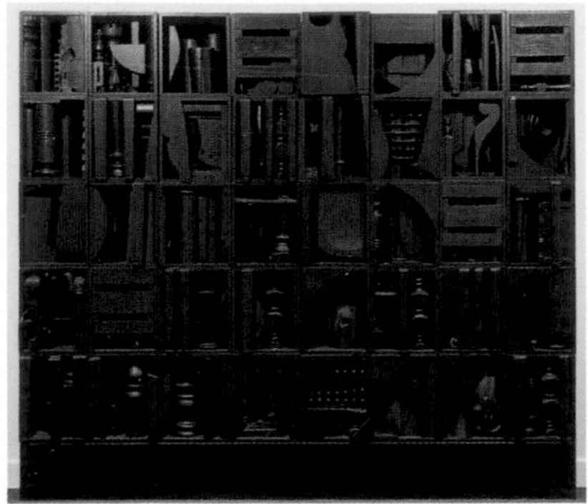

One of the foremost American sculptors of the twentieth century, Louise Nevelson is renowned for the large, monochromatic wood sculptures that she painted black, white, or gold, but mostly black. Despite the somber finish, the works seldom convey a sense of gloom or the macabre. Nevelson dismissed the Western association of black with death, often pointing out that in China white is worn at funerals. Black was a positive force for her, one that "may mean...completeness...eternity."

Nevelson began making black wood sculptures in the mid-1950s. The boxes comprising *Black Chord* are, characteristically, filled with objects found on the streets of New York City. The balusters, volutes, and brackets reflect Nevelson's particular affinity for the ornamental details of Victorian architecture. Once coated in black paint, however, these familiar objects become more evocative: urban detritus is resurrected into a mysterious shrine made dramatic and grand by the work's monumental scale.

Nevelson's largest works, or "environments," as they are often called, consist of hundreds of boxes filled with painted objects and stacked up on every wall in a room. *Dawn's Wedding Chapel II* includes elements from one such environment, titled *Dawn's Wedding Feast*, an installation of Nevelson's first white sculptures, which she created for a 1959 exhibition. The work was, in Nevelson's words, "a white wedding cake, a wedding mirror...a pillow...a kind of fulfillment, a transition to a marriage with the world." After the exhibition closed, she reassembled individual elements to form several discrete sculptures, of which *Dawn's Wedding Chapel II* is but one example. Nevelson summed up the essence of her art when she compared it to ancient Mayan ruins, which also capture "a world of geometry and magic."

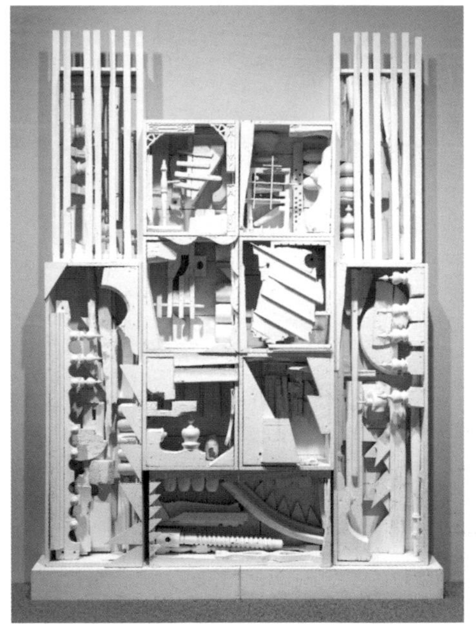

Black Chord, 1964
Painted wood, 104 1/2 x 117 3/4 x 12 1/4 in. (265.4 x 299.1 x 31.1 cm)
Gift of Anne and Joel Ehrenkranz 91.1

Dawn's Wedding Chapel II, 1959
Painted wood, 115 7/8 x 83 1/2 x 10 1/2 in. (294.3 x 212.1 x 26.7 cm) with base
Purchase, with funds from the Howard and Jean Lipman Foundation, Inc. 70.68a–m

BARNETT NEWMAN

1905–1970

In the wake of World War II, Barnett Newman found traditional subjects and styles of art incapable of expressing the feelings of horror and vulnerability elicited by the Holocaust and the creation of nuclear weapons. "You must realize," he later recalled, "that we felt the moral crisis of a world in shambles, a world devastated by a great depression and a fierce world war, and it was impossible at that time to paint the kind of paintings that we were doing—flowers, reclining nudes, and people playing the cello." Seeking an appropriate artistic response to the anxieties of the era, Newman rejected representational painting and began again, as he said, "from scratch, as if painting were not only dead, but had never existed."

The title of this painting, *Day One*, like other paintings Newman made in the late 1940s and early 1950s, evokes the idea of creation and the origins of life. These works are distinguished by large, flat, chromatic expanses, a type of painting that came to be characterized as Color Field. Newman's chromatic fields are interrupted only by bands of colors running along the edge of the canvas, usually vertically. He referred to these bands, which he often made with the aid of masking tape, as "zips." The zips allowed him to experiment with various proportions and color combinations, while keeping an all-over composition. He discovered that if he placed the zips along opposite ends of the canvas, as he does in *Day One*, he "got to the edge and didn't fall off." The unusually tall height of his works and the vertical zips enhance the sense of grandeur associated with creation myths, while reinforcing what Newman called the "uprightedness" of painting—a reference to the upright figure, which expressed Newman's belief in the dignity and positive potential of humankind.

Day One, 1951–52
Oil on canvas, 132 x 50 1/4 in. (335.3 x 127.6 cm)
Purchase, with funds from the Friends of the Whitney Museum of American Art 67.18

ISAMU NOGUCHI

1904–1988

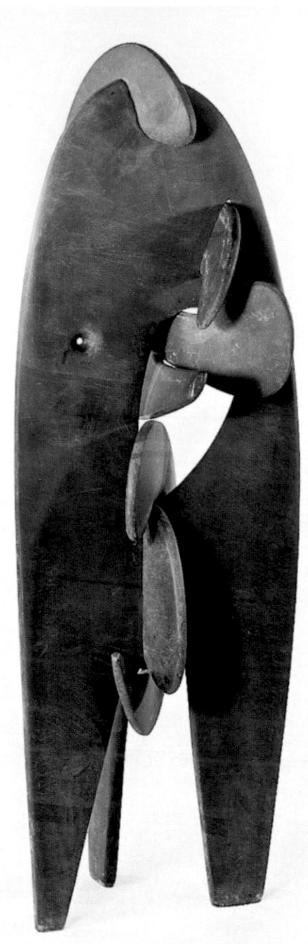

During a career that spanned more than sixty years, Isamu Noguchi created sculptures, furniture designs, dance sets, public gardens, and large-scale fountains. He drew on Eastern and Western aesthetics and traditions of craftsmanship to create highly original forms. Born to an American mother and a Japanese father, Noguchi spent most of his early childhood in Japan, where, at the age of ten, he apprenticed with a cabinetmaker—an experience that left him with a deep appreciation for his materials and tools. As an adolescent, he attended school in the United States, and he remained in this country for the rest of his life, with periodic sojourns in Europe and Japan. Before beginning medical school in 1923, Noguchi apprenticed with a sculptor in Connecticut; within a year he had abandoned medicine to take up sculpture. During a study trip to Paris in 1927 (mostly spent assisting the famed Romanian sculptor Constantin Brancusi), he began developing a style based on the reduction of forms to their barest essence—a process he called "poetic translation."

This practice of distilling forms culminated in the mid-1940s, when Noguchi began making biomorphic sculptures composed of interlocking pieces of wood or stone. *Humpty Dumpty*, an emblematic work from this period, was carefully constructed so that its five parts would fit together and stay in place without glue or screws. As Noguchi explained, "everything I do has an element of engineering in it—particularly since I dislike gluing parts together or taking advantage of something that is not inherent in the material. I am leery of welding or pasting. It implies taking an unfair advantage of nature." The title *Humpty Dumpty* playfully acknowledges the work's precarious construction, while the roundness of the forms evokes the famously plump character of the children's rhyme.

Humpty Dumpty, 1946
Ribbon slate, 59 x 21 1/2 x 19 1/2 in. (149.9 x 54.6 x 49.5 cm) overall
Purchase 47.7a–e

KENNETH NOLAND

b. 1924

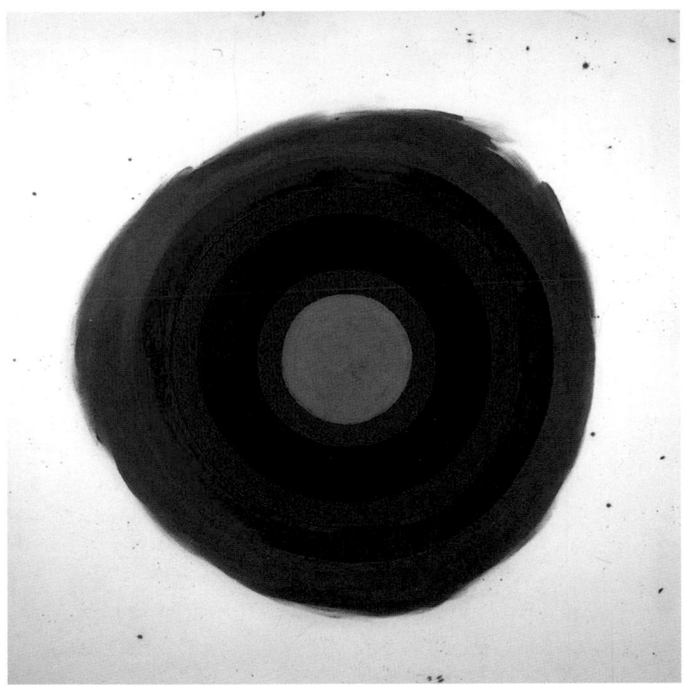

Kenneth Noland is part of the generation of American painters who emerged in the 1950s on the heels of Abstract Expressionism. His work was influenced by some artists in that movement, particularly the Color Field painters Mark Rothko and Clyfford Still (pp. 263, 300). Noland also studied with Josef Albers (p. 29) at Black Mountain College in North Carolina, where Albers taught classes in color theory. Yet the particular technique employed in *Song* and in the other *Concentric Circle* paintings Noland made between 1958 and 1963 is most indebted to his contemporary, Helen Frankenthaler (p. 110). In 1953, Noland and his colleague Morris Louis (p. 189) visited Frankenthaler's studio and saw her latest paintings, in which she had applied thinned paint directly onto unprimed canvas, allowing the colors to soak through and stain the fabric. To Noland, this staining technique was a means of developing "a less codified way of painting in which materials were dealt with in terms of texture, color, even pattern, rather than in the service of gesture or images."

The staining technique and the geometry of Noland's compositions seem to rein in the emotionalism of his Abstract Expressionist predecessors, yet their influence can still be discerned in *Song*. Tiny dots of color appear to have accidentally fallen on the unprimed canvas, interrupting its controlled geometry. These aberrations and the loose brushstrokes of the outermost ring are Noland's way of marking the emotional act of painting even in a seemingly ordered composition.

Song, 1958
Synthetic polymer on canvas, 65 x 65 in. (165.1 x 165.1 cm)
Purchase, with funds from the Friends of the Whitney Museum of American Art 63.31

GEORGIA O'KEEFFE

1887–1986

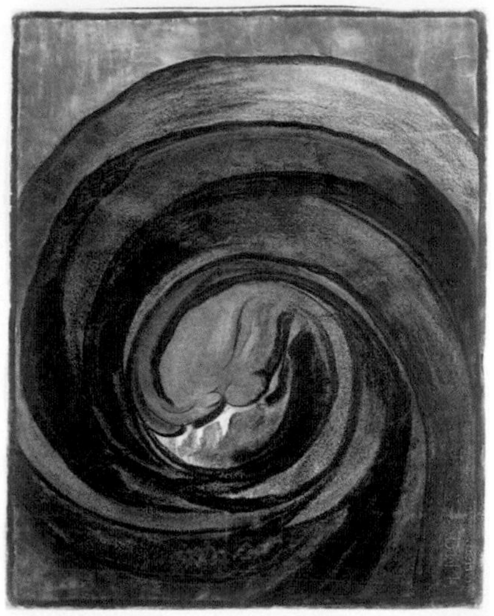

Around 1915, Georgia O'Keeffe embarked on a series of charcoal abstractions that launched her career as one of America's foremost modernists. Alfred Stieglitz premiered these works in 1917 at his famous 291 gallery in New York, an exhibition that put O'Keeffe in the company of vanguard artists such as Arthur G. Dove, Marsden Hartley, and John Marin (pp. 94, 132, 197). In the charcoal abstractions, including *Drawing No. 8*, she rejected the Cubist model in favor of her own brand of organic abstraction. The spiraling form of *Drawing No. 8* invokes the vortex as a symbol of generation, of life emerging from chaos.

O'Keeffe's abstractions suggest the forms of nature. *Music—Pink and Blue II*, for example, recalls the colors of sunset or a mountainous landscape twisted into an arc. The painting echoes O'Keeffe's description of "music that makes holes in the sky." She implies a synesthetic link between the visual and the aural, between landscape painting and music. *Black and White*, one of her most abstract paintings, relies similarly on the interaction between observation and idea. O'Keeffe may have borrowed its composition—a triangle receding into space—from her earlier landscapes of the Texas plains. But *Black and White* also elicits more formal associations, such as the contrast between light and dark or between geometric and organic.

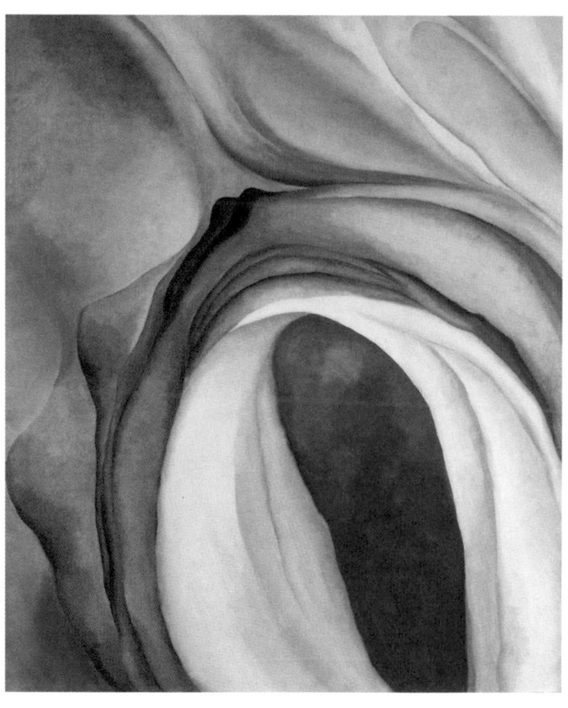

Drawing No. 8, 1915
Charcoal on paper mounted on cardboard, 24 1/4 x 18 7/8 in. (61.6 x 47.9 cm)
Purchase, with funds from the Mr. and Mrs. Arthur G. Altschul Purchase Fund 85.52

Music—Pink and Blue II, 1919
Oil on canvas, 35 x 29 1/8 in. (88.9 x 74 cm)
Gift of Emily Fisher Landau in honor of Tom Armstrong 91.90

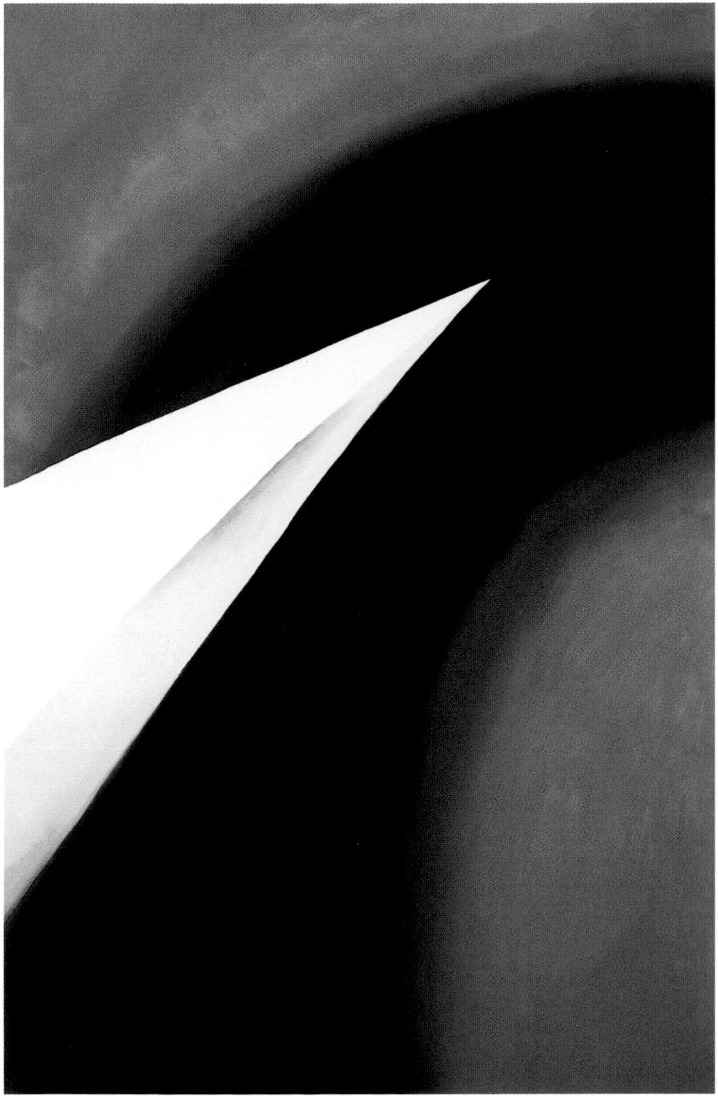

O'Keeffe was reluctant to explain the complex, layered meanings of her work, and her silence often led to misunderstandings or at least oversimplifications. Critics read paintings such as *The White Calico Flower* as emblems of female sexuality, even though these Freudian interpretations made the artist uncomfortable. Her response to nature was primarily visual, not sexual; she appreciated the form of a flower, not its generative function.

Black and White, 1930
Oil on canvas, 36 x 24 in. (91.4 x 61 cm)
50th Anniversary Gift of Mr. and Mrs. R. Crosby Kemper 81.9

GEORGIA O'KEEFFE

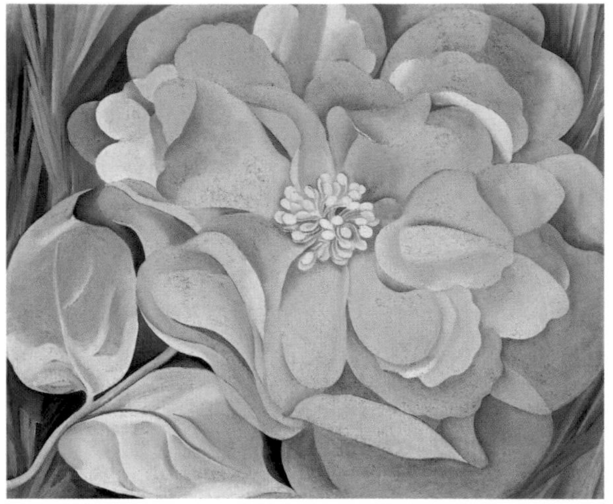

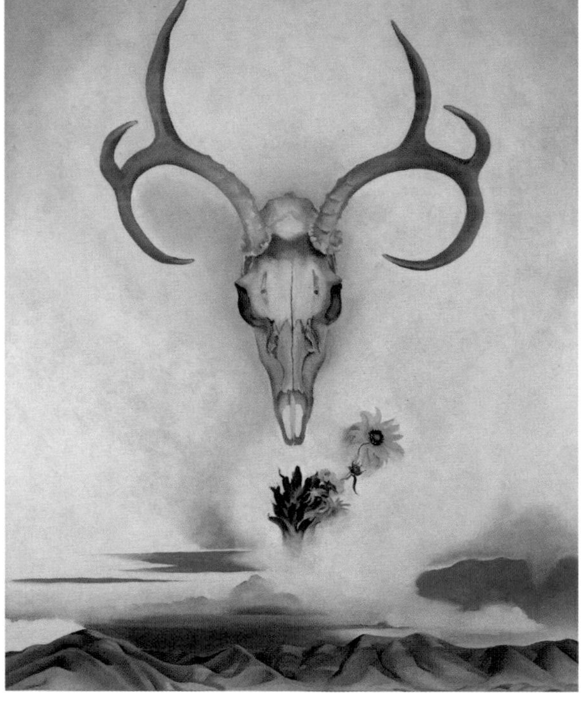

O'Keeffe was drawn to certain objects, including flowers and, later, the bones she found in the deserts of her beloved New Mexico. In *Summer Days*, a deer skull festooned with flowers floats like a mirage above distant hills. Although the painting has been described as Surrealist, O'Keeffe saw nothing incongruous or illogical in this juxtaposition of enlarged skull and diminutive landscape. As she explained, "The bones cut sharply to the center of something that is keenly alive in the desert." For O'Keeffe, objects were never simple symbols—she did not equate flowers with sexuality and bones with death. In their clarity of detail, these elements become metaphors of the life-giving rhythms of nature.

The White Calico Flower, 1931
Oil on canvas, 30 x 36 in. (76.2 x 91.4 cm)
Purchase 32.26

Summer Days, 1936
Oil on canvas, 36 x 30 in. (91.4 x 76.2 cm)
Gift of Calvin Klein 94.171

CLAES OLDENBURG

b. 1929

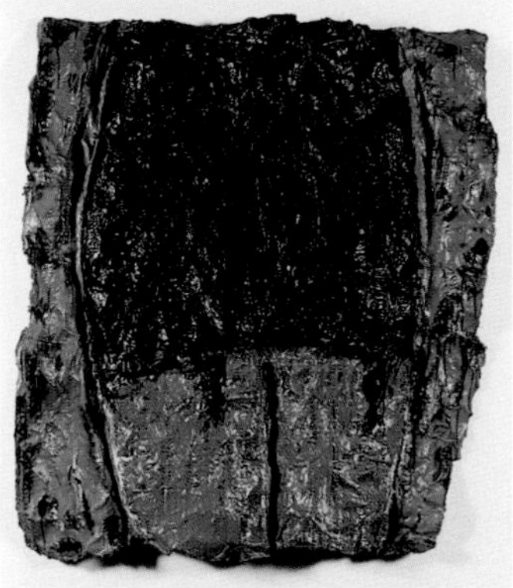

Claes Oldenburg reveals the inner life of everyday objects by defamiliarizing them—separating them from their original function, scale, or physical context. His sculptures, drawings, and large-scale projects thus disrupt our expectations of how common things "behave." As a young artist in the late 1950s and early 1960s, Oldenburg was involved in an emerging form of performance-based art called Happenings. The props, costumes, sets, and the theatricality associated with these events have continued to inform his rich body of work for the past four decades.

One of Oldenburg's most important projects was a rented storefront he transformed into a sculptural environment and "opened" in December 1961. In *The Store*, he made and sold versions of the consumer goods he saw displayed in New York's store windows—pie slices, men's shirts, and ladies' undergarments such as *The Black Girdle*. *The Black Girdle* differs from other *Store* works in that the human body is not only inferred through its tactile, corporeal surfaces, but the skin of a woman's legs is actually visible. As a creative enterprise, *The Store* circumvented the art market by offering works directly to the general public, and its innovative combination of art and commerce is often cited as a milestone in the emergence of Pop art. The works for sale were produced by dipping muslin in plaster, draping it over chicken wire, and loosely painting the rough surfaces. Exhibited from floor to ceiling, the works varied in scale not only from one another, but from the normal proportions of the object. The result was an environment replete with jagged fragments that seemed torn from their surroundings.

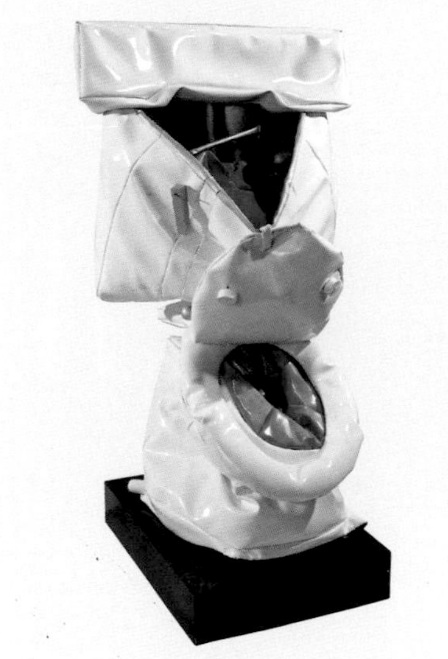

In the early 1960s, Oldenburg started to experiment with "soft" versions of quotidian objects as props for Happenings. He sometimes saved these props after the Happenings, and later began creating sculptures unrelated to performances, such as *Soft Toilet*, the fleshy version of a porcelain toilet. Made of stuffed canvas or vinyl, the soft sculptures are malleable and

The Black Girdle, 1961
Painted plaster, muslin, and wire, 46 1/2 x 40 x 4 in.
(118.1 x 101.6 x 10.2 cm)
Gift of Howard and Jean Lipman 84.60.2

Soft Toilet, 1966
Vinyl, plexiglass, and kapok on painted wood base,
57 1/16 x 27 5/8 x 28 1/16 in. (144.9 x 70.2 x 71.3 cm) overall
50th Anniversary Gift of Mr. and Mrs. Victor W. Ganz 79.83a–b

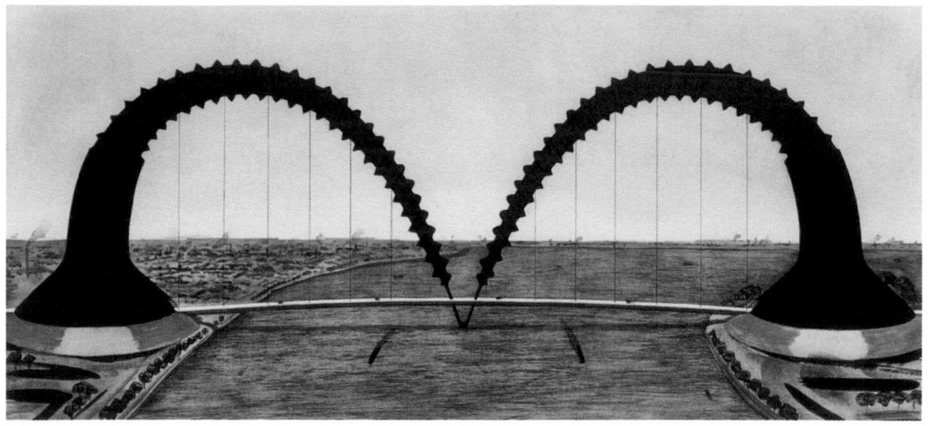

unfixed; they succumb to physical manipulation and the force of gravity. Limp and sagging like a human body, *Soft Toilet* is endowed with a personality and sense of drama all its own. Of this anthropomorphism, Oldenburg explained, "I never make representations of bodies, but of things that relate to bodies so that the body sensation is passed along to the spectator either literally or by suggestion."

In 1965, Oldenburg proposed enlarging his everyday objects to the scale of colossal monuments. He has realized a number of these playful and fantastical proposals since 1976, when he began collaborating on them with art historian Coosje van Bruggen. *Soft Shuttlecock, Raised* is a drawing for one such project, in which four enormous badminton birdies, fabricated in steel after a traditional feathered model, are scattered across the garden of The Nelson-Atkins Museum of Art in Kansas City, Missouri. Oldenburg often reworks a previously explored subject—a soft screw bowed into an arch is reconfigured years later into the proposal for *Double Screwarch Bridge*. Yet whatever the source, conceptually all the colossal works and large-scale projects defy expectations of public monuments by aggrandizing everyday objects rather than commemorating historical figures or events.

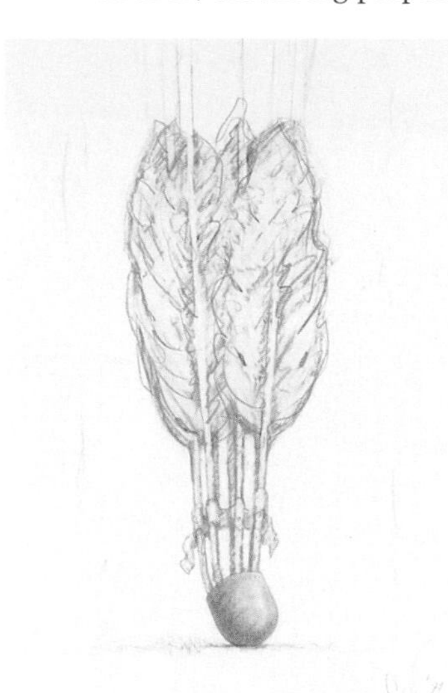

Double Screwarch Bridge, 1981
Etching and aquatint with monotype: sheet, 31 1/4 x 57 13/16 in. (79.4 x 146.8 cm); plate, 23 1/2 x 50 3/4 in. (59.7 x 128.9 cm)
Purchase, with funds from the Wilfred P. and Rose J. Cohen Purchase Fund 82.40

Soft Shuttlecock, Raised, 1994
Graphite and pastel on paper, 39 3/16 x 26 9/16 in. (99.5 x 67.5 cm)
Purchase, with funds from The Lauder Foundation, Evelyn and Leonard Lauder Fund 99.52.2

CATHERINE OPIE

b. 1961

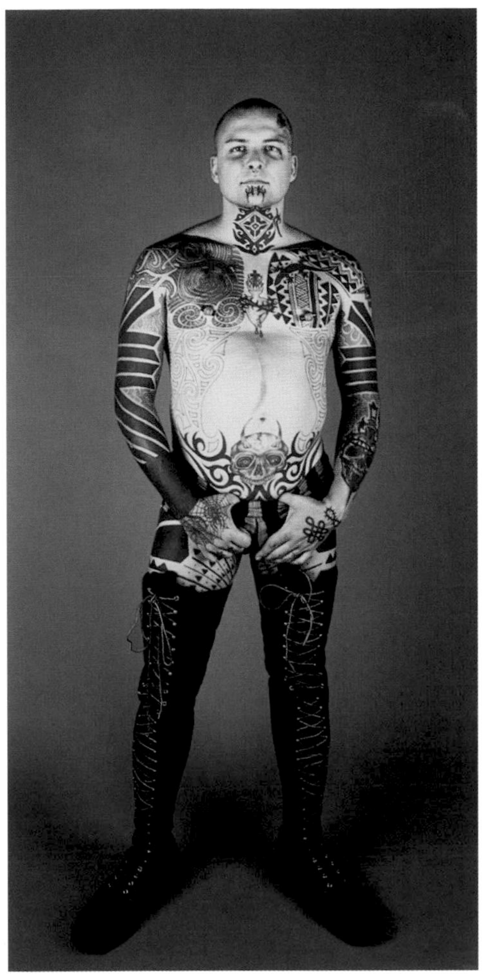

From regal studio portraits of individuals who challenge traditional definitions of gender and sexuality to photographs of Los Angeles freeways, strip malls, and domestic architectural facades, Catherine Opie's art has consistently focused on community. Combining documentary and portrait modes of photography, Opie uses the camera lens to show the many ways in which communities and individuals publicly assert their identities.

In her 1993–96 *Portraits* series, for example, she photographed members of the Los Angeles leather and S/M communities. Like Larry Clark (p. 73) and Nan Goldin (p. 118), Opie used the camera to record her own world, thereby expanding the older documentary tradition of photographing individuals from distanced or impersonal perspectives. She also departs from this tradition by taking her subjects out of their environments and isolating them against plain monochromatic backgrounds, a practice that recalls photographic studio portraiture.

In *Ron Athey*, one of the *Portraits* works, Opie positions Athey in a frontal stance before a bright aquamarine backdrop that highlights the blue undertones of his tattoos. Athey's thigh-high laced boots and suggestive briefs, along with his tattoos and piercings—the manipulations he performed on his body—express his identity as an S/M practitioner and performance artist. In works such as this, Opie inserts historically misrepresented individuals within photographic traditions, but her aim is neither to exoticize nor to normalize her subjects. Rather, she honors their individuality and celebrates their desire to exist on the outskirts of mainstream society. "The photographs stare back, or they stare through you," she says of her portraits. "They are never without dignity." Indeed, the large scale of the work transforms an individual portrait into an emblematic representation of life in a subculture.

Ron Athey, 1994
Chromogenic color print mounted on paperboard, 57 x 28 3/16 in. (144.8 x 71.6 cm) sight
Gift of Norman Dubrow 95.104

TOM OTTERNESS

b. 1952

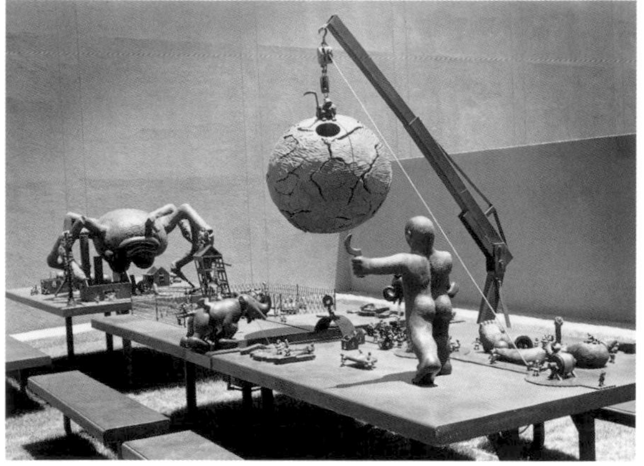

Tom Otterness has filled museums, parks, subway stations, and other civic centers with reminders of human weakness and folly. *The Tables*, made of three Cor-ten steel picnic tables, is a playful work with sinister undertones. An army of more than a hundred of the artist's signature bronze men, women, and animals covers the tables. Sculpted in varying scales, the miniature people have generalized, rounded features reminiscent of ancient Cycladic idols, along with whimsical button-smile faces typical of comic strip characters. The world they inhabit, however, is full of menace and turmoil. Otterness pits creation against destruction, with destruction taking the lead. One table hints at creation with a strand of double helix DNA, a snake, primitive hand tools, and a large, bisected cell emerging from a trap door. Other images, however, predict imminent doom: shattered eyeglasses, a teetering four-story house, a giant menacing spider, and a large, dismembered man who recalls the fallen soldier in Picasso's *Guernica*. A hooded death figure presides over a cracked globe suspended precariously above the middle table. The Apocalypse is near. Symbols of our failings abound: a skeletal fish reveals humanity's harmful impact on waterways and a large penny divided into sixteen slices suggests greedy consumption.

The sources for this ambitious tableau are as diverse as the activities it depicts. The abundance of animals reflects the five years Otterness spent in the 1970s working as a night guard at the American Museum of Natural History in New York, while the picnic tables allude to his longstanding interest in creating art for public spaces. The juxtaposition of different scales is in part influenced by the miniaturized and gigantic peoples who inhabit the imaginary lands of Jonathan Swift's *Gulliver's Travels*, which Otterness read shortly before making *The Tables*.

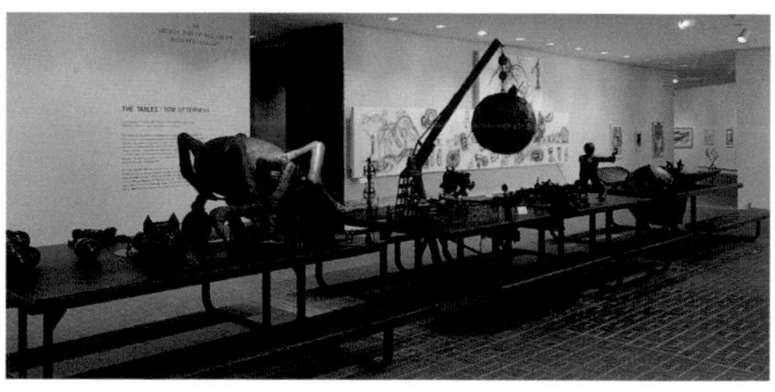

The Tables, 1986–87
Cor-ten steel and bronze, 138 x 458 x 114 in. (350.5 x 1163.3 x 289.6 cm) overall
Gift of the Lannan Foundation 96.242.16.a–kkkkkk

TONY OURSLER

b. 1957

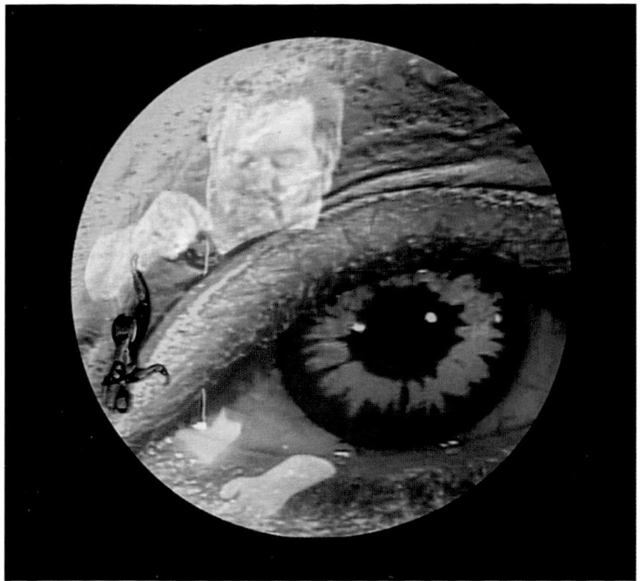

Since the late 1970s, Tony Oursler's video installations and single-channel videos have confronted our growing unease with the intrusiveness of media technology. In the video installation *The Darkest Color Infinitely Amplified*, Oursler makes use of High Definition Volumetric Display, a new imaging technology that allows both three-dimensional images and two-dimensional video projections to appear in free space, floating in midair. The installation is based on the camera obscura—a "dark room" that receives, through a pinhole, an inverted image of objects in an adjacent illuminated room (pp. 192, 211). For centuries, scientists and artists used the camera obscura to investigate vision and linear perspective, but less knowledgeable people thought it was the work of magic or devils. Fascinated by these old dialectics of good and evil, science and magic, Oursler applied them to new technologies, creating a room-sized optical illusion.

Through a large circular opening we encounter two channels of superimposed video showing imagery of flames, stage magicians, computer codes, disembodied heads, and an actress being made up into a creature reminiscent of the demon in *The Exorcist*. One channel of video is projected onto a wall behind the opening, and the other seems to hover a few feet in front of it. As we move around in the room, we see the illusion of three-dimensional glass devils floating in front of the video imagery.

In *The Darkest Color Infinitely Amplified*, perception is completely dissociated from reality. The anxiety produced by this realization has been popularized today in science-fiction accounts of the dangers of a truly virtual reality. By combining both old and new technology and imagery, Oursler's work reminds us that this anxiety has a long history.

The Darkest Color Infinitely Amplified, 2000
Multimedia installation, dimensions variable
Purchase, with funds from the Katherine Schmidt Shubert Purchase Fund, the Wilfred P. and Rose J. Cohen Purchase Fund, the Tom Armstrong Purchase Fund, the Grace Belt Endowed Purchase Fund, the John I.H. Baur Purchase Fund, The List Purchase Fund, and the Richard and Dorothy Rodgers Fund 2000.187

NAM JUNE PAIK
b. 1932

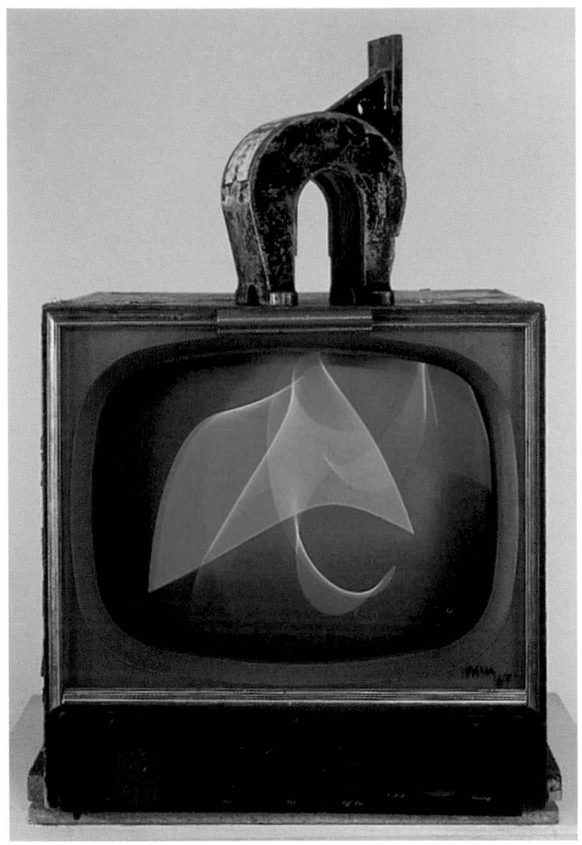

Nam June Paik is widely regarded as the foremost pioneer of video art, and he remains one of the medium's seminal figures. Korean-born, he trained as a composer in Germany, where he experimented with electronic music. He moved to New York in the early 1960s, a pivotal moment in the development of the American avant-garde, and seized on the newly emergent medium of video as an artistic tool. *Magnet TV* is one of the first examples of Paik's manipulations of broadcast television, in which he altered the television image or its physical casing. Here he placed a strong magnet on the top of a television set; the magnetic field distorts the broadcast image into an abstract form that changes, like a kaleidoscope, as the viewer moves the magnet.

Paik's radical action also undermines the seemingly inviolable power of broadcast television. The television set is transformed into a sculpture, whose moving image the viewer is able to manipulate at will. This interactivity paralled the audience participation essential to performances and Happenings of the early 1960s and anticipated the interactive art of recent years. Through his transformation of the television image, Paik challenged the idea of the art work as a self-contained entity, and established the process of instant feedback, in which the viewer's action has a direct effect on the form and meaning of the work. In fusing art with television, *Magnet TV* also predicted the widespread embrace of popular culture and technology by subsequent generations of young artists.

Magnet TV, 1965
17-inch black-and-white television set with magnet, 28 3/8 x 19 1/4 x 24 1/2 in. (72.1 x 48.9 x 62.2 cm) overall
Purchase, with funds from Dieter Rosenkranz 86.60a–b

DAVID PARK
1911–1960

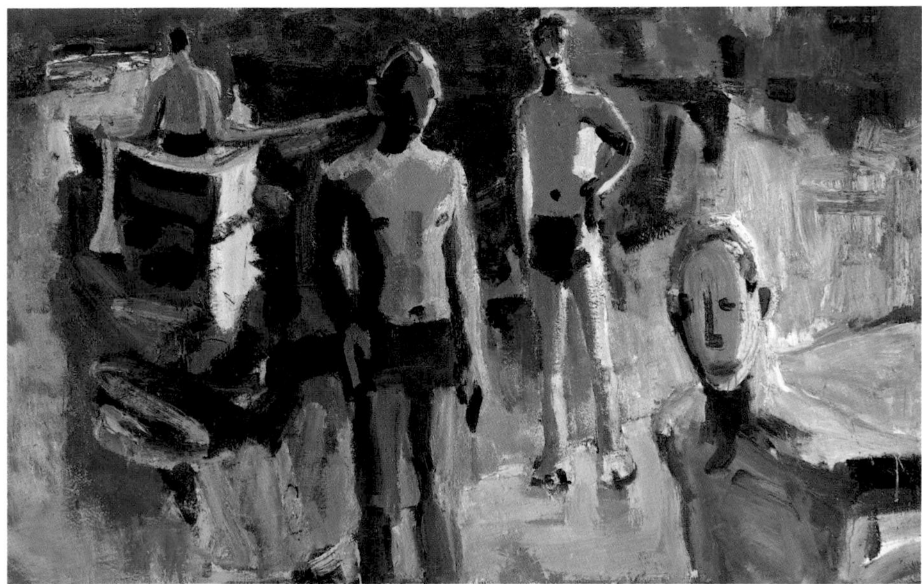

In 1951, the prominent Bay Area abstract painter David Park publicly repudiated pure abstraction by submitting a figurative scene to a San Francisco exhibition. Discouraged by the pretense and elitism associated with New York Abstract Expressionism (pp. 165, 242), he viewed figuration as a means to create works that would communicate with broader audiences, even when painted in the intuitive, gestural method advocated by the Abstract Expressionists. Park's radical break prompted other San Francisco abstract artists, including Richard Diebenkorn (p. 90), to try to reconcile recognizable subject matter with modernist compositional concerns and painting techniques. By 1957, the resolute commitment of these artists to familiar motifs—landscapes, still lifes and, for Park, the human body—had developed into a vital American movement called Bay Area Figurative art.

Four Men, a monumental painting created two years before Park's death, is one of his most accomplished canvases. It depicts a luminous landscape inhabited by four male figures wearing only bathing trunks. Three stand, rather enigmatically, on a chartreuse strip of shoreline, while a fourth rows across the sparkling, sapphire blue water. Working from observation and memory rather than preparatory studies, Park used a thick, large brush loaded with saturated pigments to create blocks of color that oscillate between descriptive references and abstract notations. His vibrant gestural strokes coalesce into a dense atmosphere that envelops the figures, who are not so much isolated from one another as disengaged. They may allude to a universal human condition, a poignant personal memory, or simply an everyday scene. In this very uncertainty lies *Four Men*'s satisfying blend of mystery and serenity.

Four Men, 1958
Oil on canvas, 57 x 92 in. (144.8 x 233.7 cm)
Purchase, with funds from an anonymous donor 59.27

PHILIP PEARLSTEIN

b. 1924

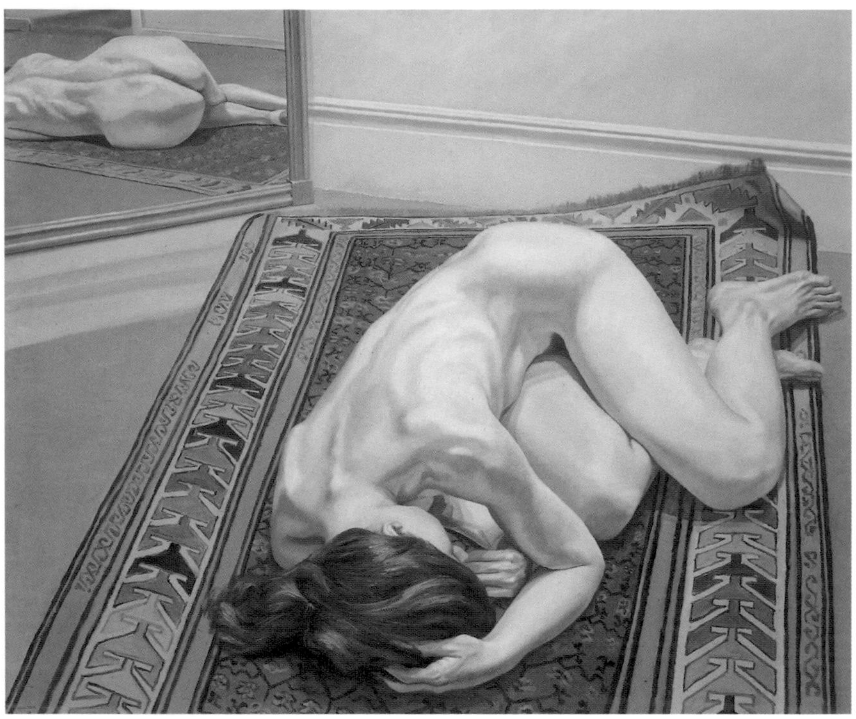

Since 1960, Philip Pearlstein has been painting male and female nudes, set in domestic interiors with scattered furniture and props. In this work—like his others, made directly from the model and scaled to life size—a woman lies on Pearlstein's own Oriental rug, her body curled inward and her hand resting on her averted head. A mirror in the painting's upper left corner expands the space rearward and reveals the other side of the figure's body. Her wavy hair and the sinuous, muscular curves of her pale flesh stand in marked contrast to the bright geometric designs on the rug and straight edges limned by the mirror, baseboard, and molding.

Pearlstein often places himself higher than his models when he paints, resulting in unexpected diagonal vantages and awkward croppings reminiscent of a photograph. His subjects' faces, moreover, are usually turned away or devoid of recognizable expression. The result is a psychological void, an impersonality and, despite the carefully articulated nudity, a complete lack of eroticism. This dispassionate assessment proposes a radical re-consideration of traditional figure painting. To Pearlstein, his models are elements in a still life, no more or less important than the rugs and wall moldings: "my art simply portrays the human figure at rest, as a kind of complex still-life object, functioning as a primary element in paintings whose basic assumptions are founded on the aesthetic relationship of the compositional elements."

Female Model on Oriental Rug with Mirror, 1968
Oil on canvas, 60 x 72 in. (152.4 x 182.9 cm)
50th Anniversary Gift of Mr. and Mrs. Leonard A. Lauder 84.69

RAYMOND PETTIBON

b. 1957

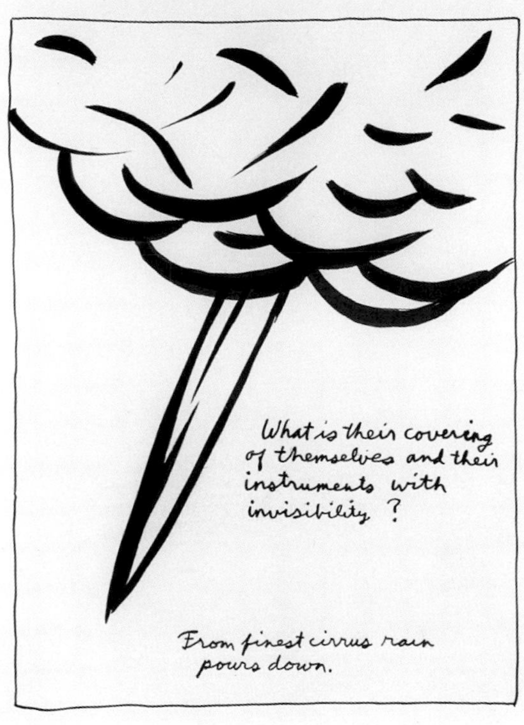

Raymond Pettibon derives his imagery from the diverse reaches of American popular culture: baseball players, surfers, children's television, psychedelia, punk and rock lore, true crime novels, hard-boiled pulp fiction, left-wing politics, political cartoons. In moods that range from the poetic to the hilarious, the scathing to the arcane, he juxtaposes these predominantly pen-and-ink drawings with hand-scrawled texts, some also borrowed, but most newly penned by Pettibon himself.

The notebook-size *No Title* consists of a broadly drawn ink likeness of a sword descending from a cloud, a motif that appears frequently in Pettibon's work, but always with different texts. In this drawing, it is accompanied by two lines of prose: "What is their covering of themselves and their instruments with invisibility?" and "From finest cirrus rain pours down." Mirroring the fugitive syntax of these lines is Pettibon's explanation of the sword-and-cloud image: it is "about the randomness of death and illness which would make you believe there is no center of fate and governing...no higher power." Although perplexing and paradoxical, the language used in Pettibon's drawings suggests complex, literary syntax. "My primary sources are the great prose writers, like Henry James and Proust and Ruskin and Pater. And Thomas Browne," he said. Like all good writers, Pettibon's voices shift in tone and style to reflect the particular narrative moment. The relationship of text to image constantly shifts, too, always defying expectations.

No Title, 1987
Ink on paper, 12 x 8 7/8 in. (30.5 x 22.5 cm)
Purchase, with funds from the Drawing Committee 97.19.1

PAUL PFEIFFER

b. 1966

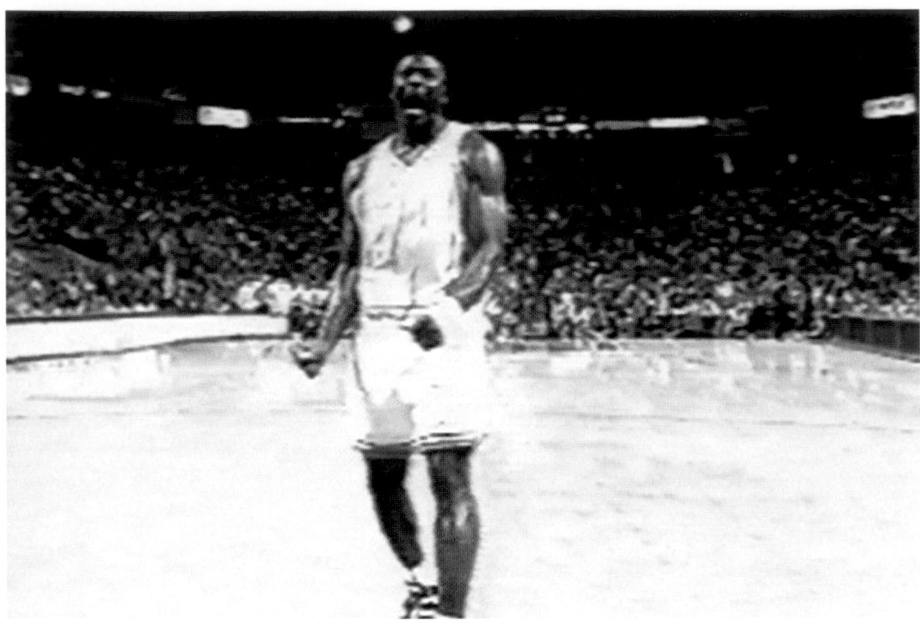

Paul Pfeiffer is a New York-based artist who uses digital technology to alter images from sports broadcasts and Hollywood cinema in sculptures, installations, and photographs. Through such alterations, and the introduction of stops, stutters, and reverse action into video sequences, he draws out subtexts, creating scenes of heightened psychological tension. In *Fragment of a Crucifixion (After Francis Bacon)*, a small-scale video projection only a few inches wide, the great basketball star Larry Johnson cries out in triumph after making a shot. Pfeiffer worked frame-by-frame on a short video clip, using digital technology to erase the other players from the court as well as the insignia from Johnson's uniform.

The title refers to a 1950 painting by British artist Francis Bacon, in which a partial, highly abstracted screaming figure is flayed on a portion of a cross. Pfeiffer's video clip is a partially erased scene in which Johnson, robbed of his teammates, forever turns to and fro, caught in a silent scream amid the cameras flashing in the crowd. By removing details from the scene, and by focusing on a narrow fragment of a larger gesture, Pfeiffer reveals the underlying aggression in the nuances of Johnson's movement. Like Sisyphus, the Greek mythological king who was condemned for eternity to push a boulder uphill, only to have to start again at bottom when the boulder rolled back down, Johnson's score has merely earned him the chance to try for another point and to play in yet another game. Pfeiffer's manipulations of the scene transform a moment of public triumph into one of lonely anguish.

Fragment of a Crucifixion (After Francis Bacon), 1999
Videotape, VHS player, projector, and metal armature, 20 x 5 x 20 in. (50.8 x 12.7 x 50.8 cm) overall
Purchase, with funds from Melva Bucksbaum and the Film and Video Committee 2000.150

JACK PIERSON

b. 1960

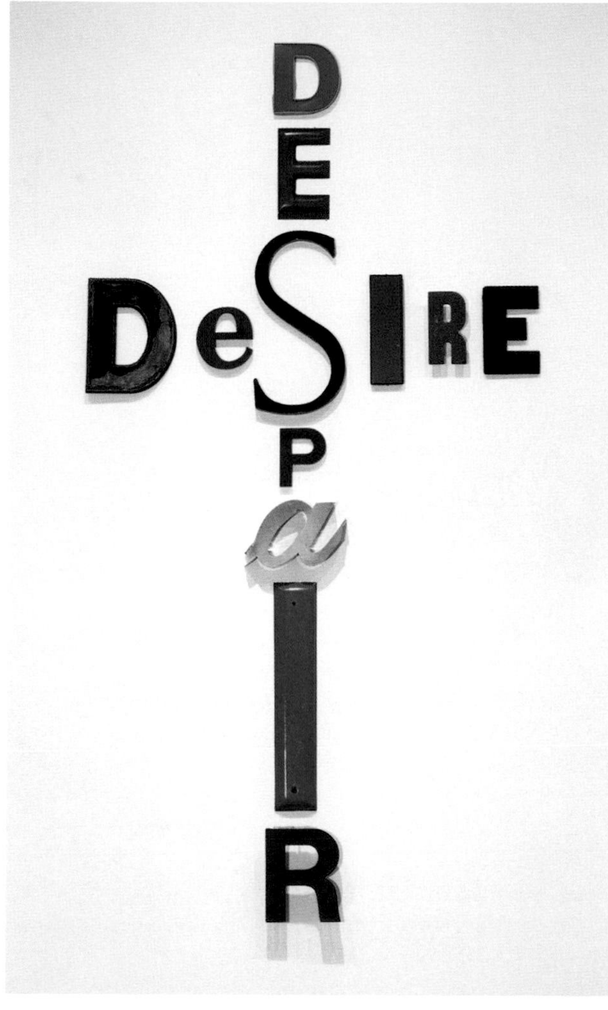

Desire, despair. The simple juxtaposition of these two words forms the basis of Jack Pierson's 1996 text-based sculpture. Pierson's work employs ready-made objects to express the pathos underlying the American dream—a pathos embodied in the mismatched letters of old movie marquees and commercial signs from which his work is created. In the opening decades of the twentieth century, Marcel Duchamp substituted mass-produced objects such as a snow shovel or bottle rack for traditionally crafted works of art, a gesture that indicated a fascination with the forces of modernity, epitomized by American industrialization and consumerism. Pierson's aesthetic recycling of the discarded remnants of popular advertisements points rather to the throwaway quality of America's consumer culture. His found letters are, in a sense, discarded dreams, their original purpose long forgotten.

In addition to Duchamp, *Desire, Despair* recalls Walker Evans' photographs of torn billboards, which evoke the lost hopes of consumer society, or Edward Hopper's paintings of half-deserted cinemas, with their poignant character of loneliness and alienation. Many viewers have also found in Pierson's elegiac tone a more contemporary reference—to the AIDS epidemic, which brought the era of liberation inaugurated by the sexual revolution of the 1960s to an abrupt and tragic halt.

Desire, Despair, 1996
Metal, plastic, plexiglass, and wood, 117 1/2 x 56 1/4 in. (298.5 x 142.9 cm) overall
Purchase, with funds from the Painting and Sculpture Committee 97.102.2a–l

ADRIAN PIPER

b. 1948

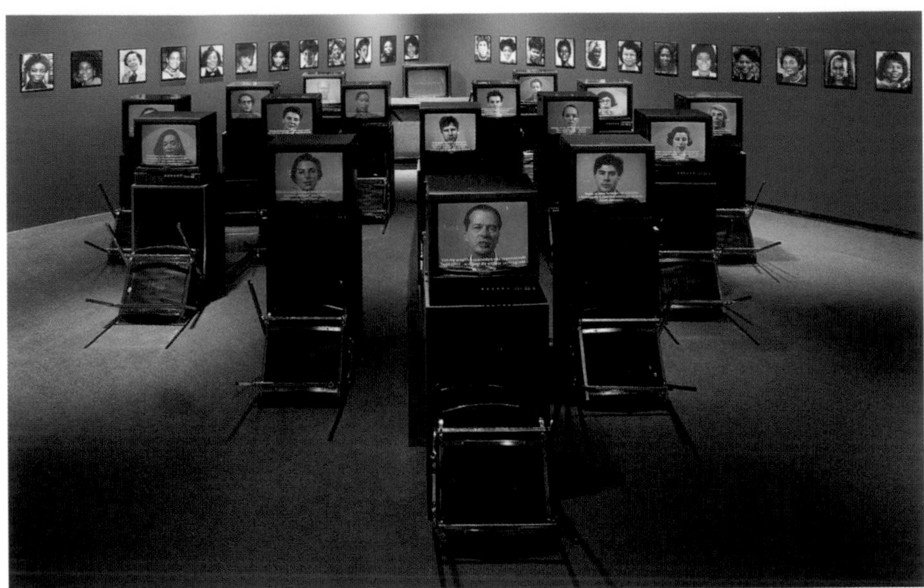

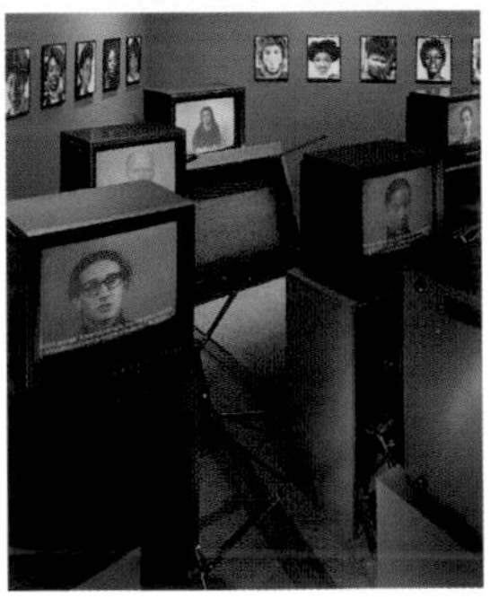

Since the mid-1960s, Adrian Piper has worked in a wide range of media, including performance, text-based projects, and video installation. All her projects expose race and racism as inherently social phenomena that can be transformed through rational analysis and critical self-awareness. In *Out of the Corner*, sixteen video monitors form a barricade in front of a single monitor, placed in the corner of a room behind an overturned table. On the walls hang sixty-four small, framed black-and-white photographs, portraits of black women from different social backgrounds that Piper rephotographed from *Ebony* magazine. Piper—whose extremely light skin confounds traditional assumptions of racial identity—appears on the "protected" corner monitor, addressing the audience with a clearly reasoned discussion of miscegenation. According to conventions of racial classification and genetic statistics, she notes, many of her "white" viewers would be considered "black." Midway through Piper's monologue, the sixteen monitors are activated in rapid succession: sixteen different figures, all apparently white, appear on the screens and repeat the following phrase, which is also printed below their faces: "Some of my female ancestors were so-called 'house niggers' who were raped by their white slave masters. If you are an American, some of yours probably were too." As Lawrence Rinder observed, with works like *Out of the Corner*, "Piper's art leaves us less certain of who we are, but more engaged in determining who we might be."

Out of the Corner, 1990
17 video monitors, 17 video playback desks, 17 videotapes, color, sound, 26 minutes; 64 gelatin silver prints, table, 16 chairs, pedestals, and specified lighting, dimensions variable
Gift of the Peter Norton Family Foundation 94.38a–ffff

LARI PITTMAN
b. 1952

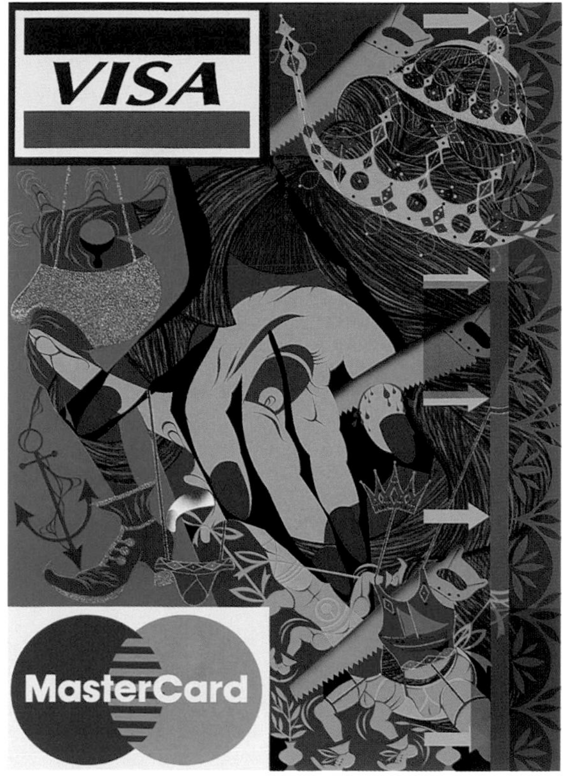

Lari Pittman likes to use the word "tableau" to describe his paintings, because it suggests "presentation, proscenium, stillness, pause...." In his art, in other words, action and calm, frontality and depth, coalesce on crowded, yet intricately organized surfaces. This sensitivity to the formal elements of composition, however, is harnessed to a resonant subject matter that encompasses aspects of Pittman's heritage and cultural identity—a gay male artist from a background combining Colombian Catholicism and Anglo-Saxon Presbyterianism. The result is an iconography deeply expressive of the principle of heterogeneity.

Untitled #16 is one of a series of paintings that Pittman began in the early 1990s. Entitled *A Decorated Chronology of Insistence and Resignation*, the series is made up of works which, like *Untitled #16*, combine exuberance with premonitions of danger or even doom. Here, two credit cards pay ironic homage to consumerist impulses, while a flock of saws seems bent on dismembering everything in their path. A bizarre collection of headless figures cavorts across the picture plane; a squadron of green arrows points insistently yet without apparent meaning at a red decorative border. With the addition of a jaunty anchor at left and a couple of crowns at right, the picture takes on a sense of carnivalesque humor and derangement.

The various elements in Pittman's painting resist easy decoding, as they resist assembling themselves in a hierarchy of importance, for their all-over dispersal draws the eye to each corner of the painting. Like the title of the series, which implies an equilibrium between opposing emotions, *Untitled #16* maintains a delicate balance of disparate icons.

***Untitled #16 (A Decorated Chronology of Insistence and Resignation)**, 1993
Synthetic polymer, enamel, and glitter on wood, 84 x 60 1/16 in. (213.4 x 152.6 cm)
Gift of Peter Norton 93.130

JACKSON POLLOCK

1912–1956

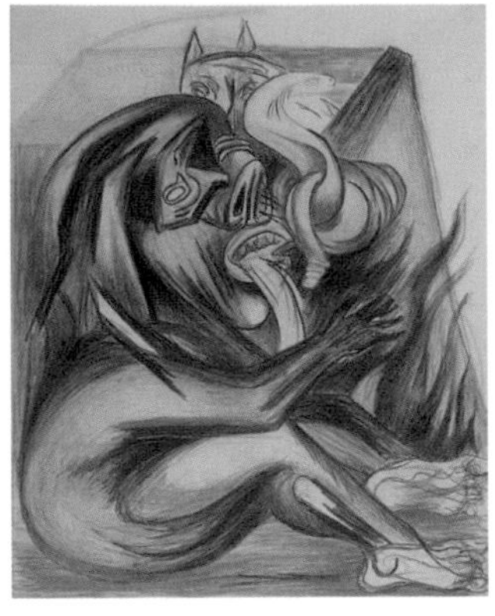

One of the pioneers of Abstract Expressionism, Jackson Pollock sought a new visual form that was both personal and relevant to his time: "It seems to me that the modern painter cannot express this age—the airplane, the atom bomb, the radio—in old forms of the Renaissance, or of any other past culture. Each age finds its own technique."

Pollock's work of the 1930s and early 1940s drew on a variety of influences, but perhaps most important was Surrealism's model of psychic automatism, which favored spontaneous expression as a means of manifesting the unconscious. Pollock's images from this period evoke mythological archetypes and totemic figures, such as the coiled snake and beastly creature sitting before the fire in the untitled drawing.

Pollock continued in this mode, his totemic figures becoming increasingly fragmented and interlocked, until 1947, when he produced his first "drip" painting. The intricate, tangled layers of paint in *Number 27, 1950* (the number refers roughly to the sequence of that year's production) record Pollock's rhythmic movements as he dripped and poured from cans of house paint onto a large, unstretched canvas laid on the floor. The calligraphic marks dissolved all discrete and figurative elements into an all-over composition that evenly covered the entire surface of the canvas. Pollock's emphasis on spontaneity and his idea that a painting revealed itself to the artist as it was being created helped elevate the act of painting to a level of importance equal to that of the finished picture. As Willem de Kooning (p. 166) famously declared, Pollock "broke the ice," clearing the way for further developments in abstraction and influencing scores of later artists.

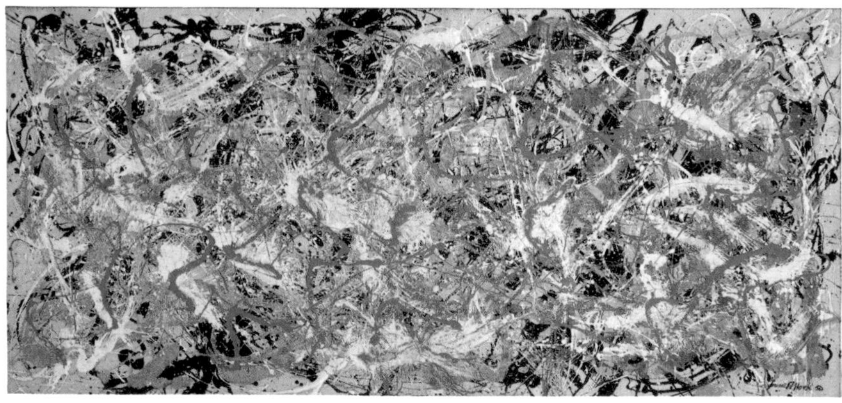

Untitled, c. 1939–42
Colored crayon and graphite on paper, 14 x 11 in. (35.6 x 27.9 cm)
Purchase, with funds from the Julia B. Engel Purchase Fund and the Drawing Committee 85.18

Number 27, 1950, 1950
Oil on canvas, 49 x 106 in. (124.5 x 269.2 cm)
Purchase 53.12

FAIRFIELD PORTER

1907–1975

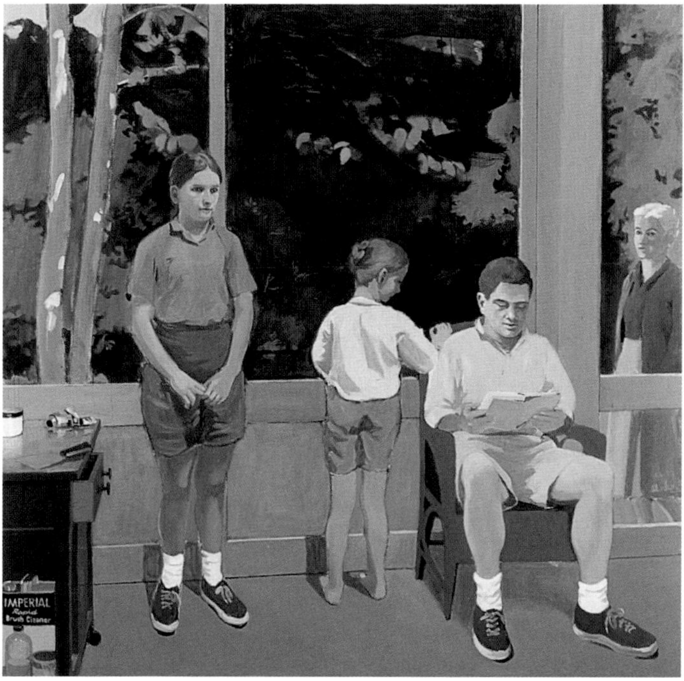

A quintessentially American painter known for his dedicated, resolute individualism, Fairfield Porter remained faithful to figuration despite his—and his generation's—schooling in vanguard abstraction. In his art criticism of the 1950s and 1960s, Porter strenuously opposed the critic Clement Greenberg, whose formalist voice and advocacy of abstraction was then dominating the American art world. Porter's own figurative painting evolved subtly and independently from his contemporaries' work, accommodating intimate subject matter with an intense focus on the atmospheric qualities of light and the visual relationships among objects.

The Screen Porch, painted in 1964 at the house Porter's father built in Great Spruce Head, Maine, depicts two of Porter's five children, Kate and Lizzie, along with his wife, Anne. The seated man is the poet James Schuyler, who arrived at the Porter household one day and stayed for twelve years. Perhaps Schuyler is reading aloud to distract the children, as he sometimes did when they posed for their father. Porter's economy with color—the unmodulated blue floor, Kate's and James' matching sneakers—accentuates other, more forceful elements, such as the contrast between Kate's bored expression and Lizzie's knock-kneed dreaminess, or the shimmer of summer light on the backyard foliage. "I paint air," Porter once remarked, but the simplicity of that statement belies his limpid vision, which elicits from ordinary objects and domestic scenes the moods—here, that of a lazy, yet anticipatory summer afternoon—that never find words.

The Screen Porch, 1964
Oil on canvas, 79 1/2 x 79 1/2 in. (201.9 x 201.9 cm)
Lawrence H. Bloedel Bequest 77.1.41

RICHARD POUSETTE-DART

1916–1992

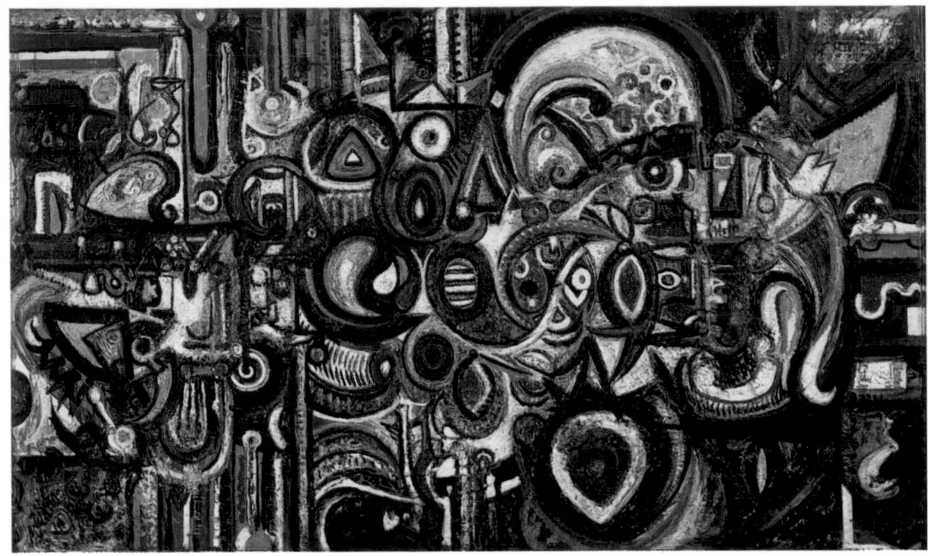

In Richard Pousette-Dart's paintings of the 1940s, the canvas becomes a stage for dramas of mythic scale. A founding member of the Abstract Expressionist movement, Pousette-Dart, like his peers, drew on Surrealist experiments with automatic writing and biomorphic forms. He also shared the Abstract Expressionists' interest in ancient mythologies and non-Western art. Unlike his peers, however, Pousette-Dart's belief in the essential truths of these myths never wavered. For the motifs in *Within the Room*, he borrowed evocative, mystical shapes and symbols from many sources, including Native American art and biomorphic Surrealism. Round, targetlike eyes stare out through a web of curves, spirals, triangles, and teardrops. Although these forms are thickly outlined, they are not visually fixed, but rather seem to be in a constant state of flux.

Pousette-Dart's compositions evolved as he worked, applying layer after layer of paint, and he never considered his canvases truly finished. In his notebooks, he described this spiritual, spontaneous approach to painting: "out of the rich inmesh of chaos unfold great order & beauty, suggesting utter simplicity in this labyrinth of all possible truths...everything is connected & is one, transmutes, transcends, is immediate." *Within the Room* suggests this labyrinth of connections, this underlying order in a complex universe. Yet the painting teeters between order and chaos; shapes coalesce into the recognizable form of a face or a fish, and then dissolve into entropy.

Within the Room, 1942
Oil on canvas, 36 x 60 in. (91.4 x 152.4 cm)
Promised 50th Anniversary Gift of the artist P.79.4

MAURICE PRENDERGAST

1858–1924

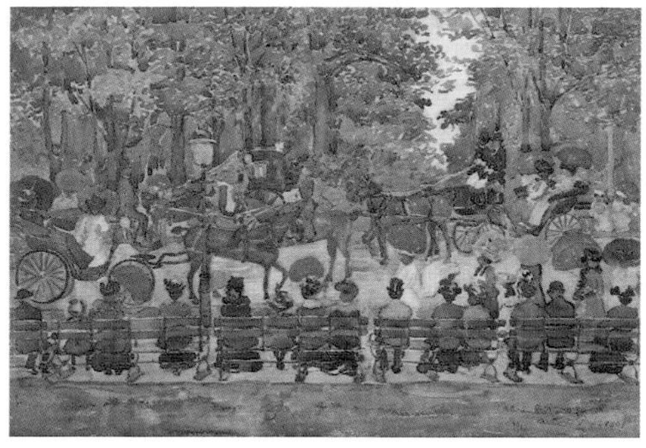

Maurice Prendergast painted bucolic visions of urban parks and beaches with an instinctive disregard for verisimilitude that led him to become a steady—if unlikely and soft-spoken—pioneer of American modernism. In 1900, he returned from a trip to Europe for his first major New York exhibition. *Central Park, 1901*, which he painted on one of his subsequent trips to New York from his home in Boston, demonstrates his remarkable technical ability as a watercolorist: delicate, loose brushwork fancifully forms a mosaic of light and color. The deliberate organization of the composition, in which figures and movement are subordinate to a friezelike hierarchy, necessitates forethought and control; in the watercolor medium, moreover, highlights are not added at the end but are created by leaving the white paper unpainted.

In 1904, through his friend William Glackens (p. 115), Prendergast met Robert Henri (p. 137). Although Glackens' paintings were, in many ways, antithetical to the gritty urban realism practiced by Henri and his circle, his interest in everyday subject matter and his nonconformist style won him entry into the group. By 1908, he was primarily making oil paintings—vibrant canvases, heavy with layers of unthinned pigment, that resemble opalescent tapestries. *The Promenade*, painted in a flat, decorative manner indebted to the French Post-Impressionists, employs contour lines and saturated, contrasting colors to distinguish figures from landscape. The pastoral seaside scene, populated with faceless women, is characteristic of Prendergast's later years, when increasing deafness prompted him to turn inward, abandoning the spectacle of public leisure for the isolated simplicity of private, arcadian fantasies.

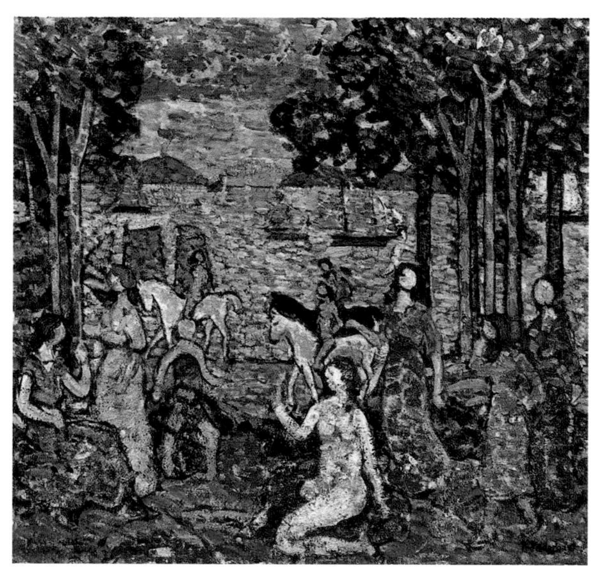

Central Park, 1901, 1901
Watercolor on paper, 15 1/16 x 22 1/8 in. (38.3 x 56.2 cm)
Purchase 32.42

The Promenade, 1913
Oil on canvas, 30 x 34 in. (76.2 x 86.4 cm)
Alexander M. Bing Bequest 60.10

STEPHEN PRINA

b. 1954

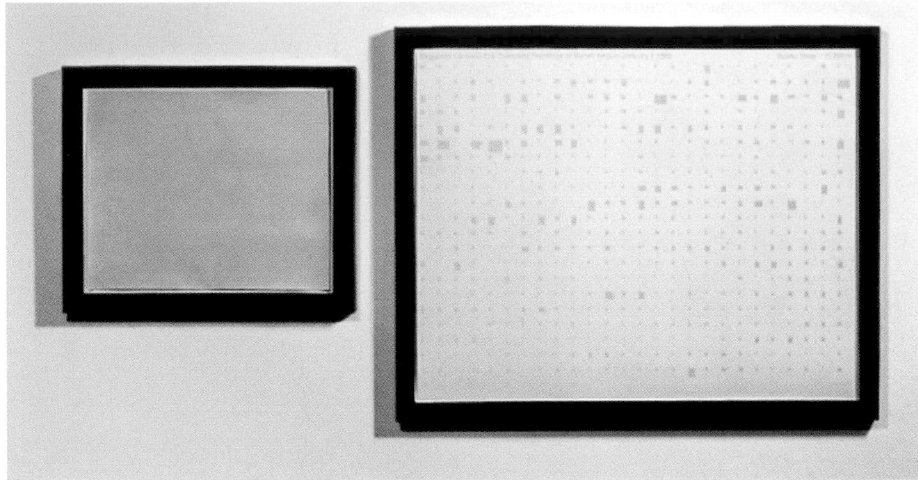

Working in a variety of media, Stephen Prina examines the systems and institutions that organize culture. Like other artists who emerged in the early 1980s, such as Louise Lawler and Fred Wilson (pp. 175, 322), Prina's work specifically investigates the role that museum contexts and art history exert on our understanding of art.

Exquisite Corpse: The Complete Paintings of Manet, 62 of 556, Huîtres (Oysters) 1862 consists of two distinct elements. At right, a framed lithographic chart presents all the paintings produced by Édouard Manet—but with the imagery blanked out, so that only relative size, shape, and chronology are indicated. At left, a framed sepia-toned ink wash on rag paper reproduces the actual scale of Manet's *Oysters*, his first still life, executed in 1862. Prina thus empties out the "original" content, while providing an equally "original" substitute.

All of the pieces in Prina's large series examine the chronological, work-by-work organization of the conventional artist's catalogue raisonné—a staple on museum and library reference shelves—and its pretense of representing the complete body of an artist's work with precision. In the series, that body becomes an "exquisite corpse," the name of a famous Surrealist writing game based on chance and unpredictable sequence. The same conditions, Prina wryly suggests through the appropriated series title, determine the contents of a monographic catalogue. Like Sherrie Levine (p. 182), he also reminds us that art viewers are increasingly more familiar with reproductions than with the aura of originals: "I work from this Cliffs Notes-type book on Manet that's riddled with inaccuracies—but I'm not interested in truth, I'm interested in representation."

Exquisite Corpse: The Complete Paintings of Manet, 62 of 556, Huîtres (Oysters) 1862, 1989
Ink wash on rag paper and offset lithograph: lithograph, 26 1/16 x 32 3/4 in. (66.2 x 83.2 cm); drawing, 14 7/8 x 18 1/16 in. (37.8 x 45.9 cm)
Gift of Pamela and Richard Kramlich 2000.273a–b

MARTIN PURYEAR

b. 1941

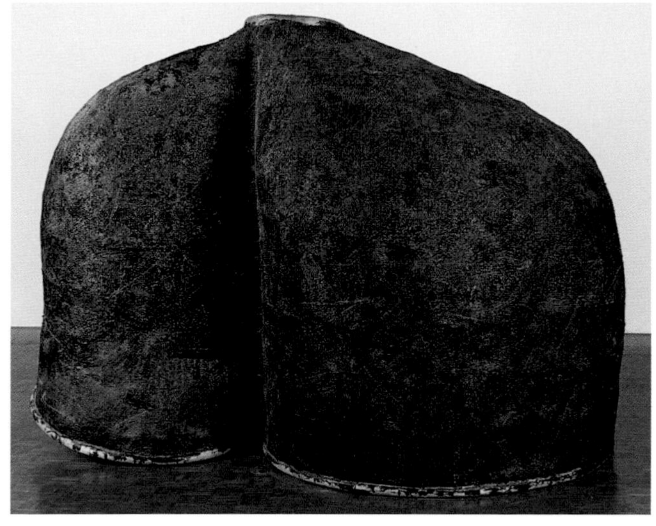

Martin Puryear's *Sanctum*, just over 6 feet tall, narrow in the neck and broad in the beam, is made with shipbuilding techniques: a wooden armature is sheathed in wire mesh and then covered with tar. As befits a structure offering sanctuary, it has a generous, embracing appearance, but it also suggests the ungainly bulk, and implicit grace, of a big boat in dry dock, or of a large sea mammal out of water. The fluidity that is latent in *Sanctum* is manifest in Puryear's untitled charcoal and graphite drawing, its paired forms descending fast and deep, heavy but oddly buoyant. There is spaciousness and protective sweep in both these works, and also a suggestion of withdrawal, of dipping below the surface for formal and psychic balance.

Puryear's eclectic education, and the interests of which it speaks, is reflected throughout his work. He spent two years with the Peace Corps in Sierra Leone, living in a village and teaching biology, English, and French. He traveled next to Sweden, where he learned furnituremaking, and concluded his education at Yale. In Africa, Puryear, who is African-American, was seeking not so much spiritual roots in tribal cultures as refined forms of craftsmanship that had been lost to or were never available in the West. In one way or another, all his sculpture integrates exacting forms of traditional handcraft—especially various methods of woodworking—with vanguard sculptural strategies, including the reductive abstraction of Minimalism. But, he explains, "I was never interested in making cool, distilled, pure objects. Associations with recognizable subject matter are inevitable human reactions."

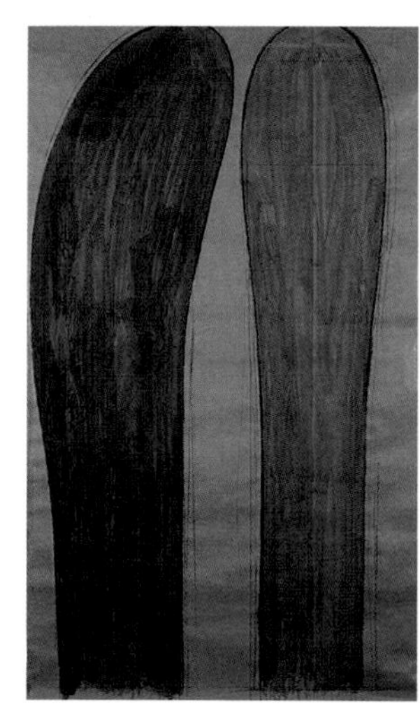

Sanctum, 1985
Wood, wire mesh, and tar, 76 x 109 x 87 in. (193 x 276.9 x 221 cm)
Purchase, with funds from the Painting and Sculpture Committee 85.72

Untitled, 1994
Charcoal, graphite, and wash on paper, 92 x 54 in. (233.7 x 137.2 cm) sight
Purchase, with funds from the Drawing Committee 98.10.1

ROBERT RAUSCHENBERG

b. 1925

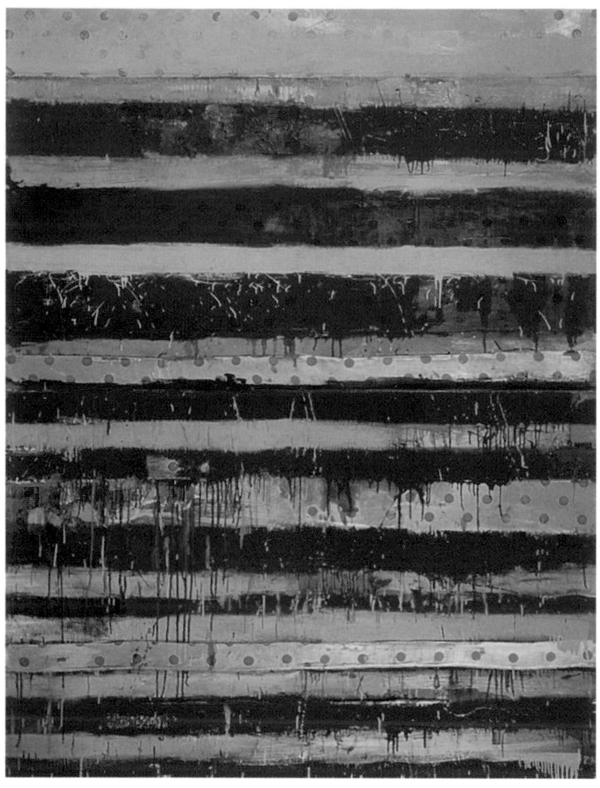

Throughout a career that spanned the second half of the twentieth century and continues into the twenty-first, Robert Rauschenberg has been one of America's most innovative and influential artists. His work defies traditional categories by combining painting, sculpture, printmaking, photography, performance, and music, and it challenges the definition of high art by incorporating everyday objects. As he famously stated in 1959, "painting relates to both art and life....I try to act in that gap between the two."

What critic Brian O'Doherty described as Rauschenberg's "vernacular glance"—his embrace of daily life—began in the early 1950s with paintings such as *Yoicks*, which included fabrics, newspapers, and found objects. The "combine paintings," as Rauschenberg called these hybrid painting-sculptures, joined the improvisatory energy of Abstract Expressionism with an exuberant proliferation of collaged elements.

Satellite, a characteristic work of the mid-1950s, includes, among other things, a stuffed pheasant, newspaper comics, doilies, and a pair of socks. "A pair of socks," Rauschenberg later asserted, "is no less suitable to make a painting with than wood, nails, turpentine, oil, and fabric." Neither in *Satellite* nor in the other combine paintings did Rauschenberg choose elements to convey a particular meaning. Meaning resides in the combination of elements, which expressed his response to postwar American society: "I was bombarded with TV sets and magazines, by the refuse, by the excess of the world.... I thought that if I could paint or make an honest work, it should incorporate all of these elements, which were and are a reality."

In the 1960s, Rauschenberg explored this collage aesthetic through transfer techniques that allowed him to appropriate found images rather than objects. He began with pictures torn from magazines and newspapers, which he combined and overlapped using silkscreen techniques. In recent works such as *Fusion*, from the *Anagrams* series, he has been

Yoicks, 1953
Oil, fabric, paper, and newsprint on two separately stretched canvases, 96 x 72 in. (243.8 x 182.9 cm)
Gift of the artist 71.210

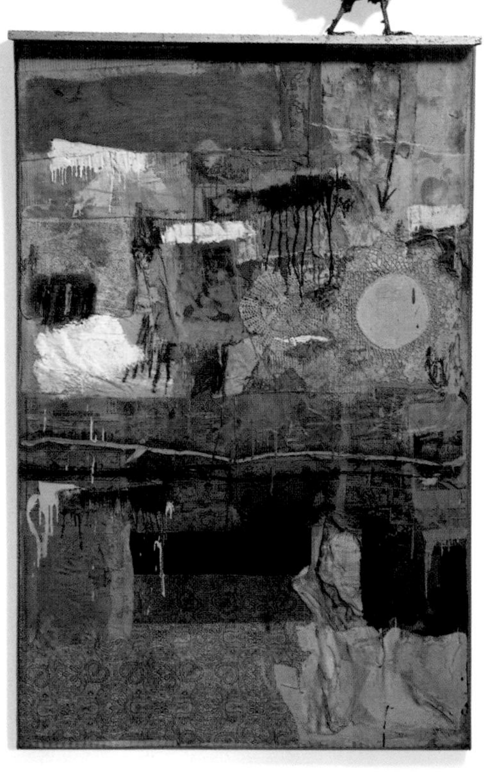

experimenting with newly developed transfer processes, specifically Iris printing (a vegetable dye digital output of photographs). He laid the Iris prints against the pulp paper, and then, with water as a solvent, transferred the images. The work fuses photographs of lightbulbs, bicycle wheels, and crates of Pepsi-Cola bottles that seem to have been taken on the streets of foreign cities. These are not, however, found images, for Rauschenberg made the photographs himself, so that the resulting accumulation represents a multifaceted engagement of the artist with his surroundings.

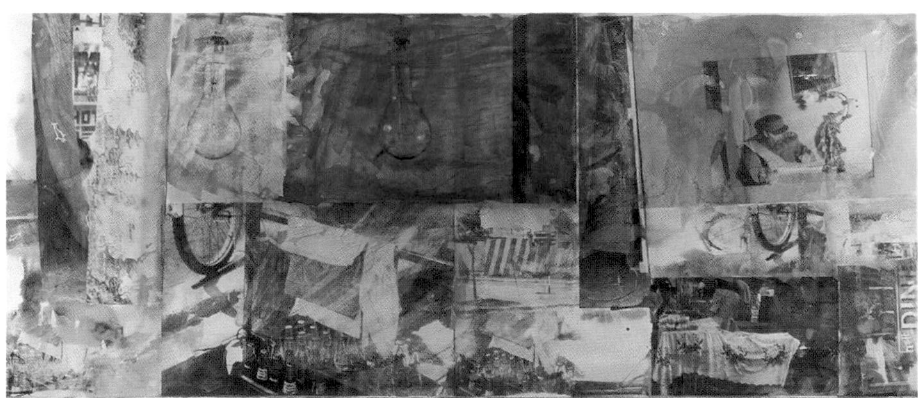

Satellite, 1955
Oil, fabric, paper, and wood on canvas with stuffed pheasant, 79 3/8 x 43 1/4 x 5 5/8 in. (201.6 x 109.9 x 14.3 cm)
Gift of Claire B. Zeisler and purchase with funds from the Mrs. Percy Uris Purchase Fund 91.85

Fusion, 1996
Color transfer drawing, 60 1/4 x 144 5/8 in. (153 x 367.4 cm)
Purchase, with funds from Leonard A. Lauder and Thomas H. Lee 96.239

CHARLES RAY

b. 1953

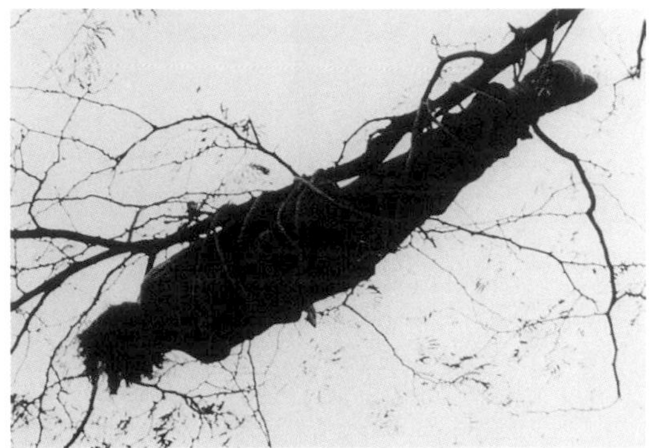

Since the early 1970s, Los Angeles-based Charles Ray has been producing perverse, surreal, hilarious, provocative, and often bizarre sculptures and performances. Although stylistically diverse, his work is unified by its theatricality, preoccupation with the body, and by Ray's ability to upset common perceptions of objects and their surroundings.

The 1978 photograph *Man in Tree* documents an early performance event in which Ray tied himself to the limb of a tree, where he hung precariously for the better half of a day. His aim was to provoke encounters with bewildered passersby, who could not have been expecting to find a man dangling from a tree above them. The photograph—all that remains to document the performance—still arrests us with its unnerving, menacing oddity.

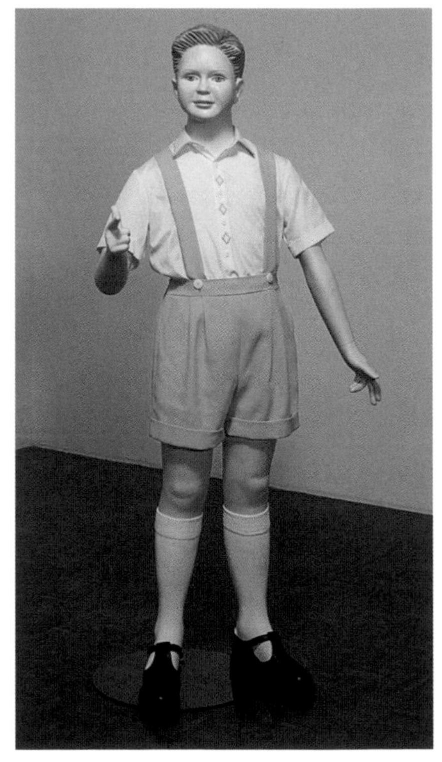

The sculpture *Boy*, made nearly fifteen years later, is Ray's illusionistic transformation of a recognizable, familiar subject—a department store mannequin—into a disturbingly unfamiliar figure. As he has done in several key works, Ray manipulates scale, in this case by making his "boy" stand as tall as a full-grown man. The figure's pose, too, has an adult cast that more readily suggests the stance of a Roman orator than the informal manner of a child in short pants. By fusing the prepubescent and the adult, Ray's sculpture treads close to the taboo territory of childhood sexuality.

Man in Tree, 1978
Gelatin silver print mounted on paperboard, 26 x 39 in. (66 x 99.1 cm)
Purchase, with funds from the Richard and Dorothy Rodgers Fund and the Photography Committee 93.74

Boy, 1992
Painted fiberglass, steel, and fabric, 71 1/2 x 27 x 34 in. (181.6 x 68.6 x 86.4 cm) overall
Purchase, with funds from Jeffrey Deitch, Bernardo Nadal-Ginard, and Penny and Mike Winton 92.131a–i

MAN RAY

1890–1976

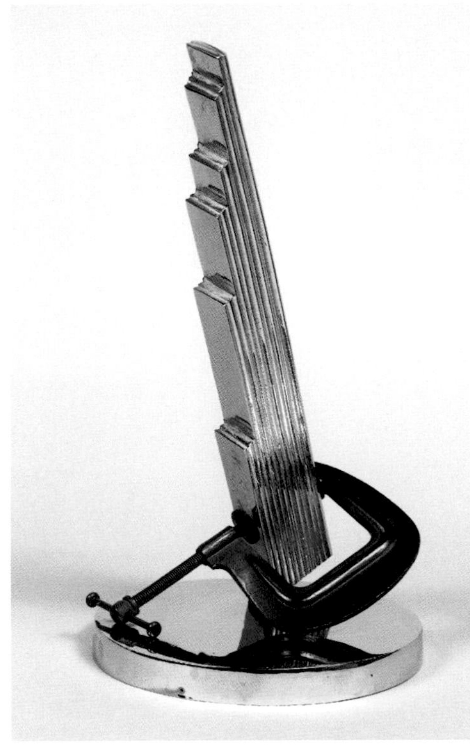

Raised in Brooklyn, New York, Emmanuel Radnitsky changed his name to Man Ray and quickly positioned himself on the cutting edge of modernism. Beginning in 1915, he evolved an American version of Dada: unlike the polemical, anti-art stance taken by Marcel Duchamp and Francis Picabia, the French Dadaists in New York, Man Ray's works were mischievous and whimsical. After moving to France in 1921, he joined the nascent Surrealist movement and worked in a wide range of media, producing sculpture, photographs, and paintings.

New York 17, Man Ray's early Dadaist construction, suggests a skyscraper, but also looks exactly like what it is: a stack of bars clamped together. (The wood original of 1917 was destroyed; Man Ray later made an identical version in chrome and bronze.) Placed on a circular pedestal, *New York 17* mocks sculptural tradition. The crude construction methods of the original disdain traditional respect for craftsmanship, while Man Ray's willingness to re-create the work in another medium denies the uniqueness of the art object.

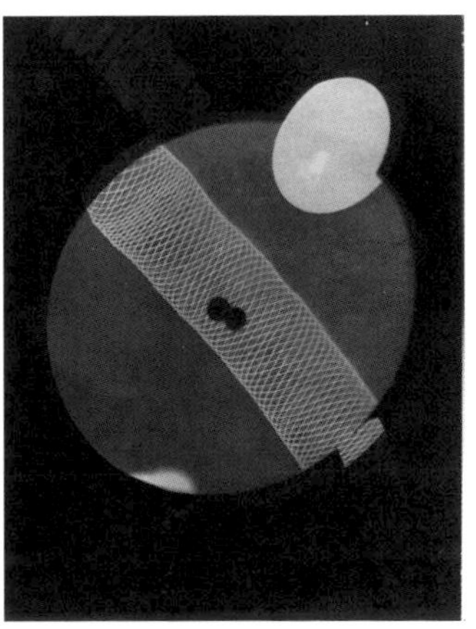

In Paris in the 1920s, Man Ray supported himself as a commercial photographer—a vocation that led to his accidental rediscovery of a nineteenth-century process known as the photogram, where objects are arranged on light-sensitive paper. Traditional photographs record the world roughly as the eye sees it. The photograms he dubbed rayographs, such as *Contrasted Circular Forms with Pair of Optical Black Dots*, were created through negation: the image resulted from the absence of light in the spaces covered by the objects or from the partial light in areas with cast shadows.

New York 17, 1917 and 1966
Chromed and painted bronze, 17 x 9 5/16 x 9 5/16 in. (43.2 x 23.7 x 23.7 cm)
Purchase, with funds from the Modern Painting and Sculpture Committee 96.174

Contrasted Circular Forms with Pair of Optical Black Dots, 1923
Rayograph, 9 3/8 x 7 1/16 in. (23.8 x 17.9 cm)
Purchase, with funds from the Simon Foundation, Inc. 72.131

MAN RAY

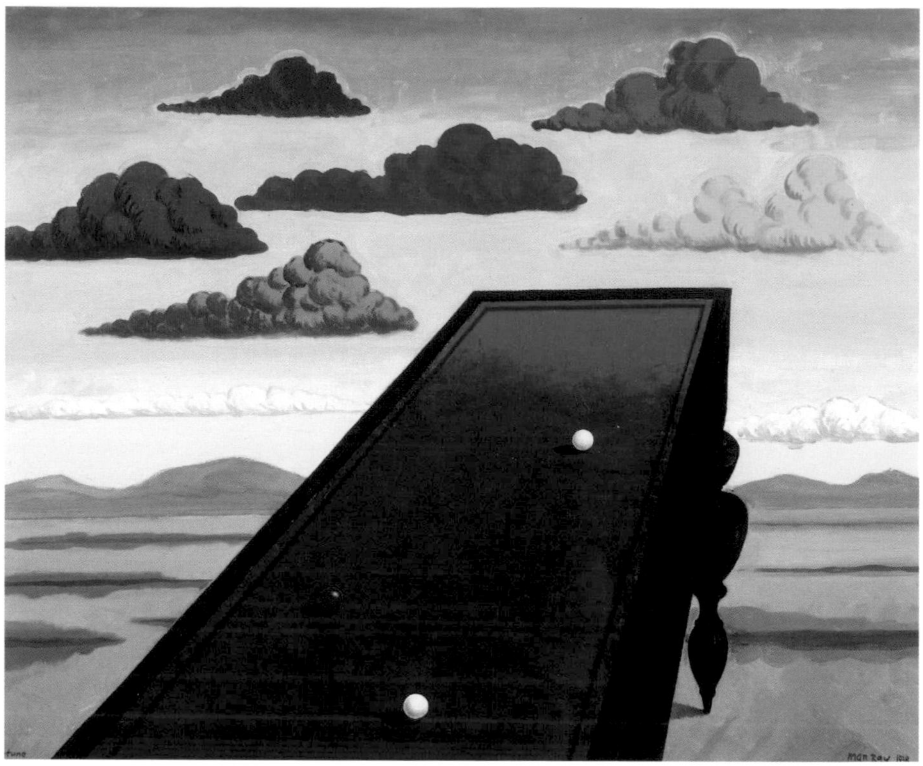

After a decade of photographic work, Man Ray returned to painting in the 1930s. On canvas, he could realize any image his mind could dream up, including the oversized pool table in his Surrealist painting *La Fortune*. The painting's attenuated perspective and oddly colored clouds defy both nature and artistic convention. *La Fortune* also defies the conventions of billiards: the table has no pockets; the game, no objective. The painting recalls the first meeting of Man Ray and Marcel Duchamp twenty years earlier, when the two played tennis without a net, making sport with the rules of tennis as they did with the rules of art.

La Fortune, 1938
Oil on canvas, 24 x 29 in. (61 x 73.7 cm)
Purchase, with funds from the Simon Foundation, Inc. 72.129

AD REINHARDT

1913–1967

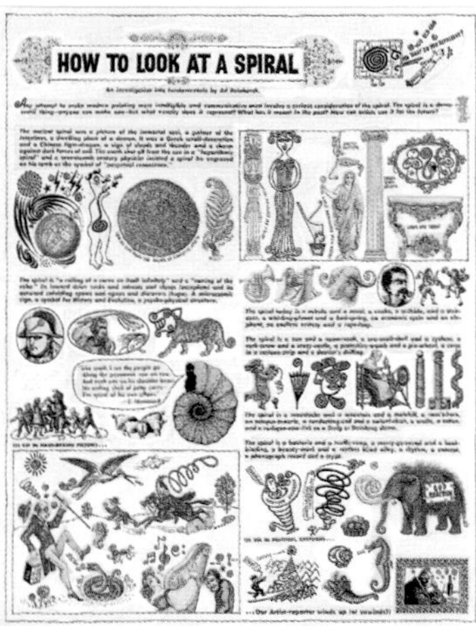

A prominent postwar painter, Ad Reinhardt was also a provocative writer and witty cartoonist on the subject of art and art history. The Whitney Museum's rich collection of Reinhardt's work, ranging from 1937 to 1966, includes nine paintings and twenty-four works on paper. *How to Look at a Spiral* (made for the left-wing newspaper *PM*) is typical of Reinhardt's waggish illustrations: it pokes fun at the significance attributed to geometric forms in modern painting by offering an absurd host of definitions and imagery associated with "spiral"; some of the collaged elements are taken from nineteenth- and twentieth-century illustrations and cartoons. Acerbic and literate, this parody is an early indicator of the profoundly skeptical distance that Reinhardt would take throughout his career from both fashionable art movements and critical authorities. During the 1950s and 1960s, he produced subtle, spare, geometric paintings, disregarding the art then being critically heralded—first the gestural brushstrokes and paint drips of Abstract Expressionism, then the deadpan, appropriated imagery of Pop art.

In *Number 18—1948–49*, an all-over format weaves together blurry, almost watercolor patches with scratched-out lines that expose the white canvas. Pure visual sensation, as opposed to defined forms, is the crux of this work, as it was in Reinhardt's paintings of the early 1950s, when he began producing canvases in a single color tone. In works such as the 1952 *Abstract Painting, Red*, a diptych of two square canvases, the composition becomes more structured and regular. Each of the canvases is composed of nine smaller squares of various shades of

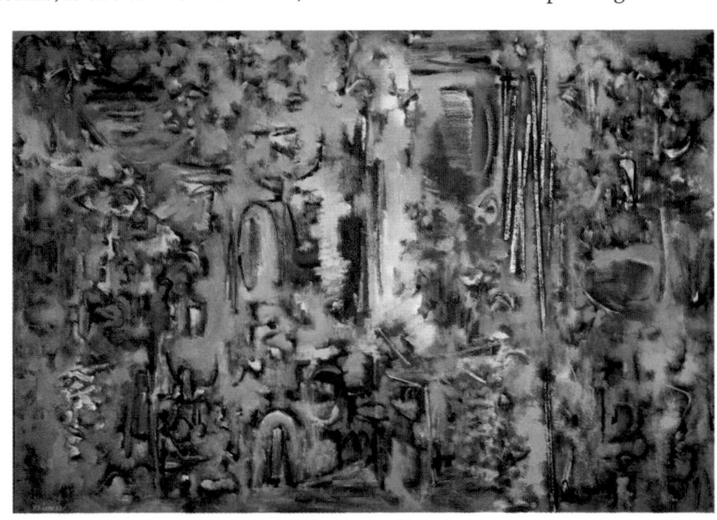

How to Look at a Spiral, 1946
Collage of ink and paper, 13 x 10 1/4 in. (33 x 26 cm)
Gift of Rita Reinhardt 76.49

Number 18—1948–49, 1948–49
Oil on canvas, 40 x 60 in. (101.6 x 152.4 cm)
Purchase 53.13

AD REINHARDT

red, creating a cruciform shape that seems to recede and project at the same time.

The long gestation of the black *Abstract Painting* reveals the extent of Reinhardt's notorious perfectionism; he only considered the painting, begun in 1960, finished in 1966, the year of his important retrospective at The Jewish Museum, New York. The somber variations of *Abstract Painting*'s extraordinarily subtle black-on-black matte squares are only perceptible through sustained, contemplative viewing. Between 1953 and his death in 1967, Reinhardt painted only black-on-black works—a total of twenty-five of them. Their exquisite subtleties are mostly lost in reproduction—as Reinhardt knew they would be; the only viable experience, he felt, was in contemplating the actual painting.

Reinhardt wanted to create "the last paintings anyone can paint," works purged of everything that was not about art. He described the black paintings in 1961 as "a pure, abstract, non-objective, timeless, spaceless, changeless, relationless, disinterested painting." Because of such outspoken positions on formal purity, as well as his reductive palette, Reinhardt set an important precedent for the Minimal and Conceptual artists of the 1960s and 1970s.

Abstract Painting, Red, 1952
Oil on canvas, 30 1/8 x 15 in. (76.5 x 38 cm)
Purchase, with funds from The Lauder Foundation, Leonard and Evelyn Lauder Fund 98.16.1

Abstract Painting, 1960–66
Oil on canvas, 60 x 60 in. (152.4 x 152.4 cm)
Purchase, with funds from The Lauder Foundation, Leonard and Evelyn Lauder Fund 98.16.3

MATTHEW RITCHIE

b. 1964

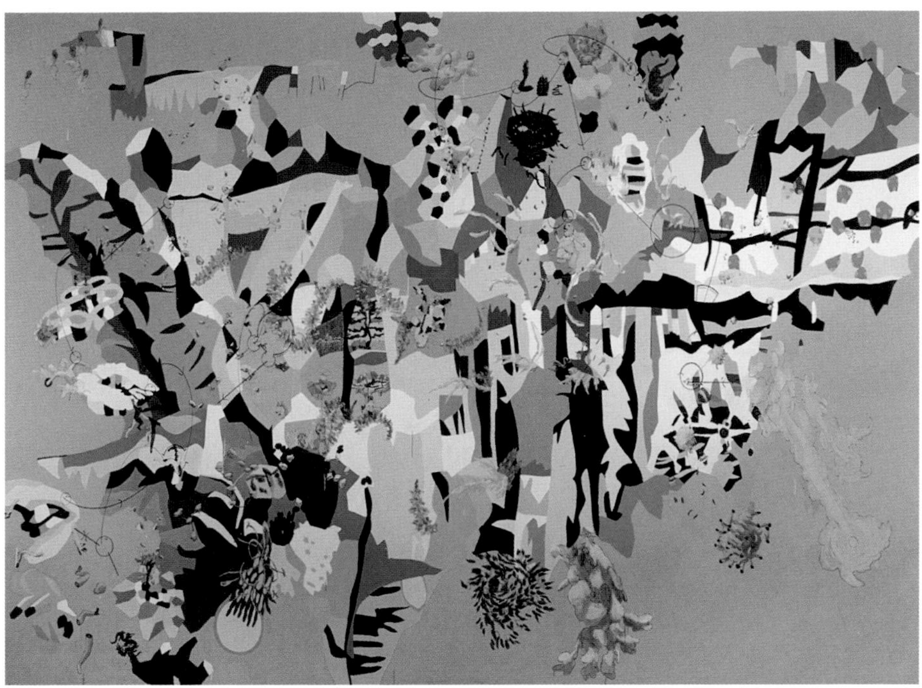

"If Einstein had been a Baroque artist, his paintings might have looked like Matthew Ritchie's," critic Roberta Smith observed. An artist of omnivorous intellectual appetite and irrepressible graphic gifts, Ritchie has developed an original universe of mythic characters, whose picaresque adventures are obliquely charted in paintings, sculptural installations, and accompanying texts. Astrophysics and evolutionary biology, the first mission to the moon and the operations of the Miami mob, as well as various fictive episodes of gambling, carousing, and more serious kinds of mayhem, all figure in his work. "The symbolic language that I use is intended to operate both independently as a pure form in itself and as a bridge between various pre-existing symbolic vocabularies," Ritchie explains.

As in the painting *Time Novel*, the confounding nature of Ritchie's worldview is formally signaled by the lack of a single spatial orientation. Emerging from a warped and buckled-looking surface, fragments of plant and animal life spin away from several possible horizon lines, appearing both upright and inverted. Positions of smaller, often subatomic, particles and their trajectories through space are indicated in black felt-tip marker. Colors as well as imagery are coded, though in a system so arcane that we have to rely on our own imaginative powers to make sense of the multifarious relationships between characters in Ritchie's complex quasi-narrative. When an interviewer asked him, "What is your work ultimately about?" he replied elliptically, "life is as complicated as it appears."

Time Novel, 1997
Oil and felt-tip pen on canvas, 100 x 160 in. (254 x 406.4 cm)
Purchase, with funds from the Contemporary Painting and Sculpture Committee 97.52

LARRY RIVERS

b. 1925

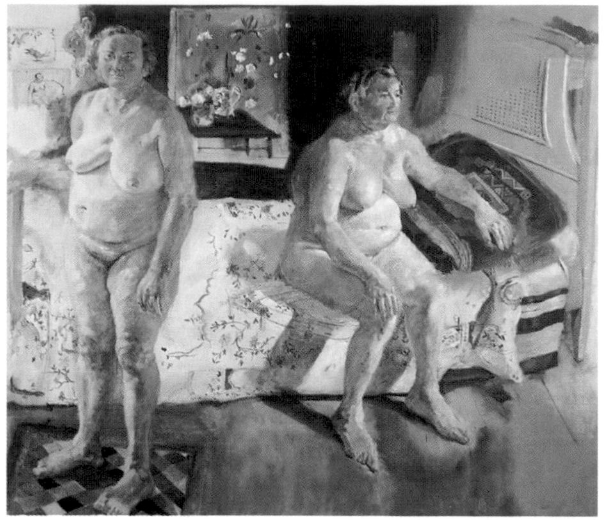

When first exhibited in 1955, Larry Rivers' *Double Portrait of Berdie* sparked controversy. Painted at the height of Abstract Expressionism, it and similar figurative tableaus were out of favor. Critics particularly objected to the artist's dispassionate rendering of his mother-in-law, Mrs. Bertha Burger, known familiarly as "Berdie." Rivers painted her nude, sixty-four-year-old body with an unapologetic realism that bared all the marks of aging flesh.

Rivers, however, had a close, affectionate relationship with his mother-in-law. From 1953 to her death in 1957, Berdie was the artist's primary model. Though Rivers was estranged from his wife, his mother-in-law lived with him in Southampton, Long Island, taking care of his son and stepson and helping him financially. In *Double Portrait of Berdie*, Rivers fused invented concepts, such as Berdie's dual image, with veristic details. And in a playful tribute to his two Berdies, in the upper left corner he painted a framed image of two small birds.

After Berdie died in 1957, Rivers moved back to New York City. In a change of artistic direction, he began welding steel into sculptures. He also collaborated with poet and critic Frank O'Hara to produce a series of lithographs entitled *Stones*. *Us*, one of the twelve works in the series, pairs images of the faces and hands of Rivers and O'Hara with fragments of O'Hara's poetry. The eclectic poems reference everything from their friendship to actor James Dean. A spirit of improvisation governs the selection of images and words on the page, and it is surely not coincidental that Rivers, before pursuing a career in art, was a professional jazz musician.

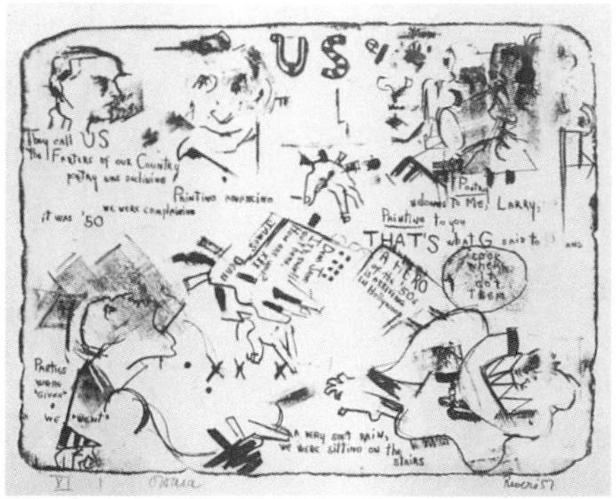

Double Portrait of Berdie, 1955
Oil on canvas, 70 3/4 x 82 1/2 in. (179.7 x 209.6 cm)
Gift of an anonymous donor 56.9

Us, 1957
Lithograph: sheet, 18 7/8 x 23 3/4 in. (47.9 x 60.3 cm) irregular; image, 13 7/8 x 18 in. (35.2 x 45.7 cm) irregular
Gift of Mr. and Mrs. Joseph L. Braun 77.123.1

LIISA ROBERTS

b. 1969

Liisa Roberts' installations invite us to question the nature of our visual and temporal perception of space. In *Blind Side*, Roberts creates a space that is both architectural and anti-cinematic. The screen operates as a device to suggest a third kind of space: neither the dark space of the cinema nor the white cube of the gallery, but an artificially constructed, metaphorical space. On a large, semitransparent screen placed inside the gallery, a film of what seems to be a nineteenth-century drawing room interior appears, activated by the entrance of the viewer into the space. The image of the drawing room was filmed over a period of twenty-four hours and compressed, through time-lapse photography, into several minutes. A mirror of identical size is situated opposite, reflecting the interior and its rapidly changing light, as day turns into night before our eyes. From a speaker above the entrance to the screening room, the live sounds of the street outside can be heard when the projection is not activated. By bringing the street sounds into the gallery space, Roberts asks us to question the parameters of museum exhibition. The viewer is caught between the space of the film, the physical space between the screens, the reflected space of both in the mirror, and the unseen, yet heard, space of the street.

In a reversal of the traditional cinematic experience, in which the viewer becomes absorbed by the film image, here the mirror structure, compressed visual time, and real-time sound make viewing a self-conscious act. The mirror invests the space of the viewer and that of the film with equal importance. We experience perceptual shifts between illusion and reality because Roberts reveals the artifice through which the images are constructed. The architecture of the screens and the actual space of the screening room cooperate with her film images, inviting us to examine the relationship between reality and representation and to pay close attention to how meaning is formulated through the interaction of viewer, space, and time.

Blind Side, 1998
16mm silent film loop in color, live outdoor sound, 16mm film projector adapted with film looper, motion detector, and projector/audio trigger device; microphone, speaker, cables, glass screen, and mirror, dimensions variable.
Purchase, with funds from the Film and Video Committee 99.99

TIM ROLLINS + K.O.S.

b. 1955

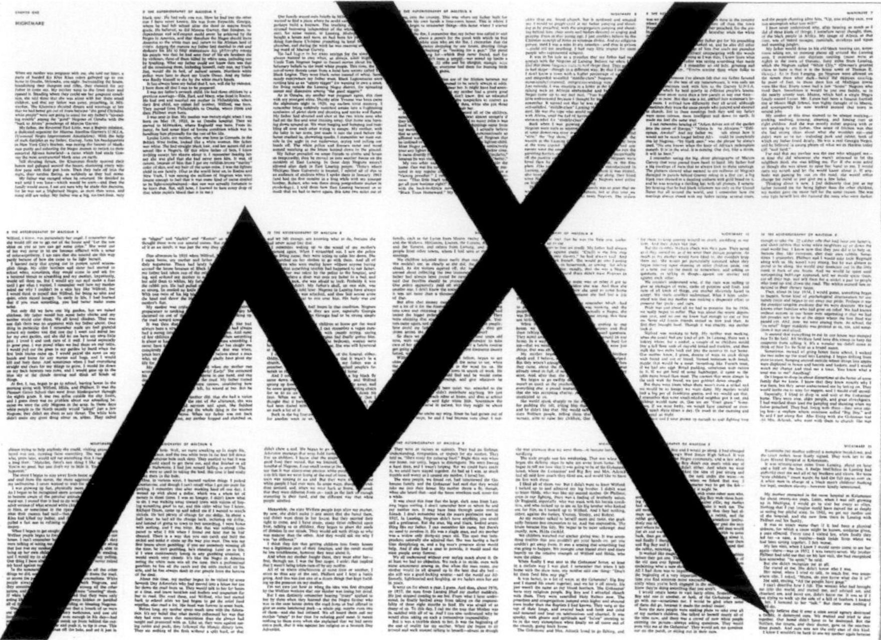

"Our art works are teaching machines," says artist-instructor Tim Rollins, who founded the art collective Tim Rollins + K.O.S. (Kids of Survival) in 1982. Rollins + K.O.S. meet at the Art & Knowledge Workshop in New York's South Bronx, a special program for about thirty academically and/or emotionally challenged teenagers with artistic talent. In a method that developed out of a unique literacy training program, Rollins + K.O.S. draw and paint images on pages torn from such modern classics as Nathaniel Hawthorne's *The Scarlet Letter*, Stephen Crane's *The Red Badge of Courage*, and Herman Melville's *Moby-Dick*. By creating works of collaborative authorship, the group also challenges the conventional notion that great art is the product of a single, isolated genius.

To make *By Any Means Necessary: Nightmare*, Rollins + K.O.S. first removed book pages from *The Autobiography of Malcolm X* and then glued them onto a canvas in a sequential grid. On top of these pages, in black gesso, they painted a logolike reduction of the slain civil rights leader's initials. The forceful, sharp, and angular character of the graphic slashing suggests a powerful and assertive analogue to the content of Malcolm X's autobiography, succinctly renewing its message of self-determination.

Along with Malcolm X, Rollins + K.O.S. make the case that the seemingly passive act of reading can also be a process of re-inscription and personal empowerment. "The work is about history," says Richie Cruz, one of the Kids of Survival. "We're taking the books and we're re-writing them, re-doing them, but in our way. And I feel like we're not just talking about history—we're making history, too."

By Any Means Necessary: Nightmare, 1986
Gesso on paper on canvas, 21 x 28 in. (53.3 x 71.1 cm)
Gift of Barbara and Eugene Schwartz 93.148

JAMES ROSENQUIST

b. 1933

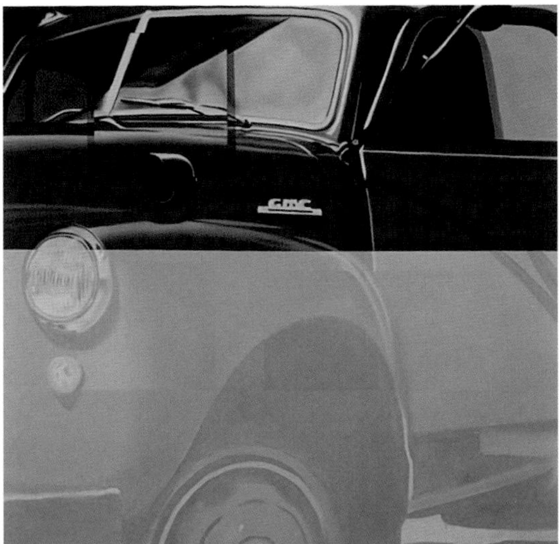

In the 1950s, James Rosenquist was a highly accomplished billboard painter, working, among other places, on the largest signs in Times Square. When he turned to fine art around 1959, he employed the vocabulary of his commercial trade for brilliantly colored, billboard-like paintings. In the spirit of Pop, his subjects included the iconic features of 1950s and 1960s American society: cars, jet fighters, dishwashing gloves, and lipstick.

Rosenquist's 6-foot square canvas *Untitled (Broome Street Truck)* depicts a cropped, alarmingly close-up image of a red 1950s GMC truck. Although a seemingly straightforward representation, the painting is in fact strangely abstracted: details are generalized, the reflections are empty, and, inexplicably, the color of the image shifts to yellow in the lower half, where the forms become even more liquid and diffuse. A small, separate canvas attached in the middle of the windshield disrupts the painting's surface and slightly fractures the image.

Rosenquist often borrows images from photographs and magazine reproductions—images, as he put it, that are "apart from nature." He then subjects them to disorienting juxtapositions and shifting scales. *Fahrenheit 1982 Degrees* is typical of his long, mural-size works, in which everyday things assume heroic proportions, such as the polished fingernail that mysteriously metamorphoses into the tip of a fountain pen. With its hot, pink and red palette and phallic lipsticks, the work is charged with erotic power. Here, as in other works, Rosenquist's defiance of pictorial convention ultimately frustrates interpretation, and his paintings remain among the most hermetic of those associated with Pop art.

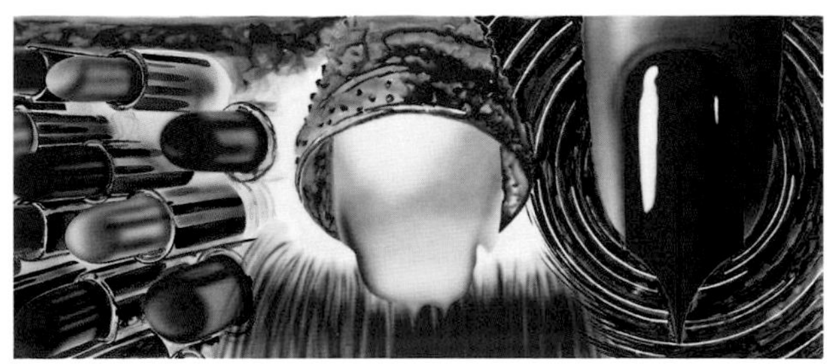

Untitled (Broome Street Truck), 1963
Oil on canvas, 72 x 72 in. (182.9 x 182.9 cm)
Purchase 64.20

Fahrenheit 1982 Degrees, 1982
Colored ink on frosted mylar, 33 1/8 x 71 1/2 in. (84.1 x 181.6 cm)
Purchase, with funds from the John I.H. Baur Purchase Fund, the Mr. and Mrs. M. Anthony Fisher Purchase Fund and The Lauder Foundation—Drawing Fund 82.35

MARTHA ROSLER

b. 1943

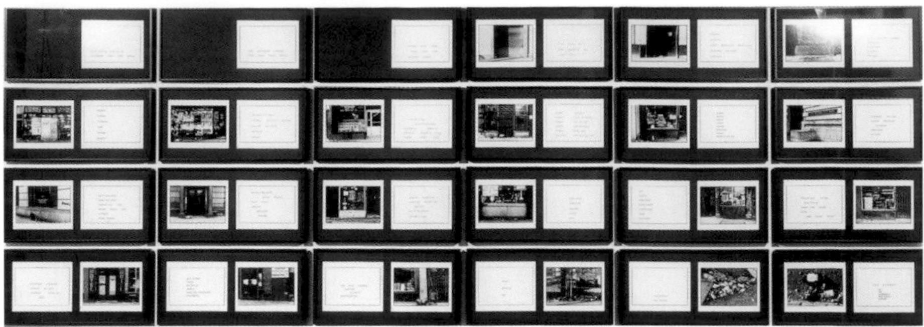

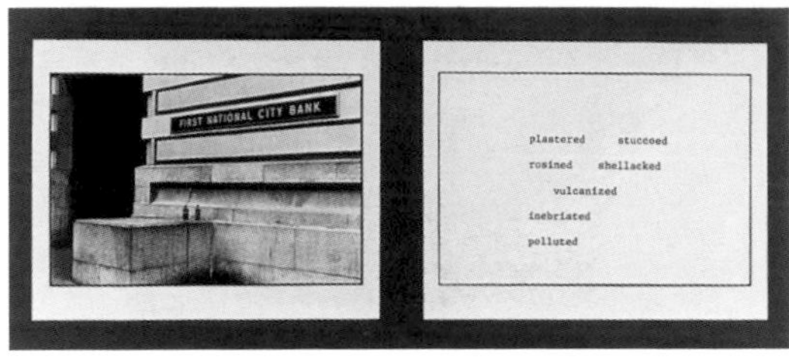

Born in Brooklyn, New York, Martha Rosler has spent much of her working life examining the authenticity and authority associated with documentary photography, especially photographs of women, the working class, and the poor. Although she remains an advocate of such documentary images, she also observes that "people without power are constantly being captured on film and their images deployed in ways that instantly become highly questionable. This is a cultural dilemma." Rosler confronts this dilemma by drawing attention to the method in which documentary photography is created, displayed, and received by the public.

In *The Bowery in two inadequate descriptive systems*, Rosler responds to earlier photographs of alcoholics and vagrants in New York's run-down Bowery neighborhood—photographs made to publicize the plight of this population. Today, she feels, such images—too often contemplated in museums and galleries—have lost the capacity to motivate social change. The initial impetus for her project came, Rosler recalled, when she "walked down the Bowery [and] was struck by the contrast of living life...to the immobilized images of the people that we often saw. I was thinking how inadequate the photos were to convey anything about the life there or, even more important, the social position of the men on that street and the circumstances that put them there."

To call into question the ability of documentary photography to adequately "convey the life there," Rosler juxtaposed photographs of Bowery storefronts with photographs of typewritten words from the lexicon of drunkenness; she intended this work to hang in museums alongside traditional documentary photographs. The disjunction between the images of inebriation conjured by the text and the unpeopled photographs suggests the limits of both language and photography, two "descriptive systems," to fully address the complex issues that have led to the destitution of those who congregate on the Bowery, or any skid row.

The Bowery in two inadequate descriptive systems, 1974–75
45 gelatin silver prints of text and image on 24 backing boards, backing boards, 11 13/16 x 23 5/8 in. (30 x 60 cm) each
Purchase, with funds from John L. Steffens 93.4.1–24a–b

THEODORE ROSZAK

1907–1981

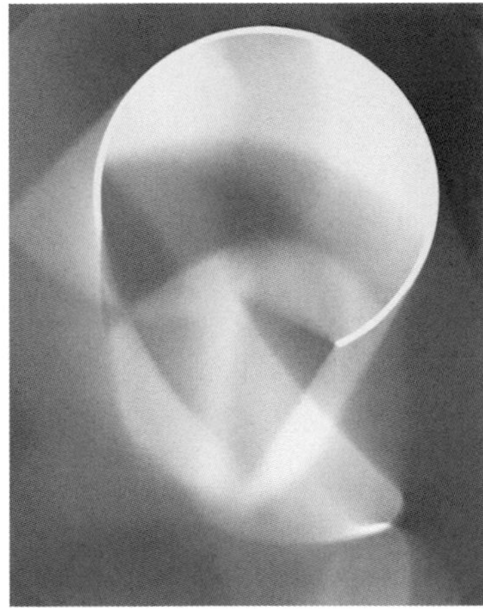

With the geometric sculptures he produced before World War II, Theodore Roszak became one of the few American artists to embrace the machine aesthetic of the Bauhaus. For the artists and architects associated with this vanguard school in Weimar, Germany, art was an ally of industry and an agent of social change.

Roszak learned of the Bauhaus through the writings of the Hungarian artist László Moholy-Nagy, who had taught at the school. The two men met after Moholy-Nagy emigrated to Chicago in 1937, and they corresponded during Roszak's tenure at the Design Laboratory in New York, an experimental school modeled after the Bauhaus. Roszak adopted one of Moholy-Nagy's teaching exercises, in which students explored the interplay of geometry and light by placing objects on light-sensitive paper. Between 1937 and 1941, Roszak experimented with this photogram technique and sent examples of his work to Moholy-Nagy.

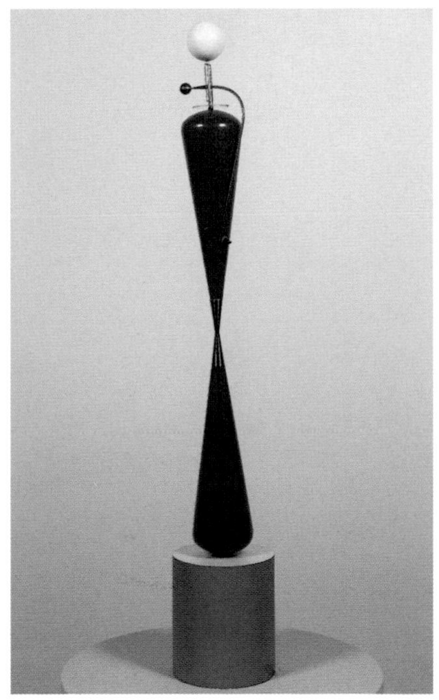

The ideals of the Bauhaus are best exemplified by Roszak's sculptures; as in *Bi-Polar in Red*, they are simple geometric forms fabricated from machine-age materials such as metal and plastic. The shapes are as precise as mathematical formulas—*Bi-Polar in Red* resembles an infinity symbol rotated on its axis. Roszak intended the sculpture to suggest scientific models, to invoke "the same natural phenomenon as north vs. south pole...male vs. female...the bi-polarity of magnetic fields in space." There is nevertheless something insistently anthropomorphic about *Bi-Polar in Red*, with its ball of a head and arm-like appendages. Roszak's sculpture is industrial, yet it remains somehow human, its wasp-waisted form pointing optimistically toward the future.

Photogram, 1937–39
Gelatin silver print, 4 15/16 x 3 7/8 in. (12.5 x 9.8 cm)
Gift of Virginia M. Zabriskie 91.100.10

Bi-Polar in Red, 1940
Metal, plastic, and wood, 54 3/16 x 8 5/8 x 8 5/8 in. (137.6 x 21.9 x 21.9 cm) overall with base
Purchase, with funds from the Burroughs Wellcome Purchase Fund and the National Endowment for the Arts
79.6a–c

SUSAN ROTHENBERG

b. 1945

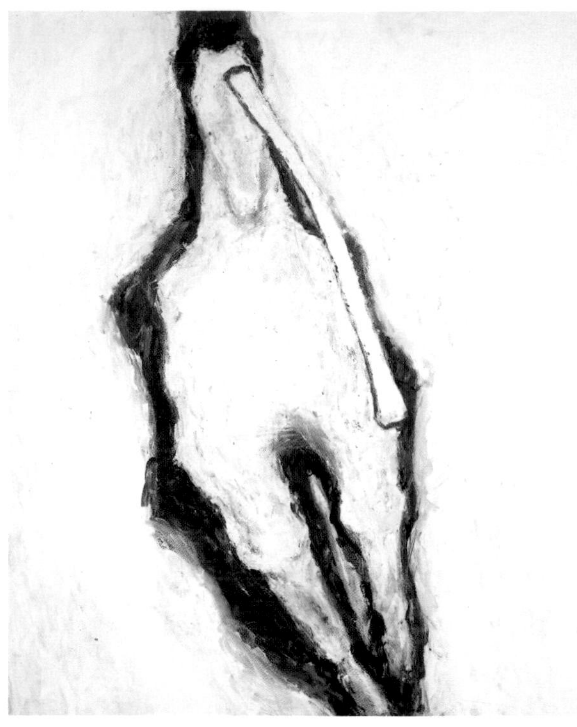

Susan Rothenberg first gained widespread recognition with paintings of horses, begun in 1973 with a casual sketch on canvas. Along with a handful of other artists in the 1970s, among them the painter Neil Jenney (p. 151) and the sculptor Joel Shapiro (p. 276), Rothenberg was instrumental in returning the figure to an art scene dominated by reductive, Minimalist abstraction. Her early horse paintings, divided across two panels, showed the animal outlined in profile. She was initially drawn to the subject for its iconic character and its regular proportions: "The horse image divides right," she said. "For the first three years that I worked with the horse, the divisions related mostly to the given of the rectangle. In 1976 I started to make the geometry relate more intensely to the horse itself."

In *For the Light*, a single panel, Rothenberg turned the horse frontally, so that it appears to be galloping into the viewer's space. As always in Rothenberg's images, the forms are suggested by expressive contours rather than filled in with detail. Here, moreover, the artist introduced a spatially and psychologically troubling device in the shape of a long white bone that descends from the horse's forehead. "That strange bone image came out as a doodle. After I got over its strangeness, I found I could use it formally." But the bone also represented a kind of introspection. "It was like digging deep in myself and pulling something out. I ended up with this bone." The emotional excavation this painting involved, and its advancing, two-legged, vaguely anthropomorphic horse, heralded Rothenberg's subsequent turn to the human figure.

For the Light, 1978–79
Synthetic polymer and vinyl paint on canvas, 105 x 87 1/4 in. (266.7 x 221.6 cm)
Purchase, with funds from Peggy and Richard Danziger 79.23

MARK ROTHKO

1903–1970

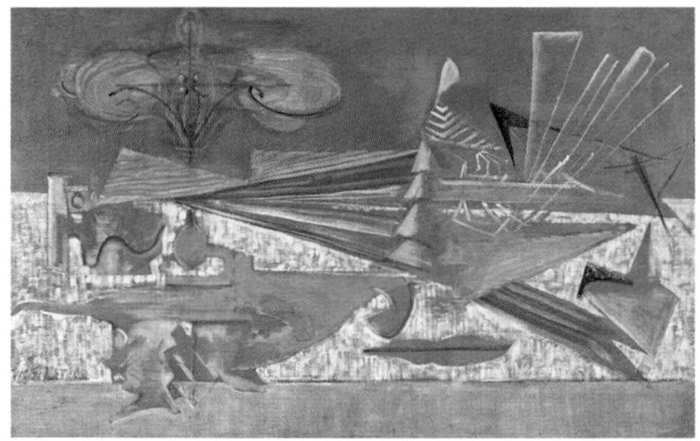

Although best known for completely abstract paintings, Mark Rothko first gained recognition in the 1940s for Surrealist-inspired representational works. The Surrealist focus on ancient myths and manifestations of the unconscious emerges in Rothko's *Agitation of the Archaic*—in the biomorphic shapes, particularly the birdlike creature hovering above at left, and the undefined landscape of muted greens and compressed space. Surrealist too is the overall effect of a mythical place or a more primitive era—although to Rothko such primitivism was also a way of addressing the destructive horrors of World War II.

Rothko's works became increasingly abstract during the 1940s until, at the end of the decade, his biomorphic forms dissolved into clouds of color. For the next twenty years, he explored compositions of subtly defined color expanses, becoming one of the key figures in the Color Field branch of Abstract Expressionism.

Four Darks in Red exemplifies the darker palette of the late 1950s, when Rothko increasingly used red, maroon, and saturated black paints. Four dark rectangular areas of different proportions dominate the composition, simultaneously emerging from and receding into a luminous red ground. Rothko's method of layering many coats of paint, along with the special reflectivity of his color mixtures, give his paintings an inimitable depth and incandescence. When this nearly 10-foot-wide canvas is seen close up (as the artist intended), the viewer is engulfed in an atmosphere of color and intense visual sensations that summon what Rothko called the "basic emotions—tragedy, ecstasy, and doom."

Agitation of the Archaic, 1944
Oil on canvas, 35 3/8 x 54 1/4 in. (89.9 x 137.8 cm)
Gift of The Mark Rothko Foundation, Inc. 85.43.1

Four Darks in Red, 1958
Oil on canvas, 102 x 116 in. (259.1 x 294.6 cm)
Purchase, with funds from the Friends of the Whitney Museum of American Art, Mr. and Mrs. Eugene M. Schwartz, Mrs. Samuel A. Seaver, and Charles Simon 68.9

MICHAL ROVNER

b. 1957

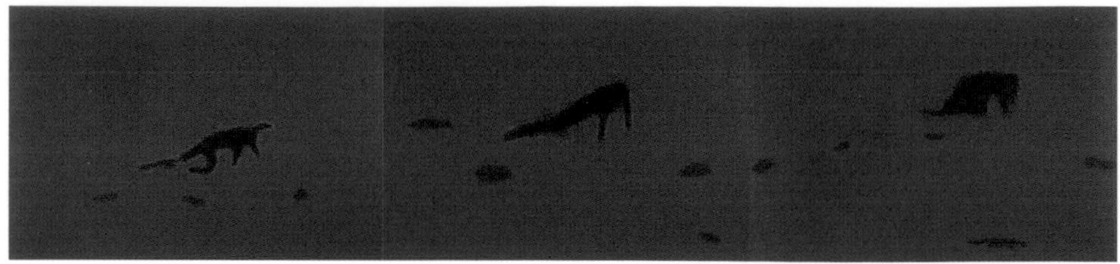

Israeli-born Michal Rovner records either staged or actual scenarios with a photographic or video camera and then alters and/or combines this material to create new photographs, videos, public installations, and films. *Red Field* consists of stills taken from video footage of a figure crawling in an Israeli desert. Before printing the images on canvas, Rovner removed the details, lowered the resolution, and infused the images with a fiery orange-red background. Each frame portrays a faint spectral being that glides in and out of existence. The figures could read as abstract marks, yet Rovner retains just enough visual information to suggest animate beings. As a whole, the horizontal format encourages the viewer to scan the work from left to right. From one image to the next, we witness the figure laboring to lift and drag itself forth. In its strained yet determined struggle to survive, it is transformed from a slim humanoid or reptilian figure on all fours to a long-beaked, long-tailed bird to a mammothlike primordial creature.

Throughout her work, Rovner probes the boundaries between reality and fiction. She uses visual and narrative ambiguity not only to shed light on the deceptive nature of visual representation, but also to explore the metaphorical possibilities of her images. In *Red Field*, she dematerializes matter in order to evoke such immaterial and universal concepts as loss, yearning, hope, and anguish. "I always have the urge to record and erase at the same time," Rovner says. "There's an almost mystical aspect to the record that's left....From one generation to another, something always remains."

Red Field, 1996
Pigmented inkjet on canvas, 40 3/16 x 169 in. (102.1 x 429.3 cm) overall
Purchase, with funds from the Harriett Ames Charitable Trust 97.77a–c

EDWARD RUSCHA

b. 1937

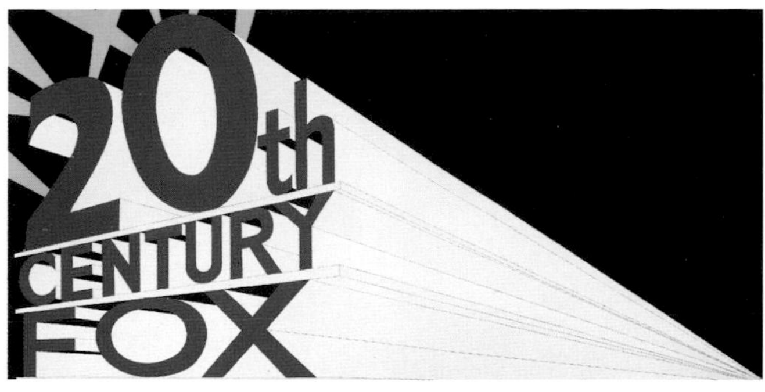

Born in Nevada and raised in Oklahoma, Edward Ruscha moved to Los Angeles in 1956. His work of the past four decades, which includes painting, film, photography, books, and prints, resists easy categorization. His straightforward depiction of subjects taken from American popular culture has earned him a reputation as a West Coast Pop artist, while his interest in language aligns him with Conceptual art of the late 1960s and early 1970s (p. 169). Ruscha's subject matter is often a single word or phrase that alludes to the culture and iconography of Los Angeles—its freeways, apartment buildings, billboards, and movie advertising. *Large Trademark with Eight Spotlights* presents one of the Hollywood film industry's best-known logos. "The subject [of Los Angeles]," Ruscha explained, "became a general metaphor for anxiety and the speed of modern life." The sign is rendered with bold primary colors in a composition cut by a dynamic diagonal. Like the company's actual logo, the letters recede in sharp perspective, illuminated by yellow spotlights against a dark triangle of night.

Hollywood to Pico is from Ruscha's recent series of aerial perspectives of Los Angeles streets and intersections, which he refers to as "Metro Plots." Its mottled gray color is both reminiscent of a sidewalk or roadway and intensely atmospheric. The reductive, regularized pattern turns the sequence of streets into a simplified city grid with horizontals but no verticals. The upside-down street names tell us that the "proper" view is from above and facing the other direction. As we mentally move ourselves around the geography of the painting, we are encompassed by the work's almost romantic atmosphere. Ruscha's emotional engagement with Los Angeles is profound: "The iconography of this place does mean something special to me. I love it, and I've always loved it, because it feeds me and it feeds my work."

Large Trademark with Eight Spotlights, 1962
Oil on canvas, 66 3/4 x 133 1/4 in. (169.5 x 338.5 cm)
Purchase, with funds from the Mrs. Percy Uris Purchase Fund 85.41

Hollywood to Pico, 1998
Synthetic polymer on canvas, 70 x 138 in. (177.8 x 350.5 cm)
Purchase, with funds from Leonard A. Lauder 99.1

ROBERT RYMAN

b. 1930

The singularly cohesive and refined work of Robert Ryman encompasses both the Chromatic Abstraction of Brice Marden and Ad Reinhardt (pp. 196, 254) and the Minimalist ethos of such artists as Sol LeWitt and Frank Stella (pp. 184, 297). Ryman has painted exclusively white-on-white paintings since the early 1960s. Far from being limiting, however, monochrome frees him to explore the infinite variations of facture—the way the paint is brushed onto the support—as well as the tactility and opacity of paint. By applying white paints and enamels to a variety of surfaces—parchmentlike paper, cotton, or steel—he reveals how a change of support can produce a different visual effect.

In the later 1960s, Ryman often insisted that his works be mounted with nothing more than tape—no frames or hanging devices; he "wanted to point out the paint and the paint surface and not so much the objectness." For the 1979 *Carrier*, he advised that "the painting depends for its aesthetic identity upon its correct installation." The instructions for this installation include the precise arrangement of the fasteners and bolts that Ryman selected and painted. *Carrier*'s puckered, stuccolike surface shows off the regular twists and flicks of Ryman's paintbrush, as does the contrast with the unpainted cotton along the edges and sides. The visible emphasis on facture thus conjoins the finished painting with the materials and process of its making.

Carrier, 1979
Oil on cotton with metal brackets, 78 x 78 in. (198.1 x 198.1 cm)
Purchase, with funds from the National Endowment for the Arts and the Painting and Sculpture Committee
80.40

ALISON SAAR

b. 1956

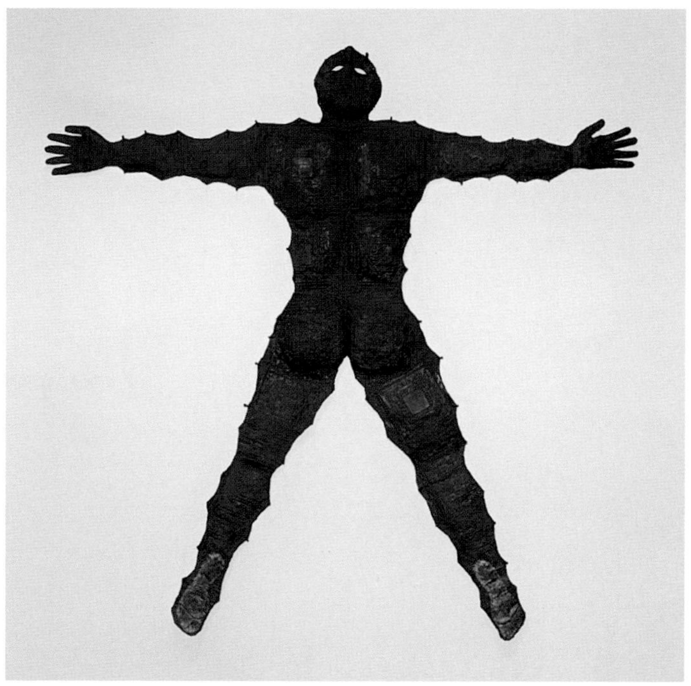

A spread-eagled human form fixed to the wall with fifty-three nails, Alison Saar's *Skin/Deep* is a brutal image that evokes the horrors of a crucifixion or the grotesque image of a flayed human body. The old stamped ceiling tin with which the figure is made connotes a sense of age, use, and reuse. The informality of the material, like the frightening appearance of the figure itself, is made to seem intentionally out of place in a genteel museum context. In this work, Saar confronts the viewer with an image of intense psychic and physical pain. Nevertheless, *Skin/Deep* may come with a subtle message of salvation and healing: not only does the figure recall a crucifix, but its flattened form also echoes the stamped metal retablos, often representing body parts, that are used in certain Latin American Catholic traditions to ward off afflictions.

Saar, whose father is of European heritage and whose mother, the artist Betye Saar (p. 268), is herself of mixed African, Native American, and European heritage, is deeply involved with notions of race. In particular, the younger Saar is intimately familiar with how attributions of racial identity can expose unexamined prejudice. Drawing on personal experience as well as her research in artistic and folkloric representations of racial stereotypes, Saar masterfully distills a multitude of images and references into a singular, searing image. *Skin/Deep* eloquently expresses the profound physical hurt and psychic damage inflicted on generations of individuals who were categorized and dehumanized because of the color of their skin.

Skin/Deep, 1993
Ceiling tin, nails, and copper, 82 x 84 x 2 1/2 in. (208.3 x 213.4 x 6.4 cm)
Purchase, with funds from the Painting and Sculpture Committee 93.34a–b

BETYE SAAR

b. 1926

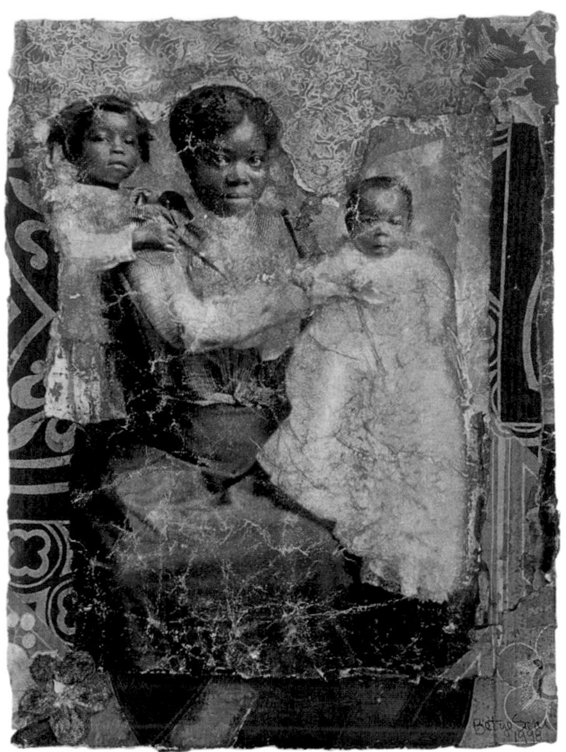

Mother and Children in Blue, a moody, psychologically nuanced collage of old photographs, takes a distinctly tender view of a traditional social role: the family matriarch. Betye Saar has often used her work to address racist stereotypes. "Yes, slavery was declared illegal in 1862," she has written, "but since then African Americans still 'served' in white homes in the form of images of cookie jars, dish towels and salt and pepper shakers." Rather than the conventional mammy figures that have appeared in Saar's previous work—most often commercial versions such as Aunt Jemima—the woman in *Mother and Children in Blue* is a fully realized subject, her bearing reflecting dignity and poise. Her children too are proud, even a little defiant. But there is undeniable melancholy wrought by the image's fractured surface and frosty blue tonality.

The African-American novelist Ishmael Reed has compared Saar's skill at finding expressive brilliance in discarded materials to the "process of making diamonds," which uses "methane gas, the stuff that emanates from junk." Saar has been influenced by a variety of spiritual practices—she has studied tarot, palmistry, voodoo, and shamanism. She has also long been interested in the assemblages and collages of the Dadaists and Surrealists. Ultimately, however, the special magic of Saar's work lies in the gemlike clarity and concentrated focus that issues a call for resurrection and renewal.

Mother and Children in Blue, 1998
Mixed-media collage on paper, 8 3/4 x 6 1/2 in. (22.2 x 16.5 cm)
Purchase, with funds from the Drawing Committee 2000.46

DAVID SALLE

b. 1952

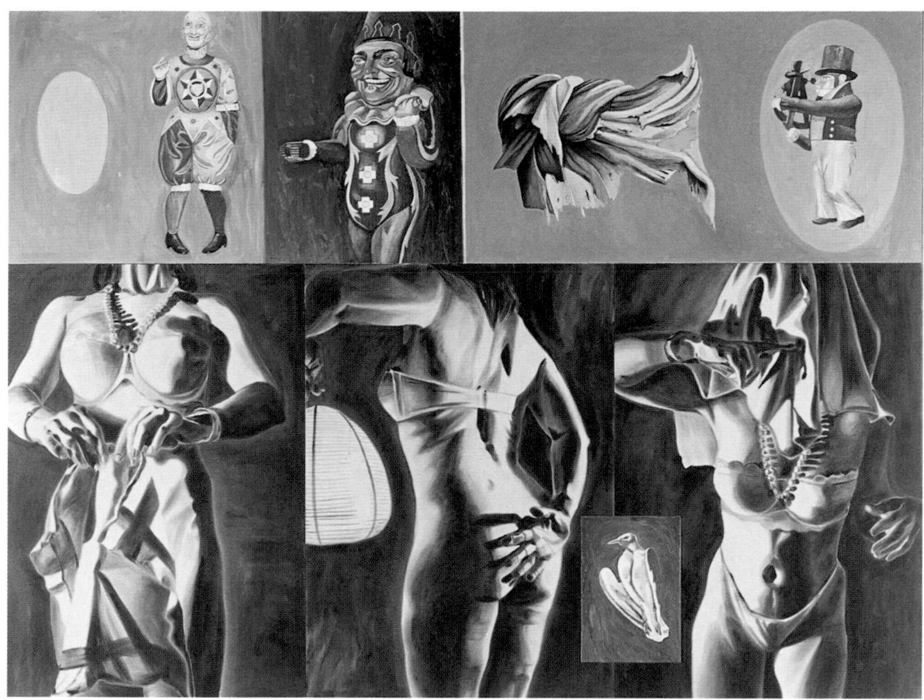

David Salle's paintings are best known for their provocative juxtapositions of disparate, often sexually explicit imagery. Culled from a wide range of popular, art historical, and pornographic sources, and combined in a manner akin to cinematic montage, Salle's subjects are locked in an enigmatic coexistence within the painting's frame. What, for example, do the toy clowns in the upper left half of *Sextant in Dogtown* have to do with the scantily clad female figures below? Is Salle alluding to these women's dehumanization as the objects of desire? The appearance of a nineteenth-century cartographer with a sextant in the upper right corner would similarly seem to equate sexual voyeurism with objectifying surveillance. But such readings, although conceivable, are nowhere confirmed. Indeed, the impossibility of locating a single verifiable meaning appears to be one of the painting's principal themes.

Salle's art is frequently associated with a renewed interest in the 1980s in figurative painting—a sharp departure from the previous decade's emphasis on ephemeral and text-based work. But he is equally linked to more conceptually based artists of the era, such as Barbara Kruger, Sherrie Levine, and Cindy Sherman (pp. 171, 182, 278), who shared Salle's interest in employing appropriated imagery to explore the relationship between vision and desire—in the realms of both fine art and our everyday, media-saturated lives.

Sextant in Dogtown, 1987
Oil and synthetic polymer on canvas, 96 3/16 x 126 1/4 in. (244.3 x 320.7 cm)
Purchase, with funds from the Painting and Sculpture Committee 88.8

LUCAS SAMARAS

b. 1936

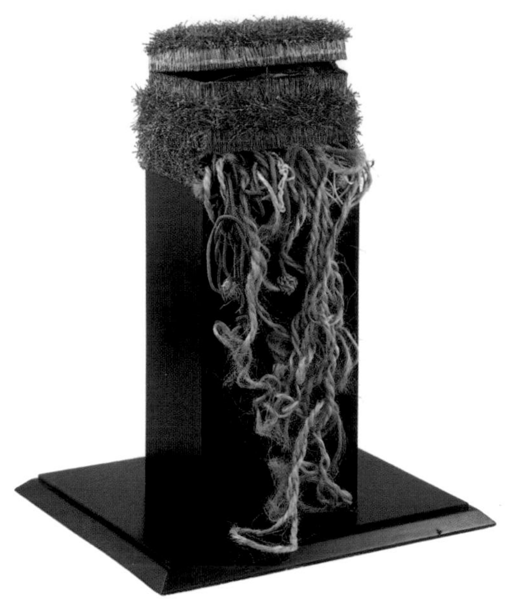

With thirty-three works by Lucas Samaras among its holdings, the Whitney Museum offers a rich selection of the artist's highly idiosyncratic inventions, particularly from the fertile period between 1963 and the late 1970s. Since he began making art in his early twenties, the Greek-born Samaras has built a diverse body of work that includes painting, pastels, photographs, exquisitely rendered ink drawings, and sculpture in a dizzying variety of media, ranging from small-scale constructions to room-sized environments.

Among the artist's best-known works are the mixed-media boxes he began to make in 1960 and the so-called *Chair Transformations* from 1969–70, of which the Whitney owns seven examples. In his studio, Samaras surrounds himself with the often prosaic ingredients of his art—cutlery, scissors, beads, yarn, sequins—and invariably transforms these everyday materials into something startlingly unexpected. *Untitled Box No. 3* typifies the obsessive deployment of such media in Samaras' many box constructions. Propped slightly ajar to reveal a stuffed mockingbird, the wooden box is covered with straight pins arranged in neat rows or glued into a prickly, threatening mass. One of the artist's favorite media, the pins are both formal devices that stand, as he says, for "marks, lines, and dots," and nostalgic emblems of his childhood (he often played with them in a relative's dress shop). They both invite and repel our desire to touch and explore this strange container that, with its poignant contents, becomes a tiny reliquary or coffin.

The pins recur in Samaras' haunting collage *Skull & Milky Way*, where they impale a profile X-ray of the artist's head and neck. Samaras, whose oeuvre has centered in many ways around his own body, said the skull image provided him with a "fresh recognizable shape to work with." For *Skull & Milky Way*, he made a cutout of his head from a positive photographic print derived from the X-ray and glued it to a large photograph of a nebula. Using pins to augment the stars and outline his own image, he created a cosmic *memento mori*, like a giant constellation in the night sky.

The more than two dozen *Chair Transformations* Samaras made represent extraordinarily inventive permutations in material and shape of this utilitarian object. But Samaras'

Untitled Box No. 3, 1963
Pins, wood, rope, wire, and stuffed bird on painted wood pedestal, 29 3/16 x 18 3/4 x 16 1/4 in. (74.1 x 47.6 x 41.3 cm) overall, with base and plexiglass case
Gift of the Howard and Jean Lipman Foundation, Inc. 66.36a-b

chairs defy their intended function; rather, they assert their presence as art and stand as poetic surrogates for the absent body. In the three examples illustrated here, the chairs morph into sculptural forms of assorted styles and moods, whether a fractured Constructivist object, a lyrically calligraphic drawing in space, or a potentially lethal weapon. Samaras was drawn to the ubiquity, variety, and power of chairs in our daily lives and throughout history, literature, and art. In one of his many written commentaries on his life and work, he listed myriad associations of the word chair, including "musical chair," "wheel chair," "person's lap," and "hot seat."

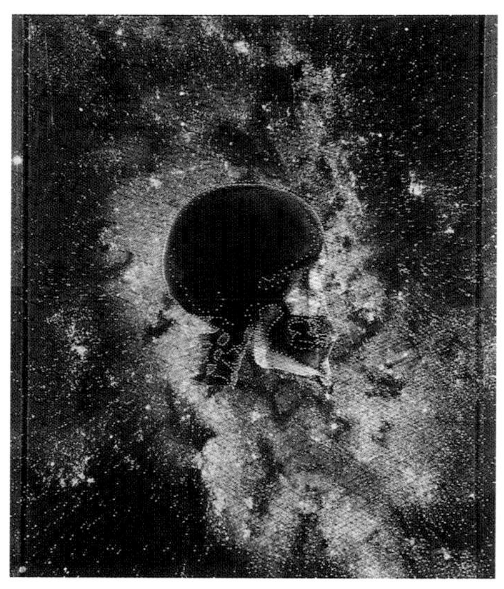

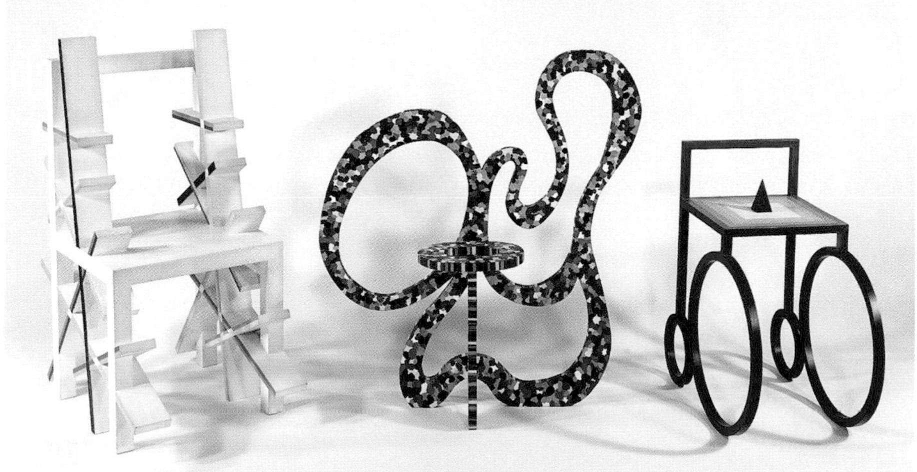

Skull & Milky Way, 1966
X-ray photograph and pins, 28 7/8 x 24 3/4 x 3 1/2 in. (73.3 x 62.9 x 8.9 cm)
Gift of Howard and Jean Lipman 91.34.6

(left to right)
Chair Transformation Number 3, 1969–70
Acrylic on wood, 43 x 20 x 29 3/4 in. (109.2 x 50.8 x 75.6 cm)
Promised 50th Anniversary Gift of Mr. and Mrs. Wilfred P. Cohen P.80.1

Chair Transformation Number 12, 1969–70
Synthetic polymer on wood, 41 1/2 x 36 x 13 in. (105.4 x 91.4 x 33 cm)
Purchase, with funds from the Howard and Jean Lipman Foundation, Inc. 70.1573

Chair Transformation Number 16, 1969–70
Synthetic polymer on wood, 30 x 14 13/16 x 28 1/4 in. (76.2 x 37.6 x 71.8 cm)
Purchase, with funds from the Howard and Jean Lipman Foundation, Inc. 70.1574

GLEN SEATOR

b. 1959

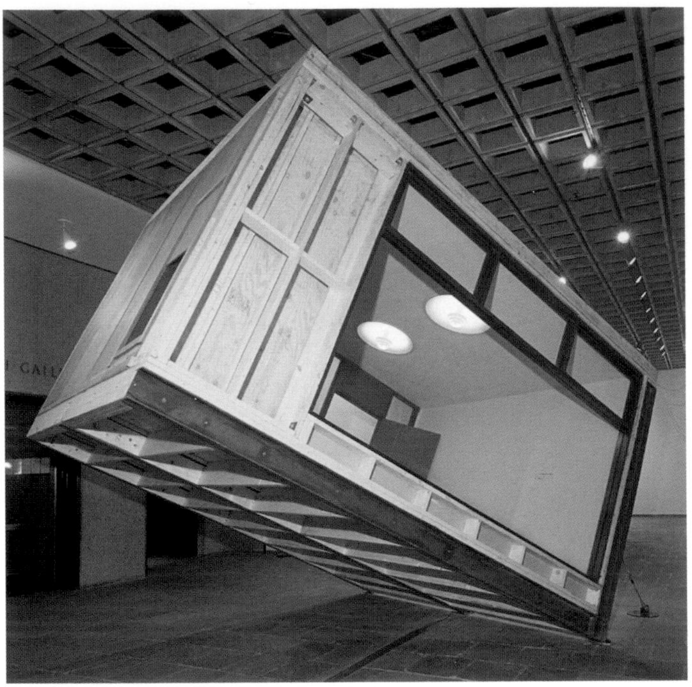

For the Whitney's "1997 Biennial Exhibition," Glen Seator dismantled the director's office (already scheduled for demolition as part of an expansion of the Permanent Collection galleries), and then meticulously rebuilt the space as a sculptural installation on the Museum's fourth floor. (The title is an abbreviation of "Biennial. Director's Office.") *B.D.O.* is characteristic of Seator's method of replicating built spaces in a slightly altered physical context in order to draw attention to their subliminal formal and social qualities. In another work, for example, he made an exact replica on a gallery floor of the street that ran outside the gallery's front window.

For *B.D.O.*, Seator tipped the boxlike, 12,000-pound structure at a 30-degree angle, creating a simultaneous illusion of weightlessness and imminent collapse. Viewers could look into the room through its doorway and window to see the office's teak wall treatments and working light fixtures, all part of Marcel Breuer's original design for the building. The geometric physicality of *B.D.O.* updates the Minimalist tradition found in 1960s sculptures by Robert Morris and Tony Smith (pp. 212, 292). Seator's subject, however, is not pure geometry, but an identifiable space. By situating the director's office in a public gallery, Seator also draws attention to the behind-the-scenes activities of the institution and to the sometimes elegant settings in which those activities take place. He also reminds us that every art work in a museum is not only an aesthetic enterprise, but a product of the place and time of its making.

B.D.O., 1997
Wood, steel, plasterboard, glass, electrical fittings, carpet, and paint, 195 x 160 x 250 in. (495.3 x 406.4 x 635 cm) overall
Purchase, with funds from the Contemporary Painting and Sculpture Committee 97.54

GEORGE SEGAL

1924–2000

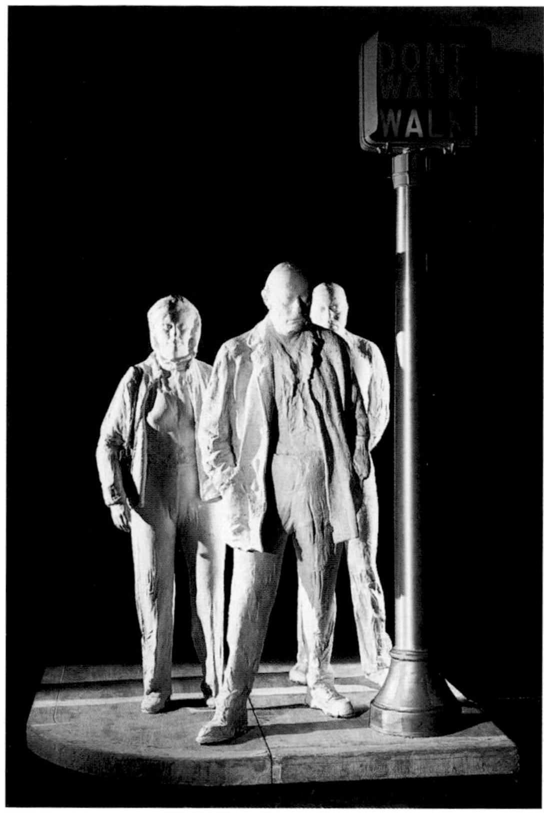

Though trained as a painter, George Segal turned to sculpture in the early 1960s. What became his signature style was the result of a fortuitous, seemingly inconsequential event: he was given a supply of medical bandaging used for setting broken bones and got the idea of wrapping live models in plaster-soaked gauze to form casts for his sculptures. When the gauze dried, Segal broke the molds off the models in sections, reassembled the parts, and then filled them with plaster. The mold of bandages was then removed.

The whiteness of the plaster lends a sense of weightlessness to the figures, usually family and friends presented as individuals or in small groups. The same uniform whiteness, however, along with the lack of detail and vacant eyes, creates ghostlike presences. This apparitional quality is balanced by the inclusion of mundane salvaged objects, such as the woman's purse and flashing traffic light in *Walk, Don't Walk.*

Though he occasionally treated religious, political, or historical themes, Segal generally set his figures in ordinary situations and occupations, expressive of what he called the "presence of man in his daily life." In *Walk, Don't Walk*, a momentary, banal experience—waiting for a traffic light to change—is forever fixed. The figures' inability to move is further emphasized by the light that continues to blink "walk" and "don't walk"—as if they are frozen by the conflicting instructions as much as by the hardness of dried plaster. Segal's haunting, motionless sculptures speak at once to the contradictory conditions that define contemporary life: the anonymous isolation of the individual in a community-driven society.

Walk, Don't Walk, 1976
Plaster, cement, metal, painted wood, and electric light, 104 x 72 x 72 in. (264.2 x 182.9 x 182.9 cm) overall
Purchase, with funds from the Louis and Bessie Adler Foundation, Inc., Seymour M. Klein, President, the Gilman Foundation, Inc., the Howard and Jean Lipman Foundation, Inc., and the National Endowment for the Arts 79.4

RICHARD SERRA

b. 1939

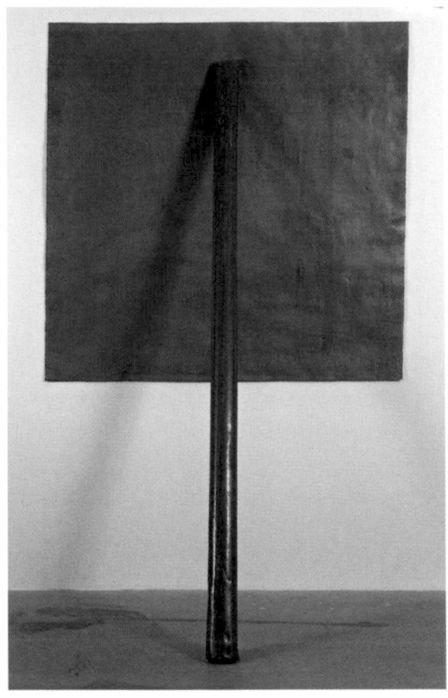

In the 1960s, Richard Serra employed the industrial materials and anti-illusionism of Minimalism to explore the physical conditions of making and viewing sculpture. Serra was particularly interested in the behavior and logic of his material, most often lead, and described his working method as "figuring out what lead does." By 1967, he had begun compiling a list of verbs—including "to roll, to crease, to fold, to bend." He then planned to subject his materials to each verbal action—rolling, creasing, folding, bending, etc.

For *Prop*, Serra rolled a sheet of lead into a pole form, which he then used to prop a square lead sheet against the wall. The work relies on the perpendicular supports of the floor and wall for its construction, creating a tenuous balance of thrust and counterthrust. This sustained tension and the possibility of collapse imposes on viewers a heightened awareness of their physical environment and personal vulnerability.

In his later work, including drawings such as *Out-of-Round IX*, Serra has continued to emphasize the physical properties of materials through his method of working. For the *Out-of-Round* series, he applied layers of oil stick, through a window screen, to paper he had placed on the floor. Working on the floor allowed him to make use of gravity. As he explained, "the compression of the materials is achieved with a gravitational load that is bearing down on them." This compression lends the drawing its uneven, tactile surface, as does the accumulative process of oil stick application. "You become the audience in reconstructing the process of their making," Serra noted, "that becomes part of the issue when you look at them."

Prop, 1968
Lead antimony, approximately 89 1/2 x 60 x 54 in. (227.3 x 154.9 x 137.2 cm) overall
Purchase, with funds from the Howard and Jean Lipman Foundation, Inc. 69.20a–b

Out-of-Round IX, 1999
Oil paint stick on paper, 79 1/2 x 79 1/2 in. (201.9 x 201.9 cm)
Purchase, with funds from James Hedges and an anonymous donor 2000.10

BEN SHAHN

1898–1969

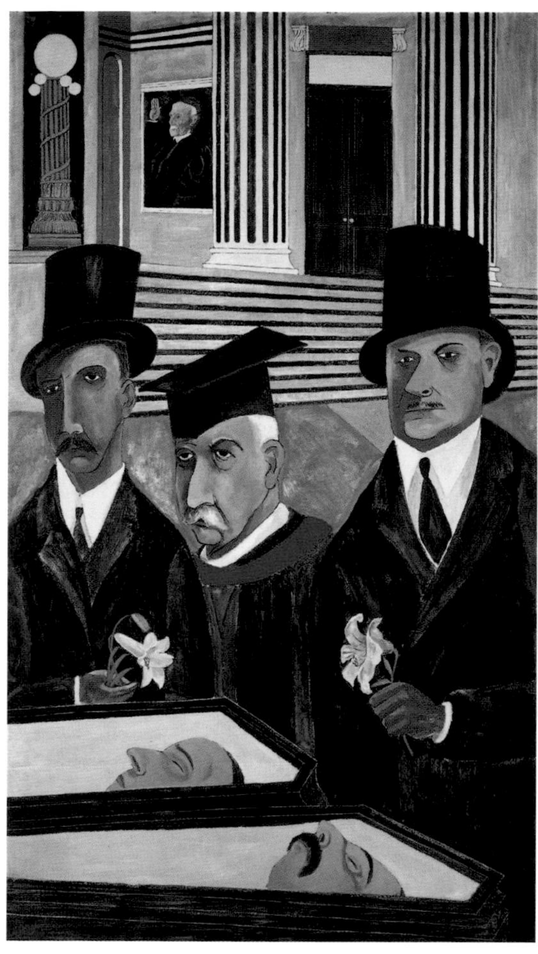

In the 1920s and 1930s, Ben Shahn was one of the foremost Social Realists—artists who used art as a vehicle to expose the grim realities of poverty and social injustice. Shahn, as a Jewish immigrant from Lithuania, had firsthand experience of discrimination in American society. In 1930, he began a series of twenty-three paintings devoted to what many considered a pulse-point of social agitation. The works told the story of two Italian immigrants, Nicola Sacco and Bartolomeo Vanzetti, who in 1927 had been sentenced to death for the murder of a shoe company employee in Massachusetts. The case against the two men was weak, and many believed they were executed because of their ethnicity and well-known anarchistic beliefs. Their execution initiated riots and protest demonstrations around the world.

Each painting in Shahn's *Sacco and Vanzetti* series presents a self-sustaining narrative. In the Whitney's large-scale canvas titled *The Passion of Sacco and Vanzetti*, Shahn depicted the immigrants lying in coffins. The judge who tried the case, Webster Thayer, appears in a background window, hand raised as if swearing in a witness—or himself swearing to tell the truth. Around the coffin stand the three members of the Lowell Committee, a group appointed by the governor of Massachusetts to determine whether the two immigrants deserved a retrial. When the committee rejected the appeal for a new trial, Sacco and Vanzetti were executed. In Shahn's biting image, two of the members proffer lilies, a fraudulent mourning gesture in view of their decision. But lilies are also a well-known symbol of the crucified Christ. Thus, with the same flower, Shahn sends another message: Sacco and Vanzetti are martyrs, punished for sins they did not commit.

The Passion of Sacco and Vanzetti, 1931–32
Tempera on canvas, 84 1/2 x 48 in. (214.6 x 121.9 cm)
Gift of Edith and Milton Lowenthal in memory of Juliana Force 49.22

JOEL SHAPIRO
b. 1941

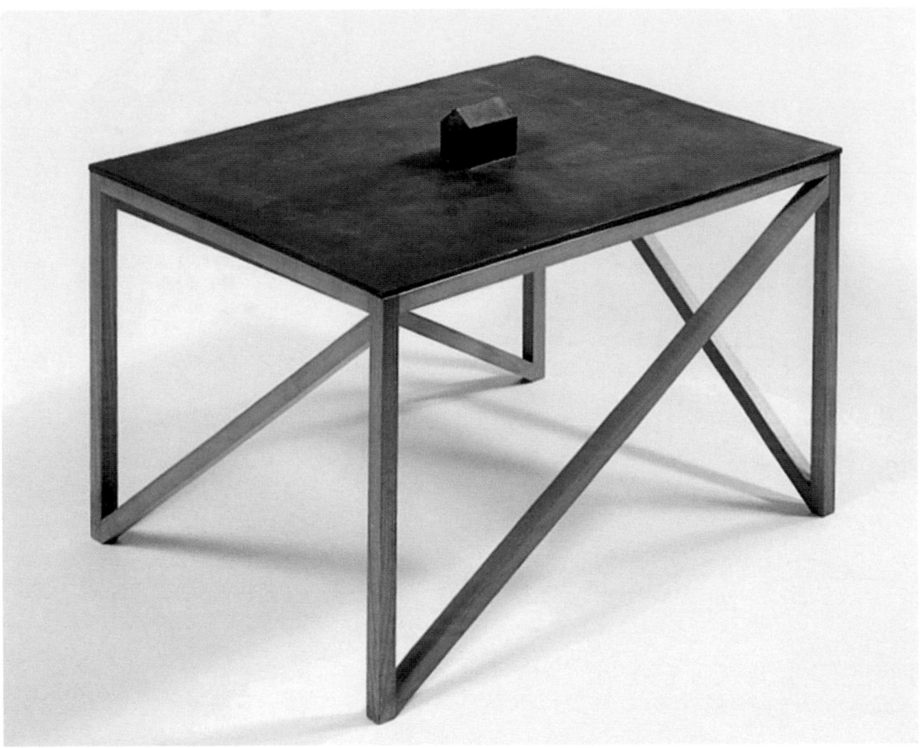

In the late 1960s, at the outset of his career, Joel Shapiro used abstract forms to explore the most basic properties of mass in space, including size and weight, gravity and inertia. By 1972, he had begun to examine the same issues by inverting the properties of simple, recognizable imagery: a chair, a horse, a bridge. All were radically reduced in scale, creating oddly powerful disturbances of the spatial dynamics in their immediate vicinity.

In *Untitled (House on Field)*, both the tiny house and its small-scale environment are subjected to this kind of distortion. Looking at this work calls for actively focused and refocused attention in order to reconcile each element with its context—house to field, field to table, table to floor. Then, in a final provocation, the whole must be reconciled to the viewer's own space and physical stature, in a body-to-body procedure that runs directly counter to the intuitive size correction we make when an object as familiar as a house is shown at the "wrong" scale, set on the "wrong" foundation. The process also has an emotional component, which Shapiro acknowledges: "This house is not engaged so much with the space that it actually occupies, but functions in a much more psychologically determined space instead. It is removed. It is very sentimental. It gives a real sense of isolation."

Untitled (House on Field), 1975–76
Bronze on wood base, 20 7/8 x 28 7/8 x 21 9/16 in. (53 x 73.3 x 54.8 cm) overall
Purchase, with funds from Mrs. Oscar Kolin 76.22a–b

CHARLES SHEELER

1883–1965

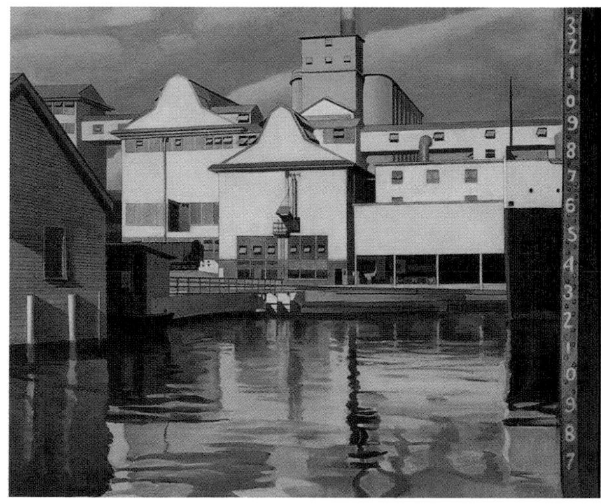

Charles Sheeler, along with fellow Precisionists Charles Demuth and Elsie Driggs (pp. 89, 96), used hard-edged forms and geometric structure to create images of order and stability that paid tribute to industrial America.

Sheeler was also a commercial photographer, and in 1927 he was hired to photograph the newly opened Ford Motor Company plant on the Rouge River, outside Detroit. His photographs and subsequent paintings of River Rouge, as it was called, ignored the automobile production at the plant and concentrated instead on the section that transformed raw materials into steel. *River Rouge Plant* depicts the facility where coal was processed into fuel; in the foreground is a boat slip and the bows of ships that transported the coal. Both the plant and the slip are reflected in the serenely still water that occupies almost the entire lower half of the painting. In Sheeler's vision, American factories and other industrial monuments were the modern equivalent of the cathedral, "our substitute," he said, "for religious experience."

Sheeler also exalted the functionalism of the simple barns of Bucks County, Pennsylvania. From 1914 to 1917, he photographed interior and exterior views of the pre-Revolutionary stone farmhouse in Doylestown, where he spent most weekends. He later translated a number of these photographs into tempera or crayon drawings. Even in densely complex works such as *Interior, Bucks County Barn*, his precise rendering reveals the inherent formal beauty in the functional carriage, tools, and other farm equipment.

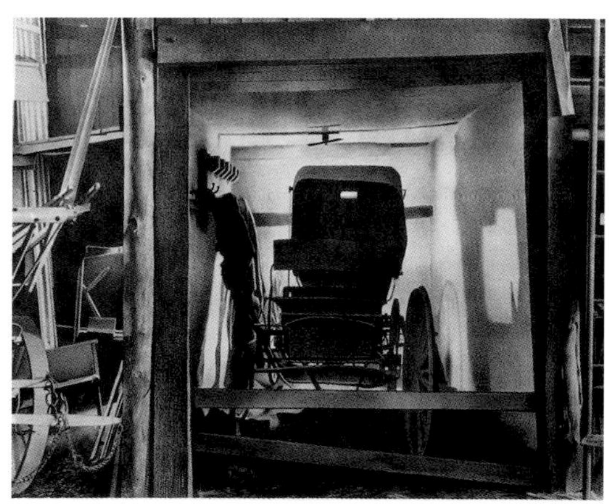

River Rouge Plant, 1932
Oil on canvas, 20 x 24 1/8 in. (50.8 x 61.3 cm)
Purchase 32.43

Interior, Bucks County Barn, 1932
Crayon on paper, mounted on board, 20 1/4 x 24 1/4 in. (51.4 x 61.6 cm)
Purchase 33.78

CINDY SHERMAN

b. 1954

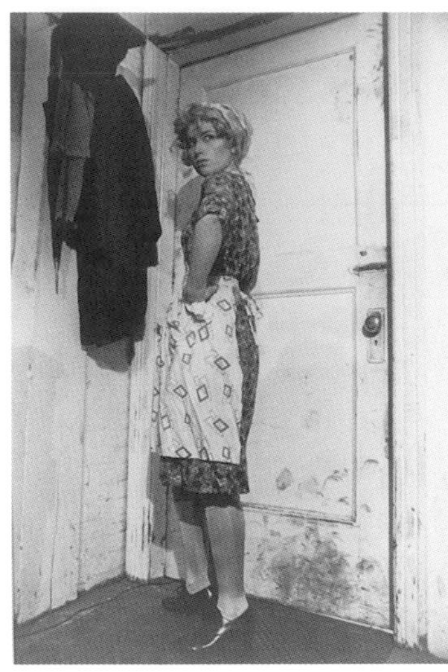

Cindy Sherman's photographs explore the ways our culture defines femininity, sexuality, fantasy, and spectatorship. Subject and object of much of her own work, Sherman uses so-called set-up photography—staged and posed studio photography—to perform the roles she both plays and photographs herself: aspiring-and-failing starlets, fake fashion models, characters in famous paintings and fairy tales.

In 1977, Sherman began her *Untitled Film Stills*, a series that eventually grew to sixty-nine black-and-white images representing an array of faux B-grade Hollywood heroines of the 1950s (all played by Sherman), each one a different female stereotype. The characters are photographed and the images crudely printed to suggest cheap, 8 x 10-inch film stills—from movies that never existed.

The dramatic, off-screen glance and low-angle shot of the woman in *Untitled Film Still #35* is typical of the way Sherman recycles the dramatic conventions of narrative cinema—we don't need a movie title to recognize a Sophia Loren-type housewife. But if the *Film Stills* suggest familiar pictures, they also speak of voyeurism: all Sherman's women direct their glances at an implied spectator out of the picture but not out of mind.

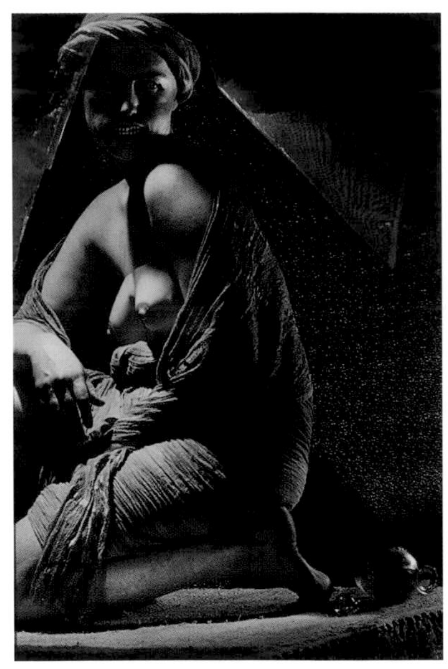

Untitled #146 belongs to a later series of color photographs in which Sherman chose deeply saturated colors to conjure up the look of cheap 1970s horror movies as well as fashion and advertising photography. Here she plays an exotic, slightly sinister *Arabian Nights* character with an oddly made-up face and gag-store breasts, the bizarre effect of the whole accentuated by the melodramatic lighting. Although we may recognize this type of vamp, here, as in all of Sherman's masquerades, the identity of the woman, as well as her narrative, remains unfixed and open-ended.

Untitled Film Still #35, 1979
Gelatin silver print, 9 7/16 x 6 3/8 in. (24 x 16.2 cm)
Gift of Barbara and Eugene Schwartz 88.50.4

Untitled #146, 1985
Silver dye bleach print (Cibachrome), 71 9/16 x 48 1/8 in. (181.8 x 122.2 cm)
Purchase, with funds from Eli and Edythe L. Broad 87.49

EVERETT SHINN

1876–1953

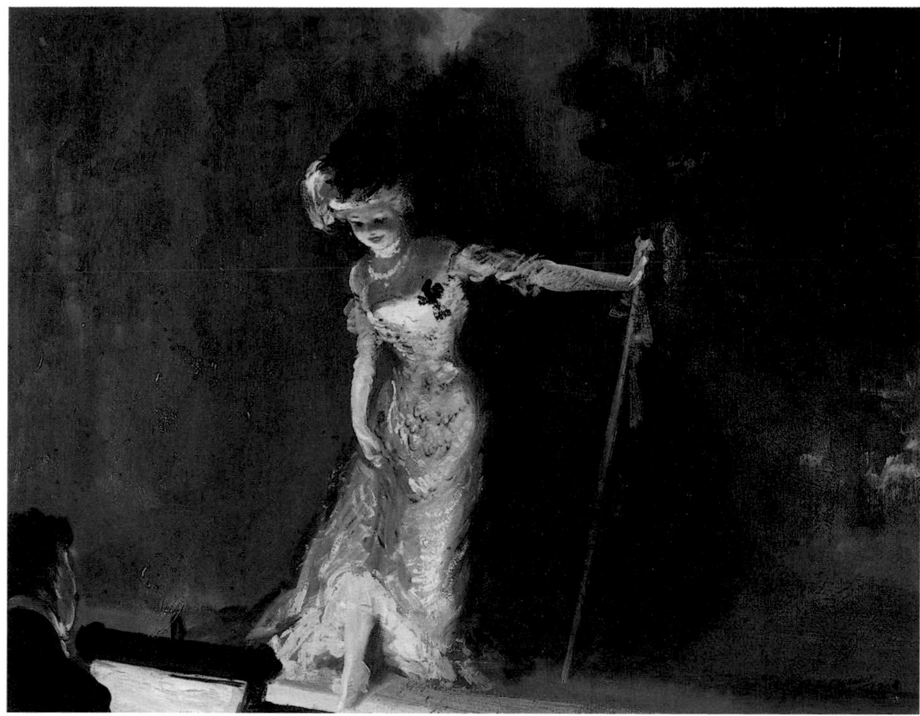

Everett Shinn developed his facility for capturing the fleeting scenes of urban life while working as a newspaper illustrator in Philadelphia, where he met Robert Henri and fellow illustrators William Glackens, George Luks, and John Sloan (pp. 115, 191, 287). The Ashcan artists, as the group later came to be known, found their subject matter in the vernacular themes and spectacles of the modern city.

By 1903, the theater had become Shinn's primary subject. He had moved to New York a few years earlier (as had Henri, Luks, and Glackens), where thriving vaudeville houses drew crowds from every social class. Shinn's paintings and drawings portray dancers kicking, orchestra leaders conducting, and trapeze artists swinging, often from angles that afford glimpses of the enrapt audience. *Revue*, however, dispenses with wild action. With broad, loose brushstrokes, Shinn reveals a dancer, her face warmly bathed by the footlights, exposing her ankle in mid-curtsy. His brushwork picks out the dainty ruffles and elaborate textures of the dancer's dress, while at lower left the gently oblique point of view admits the orchestra leader. Significantly, *Revue* was one of the paintings Shinn selected to represent his work in the landmark 1908 exhibition of urban realism organized by Robert Henri at the Macbeth Galleries in New York. The Eight, as the eight artists in the show were quickly dubbed, had individual styles, but all were rebelling against the rarefied and aristocratic themes long demanded by the academic establishment.

Revue, 1908
Oil on canvas, 18 x 24 in. (45.7 x 61 cm)
Gift of Gertrude Vanderbilt Whitney 31.346

SHAHZIA SIKANDER

b. 1969

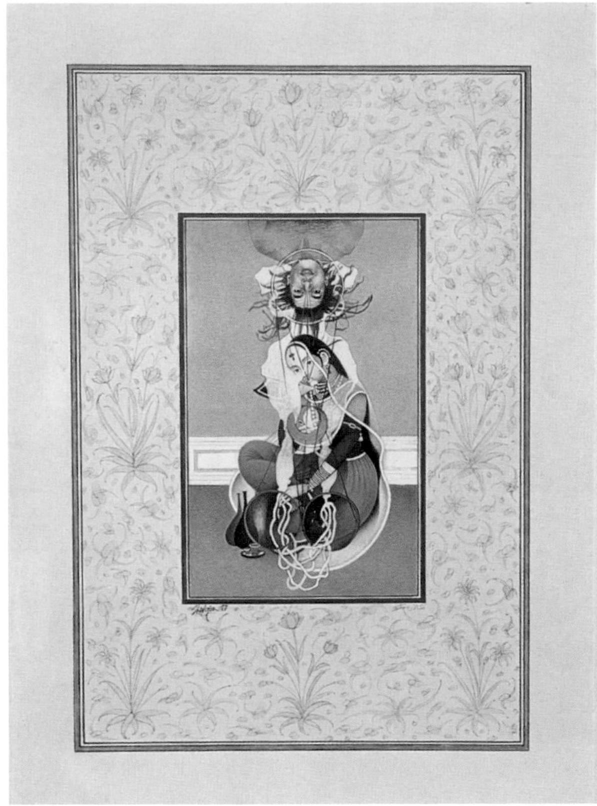

Born and raised in Pakistan, Shahzia Sikander studied first at the National College of Arts in Lahore and later at the Rhode Island School of Design. Although the National College of Arts embraced European and American aesthetics, Sikander found herself drawn to more traditional Asian forms. This interest led her to study miniature painting—an erudite form, introduced to India by Islamic conquerors, which flourished from the fifteenth through the eighteenth centuries. Sikander learned to prepare her own paper, make pigments from plants and minerals, and fashion brushes from squirrel hair. She became adept at applying multiple layers of opaque and translucent watercolors and painting foliate borders and classical figure types from Persian, Mughal, Kangra, Deccan, and Rajput sources.

Sikander's unique personal idiom exploits the fragmented forms and visual disjunctions of European modernism to introduce elements of contemporary reality into the rarefied realm of miniaturism. The seated female figure in *Reinventing the Dislocation*, for example, is an image of the artist herself. But instead of modern dress, Sikander wears traditional Persian attire. An upside-down portrait of Rick Lowe—an African-American artist and founder of a community arts center in one of Houston's poorest neighborhoods—floats improbably above her head. Although isolated in their separate spheres, Sikander and Lowe are linked through a network of thin black lines and the white cloudlike form that envelops them. In *Reinventing the Dislocation*, Sikander updates an ancient form to reflect her own past and present and give miniature painting a new—and utterly contemporary—life.

Reinventing the Dislocation, 1997
Vegetable pigment, dry pigment, watercolor, and tea water on paper,
12 15/16 x 9 1/4 in. (32.9 x 23.5 cm)
Purchase, with funds from the Drawing Committee 97.83.4

GARY SIMMONS

b. 1964

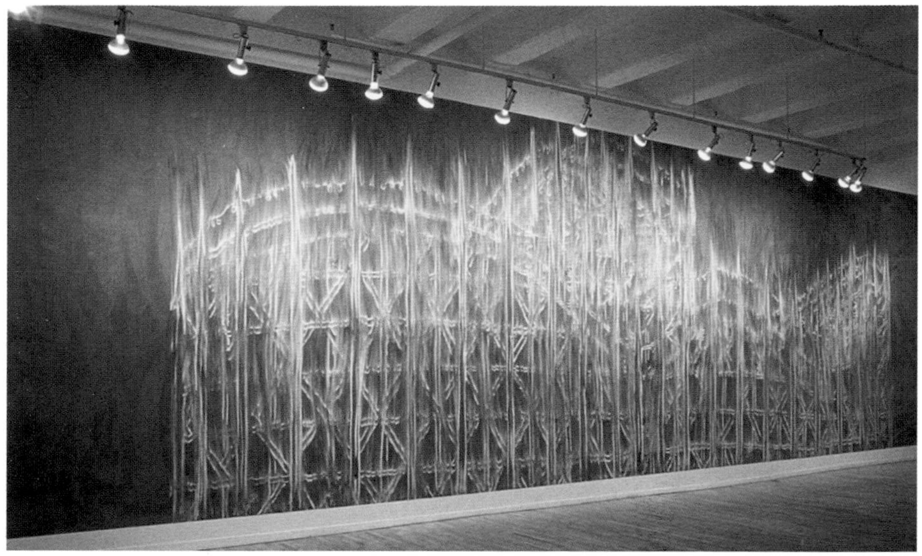

Built for speed and danger, roller coasters are nothing if not opportunities for noisy, visceral fun. On the other hand, in Gary Simmons' *Ghoster*, a roller coaster drawn with chalk on a blackboardlike surface is ghostly, silent, and still. Like all the works in this series, which is entitled *Erasure Drawings*, *Ghoster* is partly erased, as if preparation for the next day's lesson had already begun—or as if the image had been dimmed by failing memory. Simmons, who has worked in an extraordinarily wide range of media, often uses imagery of disappearance, from ephemeral stars written in smoke by airplanes, to a vacant boxing ring, to empty, child-size Klu Klux Klan robes.

The *Erasure Drawings* were inspired, in part, by the abandoned blackboards Simmons found in an old schoolhouse where he had a studio in the late 1980s. Many of the initial drawings featured racially typecast cartoon characters. "I wanted to show how we can attempt to erase a stereotype, but the image won't easily go away. It persists," says Simmons, who is African-American. Many subsequent *Erasure Drawings* have depicted images of violence or loss—a shipwreck, a vacant throne, and an empty ballroom lit by an ornate chandelier which, close inspection reveals, is made up of spinning nooses.

The *Erasure Drawings* invoke a wide range of references, from Robert Rauschenberg's notorious erasure of a drawing by Willem de Kooning and the progressively obscured texts in Glenn Ligon's work (p. 187), to Ralph Ellison's landmark 1952 novel *Invisible Man*, which linked erasure inseparably to race. Simmons himself cites the influence of sculptor Robert Irwin (p. 150), whose early work often operated, like Simmons' own, at the threshold of visibility.

Ghoster, 1997
Synthetic polymer and chalk on wall
Purchase, with funds from the Contemporary Painting and Sculpture Committee 97.100

LAURIE SIMMONS
b. 1949

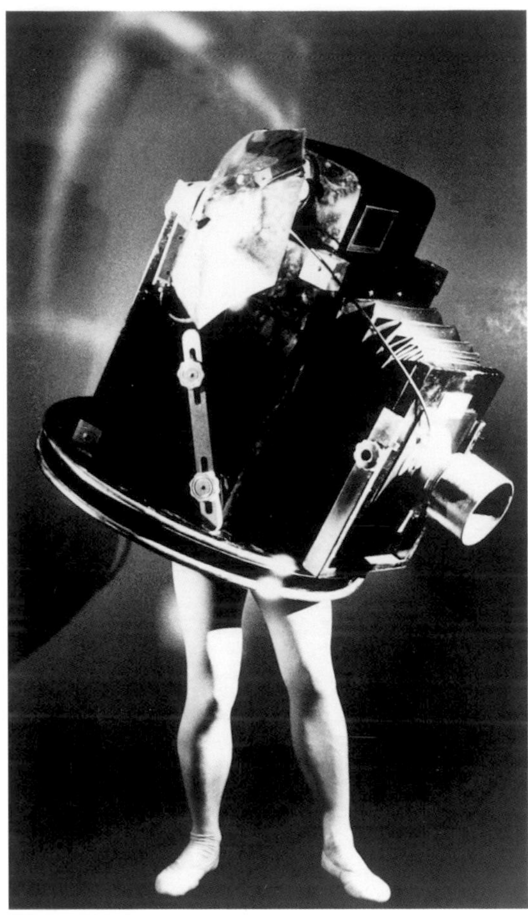

Laurie Simmons was at the forefront of a generation of artists emerging around 1980, including Cindy Sherman (p. 278), who staged and then photographed fictional scenes. Simmons' tableaux explore the ambiguities of the animate and the inanimate, incorporating dolls, dollhouse interiors, underwater ballet, ventriloquists, mannequins, walking objects, and occasionally real people. Whatever their components, the finished photographs often take their visual cues from 1950s television, advertising, and films.

To make *Walking Camera II (Jimmy the Camera)*, Simmons borrowed an oversize camera prop from a Broadway production of *The Wiz*. The result is a larger-than-life, black-and-white photograph of an anthropomorphized camera, wearing dancing tights and ballet shoes. Characteristically humorous, Simmons' hybrid is reminiscent of a mid-century advertisement for Old Gold cigarettes. But it was prompted by the artist's childhood recollection of a slightly different scene: "I had seen when I was a child in the fifties a TV show where there were dancing cigarette boxes and dancing matchboxes, and it always stayed with me as a kind of image of something that was so physical, without a brain, without a heart, without a mind—but maybe something just about joyousness and gleefulness and fun. Those ideas spawned the image of the camera on legs."

Simmons' subject is the chimerical nature of mass media imagery, and the glare of bright, studio lighting in *Walking Camera II* reflects a precious concoction of Hollywood-like artifice. But the camera's congenial pose helps create a delightful balance of magic and fancy. Such imagery, Simmons suggests, may be artificial, but it is also the stuff that dreams are made of.

Walking Camera II (Jimmy the Camera), 1987
Gelatin silver print, 82 13/16 x 47 1/2 in. (210.3 x 120.7 cm)
Purchase, with funds from the Photography Committee 94.107

JOHN F. SIMON, JR.

b. 1963

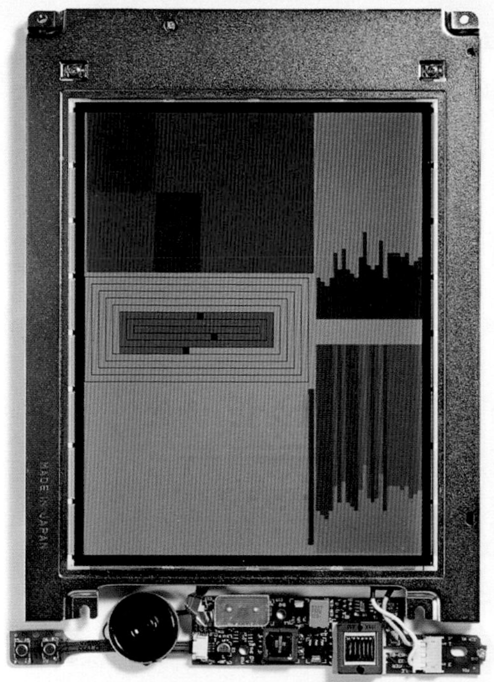

Displayed on a flat-panel computer screen, *Color Panel v1.0* is an art work in the form of a computer program. The software, which Simon wrote himself, "controls the screen, draws the composition, picks the colors, moves the colors," producing constantly evolving compositions of squares and rectangles that deliberately evoke early modernist geometric abstraction. Simon cites the influence of Johannes Itten and Josef Albers (p. 29), teachers at the Bauhaus in Germany in the 1920s and 1930s, who explored the apparent changes in hue caused by placing different colors next to each other. To this phenomenon, *Color Panel v1.0* adds the element of time and, crucially, of endless variation: its beginning is variable, and its sequences never repeat, progressing over a time frame that approaches eternity.

A native of Louisiana, Simon studied art and geology as an undergraduate; he received a master's degree in earth and planetary science before completing a second graduate degree, in fine arts. The methods and technology associated with hard science remain central to his practice, but no more so than twentieth-century art. In addition to Itten and Albers, Simon claims as "heroes" Piet Mondrian and Paul Klee, two other major abstractionists, who "showed how artists could be working analytically and still be doing art." Influential for the same reason is Sol LeWitt (p. 184): by writing directives for drawings to be executed by others, LeWitt set the precedent for Simon's end run around the conventional limitations of pictorial composition.

Color Panel v1.0, 1999
Software and synthetic polymer on Apple PowerBook 280C, dimensions variable
Purchase, with funds from the Painting and Sculpture Committee 99.88a-c

CHARLES SIMONDS

b. 1945

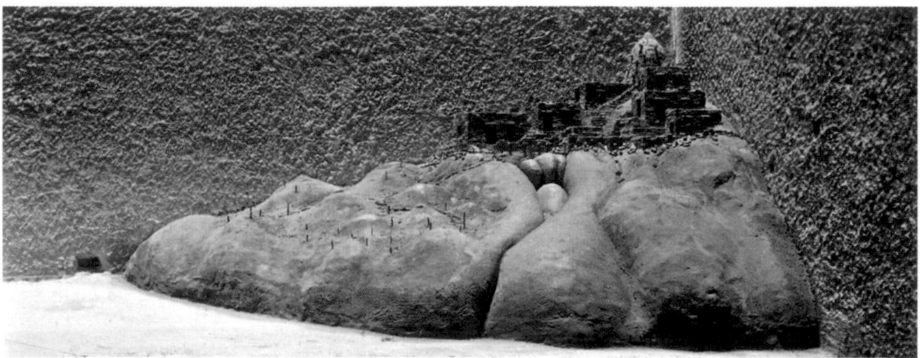

Charles Simonds' diminutive sculptures, which he calls "dwellings," began appearing in New York's SoHo neighborhood in 1970, spilling from niches of dilapidated brick buildings, perched high up on window ledges, and sunk into gutters. Simonds described these structures, which resemble miniature archaeological ruins, as part of "an endless series of dwelling places for an imaginary civilization of Little People." Each dwelling, seemingly abandoned and in disrepair, represented a different historical time and place. Constructed of earthy materials such as red clay, sand, twigs, and stone—and subject to the natural elements and the destructive whims of passersby—Simonds' dwellings were fragile, urban counterparts to the bigger, more dramatic Earth art of Robert Smithson (p. 293) and others, which transcended the physical limitations of traditional art venues.

With *Dwellings*, a three-part work commissioned by the Whitney Museum in 1981, Simonds challenges the notion of a work of art as a discrete and precious object and confronts traditional boundaries between, in his words, "inside/outside and real world/museum." The most accessible element of the work, nestled in one of the Museum's stairwell landings, is positioned above a window that looks out on the other two components; these sit on the second-story windowsill and on a rooftop chimney of the former Chemical Bank building across the street. As in his other *Dwellings*, Simonds staked out his territory by covering chicken wire with a layer of red clay, on which he crafted his Lilliputian ghost towns. By placing three of them within visual proximity, he suggests a progression of habitation and abandonment by his fictional nomads and slyly reminds viewers to look beyond museum walls. The stairwell dwelling, with its tiny organic forms, playfully exaggerates the machine-made monumentality of the Museum's building, designed in 1966 by Marcel Breuer.

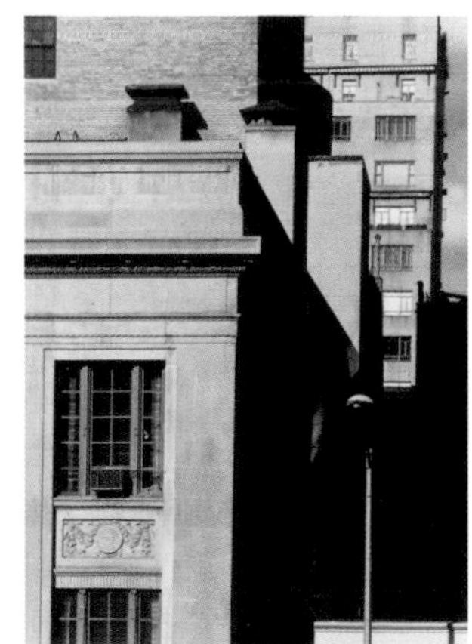

Dwellings, 1981
Clay, sand, sticks, stones, wood, plaster, cloth, and chicken wire: a) 17 3/4 x 39 1/2 x 29 in. (45.1 x 100.3 x 73.7 cm); b) 10 3/8 x 29 3/8 x 7 3/4 in. (26.4 x 74.6 x 19.7 cm); c) 8 x 29 x 13 3/4 in. (20.3 x 73.7 x 34.9 cm)
Purchase, with funds from the Louis and Bessie Adler Foundation, Inc., Seymour M. Klein, President 81.11a–c

LORNA SIMPSON

b. 1960

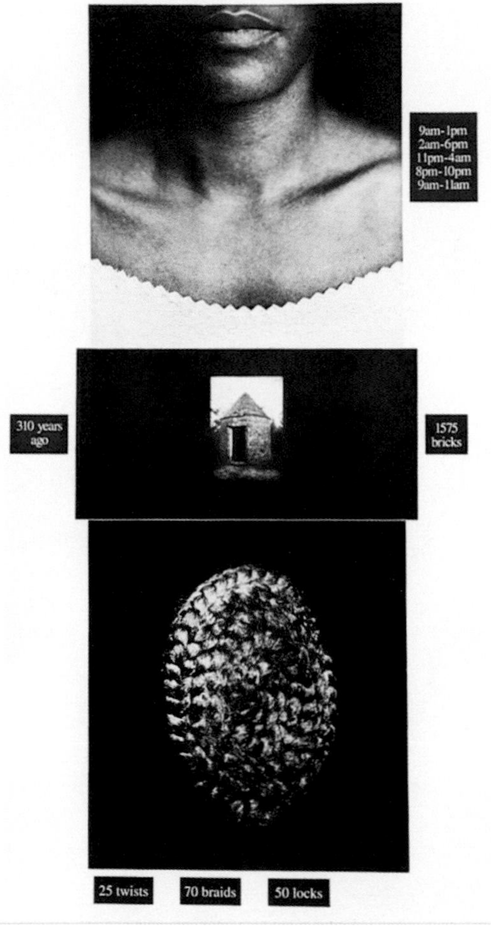

Lorna Simpson's *Counting*, a large-scale print combining photogravure and serigraph techniques, presents three evocative images, each annotated with elliptical enumerations. The top one, a closely cropped view of a woman's upper torso, neck, chin, and mouth, is accompanied by a sequence of seemingly random time periods. Are these work shifts? Appointment calendar notations? Elements of a medical chart? The piece leaves us without answers, though the profoundly anonymous character of the woman, so reduced as to be nearly genderless, ageless, and classless, endows the numerical sequence with an element of mechanization and alienation.

The central panel represents a round brick structure with a conical roof. This small building is actually a South Carolina smokehouse of the type that was sometimes used to house slaves. On either side, Simpson has placed the phrases "310 years ago" and "1575 bricks," thereby creating a poetic resonance between two systems of counting, one temporal and the other physical. Thus the artist metaphorically compares the weight of history to the physical weight of the bricks that are stacked to create a space of detention.

The bottom panel shows an oval coil of braided hair, beneath which are three text panels that enumerate the numbers of twists, braids, and locks. Here the words "twist" and "lock," which refer directly to the innocuous practice of hairstyling, also resonate with the insidious themes opened up by the image above. *Counting* deftly eludes a simplistic historical reading while evoking multiple dimensions of African-American history and daily life experience.

Counting, 1991
Photogravure and screenprint, 73 3/4 x 37 7/8 in. (187.3 x 96.2 cm)
Purchase, with funds from the Print Committee 93.94

AARON SISKIND

1903–1991

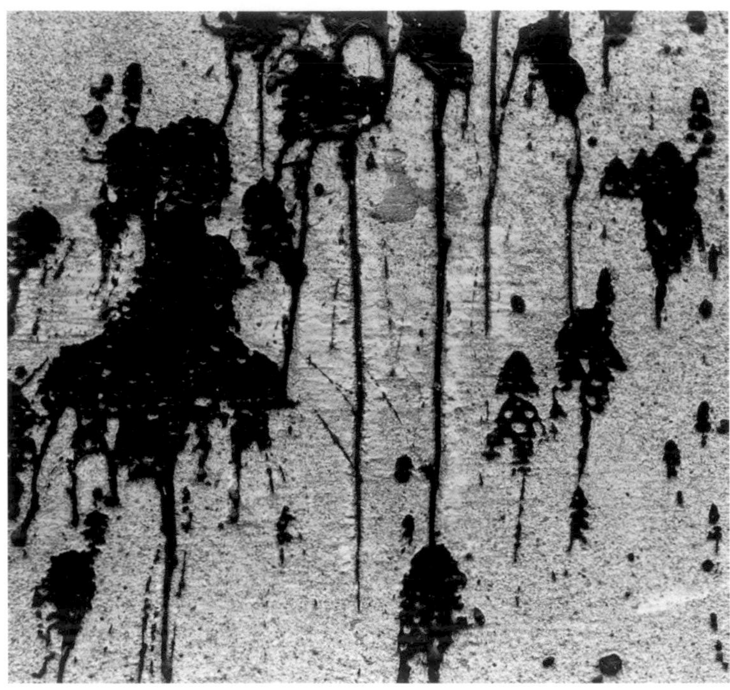

Aaron Siskind's early career as a photographer was marked by his work on *The Harlem Document* (1938–40), a social documentary project that he led under the auspices of the socialist Photo League. By 1940, however, Siskind had left the organization, and his work assumed a more abstract focus. "For some reason or other there was in me the desire to see the world clean and fresh and alive....The so-called documentary picture left me wanting something."

Over the next ten years, Siskind focused on the expressive power of inanimate urban detritus such as torn posters, graffiti, and peeling paint. *Chicago 1*, a close-up detail of a paint-splattered Chicago wall, exemplifies his technique of holding the camera perpendicular to the surface in order to collapse pictorial space into two dimensions. "First and emphatically," he said in 1950, "I accept the flat plane of the picture surface as the primary frame of reference in the picture." Not surprisingly, Siskind's calligraphic gestures have a kinship with those of the Abstract Expressionists, particularly the black-and-white abstractions of Franz Kline (p. 165). Indeed, the two artists were close friends.

The crisp focus of *Chicago 1* sensuously details the wall's rough salt-and-pepper textures, the articulated edges of its dark stains, and the softer white streaks. Siskind used deliberate cropping and high-contrast printing to create "a new object to be contemplated for its own meaning and its own beauty," a subjective expression that raises the image above its mundane origins.

Chicago 1, 1949
Gelatin silver print, 10 5/8 x 11 1/8 in. (27 x 28.3 cm)
Purchase, with funds from the Photography Committee 99.6

JOHN SLOAN

1871–1951

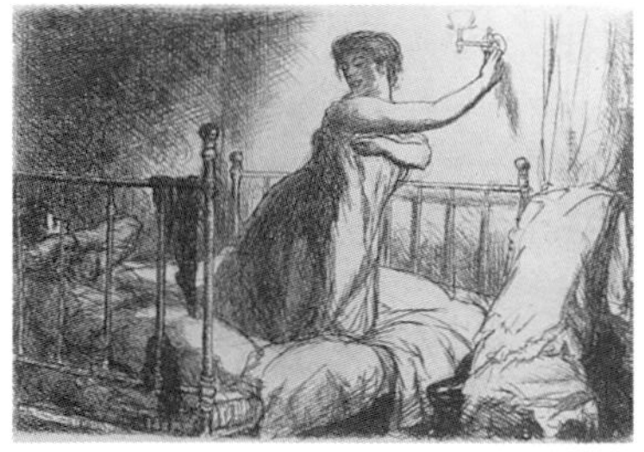

A champion of urban realism, John Sloan was one of the revolutionary artists known as The Eight, who flourished in New York in the first years of the twentieth century, painting everyday themes rather than lofty academic subjects. Sloan began his career as a staff illustrator at two Philadelphia newspapers. When he came to New York to devote himself to painting, his newspaper background served him well in works that give the commonplace a sense of dignity and even of romance.

The etching *Turning Out the Light* and the painting *Backyards, Greenwich Village* render the banal details of city life with poetic reverie. Each one also includes the viewer in private moments of the subjects' lives: a woman about to go to sleep, children engaged in backyard play—both scenes normally hidden from passersby on the street. For Sloan, making such moments public was a way of lending dignity to lives that otherwise went unnoticed.

The Picnic Grounds depicts young men and women cavorting in a wooded picnic ground on Decoration Day, 1907. The rapidity of Sloan's brushstrokes matches the animated motions of the frolicking figures. This work is particularly notable for the interaction of lively female figures with their male counterparts, in an era when normal academic practice required women to be painted as isolated, introspective beings.

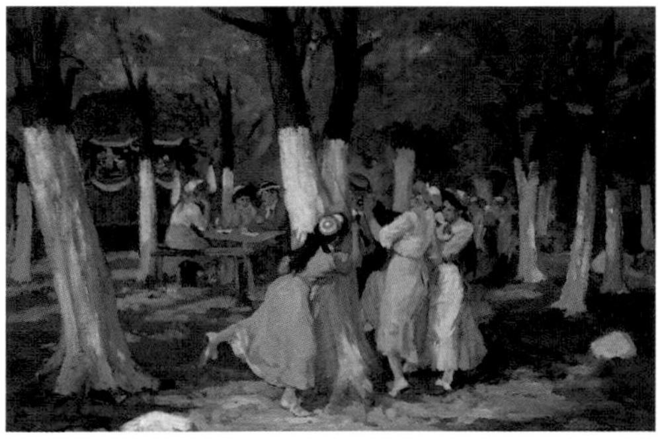

Turning Out the Light, 1905
Etching: sheet, 7 13/16 x 11 1/4 in. (19.8 x 28.6 cm); plate, 4 5/8 x 6 5/8 in. (11.7 x 16.8 cm)
Purchase 31.821

Backyards, Greenwich Village, 1914
Oil on canvas, 26 x 32 in. (66 x 81.3 cm)
Purchase 36.153

The Picnic Grounds, 1906–07
Oil on canvas, 24 x 36 in. (61 x 91.4 cm)
Purchase 41.34

DAVID SMITH
1906–1965

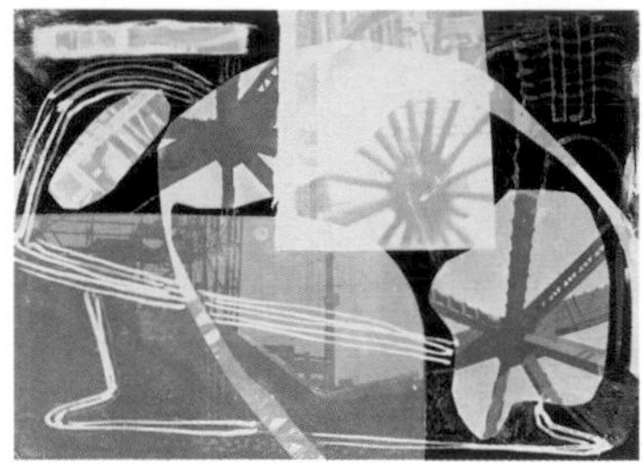

David Smith revolutionized the medium of American sculpture by fusing the methods, materials, and scale of modern American industry with the aesthetic developments of leading European avant-garde artists. In the 1930s, he was primarily a painter, but he also experimented with Cubist collage in a series of tiny photomontages such as the untitled work seen here. Layering multiple negatives and then "sandwich-printing" them onto a single sheet, he created a surreal landscape that combines multiple perspectives of industrial dockyards with abstract forms.

Smith's shift to sculpture also began in the 1930s, inspired by Pablo Picasso's and Julio González's welded metal sculptures. Under their influence, he assembled discarded scraps of iron and steel into small yet dramatic sculptures, using the welding skills he had developed one summer while employed in a Studebaker factory.

In the 1940s, Smith began working on a larger scale, seen here in the 1951 *Hudson River Landscape*. The sculpture was prompted by the view he saw on his frequent train trips between New York City and Bolton Landing, the small town in the Adirondack Mountains where he lived and worked from 1940 until his death. In this "drawing in steel," as the works in this series came to be known, Smith transformed agricultural tool fragments and foundry castoffs into a semi-abstract landscape through a direct welding process that preserved the industrial character of the individual components. He capitalized on steel's tensile strength and his own welding virtuosity to construct new sculptural forms that balanced mass and weightlessness. A free-flowing steel line sketches out an animated tableau of natural forms—clouds, rocky terrain, a river, and train tracks—around a large open space. The almost calligraphic line has an affinity with the gestural brushstrokes of Smith's Abstract Expressionist colleagues, as do the bold, swift gestures and drips of paint in the tempera drawing *Eng No. 6*, one of the thousands of drawings Smith produced. Unlike his labor-intensive sculptures, drawing—whether preliminary sketches or independent conceptions—offered Smith a sense of immediacy and spontaneity.

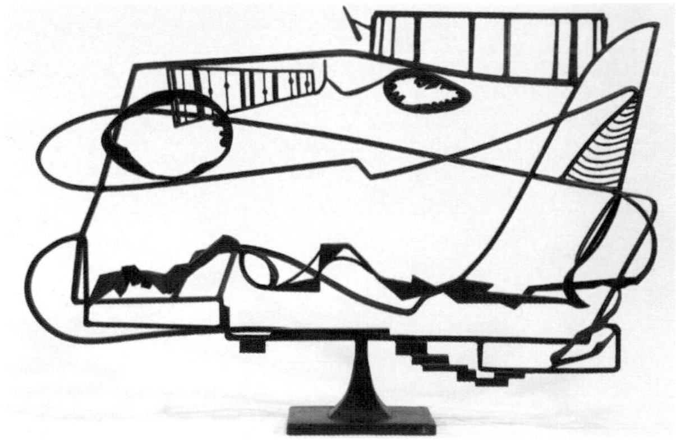

Untitled, c. 1932–35
Gelatin silver print, 3 1/2 x 4 3/4 in. (8.9 x 12.1 cm)
Purchase, with funds from the Harriett Ames Charitable Trust and the Photography Committee 98.28.4

Hudson River Landscape, 1951
Welded painted steel and stainless steel, 49 15/16 x 73 3/4 x 16 9/16 in. (126.8 x 187.3 x 42.1 cm)
Purchase 54.14

DAVID SMITH

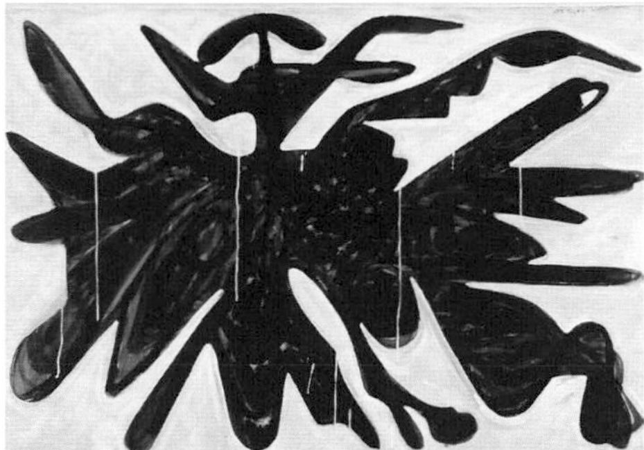

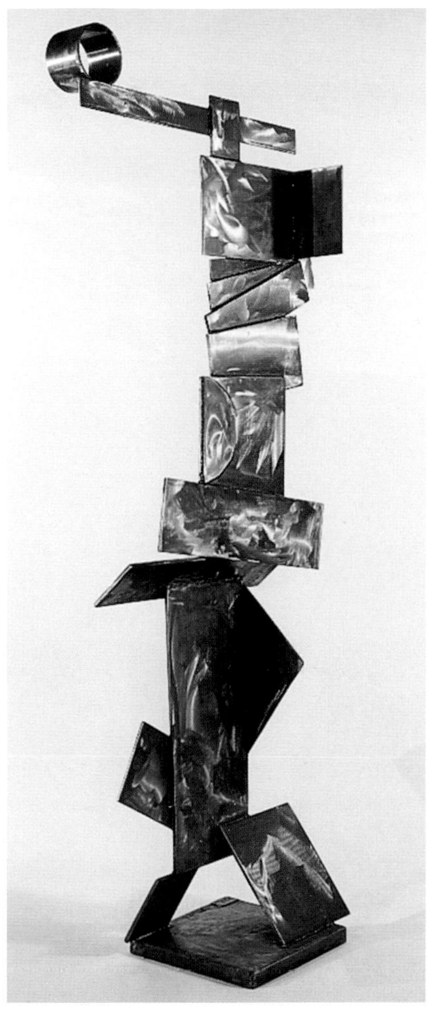

In his prolific final decades, Smith operated Terminal Iron Works, his studio in Bolton Landing, like a machine shop—complete with assistants, stockpiles of materials, and trade tools—which allowed him to develop several series of increasingly monumental sculptures at the same time. *Lectern Sentinel* (the seventh in a nine-work series) is a carefully balanced stack of shimmering planes crowned by an I-beam and cylinder—Smith's conversion of the overlapping forms of Cubist collage into large-scale sculpture. The highly reflective, crisp industrial character of stainless steel complements the work's simplified geometric form, yet Smith also lightly burnished each facet with swirling patterns that give the sculpture an organic element. Although *Lectern Sentinel* is more abstract than the earlier scrap-metal works, its vertical orientation and frontal planarity produce definite figural associations—an anthropomorphic reading reinforced by the title and by the message to his two young daughters that Smith soldered into the sculpture's base: "I greet you. Becca—Dida."

Eng No. 6, 1952
Tempera and oil on paper, 29 3/4 x 42 1/4 in. (75.6 x 107.3 cm)
Purchase, with funds from Agnes Gund and an anonymous donor 79.43

Lectern Sentinel, 1961
Stainless steel, 101 3/4 x 33 x 20 1/2 in. (258.4 x 83.8 x 52.1 cm)
Purchase, with funds from the Friends of the Whitney Museum of American Art 62.15

KIKI SMITH
b. 1954

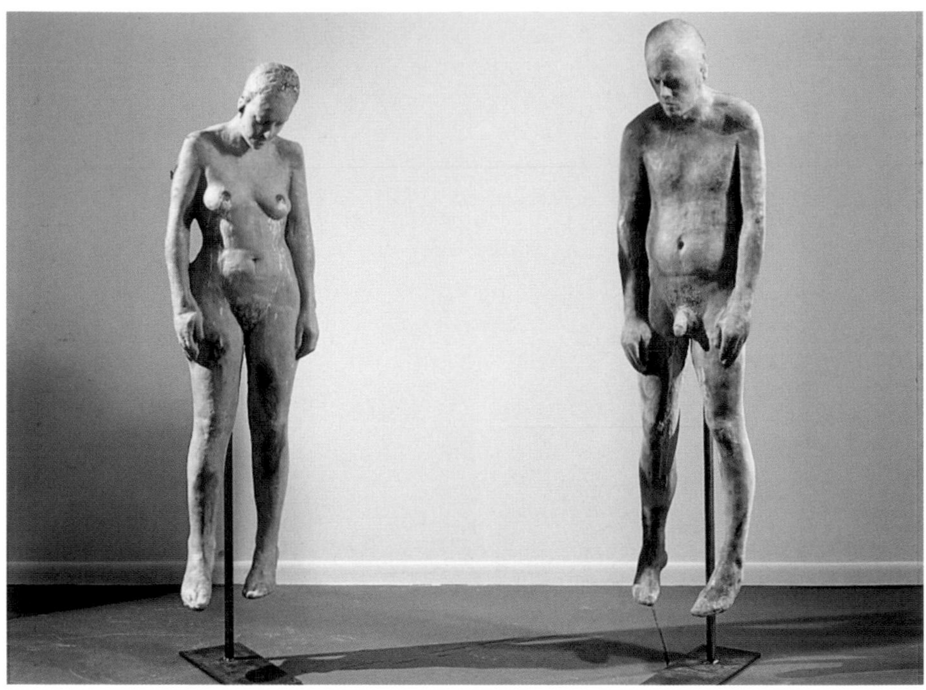

Since the 1980s, Kiki Smith has centered much of her work around the human body—distorting it, fragmenting it, making visible what is usually imperceptible or private. "I use the body because it is our primary vehicle for experiencing our lives. It's something everyone shares," she has explained. The daughter of Tony Smith (p. 292), she at one time studied to be an emergency medical technician, and her hand-wrought sculptures convey an obsessive attention to anatomical detail. Fascinated by mythologies and legends, she often draws on biblical subject matter, particularly themes that prominently involve the female body.

Untitled is one of Smith's earliest forays into large-scale wax sculpture. Two figures, one male and one female, hang limply from adjacent poles; milk drips from the woman's breasts and semen runs down the legs of the man. Although these are life-giving secretions, both figures appear suspended in a state near death. Layers of red-tinted wax suggest the vulnerable translucency of flesh and internal organs.

Untitled (from "Lot's Wife") is a photograph of one of Smith's sculptures. In Genesis, angels led Lot and his family from Sodom just before God destroyed the sinful city. But Lot's wife disobeyed the angels' instruction not to look back and was instantly turned into a pillar of salt. To Smith, Lot's wife represents a biblical female with a will of her own. But the narrative also allowed Smith to explore in sculptural terms the disintegration of a body. The photograph shows Lot's wife, caught at the moment of transformation. The left

Untitled, 1990
Beeswax and microcrystalline wax figures on metal stands:
female figure, 73 1/2 in. (186.7 cm) height; male figure, 76 15/16 in. (195.4 cm) height
Purchase, with funds from the Painting and Sculpture Committee 91.13a–d

portion of her face seems to be dissolving into salt, and, one imagines, this process will quickly overtake the untouched right side. Lot's wife is poised at a moment between two states.

In the mid-1980s, Smith began experimenting with printmaking techniques. Rather than using the printing process to make multiple examples of an image, she produced unique objects composed of repeated images. In *All Souls*, an image of five babies curled in fetal position appears thirty-six times, each on a piece of Thai tissue paper that Smith glued together. Close examination of *All Souls* reveals that each of the repeated images differs slightly from the next in density, placement, and completeness. "It's about repetition versus uniqueness," she explained. "My interest in printmaking is that prints mimic what we are as humans: we are all the same and yet everyone is different."

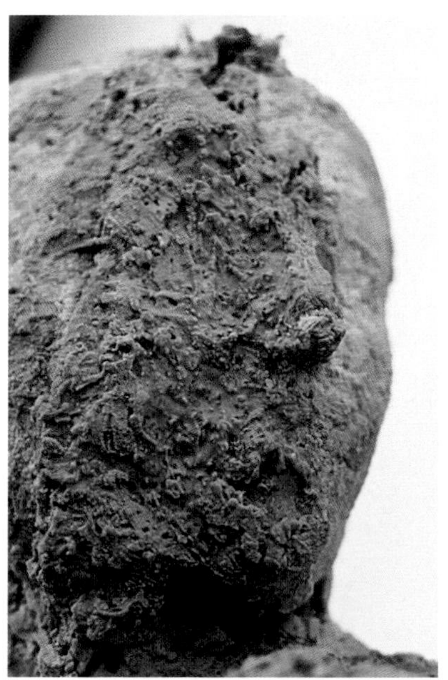

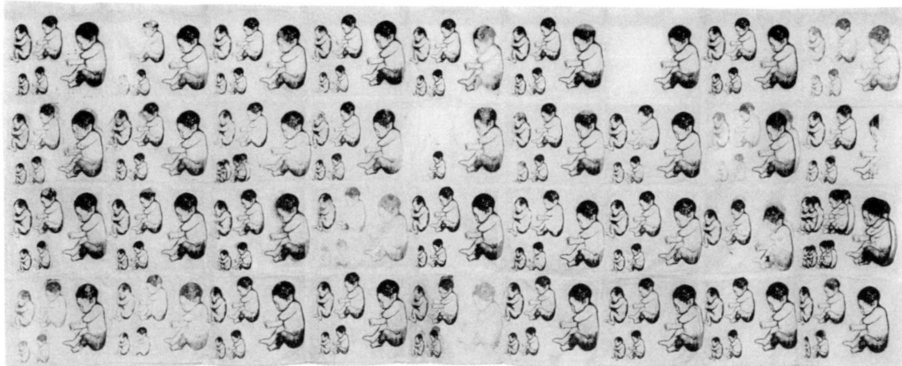

Untitled (from "Lot's Wife"), 1993
Chromogenic color print, 22 9/16 x 15 in. (57.3 x 38.1 cm)
Purchase, with funds from Anne and Joel Ehrenkranz 99.3.1

All Souls, 1985–87
Photoscreenprint, 72 1/2 x 178 1/2 in. (184.2 x 453.4 cm) irregular
Purchase, with funds from the Wilfred P. and Rose J. Cohen Purchase Fund and the Print Committee 91.20

TONY SMITH

1912–1980

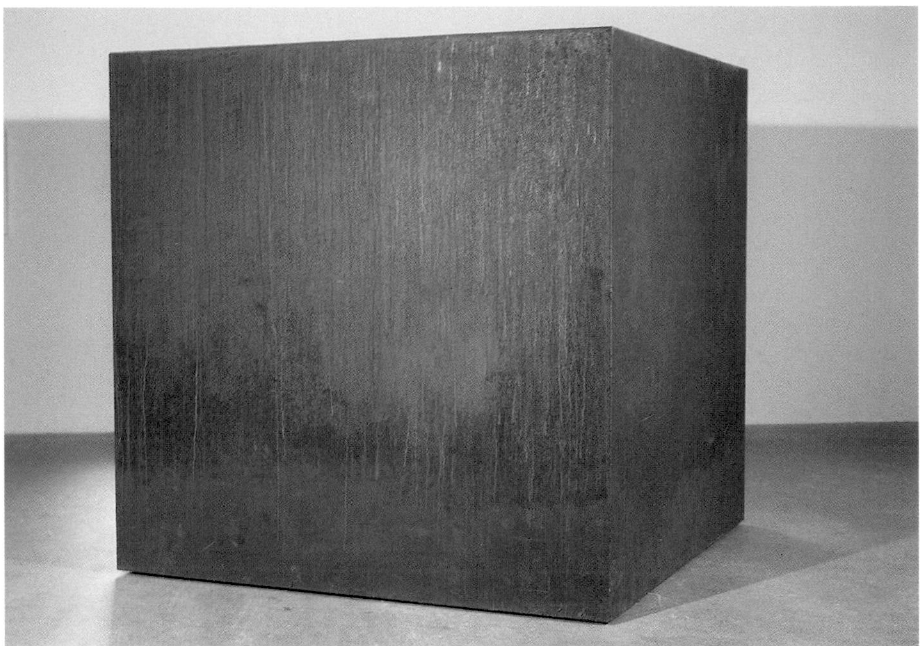

Die, a 6-foot steel cube, can be seen as the definitive, iconic Minimalist sculpture—a reduction of form to pure geometry, fabricated in industrial materials. But *Die* is also, as Smith has explained, rich in other references, a reach that violates the Minimalist mandate for opaque forms devoid of extrinsic meaning. *Die*'s human scale was inspired by Leonardo da Vinci's famous drawing of the Vitruvian man, which shows the parts of the human body in harmonic proportion to the whole—a system derived from the Roman architect Vitruvius. (Smith was trained as an architect and worked with Frank Lloyd Wright on a number of buildings.) In describing *Die*, Smith also invoked Herodotus, the ancient Greek historian, who wrote of a cubelike chapel carved from a single stone. The work's title adds further allusions—to the chance roll of the dice or the dies (manufacturing and reproduction devices) used in the waterworks-supply business run by Smith's family. Perhaps the most obvious allusion in *Die* is to death, which is reinforced by the work's dimensions. "Six feet," Smith noted, "has a suggestion of being cooked. Six foot box. Six feet under."

Smith suffered from tuberculosis as a child, and spent years living in isolation in a prefabricated house on his family's property, where the presence of a black stove had a profound effect: "If one spends a long time in a room with only one object, that object becomes a little god," he said. Despite its industrial, reproducible, heavy appearance, *Die* exemplifies Smith's ability to imbue even the coldest forms with strangely organic, allusive, even poetic energy. Hollow and slightly raised off the floor so that all twelve edges are visible, it asks us to see what is imperceptible and emotive in even the simplest object.

Die, 1962
Steel, 72 3/8 x 72 3/8 x 72 3/8 in. (183.8 x 183.8 x 183.8 cm)
Purchase, with funds from the Louis and Bessie Adler Foundation, Inc., James Block, The Sondra and Charles Gilman, Jr. Foundation, Inc., Penny and Mike Winton, and the Painting and Sculpture Committee 89.6

ROBERT SMITHSON

1938–1973

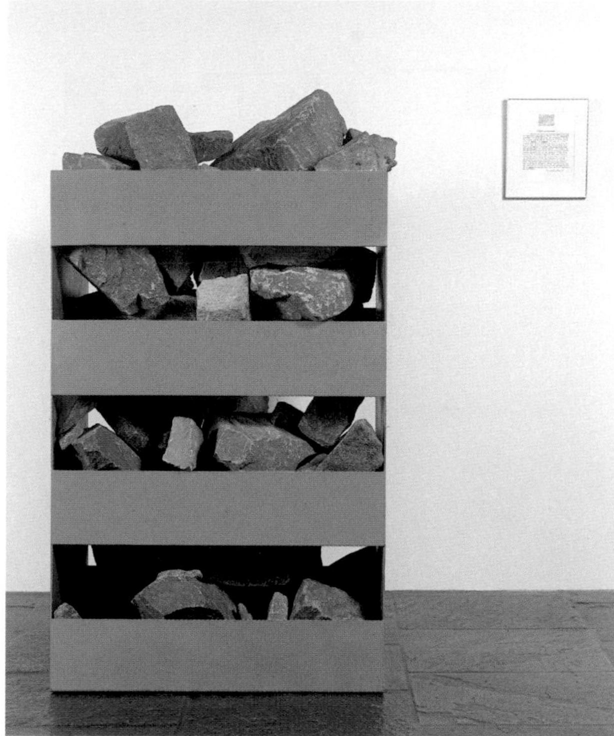

Non-sites is the all-encompassing title Robert Smithson gave to a group of geologically and geographically based works he began to make in 1968. The title refers not only to actual sites, but to what became known as "site-specific art." Taking form as performance-based installations and Earthworks—massive alterations of land, often only fully visible in aerial photographs—site-specific art probes the conventional limits we place on art, particularly regarding its location, scale, and materials. For this group of works, Smithson categorized the geographical source of his natural materials as the "site," and their packaged relocation in a museum or gallery as the "non-site."

In *Non-site (Palisades—Edgewater, N.J.)*, Smithson extracted rock from the area of an abandoned trolley system in his native New Jersey, placing the pieces in an open-slatted aluminum bin that echoes the pattern of the rail tracks. He selected the site for the way it illustrates the passage of time—through the local geology, the decay of the trolley line (what Smithson called its "de-architecturization"), and the gradual integration of nature and technology. As he explains in the accompanying text panel, "what once was a straight track has become a path of rocky crags—the site has lost its system." Smithson's container also evokes the contemporary work of Minimalist artists such as Donald Judd (p. 160), with its industrial materials and horizontal pattern.

Non-site (Palisades—Edgewater, N.J.), 1968
Enamel on aluminum with stones, 56 x 26 x 36 in. (142.2 x 66 x 91.4 cm) plus map and description of site
Purchase, with funds from the Howard and Jean Lipman Foundation, Inc. 69.6a-b

RAPHAEL SOYER
1899–1987

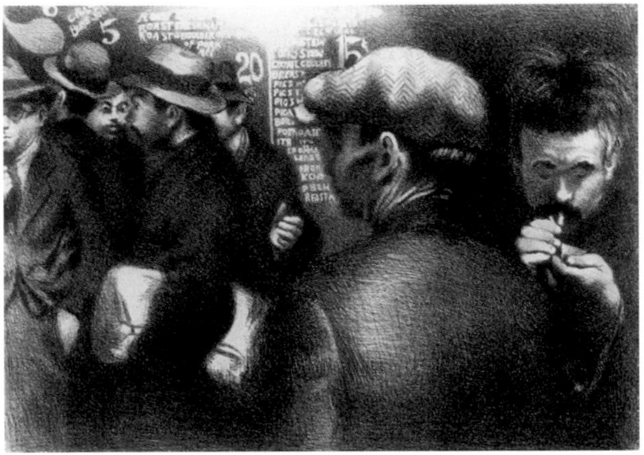

Throughout his long career as a painter and printmaker, Raphael Soyer depicted himself, a close circle of family and friends, dancers and studio models, and the ordinary men and women of New York City. Although often categorized among the Social Realists of the 1920s and 1930s, Soyer was less interested in documenting urban life, labor issues, or social reforms than in exposing the soul of his subject through a simple glance or gesture.

Two lithographs from 1933, *Bowery Nocturne* and *The Mission*, encapsulate the psychological impact of the Depression on the lives of ordinary Americans. In contrast to Reginald Marsh's *Bread Line—No One Has Starved* (p. 199), with its shambling lineup of men differentiated only by height or small details, Soyer concentrates on individuals. The denizens of *Bowery Nocturne* may be nameless, but they are distinguished from one another by their clothing, hats, gestures, physiognomies, and expressions. Although we cannot know what thoughts prompt their gestures and expressions, Soyer's careful differentiation encourages us to imagine each man's feelings, past and present.

Similarly, in *The Mission*, five impoverished men share a table, but that is the extent of their social interaction. Each drinks his coffee and munches his bread in a self-imposed isolation that accentuates their individualized faces, gestures, and actions. Soyer's ability to draw our attention to a range of physical types and responses takes his images beyond the boundaries of the 1930s into a timeless world of human emotions.

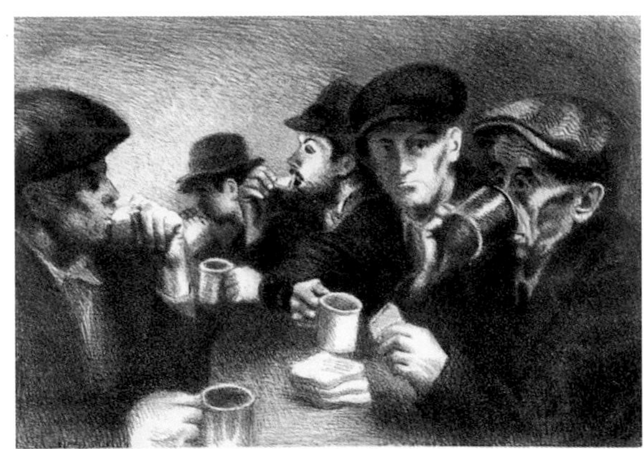

***Bowery Nocturne*, 1933
Lithograph: sheet, 15 3/16 x 21 3/8 in. (38.6 x 54.3 cm) irregular; image, 12 3/4 x 17 7/8 in. (32.4 x 45.5 cm)
Purchase, with funds from the Lauder Foundation, Leonard and Evelyn Lauder Fund 96.68.253

***The Mission*, 1933
Lithograph: sheet, 15 3/4 x 22 3/4 in. (40 x 57.8 cm);
image, 12 1/8 x 17 11/16 in. (30.8 x 44.9 cm)
Purchase 36.59

EDWARD STEICHEN

1879–1973

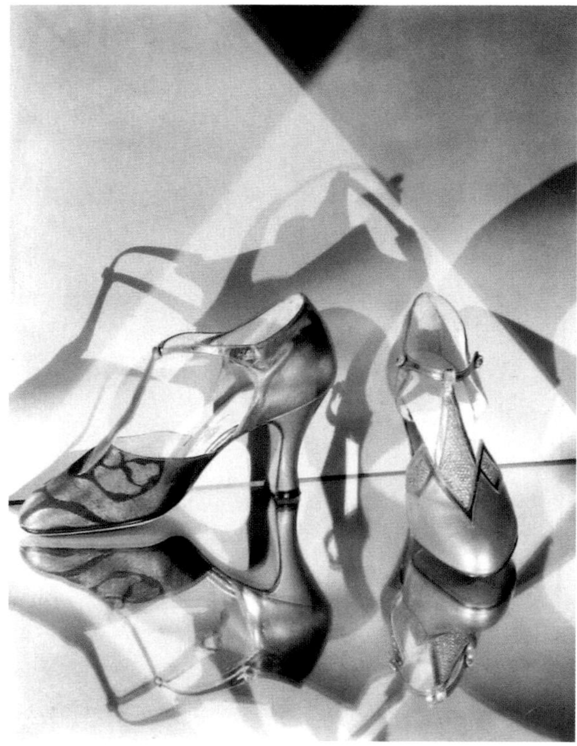

Edward Steichen began his career in the early twentieth century as a fine art photographer—indeed, his soft-focus atmospheric images were instrumental in raising the status of photography to that of painting and sculpture. In the 1920s, he shifted to commercial photography, becoming chief photographer for the popular Condé Nast publications *Vogue* and *Vanity Fair*, as well as for the J. Walter Thompson Agency, the largest advertising agency in New York. Throughout the twenties and thirties, he was the most successful commercial photographer in America—and the most influential, since his celebrity and fashion shots established an ideal that millions of women strove to attain.

Steichen's influence and success was based on the visual strategies he developed to sell his clients' products. In the photograph *Shoes*, taken for an advertisement, the elegant dress shoes cast dramatic shadows on the dynamic background arrangement of light beams. The shoes sit, moreover, on a mirror whose reflections stretch out toward our space. Raking light from the upper corners bounces off the shoes' sequins and the mirror, creating a strobe effect that gives dancelike movement to otherwise static objects. Through such strategies, Steichen made the people and products he photographed appealing, even irresistible. The glamorous, exciting lifestyle his images sold helped define consumer ideals and social norms for a generation of American women.

Shoes, 1927
Toned gelatin silver print, 9 1/2 x 7 1/2 in. (24.1 x 19.1 cm)
Promised gift of Joseph M. Cohen P.1.2001

PAT STEIR

b. 1938

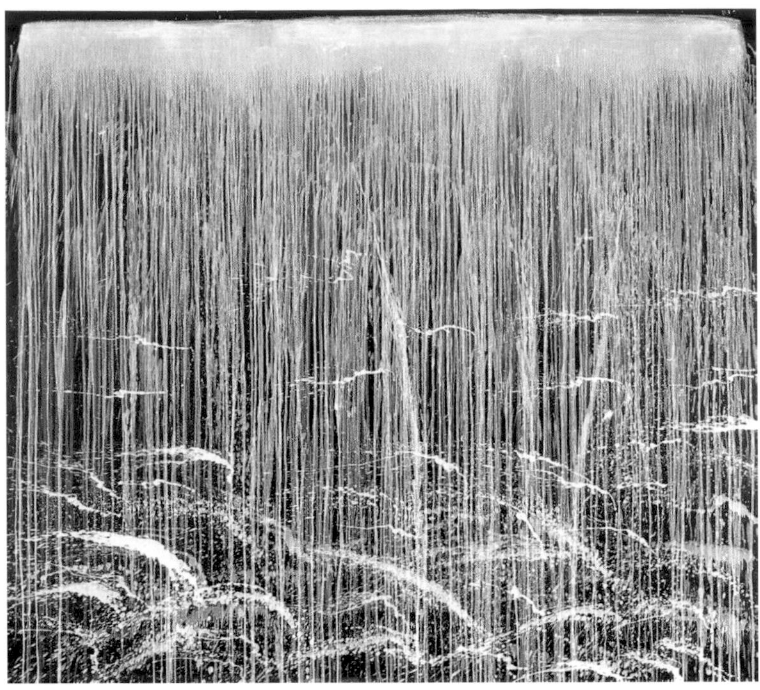

Among Pat Steir's earliest work, which dates to the late 1960s, were paintings that isolated various mark-making techniques, including brushstrokes and drips. These works, as well as her later ones, reflect Steir's acquaintance with the way contemporaneous Conceptual and Minimalist artists were dissecting the traditional techniques of art. Also relevant to Steir was the gestural method of Abstract Expressionism (including Jackson Pollock's signature drip paintings, p. 242). But it was not until 1988, when she undertook the *Waterfall* series, that she exploited the possibilities of dripping and flinging paint with full physical and expressive freedom. In *July Waterfall*, an oversaturated brushful of thinned oil paint was spread along the top of the canvas and the excess paint allowed to cascade, like a waterfall, down the surface. "Gravity," says Steir, "makes the image." The lower portion of the image gets an evocative uplift from the splashed-back skeins of paint that she produced by flinging paint from the end of the brush.

In addition to the gestures of Abstract Expressionism, Japanese "flung-ink" painting and other Japanese and Chinese ink techniques underlie Steir's waterfalls, a debt she acknowledges in other titles in the series, such as *Waterfall of the Asian Night*. But she approaches the subject with practiced delicacy, allowing the waterfalls, in effect, to paint themselves. The result, as critic Holland Cotter has described it, are paintings "in which 'masculine' strength and 'feminine' delicacy are present but unconflicted, in which turbulence and serenity balance out."

July Waterfall, 1991
Oil on canvas, 102 1/4 x 116 1/8 in. (259.7 x 295 cm)
Promised gift of Robert Miller and Betsy Wittenborn Miller P.92.3

FRANK STELLA

b. 1936

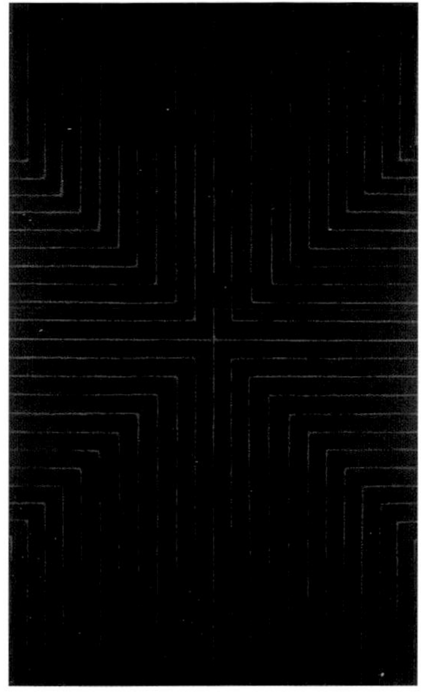

The German title of Frank Stella's *Die Fahne hoch!*, which translates as "hoist the flag," is taken from the "Horst Wessel Song," the Nazi party's marching anthem. The painting's title, cruciform configuration, and flaglike proportions call to mind not only Nazi banners, but the darkness and annihilation of the Holocaust. The title may also refer to raising the banner of a new aesthetic, one that marked a shift away from Abstract Expressionism and anticipated the geometry and rigor that would characterize Minimalism. Despite the provocative title, Stella insisted that his paintings were only about what was observable. There was nothing, he declared, "besides the paint on the canvas" and "what you see is what you see." He stretched the canvas of *Die Fahne hoch!* over an exceptionally thick stretcher, so that it asserts what he called its "objectness." The work is among a group of about twenty-four black striped paintings—the white lines are narrow areas of unpainted canvas—that Stella produced when he was twenty-three, just a year after graduating from Princeton University.

In the following years, Stella continued to explore the possibilities of striped compositions, expanding his color palette to create such vibrant works as *Gran Cairo*. One of twenty *Concentric Squares* and *Mitered Mazes* works painted in 1962 and 1963, *Gran Cairo* is made from six colors of Benjamin Moore paint, used straight from the can. The stripes follow a color-chart order from red to violet (or violet to red, depending where you begin), then reverse from violet to red and back again. The concentric squares seem to advance and recede simultaneously, and their repeated geometry underscores the square contour of the canvas, which in turn asserts the painting's objectness. As in many of Stella's works, the title refers to a place: Gran Cairo was a hotel in Spain, where Stella had traveled in 1961 and where he made the first sketches for the *Concentric Squares* and *Mitered Mazes*.

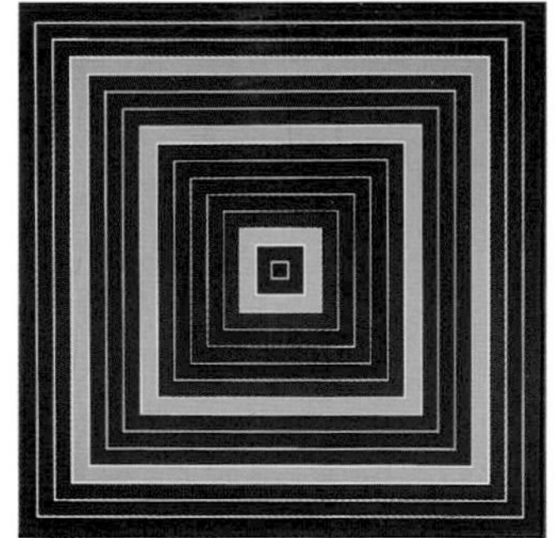

Die Fahne hoch!, 1959
Enamel on canvas, 121 1/2 x 73 in. (308.6 x 185.4 cm)
Gift of Mr. and Mrs. Eugene M. Schwartz and purchase, with funds from the John I.H. Baur Purchase Fund, the Charles and Anita Blatt Fund, Peter M. Brant, B.H. Friedman, the Gilman Foundation, Inc., Susan Morse Hilles, The Lauder Foundation, Frances and Sydney Lewis, the Albert A. List Fund, Philip Morris Incorporated, Sandra Payson, Mr. and Mrs. Albrecht Saalfield, Mrs. Percy Uris, Warner Communications Inc., and the National Endowment for the Arts 75.22

Gran Cairo, 1962
Synthetic polymer on canvas, 85 1/2 x 85 1/2 in. (217.2 x 217.2 cm)
Purchase, with funds from the Friends of the Whitney Museum of American Art 63.34

JOSEPH STELLA

1877–1946

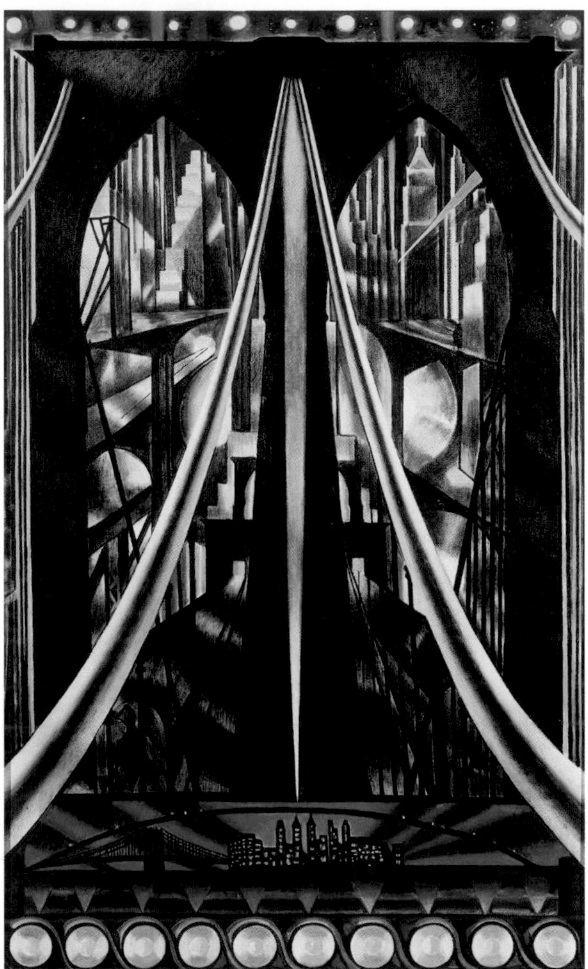

For Joseph Stella, the Brooklyn Bridge was "the shrine containing all the efforts of the new civilization, *America*—the eloquent meeting point of all the forces arising in a superb assertion of their powers, an *Apotheosis*." In this bridge and other icons of New York, Stella mined the new urban American landscape for symbols that would capture the texture and tempo of American life. To Stella, who emigrated to New York from Italy at the age of nineteen, the city was a nexus of frenetic, explosive, form-shattering power. In the engineering marvel of the Brooklyn Bridge, which he first depicted in 1918 and returned to throughout his career, he found a contemporary monument that transformed technology into an embodiment of the modern human spirit.

Across the bottom of *The Brooklyn Bridge: Variation on an Old Theme* is a frieze of headlights below a profile of the bridge's span to the Manhattan skyline, which sends out beacons into the night. The strip at the top, with white beams against a blue ground, looks like an electronically starlit sky. In the main portion of the canvas, the sweeping cables of the bridge shoot upward in dynamic elegance. The huge scale of the work—it is nearly 6 feet tall—evokes a Renaissance altar, with the narrow lower section alluding to the altar's predella, the band of small narrative scenes related to the main subject. The iconic character of the bridge is reinforced by the dominance of the massive pointed arches, whose Gothic style echoes that of medieval churches. By joining machine age steel cables with historical references, Stella turned the Brooklyn Bridge into a twentieth-century symbol of divinity, an apotheosis of modern urban life.

The Brooklyn Bridge: Variation on an Old Theme, 1939
Oil on canvas, 70 x 42 in. (177.8 x 106.7 cm)
Purchase 42.15

LOUIS STETTNER

b. 1922

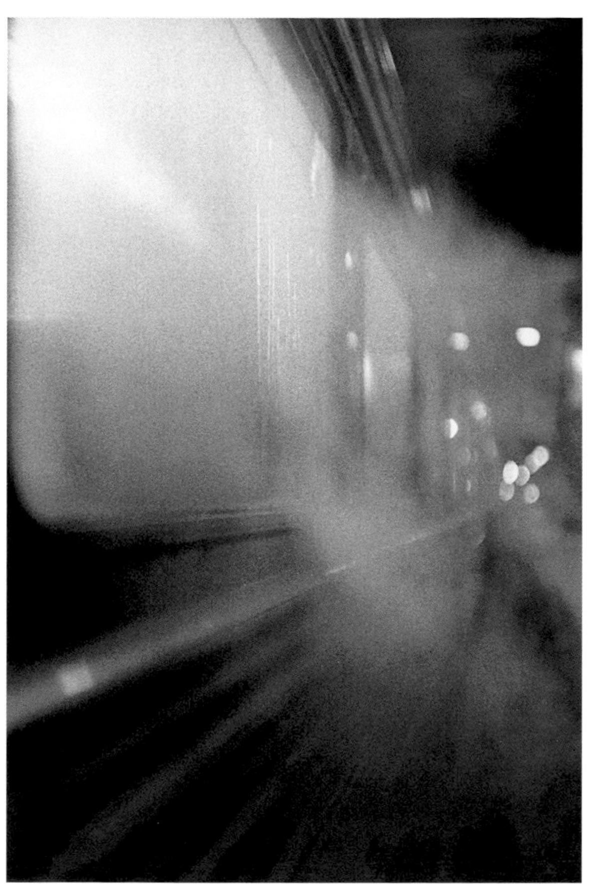

In 1958, Brooklyn native Louis Stettner made a series of photographs of New York's Pennsylvania Station, five years before the massive Neo-Roman building was torn down. Although he was drawn to the bustle of the railroad station's main terminal and waiting rooms, it was the activity on the platforms below that transfixed him. "The magic carpet was downstairs, where the trains took off," Stettner explained. "First the solitude of empty compartments, passengers settling in, then the train starting up slowly, quietly rolling out of the terminal."

Many of the works in this series depict subdued commuters, isolated and framed by the train windows, as they sleep, play cards, or otherwise while away the time. *Penn Station*, in which a train is seen pulling out of the station, only alludes to the passengers within. It is an unusually abstract image for Stettner, who had studied briefly at the socially progressive Photo League and believed that responsible photography should stay focused on people. The oblique angle suggests that Stettner leaned dangerously close to the moving train to get this exposure, an action born of his conviction that the photographer must "settle with the spontaneity of a violent embrace, capturing the split-second action and angle of view that will pull everything together." As the train gains velocity, solid forms softly dissolve in the dim light and steamy air of the platform. *Penn Station* is about atmosphere, about the camera's ability to fix the ephemeral—light, shadows, steam—and give it a tangible presence.

Penn Station, 1958
Gelatin silver print, 13 1/2 x 9 in. (34.3 x 22.9 cm)
Purchase, with funds from the Photography Committee 2000.222

CLYFFORD STILL

1904–1980

This enormous painting—more than 9 feet high and almost 13 feet long—carries Clyfford Still's trademark colored cracks that sluice the canvas vertically with sharply defined edges and strong pigments. The craggy fingers of color, however, also evoke rocky precipices or the moonlit silhouettes of trees, lending this abstraction undertones of moody landscape. Still once remarked that his work reflected "man's struggle and fusion with nature."

Still was raised and educated amid the natural grandeur of Washington State and Alberta, Canada, and he remained a man bonded to the world of nature. Even after his early semi-abstract landscapes and figurative paintings matured into pure abstraction, natural imagery lay just below the surface. In the 1950s, when New York was the center of vanguard art, Still took a decidedly anti-urban and even anti-modern stance. He called this 1957 work "an affirmation of individual responsibility...a repudiation of the mechanistic ethic and technological rationale of our culture." Such rhetoric rings with the individualism and pride in nature that is commonly associated with the Pacific Northwest; it also rejects, wholesale, the collective or consumerist character of modern culture. Insisting on a perspective that can only be unique and private, Still's words express a highly subjective search for meaning in his painting. Indeed, the somber hues and jagged edges of color convey a sense of profound isolation and solitary introspection.

Untitled, 1957
Oil on canvas, 112 x 154 in. (284.5 x 391.2 cm)
Purchase, with funds from the Friends of the Whitney Museum of American Art 69.31

JESSICA STOCKHOLDER

b. 1959

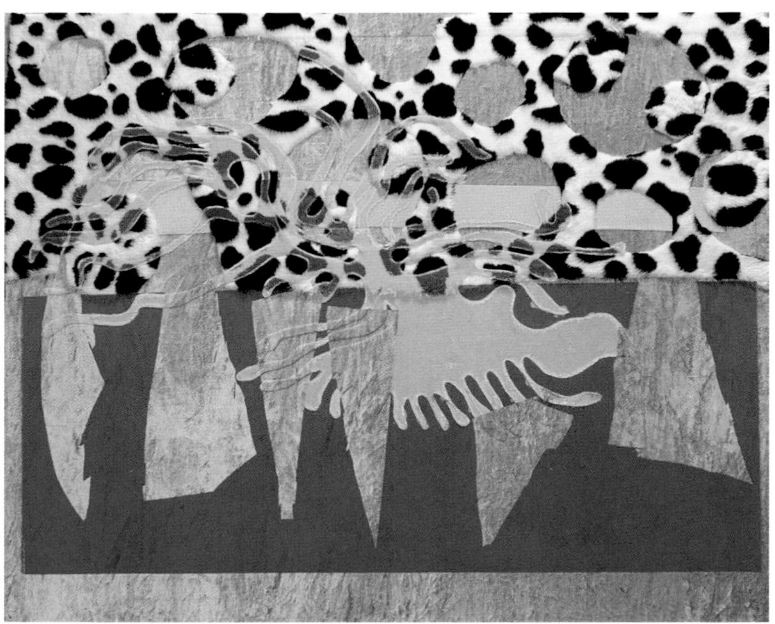

Since the mid-1980s, Jessica Stockholder has won widespread attention for her offbeat installations and sculptures, cobbled together from an extraordinary variety of ordinary materials, including two-by-fours, Sheetrock, underwear, and oranges. She brings a similar artistic sensibility to a series of monoprints produced in collaboration with David Lasry at his Two Palms Press. If her sculptures can be described as three-dimensional paintings, the prints are like sculptures flattened to hang on the wall.

In *Untitled*, reddish-orange printer's ink overlays an unconventional combination of materials, all scavenged from remnant shops in Lower Manhattan—blue upholstery fabric, spotted fake fur, and linoleum, which were then sandwiched together and placed in a hydraulic press. As in her installations, Stockholder avoids working with anything that might seem precious or rare, preferring materials that are otherwise unremarkable—materials that speak of everyday life.

In this series of monoprints, Stockholder allowed these materials to dictate compositional ideas. Although the results may seem playful and unpredictable, they also reveal her keen aesthetic sense. The tension she creates between spontaneity and discipline, chaos and order, is central to her work. For Stockholder, "things that are beautiful are things that are awkward and shake things up, and stretch how I can understand things as complete." This rejection of rarefied notions of beauty is evident in the monoprint. With a bold palette of primary colors and a jumble of overlapping shapes, it aspires to the kind of beauty found in the real world, where colors sometimes clash and not every juxtaposition is neatly resolved.

Untitled, 2000
Monoprint with woodcut, fake fur, linoleum, and blue fabric, 41 x 51 in. (104.1 x 129.5 cm)
Purchase, with funds from the Print Committee 2000.256

JOHN STORRS

1885–1956

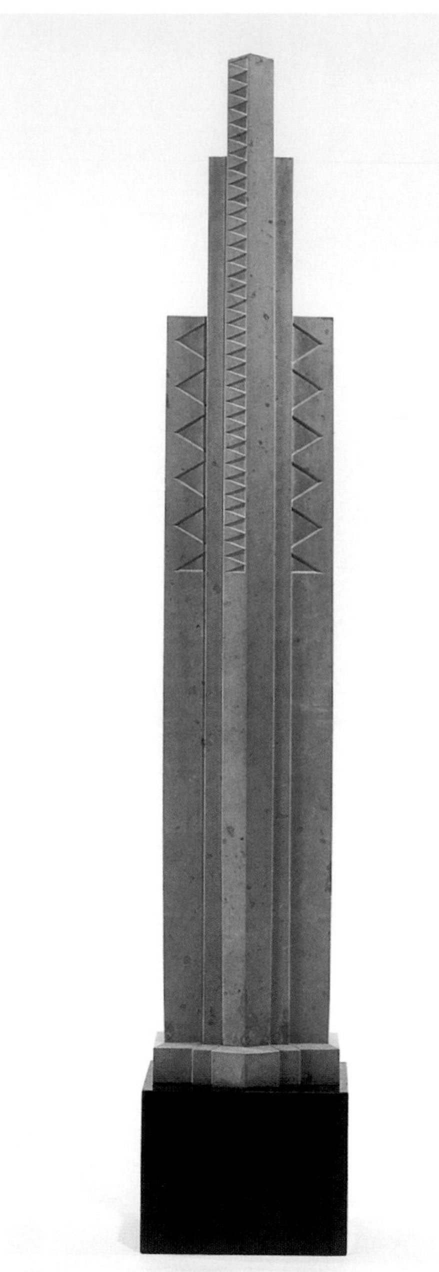

John Storrs' 1920 show at New York's Folsom Gallery was one of the first exhibitions of modernist sculpture by an American artist. Although he began his career making figurative work under the tutelage of Auguste Rodin, by the early 1920s Storrs was producing a series of sculptures that followed the essential contours of the modern skyscraper. *Forms in Space #1* is a solid, vertical block of marble, more than 7 feet tall, with the multiplaned facade and stepped silhouette of a skyscraper. Storrs embellished this symmetrical, angular form with shallow, sharp-edged zigzags that anticipate the Art Deco style of the Chrysler Building, completed just a few years later in 1930.

The son of a Chicago architect and real estate developer, Storrs chose to become a sculptor over his father's objections, but maintained his ties to architecture. His numerous architectural commissions included the Art Deco sculpture of Ceres atop the Chicago Board of Trade. Although he spent at least part of each year in France, Storrs knew many of the Chicago architects associated with Frank Lloyd Wright, and met Wright himself in the late 1920s or early 1930s. Storrs, however, was a sculptor, not an architect, and *Forms in Space* is not a proposal for a skyscraper. Nor does it depict any existing building. Instead, stripped of practical features such as windows and doors, *Forms in Space* is a tribute to the essential idea of a skyscraper and to the soaring promise of the machine age.

Forms in Space #1, c. 1924
Marble, 88 5/8 x 15 1/4 x 9 5/8 in. (225.1 x 38.7 x 24.4 cm) with base
50th Anniversary Gift of Mr. and Mrs. B.H. Friedman in honor of Gertrude Vanderbilt Whitney, Flora Whitney Miller, and Flora Miller Biddle 84.37a–b

SARAH SZE

b. 1969

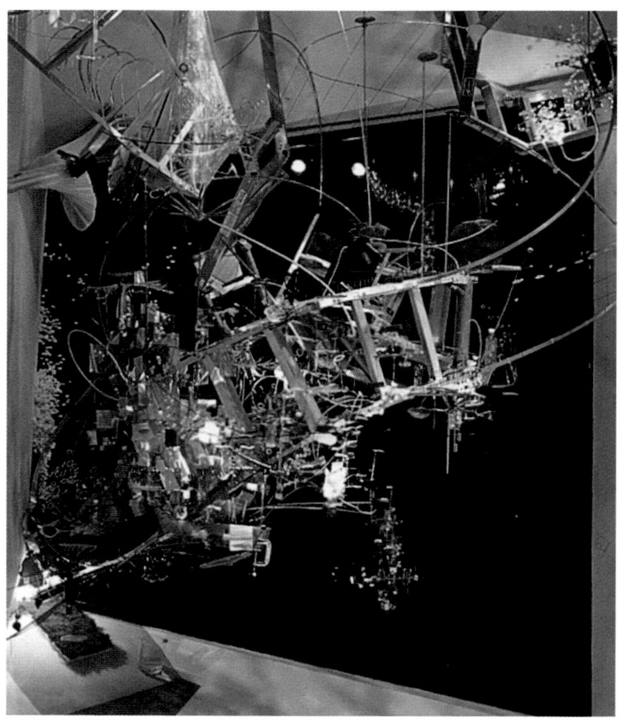

Sarah Sze transforms the miscellany of everyday life into astonishing site-specific installations made up of hundreds, sometimes thousands, of everyday objects. *Strange Attractor* was originally commissioned for the monumental fourth-floor window of the Whitney Museum for the "2000 Biennial Exhibition." It was meant to be seen in two ways: by walking around it in the gallery space, and by looking at it from street level 75 feet below. To construct the piece, Sze used a large array of common objects—all purchased in the neighborhood around the Whitney Museum—including balsa wood, aspirin tablets, plastic spoons, tickets, artificial plants, and a twisting conglomeration of ladders. Mirrors reflect both the gallery space and, through the window, the sidewalk below.

Sze's collection of unrelated parts comes together to form a sort of ecosystem or model universe, with every object somehow dependent on every other. Mimicking the top-heavy structure of the Whitney Museum itself, *Strange Attractor* has a strong upward thrust, with more ladders and mirrors and even a box of tissue paper visible through the open gridwork of the gallery ceiling. Small fans cause bits of paper to flutter, an air humidifier creates a constant cloud of steam, and a set of clear plastic tubing circulates water throughout the work, thus adding a delicate motion and dynamism to the massive piece. In the midst of frantic chaos, Sze creates a sensation of unity and balance.

****Strange Attractor***, 2000 (detail)
Mixed media, dimensions variable
Gift of Marianne Boesky, Ed Cohen, and Adam Sender 2001.1

YVES TANGUY

1900–1955

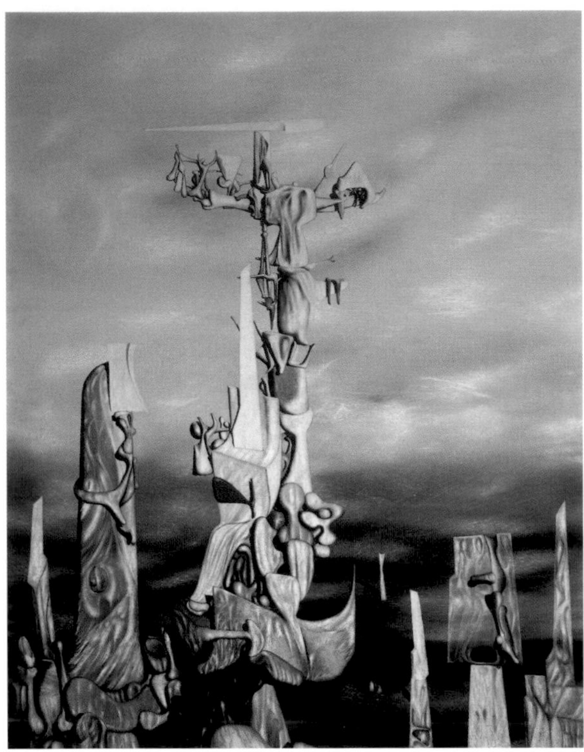

Early on in his career, Yves Tanguy formulated his signature technique of covering canvas with paint thinned to an almost liquid consistency, which allowed an extraordinarily subtle and controlled gradation of tones. This tonality helps create the macabre effect of *The Wish*, where ossified, almost sculpturally totemic formations populate a primeval landscape. The absence of any fixed horizon between spongy sky and misted ground invokes an atmosphere of foreboding and isolation. The twisted Surrealist structures seem to exist in a world without time, their stark presences providing visual analogies not to landscape or architecture but to atavistic urges. While still living in France, Tanguy returned often to the Breton coastline, near his childhood home, where the haunting menhirs—upright stone structures used in prehistoric worship and burial practices—bear a distinct resemblance to his own painterly forms.

Tanguy was one of the few Surrealist painters who labored to translate unconscious knowledge into visual form. Along with other important French Surrealists, he emigrated to New York during World War II. Together, this group of artists, with their emphasis on art as a manifestation of the unconscious, exerted a profound influence on the Abstract Expressionist paintings of American artists such as Robert Motherwell and Jackson Pollock (pp. 213, 242).

The Wish, 1949
Oil on canvas, 36 x 28 in. (91.4 x 71.1 cm)
Kay Sage Tanguy Bequest 63.46

DIANA THATER

b. 1962

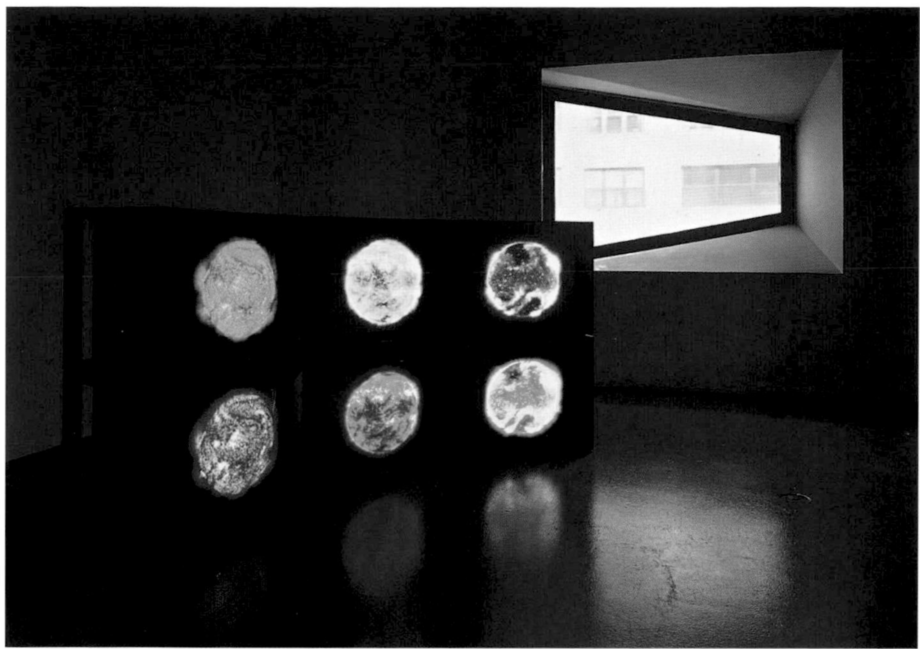

Since the early 1990s, Diana Thater has been exploring the nature of video light and the colors that compose it. Working with video monitors, video projection, and light filters, she strives to maintain correspondences among the forms of her installations, the material properties of video light, and the content of her video imagery. Thater used digital photographs of the surface of the sun to create *Six-Color Video Wall*, an analytical yet exceptionally lyrical exploration of the relationship between the light of video and its origins in the burning star at the center of our solar system.

She began by transforming three series of NASA photographs taken with red, blue, and green filters—also the component colors of video—into three animated sequences of the sun in motion. She then paired these animations with another set of photographs, identical except that the red, blue, and green have been reversed into their complements of cyan, yellow, and magenta. Mimicking the color-filtration process used to make the videos, all the lights and windows are covered in an array of colored gel filters that produce a painterly fade from deep blue to lavender across the room. In this way, Thater extends the boundaries of the work beyond the video monitors to encompass their surrounding space as well as the physical and perceptual environment of the viewers. Ultimately, *Six-Color Video Wall* addresses how our experience of nature is mediated by layers of representational technologies and by culturally specific ways of seeing.

Six-Color Video Wall, 2000
6 video monitors, 6 DVDs, and 6 DVD players, dimensions variable
Purchase, with funds from the Contemporary Committee and the Film and Video Committee 2000.193

PAUL THEK

1933–1988

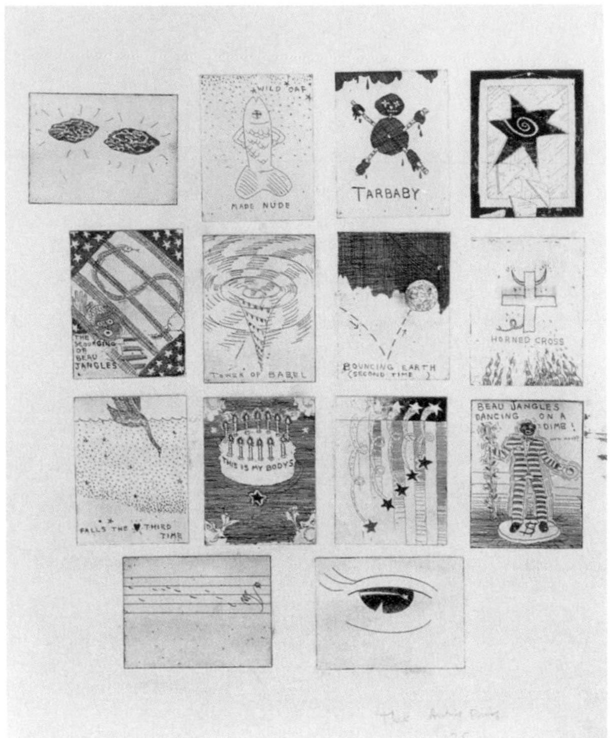

Paul Thek first gained recognition in the 1960s, even though he rejected the prevalent art movements of the decade: the cold, industrial aesthetic of Minimalism and Pop's embrace of consumerism. Instead, he drew on the rituals of his Catholic boyhood to weave a highly personal network of symbols and associations. Yet his work also reflects the wider political and social conflicts of the era: the Vietnam War, the struggle for civil rights, and the Watergate scandal.

Although Thek is perhaps best remembered for his installations and for sculptures of meat fashioned from wax and other materials, he was also a printmaker. His untitled etched sheet of 1975, an artist's proof for an edition that was never completed, merges American icons with Christian symbolism. The fourteen etched plates include a Tower of Babel whirling like a tornado, a crucified tar baby, and stars falling off an upturned American flag. A birthday cake with thirteen candles bears the inscription "This is my bodys," an ambiguous misspelling—or misquotation—of Christ's words at the Last Supper.

The famous minstrel performer Bo Jangles is an important figure in Thek's personal cosmology, which he envisioned as a reinterpretation of Catholicism's Stations of the Cross. Bo Jangles, rechristened "Beau" (Thek was living in Paris at the time), becomes the artist's alter ego. Thek described Beau as "a poor clownish collaborator—as we all are—in a hopelessly lethal, totally inhuman system." Whether imprisoned behind the stars and stripes—the stripes here conflated with a dollar sign—or dancing on a dime, Beau Jangles was, for Thek, an embodiment of America's sins.

Untitled, 1975
Etching: sheet, 25 3/4 x 19 9/16 in. (65.4 x 49.7 cm); 14 plates, approximately 4 5/8 x 3 1/2 in. (11.7 x 8.9 cm) each
Purchase, with funds from the Print Committee 95.10

WAYNE THIEBAUD

b. 1920

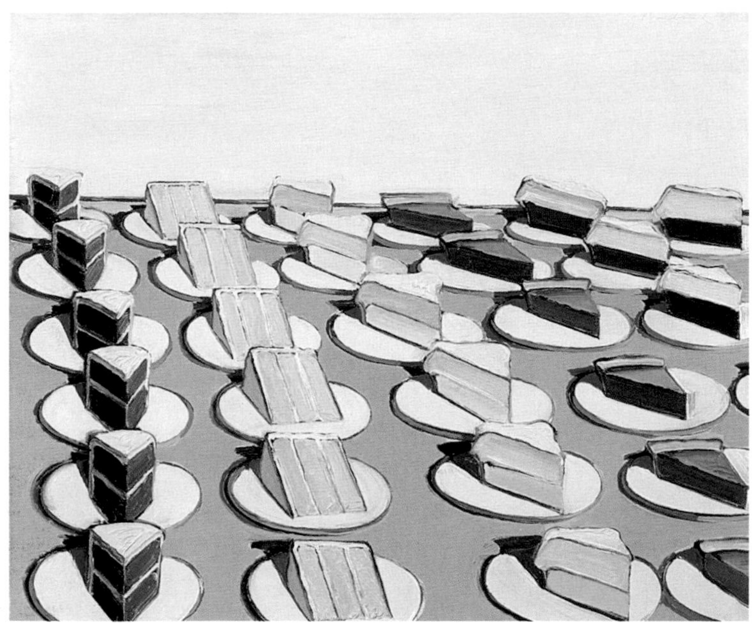

Wayne Thiebaud is best known for the richly impastoed still lifes—paintings of cakes, hot dogs, gumball machines, and pastry counters—that he began in the early 1960s. His depictions of these typically American foods reflect the nation's culture of consumption, an integral part of the dialogue of artmaking in America in the 1960s. Yet Thiebaud selected the iconography for works such as *Pie Counter* for their ritualistic associations as well. As he explained, "Pie has a long history and it has other implications: the idea of 'Pie in the Sky,' the old American preoccupation with Mom and Apple Pie, pie throwing contests, pie throwing in Chaplin films. One makes a pie out of ordinary stuff, like raisins, squash or apples and gift wraps it, in a sense with a crust. It's very magical, very special."

Because of his choice of subject matter in the 1960s, Thiebaud has often been tied to Pop art. But unlike Pop artists, who preferred the slick effects of mechanical reproduction, Thiebaud used his slices of pie and other foodstuffs to explore composition, color, light, and texture. He exploited the physical properties of paint to mimic the look and feel of the substance depicted, so that in *Pie Counter* the paint imitates the gestural strokes a baker might make when frosting a cake or spreading whipped cream across a pie. Thiebaud has described this palpable, sensuous employment of paint as "object transference." By combining the physical treatment of paint with the rigid geometry of triangular pie slices and circular plates, he makes his works simultaneously representational and abstract—"organic messiness combined with the geometric clarity," as he put it. The often appetizing results of this painterly alchemy and careful composition have become hallmarks of his style.

Pie Counter, 1963
Oil on canvas, 30 x 36 in. (76.2 x 91.4 cm)
Purchase, with funds from the Larry Aldrich Foundation Fund 64.11

BOB THOMPSON

1937–1966

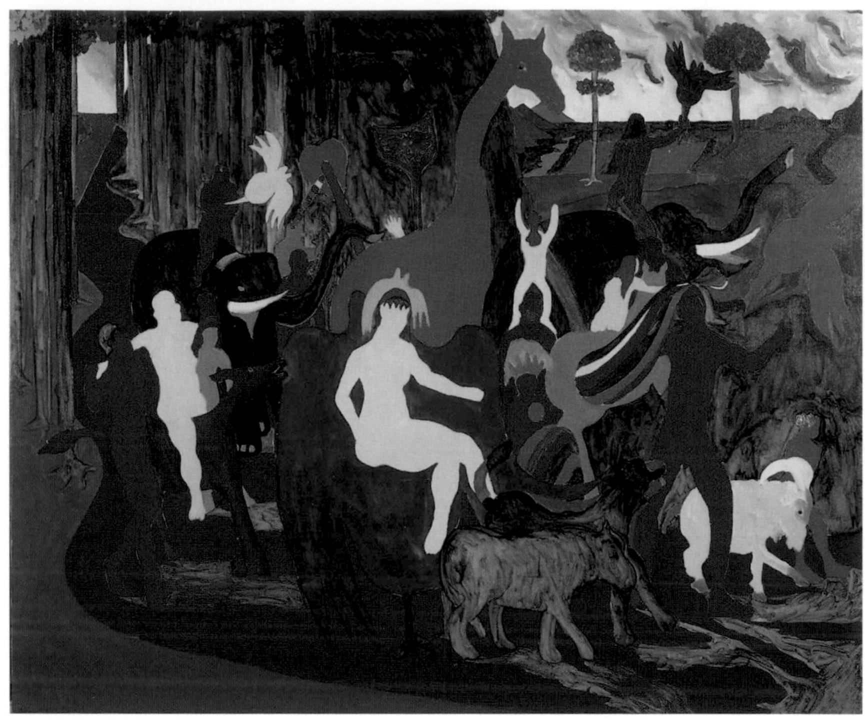

Bob Thompson's painting presents a jubilant procession in honor of Bacchus, the pagan god of wine. Seated cross-legged at center, Bacchus is a yellow silhouette surrounded by celebratory attendants, including satyrs, nymphs, and fantastical animals. Thompson used flat, bold, unmodulated colors to render this bacchanalia, in which humans, gods, and animals interlock chromatically, creating a dense surface that discourages focus on any one part.

Thompson's subject matter was often taken from Greek and Roman mythology as well as from the religious themes of Renaissance masters. Though based in New York, the African-American artist spent periods living and working in Europe, where exposure to the museums of Paris, Rome, and Madrid solidified his keen knowledge of Western painting. Thompson appears to have followed the advice of his friend the artist Jan Müller, who told him, "Don't ever look for your solutions among the work of your contemporaries—look to the Old Masters."

Thompson was one of several artists in the 1960s who reintroduced figurative representation to American art, which had been dominated since the late 1940s by Abstract Expressionism. Among his friends outside the art world were the jazz musicians Charlie Parker, Dizzy Gillespie, and Ornette Coleman; indeed, this animated, color-saturated canvas conveys a sense of the undulating rhythms and syncopated movement found in jazz.

Triumph of Bacchus, 1964
Oil on canvas, 60 x 72 1/16 in. (152.4 x 183 cm)
Purchase, with funds from the Painting and Sculpture Committee and The Lauder Foundation, Leonard and Evelyn Lauder Fund 98.19

MARK TOBEY

1890–1976

In *Universal Field*, Mark Tobey employed his signature "white writing" technique, incising a labyrinth of delicate lines against a mottled background of pinks, grays, and browns. The wiry lines form geometric shapes, crisscross, and interlace, creating an all-over pattern that seems to move as the eye traverses its tight skeins of paint and intricate meshes. One critic, describing the effect of Tobey's white writing, observed that the lines "cause the picture surface to vibrate in depth—or, better, toward the spectator." Indeed, Tobey said that his paintings "do not allow the viewer to rest on anything. He is bounced off it or he has to keep moving with it."

Although Tobey was a contemporary of the Abstract Expressionists and his work is without recognizable imagery, he was principally inspired by Eastern calligraphy, Zen Buddhism, and his own Baha'i faith, which emphasizes the spiritual unity of all religions and a oneness between man and the world. Tobey spoke of his attempts to reflect this balance by giving equal value to the component parts of his paintings. He conceived of space not as a vacuum but as a vital field charged with spiritual and material energy. "There's no such thing as empty space," he said. "It's all loaded with life." Tobey's early work depicted naturalistic images of animals and landscapes, but he found abstract painting the best way to convey the intangibility of the human spirit. His art at once pulsates with whirling dynamism and inspires quiet meditation.

Universal Field, 1949
Tempera and pastel on cardboard, 28 x 44 in. (71.1 x 111.8 cm)
Purchase 50.24

FRED TOMASELLI

b. 1956

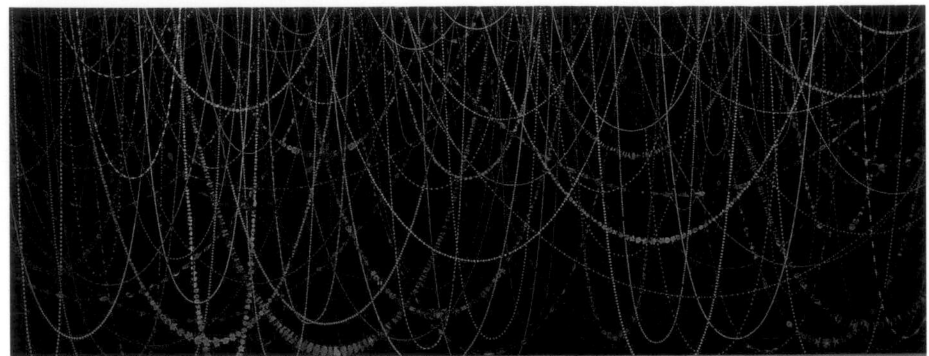

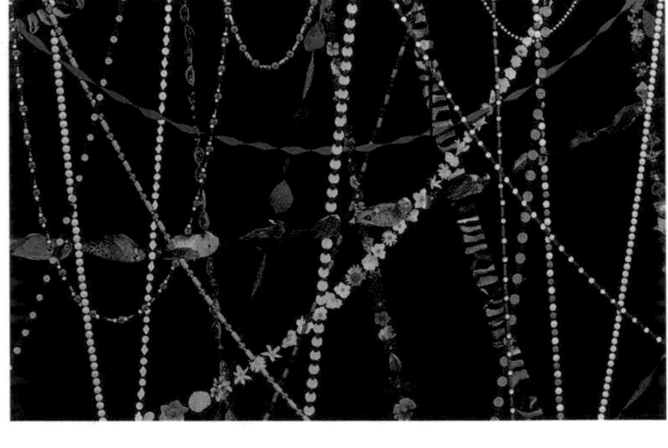

Strands of bright jewel-like colors dance in arcs across the lustrous black surface of *Gravity's Rainbow (Large)*. Closer inspection reveals that the arcs are composed of hundreds, sometimes thousands, of individual elements, painstakingly attached to panels and coated in resin: magazine cutouts of eyes, mouths, hands, and feet; images of insects, flowers, and birds culled from field guides; real hemp leaves as well as pills, ranging from aspirin to Prozac, along with painted placebos of every color and size. This dazzling pharmaceutical array alludes to the power of art, like that of drugs, to alter our perceptions and transport us to other worlds. But for Fred Tomaselli, the abundance of pills also provides a cautionary metaphor for our escapist culture: "Drugs may promise transcendent visions or relief from pain, but they also deliver addiction and death."

To create the arced strands of *Gravity's Rainbow (Large)*, Tomaselli suspended different lengths of lightweight chain between two points on a wall, traced the arcs the chain created onto panels, set the panels on the floor, and then affixed his images and objects to the traced arcs. Gravitational pull thus produced the wide range of arcs that forms the composition. The specific reference in the title, however, is to *Gravity's Rainbow*, the 1973 Thomas Pynchon novel, in which the phrase "gravity's rainbow" refers to the arced trajectory of a V-2 rocket falling on World War II London. This sense of impending destruction parallels the metaphorical implications of Tomaselli's pharmaceutical chains: the beauty that transports us in *Gravity's Rainbow (Large)* has a dark, toxic underside.

Gravity's Rainbow (Large), 1999
Leaves, pills, flowers, photocollage, synthetic polymer, and resin on wood panels, 96 x 240 in. (243.5 x 609.6 cm) overall
Purchase, with funds from the Jack E. Chachkes Endowed Purchase Fund, Saul Rosen Fund on behalf of Arthur G. Rosen, James Cohan, and Anthony d'Offay 2000.9a–e

GEORGE TOOKER

b. 1920

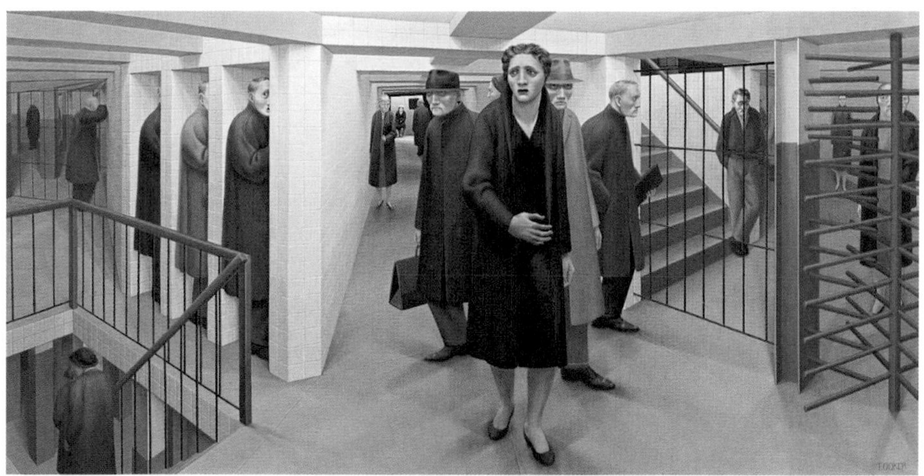

George Tooker painted *The Subway* in 1950, the same year that he was included in critic Lincoln Kirstein's landmark exhibition "Symbolic Realism." Kirstein, an early champion of Tooker's work, had placed him among a small group of artists—including Tooker's close friends Paul Cadmus and Jared French (pp. 61, 111)—whose precise, psychologically charged representations set them apart from the era's mainstream practitioners of Abstract Expressionism. Tooker had learned to paint in egg tempera in the traditional Renaissance manner from Cadmus. The medium, which necessitated a slow painting process, suited Tooker's deliberate, intellectual approach to artmaking; he seldom produced more than four paintings a year.

The Subway is the most famous of several paintings that he made as a distressed outcry against the social injustices and isolation of contemporary urban society. Most of his watchful figures have similar, androgynous faces that deny them individuality. Moreover, whether closed off in tiled niches or walking down the passageway, they remain hopelessly and pitifully alone. The central group is locked in a grid of shadows cast by the nearby metal grating while the labyrinthine passages of this claustrophobic environment lead nowhere. Tooker employs multiple vanishing points and sophisticated modeling to create an imagined world that is nevertheless set in a familiar urban terrain. *The Subway* gives visual form to cold war America's existential despair, suspending the city's inhabitants in a modern purgatory.

The Subway, 1950
Egg tempera on composition board, 18 1/8 x 36 1/8 in. (46 x 91.8 cm)
Purchase, with funds from the Juliana Force Purchase Award 50.23

JAMES TURRELL

b. 1943

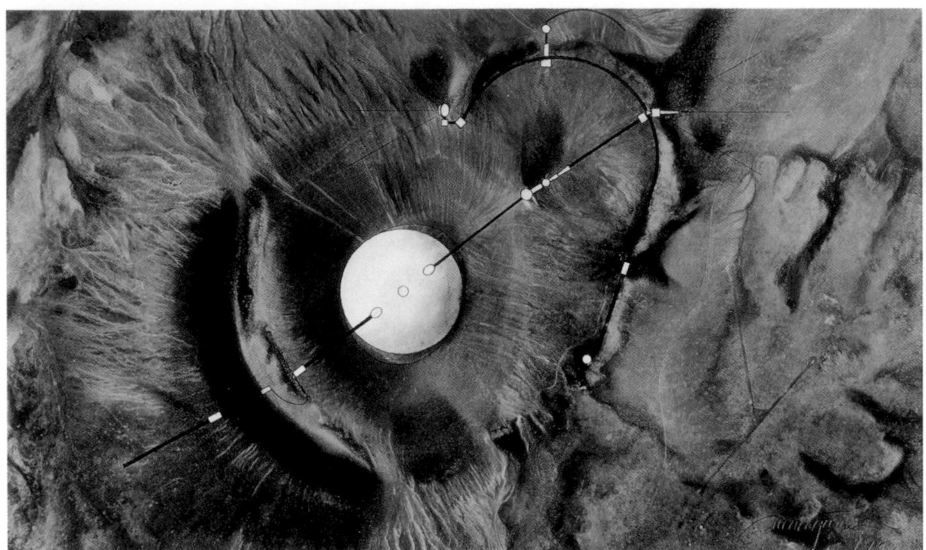

Born in Los Angeles, James Turrell is one of the so-called light and space artists who emerged in the late 1960s in California. In his gallery-based work, he explores the play of light, natural and artificial, in controlled architectural spaces. These works defy description. "There is no object and there is no image," says Turrell, speaking as both engineer and philosopher. "I use the material of light in its tangible, physical presence, [but] my medium is your perception."

The perception of light is also the subject of a work that has consumed decades of Turrell's career—the Roden Crater Project. This ongoing project is a celestial observatory Turrell built in an extinct Arizona volcano. He discovered the Roden Crater while performing an aerial survey in 1974 and has been engaged with the project for more than twenty years. *Site Plan, Roden Crater II* is a composite of the crater. The photography-based, aerial perspective opening is 3,000 feet in diameter and incorporates underground viewing chambers built inside the volcano. From within the crater, visitors can see light from stars billions of years old creating an array of perceptual and spatial illusions.

***Site Plan, Roden Crater II*, 1990**
Photo emulsion, wax, synthetic polymer, and ink on mylar and paper, 16 x 25 3/4 in. (40.6 x 65.4 cm)
Jack E. Chachkes Bequest 95.156

RICHARD TUTTLE

b. 1941

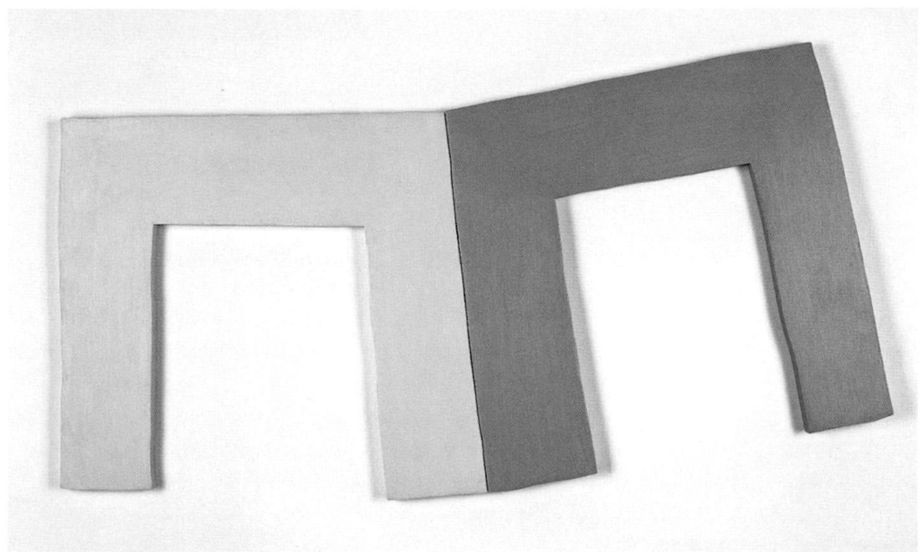

Richard Tuttle was one of a number of artists in the mid-1960s who had reservations about the media-oriented imagery of Pop as well as the industrial precisionism of Minimalism, the two dominant art forms of the decade. Instead, he concentrated on more organic sources of inspiration—landscape and the natural elements—and used imprecise shapes and, sometimes, ephemeral materials.

From 1964 to 1965, Tuttle created approximately 130 small-scale, irregularly shaped objects made of painted plywood. The works, with titles like *Fountain*, *Fire*, and *Hill*, were installed in a gallery in 1965, covering both the floors and the walls. *Drift III*, the third in a series of six, is one of these works. It transgresses the usual boundaries between sculpture and painting: although it hangs on the wall like a painting, it hangs askew, and its two-part wooden structure creates unusual negative spaces, engaging the surrounding area in the manner of a sculpture. Tuttle drew the irregular shape on paper, made a paper template, and then carefully cut the form from wood. As a result, *Drift III* possesses the idiosyncratic contours of his drawing. Although Tuttle usually avoids identifying the sources for his work, he has explained that the *Drift* series reminds him of the colored cloud formations he observed while briefly serving in the United States Air Force. The title evokes not the clouds themselves but their wandering movements as they respond to natural forces.

Drift III, 1965
Painted wood, 24 1/4 x 52 3/4 x 1 1/4 in. (61.6 x 134 x 3.2 cm) overall
Purchase, with funds from Mr. and Mrs. William A. Marsteller and the Painting and Sculpture Committee
83.18a–b

CY TWOMBLY

b. 1928

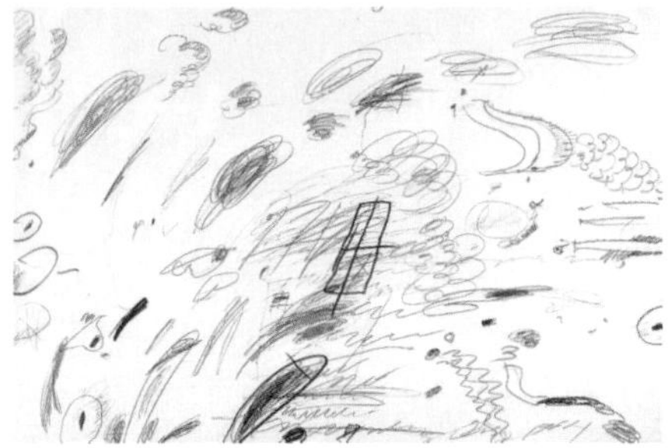

Cy Twombly's painting began to develop during the 1950s, when Abstract Expressionism held sway. Although he studied with some of the movement's key figures, such as Franz Kline (p. 165), he maintained an idiosyncratic independence from all defined styles—and continues to do so today. The graffiti-like appearance of his marks, for example, as in the Whitney's untitled work of 1964, is related to the gestural strokes of Abstract Expressionism, as is the all-over spread of the composition. But Twombly drew inspiration more directly from classical rather than contemporary sources. His real model, as critic Robert Hughes observed, is the palimpsest, an image or document in which a later text effaces an earlier one. In this way, his works convey a sense of the passage of time. Twombly's move to Rome in 1957, a city filled with ancient monuments, heightened this temporal aspect of his work and extended his range of references to the lyric poetry and classical mythology of Italy.

In the late 1960s, Twombly worked primarily against a slate-gray ground, and his white markings grew more diagrammatic in appearance—the paintings from this period, including the 1969 *Untitled*, are often referred to as the "blackboard" works. The diagram effect can in part be attributed to Twombly's fascination with the drawings in Leonardo da Vinci's notebooks, in particular the sketches and notations about maelstroms and water currents. In *Untitled*, the chalky white scribblings and rectangular smears become pliable, curving diagonally down the picture like miniaturized versions of the slope of the composition, while dripping gray washes become a graphic torrent. The words "water chart" scrawled at upper right may refer to Leonardo's drawings or to the remains of the ancient aqueducts that surround Rome.

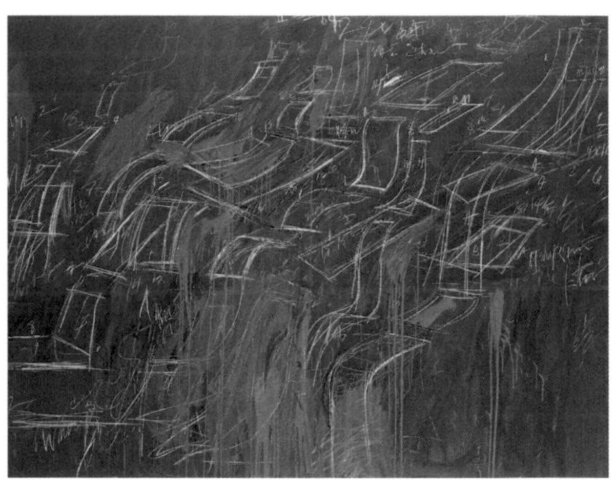

Untitled, 1964
Graphite, colored pencil, and crayon on paper, 27 1/2 x 39 3/8 in. (69.9 x 100 cm)
Purchase, with funds from the Drawing Committee 84.21

Untitled, 1969
Oil and crayon on canvas, 78 x 103 in. (198.1 x 261.6 cm)
Purchase, with funds from Mr. and Mrs. Rudolph B. Schulhof 69.29

BILL VIOLA

b. 1951

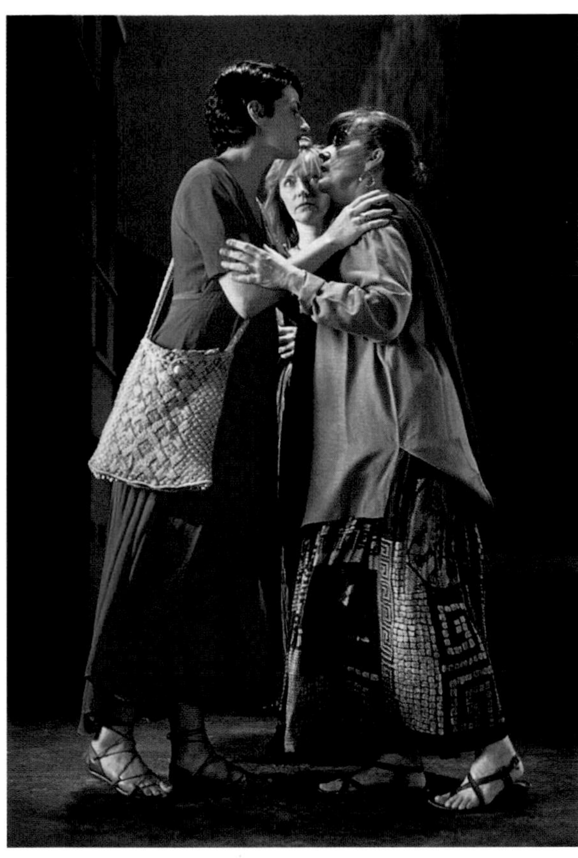

Bill Viola began working in video in the early 1970s and is now one of the preeminent figures in video art. His recent video installations evoke the language of painting and classical architecture. *The Greeting* was inspired by the *Visitation*, painted in 1528–29 by Italian Mannerist Jacopo Pontormo. The sixteenth-century work depicts a familiar theme of Christian iconography: the visit of the Virgin Mary to her older cousin Elizabeth, who acknowledges that the child Mary is carrying is the Son of God. The theme of birth as a symbolic journey has been important to Viola since the early 1980s. *The Greeting* takes off from the composition of Pontormo's painting, but secularizes the narrative. In the frame reproduced here, three women are dressed in long flowing garments and standing in an Italianate architectural setting not dissimilar to that in the Pontormo painting. The woman in the orange dress has just entered the scene from the left, interrupting a conversation between an older woman on the right and a younger woman, who has now retreated into the background. The newcomer, whose stomach is visibly swollen, is perhaps conveying to the older woman in a confidential whisper the news of her pregnancy. The woman pushed aside appears to eye the meeting with a tinge of resentment or jealousy.

Viola slows the charged encounter between the three women almost to a standstill. Within the extended time frame of extreme slow motion, the women's gestures and glances render the psychological dynamic of the exchange visible. A rumbling sound becomes increasingly loud, reflecting the growing emotional intensity of the tableau. Viola's sequence echoes the drama of Pontormo's painting, but transforms the ancient Christian moment into an enigmatic contemporary narrative.

The Greeting, 1995
Video-sound installation, dimensions variable
Promised gift of Marion Stroud in honor of David A. Ross 95.261

ANDY WARHOL

1928–1987

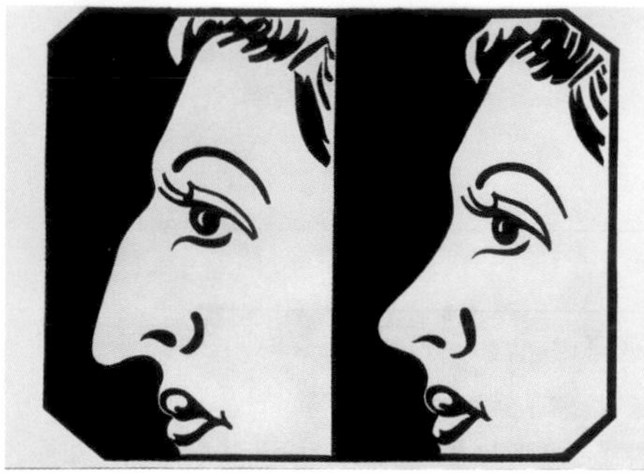

Andy Warhol, a pivotal figure in the development of Pop art, has become one of the most influential artists of the second half of the twentieth century. During the 1950s, Warhol was a commercial illustrator, acclaimed for his playful advertisements. When he turned to fine art in 1960, he employed the methods of commercial art as he mined America's fast-growing consumer and media culture for his imagery.

The graphic for *Before and After, 3* was borrowed from a crudely drawn advertisement for cosmetic surgery, the type found in the back of newspapers. Warhol rendered the faces in the flat, impersonal character of commercial art—no brushstrokes visible—but on a canvas more than 8 feet wide. In this sense, *Before and After, 3* constitutes a hilarious riposte to the grand painterly gestures and heroic size of Abstract Expressionist canvases. The painting also signifies the promise of magical transformation that became such a large part of American postwar consumer society, a promise with which the artist himself was unabashedly obsessed. Warhol was fascinated by makeovers and reinvention, whether epitomized by Hollywood starlets or drag queens. He had plastic surgery on his own nose in the 1950s.

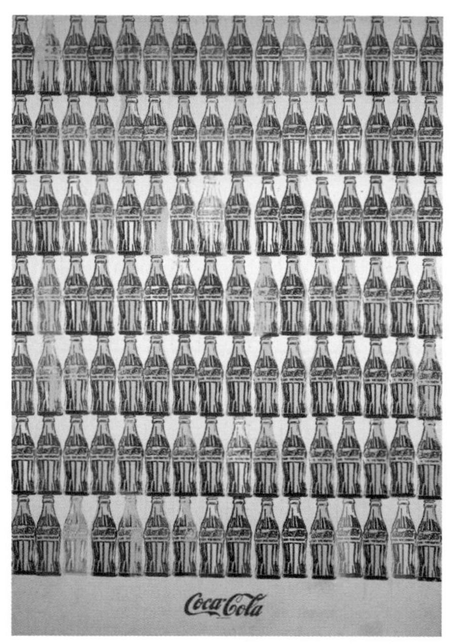

Green Coca-Cola Bottles consists of a grid of 112 bottles of Coca-Cola aligned above the company's logo. The repetitive imagery evokes the look of mechanical reproduction, but the bottles were most likely stamped individually from a single carved woodblock, leaving variously weighted and inked impressions. In his deadpan and ironic way, Warhol both criticized and celebrated the consumerist idols and surface values of America's media-saturated culture. "A Coke is a Coke," he explained, "and no amount of money can get you a better Coke than the one the bum on the corner is drinking."

Before and After, 3, 1962
Synthetic polymer and graphite on canvas, 72 x 99 5/8 in. (182.9 x 253.1 cm)
Purchase, with funds from Charles Simon 71.226

Green Coca-Cola Bottles, 1962
Acrylic, silkscreen ink, and pencil on canvas, 82 1/2 x 57 in. (209.6 x 144.8 cm)
Purchase, with funds from the Friends of the Whitney Museum of American Art 68.25

MAX WEBER
1881–1961

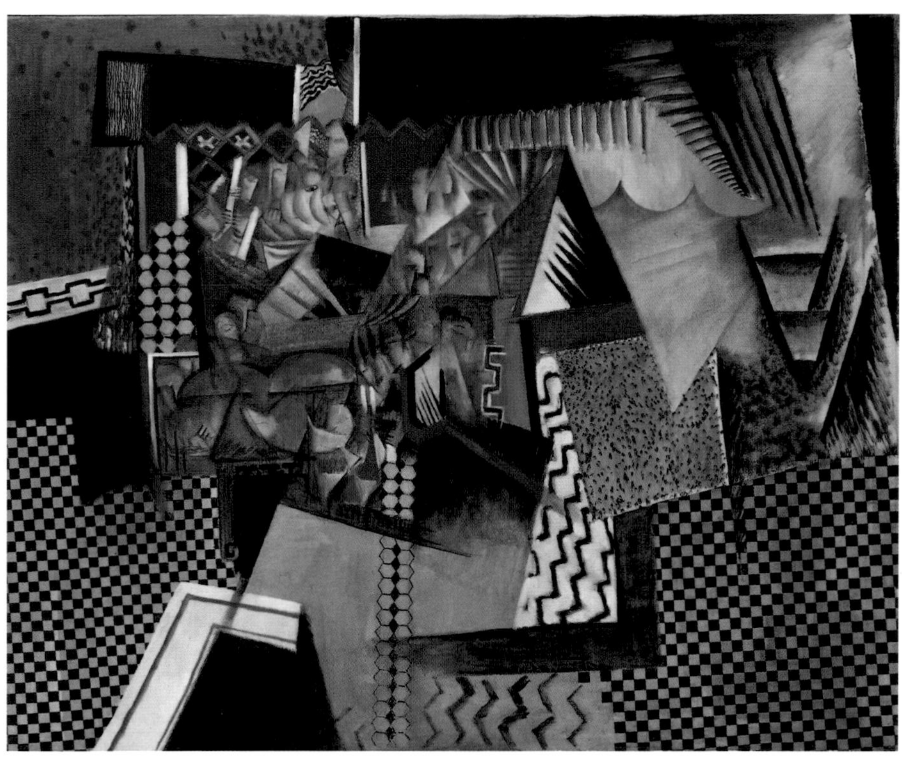

As the title declares, this work depicts a Chinese restaurant, one of the many that were opening in New York in the early twentieth century, as a growing number of immigrants from Asia settled in America. Max Weber loved these restaurants, and his painting seeks to evoke the sense of entering one of the brightly lit and ornately decorated establishments. Weber, himself an immigrant (he was born in Białystok, Russia), wanted to capture the collective sensations of dining amid the hustle and bustle typical of New York's Chinese restaurants. He achieved these dynamic effects by assimilating the high-pitched palette of the Fauves and the lessons of French Cubism, here evident in the fragmentation of forms combined with patterned sections that recall the wallpaper incorporated in Cubist collage.

Although *Chinese Restaurant* is rendered abstractly, Weber gives the viewer clues to the realistic subject matter: the repeated pattern of the restaurant floor, the scrolled leg of a table, the Chinese red-black-and-gold color scheme, and the suggestion of tabletops. *Chinese Restaurant* was exhibited in the first annual exhibition of the Society of Independent Artists, held in New York in April 1917, and served as an example of how thoroughly Weber had absorbed European modernism. In this and other canvases of the period, he translated a European style into a potent vehicle for expressing the dynamism of the new American urban landscape.

***Chinese Restaurant*,** 1915
Oil on canvas, 40 x 48 in. (101.6 x 121.9 cm)
Purchase 31.382

WEEGEE (ARTHUR FELLIG)

1899–1968

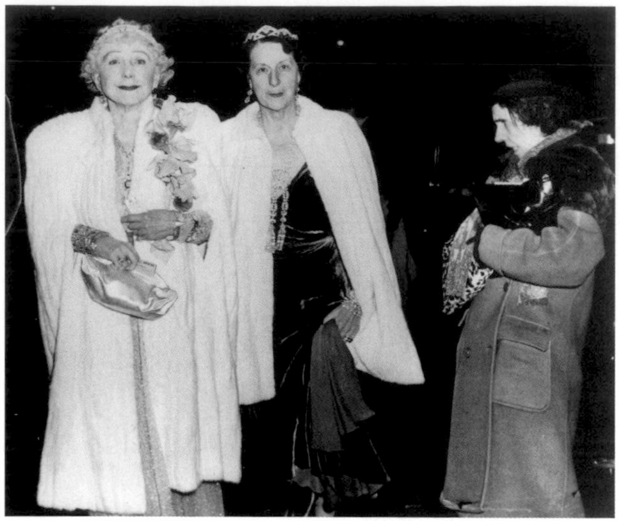

Weegee's sensational career as a freelance photographer started in 1935, when he abandoned his graveyard-shift darkroom job and began driving around nighttime New York taking hard-boiled pictures of car accidents, gangster murders, tenement fires, and other nocturnal tragedies. His photographs, which he hustled to local newspapers the following morning, revealed a vibrant Gotham bursting with chaos and macabre drama. But Weegee's preoccupation with the gritty adventure of city life extended beyond his tabloid-style crime pictures. Roaming the city with his Speed Graphic camera, he also photographed summertime Coney Island's teeming crowds and the raunchy flock of misfits at Sammy's, a club he frequented on the Bowery, along with photographer Lisette Model (p. 210).

Weegee's reputation (and his nickname, a phonetic approximation of "ouija" board) was earned because of his uncanny knack for anticipating disasters and climactic moments. However, he was also an unrepentant showman and self-advertiser, and his most famous image, *The Critic*, was the result of a carefully orchestrated scenario. On the opening night of the Metropolitan Opera House's sixtieth season, an occasion advertised as a Diamond Jubilee, Weegee brought along a regular from Sammy's club, whom he plied with cheap wine and coaxed into this photograph of two of New York's most famous benefactors, Mrs. George W. Kavenaugh and Lady Decies. Weegee's trademark explosive flash, which allowed him to photograph at night and gave a floodlit effect to the exposure, bleached out skin tones and set up stark contrasts between the white-clad rich and the grubby poor. To further intensify his manufactured confrontation, he dramatically cropped the print to eliminate sideline spectators. When Acme Newspictures ran the photo, a caption was added that turned Weegee's sardonic commentary on ostentatious wealth into moral indignation: "She is aghast at the quantity of diamonds in evidence at a wartime opening of the Met, but the bejeweled ladies are aware only of Weegee's clicking camera."

The Critic, 1943
Gelatin silver print, 10 1/2 x 12 1/2 in. (26.7 x 31.8 cm)
Gift of Denise Rich 96.90.2

CARRIE MAE WEEMS

b. 1953

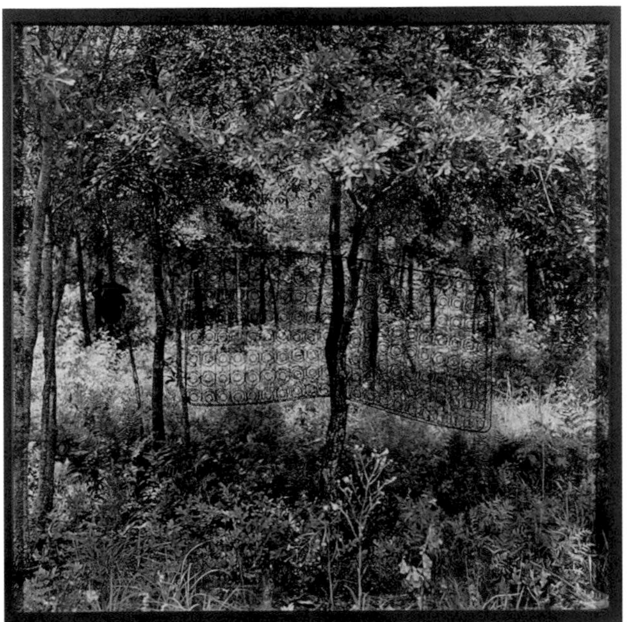

Carrie Mae Weems' *Sea Island Series*, to which this photograph belongs, celebrates a group of isolated African-American communities off the coasts of Georgia and South Carolina. On these remote islands, Gullah, a culture (and a name) derived from the Gola tribe of West Africa, still survives. Inhabitants of the islands are descendants of Gola tribespeople who were brought to this country as slaves as early as the seventeenth century. In addition to straightforward photographs of various sites such as this one, the *Sea Island Series* includes staged photographs, rephotographed ethnographic images, and ceramic plates bearing texts that all begin, "Went looking for Africa." Indeed, Weems' involvement with this series eventually led her to visit Africa for the first time. This photograph affirms the strength of Gullah ties to traditional belief systems. It depicts a bedspring wedged into the fork of a tree—which Weems says is meant to ensnare evil spirits. But the image also sustains a delicate, mournful beauty that transcends time and place.

A daughter of sharecroppers who moved in the 1950s to Portland, Oregon, where she grew up, Weems made her first photographs when she was in her twenties. Her academic training is in both fine art and folklore (she has graduate degrees in both). Political conviction drives her work, but not exclusively. "I'd come out of a serious political background," she says, "and I'm always thinking about political issues. But being politically correct has a very narrow margin for failure." Nevertheless, Weems' work is related to that of other artists, including Catherine Opie, Lorna Simpson, and David Wojnarowicz (pp. 231, 285, 327), who in the late 1980s and 1990s made photographic work that dealt with social or identity politics.

Untitled, 1992
Gelatin silver print, 19 3/4 x 19 3/4 in. (50.2 x 50.2 cm)
Gift of Carrie Mae Weems and P.P.O.W. 97.97.1

LAWRENCE WEINER

b. 1942

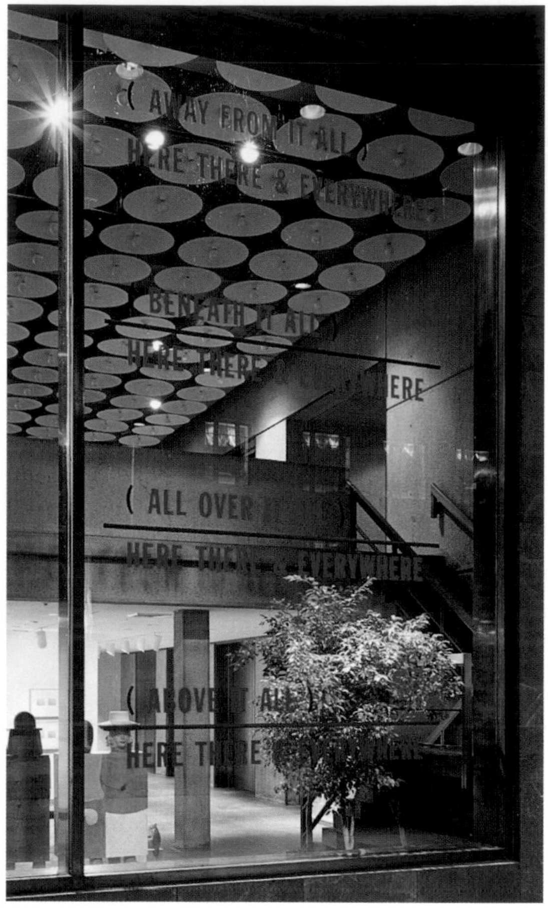

Lawrence Weiner was among the first generation of Conceptual artists, a group that also included Joseph Kosuth (p. 169). These artists gave priority to ideas over visual images and forms, transforming the traditional art object into a site for the presentation of concepts. Weiner's work teaches us, quite literally, how to read art. He uses language to refer to materials, procedures, conditions, and actions, but emphatically calls this language-based activity sculpture rather than poetry or literature. His work appears in varying formats and contexts, including wall texts, books, posters, films, videos, public sculpture, exhibition announcements, stickers, and even pop songs. Constructing art out of shifting statements and propositions, Weiner explores the way that language mediates things, contexts, and experiences, raising questions about how viewers relate to art, objects, places, and each other.

Here There & Everywhere consists of eight lines of text, comprising a chorus and refrain of four directionally related statements: (AWAY FROM IT ALL)/HERE THERE & EVERYWHERE; (BENEATH IT ALL)/HERE THERE & EVERYWHERE; (ALL OVER IT ALL)/HERE THERE & EVERYWHERE; (ABOVE IT ALL)/HERE THERE & EVERYWHERE. The open-ended concept is characteristic of Weiner's art. In the same expansive spirit, he allows the work to be installed either on four separate walls or, as in the Whitney Museum installation pictured here, together on a single window: the decision, like the installation itself, is up to the curator. Art is like language, Weiner reminds us, and is not fixed in its significance, but subject to change according to "various manners with various things."

Here There & Everywhere, 1989
Vinyl lettering on wall/glass, dimensions variable
Purchase, with funds from the Contemporary Painting and Sculpture Committee 94.136

H.C. WESTERMANN

1922–1981

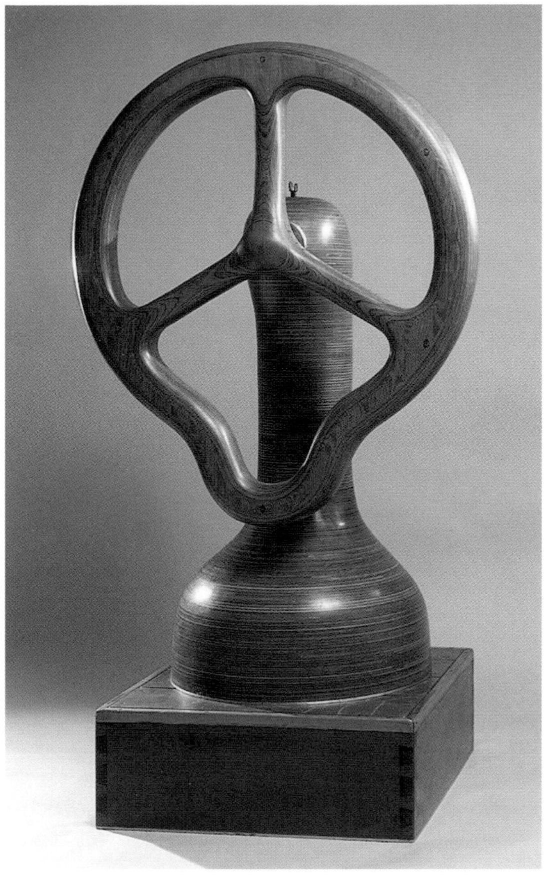

Flawlessly constructed of marine plywood and Douglas fir, *Antimobile* is made to move: the wheel turns on an axle fashioned from a bicycle pedal with a ball-bearing mechanism. But everything about *Antimobile*, from its name to its drooping contour, suggests immobility. This evocative subversion of functionalism can be linked to Surrealism—the molten form recalls, in particular, Salvador Dalí's famous dripping watches, though the Surrealist with whom H.C. Westermann is most often compared is the master assemblagist Joseph Cornell (p. 79).

Westermann's development as an artist, however, was far more complex than such a genealogy suggests. His imagery was originally inspired by his service in the Marine Corps during World War II (and later the Korean War). As an anti-aircraft gunner on the U.S.S. *Enterprise*, he watched ships being destroyed by suicide attacks from the air. He also acquired professional skills in carpentry and acrobatics—in 1947, he toured Asia as part of a USO acrobatic act—and attended art school. His impeccable craftsmanship and attention to detail, the physical poise of his work, and its highly developed sense of the absurd can be traced to these varied experiences.

Just below the mordant humor that characterizes Westermann's work there is often anger at the crass consumerism he saw overtaking American culture: "everything is on wheels...a hundred million cars...and everything turns and it's all a bunch of junk....I wanted to make something that was just completely anti-wheel, anti-mobile." Though in scale and material more like a ship's wheel than a car's—an allusion to Westermann's wartime experiences—*Antimobile* remains a penetrating expression of his belief that rampant industrialization had run amok in American society.

Antimobile, 1966
Laminated plywood, 67 1/4 x 35 1/2 x 27 1/2 in. (170.8 x 90.2 x 69.9 cm) overall
Purchase, with funds from the Howard and Jean Lipman Foundation, Inc. and exchange 69.4a–b

FRED WILSON
b. 1954

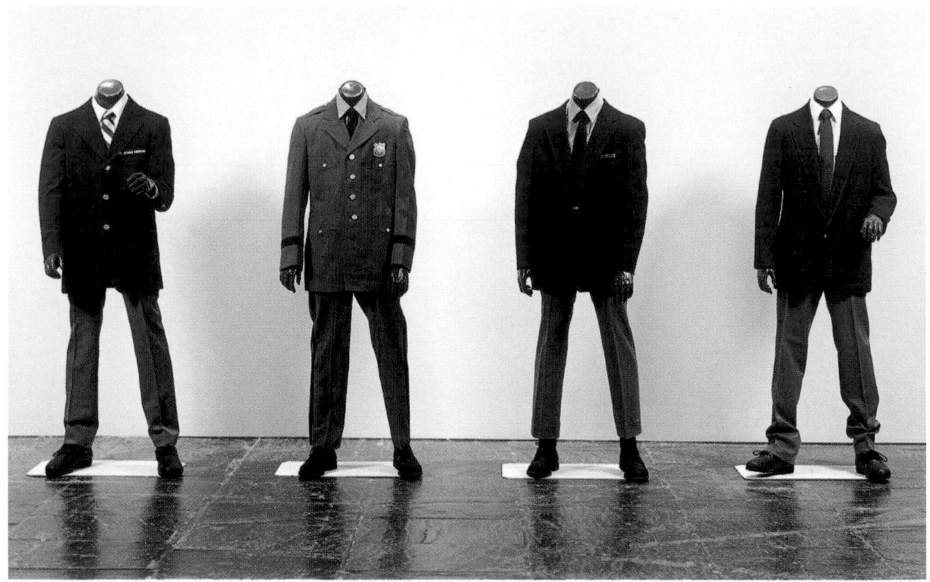

In an approach initiated by Conceptual artists in the 1960s and now referred to as "institutional critique," Fred Wilson's sculptures and installations reveal the ideological biases and presumptions implicit in the everyday practices of museums. The artist's initial installations in the late 1980s consisted of simulations of ethnographic displays in museumlike settings, including arrangements of tribal objects accompanied by fictional museum labels. Through creative and incisive use of these text labels as well as unexpected juxtapositions of objects and images, Wilson confronts issues of museology, racism, ethnography, and colonialism. Since the early 1990s, this institutional scrutiny has taken place within the context of actual museums. Conflating the roles of artist, activist, and curator, Wilson raises questions about the politics of race, representation, and history through an examination of cultural institutions and their narratives of collecting and exhibiting.

Guarded View consists of four black, headless mannequins wearing the distinctive uniforms of security guards at four Manhattan museums—the Whitney, The Museum of Modern Art, The Metropolitan Museum of Art, and The Jewish Museum. In this work, Wilson departs somewhat from his usual area of investigation to explore the nature of the museum's own workforce. Evoking a historical costume room display, *Guarded View* expresses Wilson's perspective that in museum hierarchies, people of color are most often found in the role of security guards. By creating an ironic distance from something we often see but may never really perceive, Wilson challenges us to respond to entrenched social and economic inequities. "I believe a critique of the system is possible within the institution itself," he asserts.

Guarded View, 1991
Wood, paint, steel, and fabric, dimensions variable
Gift of the Peter Norton Family Foundation 97.84a–d

ROBERT WILSON

b. 1941

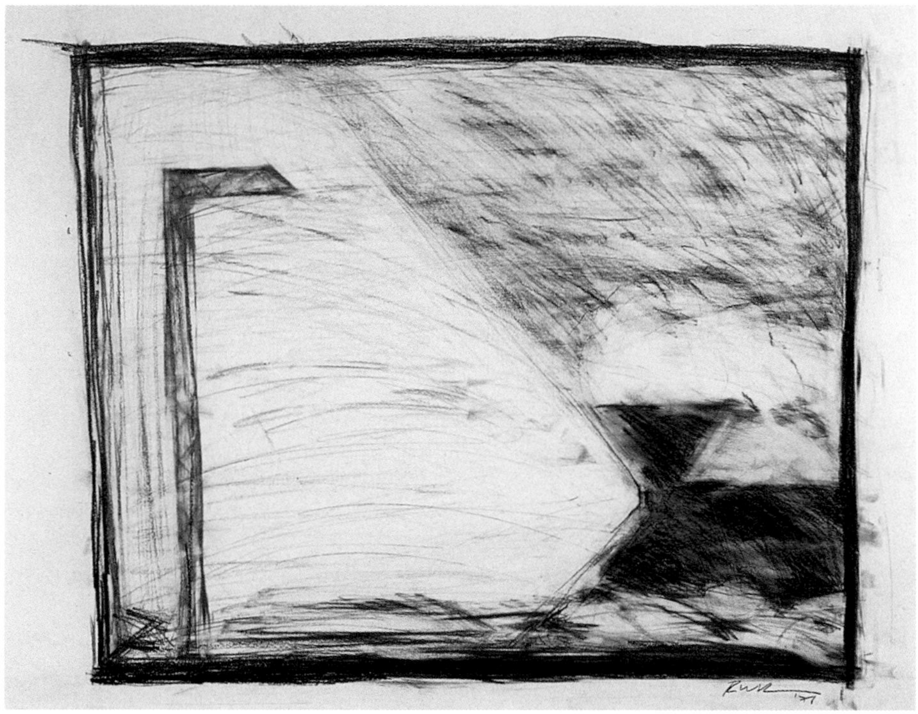

The reach of Robert Wilson's avant-garde art is so long that normal categories such as sculptor, video artist, draftsman, or designer are too limiting. He has worked in all these media as well as designed, produced, and directed experimental theater and opera.

Einstein on the Beach, a landmark work of 1976, with music by Philip Glass, was the first of Wilson's massive operatic productions to treat a biographical subject. The opera takes off, in Wilson's vanguard manner, from a famous anecdote about the young Albert Einstein. Einstein dreamt he was lying on a hill, watching a man above him flying on a beam of light and carrying a mirror held in front of him. Because he is moving at the speed of light, the man can never see his reflection; only Einstein, dreaming on his back, can observe both the man and his mirror reflection. Time, space, and velocity resurface in Wilson's 108 graphite illustrations of the opera's scene-by-scene progression. The progression from image to image—of a barely etched approaching train, of light dispersing over moving figures—can be subtle, almost neutral; at other times an abrupt shift signals the start of a new scene. In the drawing here, a volume of space animated by soft, crystalline lines simultaneously evokes the space of the theater and that of Einstein's profoundly abstract imagination. In Wilson's vision, the two registers collapse, giving back to Einstein's mathematical formulations the clarity of a dream.

Einstein on the Beach, 1976
Graphite on paper, 29 7/8 x 35 3/4 in. (75.9 x 90.8 cm)
Gift of an anonymous donor 98.87

GARRY WINOGRAND

1928–1984

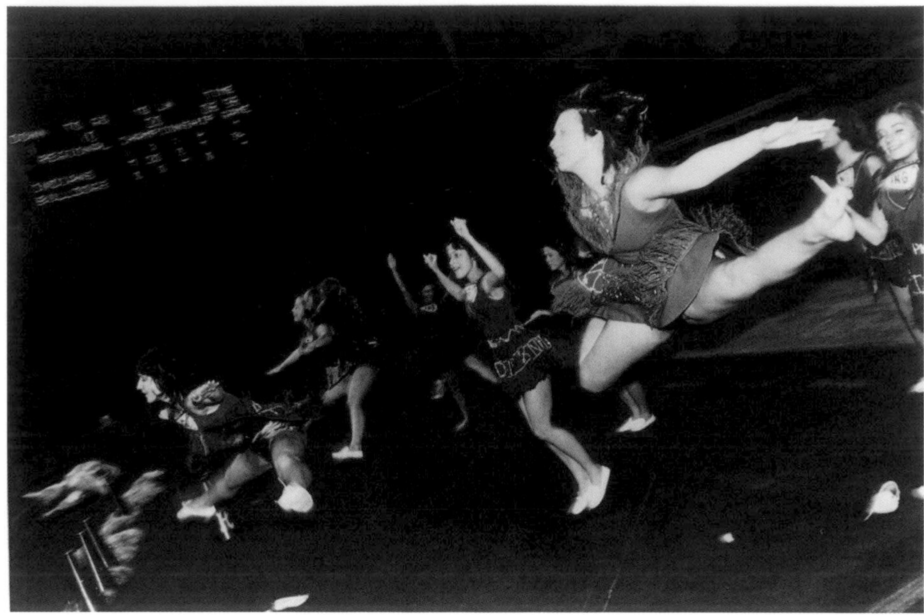

Garry Winogrand's forceful photographs, taken on city streets and in other public places, visually transcribed the off-kilter, energetic pace of America in the 1960s and 1970s. A native New Yorker, Winogrand felt most at home when surrounded by the vigorous crush of life, which he photographed voraciously. But his was not a documentarian's approach: he understood that the fugitive narratives he registered with his 35mm camera were an "illusion of a literal description of a piece of time and space." What fascinated him were not social or historic facts, but rather the formal relationships that could be glimpsed in casual, public encounters.

Winogrand's choice of vernacular subject matter was deeply influenced by the work of Walker Evans and Robert Frank (p. 109), but his unorthodox approach to pictorial composition—evident in *Houston, Texas*—was novel. Within the picture frame, he established a vertical axis (here, the invisible line falling from the main cheerleader's face down to her bent knee), which forced the horizon to tilt dizzyingly. Such tilted horizons, characteristic of Winogrand's work, add energy and a sense of spontaneity to the picture. In *Houston, Texas*, the extended legs of the cheerleader parallel the angle of the tilt, as if frenzied acrobatics rather than artistic will had determined the dynamics of the composition.

Although he was a capable darkroom technician, Winogrand was infinitely more passionate about making his images than printing them, a task he often left to others. When he died in 1984, he left more than 300,000 unexamined, unprinted negatives from the last years of his life.

Houston, Texas, 1977
Gelatin silver print, 8 7/8 x 13 5/16 in. (22.5 x 33.8 cm)
Gift of Mr. and Mrs. Raymond W. Merritt 98.40.3

JACKIE WINSOR

b. 1941

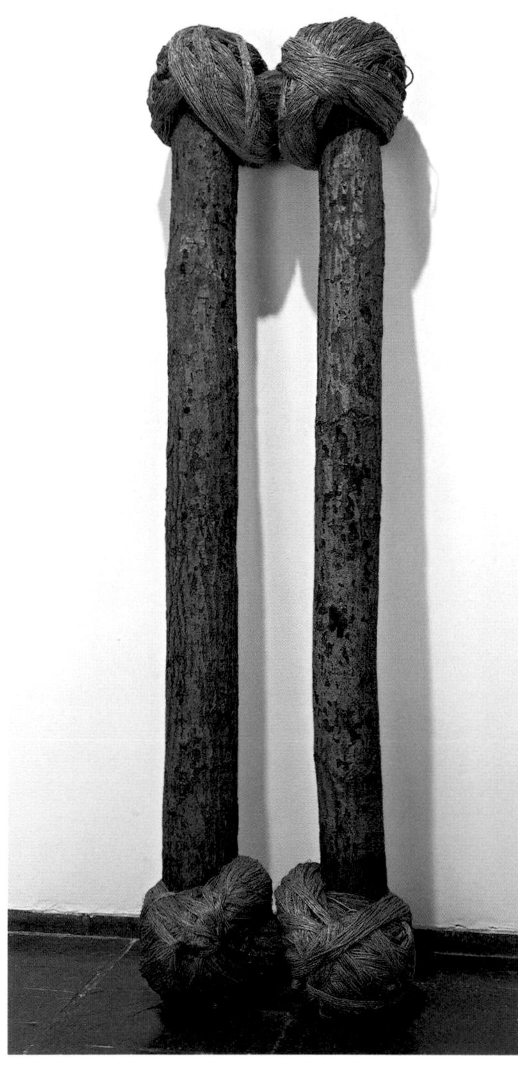

The raw tree trunks and hemp twine of *Bound Logs* reflect Jackie Winsor's resistance, in her early work, to the industrial fabrication techniques associated with Minimalism (pp. 160, 292). Winsor's sculptures of this period, by contrast, brandish their rough, unpolished surfaces and the evidence of the artist's hand. The abundant twine joining the corners of *Bound Logs* exceeds functional requirements, and in this surplus of repetitive effort there is a connection with the meditative practices of ritual—albeit ritual of a decidedly secular variety. As in the contemporaneous work of Eva Hesse (p. 138) and other like-minded artists, the time-consuming, contemplative wrapping involved in making *Bound Logs* represented a new emphasis on process rather than finished product. As critic Mark Stevens wrote, "Jackie Winsor's sculpture celebrates it own making: it's as much verb as noun."

Winsor grew up in coastal Newfoundland, a landscape she remembers as "made barren both by civilization, when farmers cleared the land, and by nature, the wind and the sea." The simplified structure of her work and the physically demanding, deliberate character of her working methods suggest an internalization of these conditions. *Bound Logs* also addresses the uncertain boundary between inside and out—what in this piece is the contour and what conveys its volume? Equally ambivalent is Winsor's attitude toward nature. The heavily articulated joints of *Bound Logs*, she says, were a means of "subduing" the aggressive presence of the trunks, so that they wouldn't look "like all outdoors." Yet in their related coloring and texture, the logs and hemp are symbiotic, signaling a confluence of nature and the artist's handiwork.

Bound Logs, 1972–73
Wood and hemp, 114 x 29 x 18 in. (289.6 x 73.7 x 45.7 cm)
Purchase, with funds from the Howard and Jean Lipman Foundation, Inc. 74.53

TERRY WINTERS

b. 1949

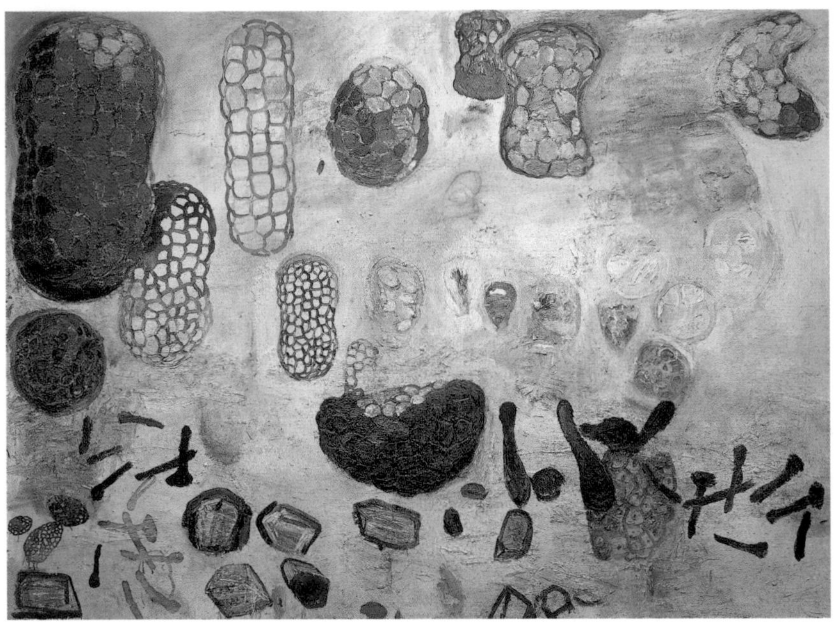

Terry Winters, along with Carroll Dunham (p. 98) and other artists, reinvigorated the language of organic abstraction in the 1980s. A methodical craftsman, Winters ground his own paint pigments; by 1980 he was painting representations of the crystalline structure of the minerals in the pigments, the first of many metaphors he has used for articulating the most fundamental properties of painting. Working from nature itself and in natural history museums, he was soon drawing spores, pollen, ova, and embryos, as well as microscopic organic structures. At first these elements were rendered schematically, isolated in barren fields of paint, but by the early 1980s they began to come together to suggest an incipient landscape—or the populace of a nascent society.

In *Good Government*, the forms include crystals, chromosome fragments, dividing cells, and indeterminate bits of organic matter. This large painting occupied Winters for three months, reaching resolution when he "thought it looked like one of those maps you saw in grammar school and it said 'good government' and everything was working together." Also relevant to Winters' concept is the famous fourteenth-century fresco of the same title by Ambrogio Lorenzetti in the Palazzo Pubblico, Siena. An allegory of enlightened civic rule, it is partly based on Aristotelian ideals and, as in Winters' painting, the elements are seen from several independent perspectives. An artist of considerable erudition, Winters had named a previous series of paintings for Theophrastus, a disciple of Aristotle. But such references explain, at most, only the inception of a work. "I always start from someplace outside myself," Winters has said, "and end up someplace inside myself."

***Good Government**, 1984
Oil on canvas, 101 1/4 x 137 1/4 in. (257.2 x 348.6 cm)
Purchase, with funds from The Mnuchin Foundation and the Painting and Sculpture Committee 85.15

DAVID WOJNAROWICZ

1954–1992

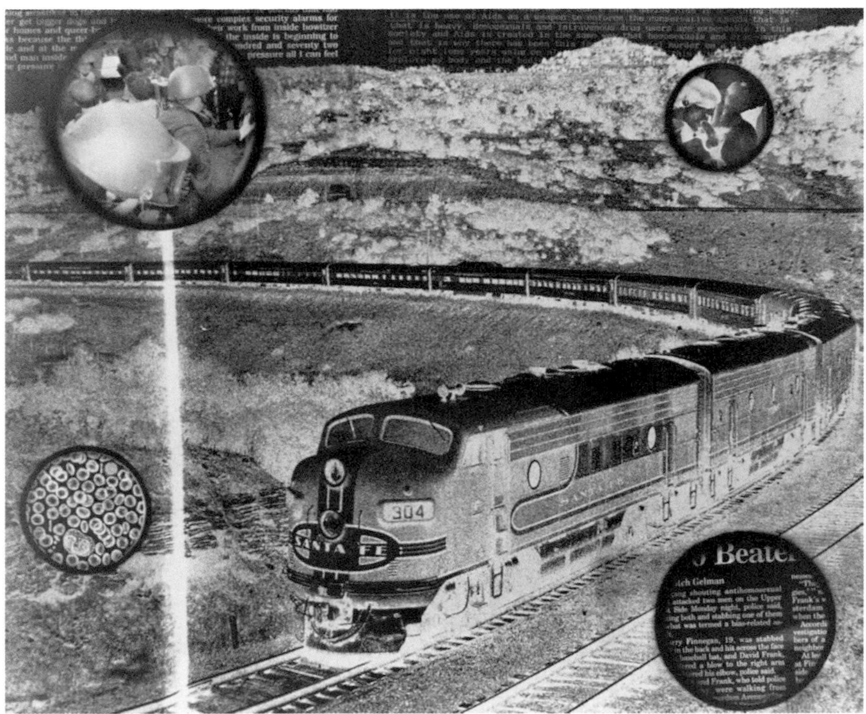

Like David Wojnarowicz's work in other, widely varied media, the eight large, heavily layered and manipulated photographs in the *Sex Series* express outrage at homophobia and classism, militarism and environmental irresponsibility, and, especially, indifference to AIDS (of which the artist died). The prints were made by putting color slides in an enlarger and exposing them directly onto black-and-white photographic paper, producing a reversal of negative and positive tonal values. Dropped into these stock photographs—of cityscapes and landscapes, trains and planes—are secondary images, whose tonal values are also reversed. These circular cameo shots feature a variety of subjects: explicit sex, cellular life, and riot police in action against demonstrators. In three of the *Sex Series* prints, a third layer of representation takes the form of texts printed in ghostly white. Those used here—two across the top and another in the cameo at bottom right—refer to gay bashing and other homophobic activities, including an invective against the "use of AIDS as a weapon to enforce a conservative agenda."

With varying degrees of explicitness, Wojnarowicz's work reflects a desperately difficult youth and a lifelong anger at the way the homosexual world that framed his early experiences remains invisible to mainstream culture. Along with other activist artists of his generation, Wojnarowicz used his art as a tool of education and resistance.

Untitled, 1989
Gelatin silver print, 14 7/8 x 17 11/16 in. (37.8 x 44.9 cm)
Purchase, with funds from The Sondra and Charles Gilman Jr. Foundation, the Robert Mapplethorpe Foundation, Inc., and the Richard and Dorothy Rodgers Fund 92.75.5

STEVE WOLFE

b. 1955

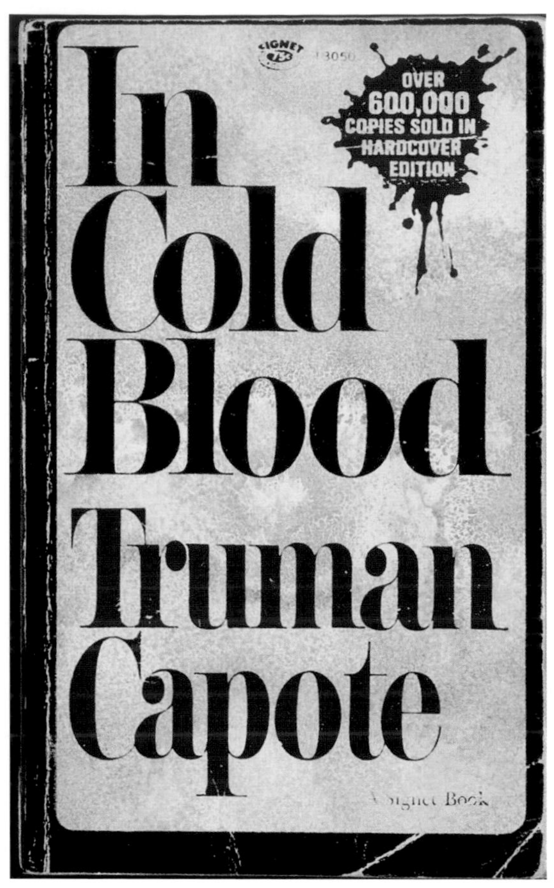

Since 1986, Steve Wolfe has made enigmatic painted sculptures that physically simulate selected books. As with his other works based on record and album covers, Wolfe deploys a *trompe-l'oeil* technique involving a variety of sculptural, painterly, and commercial printing processes. Creating a dialogue between the mass-produced and the fastidiously handcrafted, Wolfe remakes, to original scale, such books as Marcel Proust's *Remembrance of Things Past* and Michel Foucault's *This Is Not a Pipe*, transforming them into uncanny aesthetic objects.

All of Wolfe's sculptures are based on books he has owned and/or read. *Untitled (In Cold Blood)* replicates the hardcover edition of Truman Capote's 1965 work *In Cold Blood*, the popular novelistic account of a family murdered shotgun-style and the killers' trial. This painted work, fashioned of wood and modeling paste, is a meticulous simulation of a well-worn, dog-eared, and even dirtied copy, suggesting both avid use and age. But this is not, of course, a book. *Untitled (In Cold Blood)* hangs on the wall like a painting; it can neither be opened nor read. Lacking this fundamental character of books, it evokes a sense of loss or absence. As writer Todd Alden observed, Wolfe's object offers "a wry, dispassionate commentary on the current predicament of books (and art) in late capitalist media culture—a society that often seems to value not what collectors have to say about books and culture, but what books (or art) have to say about collectors."

Untitled (In Cold Blood), 1992
Oil, screenprint, and modeling paste on wood, 7 x 4 1/4 x 3/4 in. (17.8 x 10.8 x 1.9 cm)
Purchase, with funds from Arthur Goldberg and The List Purchase Fund 92.115

MARTIN WONG

1946–1999

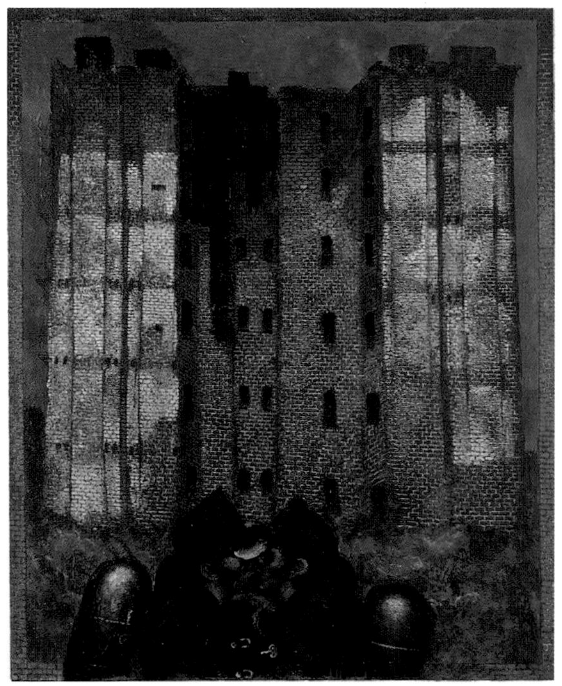

In 1981, Martin Wong moved from San Francisco to New York's Lower East Side, an area known as "Loisaida" by its predominantly Hispanic residents. A self-taught painter with a degree in ceramics, he began to chronicle the neighborhood's people, run-down buildings, and storefronts with a straightforward, naturalistic approach, reminiscent of the Ashcan School painters of the early twentieth century and the urban realists who succeeded them in the 1930s. Like Paul Cadmus and Reginald Marsh (pp. 61, 198), among others, Wong infused his "realism" with healthy doses of fantasy and desire.

In *Big Heat*, a typical brick tenement of the Lower East Side is the backdrop for a striking image of two firemen kissing. The ethereal sensations of romance are contrasted with the stark physicality of the tenement bricks, which Wong has rendered with thick deposits of acrylic paint that give them a palpable presence, even to the brick-painted frame around the canvas. Wong often enclosed his pictures in a variety of elaborate frames—from gilt Baroque extravaganzas to *trompe-l'oeil* borders simulating wood or, as in *Big Heat*, brick.

The passages of green spray paint on the frame of *Big Heat* are a reminder that Wong was an avid collector and supporter of graffiti art. He saw graffiti as tangible evidence that art and beauty can flourish in even the most unexpected, squalid urban places. *Big Heat* is Wong's utopian vision of hope, love, and redemption within the crumbling environs of what was once one of New York's poorest neighborhoods.

Big Heat, 1988
Synthetic polymer on canvas, 60 1/8 x 48 in. (152.7 x 121.9 cm)
Purchase, with funds from the Painting and Sculpture Committee 99.89

GRANT WOOD

1892–1942

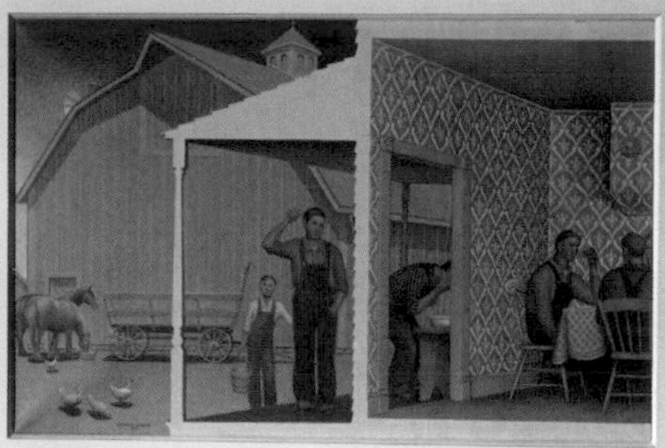

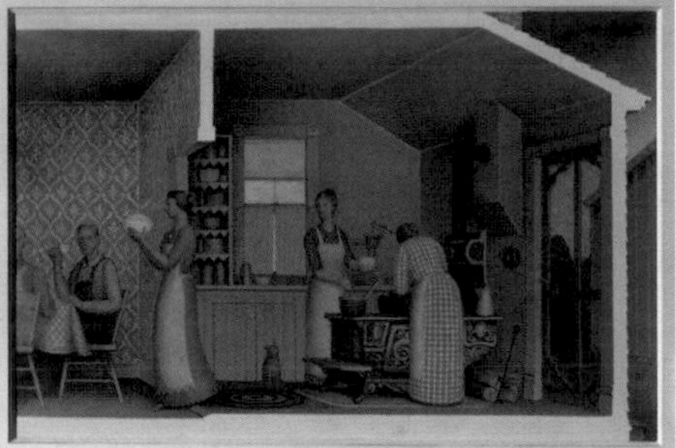

These two parts of a preparatory drawing for Grant Wood's *Dinner for Threshers* depict an annual rite in the rural Iowa of the artist's youth: neighbors would travel from farm to farm threshing grain, and then gather together for a bountiful meal served on the host family's finest china. Wood and his Regionalist contemporaries, among them Thomas Hart Benton and Joe Jones (pp. 49, 158), celebrated the work ethic and communal values of the nation's heartland, but drew criticism for ignoring the bitter realities of the Depression.

Dinner for Threshers, however, is not set in the 1930s, but in the 1890s. The women wear long skirts and cook on a cast-iron stove; horses, not engines, power the farm equipment. Wood, who was born in 1892, spent the first ten years of his life on a farm, until his father's death forced his mother to sell their land. Although his family moved to the town of Cedar Rapids, Wood never forgot his idyllic youth: "Alexander, Caesar, Napoleon, you all had your great moments, but you never tasted the supreme triumph; you were never a farm boy riding in from the fields on a bulging rack of a new-mown hay."

Wood's childhood journey from farm to town mirrored the nation's transformation from an agrarian society to an industrial one. *Dinner for Threshers* eulogizes a way of life that was gradually disappearing. Inspired by late medieval panel paintings of biblical narratives, Wood has created his own version of the Last Supper. Even in the depths of the Depression, even as industrialization threatened America's rural landscape, salvation, Wood suggests, could be found in a simple repast.

Dinner for Threshers (left section), 1933
Graphite and gouache on paper, 17 3/4 x 26 3/4 in. (45.1 x 68 cm)
Purchase 33.79

Dinner for Threshers (right section), 1933
Graphite and gouache on paper, 17 3/4 x 26 3/4 in. (45.1 x 68 cm)
Purchase 33.80

CHRISTOPHER WOOL

b. 1955

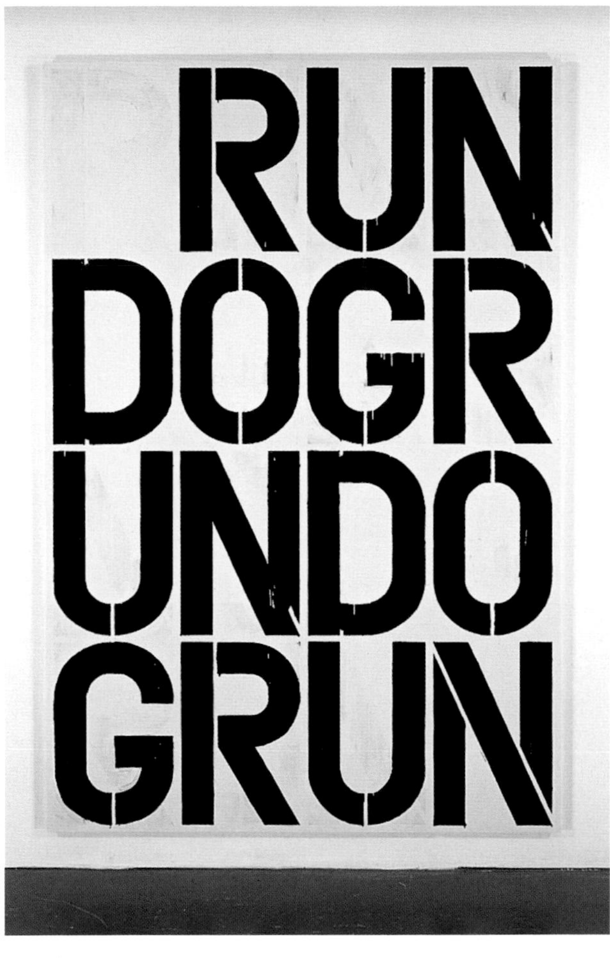

Christopher Wool works with familiar words and phrases excerpted from American popular culture. Like many contemporary artists, he draws freely from an unprecedented array of source materials, including films, magazines, books, and even other art works. In this untitled painting, "Run Dog Run," the timeworn, three-word sentence from elementary school textbooks, becomes humorous and absurd through Wool's 9-foot-high, deadpan presentation. The childhood idiom, however, simultaneously conveys anxiety and danger, its repetition in bold capital letters reading like a warning sign on packaging or at a construction site. Wool heightens the work's sense of urgency and alarm by running the words together into a single compressed sequence. The arbitrary line breaks, moreover, make it difficult to distinguish basic syntax from the overall pattern of letters.

Wool paints on large sheets of aluminum with common industrial materials, such as paint rollers, rubber stamps, stencils, and a limited palette of the enamel paints used by commercial sign painters. With their crisp graphics, sleek surfaces, and standardized grid formats, his text-based paintings emit a cool, clean, machine-made quality. Only a few purposeful imperfections—a drip of pigment here or a minor textural irregularity there—blemish the mechanical evenness of Wool's compositions and reveal the artist's hand.

Untitled, 1990
Alkyd enamel on aluminum, 108 x 72 in. (274.3 x 182.9 cm)
Purchase, with funds from the Painting and Sculpture Committee 91.2

ANDREW WYETH

b. 1917

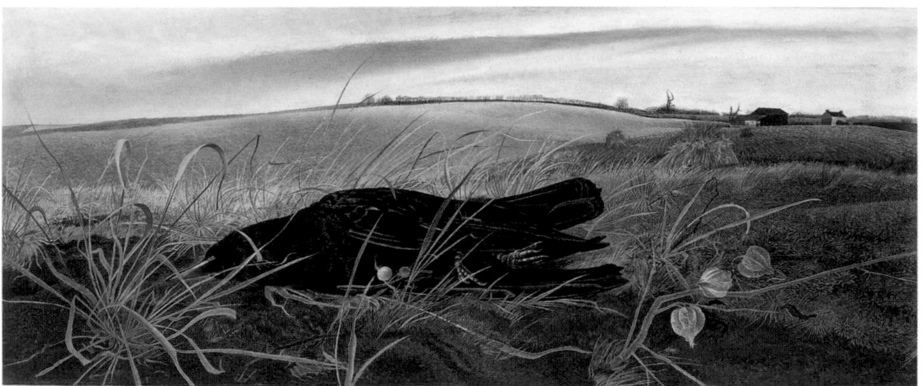

When the tide of American art was turning toward abstraction, Andrew Wyeth remained a realist, producing precise, evocative paintings of the places he knew best. *Winter Fields* depicts a dead crow Wyeth found near his home in Chadds Ford, Pennsylvania. He took the bird into his studio and made several sketches of its lifeless form. These drawings evolved into *Winter Fields*, which depicts the crow in exquisite detail, down to its twisted feet. Seen from a worm's-eye view, the body rests stiffly amid twisting blades of grass. From this perspective, the bird seems larger and its death assumes a wider significance. Completed during World War II, *Winter Fields* recalls photographs of corpses lying on battlefields. The painting, like the photographs, is a haunting, unflinching image of death.

Yet Wyeth resented comparisons of his work to photography and said he despised cameras. In fact, despite its apparent precision, *Winter Fields* subtly distorts reality. The distant trees are as sharply focused as the crow in the foreground—an impossibility for both the human eye and the camera lens. The visual effect is to compress the sense of space toward the surface, an effect accentuated by the lacelike, overlapping blades of grass, which create a delicate surface pattern. Wyeth lingers over each detail, carefully inscribing the bird's striated plumage or the delicate form of a Chinese lantern plant. *Winter Fields* does not simply record Wyeth's discovery of the dead crow; instead, each meticulous stroke of the brush memorializes the moment.

Winter Fields, 1942
Tempera on canvas, 17 1/4 x 41 in. (43.8 x 104.1 cm)
Gift of Mr. and Mrs. Benno C. Schmidt in memory of Mr. Josiah Marvel, first owner of this picture 77.91

MARGUERITE ZORACH

1887–1968

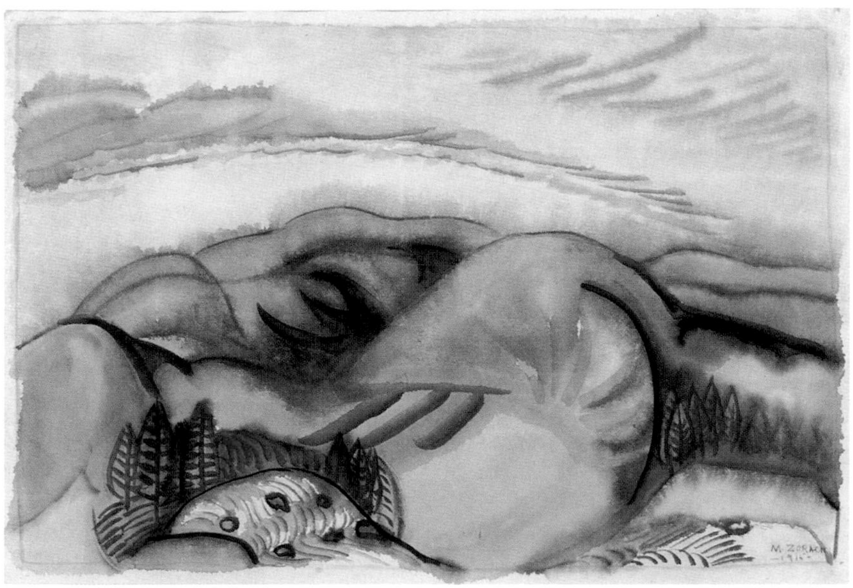

"Climb the mountains and get their good tidings. Nature's peace will flow into you as sunshine flows into trees." Marguerite Thompson tacked this passage from John Muir, the pioneer ecologist, to the wall of her Paris studio. For the young artist, born in Fresno, California, mountains represented the freedom to paint, to escape the confining world women of her generation were expected to inhabit. She had left that world in 1908, when she accepted an invitation to join an aunt in Paris. She spent the next three years studying art, and soon adopted the brilliant palette of the Fauves.

In 1911, Thompson and her aunt left Paris, traveling through the Middle East and Asia en route home to California. In her letters, she wrote often of the landscape, and especially admired the mountainous terrains of Switzerland, Palestine, and China. When she finally returned home, her family tried to dissuade her from a career in art, but while on vacation in the Sierra Mountains, she painted a series of bold Fauvist landscapes.

In 1912, Thompson married the artist William Zorach, whom she had met in Paris. Although career considerations compelled the Zorachs to live in New York, Marguerite detested the city, and insisted on spending summers elsewhere. During these productive summer months, she turned frequently to her beloved mountains. In *White Mountain Landscape, Number 1*, painted in New Hampshire, the vivid, Fauvist palette of her Parisian days is gone, replaced by subdued, almost gloomy colors. Yet Zorach's approach to the landscape, although emphatically modernist, still resists conventional categories. The loose, inventive brushwork follows the contours of the hills, creating, along with the stylized triangulation of the trees, patterns that are more descriptive of the artist's emotional response than of the setting itself.

White Mountain Landscape, Number 1, 1915
Watercolor on paper, 10 1/2 x 15 in. (26.7 x 38.1 cm)
Gift of the artist's children 71.158

WHITNEY MUSEUM OF AMERICAN ART OFFICERS AND TRUSTEES

ACKNOWLEDGMENTS

The curatorial staff of the Whitney Museum of American Art selected the works for this volume, with the assistance of Maxwell L. Anderson, Alice Pratt Brown Director, and Mary E. DelMonico, Project Director. The curators also contributed to the development of the content and offered invaluable suggestions at all stages of the manuscript: Barbara Haskell, curator of prewar art; Chrissie Iles, curator of film and video; David Kiehl, curator, prints; Janie C. Lee, curator, drawings; Dana Miller, assistant curator, postwar art; Christiane Paul, adjunct curator of new media arts; Marla Prather, curator of postwar art; Lawrence R. Rinder, Anne and Joel Ehrenkranz Curator of Contemporary Art; and Sylvia Wolf, Sondra Gilman Curator of Photography.

Individual texts were contributed by: Todd Alden, Rachel Haidu, Angela Kramer Murphy, Lisa Pasquariello, Nancy Princenthal, Veronica Roberts, Margaret Sundell, Anne Wehr. Whitney Museum staff: Christopher Eamon, Evelyn Hankins, Henriette Huldisch, Chrissie Iles, David Kiehl, Anne Lampe, Yvette Lee, Dana Miller, Jennifer Palladino, Christiane Paul, Glenn Phillips, Marla Prather, Lawrence R. Rinder, Debra Singer, and Yukiko Yamagata.

This book is a publication of the Whitney Museum of American Art
Director of Publications and New Media, Garrett White

Project Director: Mary E. DelMonico
Editor: Sheila Schwartz
Designer: Makiko Ushiba
Proofreaders: Elaine Koss and Susan Richmond
Research: Jennifer Brennan, Kenneth Fernandez, Henriette Huldisch, Jennifer Palladino, Veronica Roberts, and Yukiko Yamagata
Rights and Reproductions: Jennifer Belt, Anita Duquette, and Judy Greene
Curatorial Coordination: Henriette Huldisch

Printing: Dr. Cantz'sche Druckerei, Ostfildern, Germany
Color Separations: C+S Repro, Filderstadt, Germany
Binding: Kunst- und Verlagsbuchbinderei, Leipzig
Printed and bound in Germany

PHOTOGRAPH AND REPRODUCTION CREDITS

The Artists' Museum
All photographs on pp. 6–23 are in the collection of the Whitney Museum of American Art and the Frances Mulhall Achilles Library Archives, Whitney Museum of American Art, unless otherwise noted. Additional credits are acknowledged below.

6: Walt Kuhn, Kuhn Family Papers, and Armory Show Records, 1882–1996, Archives of American Art, Smithsonian Institution, Washington, D.C.; 7 (top): Reprinted with permission of Joanna T. Steichen; (bottom): Photo copy print by Geoffrey Clements; 9 (top): Fay S. Lincoln; (bottom): Samuel H. Gottscho; 11: © Walt Sanders/Black Star, New York; 12: © Arnold Newman/Getty Images; 13 (top and middle): Brooks Edler; (bottom): Ezra Stoller © Esto. All rights reserved.; 14 (top): Brooks Edler; (second from top): *Women's Wear Daily* photograph, Fairchild Publications, Inc., N.Y.; (second from bottom): Ezra Stoller © Esto. All rights reserved.; (bottom): Brooks Edler; 15: Art © Richard Serra/Artists Rights Society (ARS), New York; photograph © The Estate of Peter Moore/Licensed by VAGA, New York, NY; 16: Jeanne Trudeau; 17: Helaine Messer; 18 (top): Kira Perov; (bottom): Geoffrey Clements; 19: Paschall/Taylor; 20 (top): © Star Black; (middle): Jerry L. Thompson; (bottom) Paul Rocheleau; 21 (top): Matt Flynn; courtesy of Office of Metropolitan Architecture; (middle and bottom): © Patrick McMullan

The Artists and Their Works
Photograph and Reproduction Credits:
Peter Accettola: 45, 199 (top), 219 (right); David Allison: 39, 125, 204, 233, 240; Archival Color, New York: 181; Larry Barns: 221; Ben Blackwell: 87; Geoffrey Clements: 26, 27, 29, 30, 34, 37, 38, 41, 44, 46, 47, 48, 49 (bottom), 51, 52, 55, 57 (bottom), 58, 59, 61, 64, 68, 69, 70 (bottom), 73, 74, 75, 77, 79, 82, 83, 84, 85 (top), 86, 90, 91, 92 (top), 94 (top), 96, 97, 98, 103, 104, 106, 107, 108, 110, 114, 115, 116, 117 (top), 122 (bottom), 123 (bottom), 124, 128, 129, 131, 132, 137, 138 (bottom), 140, 142 (bottom), 144, 145 (top), 147, 149, 150, 151, 153, 154 (top), 155, 158, 161 (top), 162, 163 (top), 169, 170, 172, 176, 178, 182, 183, 185, 187, 189, 190, 191, 193, 195, 196 (bottom), 197, 198, 199 (bottom), 203, 210, 213, 215, 218, 220, 225, 229 (top), 239, 243, 244, 245 (top), 247, 249, 250 (top), 251, 252, 254 (top), 255, 256, 258, 259 (top), 260, 261, 263 (top), 264, 265 (bottom), 269, 271 (top), 272, 274 (top), 275, 277, 278, 279, 280, 282, 285, 286, 287 (top), 290, 291, 292, 293, 294, 297 (top), 298, 306, 307, 308, 309, 311, 313, 316 (bottom), 318, 319, 322, 323, 324, 327; Sheldan C. Collins: 31, 40, 42 (bottom), 50, 76, 78, 81 (bottom), 85 (bottom), 88, 89, 92 (bottom), 100, 102, 105, 112, 113, 119, 133 (bottom), 135, 152, 156, 159, 166 (top), 167, 171, 175, 177, 188, 192, 206, 207, 211, 219 (left), 230, 245 (bottom), 246, 253 (top), 268, 274 (bottom), 283, 287 (middle and bottom), 288 (top), 299, 301, 312, 314, 317, 320, 328, 329, 331, 332, 333; Charles W. Crist: 262; Pierre Dupuy: 139; Electronic Arts Intermix: 157, 202; Erma Estwick: 101, 310; Gamma One Conversions: 123 (top), 126 (top), 259 (bottom), 289 (left); George Hirose: 180, 303; Bill Jacobson: 43, 94 (bottom), 143 (top), 201, 212, 254 (bottom), 326; Jennifer Kotter: 33; Matthew Marks Gallery: 146; Robert E. Mates: 49 (top), 53, 54, 111, 142 (top), 154 (bottom), 160 (bottom), 234, 235, 236, 242 (top), 253 (bottom), 266, 297 (bottom), 304; Metro Pictures: 281; Richard Nicol: 121; Fredrik Nilsen: 305; Greta Olafsdottir: 257; Douglas M. Parker Studio: 241; Kira Perov: 315; Beth Phillips: 296; Shelby Roberts: 62; Paul Rocheleau: 184; Sandak, Inc.: 67 (bottom), 72, 148, 160 (top), 194, 231, 267, 284, 300, 316 (top), 330; Dimitris Skliris: 232; Steven Sloman: 35, 81 (top), 95, 126 (bottom), 127, 143 (bottom), 145 (bottom), 163 (bottom), 165, 166 (bottom), 196 (top), 209, 216, 223, 242 (bottom), 263 (bottom), 265 (top); Videography by Peter Strietmann: 42 (top); Jerry L. Thompson: 57 (top), 60, 63, 65, 66, 67 (top), 71, 93, 117 (bottom), 130, 138 (top), 164, 173, 214, 217, 222, 224, 229 (bottom), 238, 250 (bottom), 270, 271 (bottom), 273, 276, 288 (bottom), 289 (right), 290, 302, 325; Michael Tropea: 248; Malcolm Varon: 186, 321
Copyright Credits:
© 2001 The Josef and Anni Albers Foundation/Artists Rights Society (ARS), New York; Art © Carl Andre/Licensed by VAGA, New York, NY; © 1972 The Estate of Diane Arbus, LLC; © 2001 Richard Artschwager/Artists Rights Society (ARS), New York; © 1980 Richard Avedon; © 2001 Estate of Milton Avery/Artists Rights Society (ARS), New York; © Matthew Barney; © 2001 Artists Rights Society (ARS), New York/ADAGP, Paris (Jean-Michel Basquiat); © Romare Bearden Foundation/Licensed by VAGA, New York, NY; © Lynda Benglis/Licensed by VAGA, New York, NY; © T.H. Benton and R.P. Benton Testamentary Trusts/Licensed by VAGA, New York, NY; © Estate of Peter Blume/Licensed by VAGA, New York, NY; © Louise Bourgeois/Licensed by VAGA, New York, NY; © 2001 Estate of Alexander Calder/Artists Rights Society (ARS), New York; © Estate of Federico Castellon, Courtesy of Michael Rosenfeld Gallery, New York City; © 2001 John Chamberlain/Artists Rights Society (ARS), New York; © Christo 1973; Copyright © 1991 Sue Coe; © The Joseph and Robert Cornell Memorial Foundation/Licensed by VAGA, New York, NY; © John Currin, courtesy Andrea Rosen Gallery; © Estate of Stuart Davis/Licensed by VAGA, New York, NY; © 2001 Estate of Jay DeFeo/Artists Rights Society (ARS), New York; © Estate of Burgoyne Diller/Licensed by VAGA, New York, NY; © 2001 Jim Dine/Artists Rights Society (ARS), New York; © Richard Estes/Licensed by VAGA, New York, NY/Marlborough Gallery, NY; © 2001 Estate of Dan Flavin/Artists Rights Society (ARS), New York; Copyright Robert Frank, courtesy Pace/MacGill Gallery, New York; The Estate of Fritz Glarner, © 2001 Kunsthaus Zürich. All rights reserved.; © Nan Goldin, courtesy Matthew Marks Gallery, New York; © Estate of Félix González-Torres, courtesy Andrea Rosen Gallery; © 2001 Estate of Arshile Gorky/Artists Rights Society (ARS), New York; © Adolph and Esther Gottlieb Foundation/Licensed by VAGA, New York, NY; © Estate of Duane Hanson/Licensed by VAGA, New York, NY; © Estate of Keith Haring; Reproduced with the permission of the Estate of Eva Hesse; © 2001 Jenny Holzer/Artists Rights Society (ARS), New York; © 1981 The Estate of Peter Hujar, courtesy Matthew Marks Gallery, New York; © 2001 Robert Indiana–Morgan Art Foundation/Artists Rights Society (ARS), New York; © 2001 Robert Irwin/Artists Rights Society (ARS), New York; © 2001 Estate of Alfred Jensen/Artists Rights Society (ARS), New York; © Jasper Johns/Licensed by VAGA, New York, NY; Art © Donald Judd Estate/Licensed by VAGA, New York, NY; © Alex Katz/Licensed by VAGA, New York, NY/Marlborough Gallery, NY; © 2001 The Franz Kline Estate/Artists Rights Society (ARS), New York; © 2001 Willem de Kooning Revocable Trust/Artists Rights Society (ARS), New York; © Jeff Koons; © 2001 Joseph Kosuth/Artists Rights Society (ARS), New York; © 2001 Pollock-Krasner Foundation/Artists Rights Society (ARS), New York; © Gwendolyn Knight Lawrence, courtesy of the Jacob and Gwendolyn Lawrence Foundation; © 2001 Sol LeWitt/Artists Rights Society (ARS), New York; © Estate of Roy Lichtenstein; © 1958 Morris Louis; © 2001 Robert Mangold/Artists Rights Society (ARS), New York; © The Estate of Robert Mapplethorpe. Used by permission.; © 2001 Brice Marden/Artists Rights Society (ARS), New York; © 2001 Estate of John Marin/Artists Rights Society (ARS), New York; © 2001 Estate of Reginald Marsh/Art Students League, New York/Artists Rights Society (ARS), New York; © Estate of Gordon Matta-Clark/Artists Rights Society (ARS), New York; © Susan Meiselas/Magnum Photos, Inc.; © The Estate of Joan Mitchell; © 2001 Robert Morris/Artists Rights Society (ARS), New York; © Dedalus Foundation, Inc./Licensed by VAGA, New York, NY (Robert Motherwell); © Vik Muniz/Licensed by VAGA, New York, NY; © 2001 Bruce Nauman/Artists Rights Society (ARS), New York; © 1999 Shirin Neshat, courtesy Barbara Gladstone; © 2001 Estate of Louise Nevelson/Artists Rights Society (ARS), New York; © 2001 Barnett Newman Foundation/Artists Rights Society (ARS), New York; © Kenneth Noland/Licensed by VAGA, New York, NY; © 2001 The Georgia O'Keeffe Foundation/Artists Rights Society (ARS), New York; © Tom Otterness/Licensed by VAGA, New York, NY/Marlborough Gallery, NY; © 2001 Pollock-Krasner Foundation/Artists Rights Society (ARS), New York; © Robert Rauschenberg/Licensed by VAGA, New York, NY; © 2001 Man Ray Trust/Artists Rights Society, NY/ADAGP, Paris; © 2001 Estate of Ad Reinhardt/Artists Rights Society (ARS), New York; © Matthew Ritchie, courtesy Andrea Rosen Gallery; © Larry Rivers/Licensed by VAGA, New York, NY; © James Rosenquist/Licensed by VAGA, New York, NY; © Estate of Theodore Roszak/Licensed by VAGA, New York, NY; © Susan Rothenberg/Artists Rights Society (ARS), New York; © 2001 Kate Rothko Prizel & Christopher Rothko/Artists Rights Society (ARS), New York; © Betye Saar, courtesy of Michael Rosenfeld Gallery, New York City; © David Salle/Licensed by VAGA, New York, NY; © 1963, 1966 Lucas Samaras; Art © The George and Helen Segal Foundation/Licensed by VAGA, New York, NY; © 2001 Richard Serra/Artists Rights Society (ARS), New York; © Estate of Ben Shahn/Licensed by VAGA, New York, NY; © 2001 Joel Shapiro/Artists Rights Society (ARS), New York; Art © Estate of David Smith/Licensed by VAGA, New York, NY; © 2001 Estate of Tony Smith/Artists Rights Society (ARS), New York; Art © Estate of Robert Smithson/Licensed by VAGA, New York, NY; © Estate of Raphael Soyer, courtesy of Forum Gallery, New York; Reprinted with permission of Joanna T. Steichen, courtesy Howard Greenberg Gallery; © 2001 Frank Stella/Artists Rights Society (ARS), New York; © 2001 Artists Rights Society (ARS), New York/ADAGP, Paris (Louis Stettner); © Estate of Yves Tanguy/Artists Rights Society (ARS), New York; © Wayne Thiebaud/Licensed by VAGA, New York, NY; © 2001 Artists Rights Society (ARS), New York/Pro Litteris, Zurich (Mark Tobey); © 2001 Andy Warhol Foundation for the Visual Arts/Artists Rights Society (ARS), New York; © Arthur Fellig (Weegee)/Getty Images; © 2001 Lawrence Weiner/Artists Rights Society (ARS), New York; © Estate of H.C. Westermann/Licensed by VAGA, New York, NY; © Estate of Grant Wood/Licensed by VAGA, New York, NY